AF473751

Remarkable Graphic Styles

ROUGH

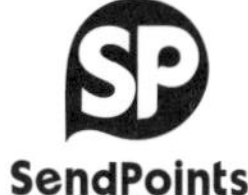

SendPoints

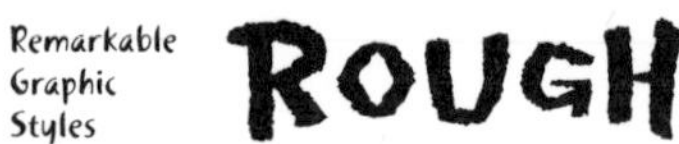

Second printing of the first edition, April 2020

EDITED & PUBLISHED BY SendPoints Publishing Co., Ltd.
PUBLISHER: Lin Gengli
PUBLISHING DIRECTOR: Lin Shijian
ASSISTANT PUBLISHING-DIRECTOR: Chen Ting
CHIEF EDITOR: Lin Shijian
LEAD EDITOR: Li Weiji
EXECUTIVE EDITOR: Huang Qian
DESIGN DIRECTOR: Lin Shijian
EXECUTIVE ART EDITOR: Ding Jiaxin
PROOFREADING: James N. Powell, Li Weiji

REGISTERED ADDRESS: Room 15A Block 9 Tsui Chuk Garden, Wong Tai Sin, Kowloon, Hong Kong
TEL: +852-35832323 / FAX: +852-35832448
OFFICE ADDRESS: 7F, No.9-1 Anning Street, Jinshazhou Road, Baiyun District, Guangzhou, China
TEL: +86-20-89095121 / FAX: +86-20-89095206
BEIJING OFFICE: Flat 1701, Block C, BBMG International, Wangjing West Road no.48, Chaoyang District, Beijing, China
TEL: +86-10-84139071 / FAX: +86-10-84139071
SHANGHAI OFFICE: Room 302, Floor 3, Ningbo Road no.349, Huangpu District, Shanghai, China
TEL: +86-21-63523469 / FAX: +86-21-63523469

SALES TEAM
UK, Europe, Africa, Oceania: Sunnie sales02@sendpoints.cn
America, the Middle East: Mia sales03@sendpoints.cn
Asia: Hedy sales01@sendpoints.cn
TEL: +86-20-81007895
EMAIL: sales@sendpoints.cn
WEBSITE: www.sendpoints.cn / www.spbooks.cn

ISBN 978-988-78494-5-2

Printed and bound in China

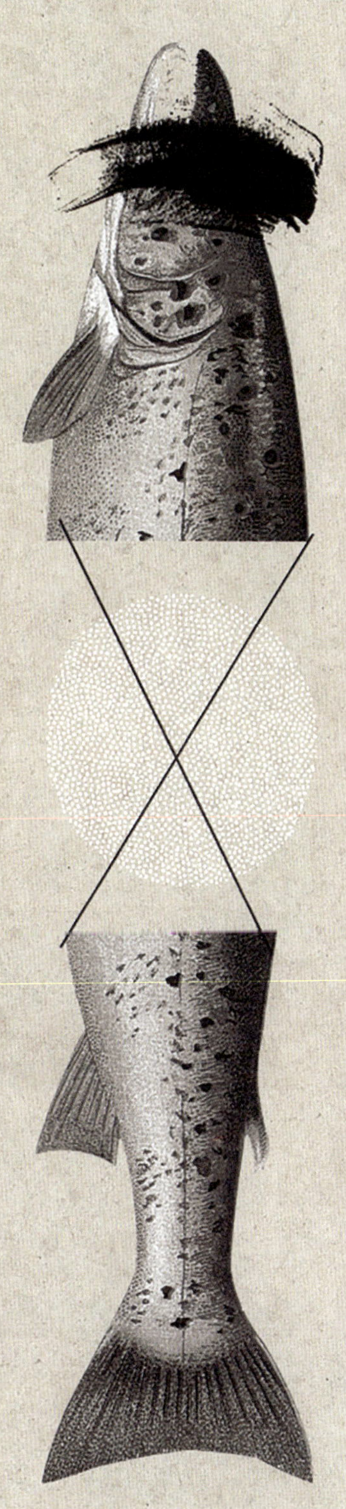

CONTENTS

ROUGH HERITAGE

We can take advantage of tools and techniques to create more and more delicate objects, but why have rough and crude qualities in art not disappeared?

There is no lack of roughness in the history of aesthetics. Though never intended for visual pleasure, African sculpture had been an art for the sake of the meanings endowed as well as practicality, until modern Western artists brought a new perspective to it. This figurative art, which dominated Western art history, began to face threats from groups of avant-garde artists in the 19th century. Among avant-garde artists, Picasso, Matisse, and others applied rough and naive brushstrokes to express a new visual philosophy—"I do not literally paint that table, but the emotion it produces upon me," said Matisse. Such a rough style of painting was long before practiced by the sketchy style of painter Liang Kai, in China's Song dynasty, while in Japan the aesthetics of wabi-sabi eulogizes imperfection, confronting extravagant fashion for centuries. In terms of technique, there are color field painters, action painters, and pop artists who simply fill in or drop the paint or duplicate or put together raw materials. Can't anyone do that?

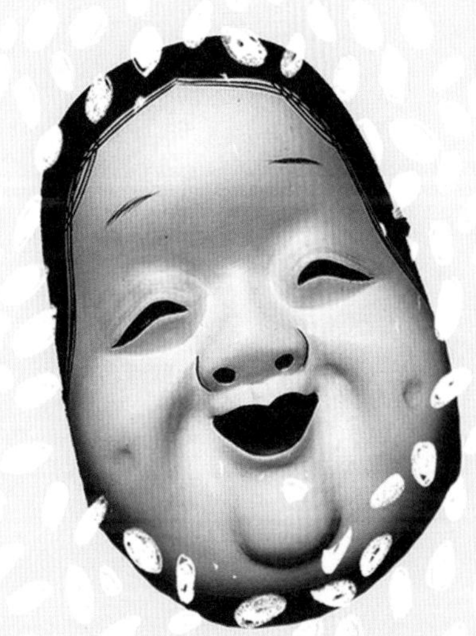

In the field of graphic design today, on which this book focuses, rough visuals keep popping up—with primitive textures, crude materials, clumsy lines, non-matching colors, unthoughtful composition, and so on. These courageous attempts, pursuing beauty not for beauty itself, are interesting. But at the same time they make us ponder over the dividing line between vulgarity and elegance, and the possibilities of art and design.

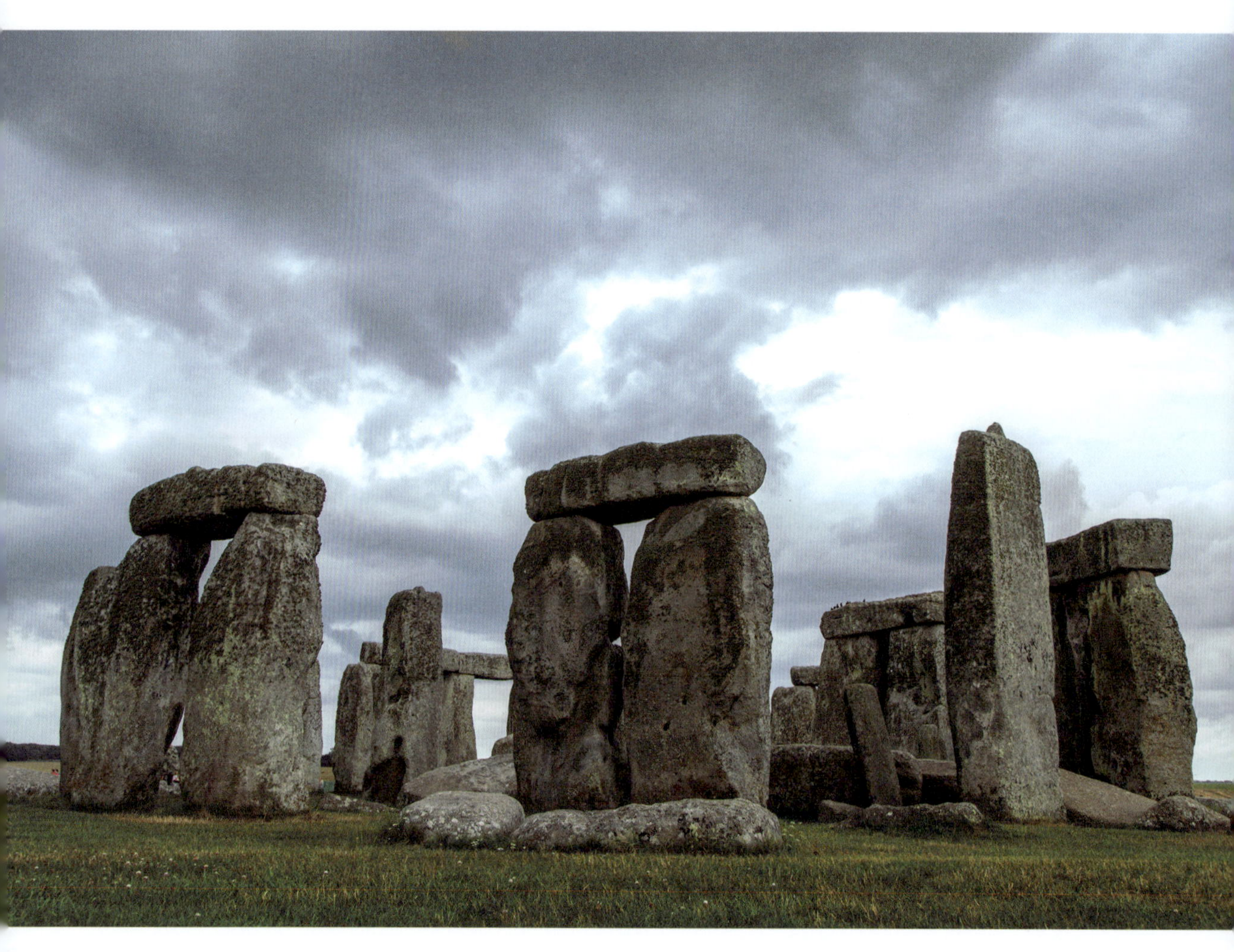

Stonehenge. Photo courtesy: www.twin-loc.fr

Prehistoric Art—Stonehenge

Located on the Salisbury Plain in England, Stonehenge is a prehistoric and massive stone circle: a monument built in several phases, with the earliest phase dated at about 3100 BC. The ruins of this now incomplete circle consist of huge oblong stones in an upright position, some pairs topped with lintel stones, forming an outer ring, and an inner ring: with the largest remaining stone of about 6.7 meters tall and more than 45 tonnes in weight. Although Stonehenge is not the largest stone circle in Britain, its complexity of design and the weight of the stones are remarkably incomparable.

The mysteries of Stonehenge have been puzzling historians and archeologists for centuries. Who built it? How and why was it built? Some have speculated that its function was that of a burial site or an astrological observatory. Regardless of its archeological values, it is doubtlessly a representation of megalithic architecture, a piece of prehistoric art. Its grandeur, under a veil of roughness, must have been a result of the power of resource manipulation and organization, whereas its precise solar and lunar alignments reflect the designer's thinking about and interaction with their world.

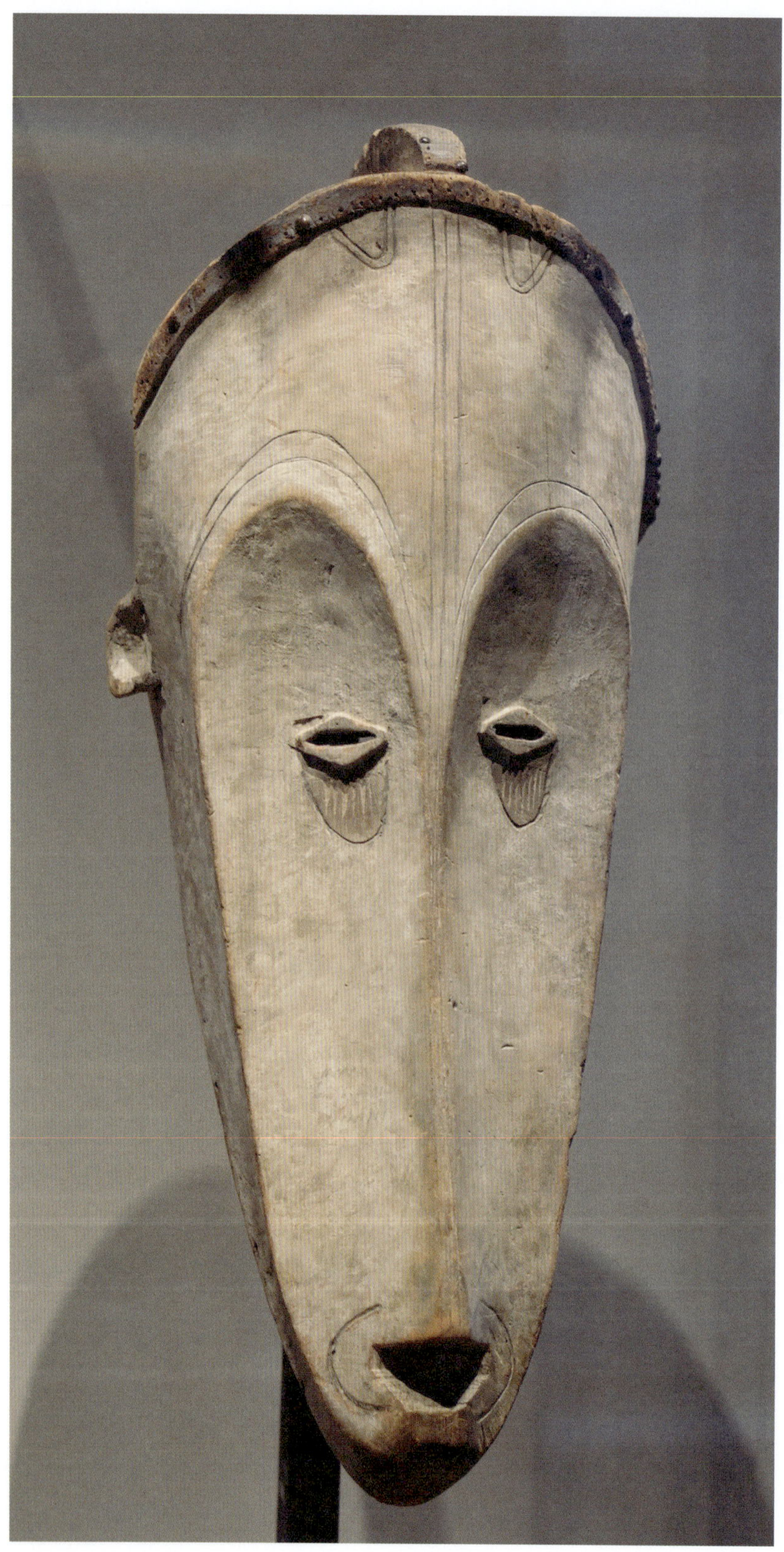

A mask of the Fang people, 19th century

African Sculpture

Historically, sculpture is a prestigious art form in most sub-Saharan African countries. Due to the relatively high temperature and humidity in the area, wood is an abundant source and became the most accessible material for making sculptures, but is difficult to preserve. Other primary materials of African sculpture include clay, stone, ivory, and metal. Though the time of origin is not clear, African sculpture has proved to have a long history thanks to the unearthed remains of sculptures.

African sculpture can be divided into two forms: human figures and masks, which are mostly for religious or social purposes. The craftsmen created without model or sketches, combining creativity and skill, and produced works that distinguish themselves through their bold abstraction. The rough and mysterious art enchantment of the African sculpture even had a profound impact on European Modernist art, with, for instance, the prominent artist Pablo Picasso finding tremendous inspiration in it.

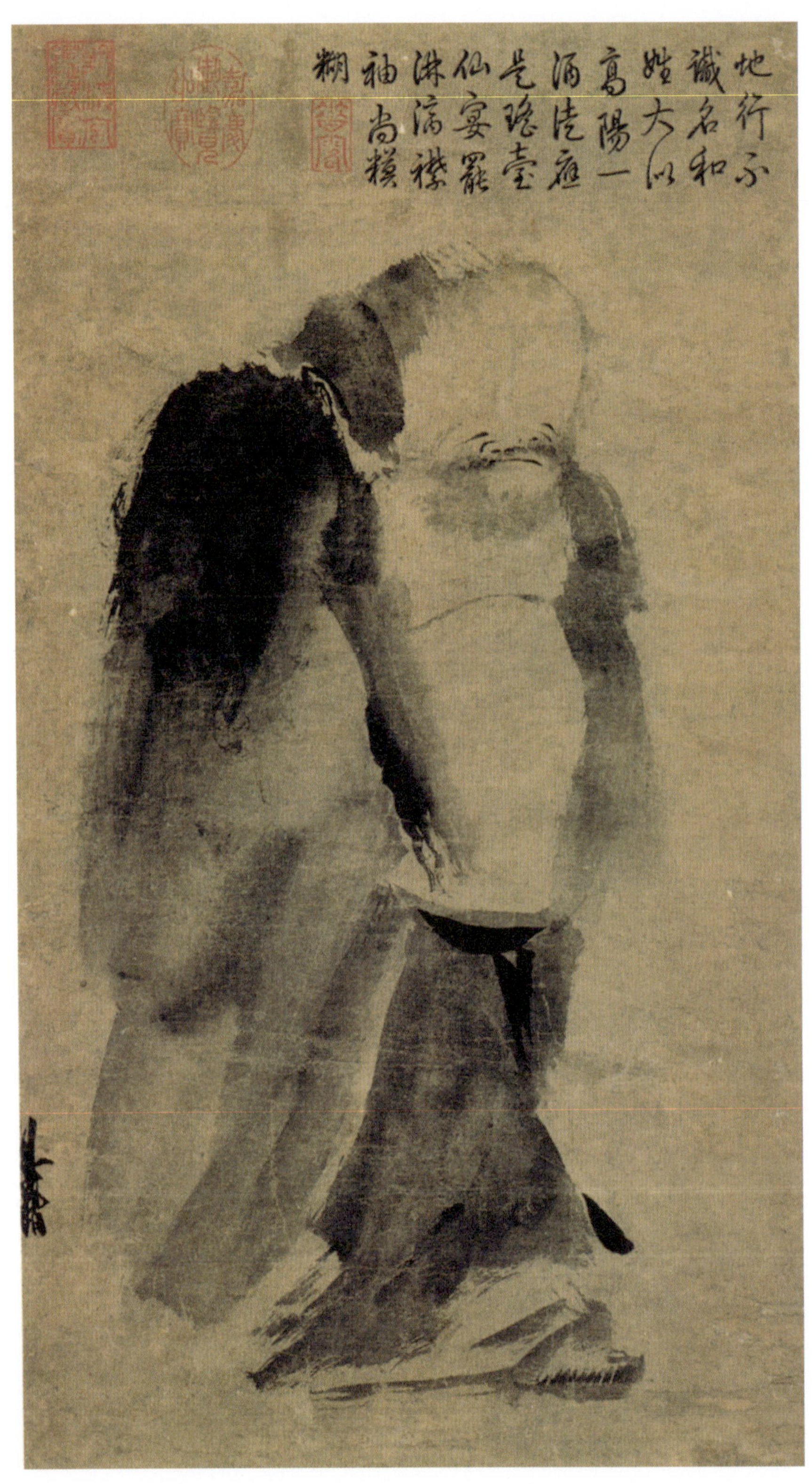

Immortal in Splashed Ink by Liang Kai

Chinese Splashed-Ink Painting

Chinese splashed-ink painting is a form of brush painting, similar to Chinese cursive script, both practiced by intellectuals using black ink of varied density to capture the spirit of objects instead of faithful representations.

Immortal in Splashed Ink is the earliest available figure painting of splashed-ink free-hand and has been honored as an outstanding example of Chinese traditional xieyi or sketchy style. The painter, Liang Kai, a leading artist of the Southern Song Dynasty (1127-1279) is said to have created this painting while drinking. The immortal in the work seems to be staggering, with his robe dangling. The artist painted the figure in light ink at the very beginning, then applied darker ink when the light ink was half dried, with the intention of expressing the immortal's body weight. He used a few short and swift strokes rather than lines to depict even some details of the figure, such as the belt. This kind of technique of reducing brushstrokes is so-called "abbreviated brush," perfected by Liang Kai.

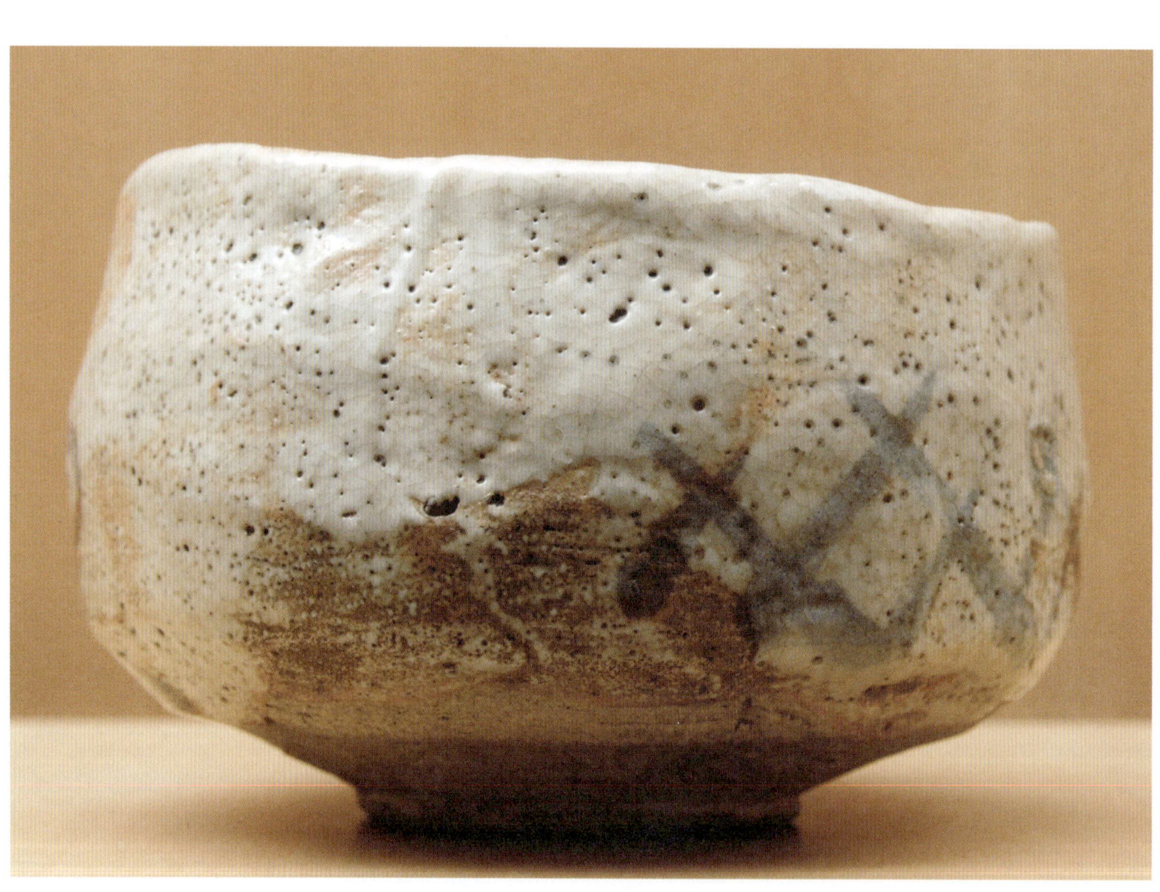

Japanese tea bowl. Photo courtesy: Marie-Lan Nguyen

Wabi-Sabi

In Japanese culture, wabi-sabi, a unique aesthetic concept derived from the philosophy of Buddhism, represents the acceptance of imperfection and ephemerality. Originally, the word *wabi* referred to "solitude" and *sabi* meant "withered" and "lean." The connotations of these words became more positive in the 14th century. Gradually wabi assumed the meaning of "roughness," "simplicity," "modesty" and "quietness" of both natural matters and artifacts, whereas sabi came to be the beauty brought by the passage of time.

The Japanese tea ceremony is a typical example of wabi-sabi. Sen no Rikyū, a master of the Japanese Way of Tea, had a profound impact on wabi-sabi impelling it to reach a zenith during the 16th century. He expanded the wabi-sabi aesthetic in the tea ceremony, advocating the use of black pottery bowls, bamboo cushions and teaspoons, as well as rustic and tiny tea houses to contradict the extravagant fashions at that time. Legend has it that he once cleared the fallen leaves in a courtyard, and after that he shook a tree to make some leaves fall off on the ground. This is this kind of flawed beauty drawn from nature that brings inner peace.

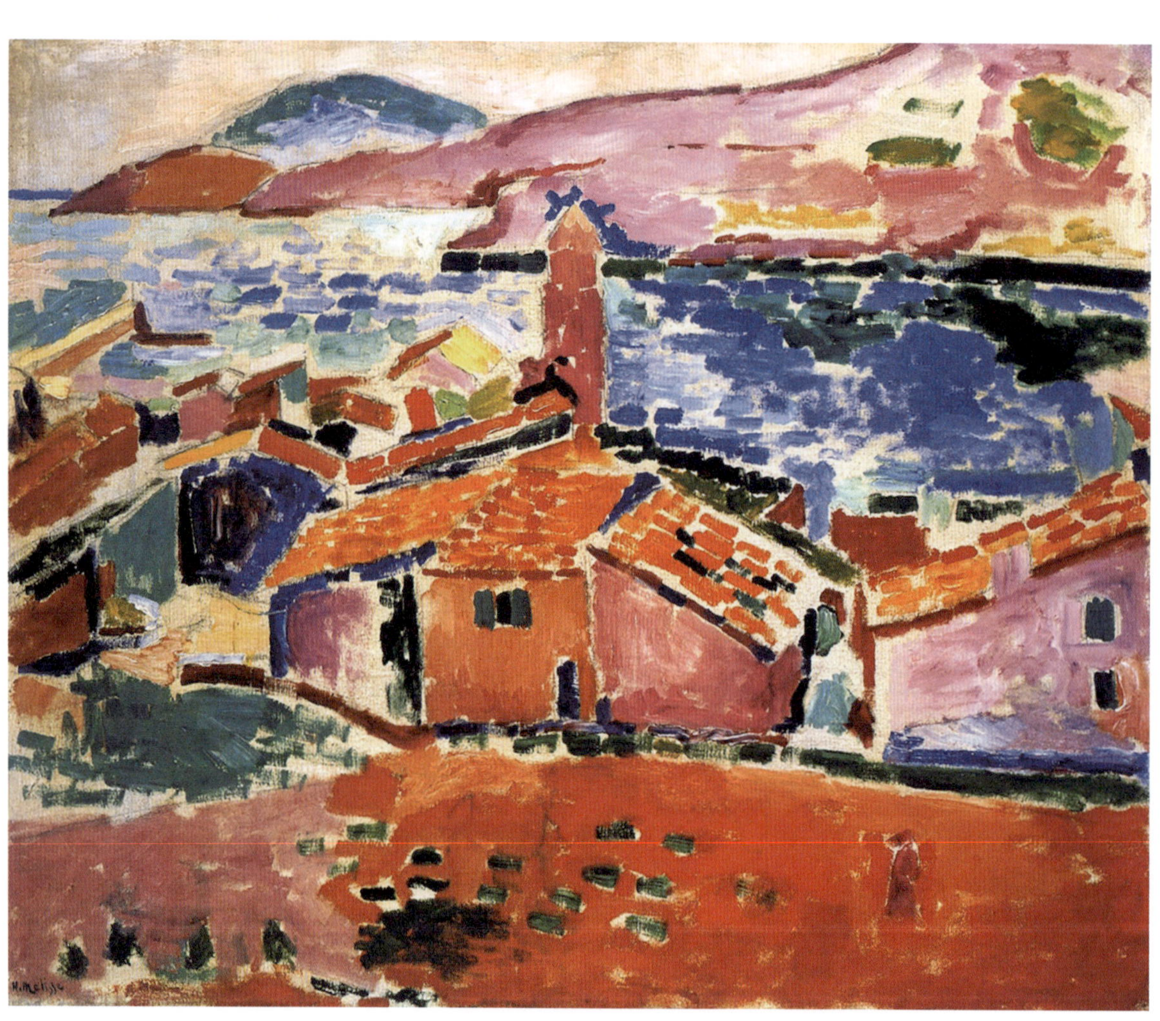

Les toits de Collioure by Henri Matisse

Henri Matisse and Fauvism

Henri Matisse (1869–1954) was a French artist who has been widely acknowledged as a leader of the Fauvism—the style of "the wild beasts" originated in the early 20th century, emphasizing characteristics of painting and the use of intense color.

Matisse has often been compared with Pablo Picasso, for their epoch-making contributions to modern art. Whereas Picasso was known for his deconstruction via cubist planes, Matisse is known as a colorist for his "construction by means of color," retaining the impressionistic way of using color and loose application. Like Picasso, the aesthetics of Japanese prints and African sculpture were also important influences for Matisse. The contrasting pure colors on Matisse's paintings offer structure and volume, while the rough brushstrokes and vigorous colors lend them a sense of naivety. His unique artistic view and love for color and line were continued in another form of art — the cut outs, in the 1940s when the elderly artist had to work on a chair or bed.

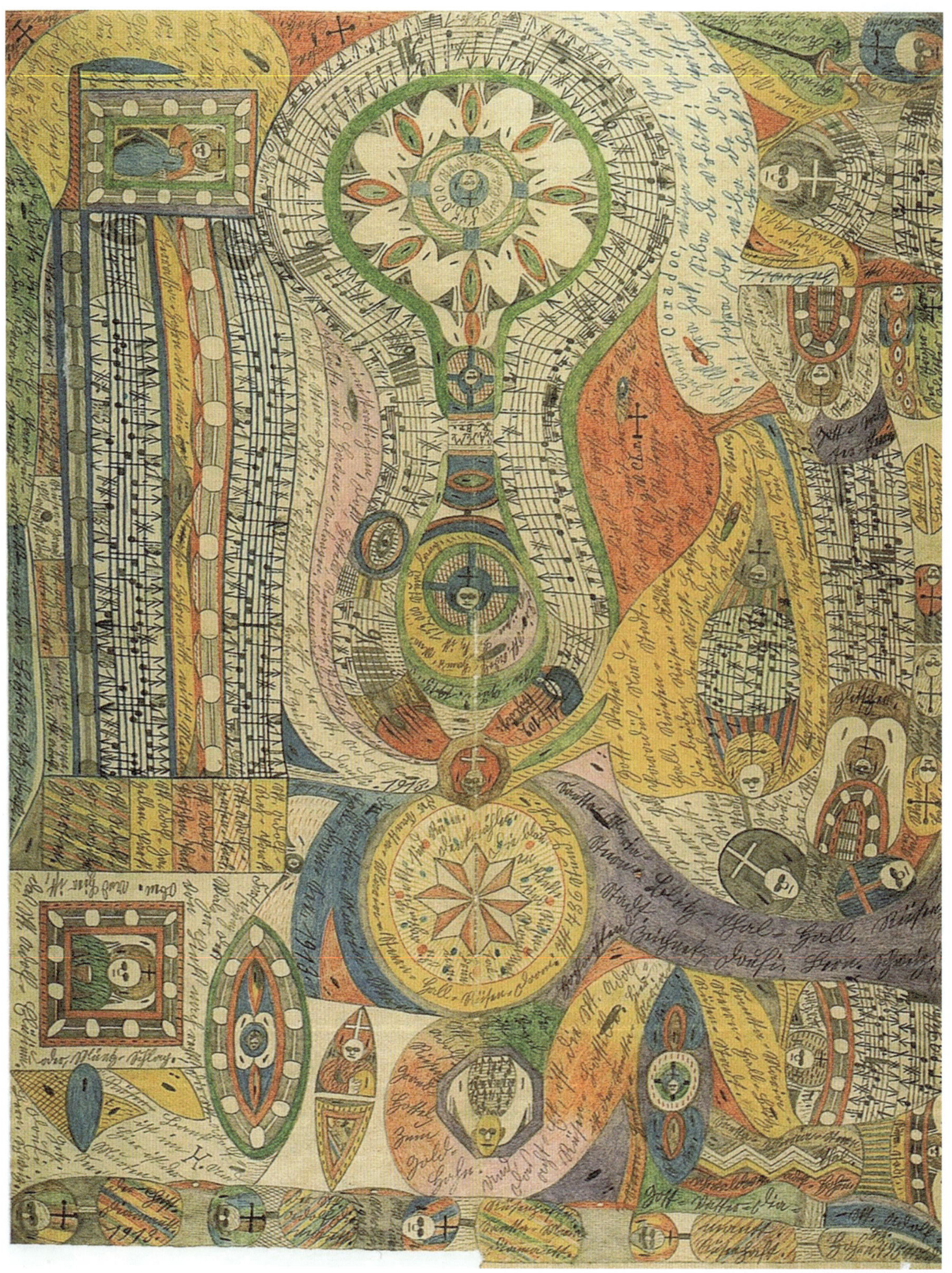

Drawing by Adolf Wölfli

Outsider Art

Outsider art, or art brut, refers to art created by individuals who create outside the mainstream art world. Such artists are usually self-taught, alienated from art education, and in earlier times were always marginal figures in society. The works of these outsiders are appreciated for their primitive creativity and uninfluenced authenticity. Founded and championed by French artist Jean Dubuffet, this "raw art" or "rough art" is another avant-garde art movement that confronted conventional artistic values in the 20th century.

Swiss outsider Adolf Wölfli (1864-1930) was one of the genre's key figures. His large volume of paintings was done in a psychiatric hospital and caught the attention of a doctor, Walter Morgenthaler, who later published a monograph on Wölfli and his creations. The most impressive body of works by Wölfli is believed to be his imaginary autobiography, a 25,000-page illustrated narrative, combining drawings, writing, musical compositions, and even collages. His art is noticeable for its intricacy, surrealist quality, and intensity of feeling, with a strong focus on geometric symmetry and use of color.

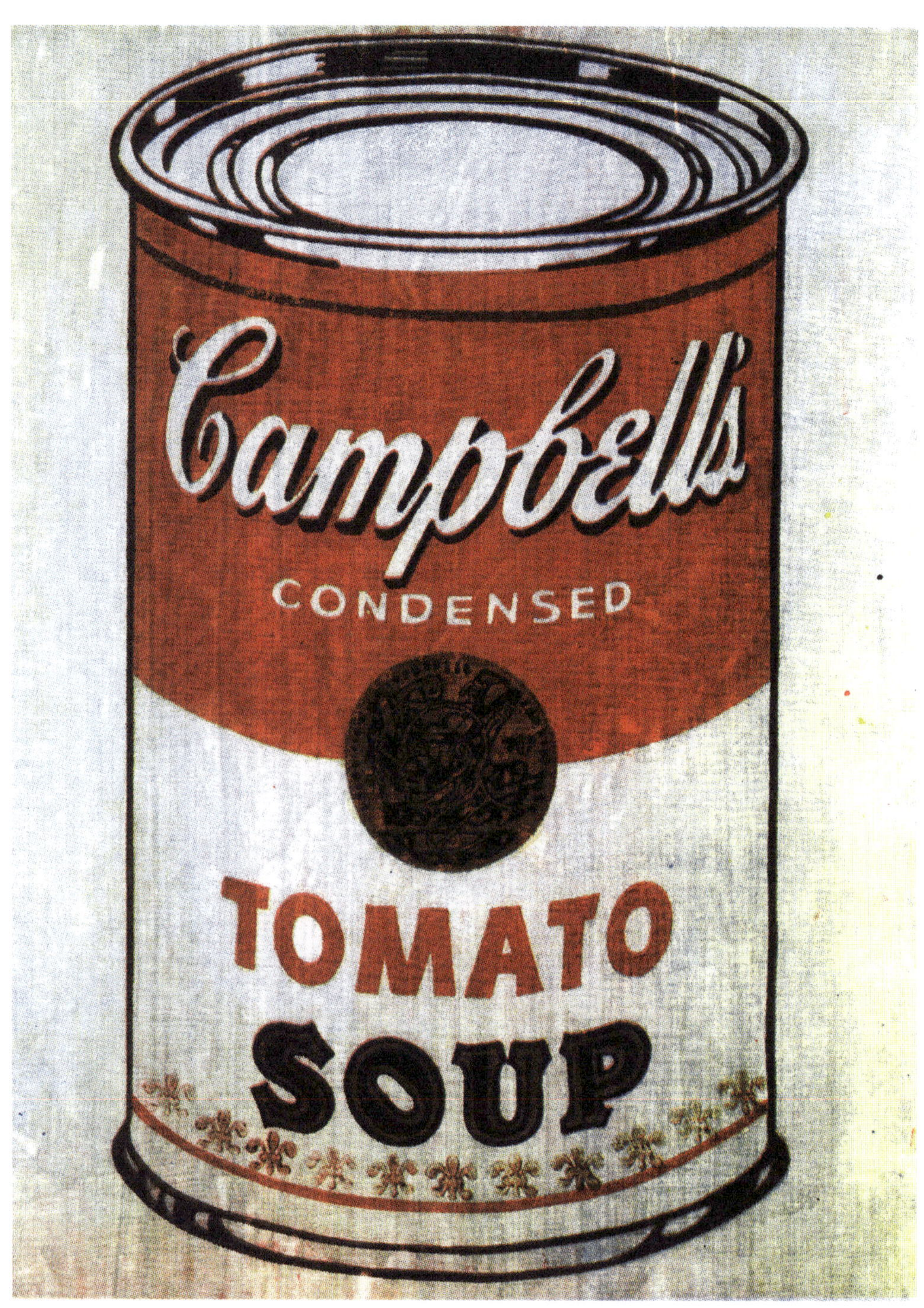

Campbell's Soup Cans (detail) by Andy Warhol

Andy Warhol and Pop Art

"It is the idea that matters, not the production of it," said Andy Warhol (1928-1987), an iconic Pop artist of 20th century America. His early experience as an advertisement illustrator is believed to be important for Warhol's ingenuity of transferring everyday items and popular subjects into art. His non-painterly and effortless-repetition approach realized by silk-screening seemed to mimic the mass production and blooming consumerism in the 1960s. While abstract expressionism was unintelligible to the general public, Pop art, with its root in popular culture, attracted a wider audience.

Popular American symbols such as the Coca-Cola bottle, the Campbell's soup can, and screen star Marilyn Monroe were recurrent subjects in Warhol's works. Even a simple image of a banana became a legendary graphic, after being featured on an album cover of the rock band managed by Warhol himself. The integration of ordinary objects in life with mechanized aspects did challenge the beholder's nerves, but more important, Warhol upended deep-rooted ideas about art, which earned him the name of the "Pope of Pop."

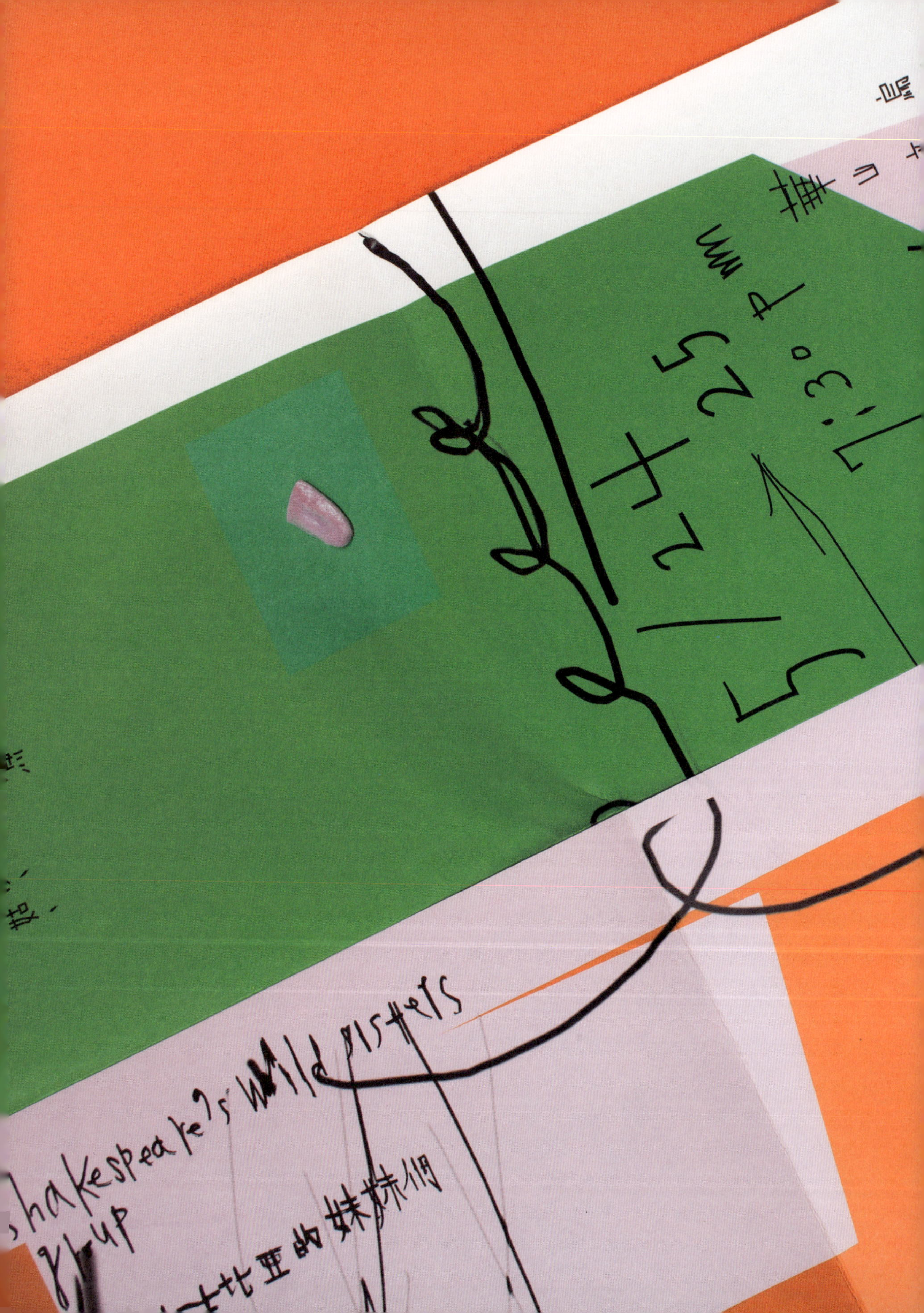

5/27 2025
1:30 pm
Shakespeare's Wild Sisters
group
士比亞的妹妹們

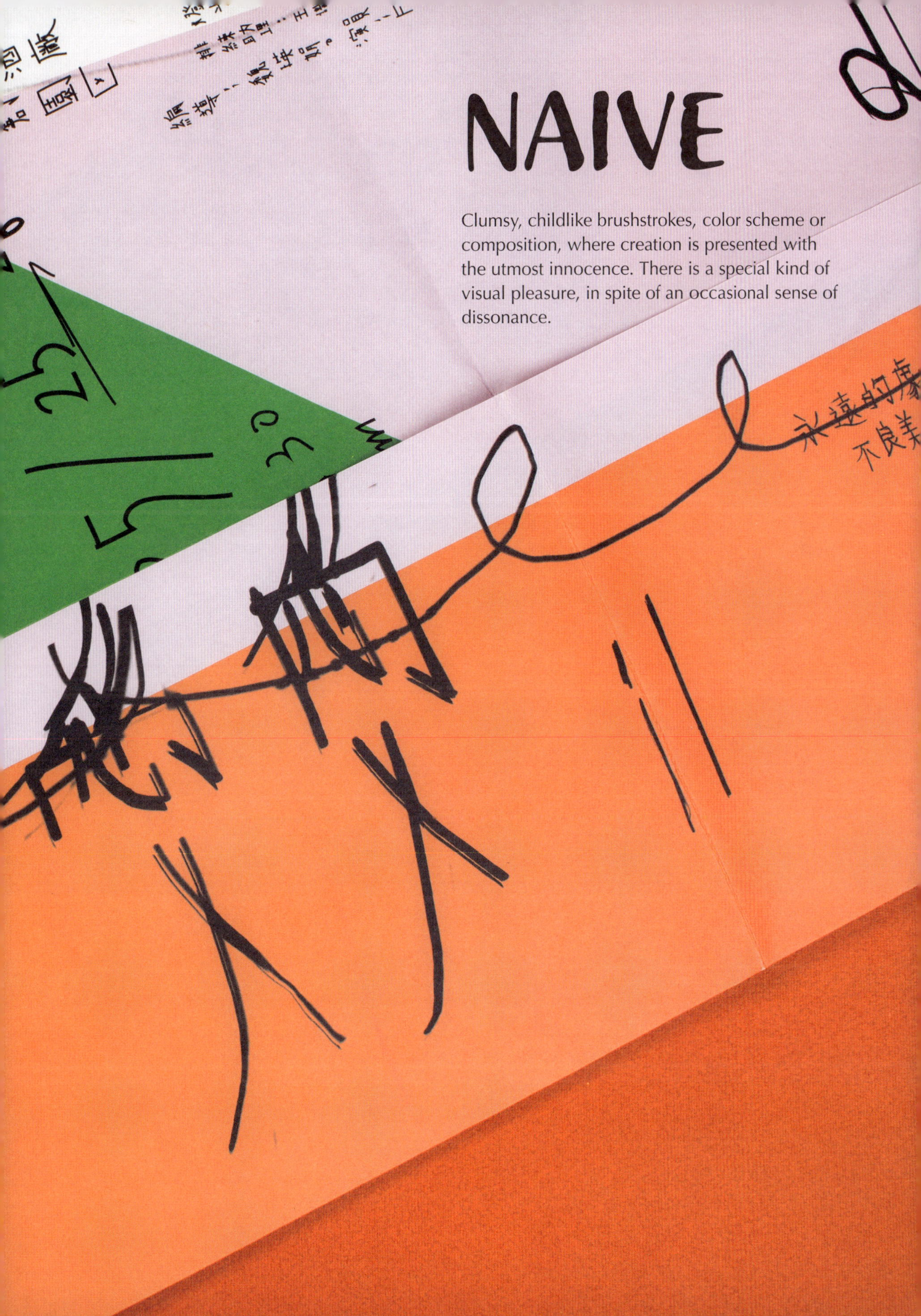

NAIVE

Clumsy, childlike brushstrokes, color scheme or composition, where creation is presented with the utmost innocence. There is a special kind of visual pleasure, in spite of an occasional sense of dissonance.

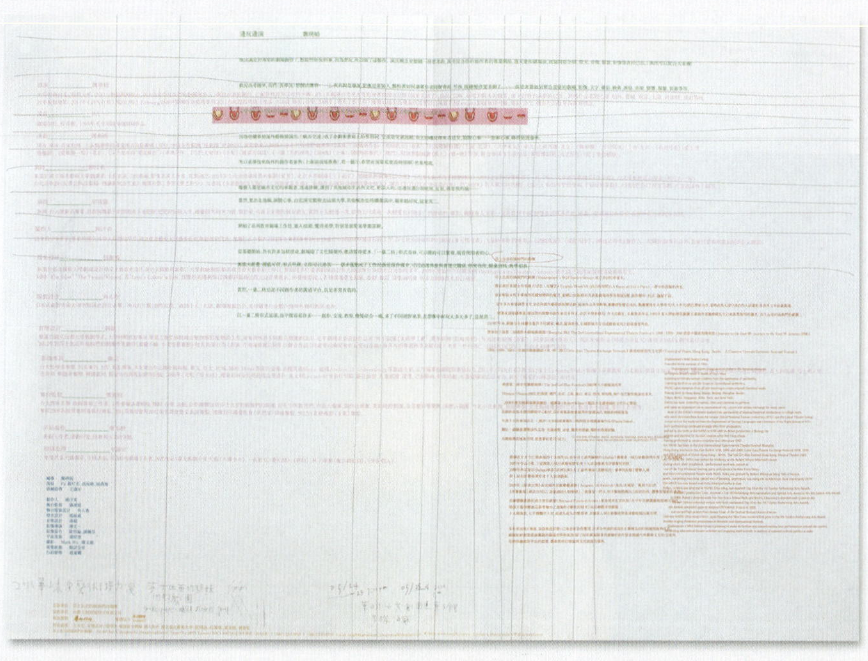

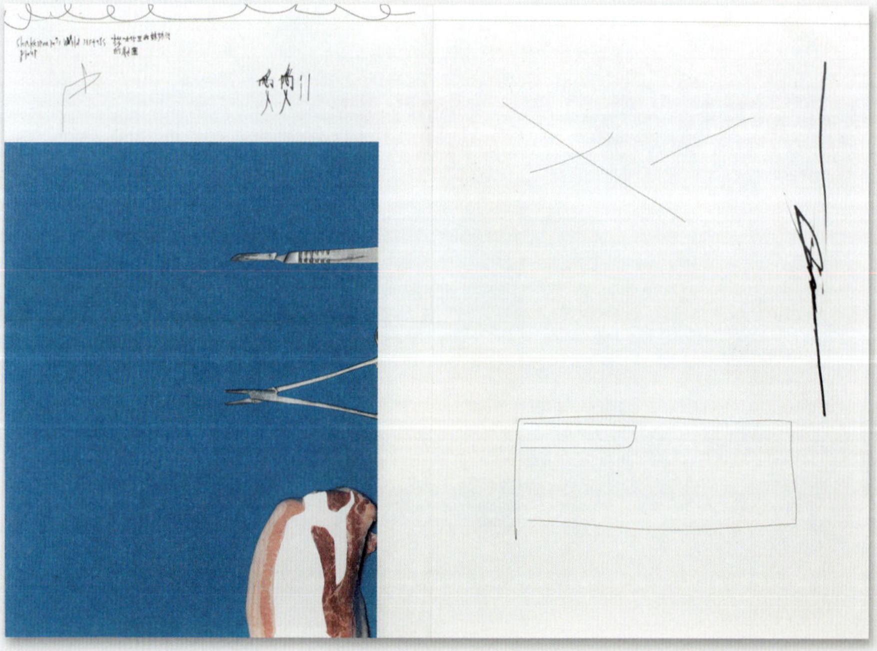

II

Designer : YuehYueh Liu

These poster designs for Shakespeare's Wild Sisters Group are characterized by willful brush strokes and enveloping color schemes. The designer believes that there is no need to define the differences among words, images and colors. These materials are just like everything else on earth—all the connections could be interesting. What appeals to her most is to find the "just good enough" among those connections.

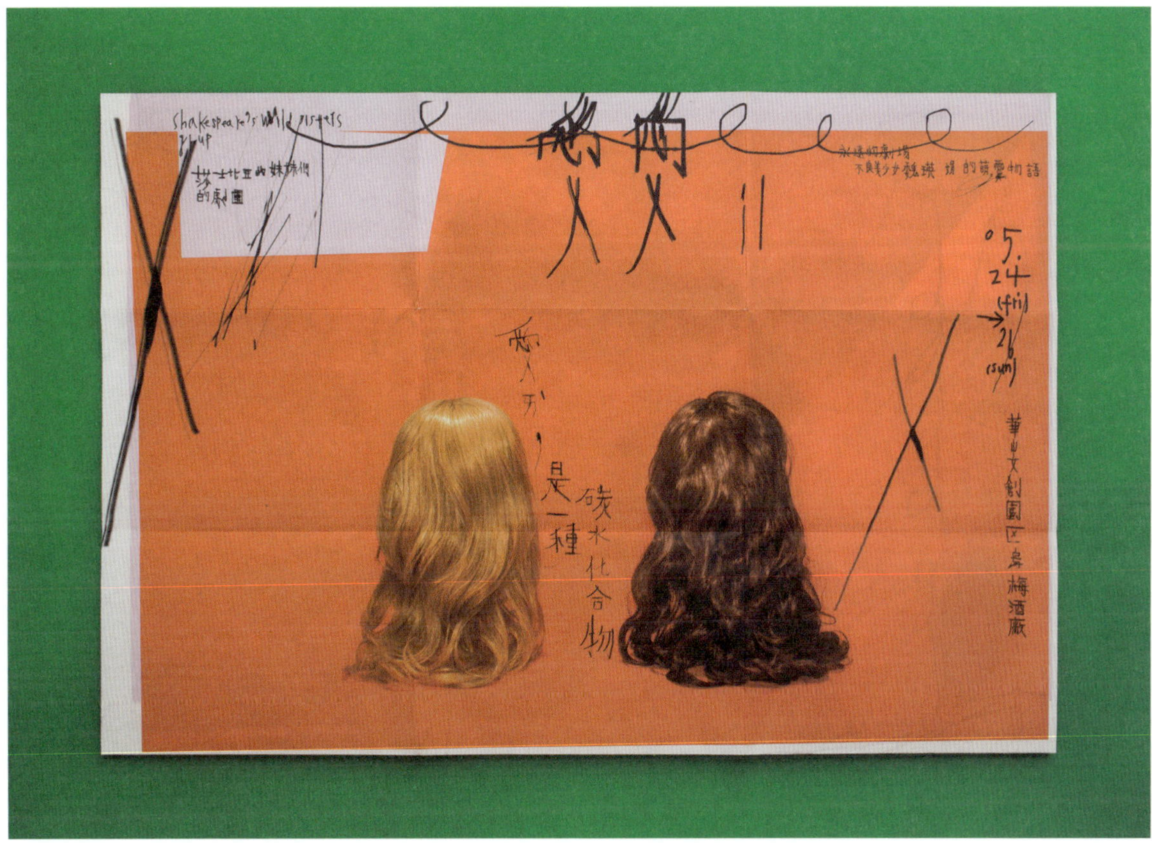

As a kind of visual experience, what do you think about the "roughness" in graphic design ?

Straightforward, unaffected, beautiful but not for beauty itself.

What are your common approaches to produce a "rough" visual effect ?

To me, visual design means exploring the beauty of anti-beauty. I am fond of techniques like collage and graffiti, willfully piling, cutting, rearranging or hollowing out the visuals, and then eventually come to an exact counterbalance. It is always an approach full of coincidences, no default norms. When it comes to that visual, it seems an unnecessary discussion of whether it is beautiful or not.

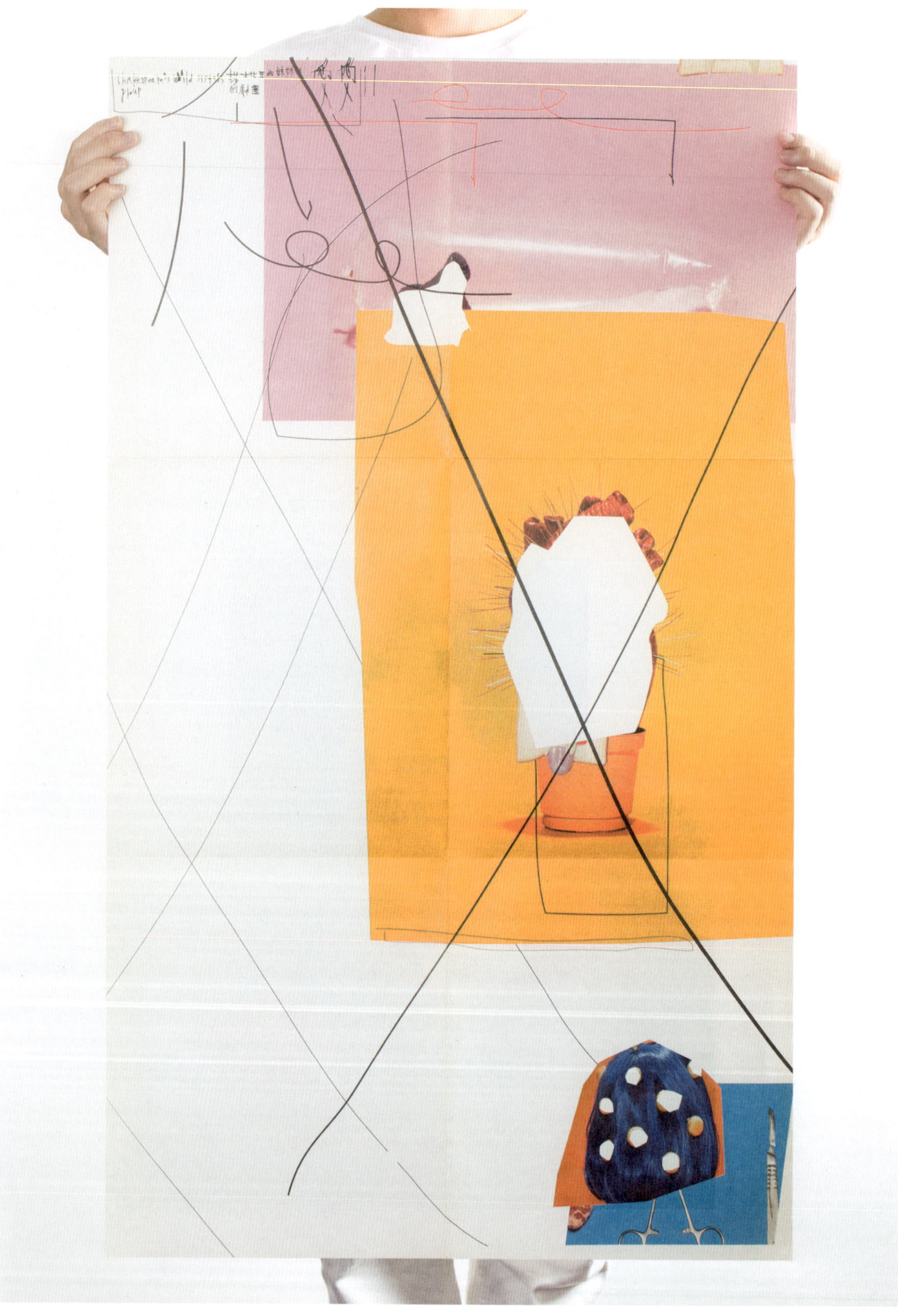

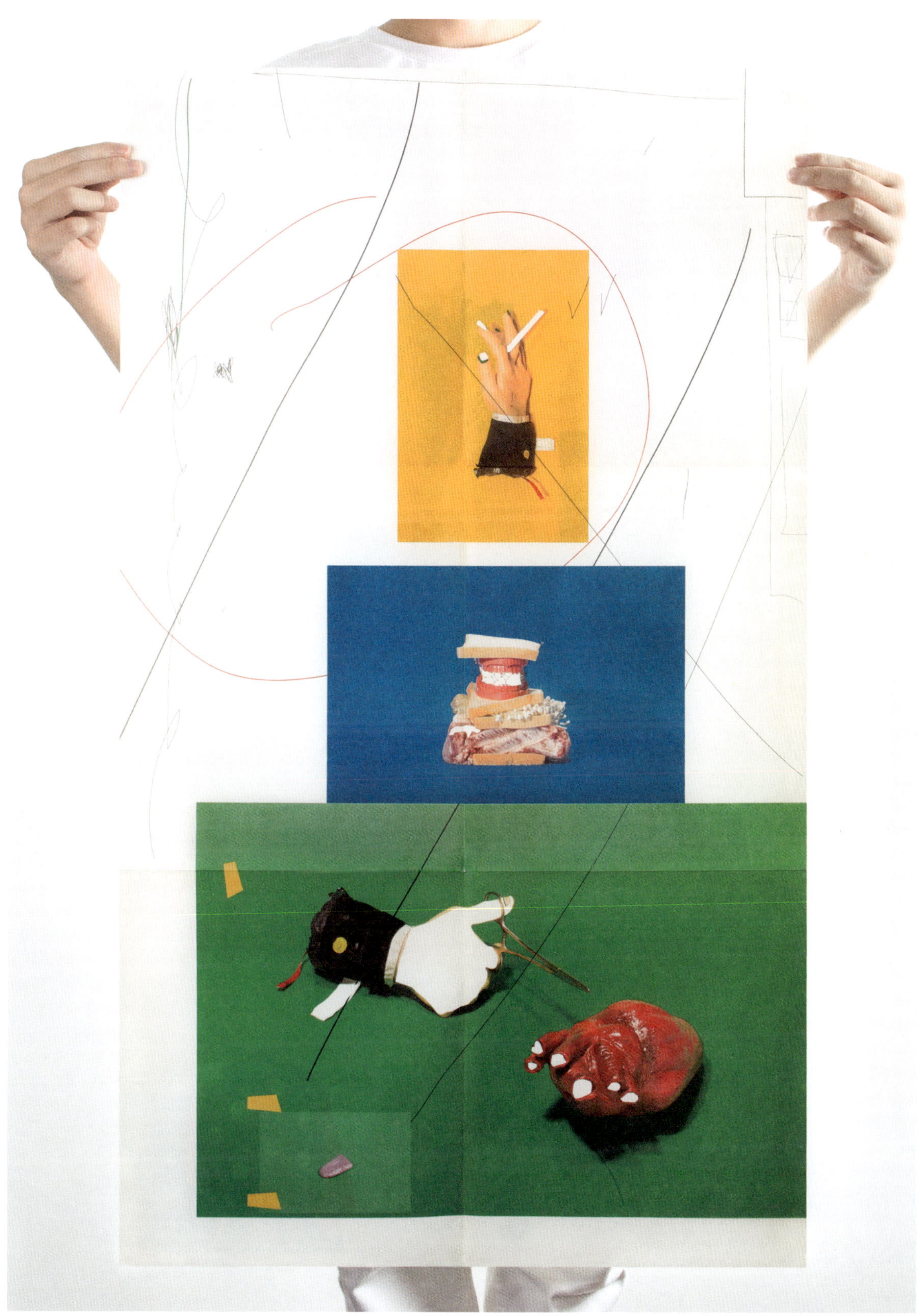

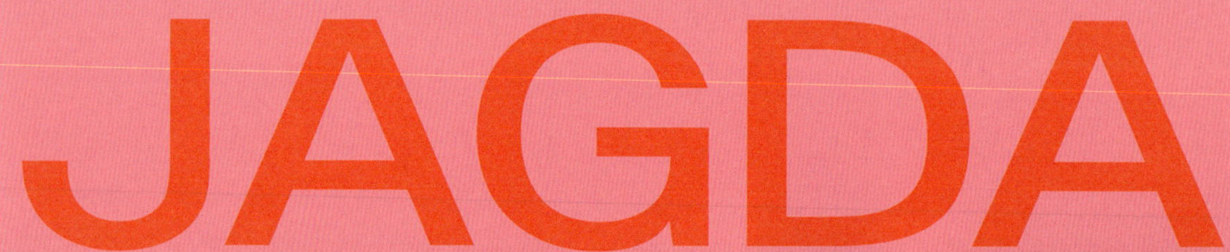

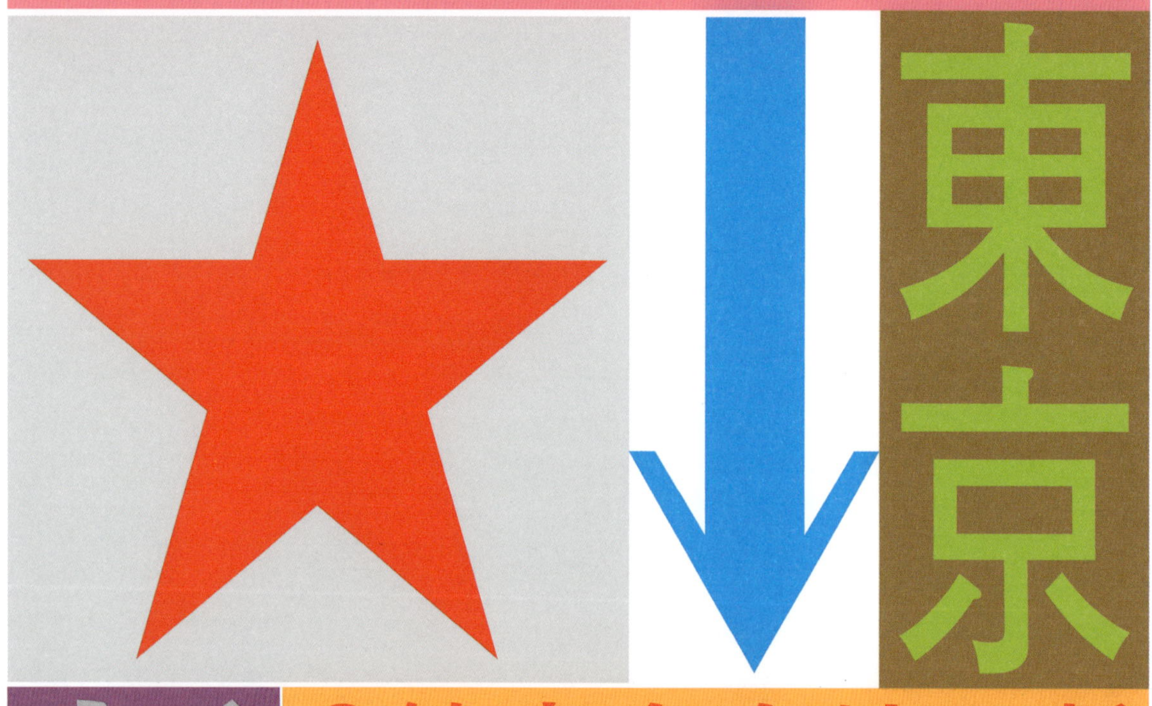

新歓

新入会員の皆さまはもちろん、東京の会員の皆さまも大歓迎です!

コンパ（勉強会）

JAGDA TOKYO
—FRESHMEN WELCOME PARTY

Art Director & Designer : Yui Takada

Poster for the Freshmen Welcome Party of JAGDA (The Japan Graphic Designers Association) in Tokyo. In the designer's work, expression is considered prior to beauty. The color scheme was a technique often used by postwar designers and at the same time was inspired by packages such as snacks.

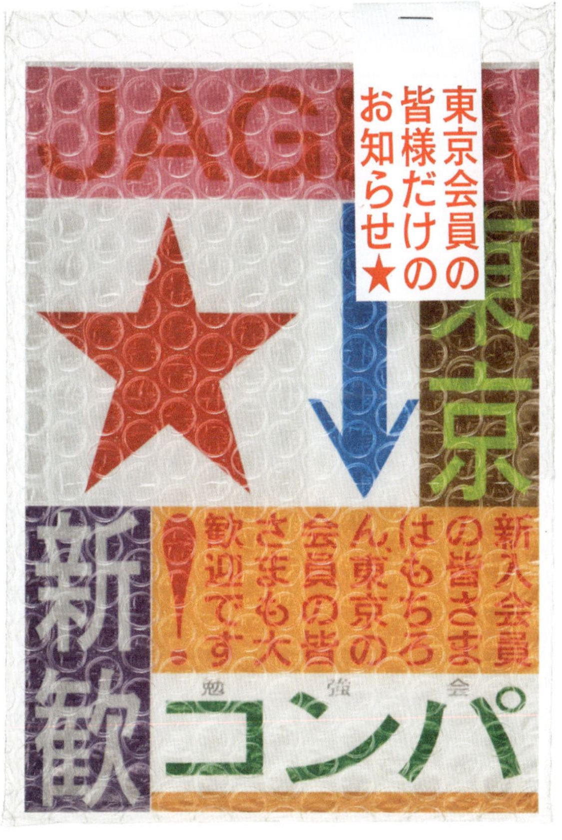

As a kind of visual experience, what do you think about the "roughness" in graphic design?

First of all, I doubt the preconception of "well arranged= beautiful". Sophisticated sharp design is good, but sophisticated "rough" design is also good.

When trying to fully convey earnest and honesty, the questions like "Really?" comes up conversely. By daringly bringing "looseness" or something "removed" into expressions, I think we can make the audience reassured. And if only the concept goes first, expression will be lagged. What I meant is that expression can go first. That is why graphic designers like us are for. However, we do not just seek for "roughness", but we try to make it "clean roughness" to avoid giving uncomfortable feeling to the audience.

What are your common approaches to produce a "rough" visual effect?

There are two things I rely on when making "rough graphic".

The first thing is to borrow the power of other people. In order to have a rich, "unexpected" effect, I rely on others who are able to propose images that I can't imagine by myself. The second thing is the unrefined signboards in the city made by amateurs. By taking hints from such things, we produce a sense of strangeness or incompatibility.

However, I do not always aim for "rough graphic". I think that it is meaningless unless the "rough graphic" is mixed as a foreign matter in a place where the surroundings are well arranged.

JAGDA

東京

新歓

コンパ

YUI TAKADA EXHIBITION

Art Director & Designer : Yui Takada
Art Work : Masanao Hirayama, Ikki Kobayashi, Hiroyuki Nakagawa

A poster for the designer's solo exhibition which summarizes 11 years of work. The exhibition was named "Swimming Graphic" as a hint that the designer will go on with his creative designs that seem to be swimming.

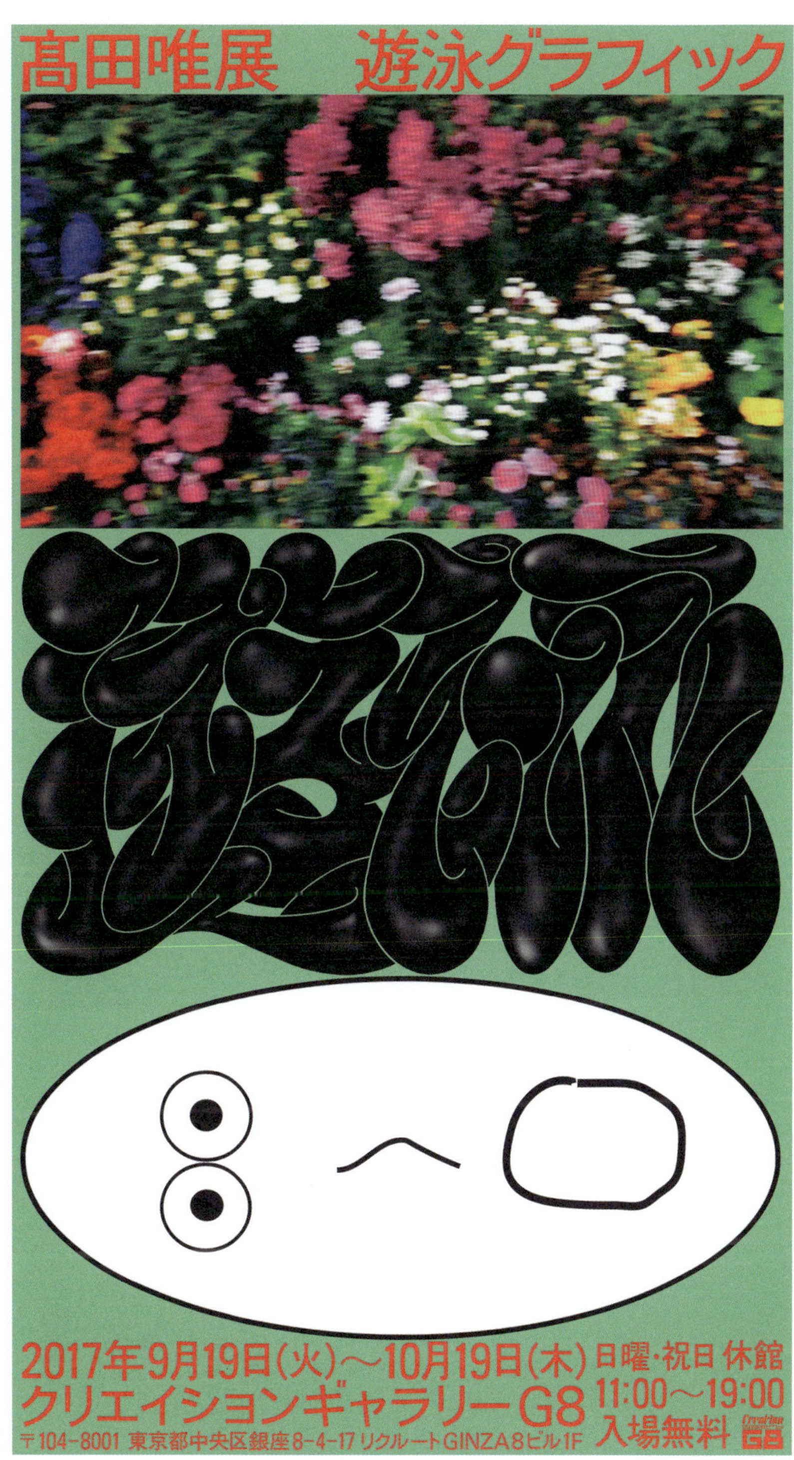

BOX EXHIBITION

Art Director & Designer : Yui Takada
Art Work : Masanao Hirayama

Graphic design for the Box Exhibition hosted by Tokyo Paper Manufacturers Association.

BOX

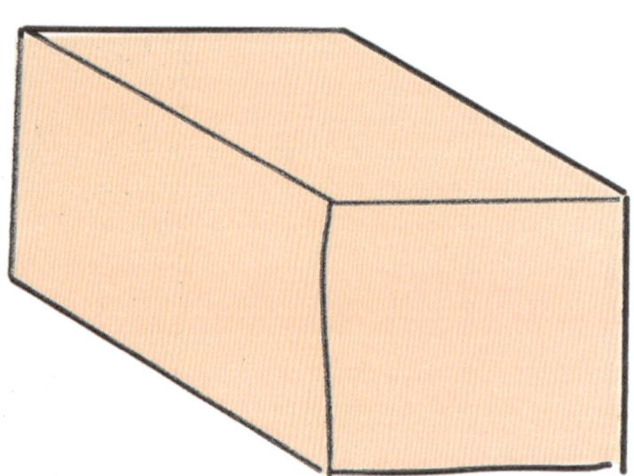

2012

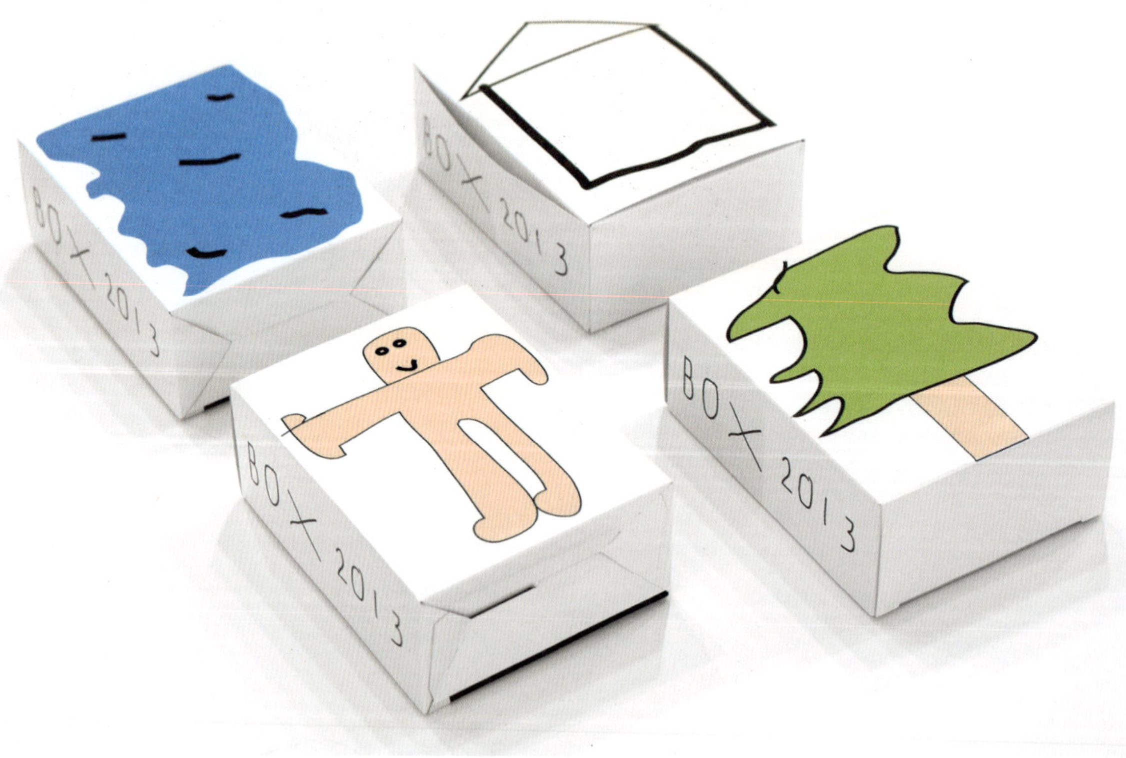

BOX 2012

年に一度のハコのお祭り!

貼箱・段ボール箱等、最新の紙器技術が展示されます!

日時	8月10日(金) 10:00—18:00 8月11日(土) 10:00—16:00
会場	墨田区役所庁舎1階ギャラリー 〒130-8640 東京都墨田区吾妻橋1-23-20

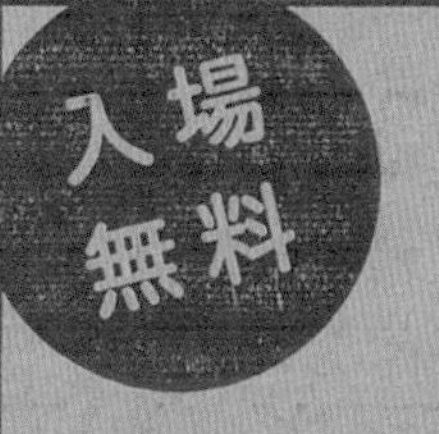

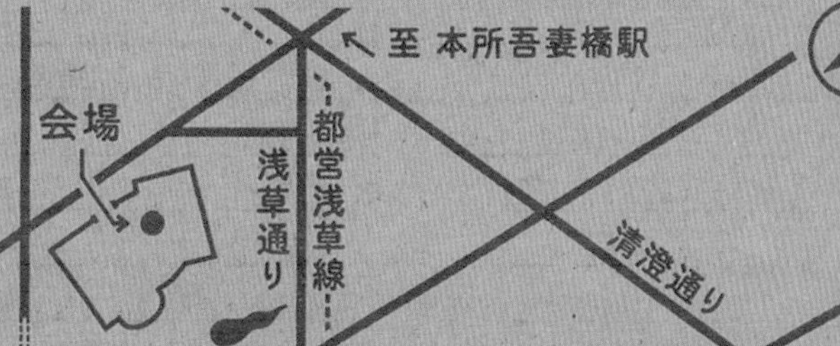

東武伊勢崎線「浅草駅」正面口から約5分/東京メトロ銀座線「浅草駅」5番出口から約5分/都営地下鉄浅草線「浅草駅」A5出口から約5分/都営地下鉄浅草線「本所吾妻橋駅」A3出口から約5分

主催	東京紙器工業組合	協賛	関東甲信越静紙器段ボール箱工業連合会

お問合せ・BOX 2012(ハコの日)イベント実行委員会 事務局 〒130-0005
東京都墨田区東駒形1-16-1 東京紙器工業組合 事務局(東京紙器センタービル5F)
TEL・03-3624-2683 FAX・03-3624-7184 E-mail・info@tokyoshiki.or.jp

イベントの詳細は、東京紙器工業組合のHP(www.tokyoshiki.or.jp)をご覧ください。

Main visual by Masanao Hirayama

FOR STOCKIST EXHIBITION 2017

Art Direction & Design : Yui Takada
Art Work : Ikki Kobayashi

For Stockist Exhibition is a trade fair of furniture, home accessories, apparel, food, jewelry, etc.

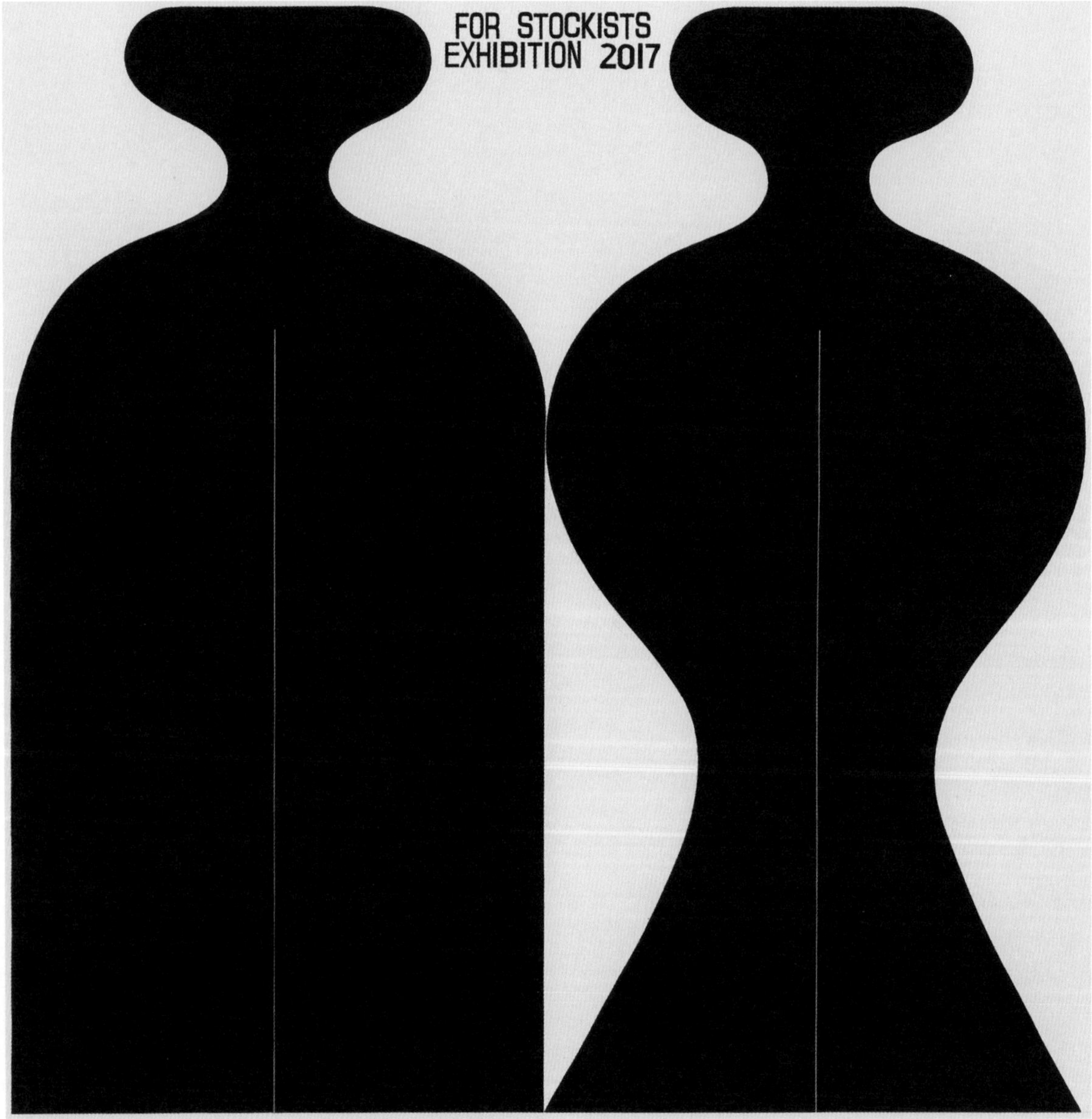

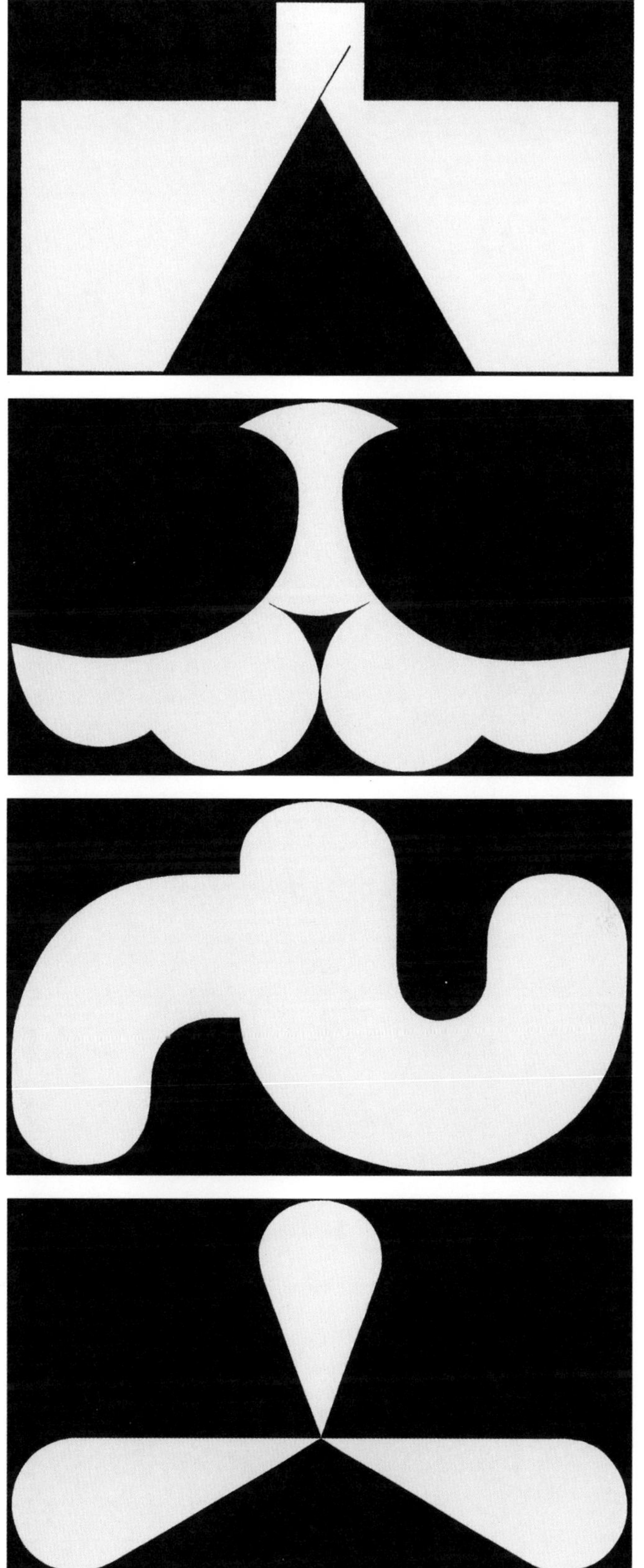

LOOKING FOR.

Designer : Pasha Bumazhniy

The designer used second hand stickers, spray paint, pencil, brush and two Chinese knives to make this design. This is a process of enjoying creation itself without thinking too much. Here, roughness is fast and good.

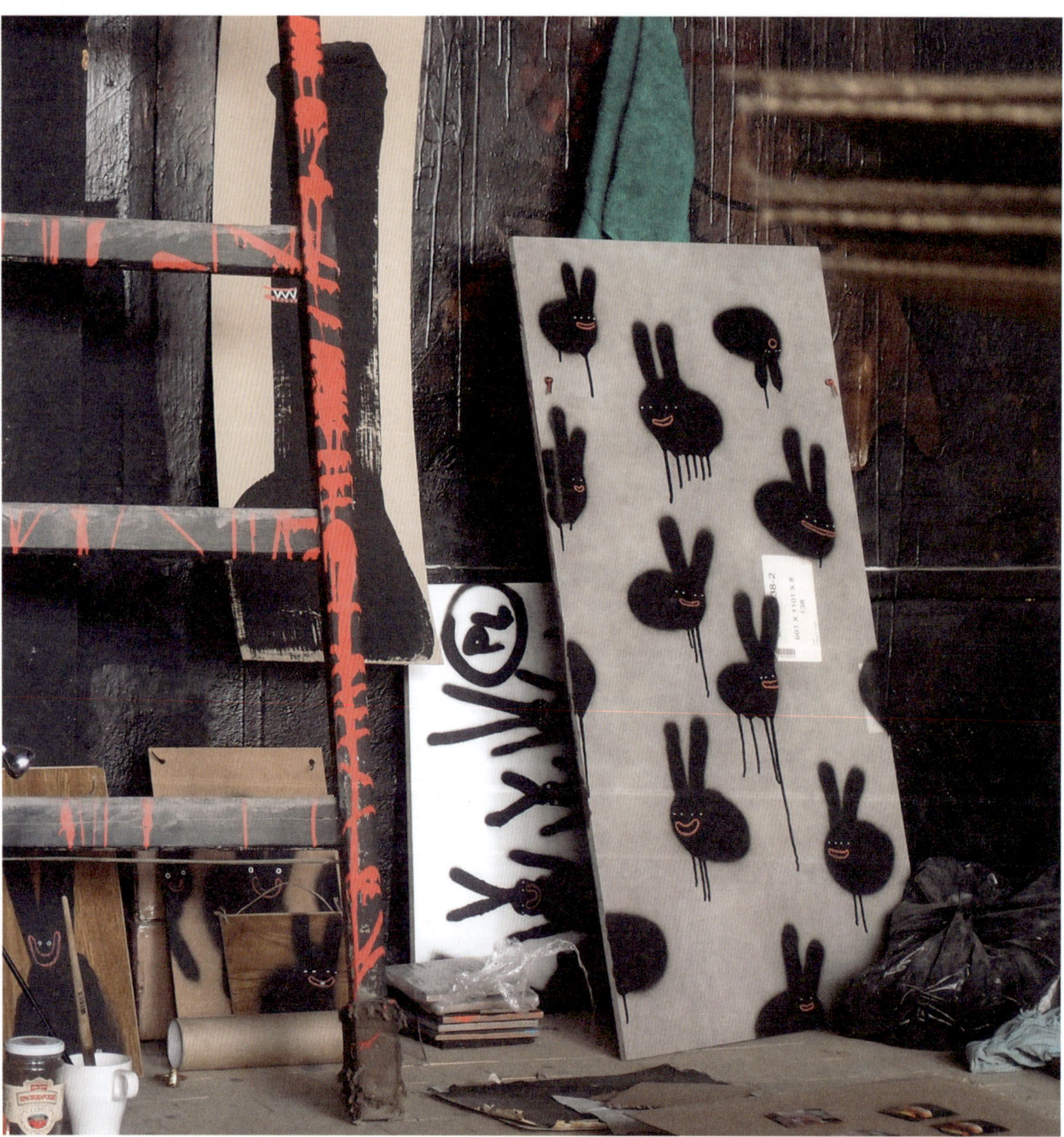

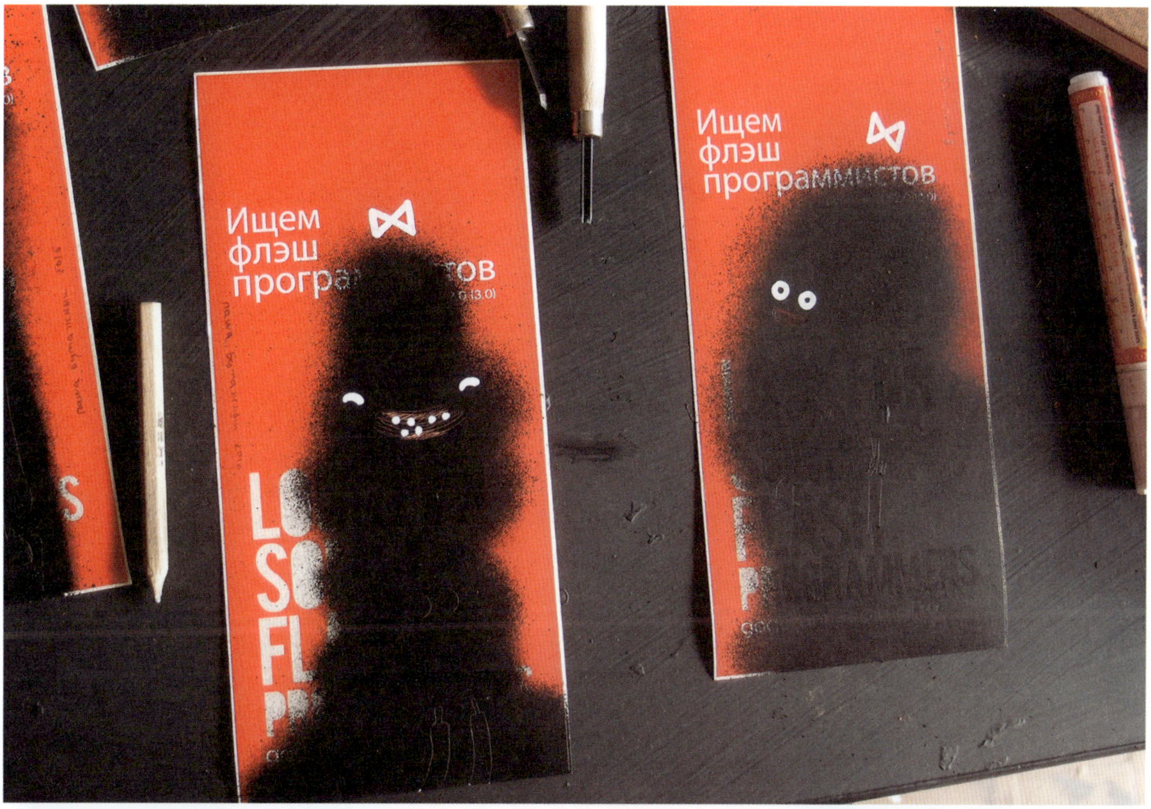

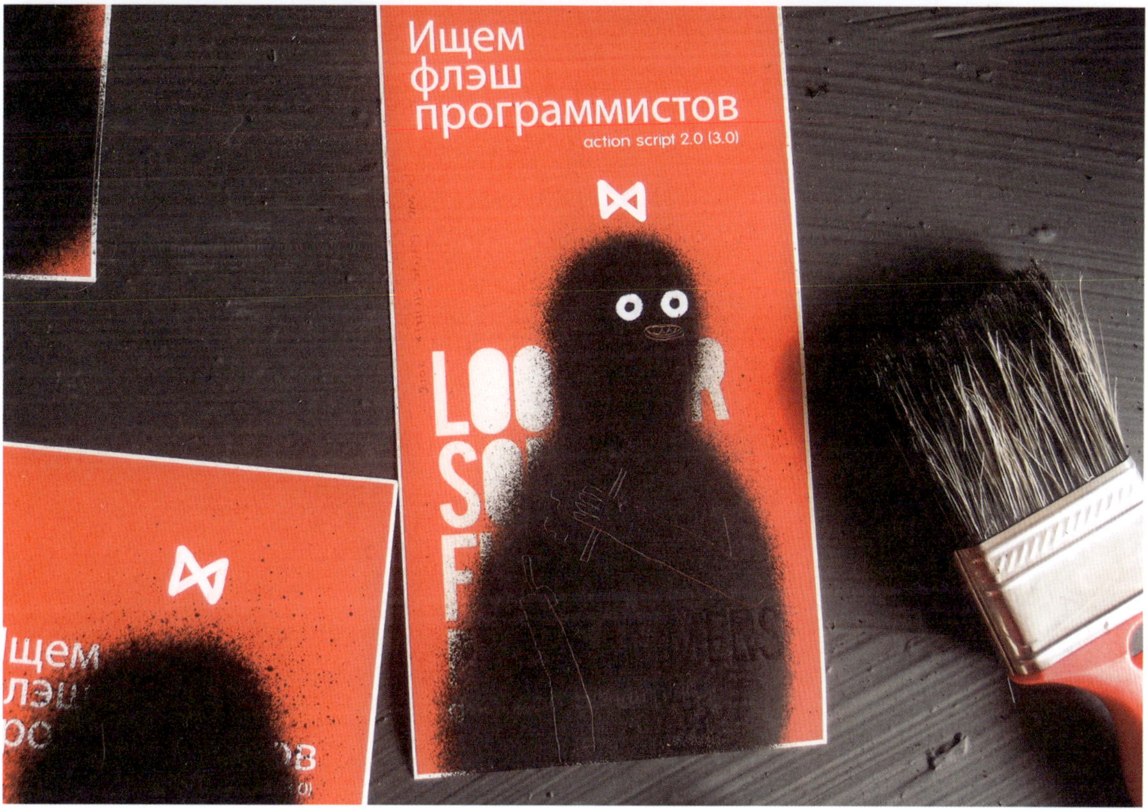

Ищем
флэш
программистов
action script 2.0 (3.0)

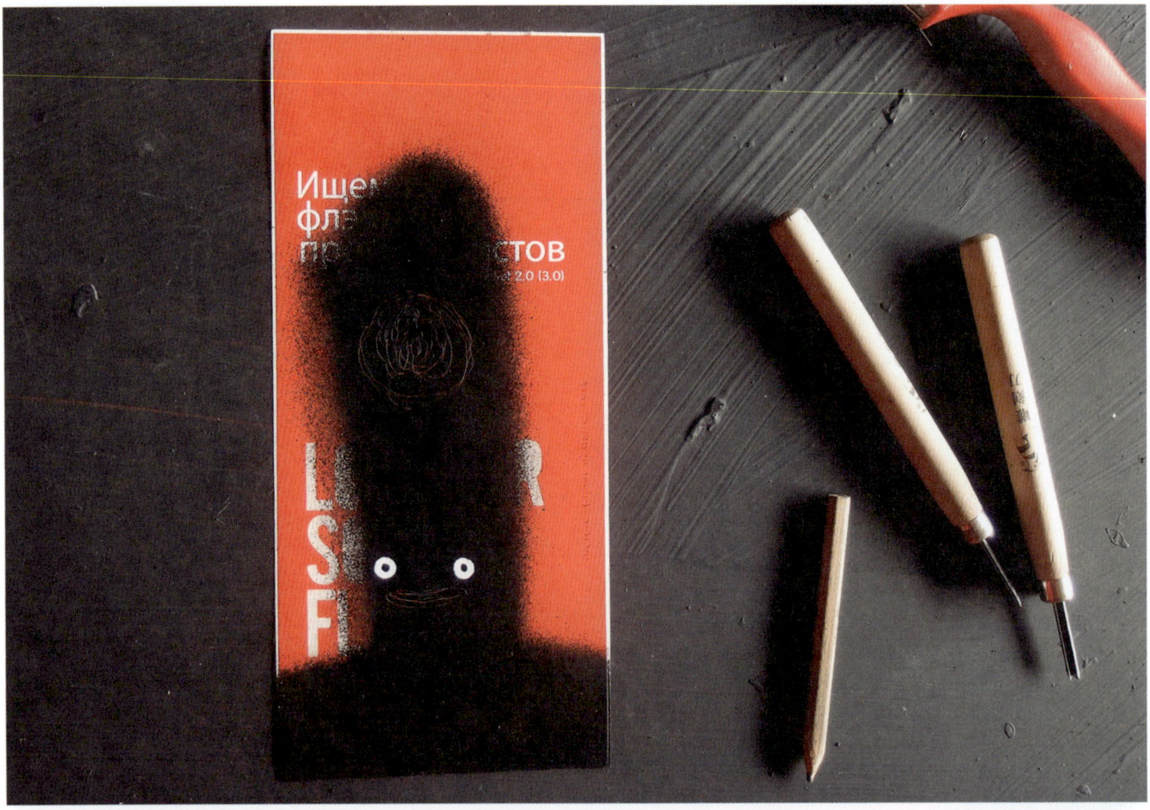

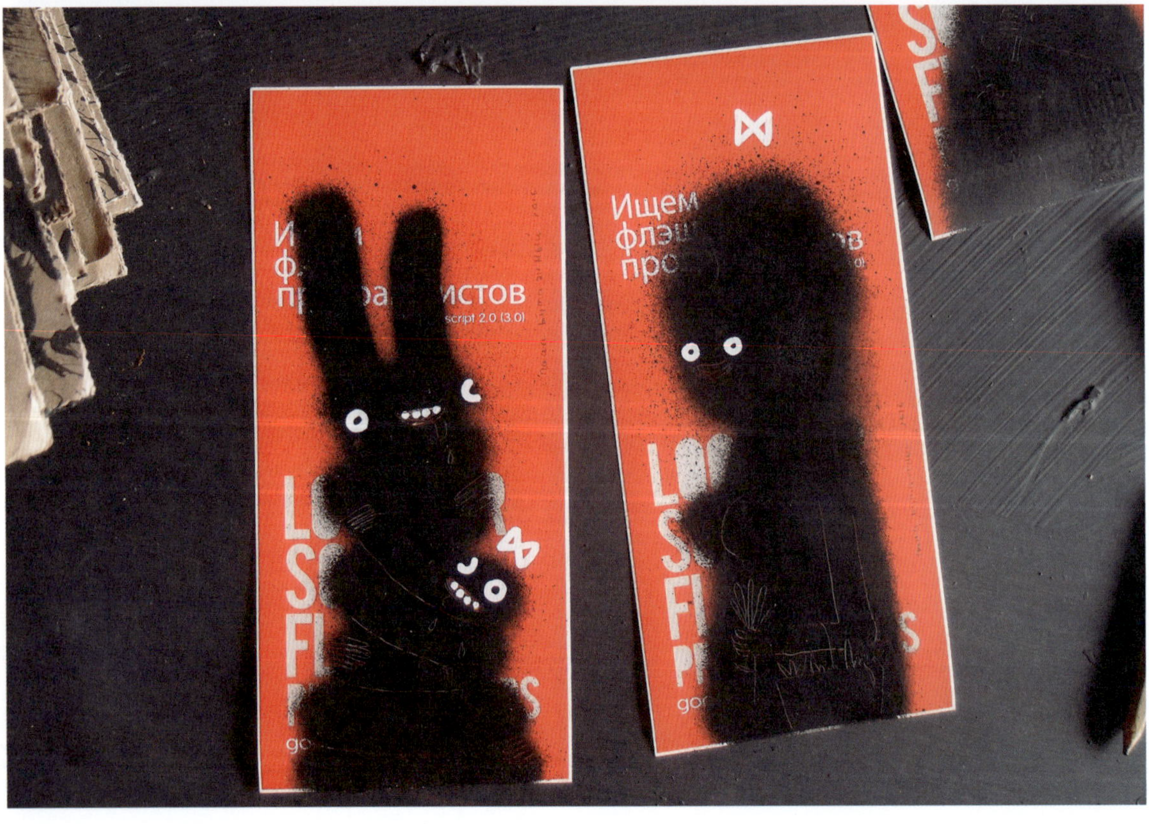

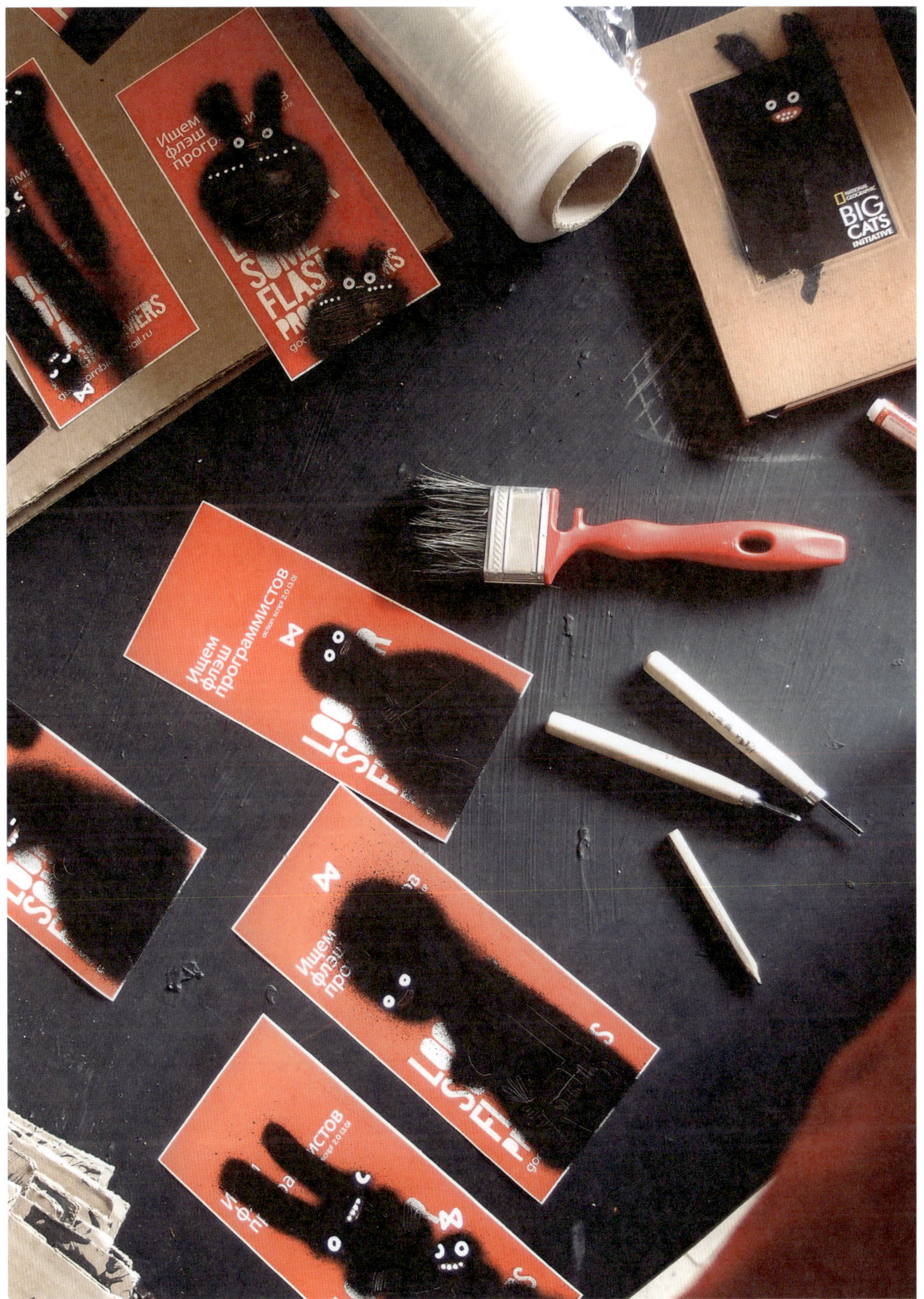
Ищем флэш программистов
action script 2.0 (3.0)
BIG CATS INITIATIVE

REMEMBER THE CHILDHOOD

Designer : Wang Bowei

This project, themed "Remember the Childhood", showcased the designer's memories of his close contact with family members, nature and the world, together with his introspection on today's social problems like war, interpersonal relationship and environment.

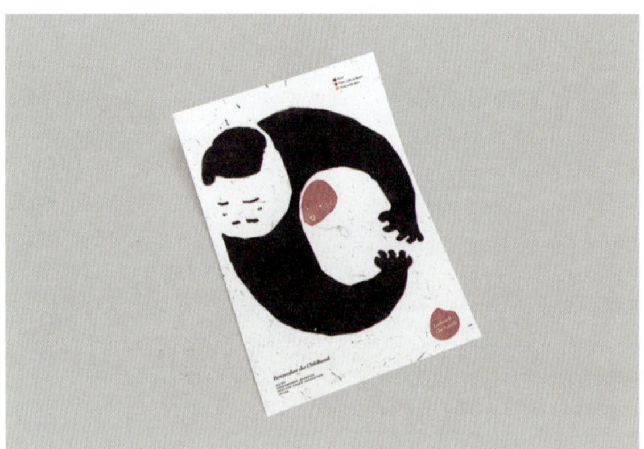

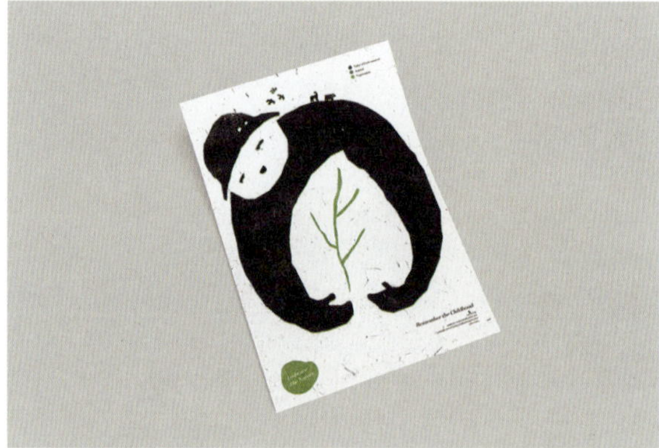

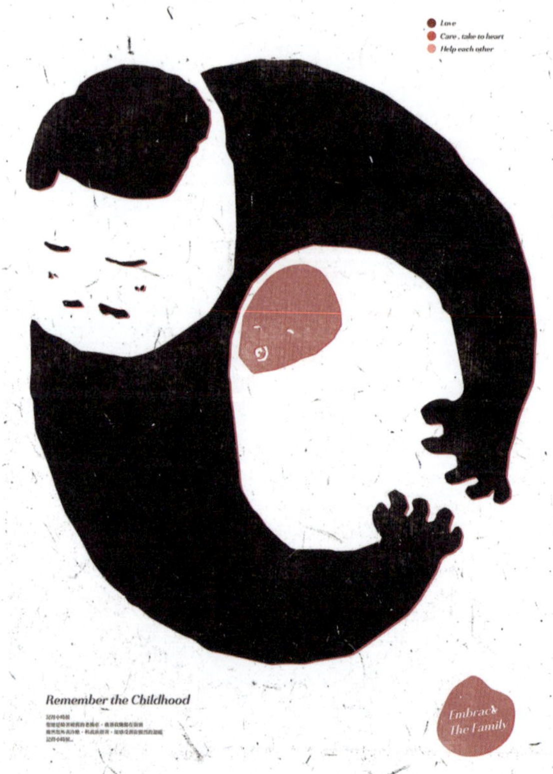

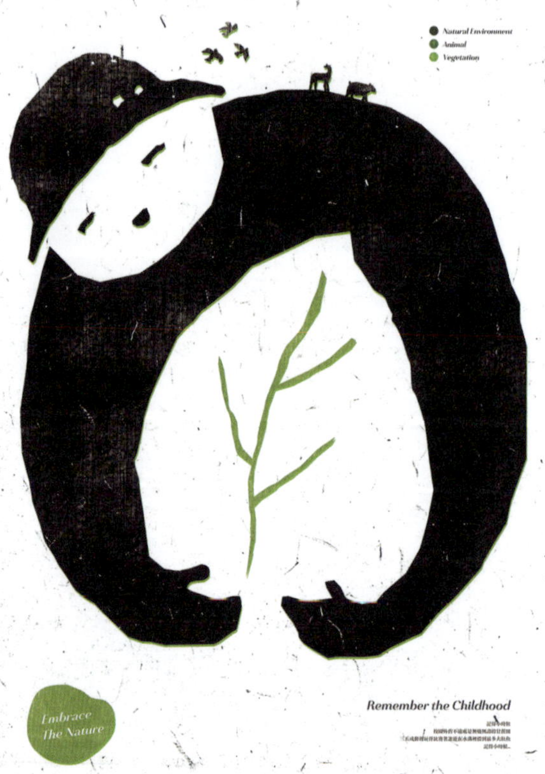

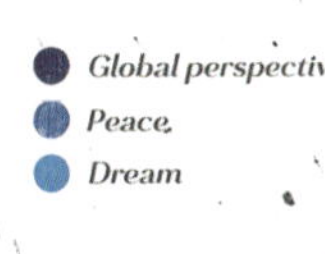

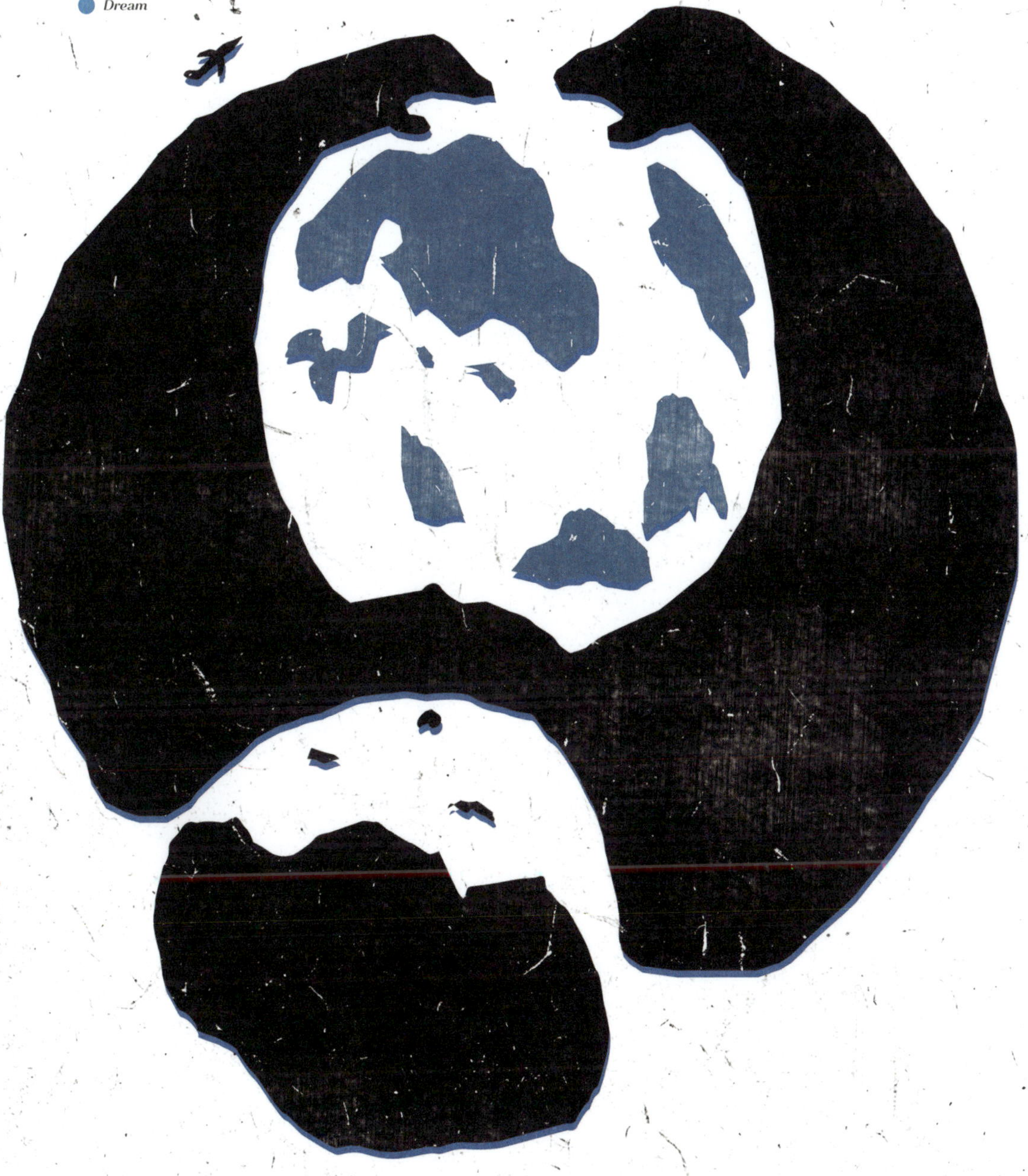

Remember the Childhood

記得小時候
看著電視機裡的世界非常奇妙幻想在腦海打轉
大一點時吃著出國回來同學帶回的珍貴零食
記得小時候...

Embrace The World

FAST SOUL, SLOW BODY, BROKEN HEART

Designer : Shu Yu Tsai

The designer believed that what was lost couldn't be as perfect as it once was even after its return, just like a body without a soul that couldn't be as clean as before. He put irregular concave lines on the album cover, producing seemingly imperfect perfection.

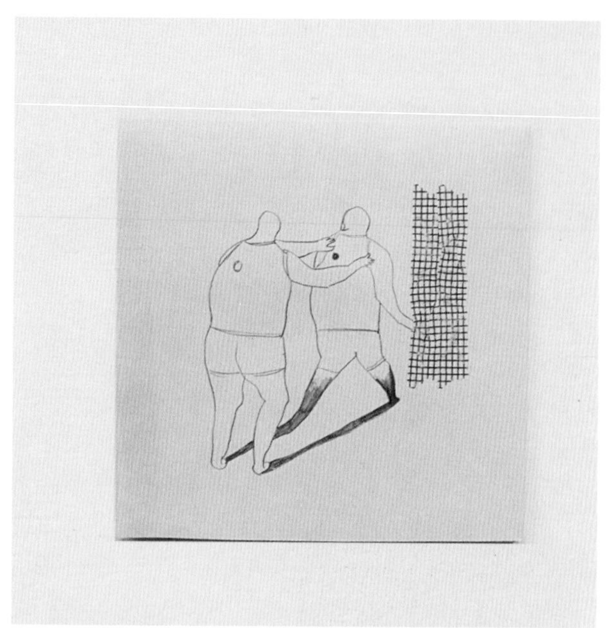

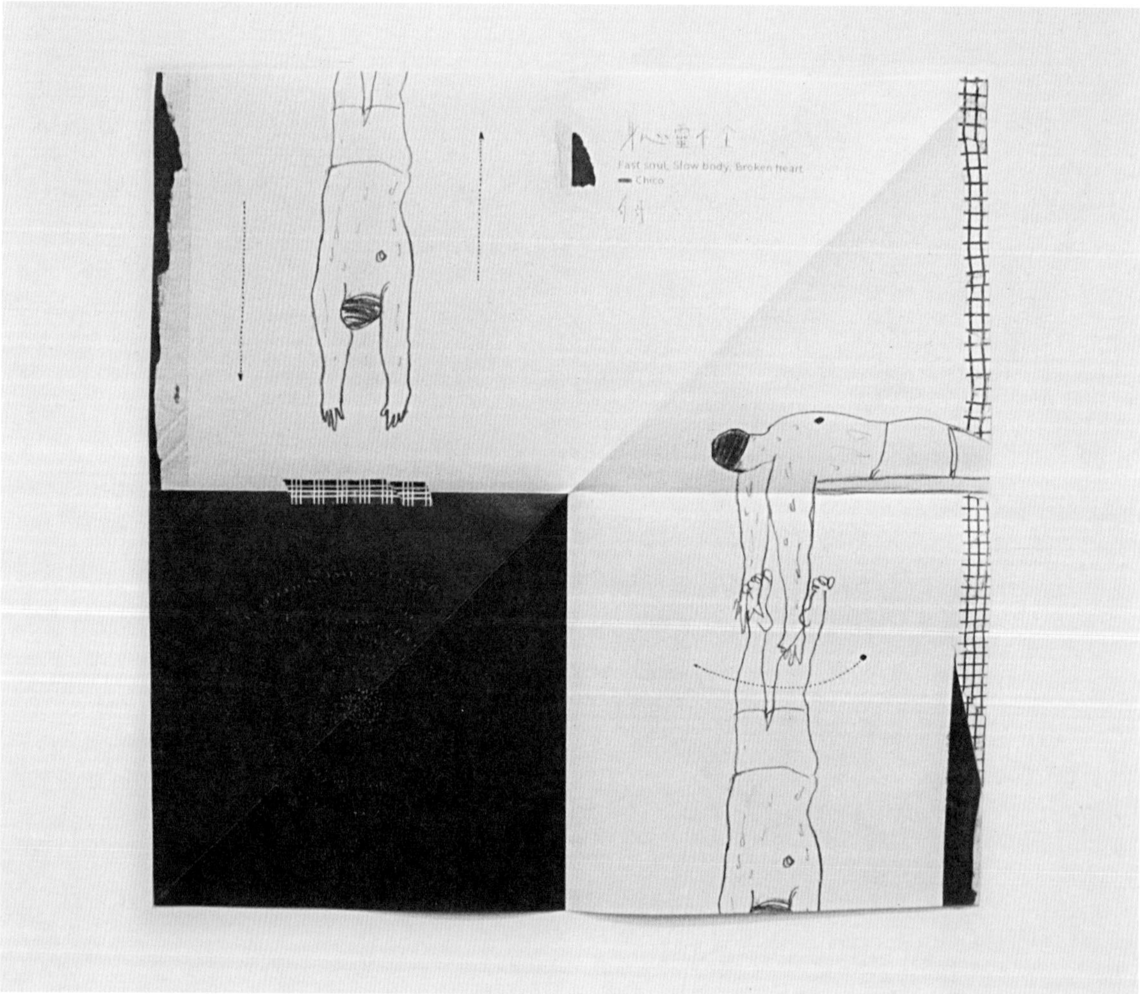

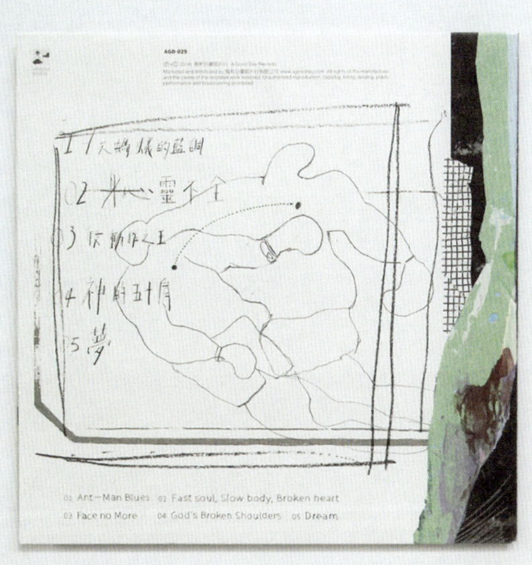

01 Ant-Man Blues
02 Fast soul, Slow body, Broken heart
03 Face no More
04 God's Broken Shoulders
05 Dream

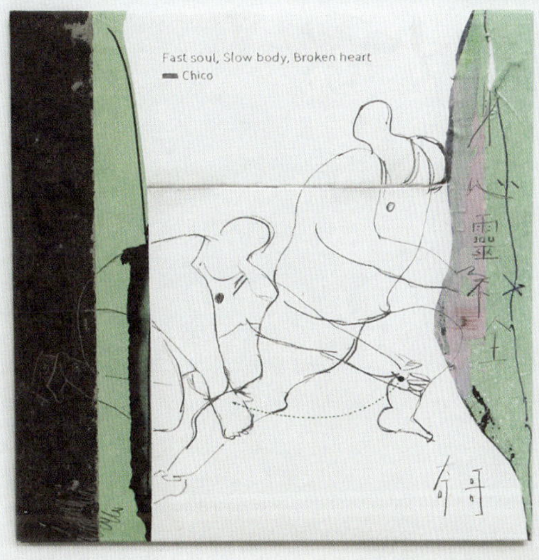

Fast soul, Slow body, Broken heart
Chico

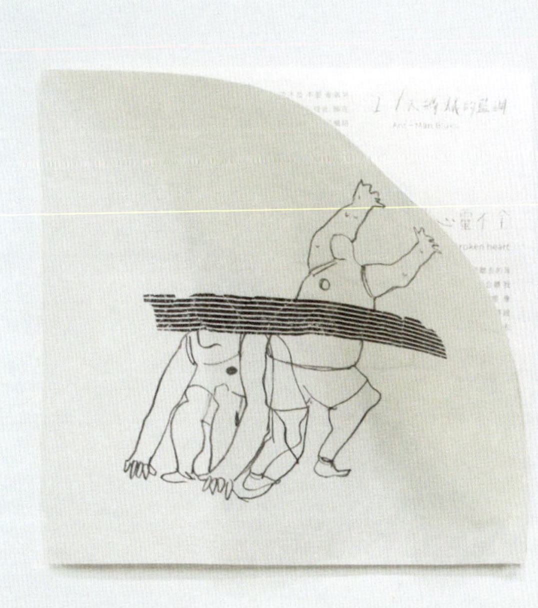

Ant-Man Blues

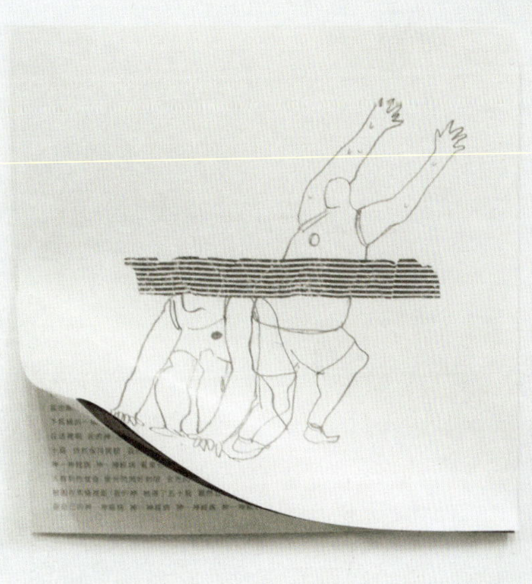

PIBU

Designer : Yeonjin Park

Pibu (pee-bu, means skin in korean) is an education kit that deals with skin to skin contact, namely sexual activity. The most important factors that the designer took into account while making Pibu were metaphor of design and portability, because the main goal was to make a product that can be put near bed or desk and to help grown-ups explore and love their own body much more.

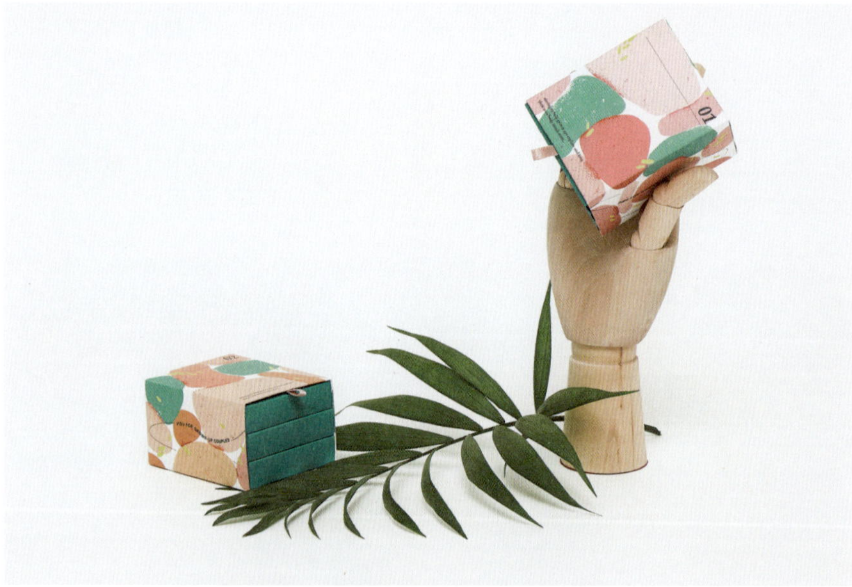

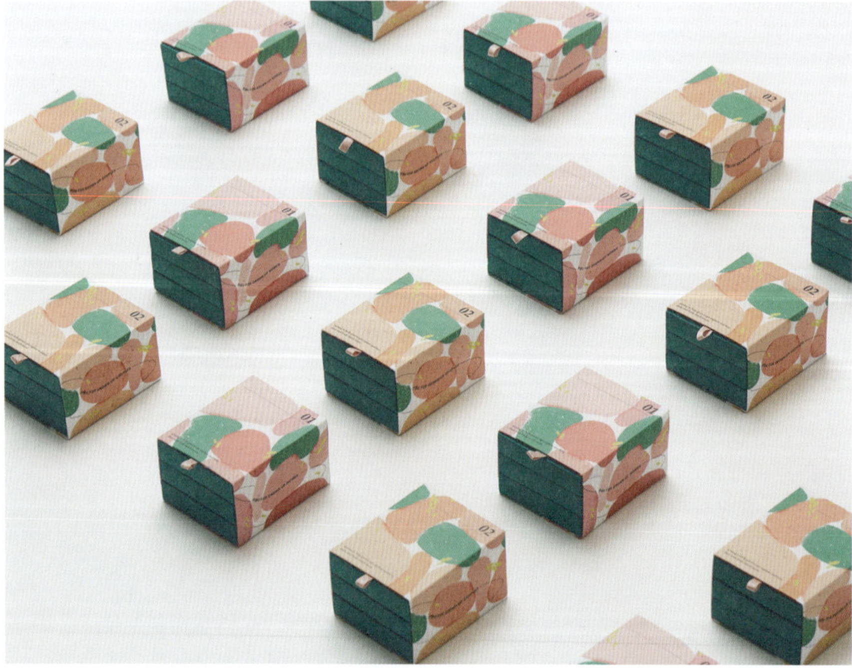

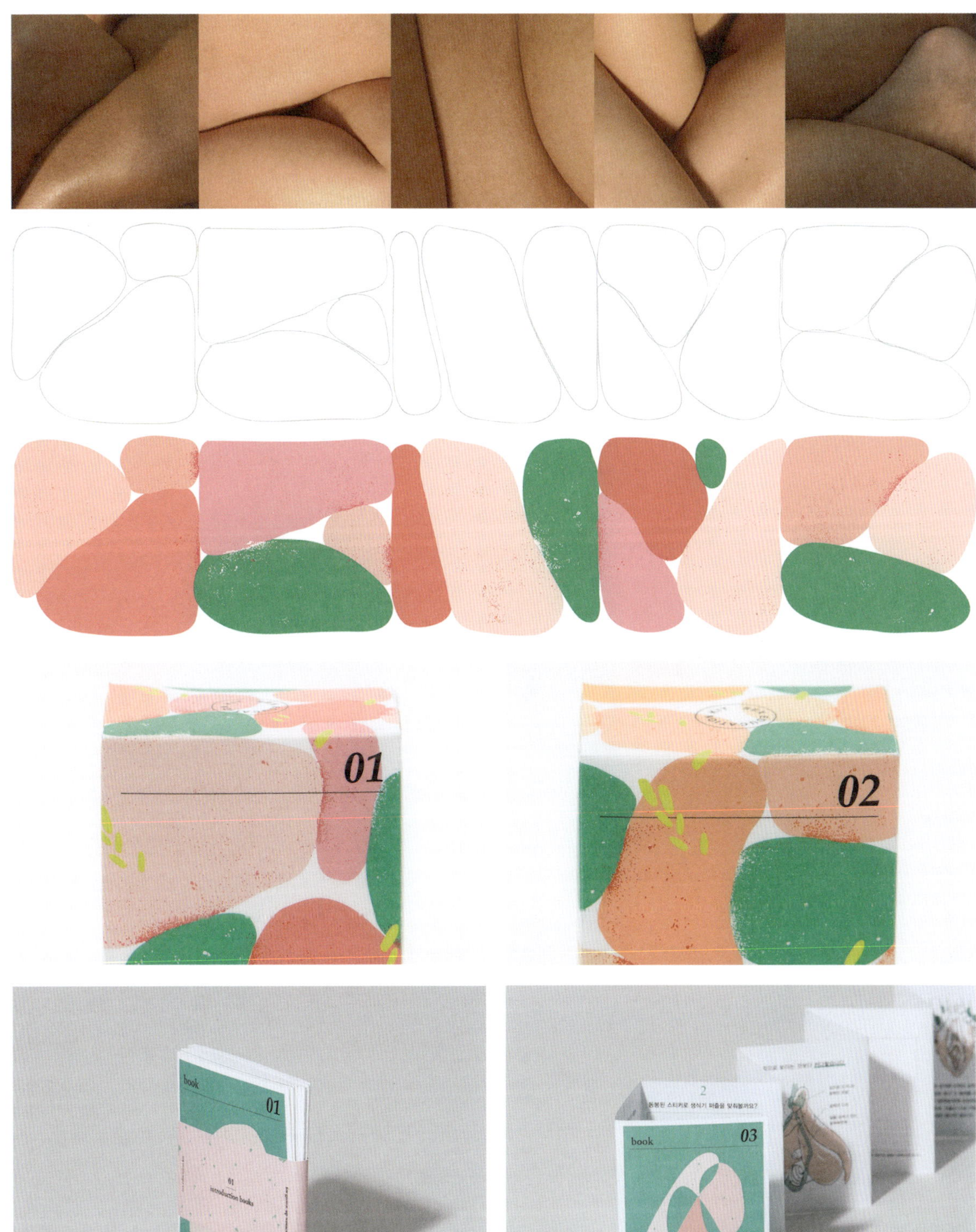
01
02
book
01
01
introduction books
2
동봉된 스티커로 생식기 퍼즐을 맞춰볼까요?
book
03

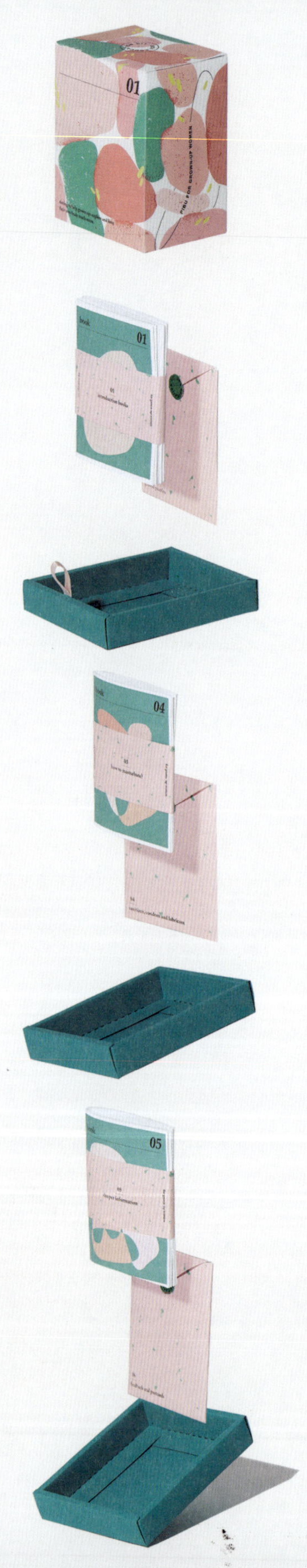

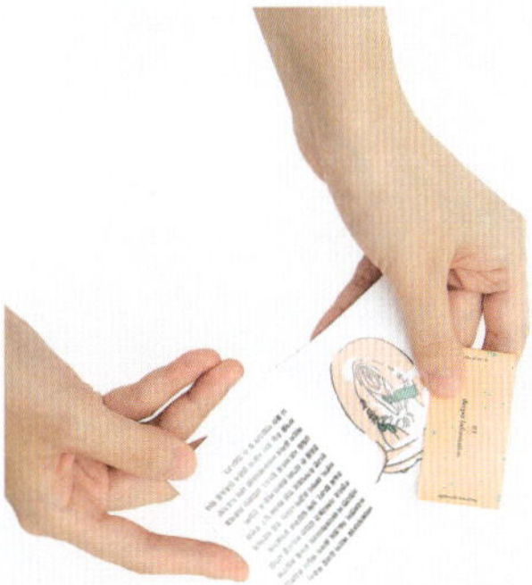

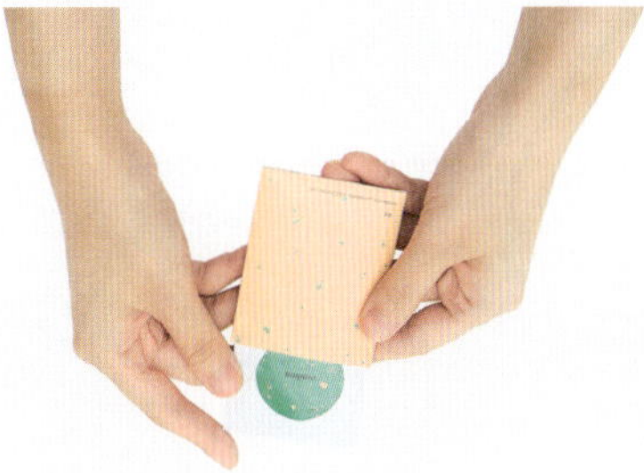

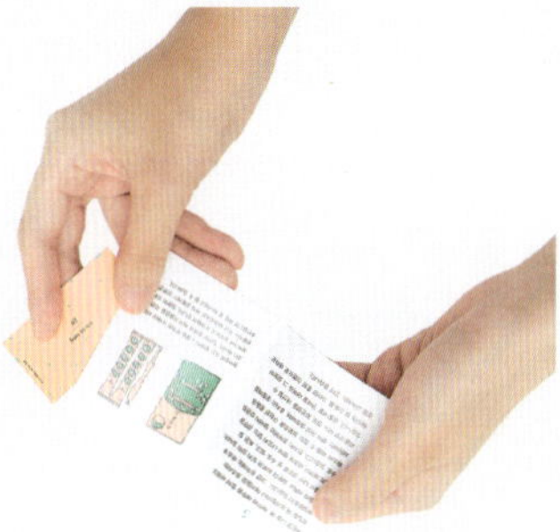

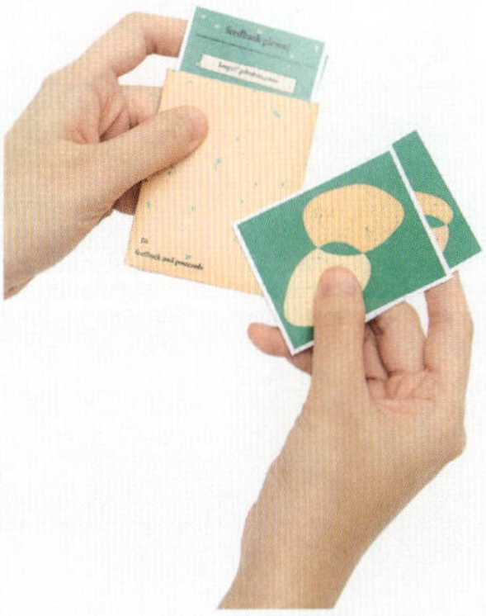

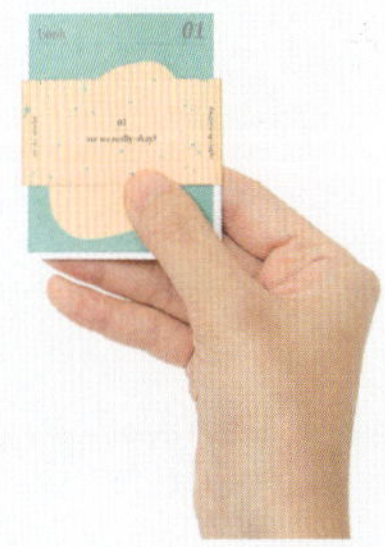

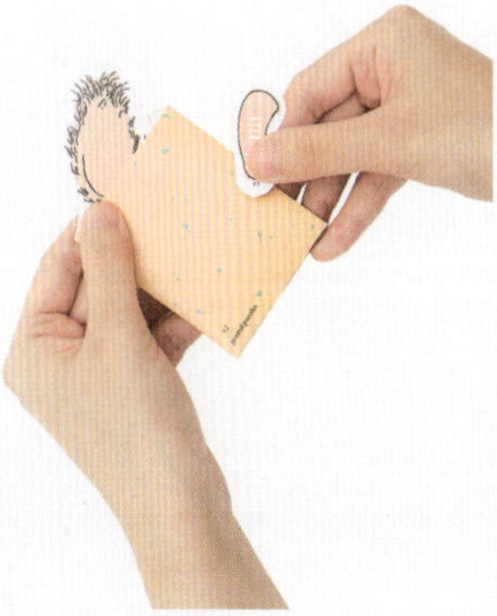

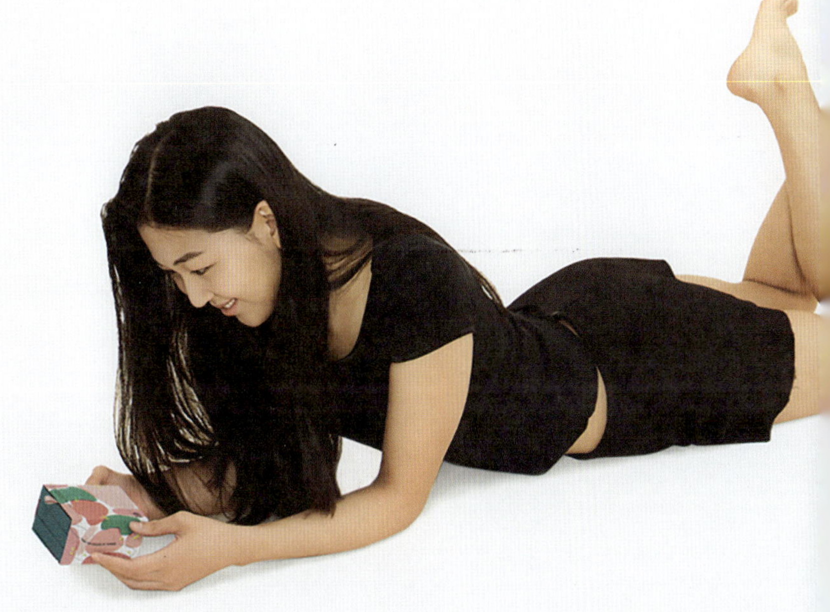

HI, BAYEN!

Designer : Lan-Zi sin

This is a record of a rural settlement with only 9 households in it. The designer believes that everyone's life is like a song that can be memorized forever. Thus she chose to present the design in the specific way of "silent album".

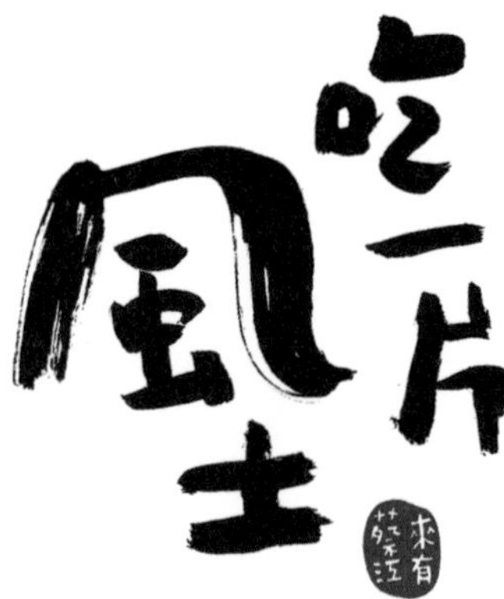

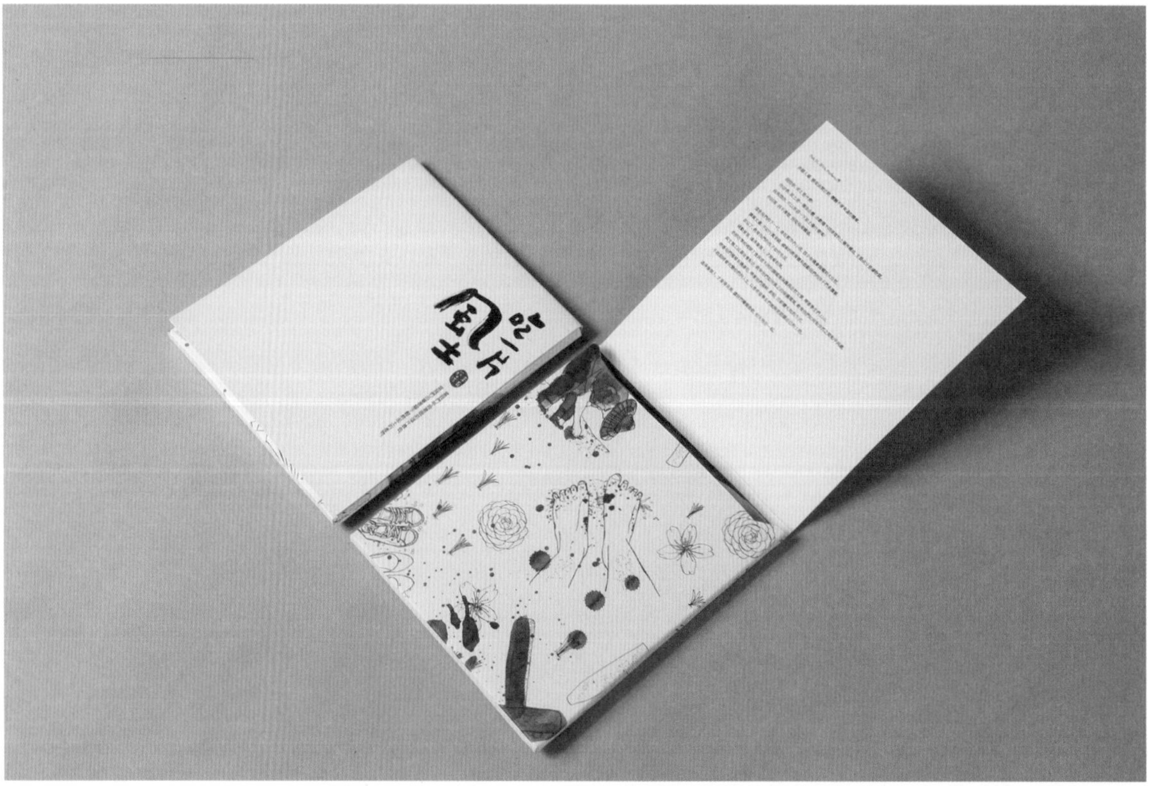

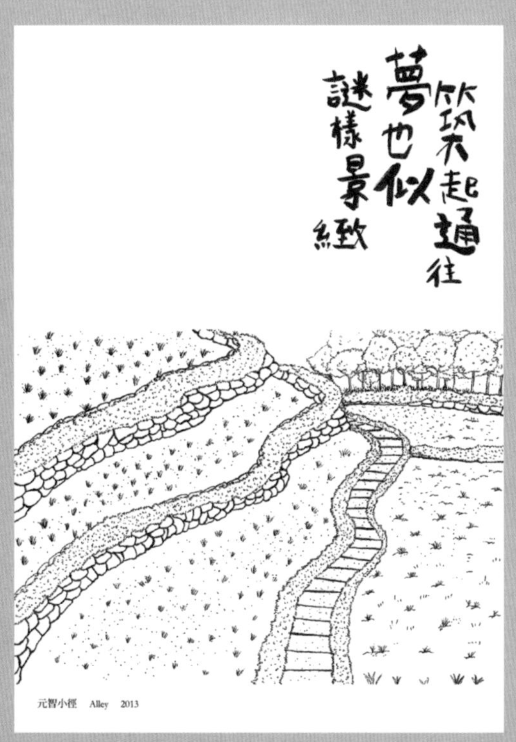

元智小徑　Alley　2013

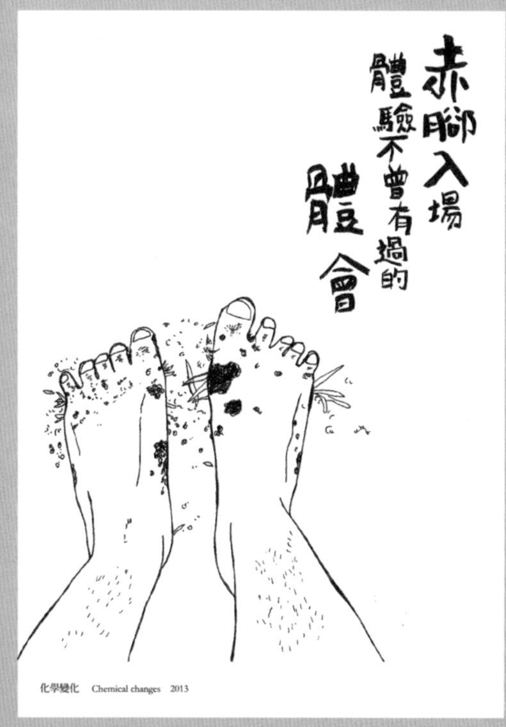

化學變化　Chemical changes　2013

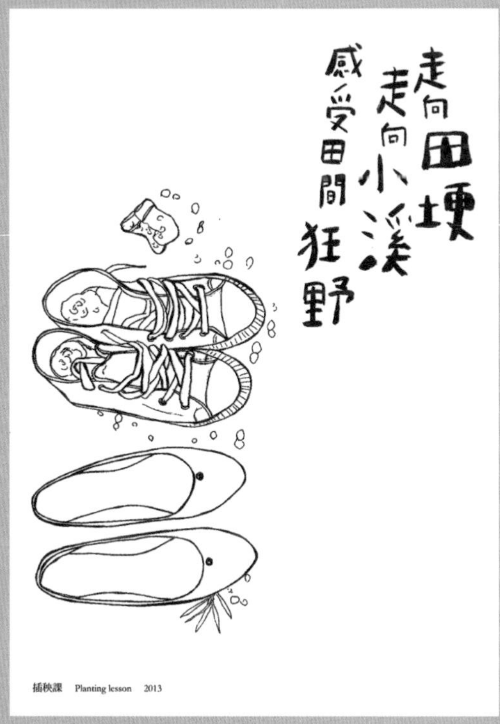

插秧課　Planting lesson　2013

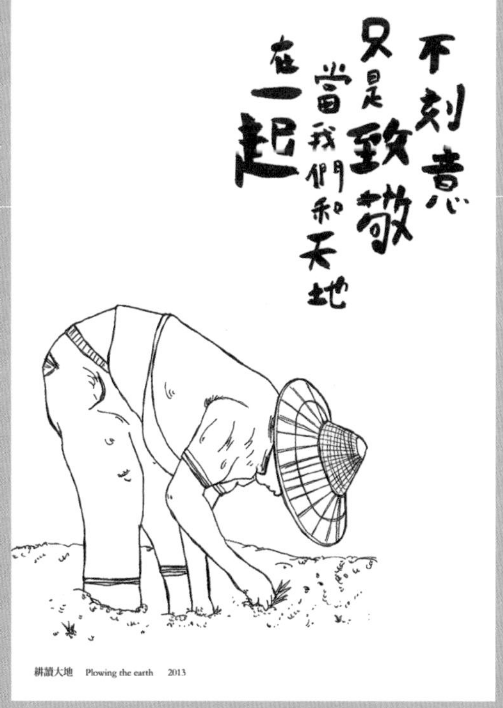

耕讀大地　Plowing the earth　2013

耕讀大地

環境保護和自然文學開課了
在五年前　學究裡的服務課程不免俗的
以服務人群為志向　老師希望這堂課不同以往
沒有設限　去親近大地　了解大地　耕讀大地
學習人與環境和諧共存的方式
賴以生存的土地同一本厚實的書
那麼置身其中　就是了解這本書最好的方式
彎腰生活　懂得感謝
彎腰生活　懂得知足
彎腰生活　懂得常樂
不刻意佈道　只是低頭彎腰像土地致敬
這種虔誠會傳染　當我們和天地在一起

元智小徑

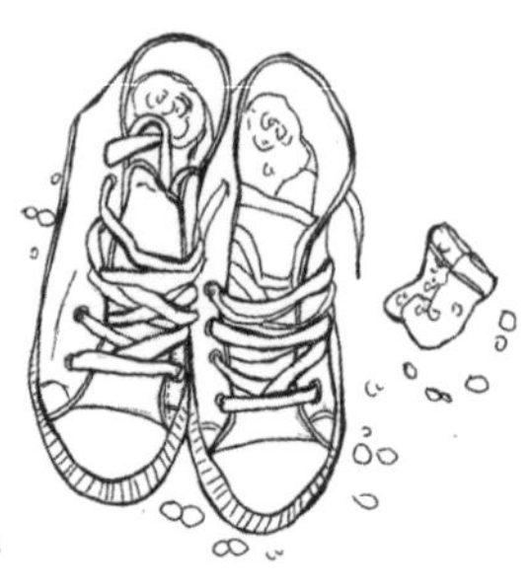

阡陌縱橫　蜿蜒的石板小路
阡陌縱橫　斗大的蓮花露珠
在下著滂沱大雨的早晨
窸窸窣窣的黃色雨衣 列隊進入泥地
從無到有　片片厚重石板
築起通往夢也似謎樣景致
從無到有　多多含苞蓮花
築起通往夢也似謎樣景致
親手種下　只為腳下那片風土
所謂前人種樹　後人乘涼
我想是這樣形容的吧　感謝他們
感謝這群默默的無名英雄
小徑也是無名的
腳下的石板　沒有人知道是誰的汗
腳下的石板　沒有人知道是誰的淚

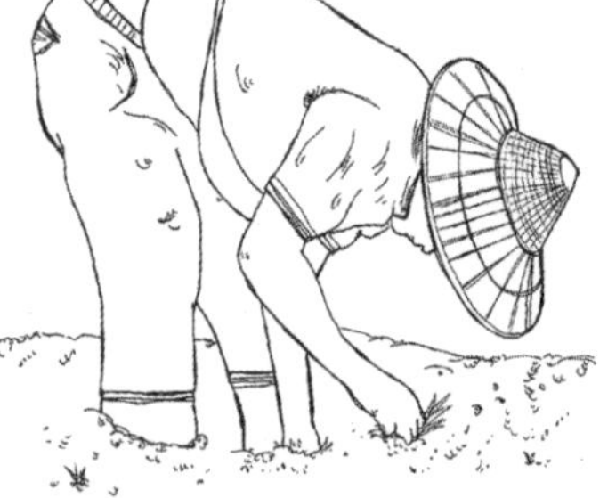

插秧課

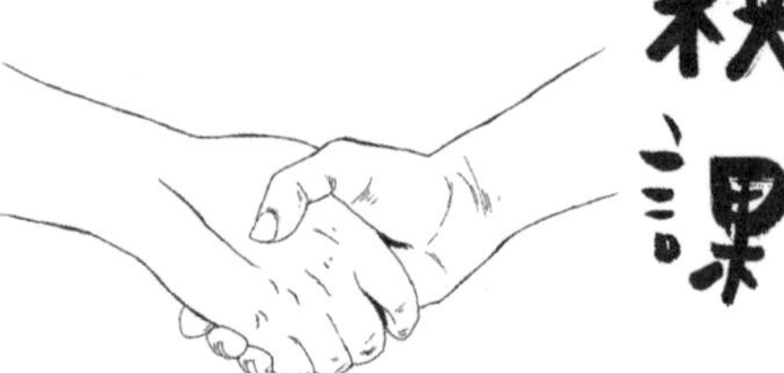

同學　你上過插秧課了嗎
真是有趣的對白
老師所開的這門課可炙手著
選課是場征戰
同學們總不記得課程名稱
只想著插秧
對城市長大的我們來說　是最新鮮不過的
向第一次穿著會發出啾啾聲的鞋子一樣
開心地蹦蹦跳跳
脫下你的鞋　脫下你的襪
走向田埂　走向小溪
感受田間狂野　蛙鳴　鳥叫
交響樂順勢而起　在田間

化學變化

應該這樣講
讓學生對於自己的土地比從前深刻許多
讓學生明白基金會的努力為何
認識起土地　關心起土地　參與起土地
赤腳入場　體演不會有過的體會
人生應該要多點眼界
要過得像個人　看得見美
學生們透過這堂課　認識自己的土地
雖然土生土長　但卻陌生
對很多事物都是
藉由這次的體驗　或許會起些化學變化
深化自己生命的養分

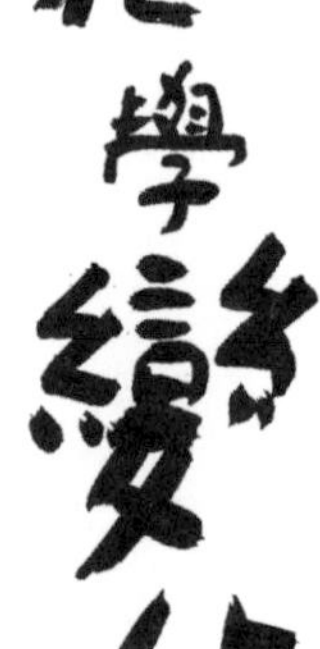

維繫

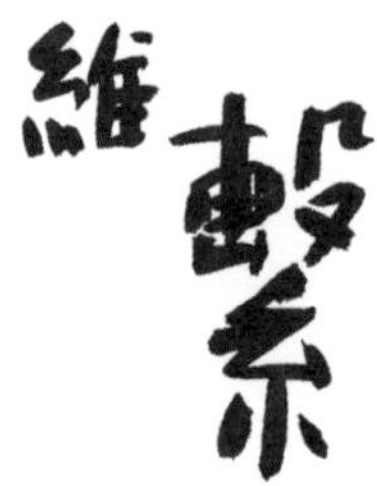

一段關係的建立　需要長久的經營
深耕方能永續
對老師而言　不為去而去
不打擾居民的生活
只為獻上單純的心　去感受大地
請基金會執行長先給學生上堂行前課
向學子們傳達基金會對於這片土地的執著
辛苦耕耘　只為無憾的心
學生的回饋是一直做下去的動力　不是為了做而做
看著學生滿車收穫　老師也好欣慰
每每上山　都是一趟舟車勞頓
苦是一定有的
但跟基金會所做的努力比起來　這些不算什麼
只願彼此都滿有收穫

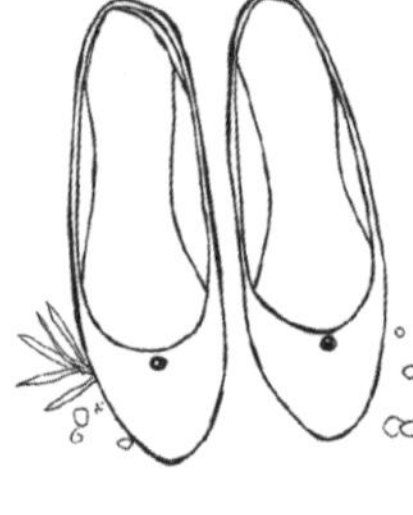

五天幾年

鋪路　顆顆斗大汗珠
分不清是雨水還是汗水
割稻　層層隨風搖曳稻浪
插秧　株株青禾期待茁壯
種蓮　朵朵蓮花期待綻放
五年青春　只換不悔
用心感受　滿車收穫　驀然回首
明白自己得到好多

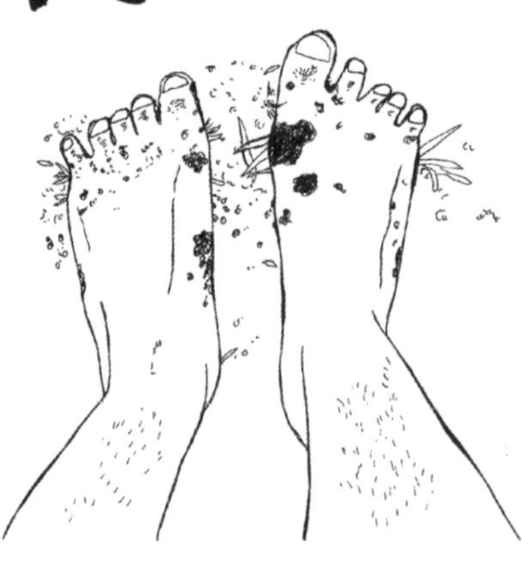

回家

回家吧　大地母親正聲聲呼喚著
回家二字對一般人來說是句再普通不過的話了
但對於十幾歲就離開家鄉在外打拚十多年的蔡文照來說
不知在心理歷經多少次的天人交戰
故鄉人　或許近鄉情更怯吧
當初　機緣是生態工法基金會要請我一起復育家鄉的水梯田
由於人口的外移　年長者選擇較不費工且高經濟價格的作物
如番薯　花卉　樹栽　蔬菜　因此水田便漸漸消失了
現實面來說　八煙一年一獲　種稻需要大量的人力
八煙的年輕人都到外地去討生活了
只剩下老人家　稻子又很怕颱風
颱風一來　一年的心血也就作廢了
不得已才改種旱作
基金會的熱情讓蔡文照好不感動
經多番考慮　辭去原本相對安定穩妥的工作　回家去
八煙是我的故鄉　我的家　我要回來盡自己微薄的心力　他說
眼神透露他堅定的心
台灣人骨子裡總橫著毅力　傻氣　單純卻有力量

歡迎來坐

霜降　天微亮的清晨六點
我們驅車前往台北後花園　陽明山
草山風　竹子湖雨　金包里大路
向來是形容陽明山景物的台灣諺語
很少人知道在陽金公路七點二公里處有一小入口
通往一小聚落
那裏保留了台灣傳統的農村生活
其純樸的自然景觀與在地鄉土人文足以令人醉心
入口處有著一塊不明顯的木製招牌
斑駁的字跡　寫著
八煙聚落歡迎來坐
旅人們旅行的意義不外乎發現難得驚喜
來趟八煙　你就明白

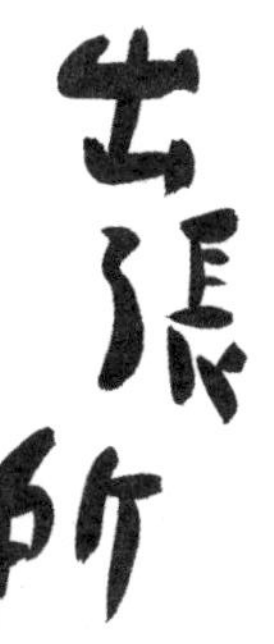

出張所

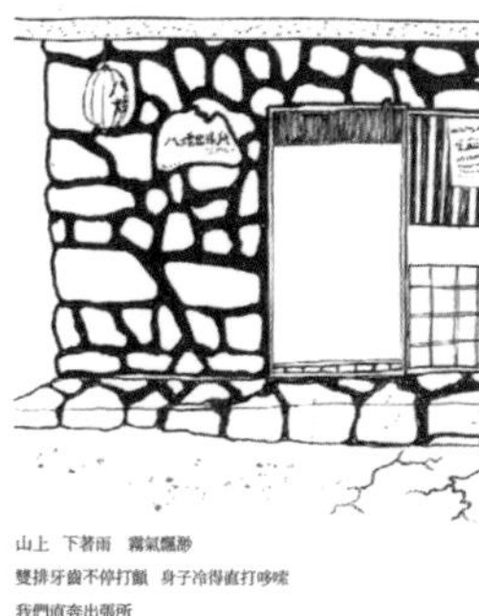

山上　下著雨　霧氣飄渺
雙排牙齒不停打顫　身子冷得直打哆嗦
我們直奔出張所
這是我們第三次造訪了
蔡先生依舊熱情的招呼我們
來　喝茶　剛燒得
出張是日語　指在地服務站之意
基金會租下這古老的砌石屋 做為展示當地人文生態的地點
所裡總飄散著陣陣茶香
是田間野草　大葉田香　真的好香
在冷冷的冬日　一杯熱茶　溫暖訪客的心

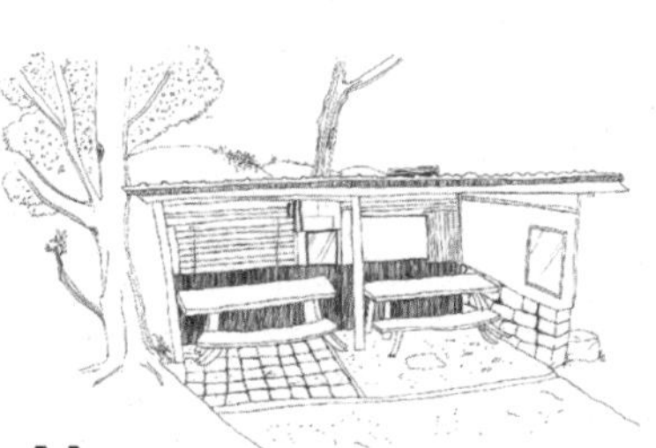

共享

日日　從日出到日落
和泥土親密為伴的母親
這樣講
清爽的風　是最好的電扇
稻田　是最好看的風景
水聲和鳥聲　是最好聽的歌
蔡先生和村民們想與大伙共享八煙的美好
八煙的水　八煙的田　在這片田地上
用一生的汗水　灌溉

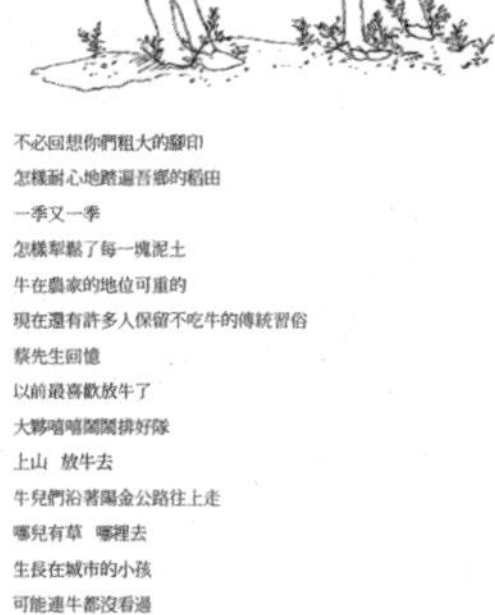

放牛去

不必回想你們粗大的腳印
怎樣耐心地踏遍吾鄉的稻田
一季又一季
怎樣犁鬆了每一塊泥土
牛在農家的地位可重的
現在還有許多人保留不吃牛的傳統習俗
蔡先生回憶
以前最喜歡放牛了
大夥嘻嘻鬧鬧排好隊
上山　放牛去
牛兒們沿著陽金公路往上走
哪兒有草　哪裡去
生長在城市的小孩
可能連牛都沒看過
只能從網路圖片或書本認識他們
殘酷點的
是從超市的生鮮販賣區看見它們部分的身驅
說起來有點感傷

導覽人

導覽員
似乎是個常見的職業
博物館導覽員　景點導覽員
而蔡先生現在的身分
也是一名導覽員
特別的是　他是
故鄉的導覽員
導覽八煙的美　八煙的水
導覽八煙的生態　導覽八煙的好
能為故鄉盡一份力
蔡先生好高興
閒暇之餘
整整地　除除草
能讓更多的人知道八煙　了解八煙
好不快樂

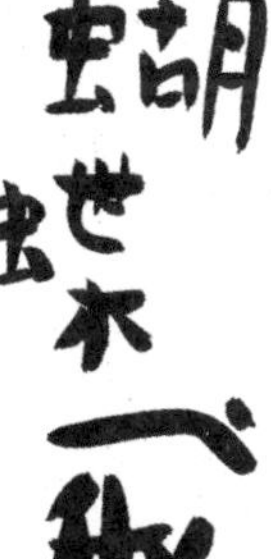

蝴蝶飛

蝴蝶在飛
飛在田埂間　飛在稻浪中
飛在花與花之間
仲夏是蝴蝶最多的時節
翩翩起舞在這山谷
夏季特別的導覽課程主角是蝴蝶
鳳蝶和青斑蝶是八煙最常見的種類
出張所還有著逗趣的標語
小心　蝶出沒
蝴蝶的魅力是大小朋友都無法抵擋的吧
蝴蝶在飛
飛在田埂間　飛在稻浪中
飛在花與花之間

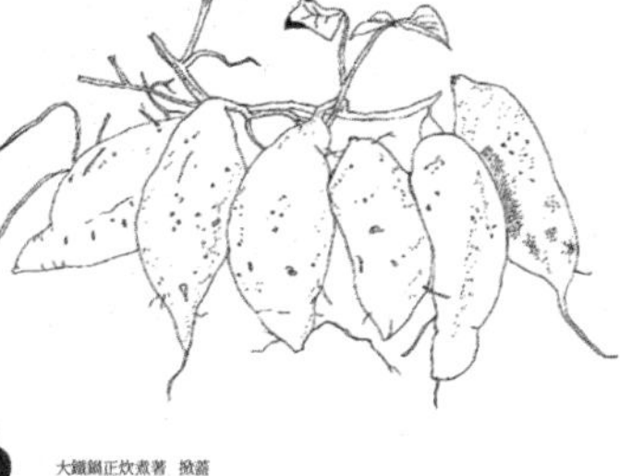

故鄉味

大鐵鍋正炊煮著　掀蓋
撲鼻的地瓜香
台農57號　黃皮黃肉　鬆軟的口感　濃郁的香味
台農66號　紅皮紅肉　綿密的口感　很甜
台北打拼數十載　每回吃到外頭的地瓜
總會讓蔡先生想起八煙
想起滿身汗　滿身泥
在田地挖起地瓜的感動
八煙受地形及氣候影響
地下水位高　水質清澈
因此許多農作都很好吃
打哪都有地瓜　沒有好壞　只有不同
但還是最愛八煙那一味
那味　甚好

O'PHELIA CRAFT BEER

Studio : VOLTA Brand Shaping Studio

The label for O'phelia was designed to reflect a young Celtic woman's life. The daughter of a warrior and master brewer, O'phelia decided to surprise her father with a perfect beer formula. But her father did't return from his quest and she died, sad and somber, next to her precious beer barrels. The label as well as the box mirror O'phelia's personality: strong on the outside but gentle and pure inside.

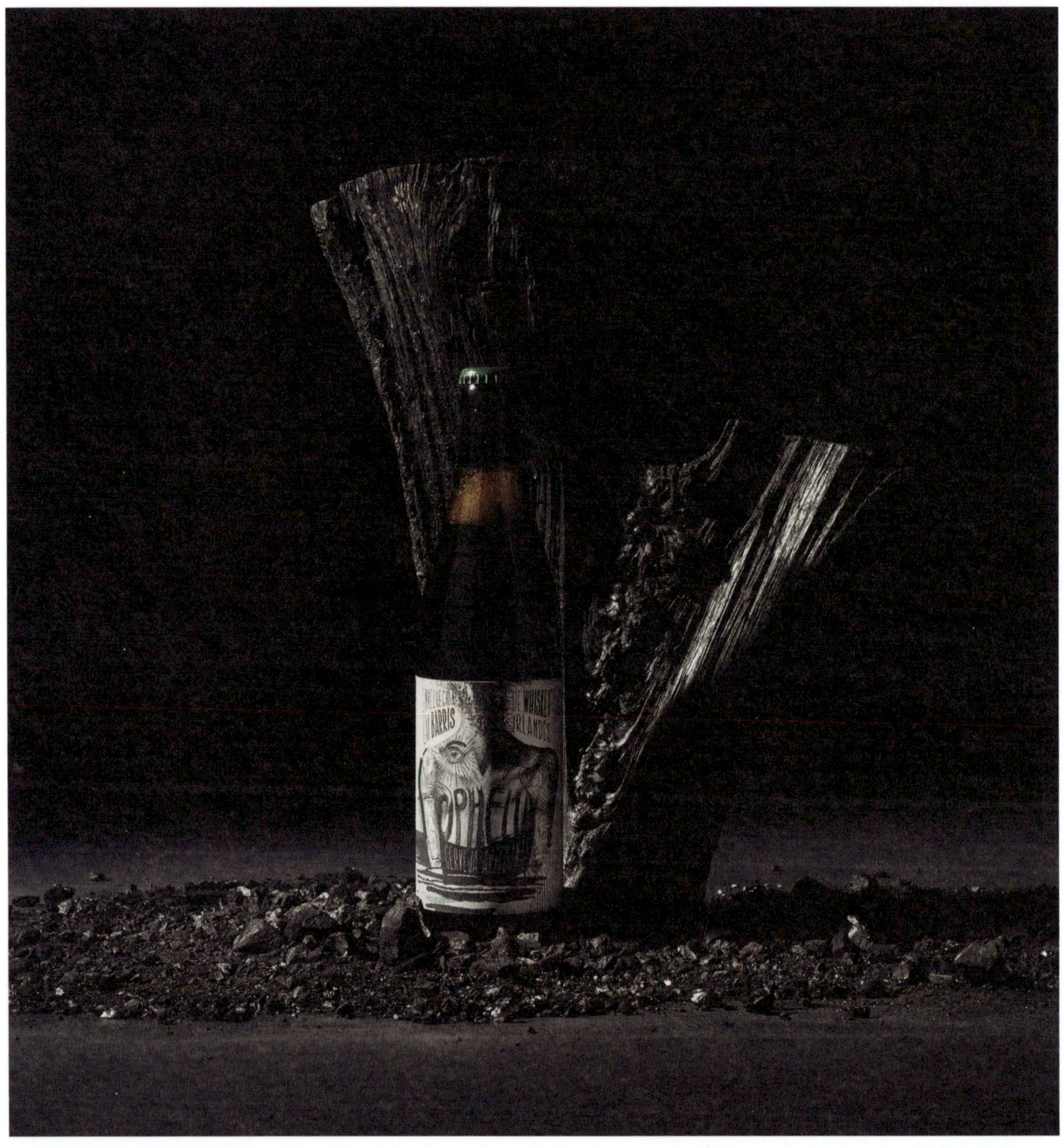

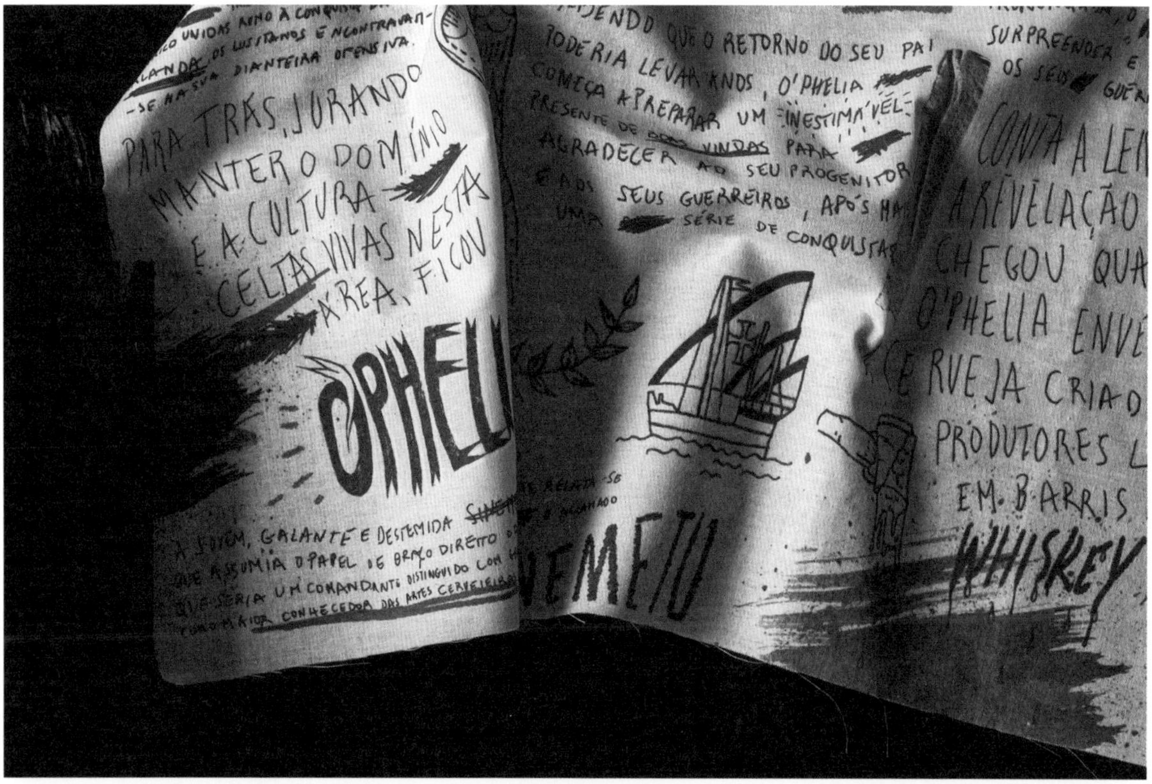
PARA TRÁS, JURANDO
MANTER O DOMÍNIO
E A CULTURA
CELTAS VIVAS NESTA
ÁREA, FICOU
A JOVEM, GALANTE E DESTEMIDA
PODERIA LEVAR ANOS, O'PHELIA
COMEÇA A PREPARAR UM INESTIMÁVEL
AGRADECER AO SEU PROGENITOR
SEUS GUERREIROS
SURPREENDER
A REVELAÇÃO
PRODUTORES
EM BARRIS
WHISKEY

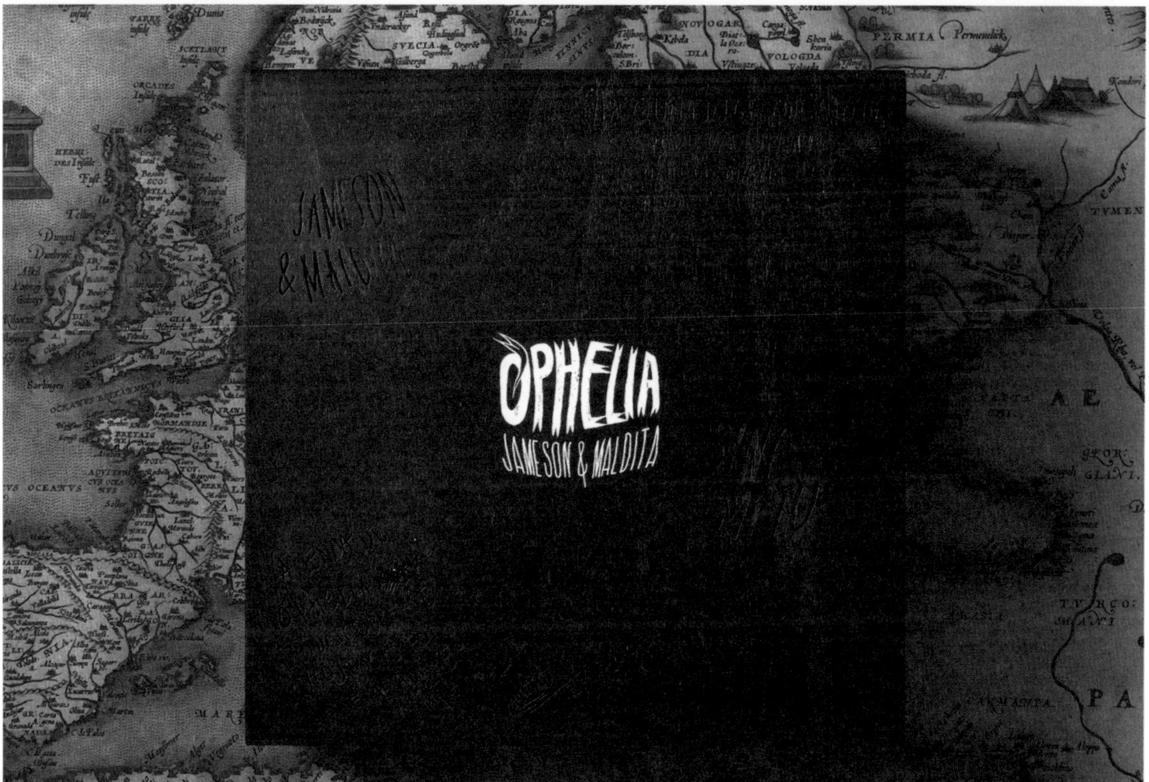
OPHELIA
JAMESON & MALDITA

ONEGROOVE

Designer : Yeye Weller

This is a series of LP cover design for a German record label who was in need of a conspicuous artwork instead of the commonly clean design. To further this idea, every release has a new color scheme and a high recognition factor.

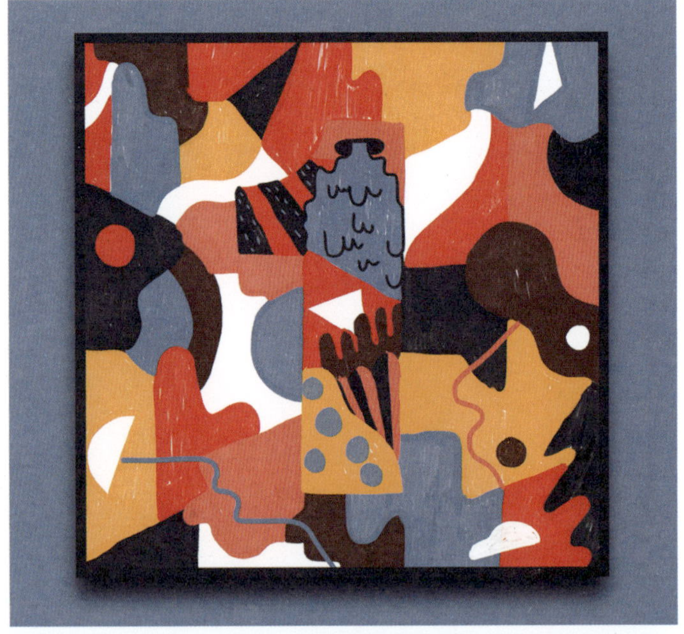

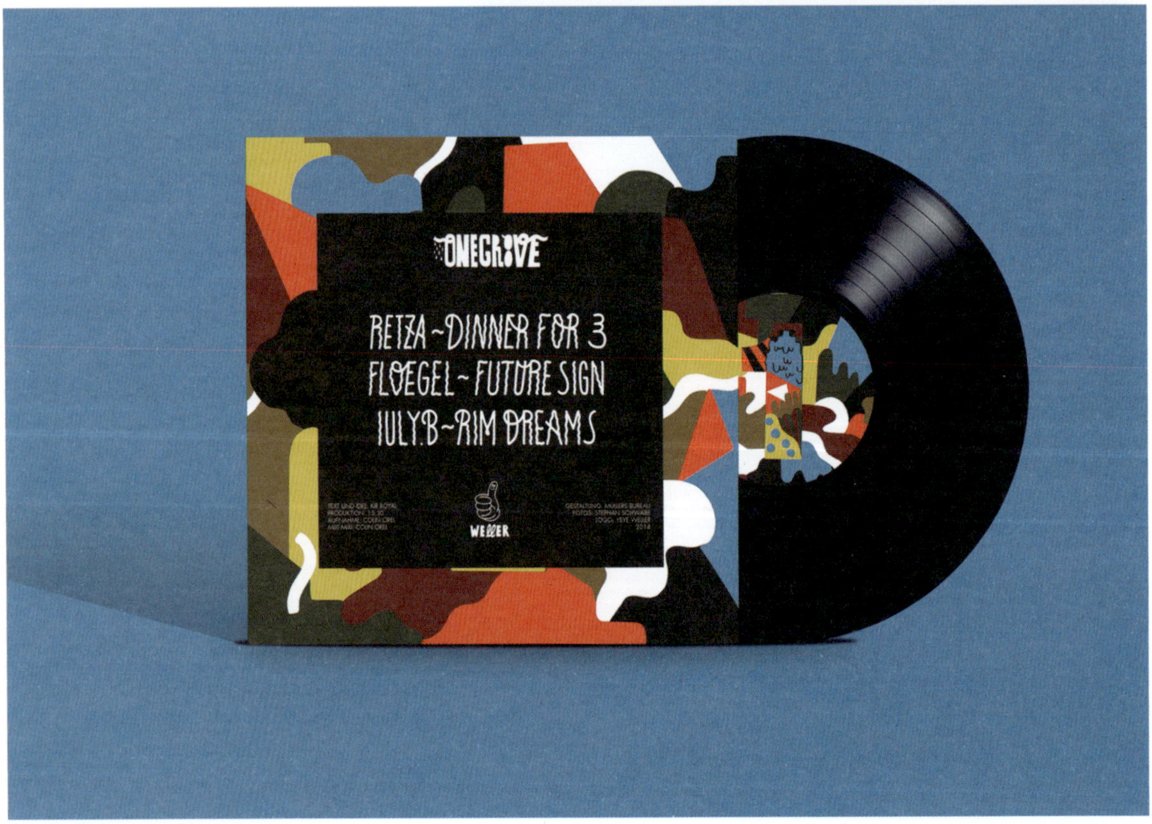

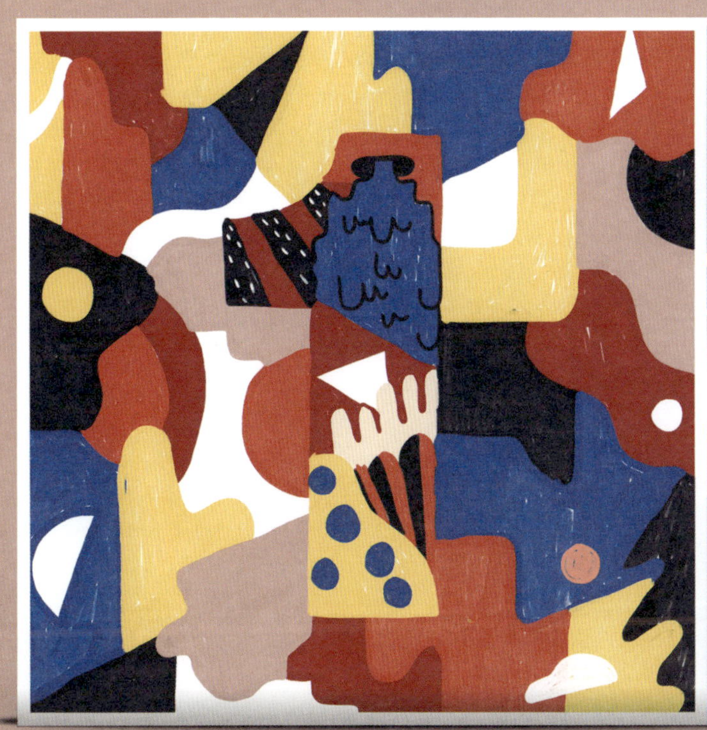

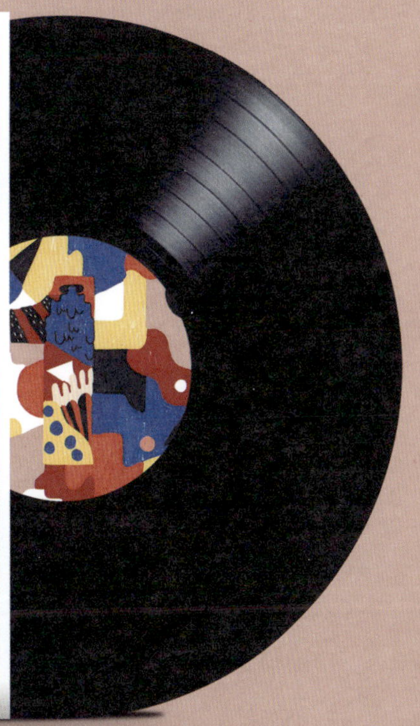

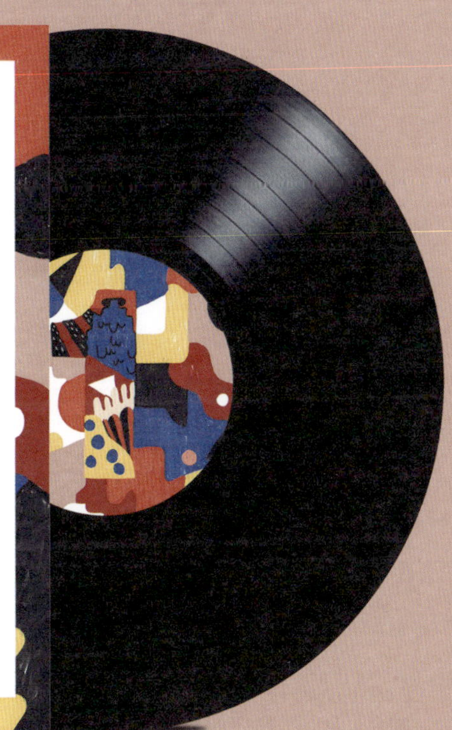
ONEGROOVE
a
RETZA ~ DINNER FOR 3
b
FLOEGEL ~ FUTURE SIGN
IULY.B ~ RIM DREAMS
TEXT UND IDEE: KIR ROYAL
PRODUKTION: 15:30
AUFNAHME: COLIN OREL
MIXI MIXI: COLIN OREL
GESTALTUNG: MÜLLERS BUREAU
FOTOS: STEPHAN SCHWABE
LOGO: YEYE WELLER
2014

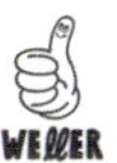
WELLER

MOE MEGURO

Designer : Chou Yi

The concept of this cover design was to visualize the impression of Moe Meguro's music—roughness, clumsiness, and freedom.

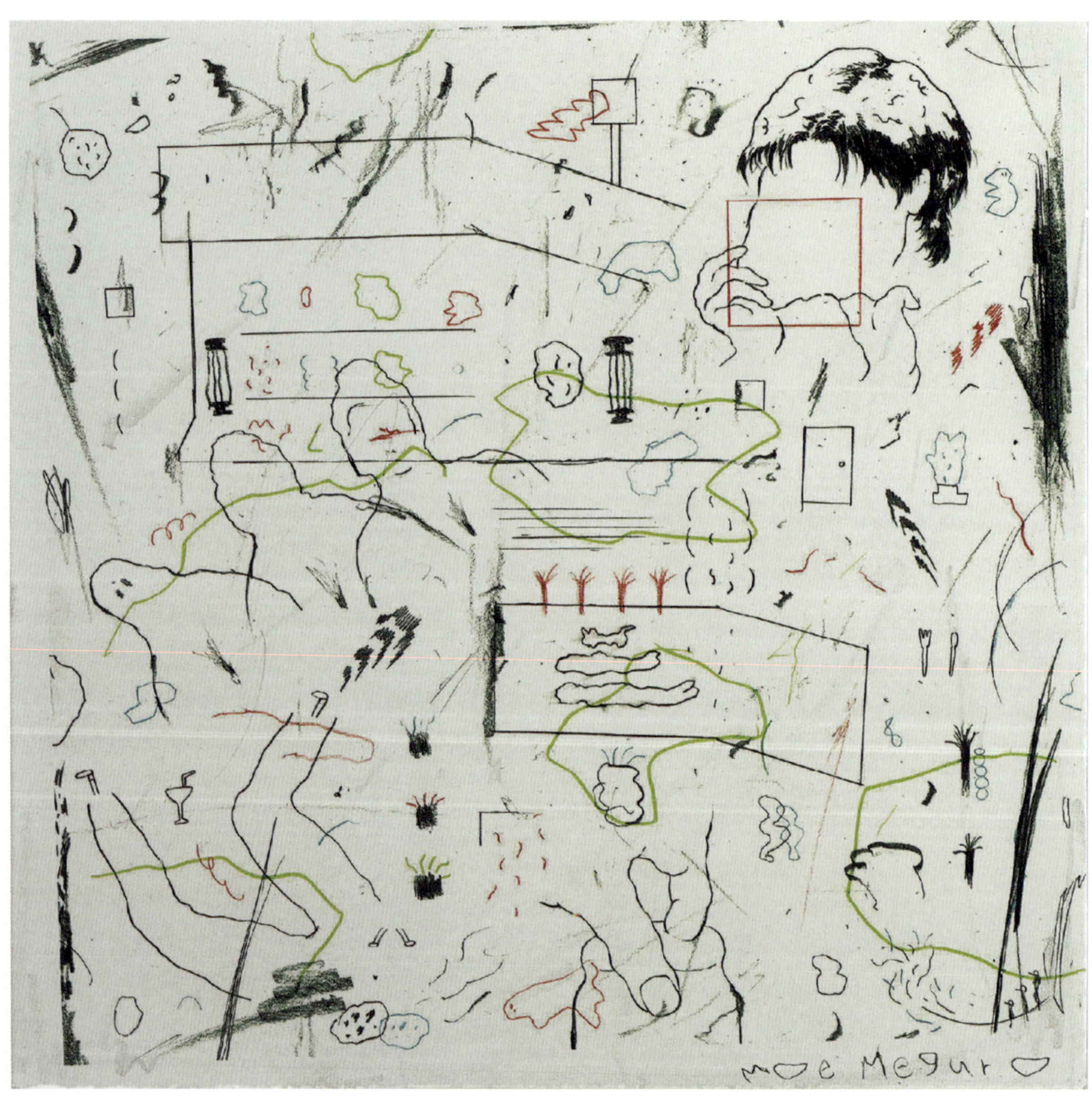

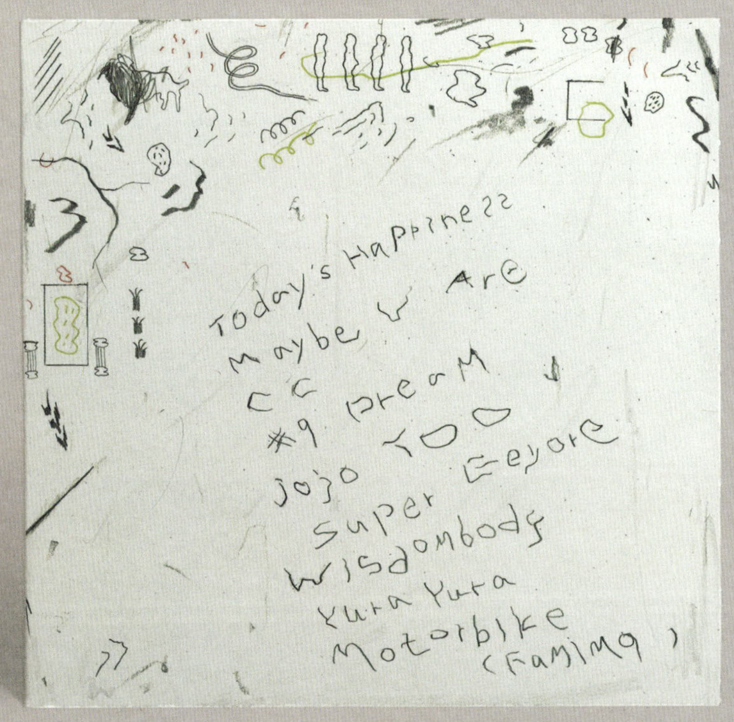
Today's Happiness
Maybe U Are
CC
#9 Dream
TOO
jojo
Super Eeyore
Wisdombody
Yura Yura
Motorbike
(Famima)

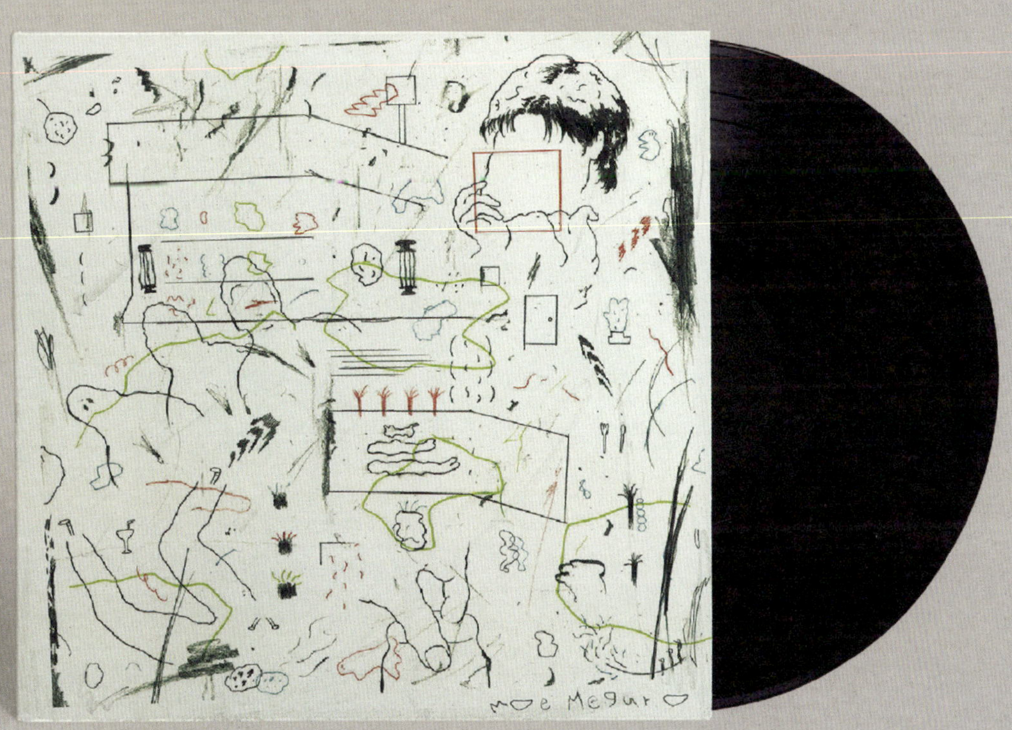
moe Meguro

DECISION TEXTBOOK

Designer : Sieun Baek

This textbook was created to help the irresolute people, for many of us are having trouble making choices and decisions in the age of information explosion.

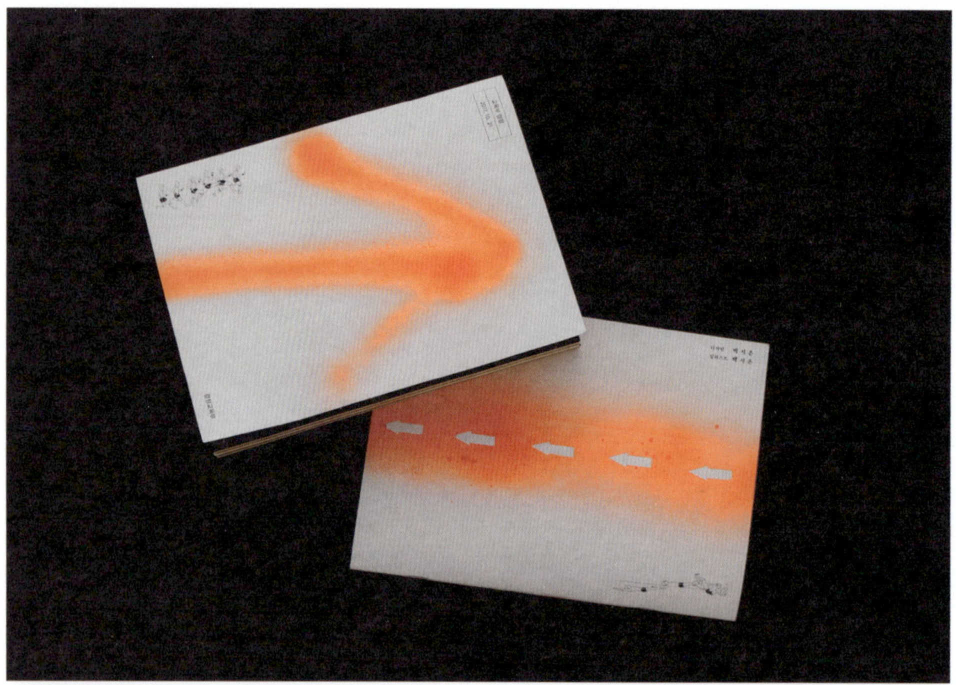

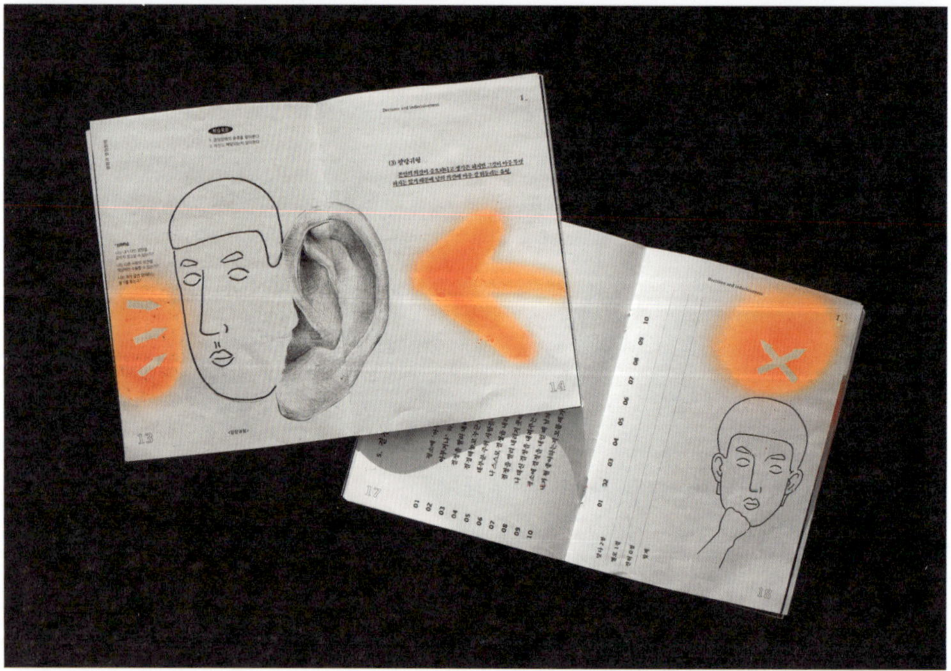

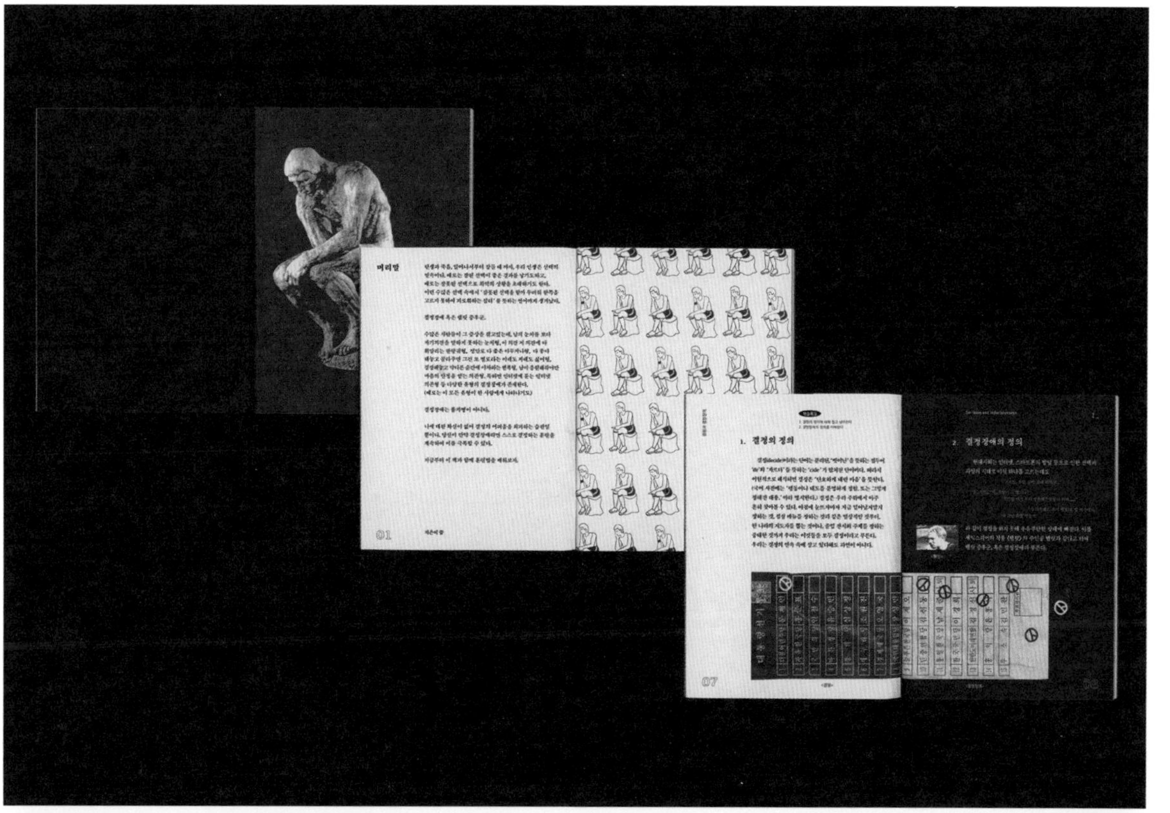

머리말

1. 결정의 정의

2. 결정장애의 정의

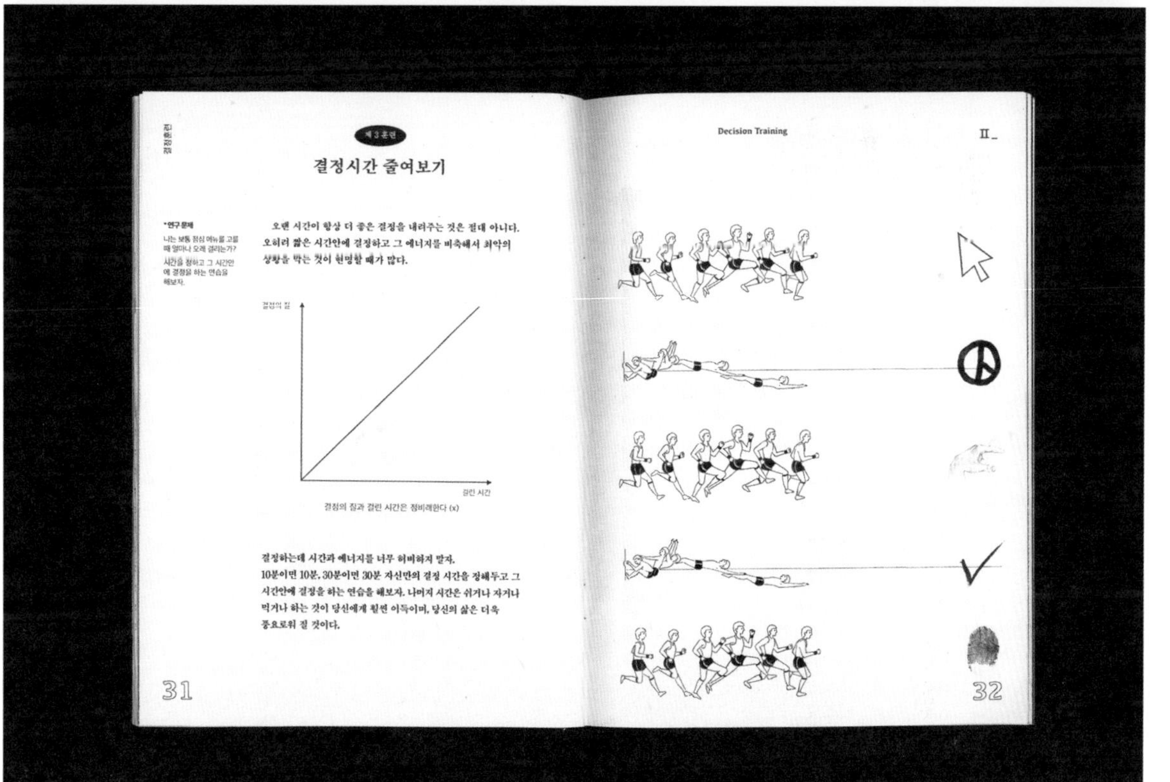

결정훈련

제 3 훈련

결정시간 줄여보기

*연구문제

나는 보통 점심 메뉴를 고를 때 얼마나 오래 걸리는가? 시간을 정하고 그 시간안에 결정을 하는 연습을 해보자.

오랜 시간이 항상 더 좋은 결정을 내려주는 것은 절대 아니다. 오히려 짧은 시간안에 결정하고 그 에너지를 비축해서 최악의 상황을 막는 것이 현명할 때가 많다.

결정의 질

걸린 시간

결정의 질과 걸린 시간은 정비례한다 (x)

결정하는데 시간과 에너지를 너무 허비하지 말자.
10분이면 10분, 30분이면 30분 자신만의 결정 시간을 정해두고 그 시간안에 결정을 하는 연습을 해보자. 나머지 시간은 쉬거나 자거나 먹거나 하는 것이 당신에게 훨씬 이득이며, 당신의 삶은 더욱 풍요로워 질 것이다.

31

Decision Training

II_

32

FADE TO BLUE

Studio : Onion Design Associates
Creative Director : Andrew Wong   Designer : Karen Tsai, Fong Ming Yang

Chung Yufeng, a pipa player, and David Chen, an American guitarist, collaborated in the music project called "Fade to Blue". To capture the essence of their collaboration, only two colors of ink were used for the album: red for the pipa, the female musician and the East, and blue for the guitar, the male musician and the West. Letterpress printing was used on the entire cover to reinforce the raw and organic nature of their performance.

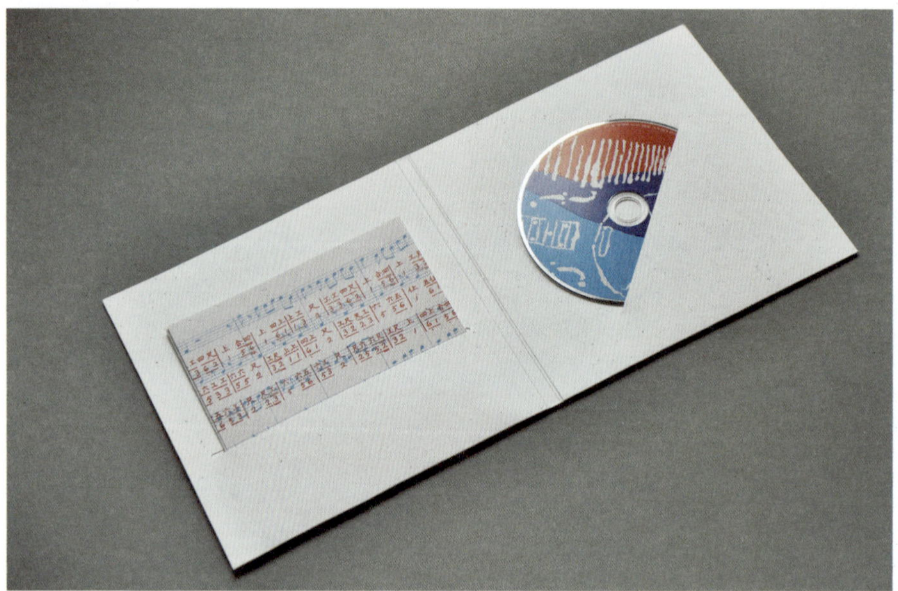

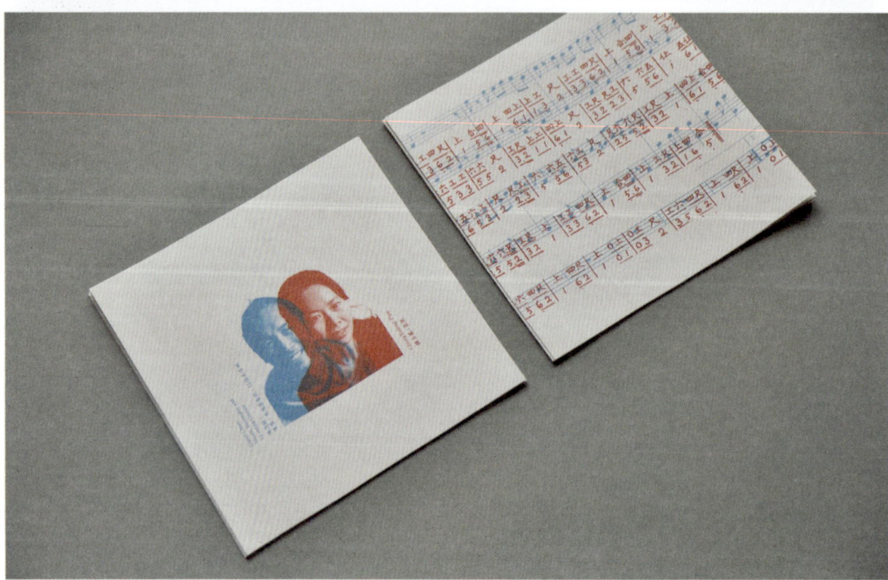

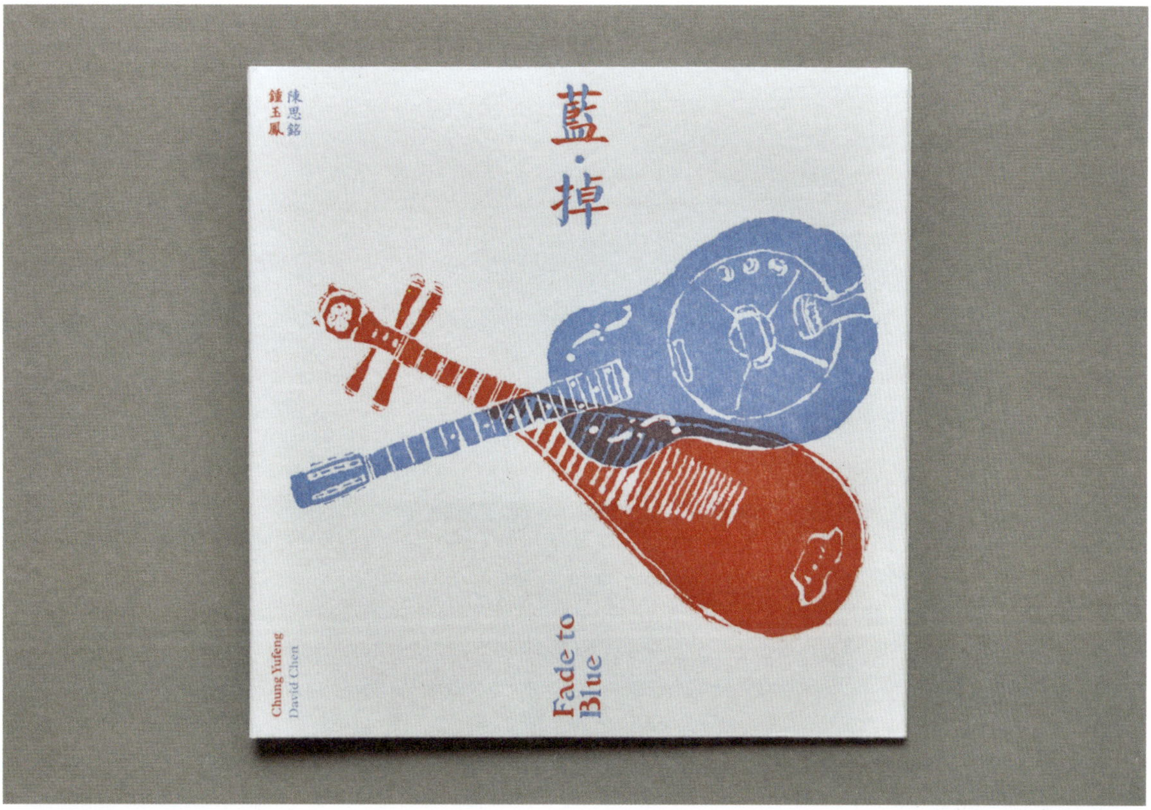

陳思銘
鍾玉鳳

藍·掉

Fade to Blue

Chung Yufeng
David Chen

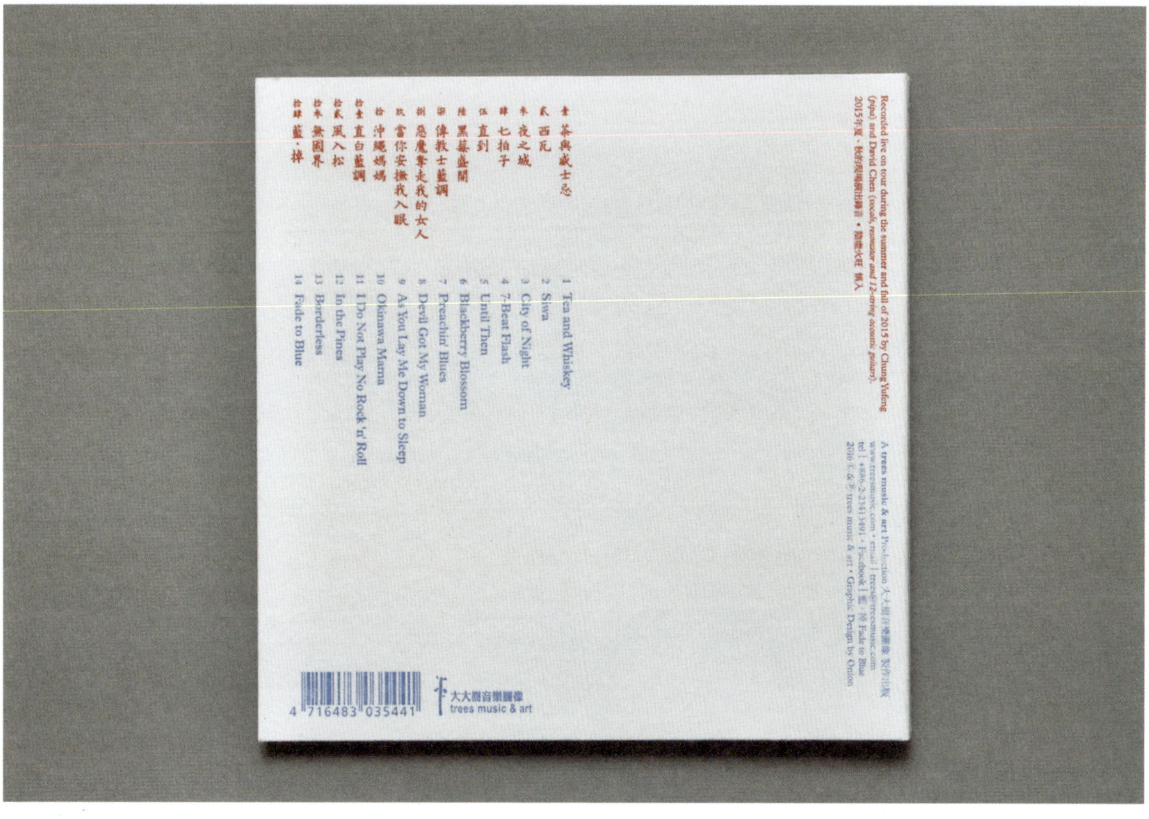

Recorded live on tour during the summer and fall of 2015 by Chung Yufeng (pipa) and David Chen (vocals, resonator and 12-string acoustic guitars).

壹 茶與威士忌
貳 西瓦
叁 夜之城
肆 七拍子
伍 直到
陸 黑莓盛開
柒 傳教士藍調
捌 惡魔奪走我的女人
玖 當你安撫我入眠
拾 沖繩媽媽
拾壹 直白藍調
拾貳 風入松
拾叁 無國界
拾肆 藍·掉

1 Tea and Whiskey
2 Siwa
3 City of Night
4 7-Beat Flash
5 Until Then
6 Blackberry Blossom
7 Preachin' Blues
8 Devil Got My Woman
9 As You Lay Me Down to Sleep
10 Okinawa Mama
11 I Do Not Play No Rock 'n' Roll
12 In the Pines
13 Borderless
14 Fade to Blue

A trees music & art Production

4 716483 035441

大大樹音樂圖像
trees music & art

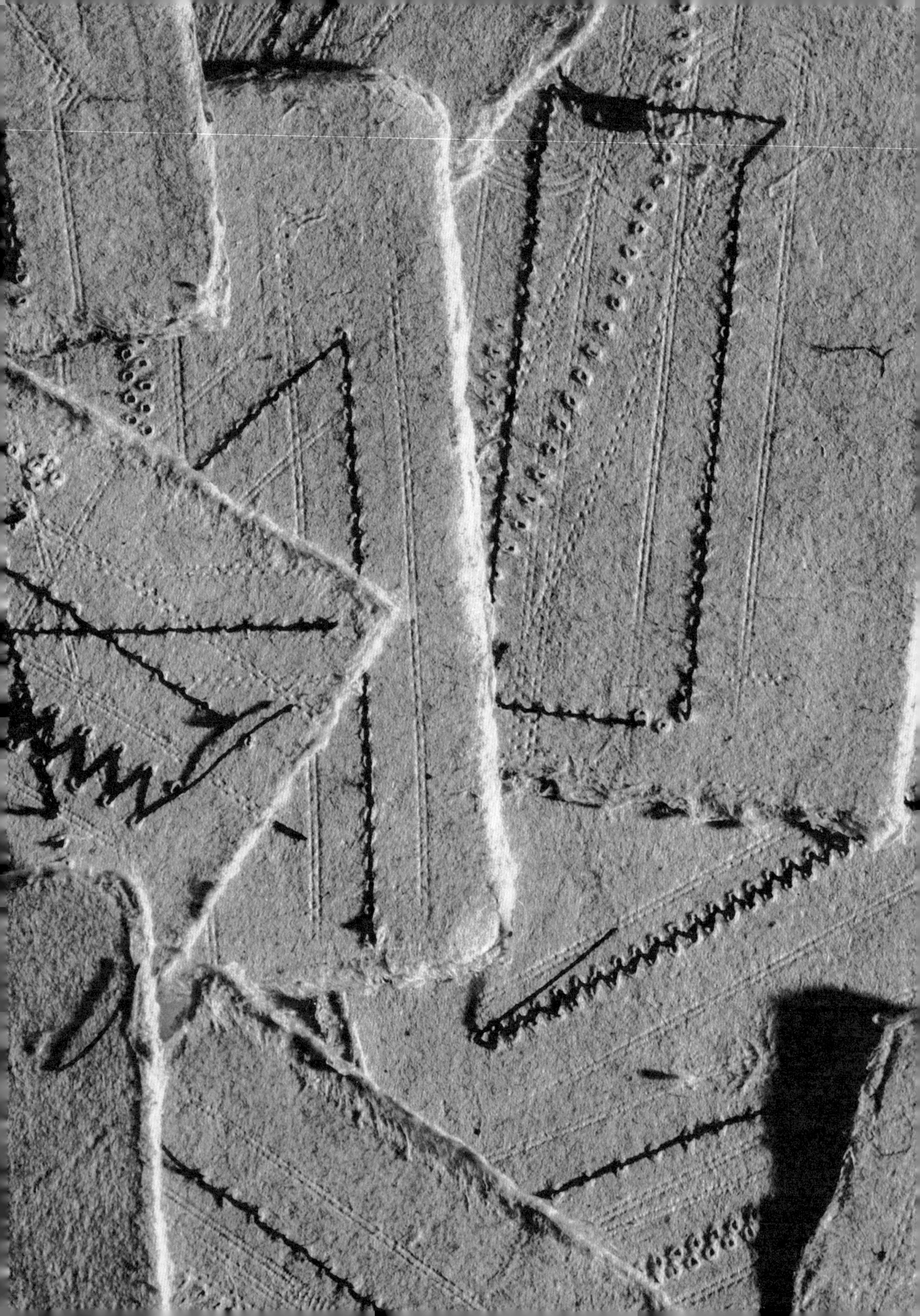

CRUDE

Crude making process involving roughly made materials or rough means such as tearing, crumpling, poking, burning, scanning or recycling. Crude visuals possess a unique wild beauty—beautiful but not for beauty itself.

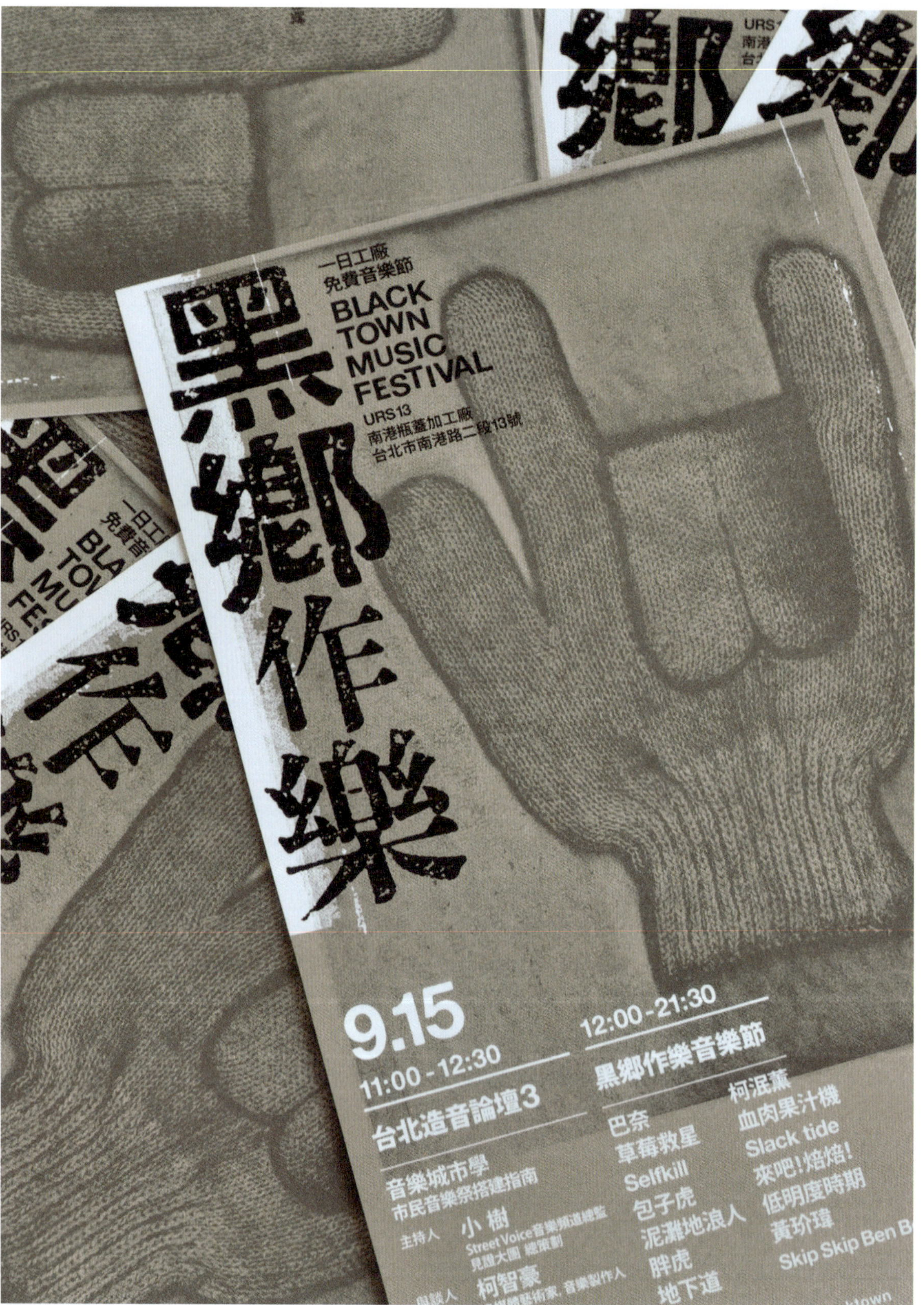
一日工廠
免費音樂節
BLACK TOWN MUSIC FESTIVAL
URS13
南港瓶蓋加工廠
台北市南港路二段13號
黑鄉作樂
9.15
11:00 - 12:30
台北造音論壇3
音樂城市學
市民音樂祭搭建指南
主持人 小樹
Street Voice音樂頻道總監
見證大團 總策劃
與談人 柯智豪
12:00 - 21:30
黑鄉作樂音樂節
巴奈
草莓救星
Selfkill
包子虎
泥灘地浪人
胖虎
地下道
柯泯薰
血肉果汁機
Slack tide
來吧!焙焙!
低明度時期
黃玠瑋
Skip Skip Ben

BLACKTOWN MUSIC FESTIVAL

Studio : Onion Design Associates   Creative Director : Andrew Wong
Designer : Andrew Wong, Charly Chen

The Festival was located in an abandoned factory in Nangang, Taipei. The town was known as "Black Town" in the post war era, bristled with various heavy industrial plants and factories in the past—hence, the term "Dirty Hands." The designers chose an ordinary cheap industrial glove to be the main visual of the festival, representing the industrial location and its working class inhabitants.

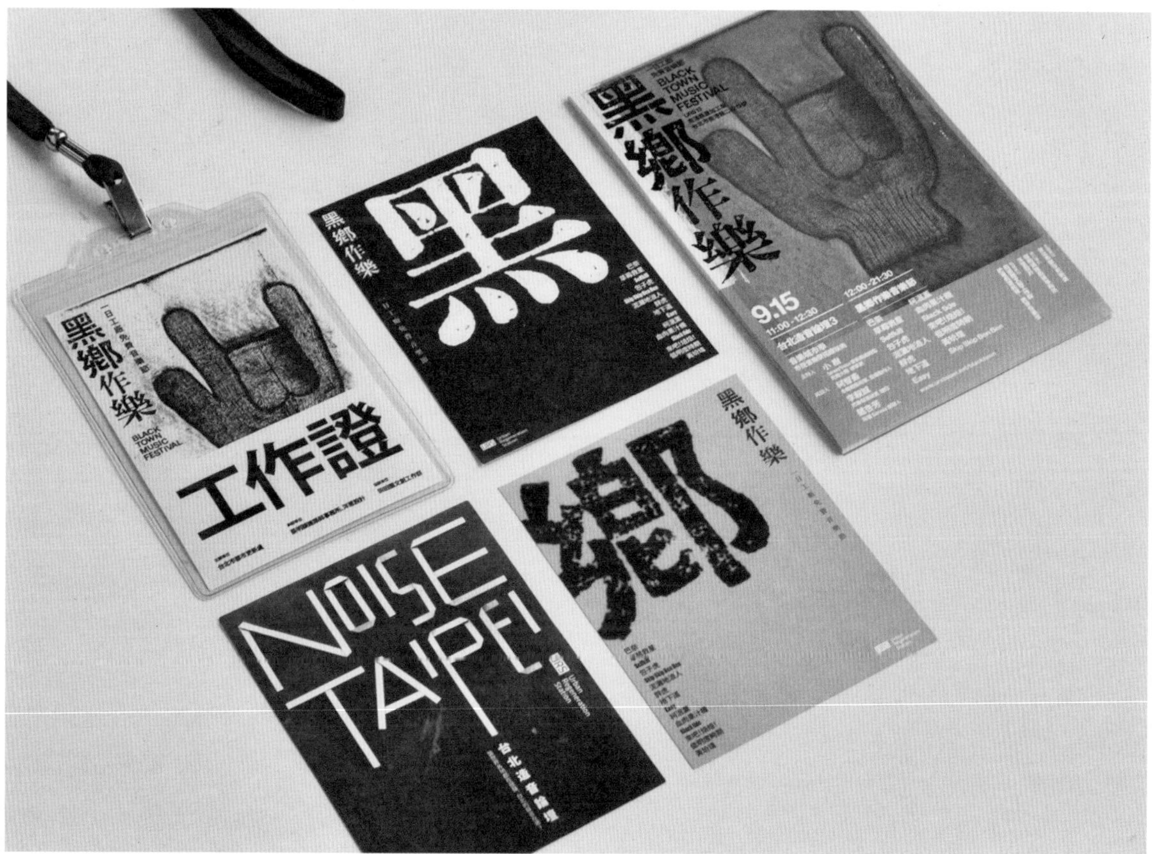

As a kind of visual experience, what do you think about the "roughness" in graphic design?

Today, young designers are using the same digital software. Making perfect, clean, minimal design layout is too easy. Eventually, all the works look the same. If we can stay away from the computer, using our hands to experiment with different textures and scan them in, you can create design work with high personal character that is like no one else.

What are your common approaches to produce a "rough" visual effect?

Find everyday object that you can feel a connection to the theme and communicate your concept, play with them, experiment and manipulate them with different lo-fi techniques, until they are not clean anymore, then make a photograph or scan them in.

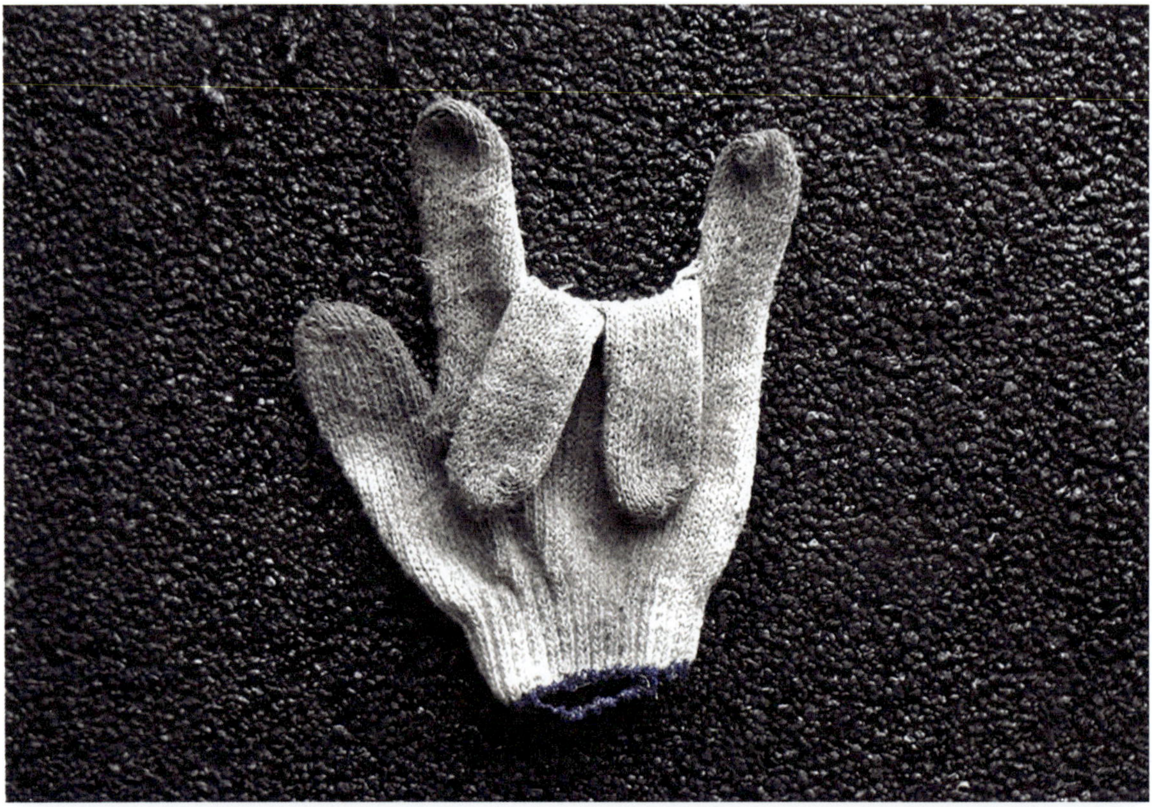

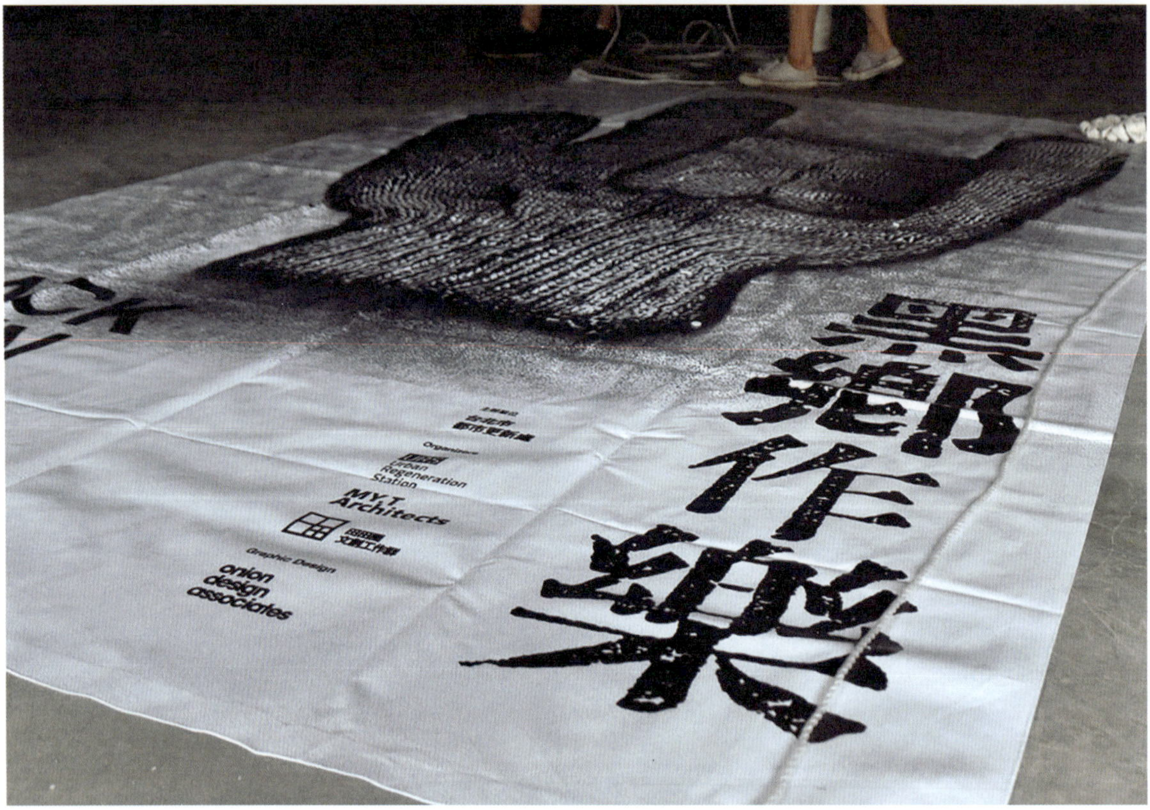
黑鄉作樂
Organisers
Urban Regeneration Station
MY.T Architects
Graphic Design
onion design associates

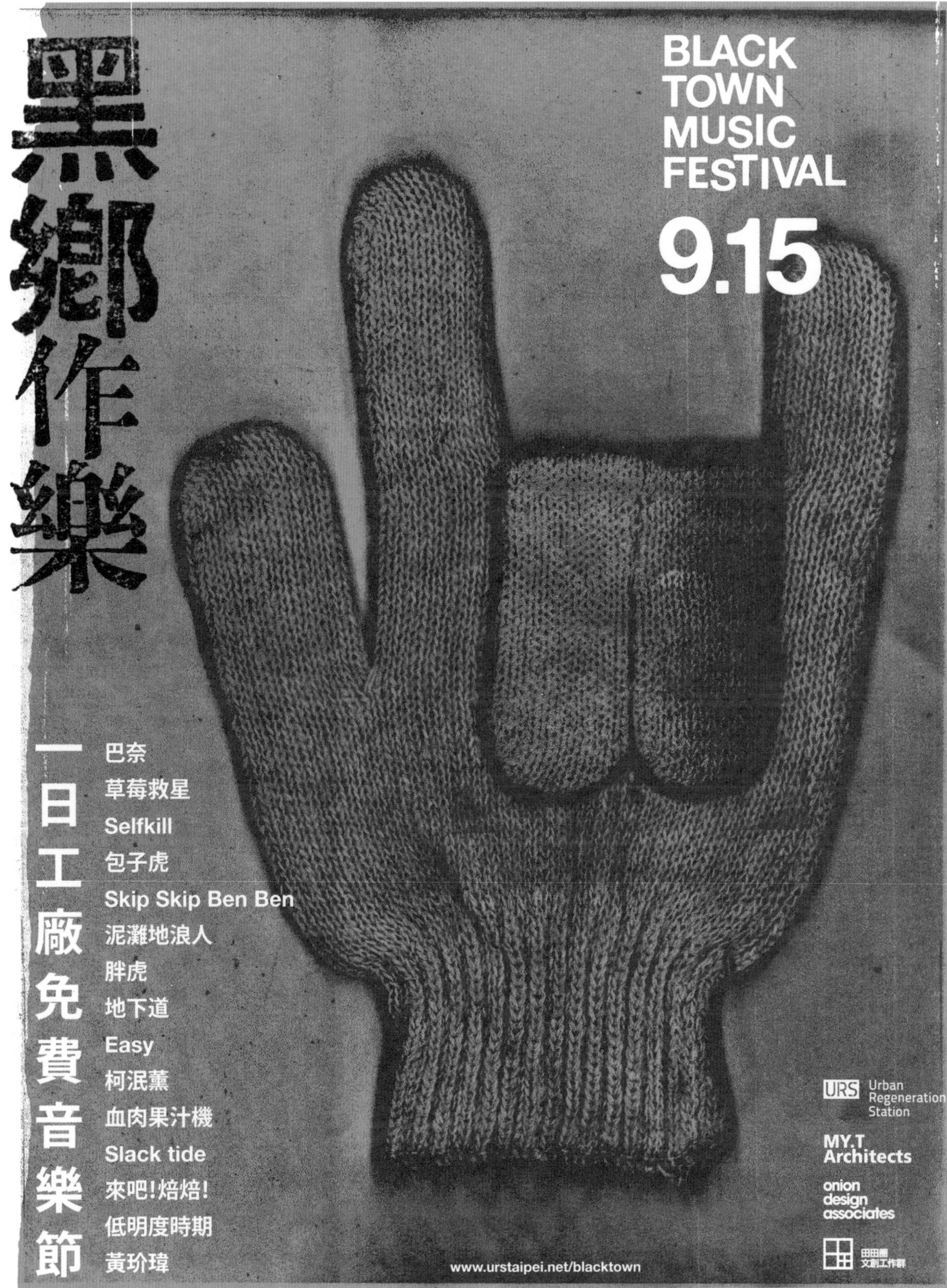
黑鄉作樂
BLACK
TOWN
MUSIC
FESTIVAL
9.15
一日工廠免費音樂節
巴奈
草莓救星
Selfkill
包子虎
Skip Skip Ben Ben
泥灘地浪人
胖虎
地下道
Easy
柯泯薰
血肉果汁機
Slack tide
來吧!焙焙!
低明度時期
黃玠瑋
www.urstaipei.net/blacktown
URS Urban Regeneration Station
MY.T Architects
onion design associates
田田圈 文創工作群

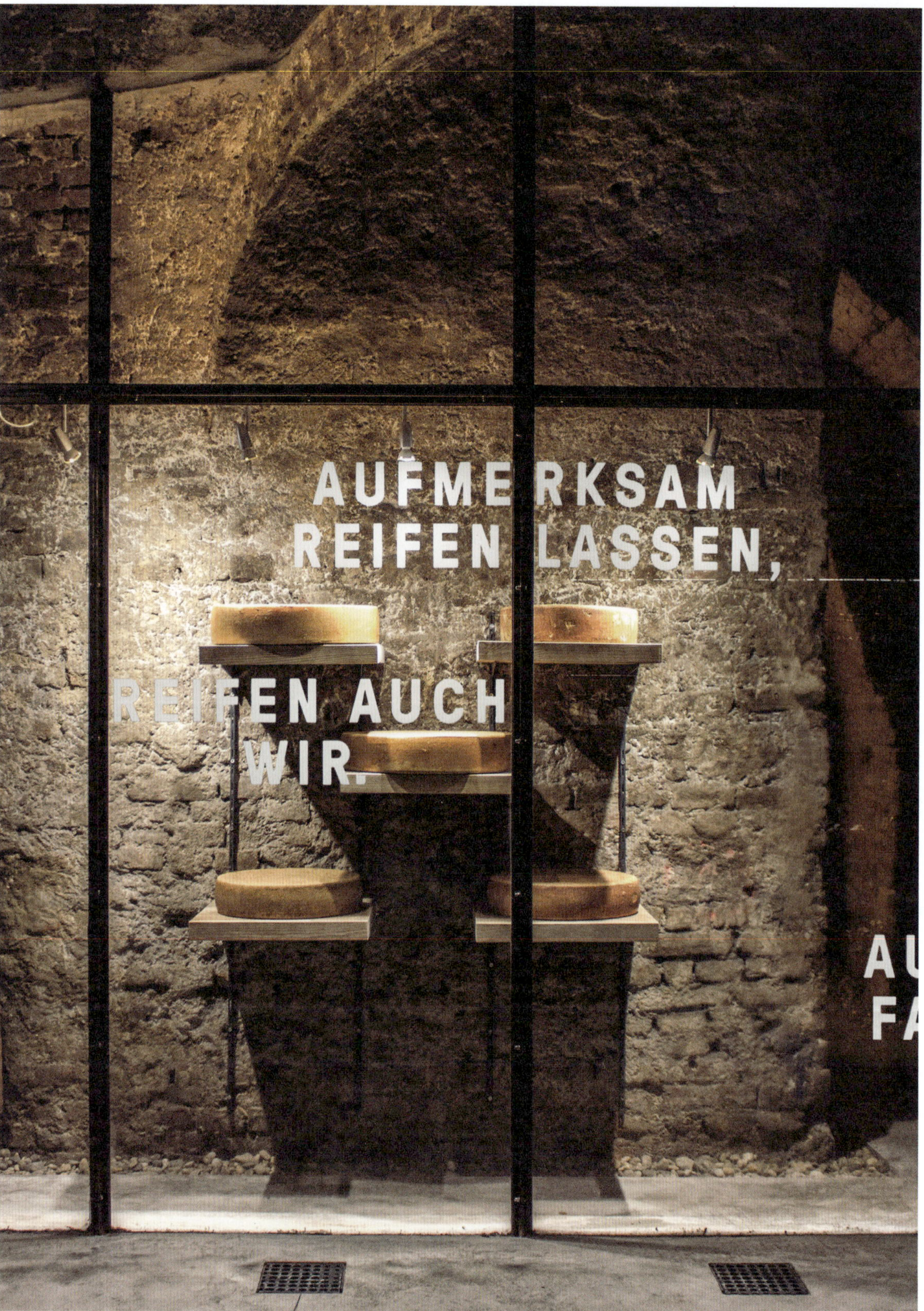
AUFMERKSAM
REIFEN LASSEN,
REIFEN AUCH
WIR.

ANTON MACHT KE:S

Studio : Studio Riebenbauer   Designer : Rui Magalhães, Denise Schindele, Franz Riebenbauer

This is the identity design for Anton Macht Ke:s. Anton has been making Ke:s (Voralberg dialect for cheese) since he was a child. Hence, the maturing of the cheese is closely connected with his own maturity. The designers used the very same words from Anton in their first meeting as the centerpiece of the identity, without logo or any graphic elements.

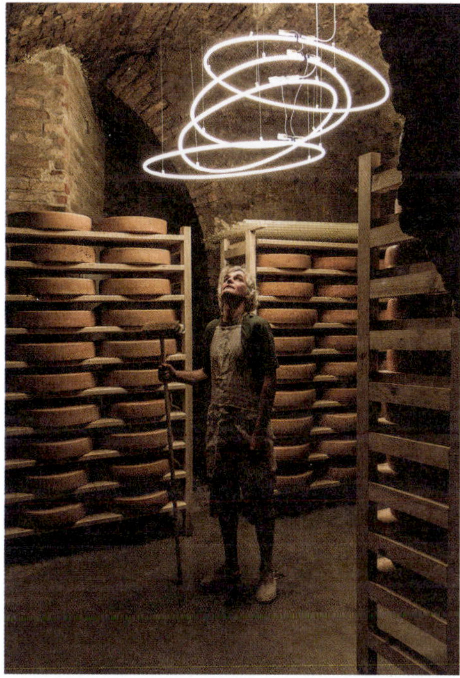

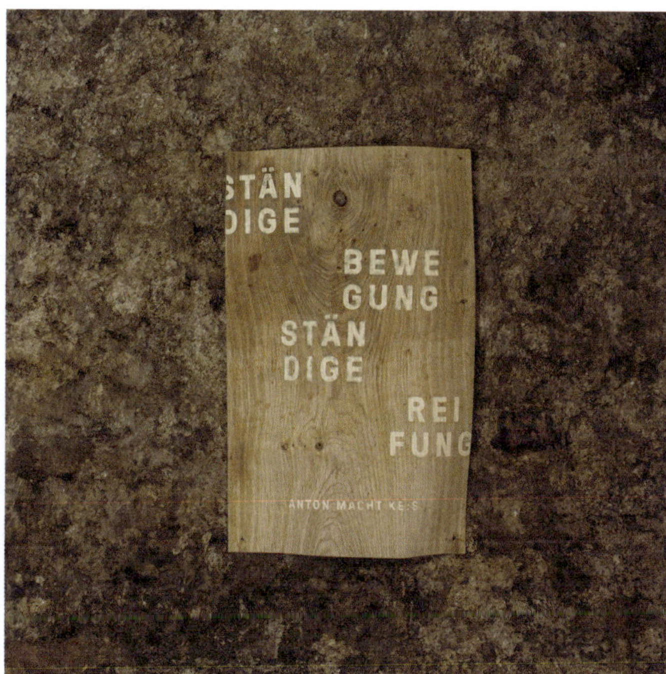

As a kind of visual experience, what do you think about the "roughness" in graphic design?

Roughness is a consequence, not a goal. As a design studio we try to focus on expressing a brand through all possible channels in order to make it experienceable with all senses. This also means focusing on every other small detail besides "traditional" graphic design. A big part of this is materiality. To choose the materials that, like the rest of the details, convey the message of the brand we are working on. When we create brands for clients like Anton macht Ke:s, that roughness comes as a natural consequence of that approach, trying to express the craft and passion they put into their work.

What are your common approaches to produce a "rough" visual effect?

Honesty. Above all, branding is about honesty. We strive for the perfect expression of a brand's true identity, choosing every detail, material, smell or sound according to that. A lot of it comes from the client themselves: what they do, how and where they do it, and their craft and traditions. Only in those cases one can get an authentic "rough" feeling.

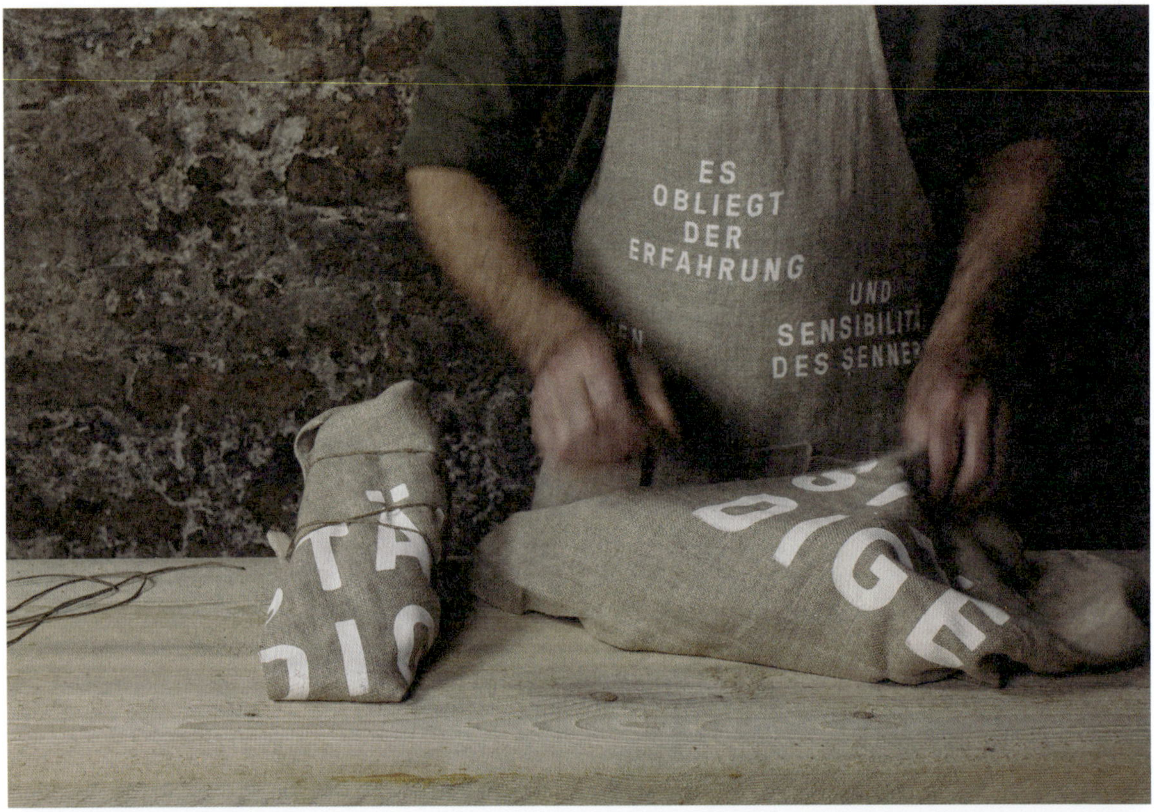

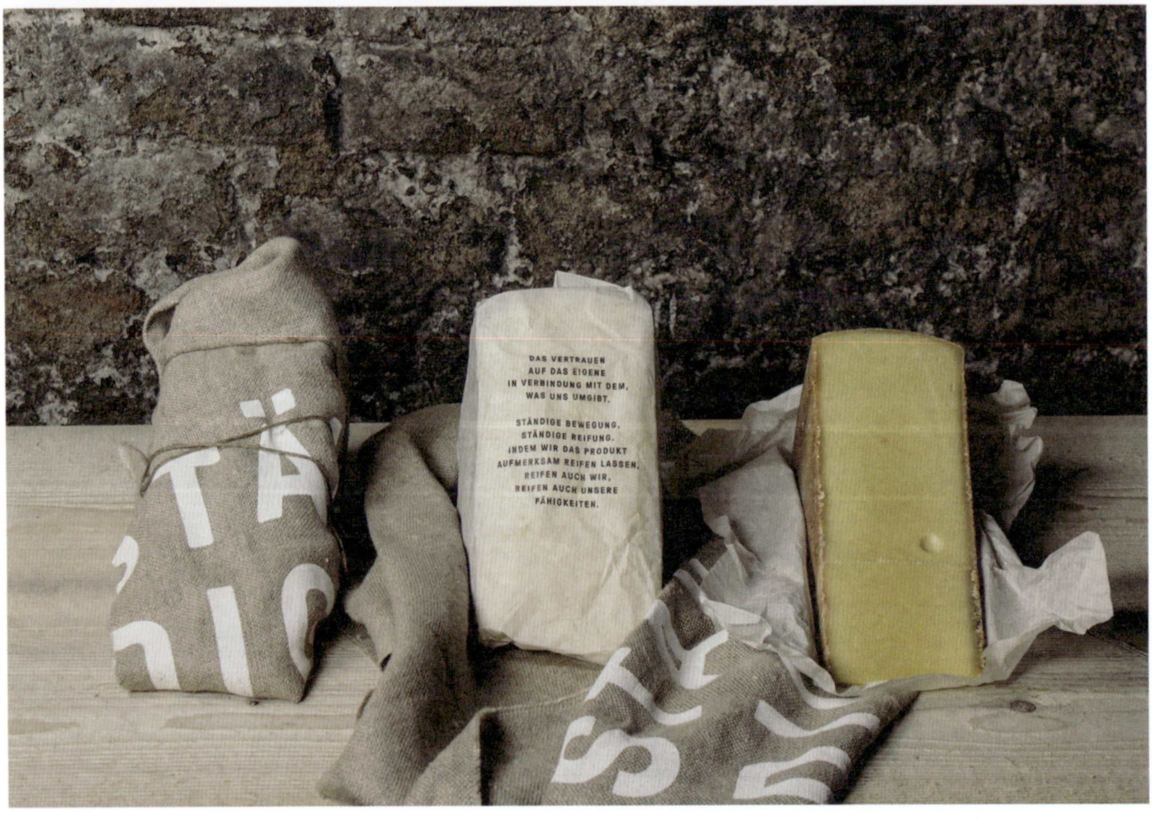

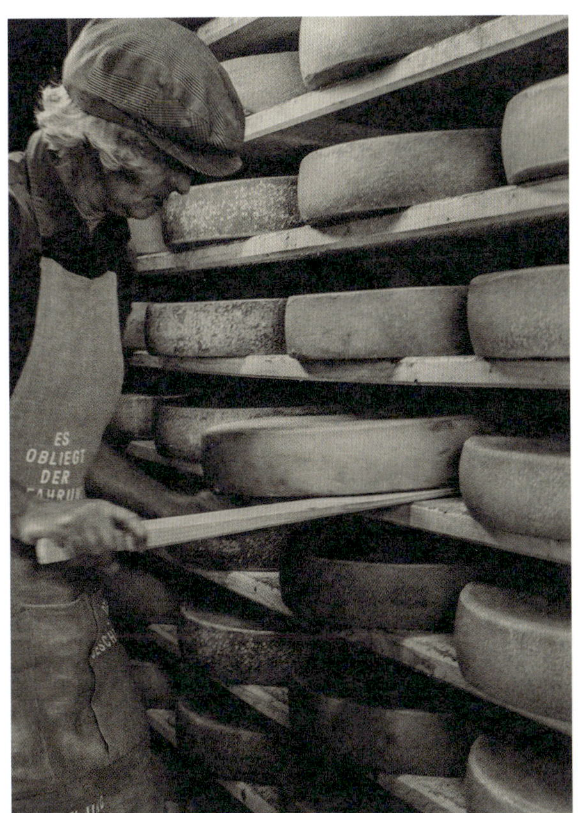
ES
OBLIEGT
DER

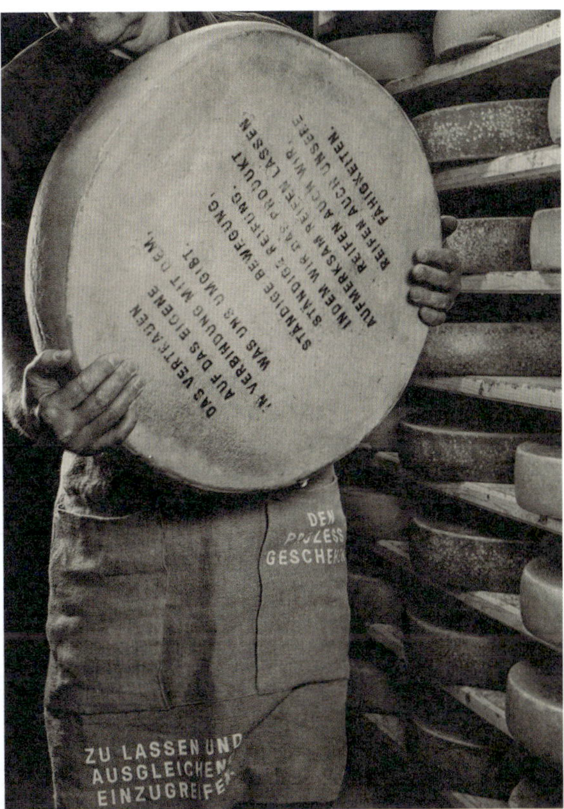
DAS VERTRAUEN
AUF DAS EIGENE
IN VERBINDUNG MIT DEM,
WAS UNS UMGIBT.
STÄNDIGE BEWEGUNG,
STÄNDIGE REIFUNG,
INDEM WIR DAS PRODUKT
AUFMERKSAM REIFEN LASSEN
REIFEN AUCH WIR,
REIFEN AUCH UNSERE
FÄHIGKEITEN.
ZU LASSEN UND

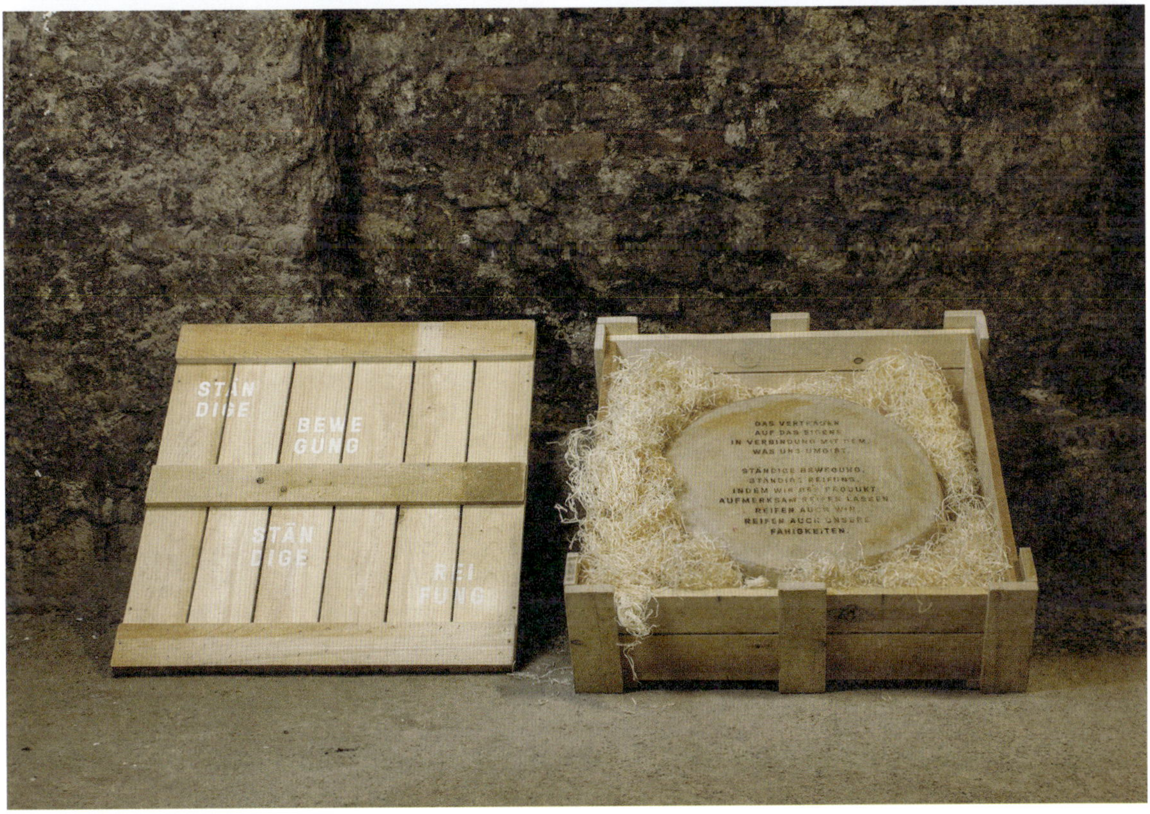

KAISER

Studio : Estudio Yeyé

Kaiser is a barbecue restaurant which inherited the traditions of ancestors and brings together the grills of Germany and Mexico. The visual identity design was based on an imaginary tavern in First World War Germany, where soldiers assemble for meal and drink after a battle. The images of German generals were inspired by the owner's memory of his grandfather—a tough, old gentleman who was experienced in his craft.

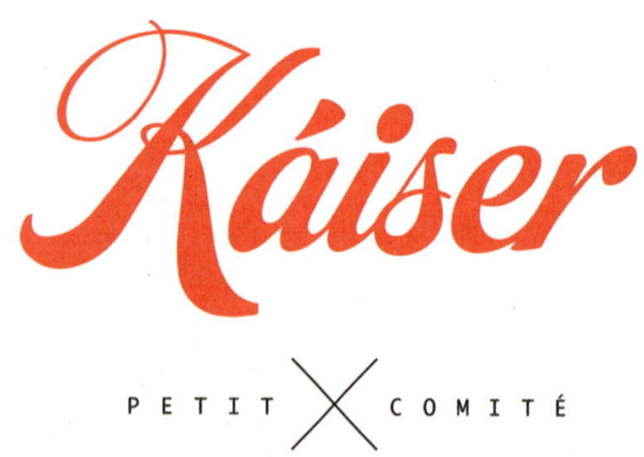

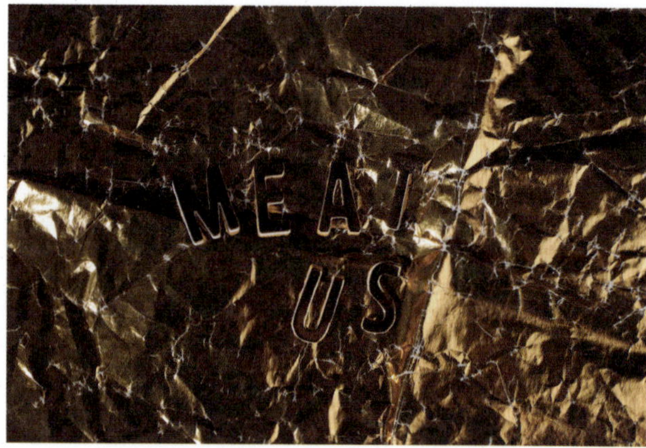

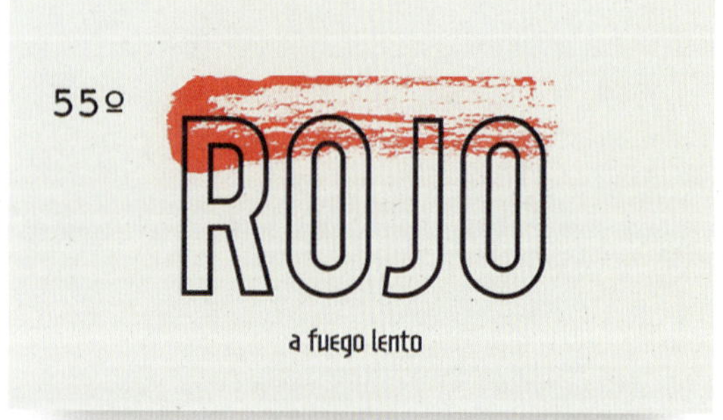

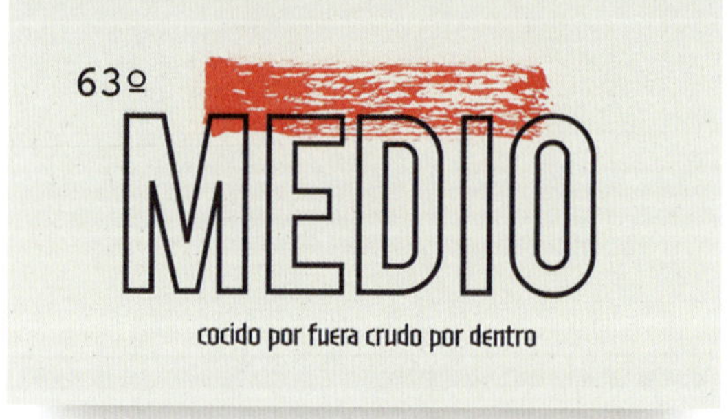

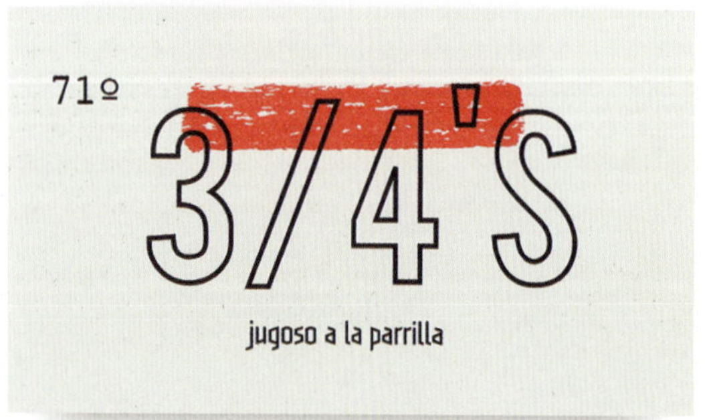

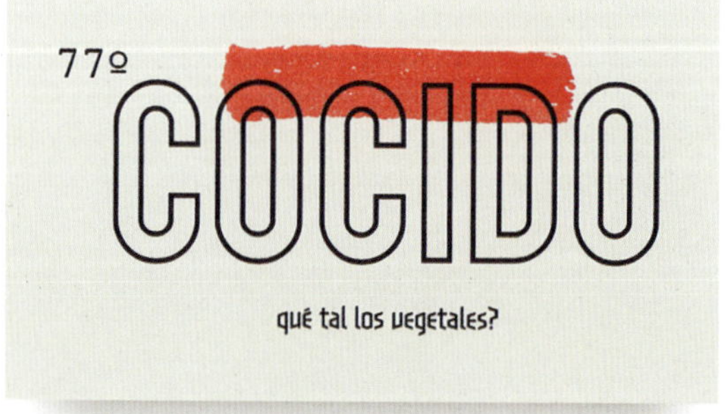

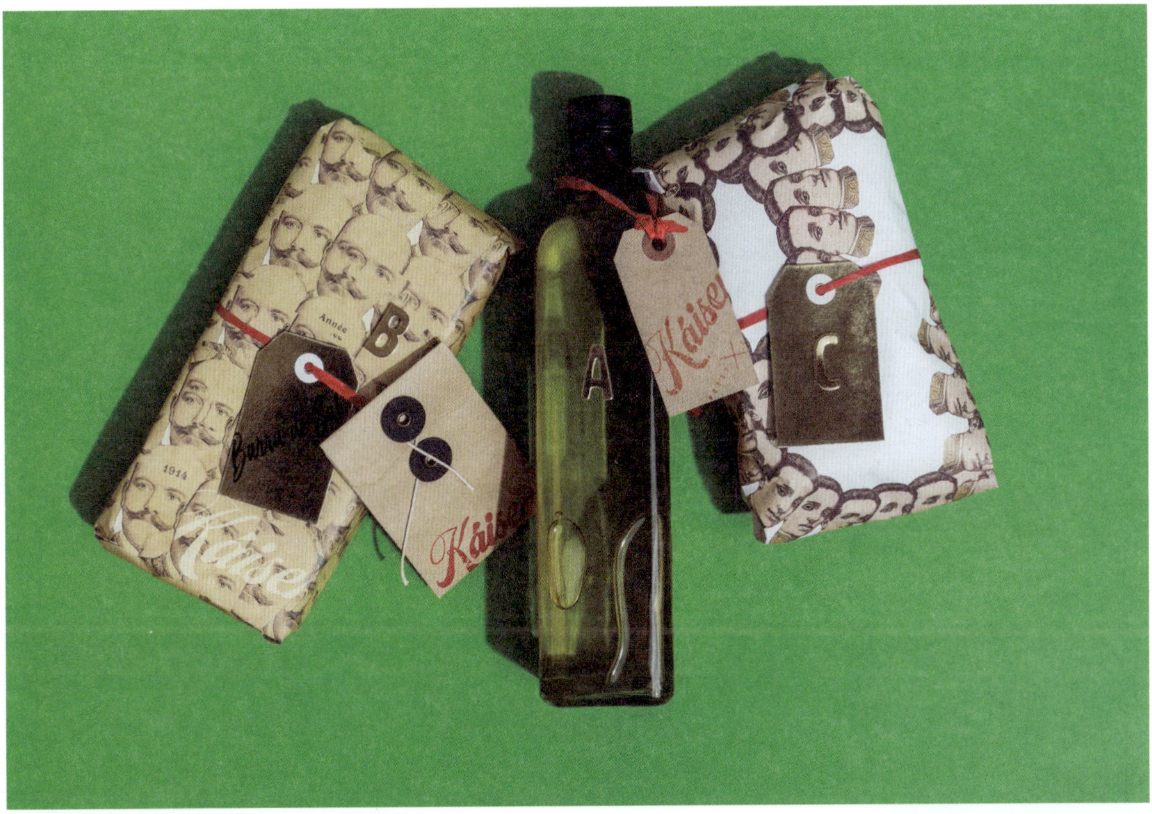
Káiser
1914
Année
B
A
C
Káiser

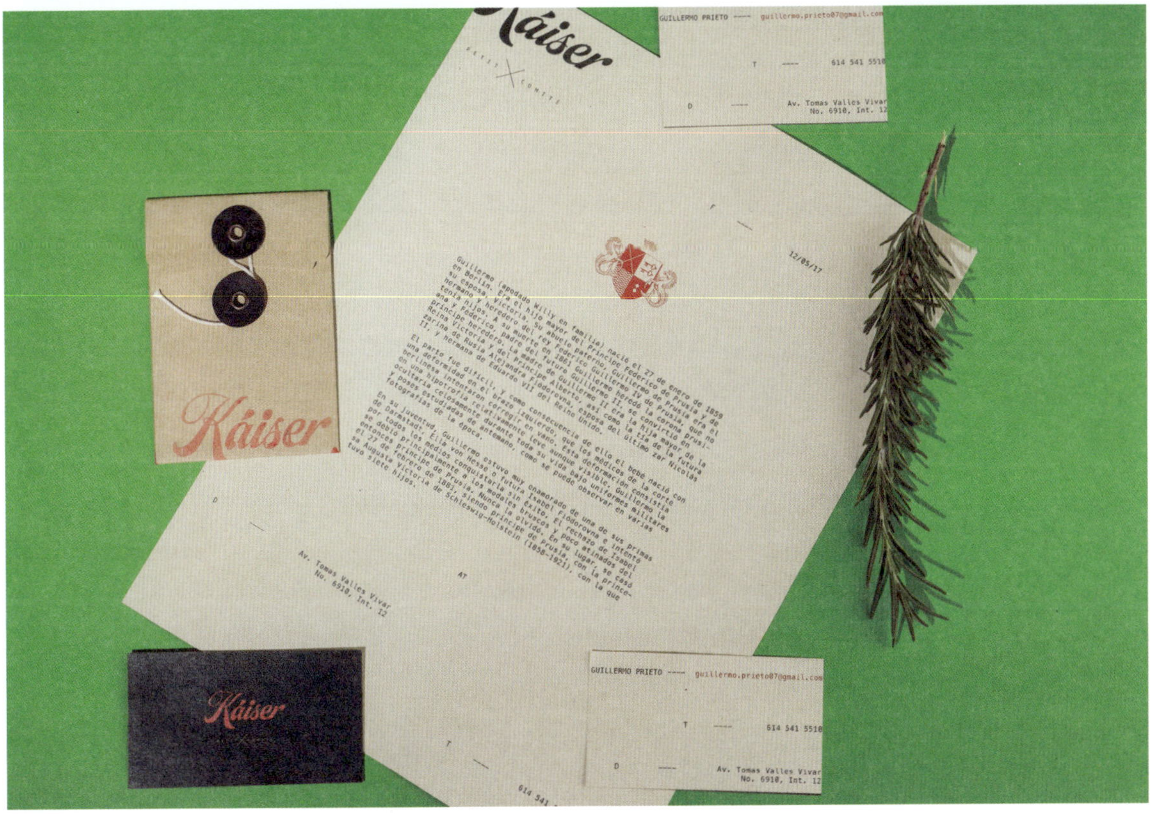
Káiser
GUILLERMO PRIETO
guillermo.prieto07@gmail.com
614 541 5510
Av. Tomas Valles Vivar
No. 6910, Int. 12
12/05/17
Káiser
Káiser

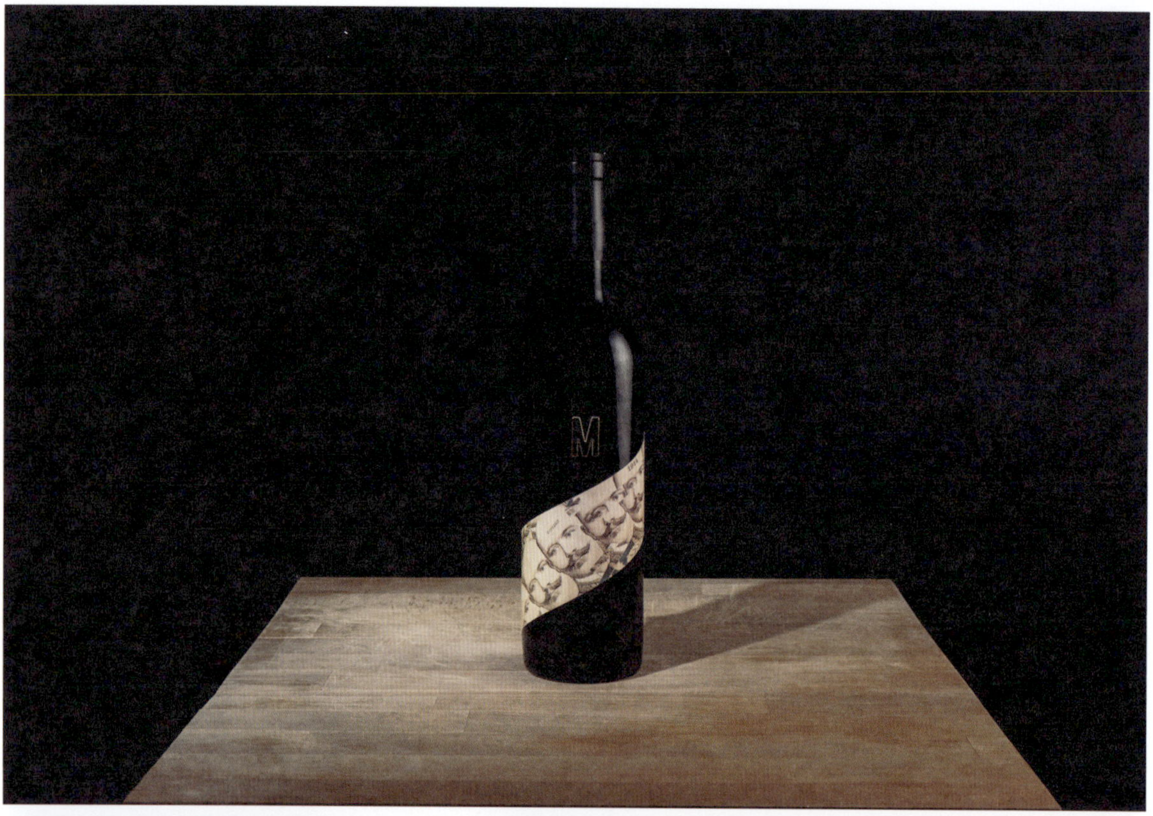

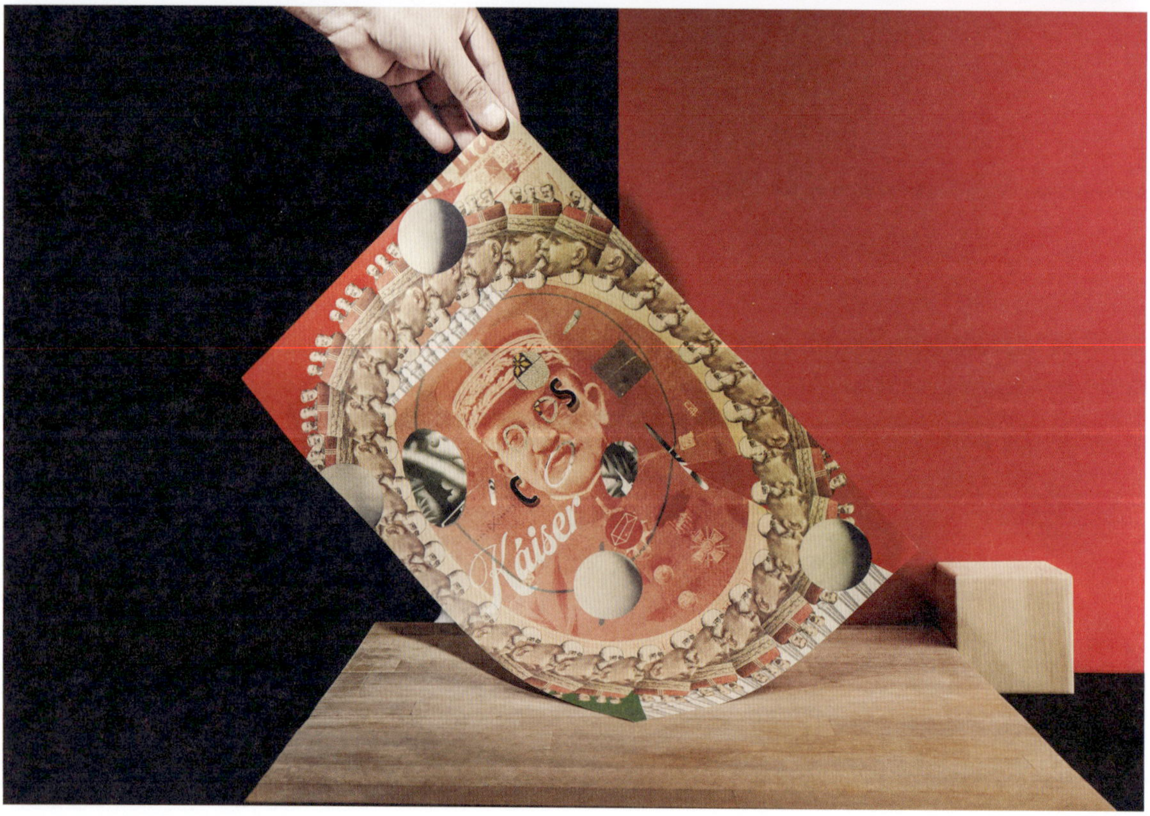

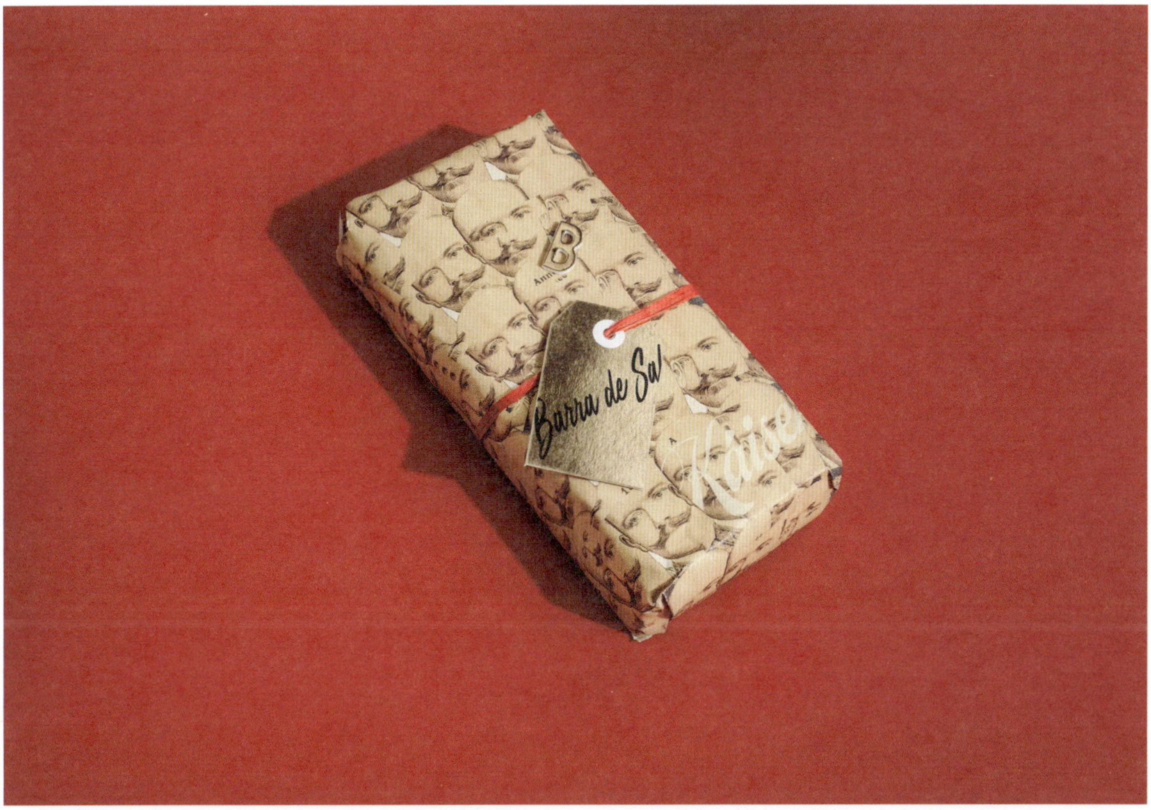

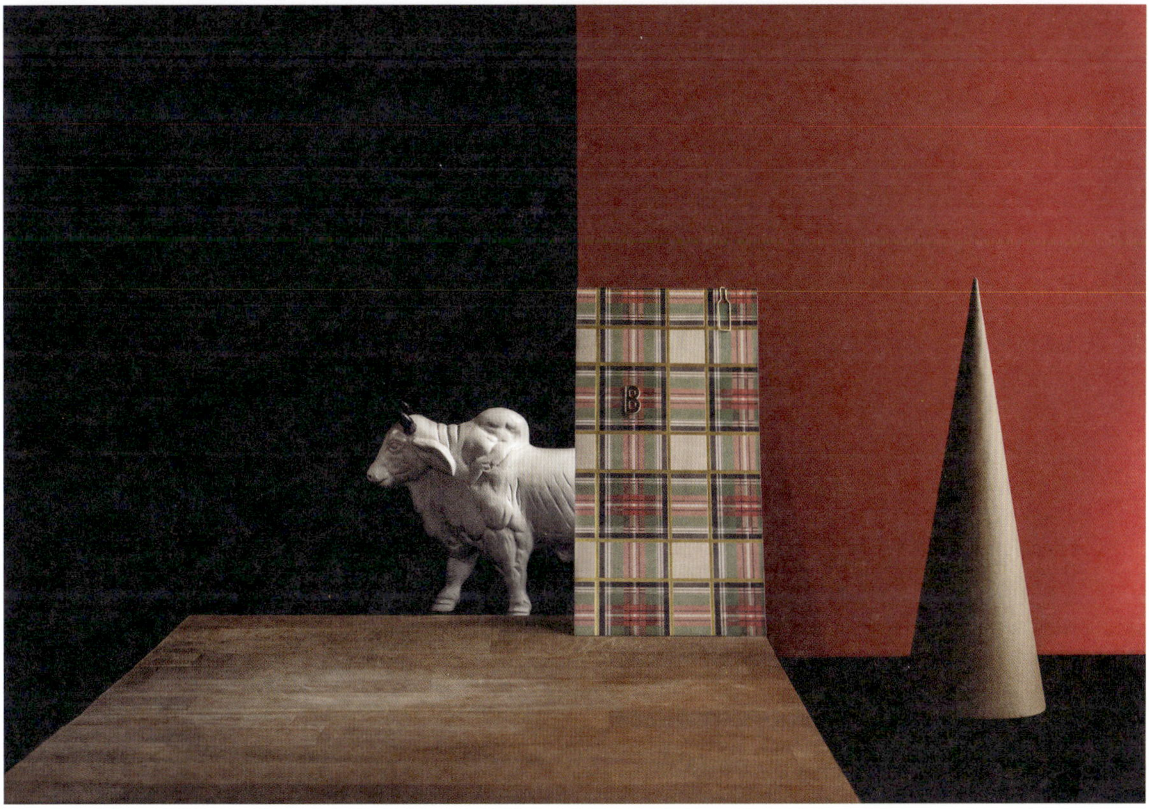

MY MOTHER IN PADDY FIELD

Studio : mistroom

The author of this double-volume book tells his family's vagrant story spanning more than a century. The cover design works in concert with the story, showing the dedication and persistence of the author's mother to supporting the whole family. It visually presents the chapter "Exile at Night", narrating how the mother hid into a paddy field to elude cops, by muddy footprints. The embossed pattern symbolizes the mother's heavy burden and deep love for her children.

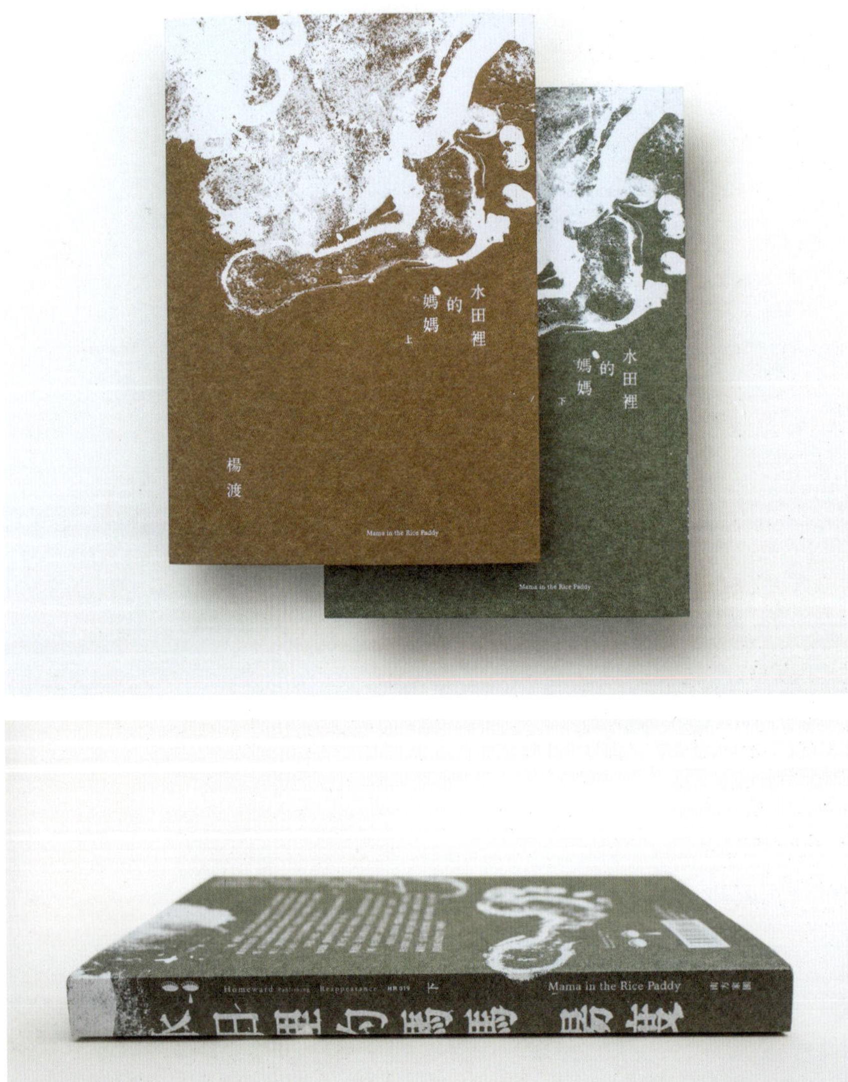

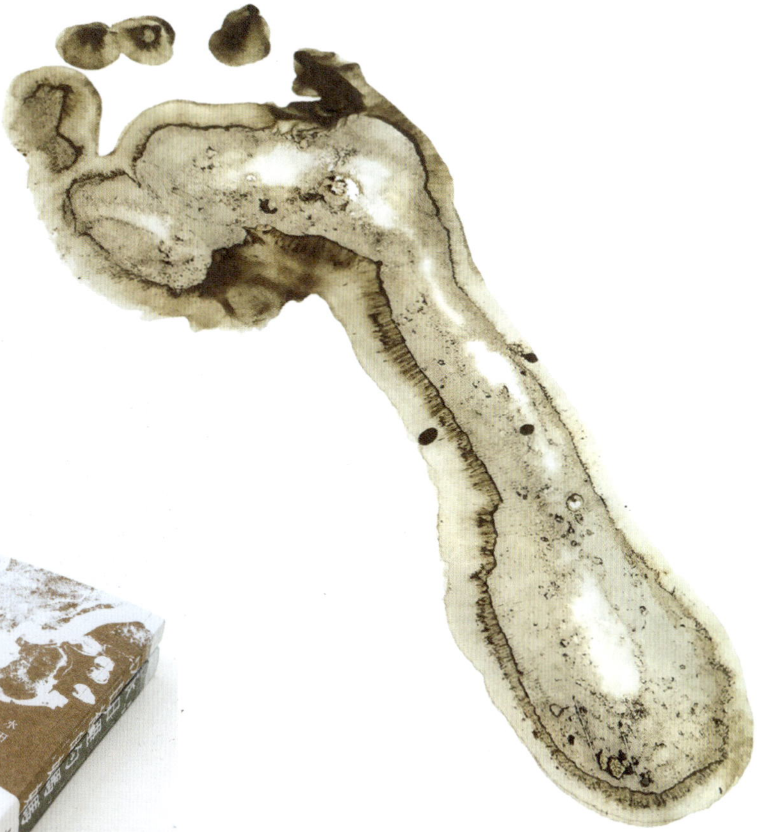

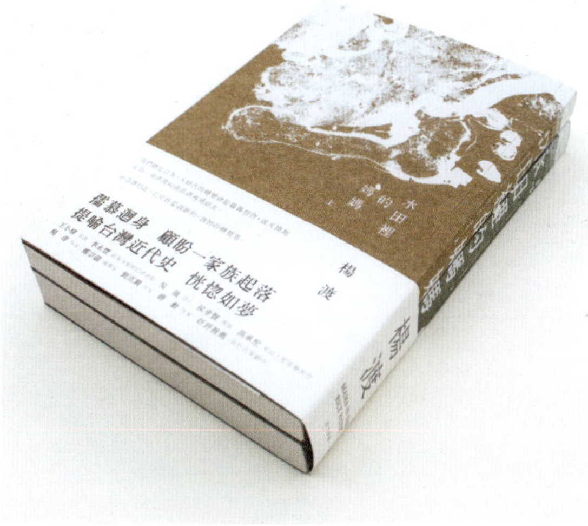

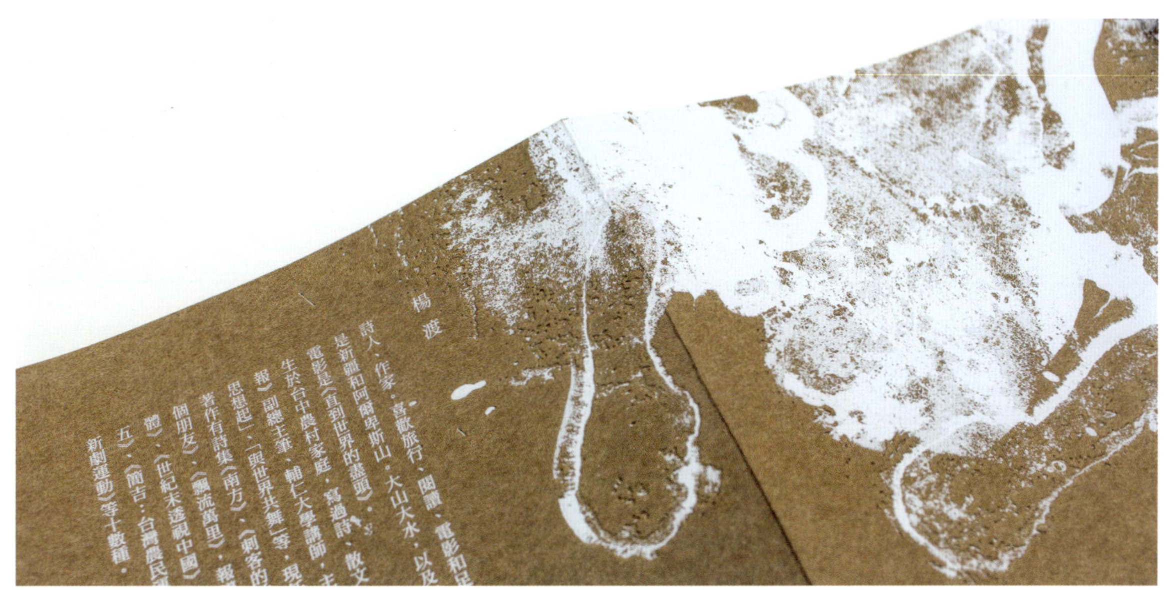
楊渡
詩人、作家。喜歡旅行、閱讀、電影和
是新疆和阿爾卑斯山。大山大水，以
電影是《直到世界的盡頭》。
生於台中農村家庭，寫過詩、散文
報》副總主筆，輔仁大學講師，
思想起」、「與世界共舞」等，現
著作有詩集《南方》、《刺客的
個朋友》、《飄流萬里》，報
體》、《世紀末透視中國》
五》、《簡吉：台灣農民
新劇運動》等十數種。

RIPPED PAPER

Designer : Jules Tardy

This project is a series of illustrations entirely made out of ripped color paper. The illustrations are designed as layered sheets placed on top of each other to create a character or landscape.

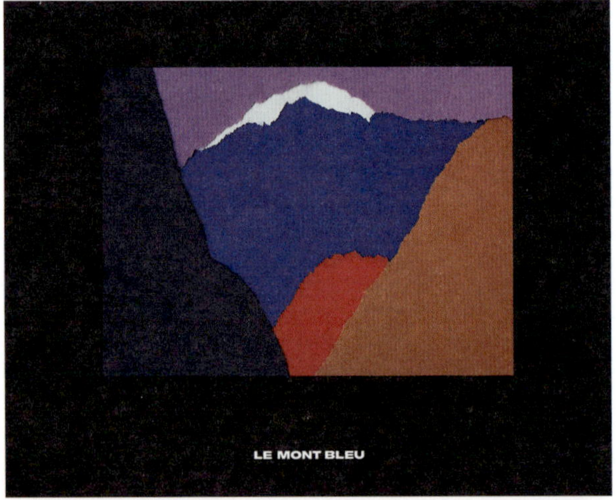

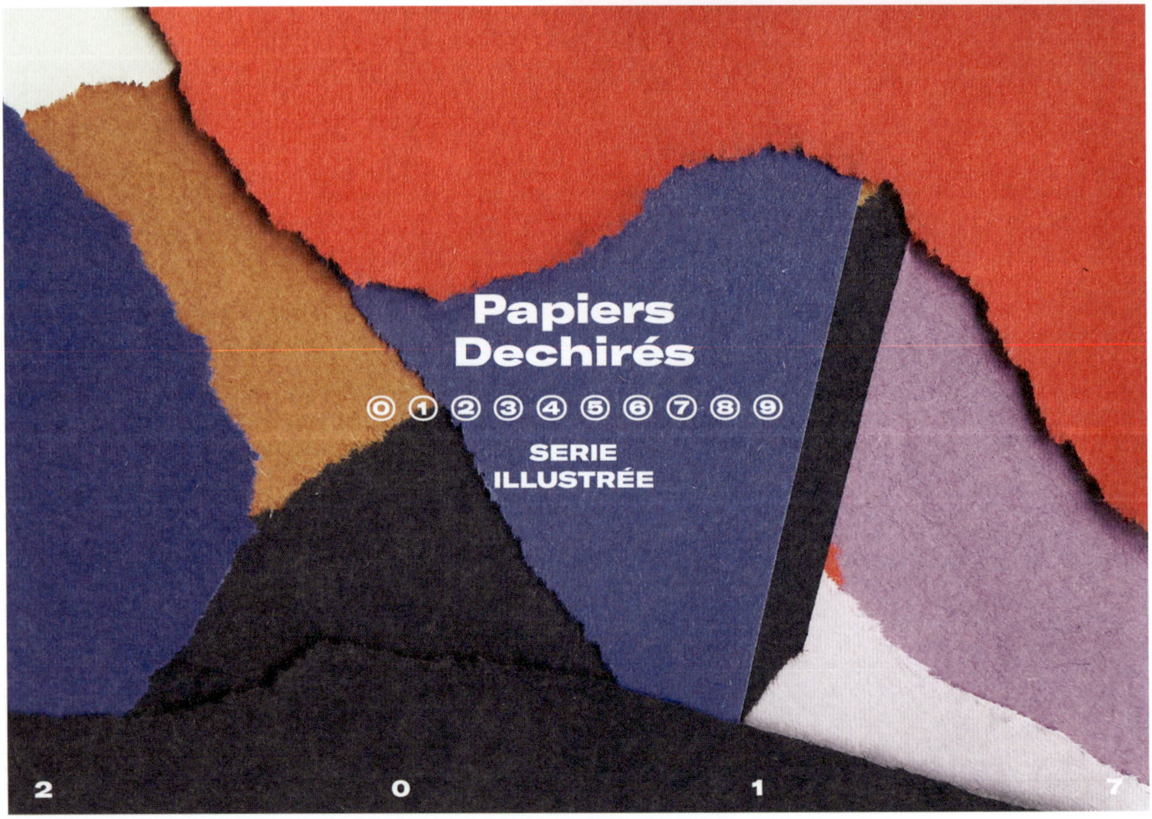

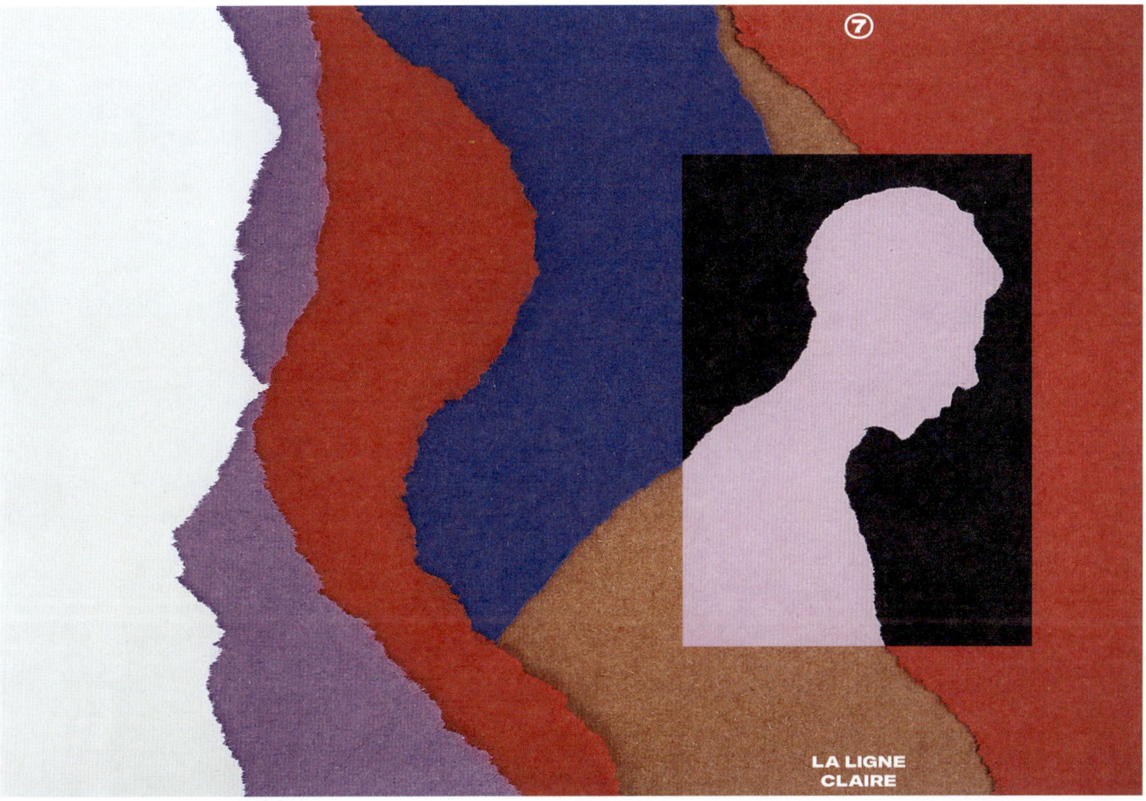

⑦

LA LIGNE
CLAIRE

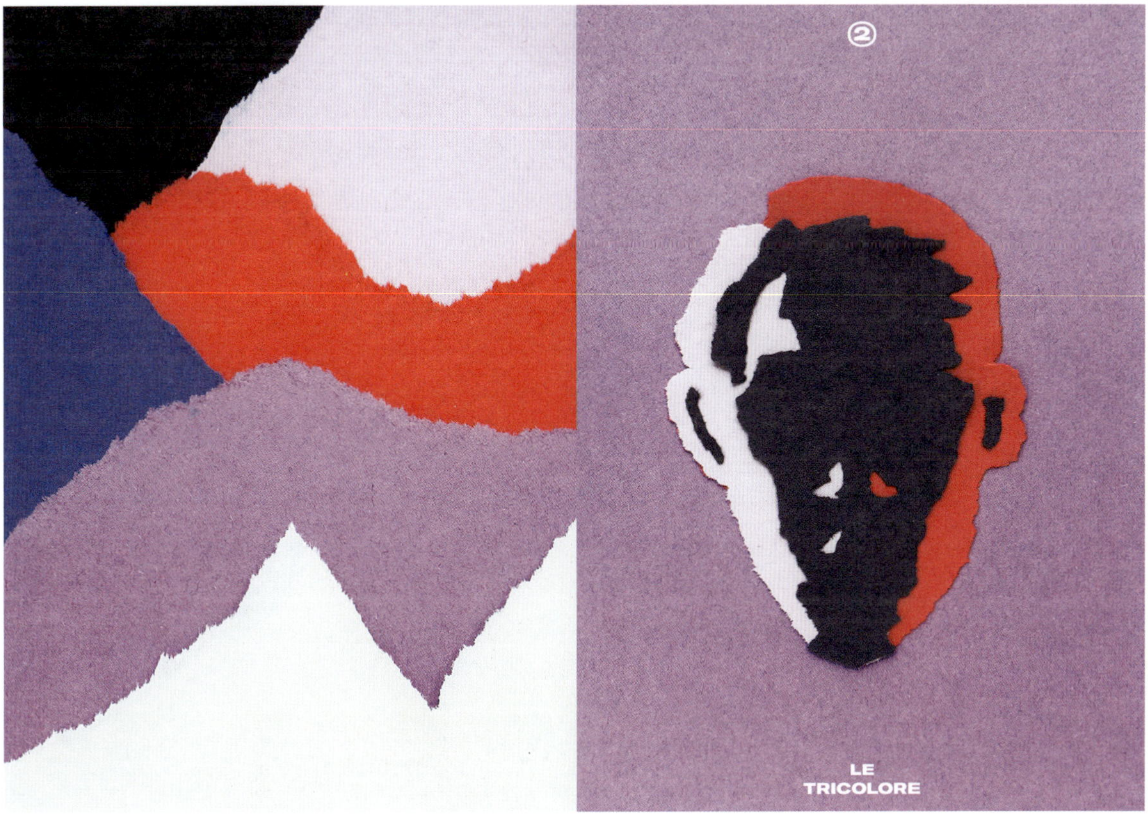

②

LE
TRICOLORE

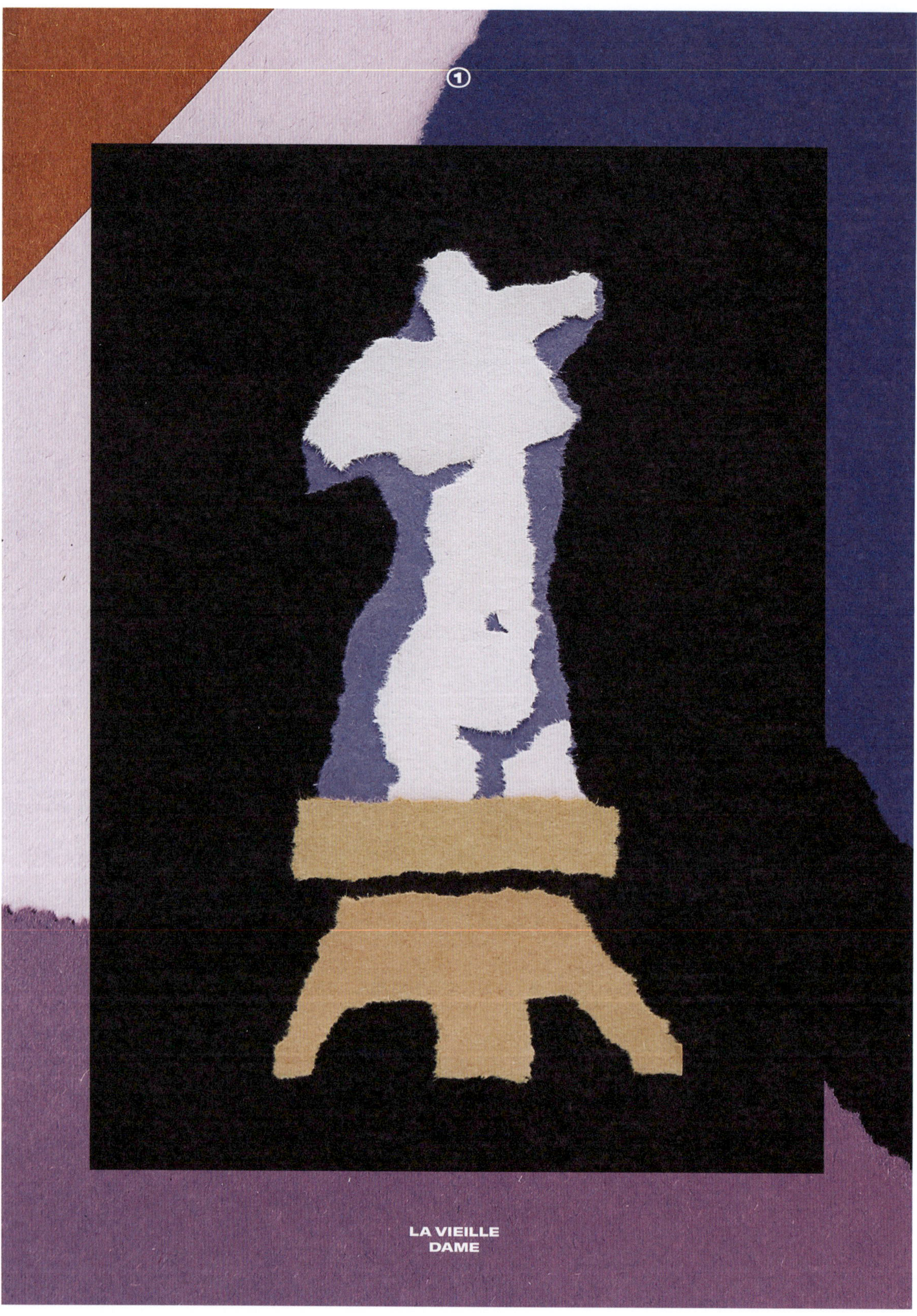
①
LA VIEILLE
DAME

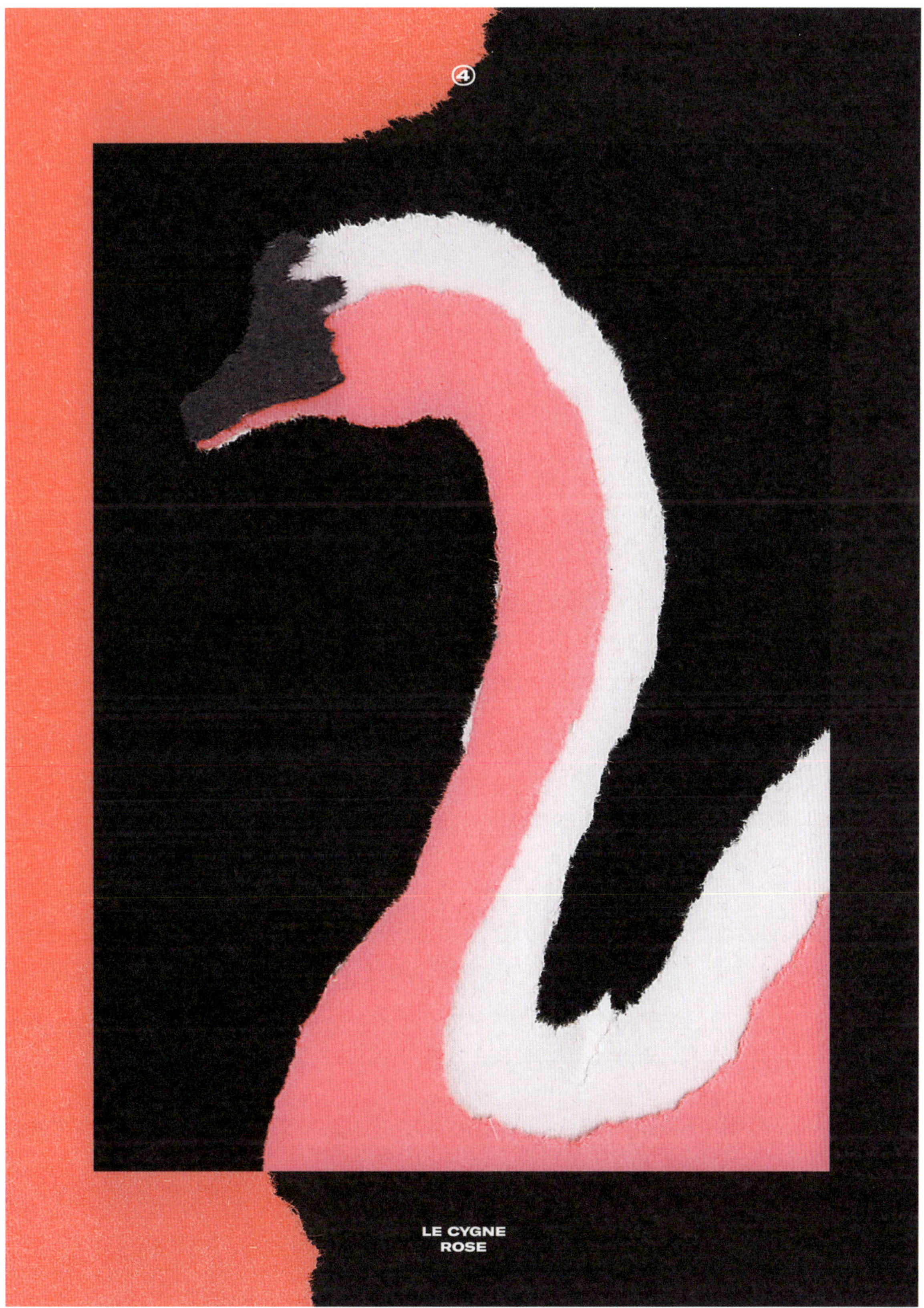
④
LE CYGNE
ROSE

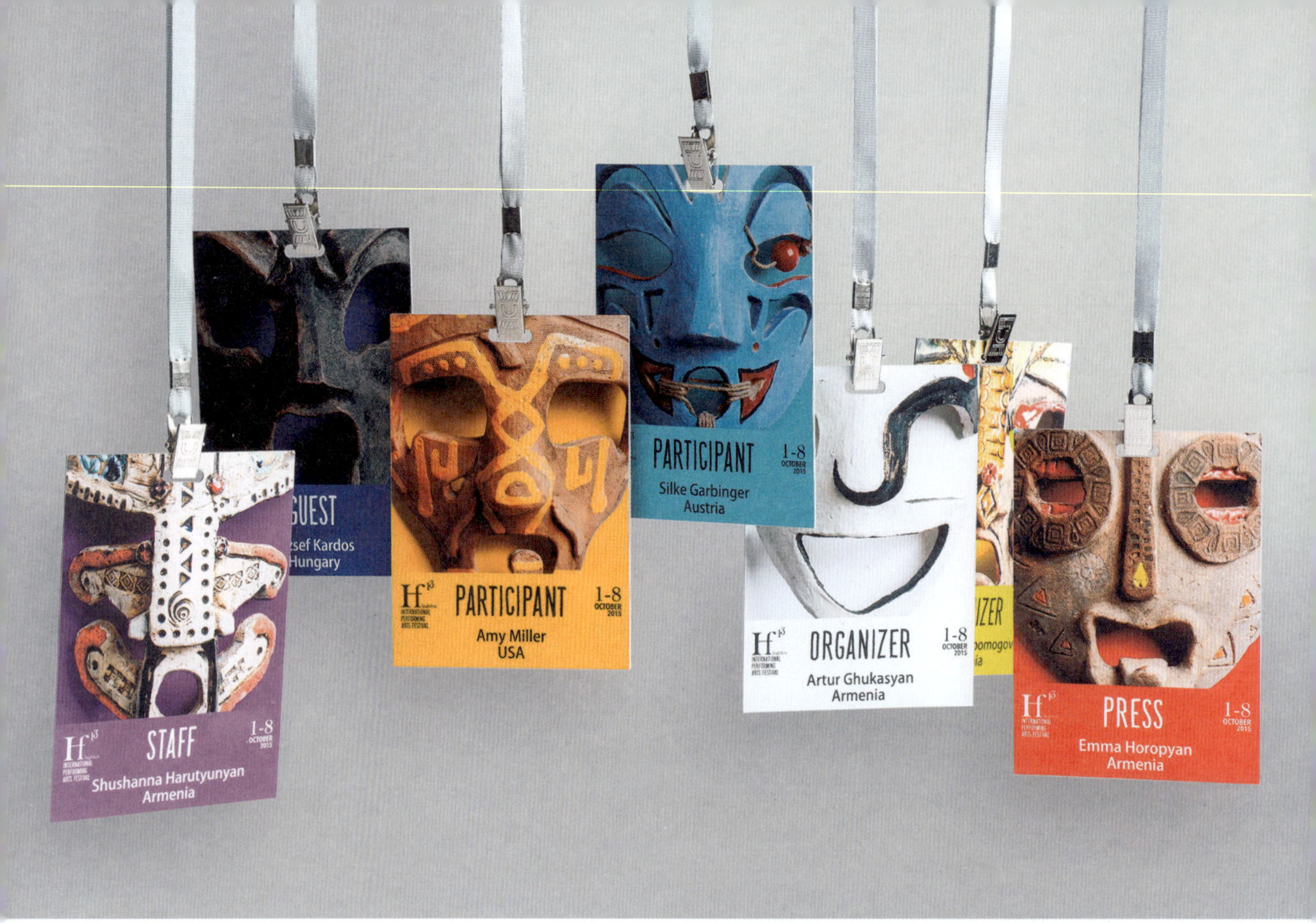

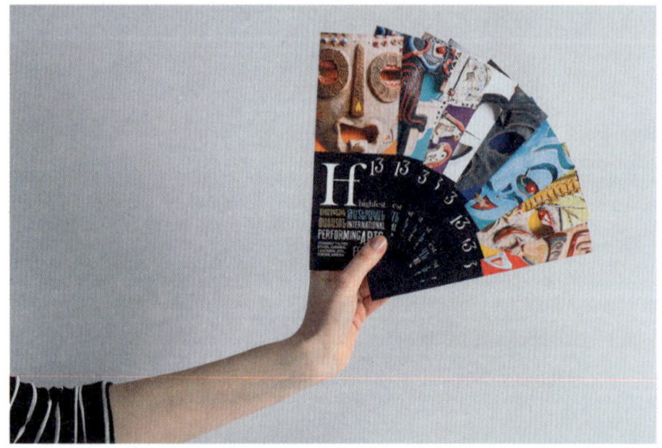

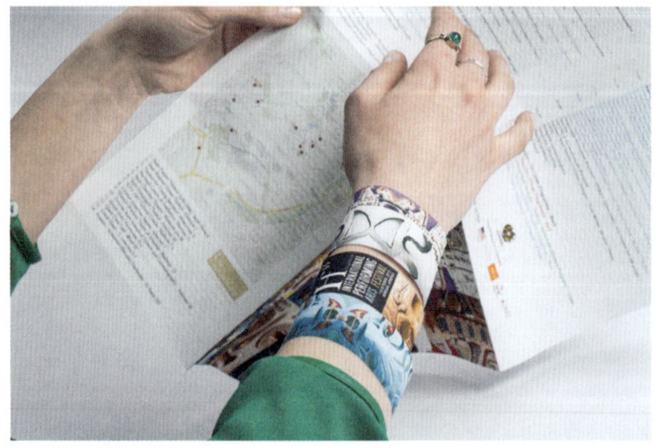

HIGH FEST

Studio : Backbone Branding
Designer : Stepan Azaryan
Ceramic Artist : Vache Manukyan

The visual identity of the 13th HIGH FEST International Performing Arts Festival was based on the ceramic masks created by Vache Manukyan. The idea was to maintain the significant role of masks as a symbol of the history of performing arts through the unique masks made of clay and glaze. The masks were presented with colored backgrounds to express the main theme of the year: The Gallery of Emotions.

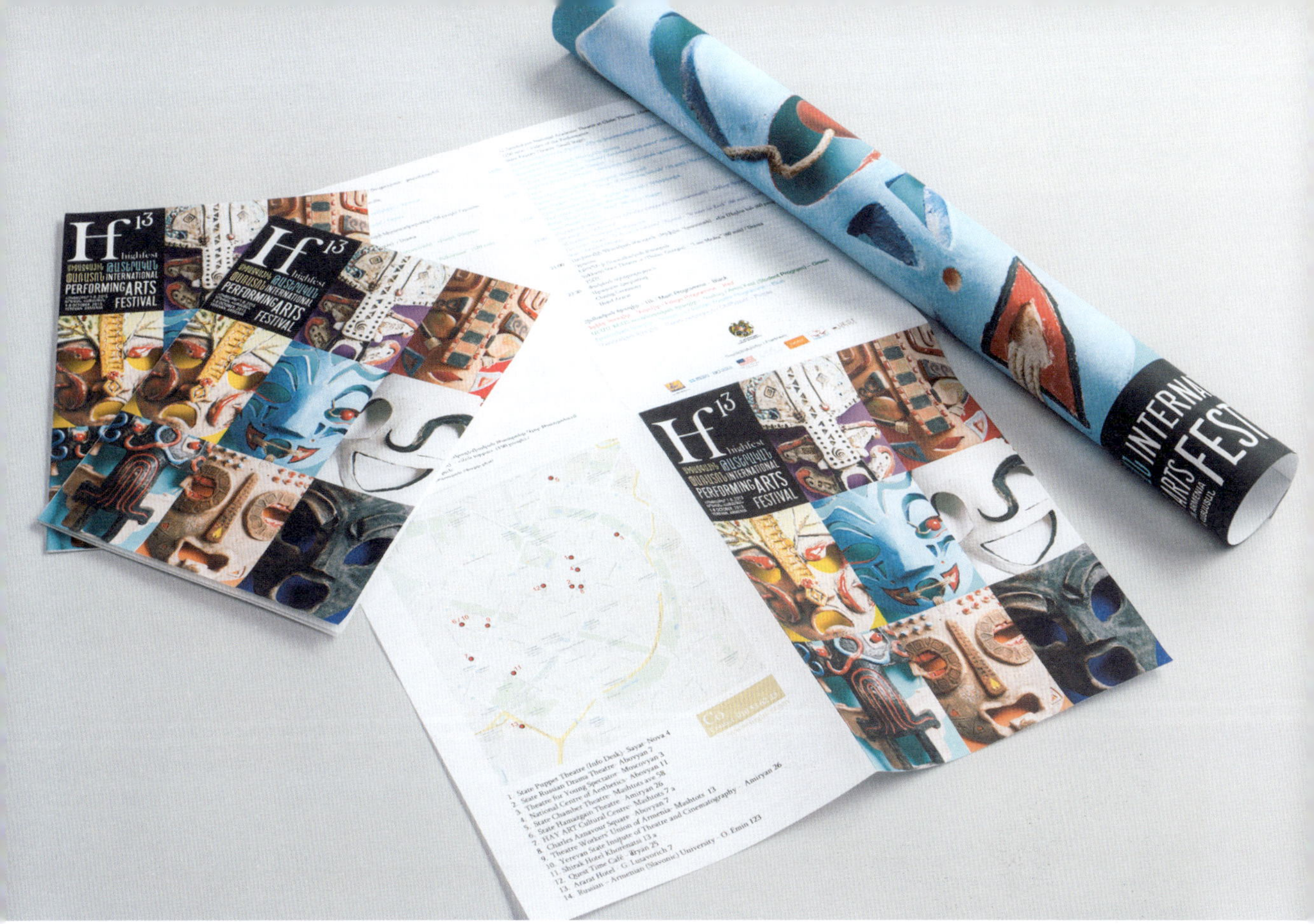

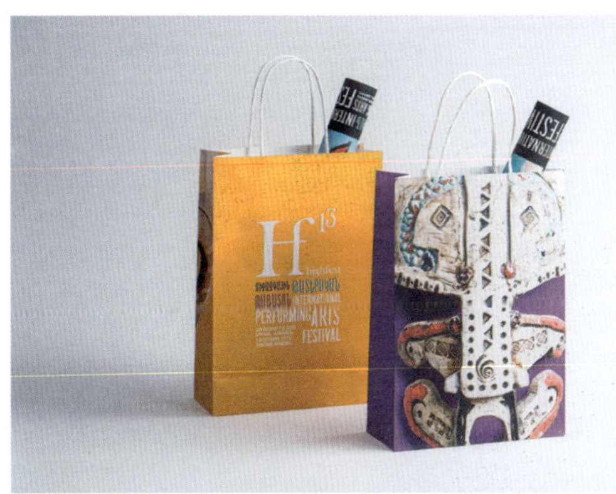

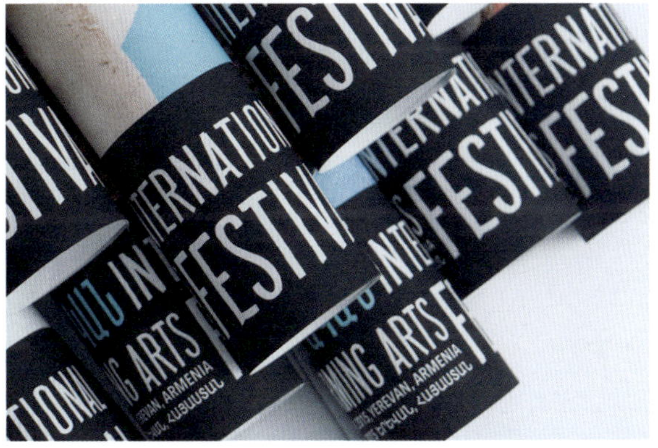
FESTIVAL
INTERNATIONAL
ARTS
YEREVAN, ARMENIA

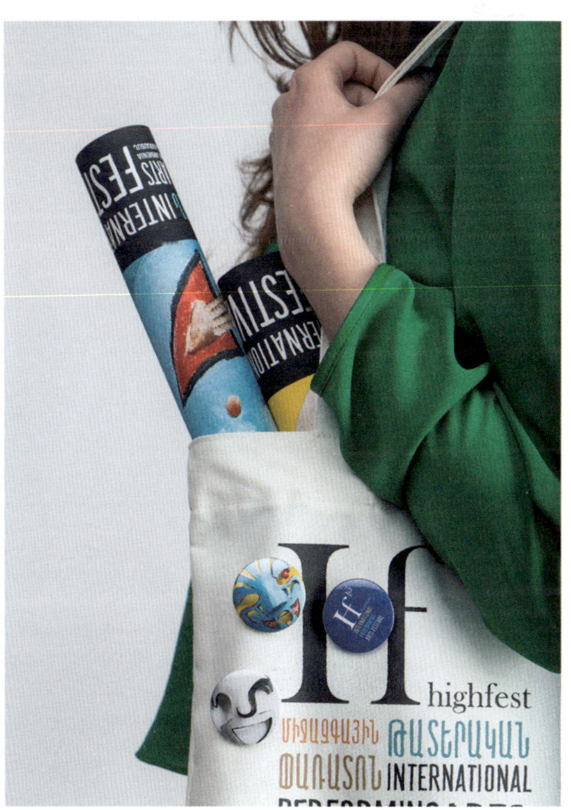
Hf
highfest
ՄԻՋԱԶԳԱՅԻՆ ԹԱՏԵՐԱԿԱՆ
ՓԱՌԱՏՕՆ INTERNATIONAL

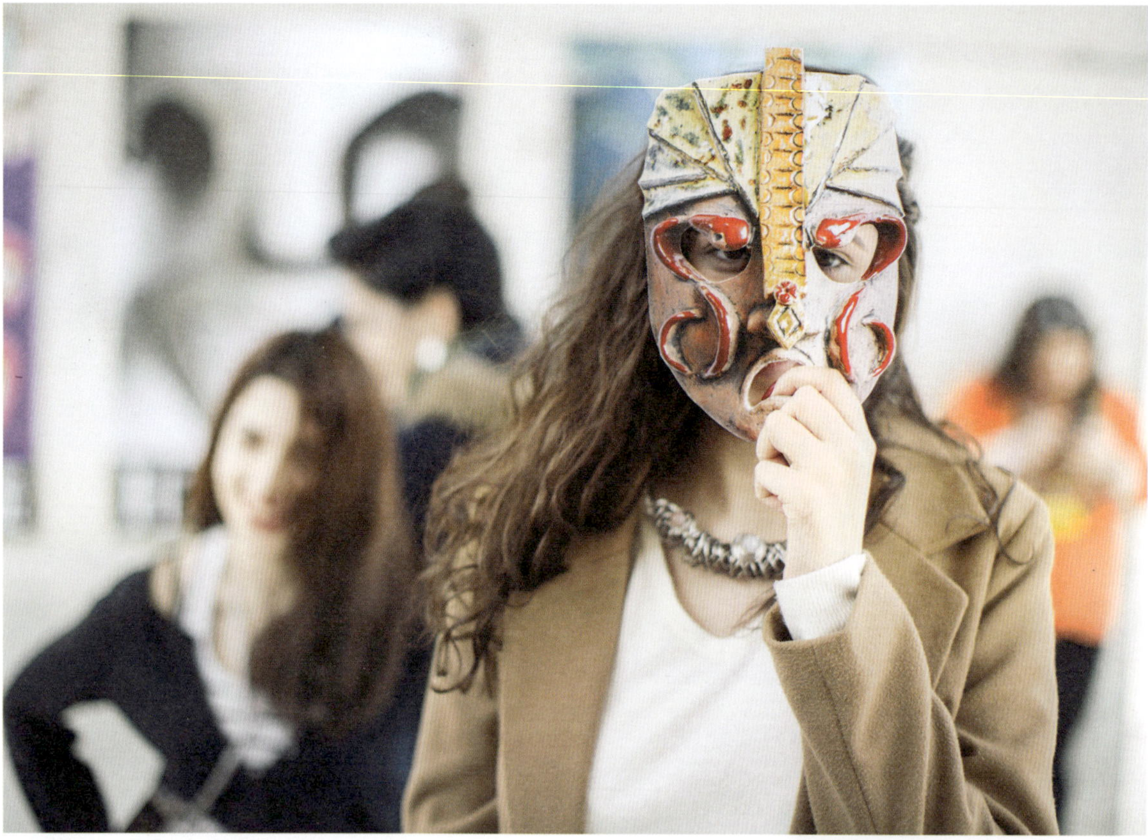

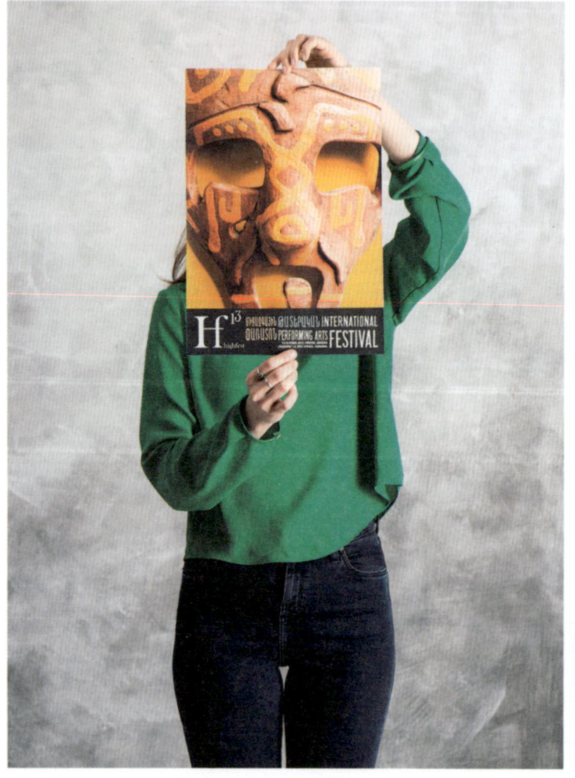

Hf 13
highfest
ՄԻՋԱԶԳԱՅԻՆ ԹԱՏԵՐԱԿԱՆ INTERNATIONAL
ՓԱՌԱՏՈՆ PERFORMING ARTS FESTIVAL

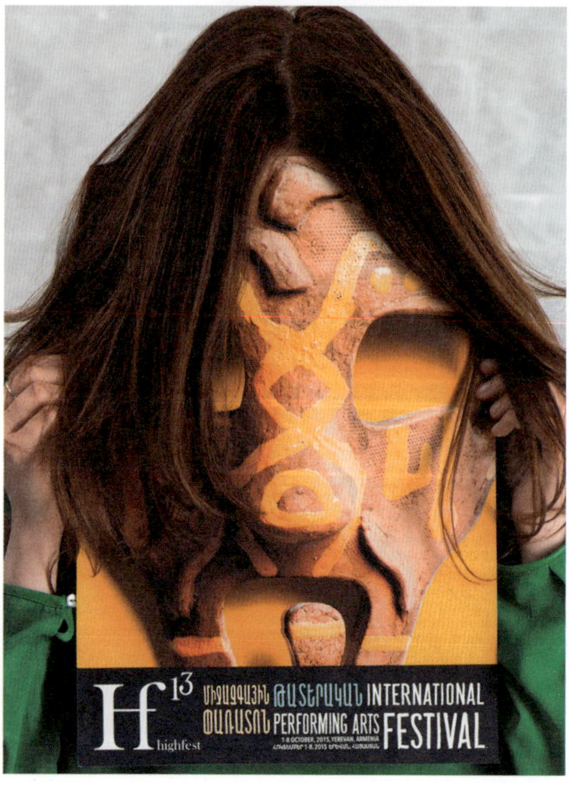

Hf 13
highfest
ՄԻՋԱԶԳԱՅԻՆ ԹԱՏԵՐԱԿԱՆ INTERNATIONAL
ՓԱՌԱՏՈՆ PERFORMING ARTS FESTIVAL
1-8 OCTOBER, 2015, YEREVAN, ARMENIA

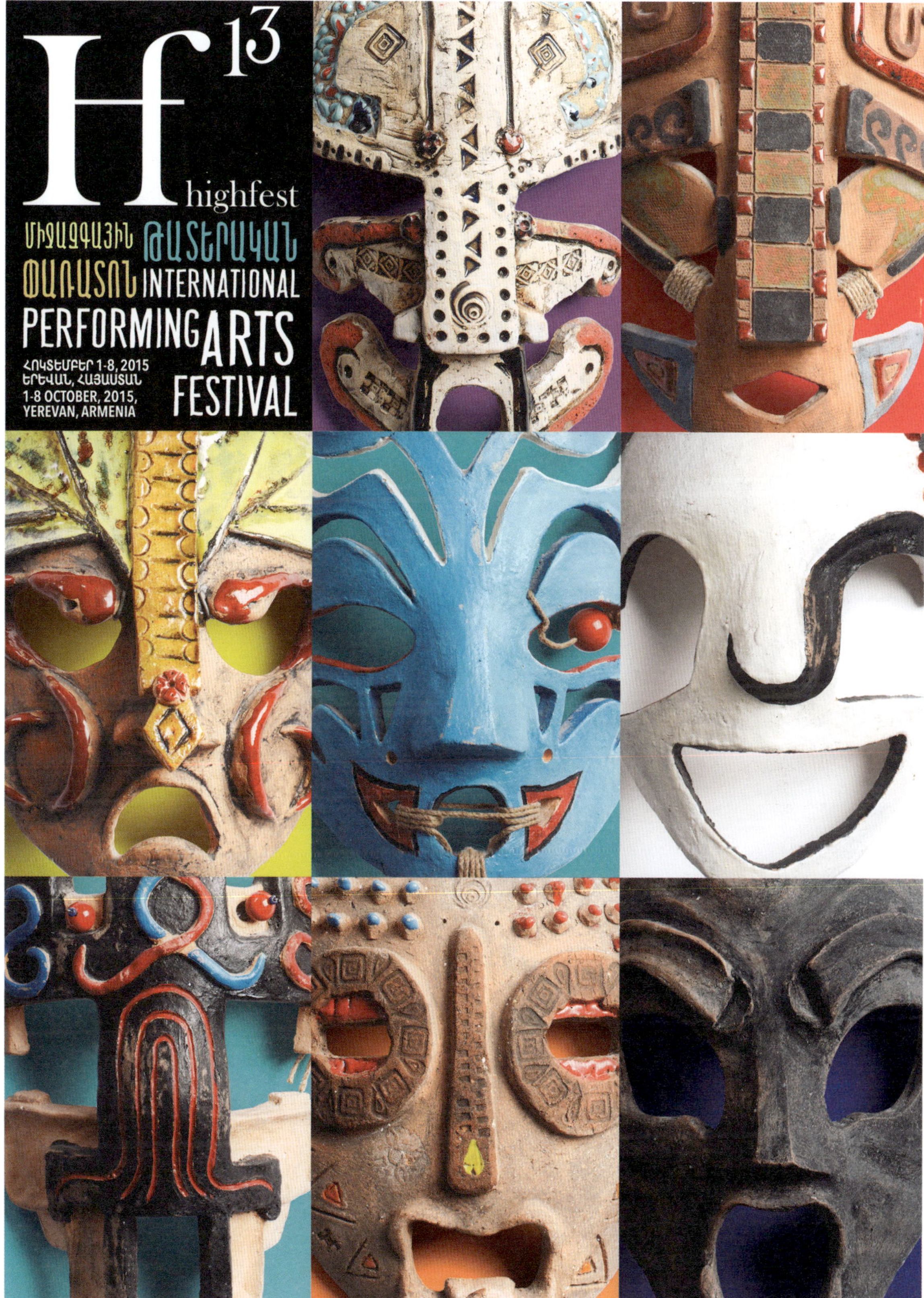
Hf 13
highfest
ՄԻՋԱԶԳԱՅԻՆ ԹԱՏԵՐԱԿԱՆ ՓԱՌԱՏՈՆ
INTERNATIONAL PERFORMING ARTS FESTIVAL
ՀՈԿՏԵՄԲԵՐ 1-8, 2015
ԵՐԵՎԱՆ, ՀԱՅԱՍՏԱՆ
1-8 OCTOBER, 2015,
YEREVAN, ARMENIA

©THE TRASH BOOK

Studio : Amateur(dot)rocks
Designer : Ivo Pallucchini, José Bessega

The Trash Book is an editorial project which is a "not so clean" way to explore cities and to understand their communities, with all their complexities and different manners of living. New York is the first city for this project. The book was made and bound exclusively with waste material found on the streets. It is a tour through different cultures, American consumerism and capitalism, all living together in the most cosmopolitan city of the world.

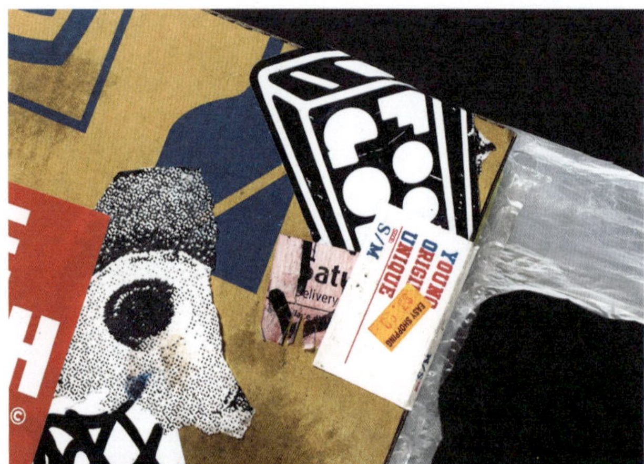

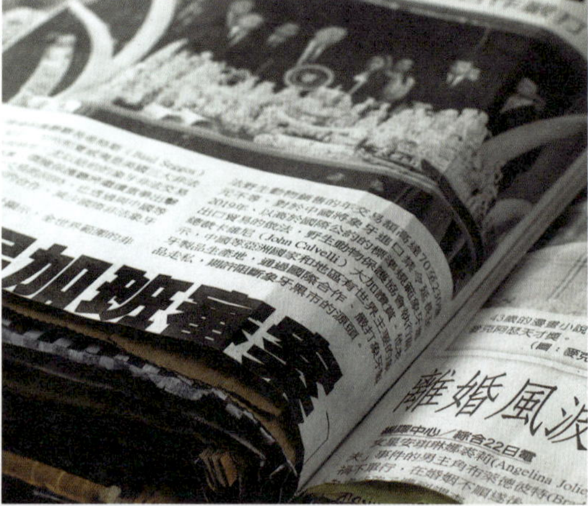

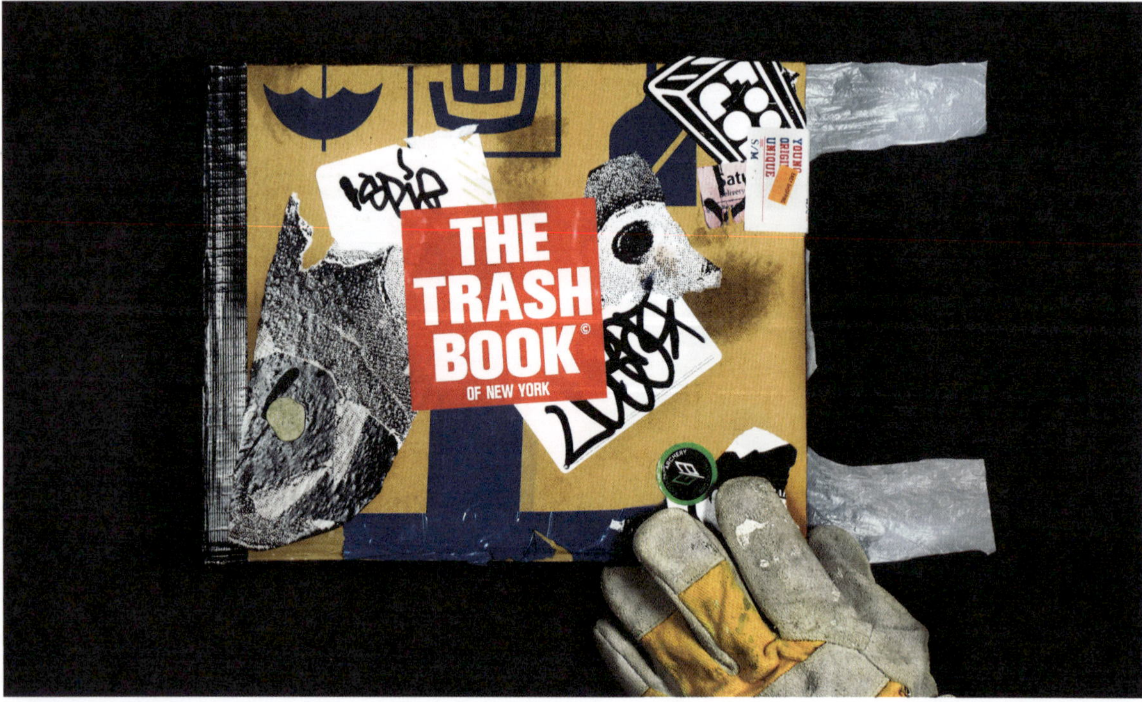

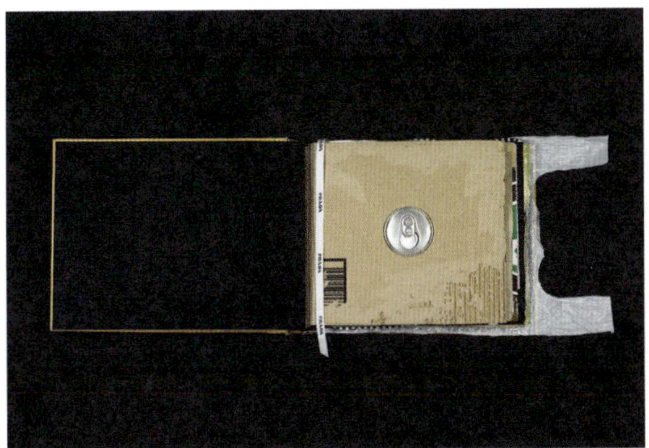

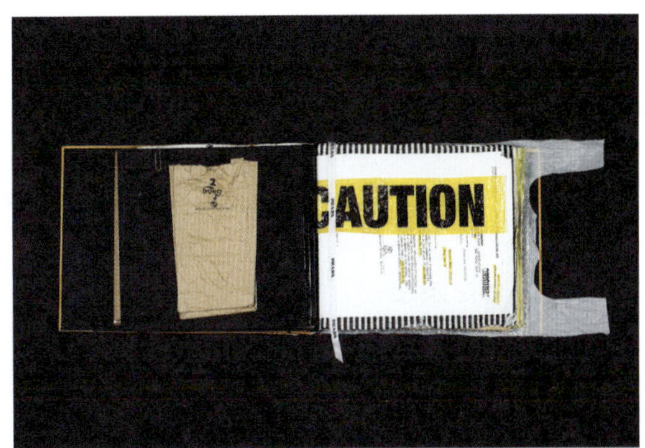
CAUTION

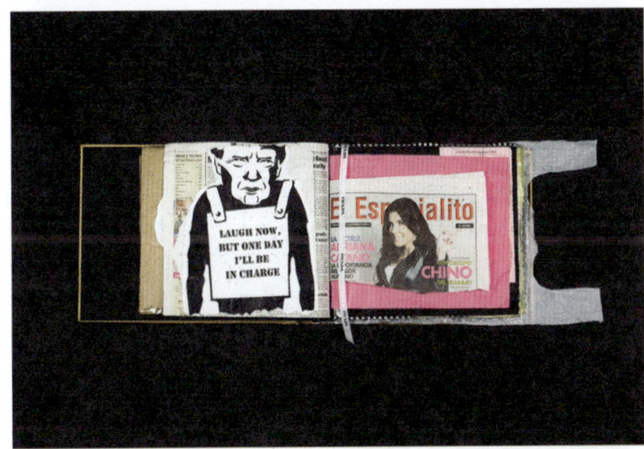
LAUGH NOW,
BUT ONE DAY
I'LL BE
IN CHARGE
CHINO

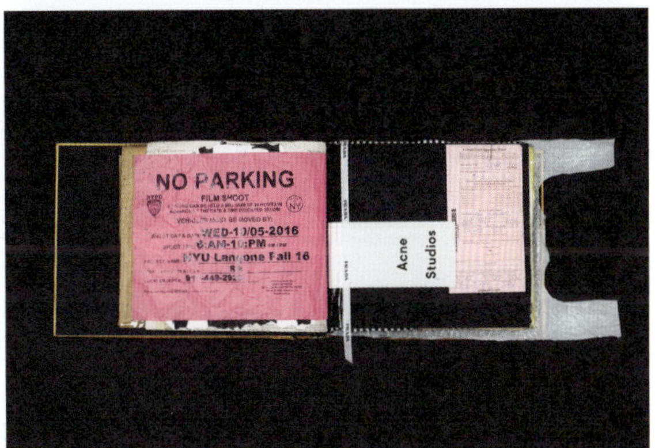
NO PARKING
FILM SHOOT
Acne
Studios

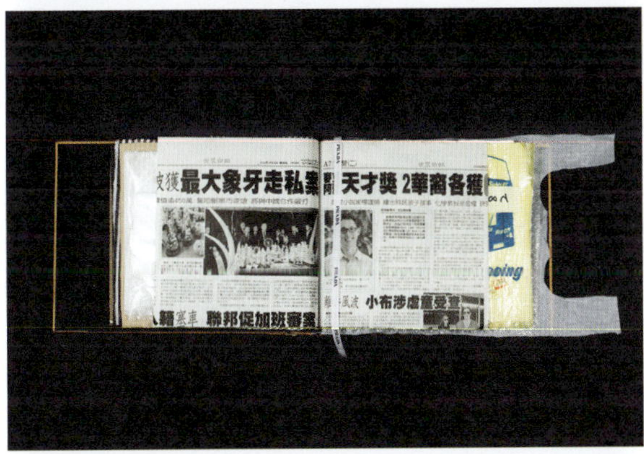
最大象牙走私案
天才獎 2華裔各獲

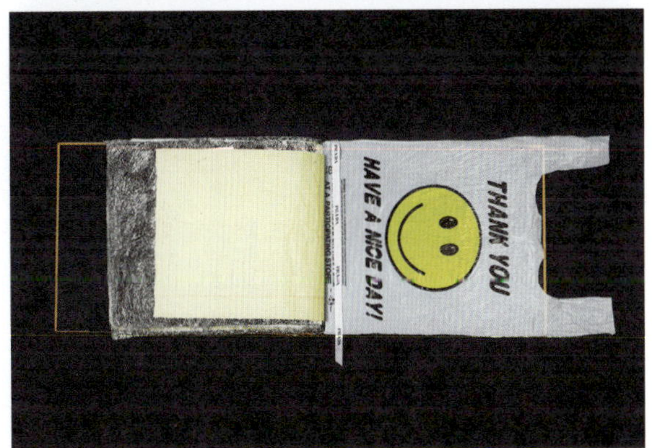
HAVE A NICE DAY!
THANK YOU

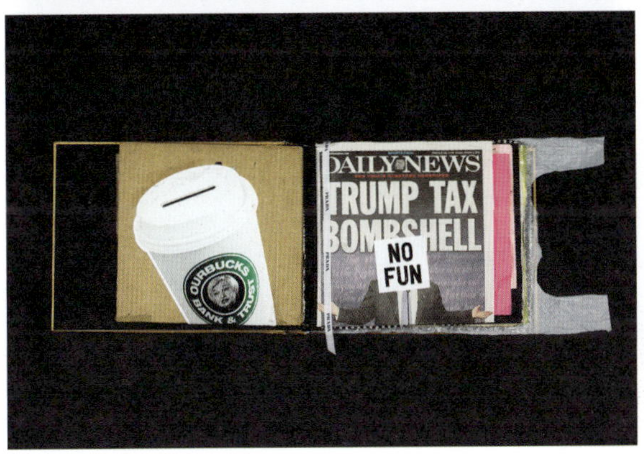
DAILY NEWS
TRUMP TAX
BOMBSHELL
NO
FUN

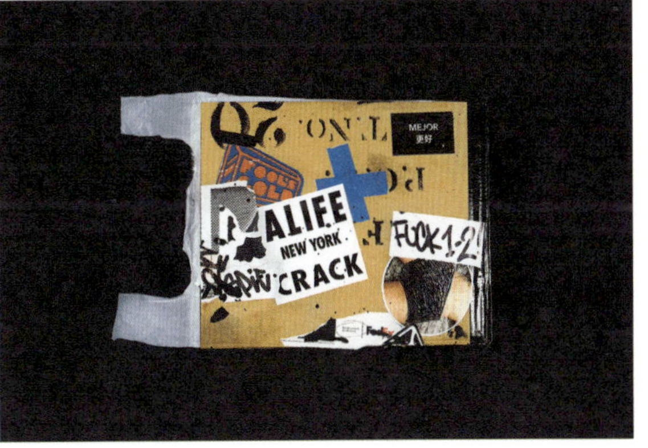
MEJOR
ALIFE
NEW YORK
CRACK

CONCEPTUAL POSTERS

Studio : Amateur(dot)rocks
Designer : Ivo Pallucchini, José Bessega

This is a reactive idea to the intense and constant insistence of drug-dealers to sell substances to anyone in some neighborhoods in Lisbon. The designers designed a series of drug-dealer flyers and spread them all over the city. The main objective was to reduce the unwanted harassment by changing the verbal communication channel to a visual and graphic one, adopting in each piece the persuasive expressions that the dealers use.

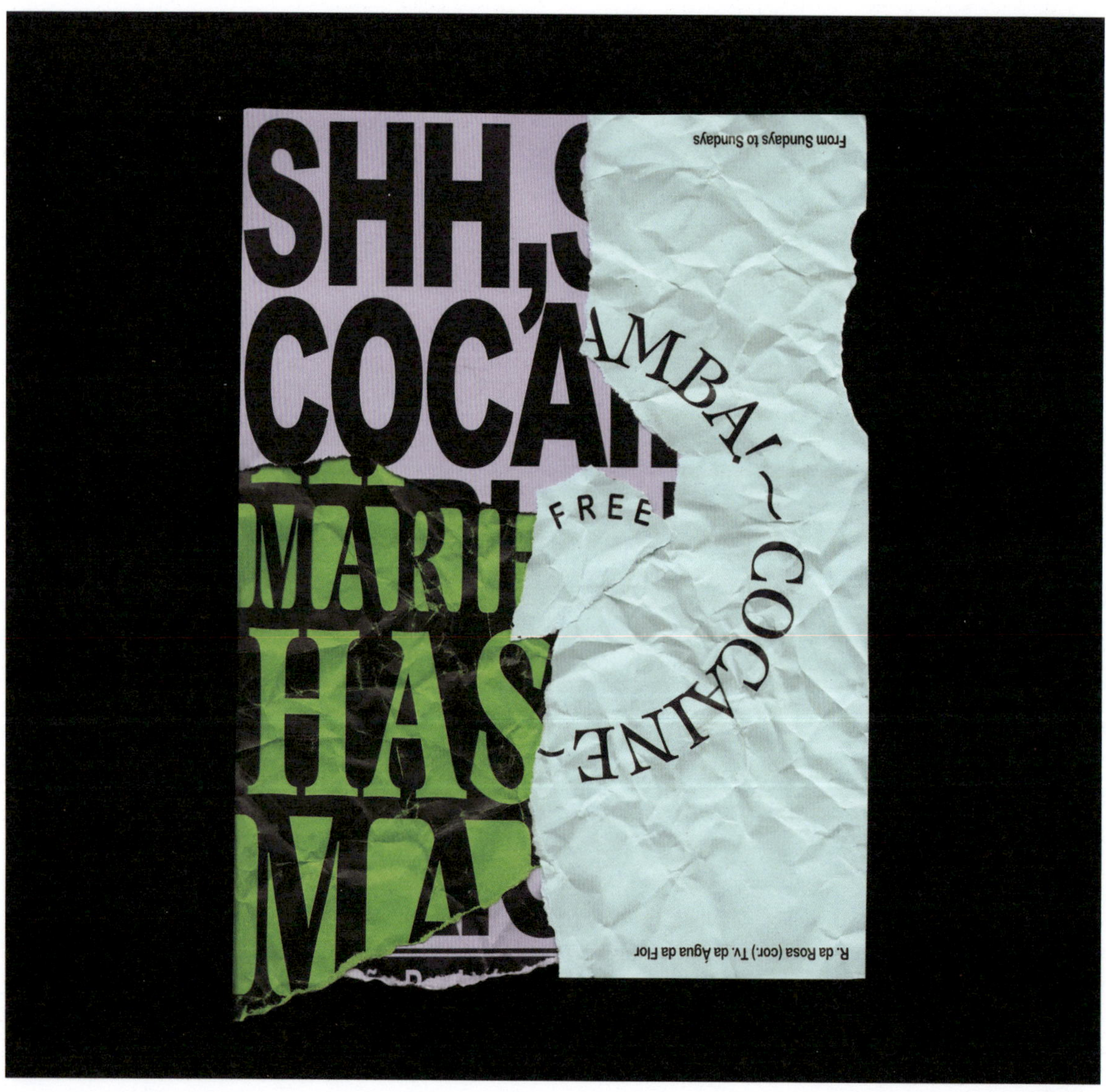

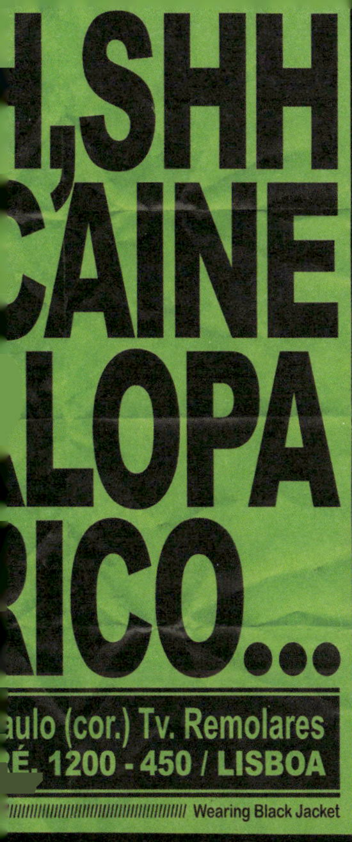
H,SHH
CAINE
LOPA
RICO...
aulo (cor.) Tv. Remolares
É. 1200 - 450 / LISBOA
Wearing Black Jacket

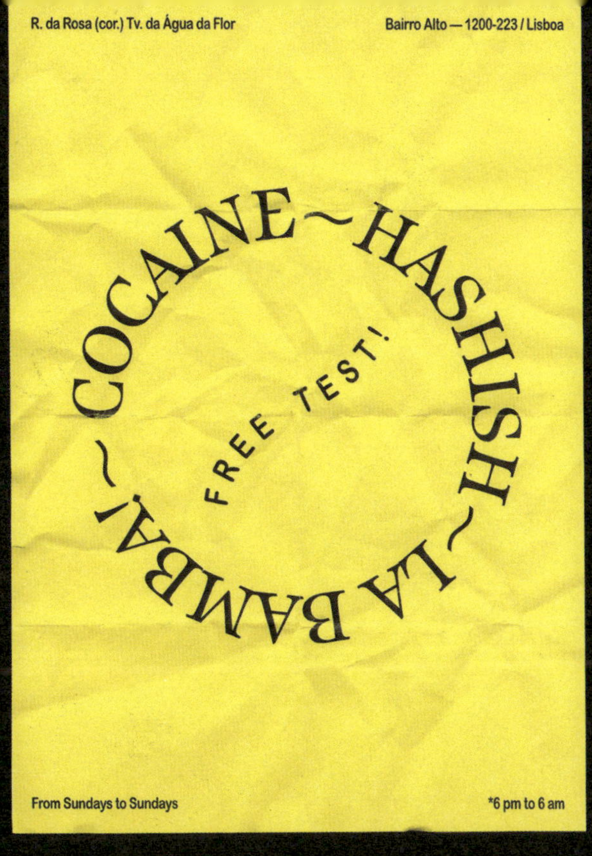
R. da Rosa (cor.) Tv. da Água da Flor
Bairro Alto — 1200-223 / Lisboa
COCAINE~HASHISH~LA BAMBA!~
FREE TEST!
From Sundays to Sundays
*6 pm to 6 am

COCA
100m
Good!
It's Ok!
Gypsy Shit!
Cc. do Tijolo
R. do Século
R. Nova do Loureiro
R. da Rosa
R. da Rosa
R. da Atalaia
Fiéis de Deus
R. da Barroca
From Sundays to Sundays / 6 pm to 6 am
BAIRRO ALTO —1200

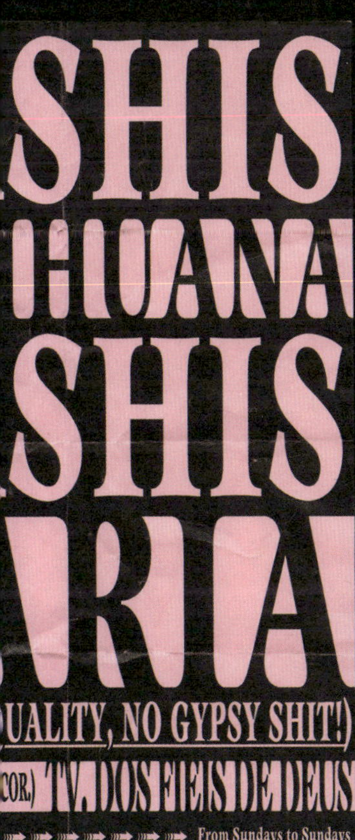
SHIS
HUANA
SHIS
RIA
UALITY, NO GYPSY SHIT!)
COR.) TV. DOS FIEIS DE DEUS
From Sundays to Sundays

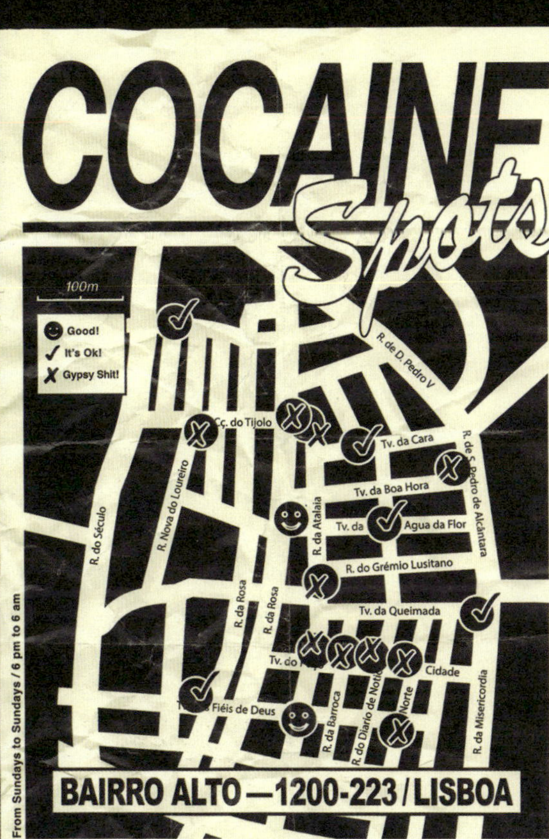
COCAINE
Spots
100m
Good!
It's Ok!
Gypsy Shit!
R. de D. Pedro V
Cc. do Tijolo
Tv. da Cara
R. de S. Pedro de Alcântara
Tv. da Boa Hora
Tv. da
Água da Flor
R. do Século
R. Nova do Loureiro
R. da Atalaia
R. do Grémio Lusitano
Tv. da Queimada
R. da Rosa
R. da Rosa
Cidade
Fiéis de Deus
R. da Barroca
R. do Diário de Notícias
Norte
R. da Misericórdia
From Sundays to Sundays / 6 pm to 6 am
BAIRRO ALTO —1200-223 / LISBOA

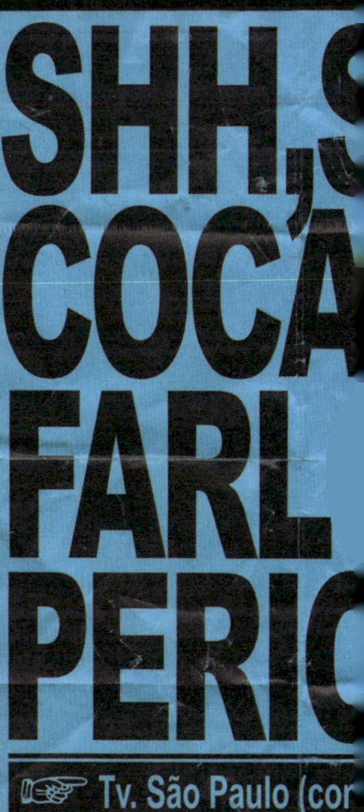
SHH,
COCA
FARL
PERIC
Tv. São Paulo (cor
CAIS DO SODRÉ, 1200
From Sundays to Sundays

COCAINE *Spots*

100m

Good!

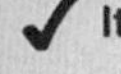
It's Ok!

Gypsy Shit!

R. de D. Pedro V

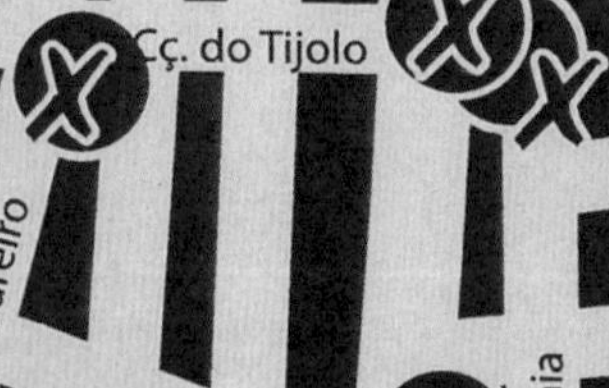

Cç. do Tijolo

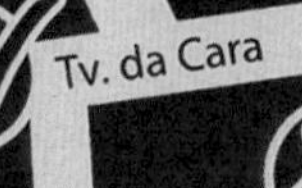

Tv. da Cara

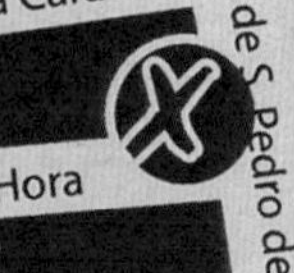

R. de S. Pedro de Alcântara

Tv. da Boa Hora

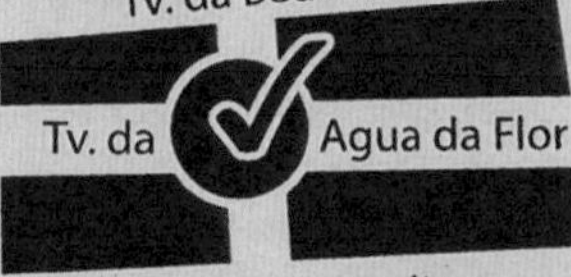

Tv. da Agua da Flor

R. do Século

R. Nova do Loureiro

R. da Atalaia

R. do Grémio Lusitano

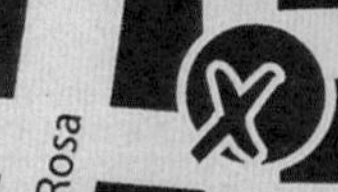

Tv. da Queimada

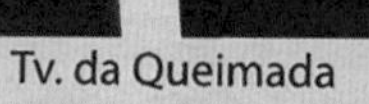

R. da Rosa

R. da Rosa

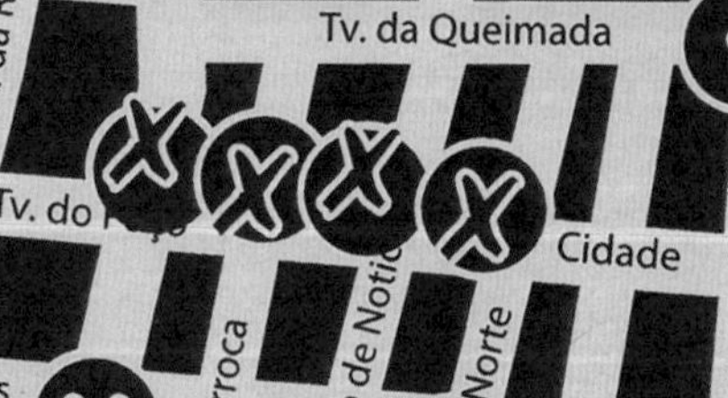

Tv. do Poço

Cidade

Tv. dos Fiéis de Deus

R. da Barroca

R. do Diario de Notícias

R. do Norte

R. da Misericordia

From Sundays to Sundays / 6 pm to 6 am

BAIRRO ALTO — 1200-223 / LISBOA

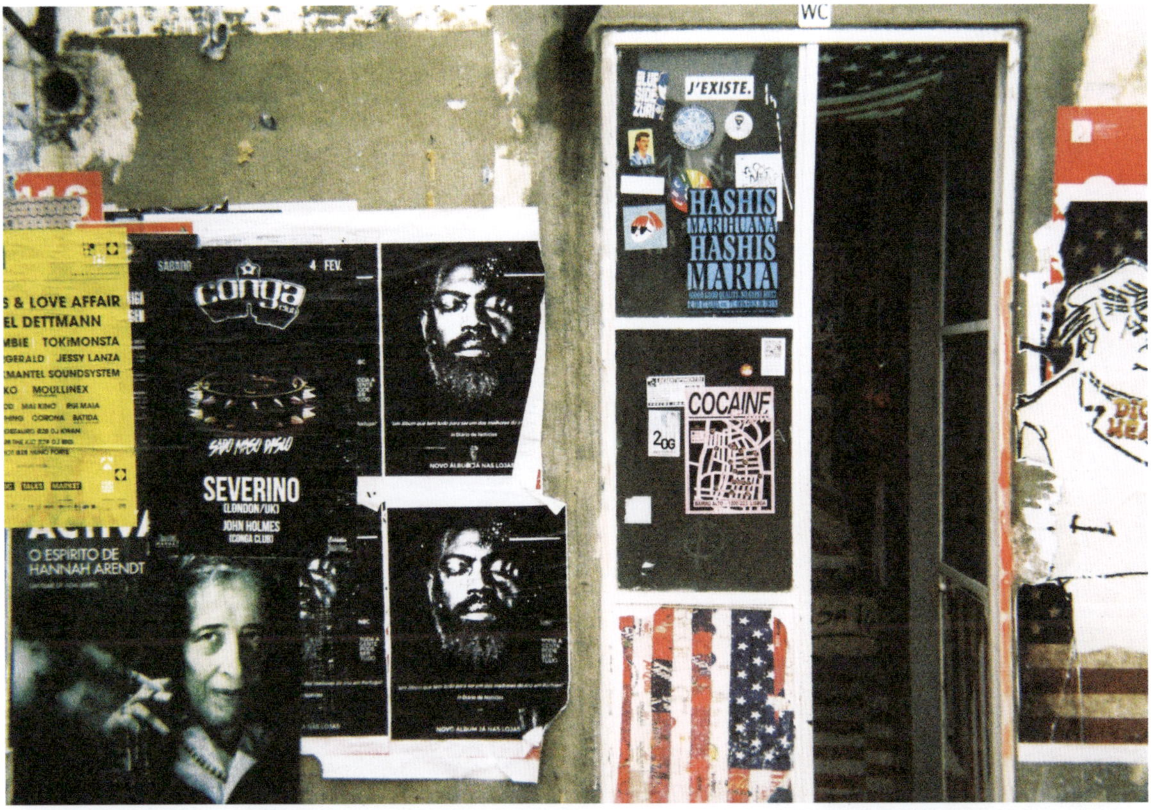

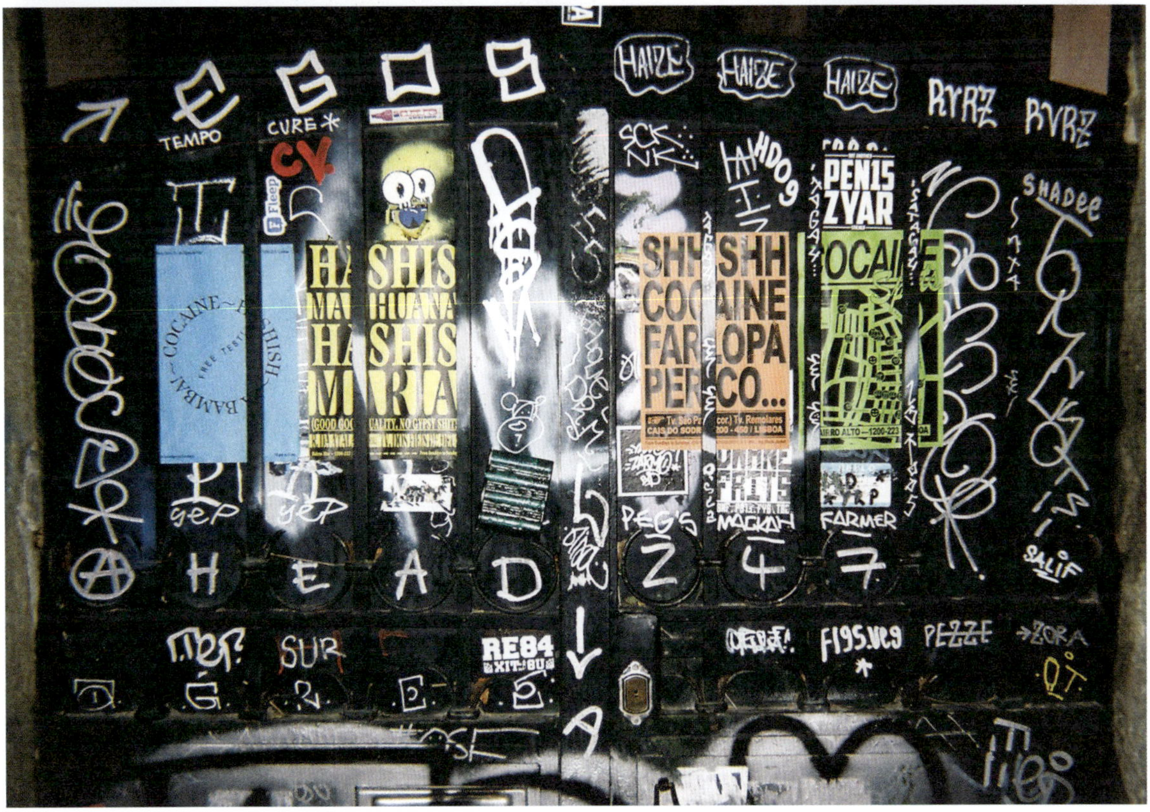

FOUR ELEMENTS TEXTURES

Studio : Yambalaya estudio
Designer : Silvia G. Guerra

This is an experimental project where the designer improvised with the four elements—water, air, soil, and fire. Sometimes it is pleasing and useful to create as nature and its spontaneity do: to embrace the graphic surprise without prior knowledge of the final result.

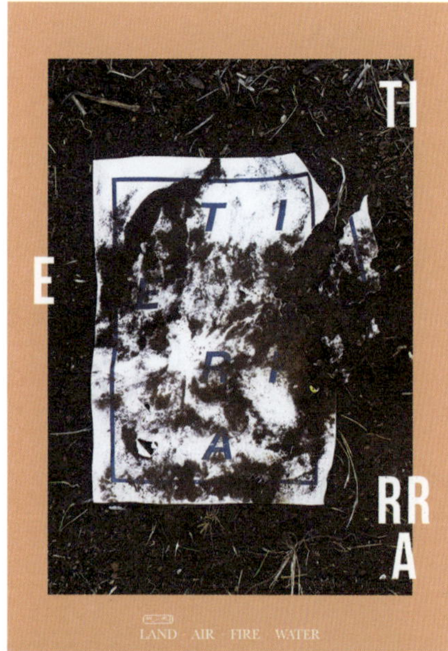

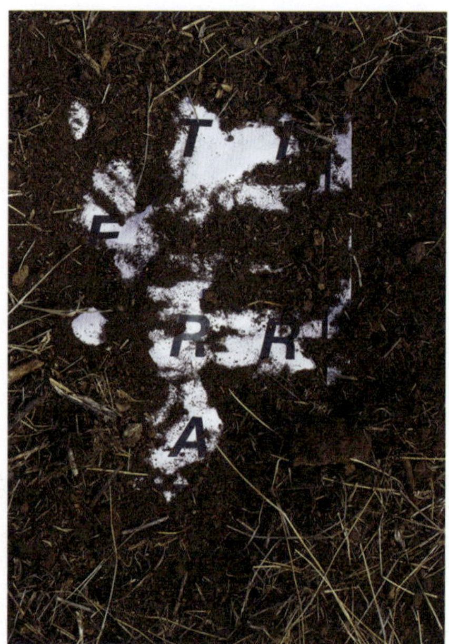

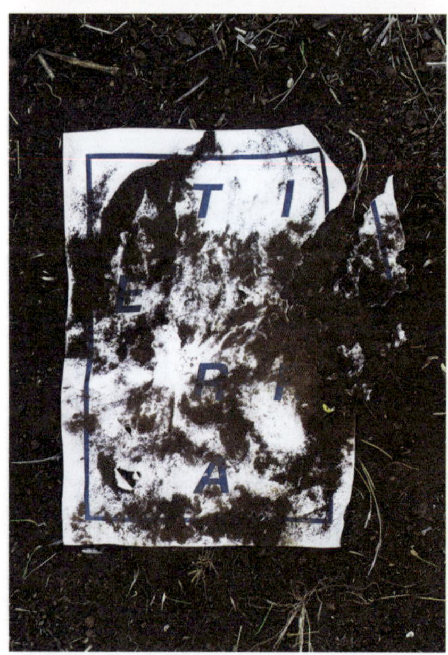

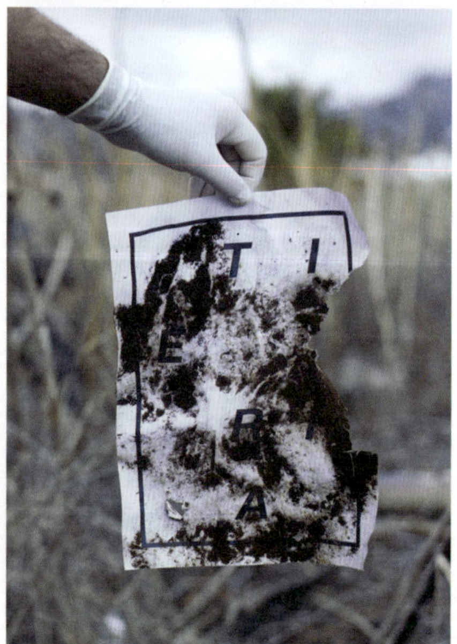

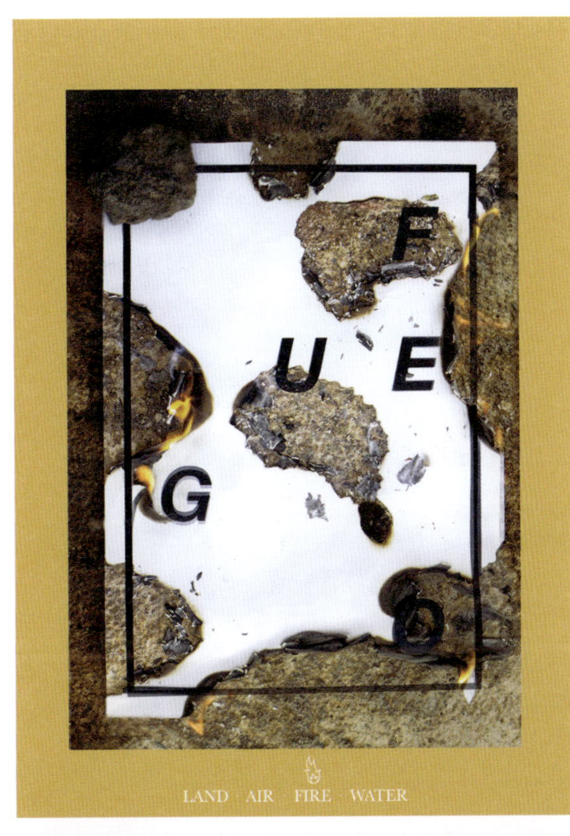
F
U E
G
O
LAND AIR FIRE WATER

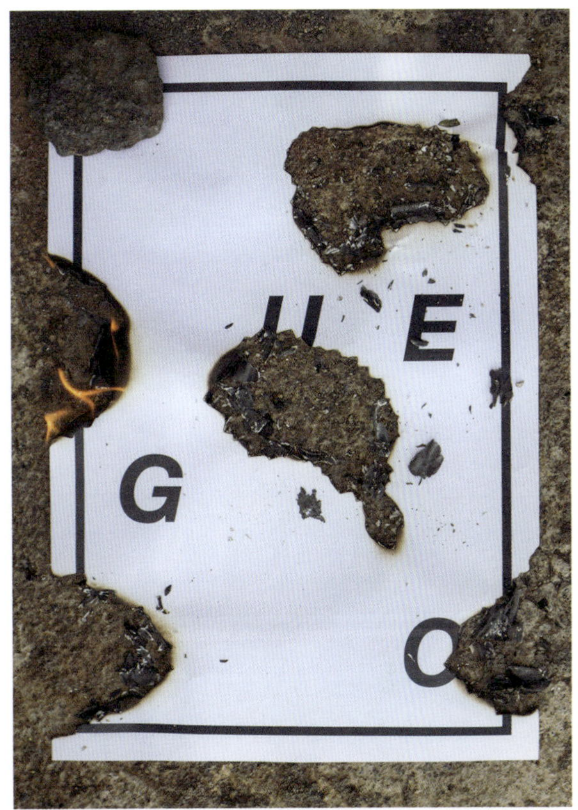
U E
G
O

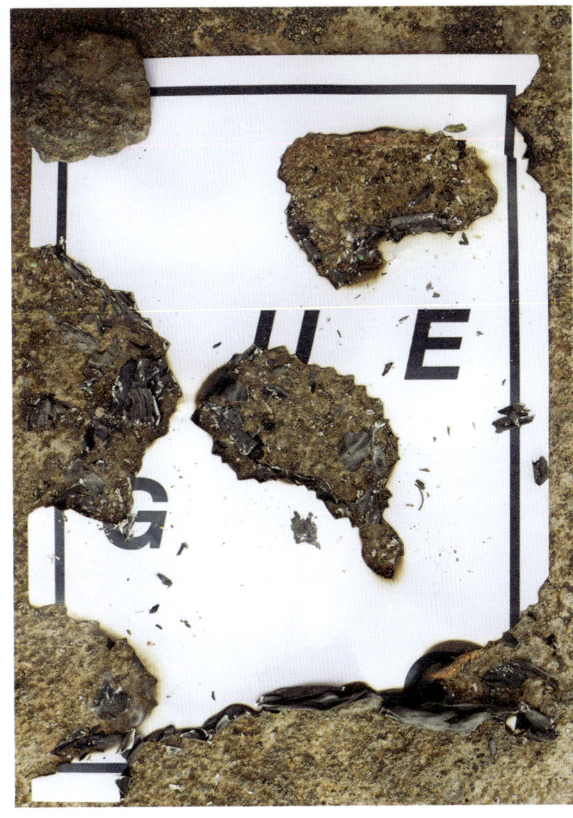
U E
G

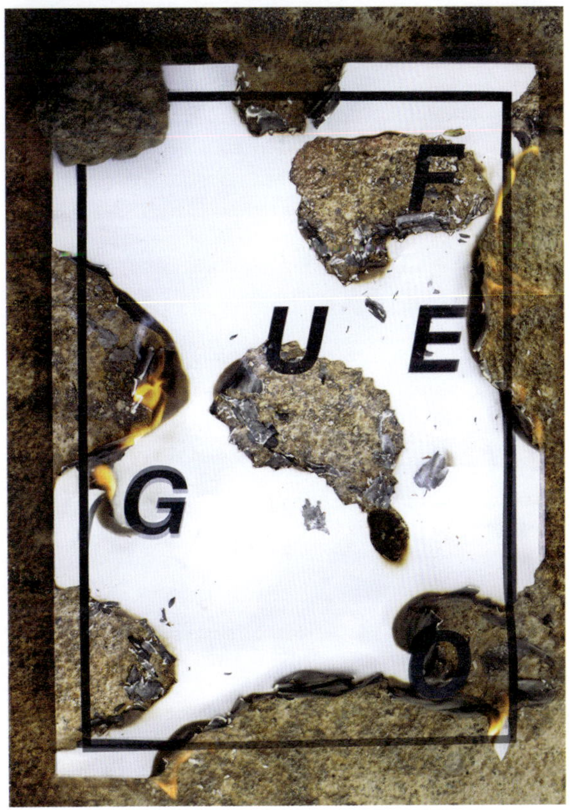
F
U E
G
O

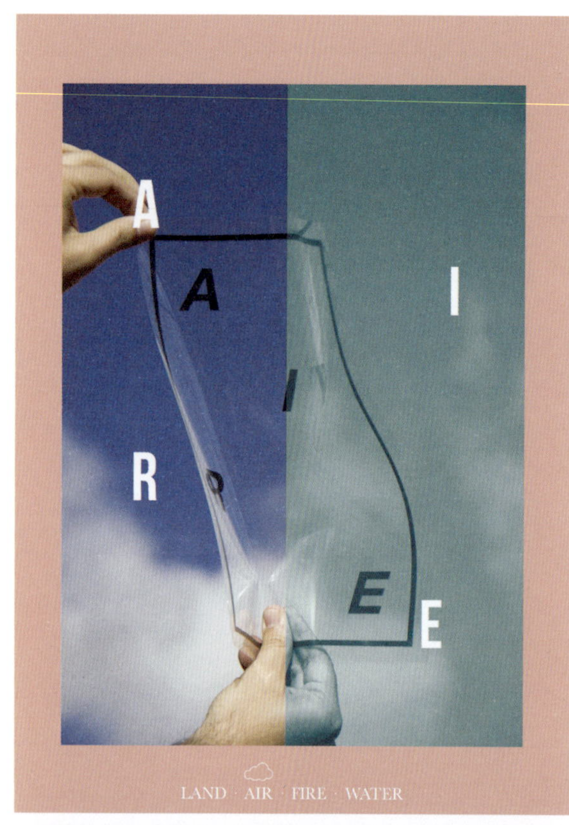
A
I
R
E
A
I
E
LAND · AIR · FIRE · WATER

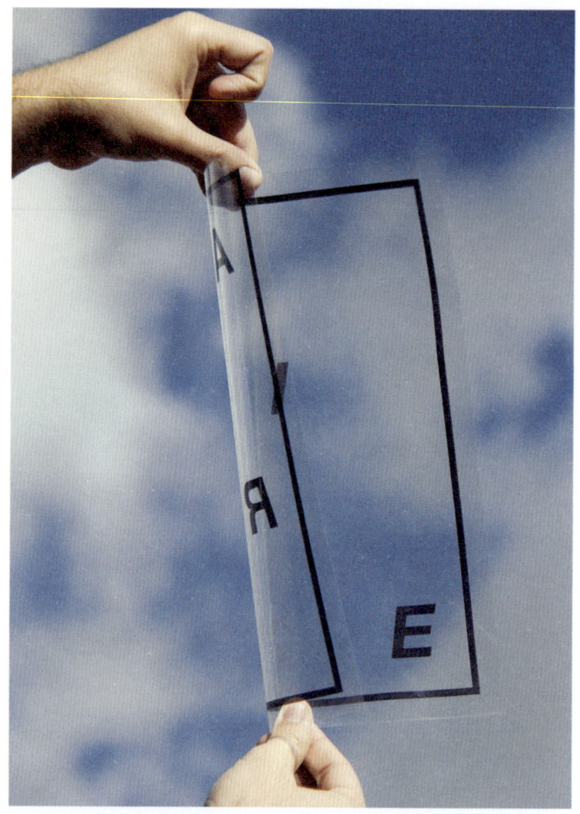
E

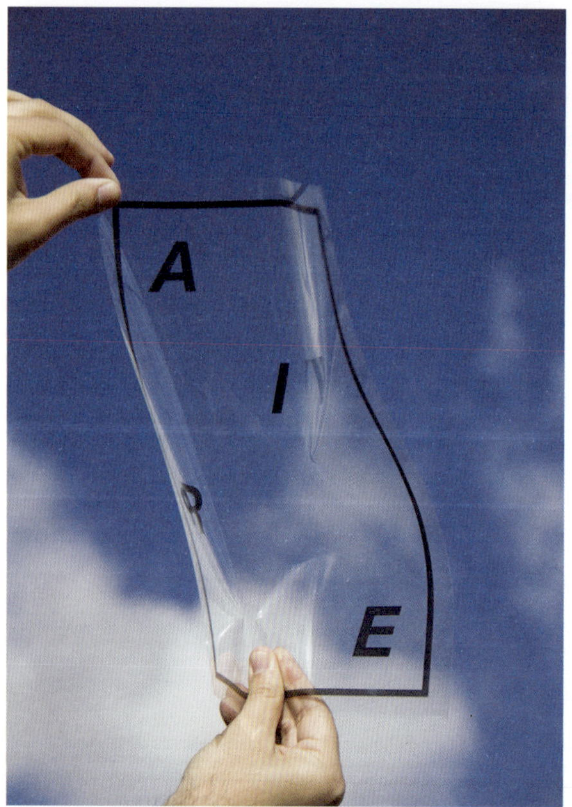
A
I
E

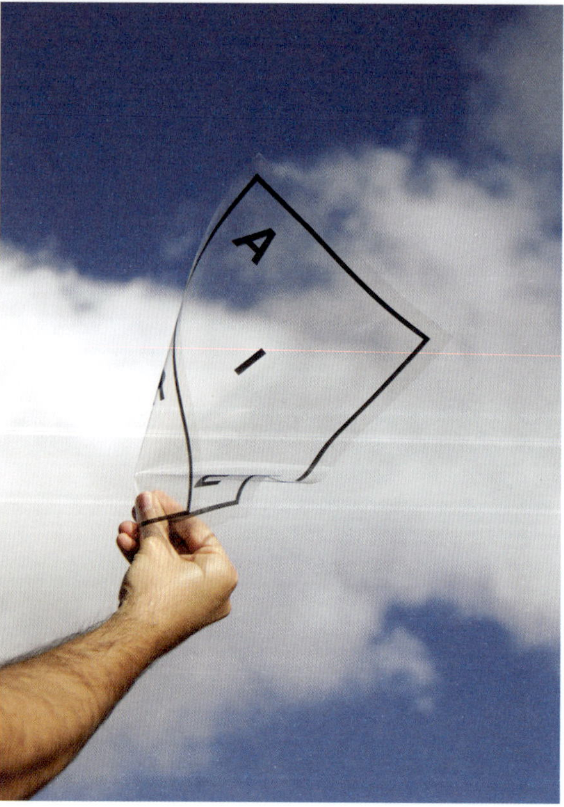
A

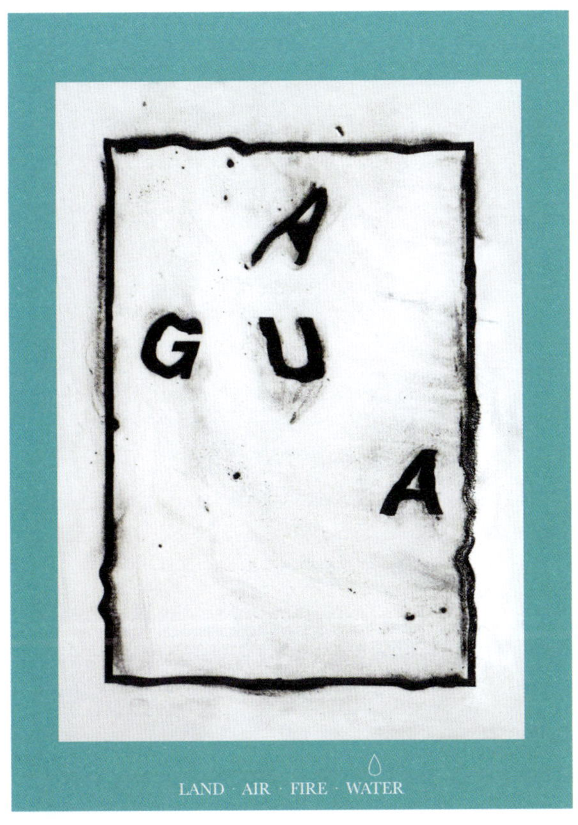
A
G U
A
LAND · AIR · FIRE · WATER

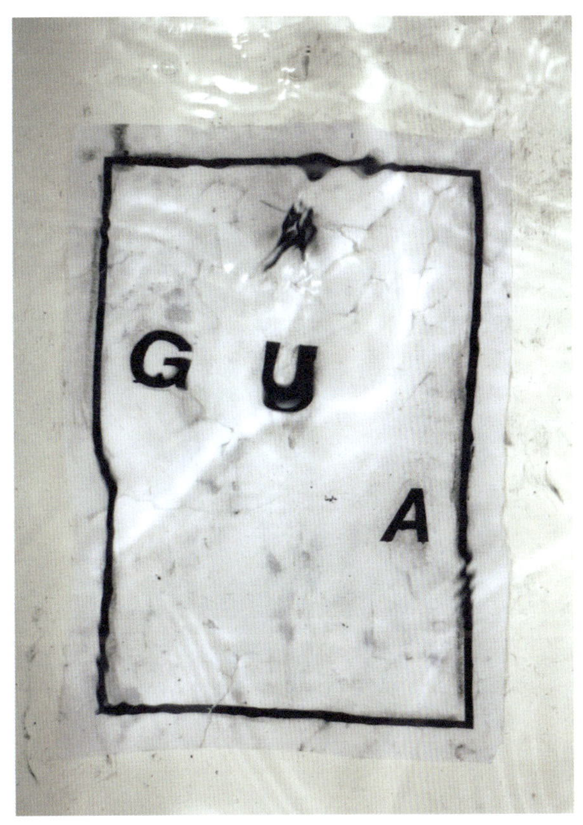
G U
A

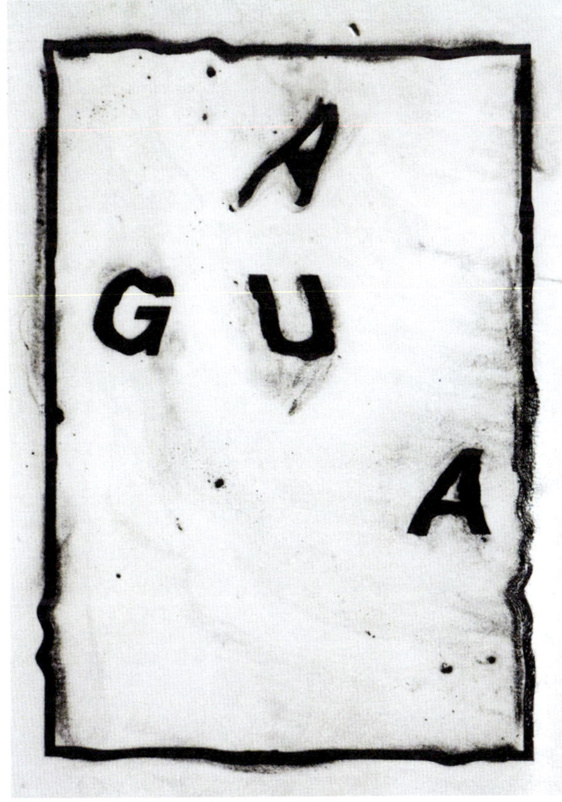
A
G U
A

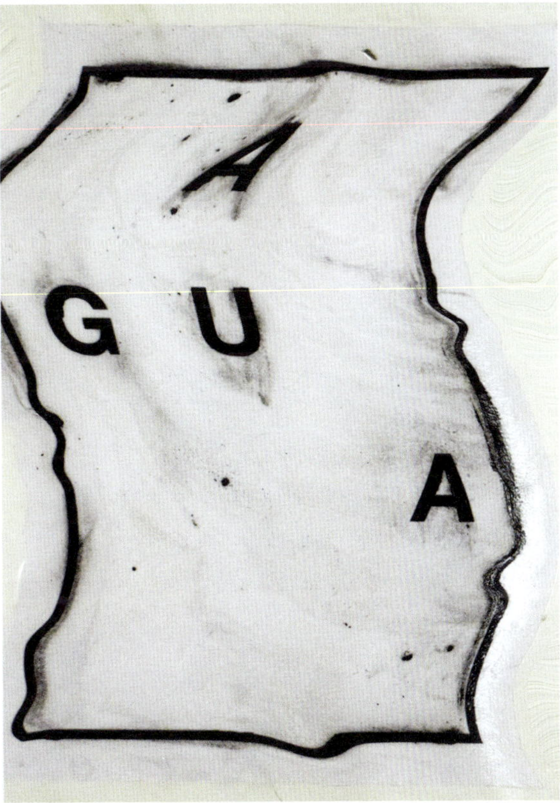
A
G U
A

PAU BRUGADA

Studio : Enserio   Designer : Miquel Amela, Ferran Rodríguez

This was designed for the first solo album of the musician Pau Brugada. This simple but delicate pack has included all the materials, such as the song, videoclips, and the musician's thoughts.

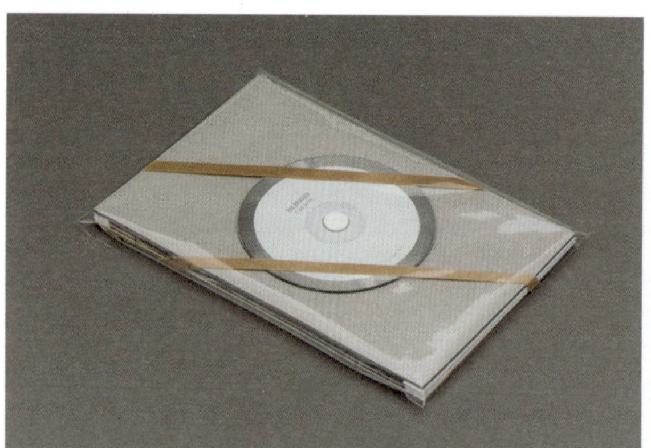

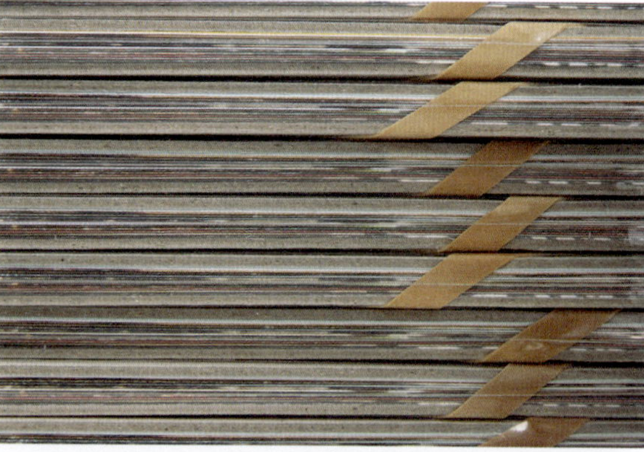

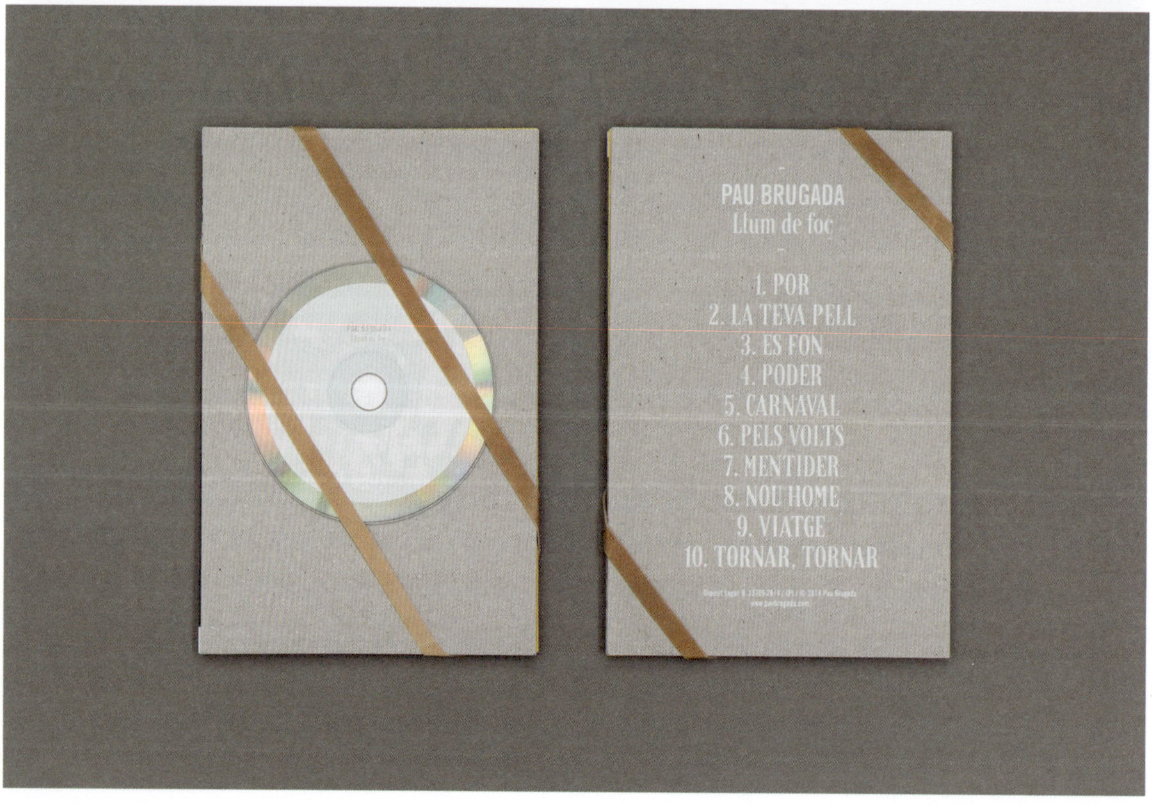

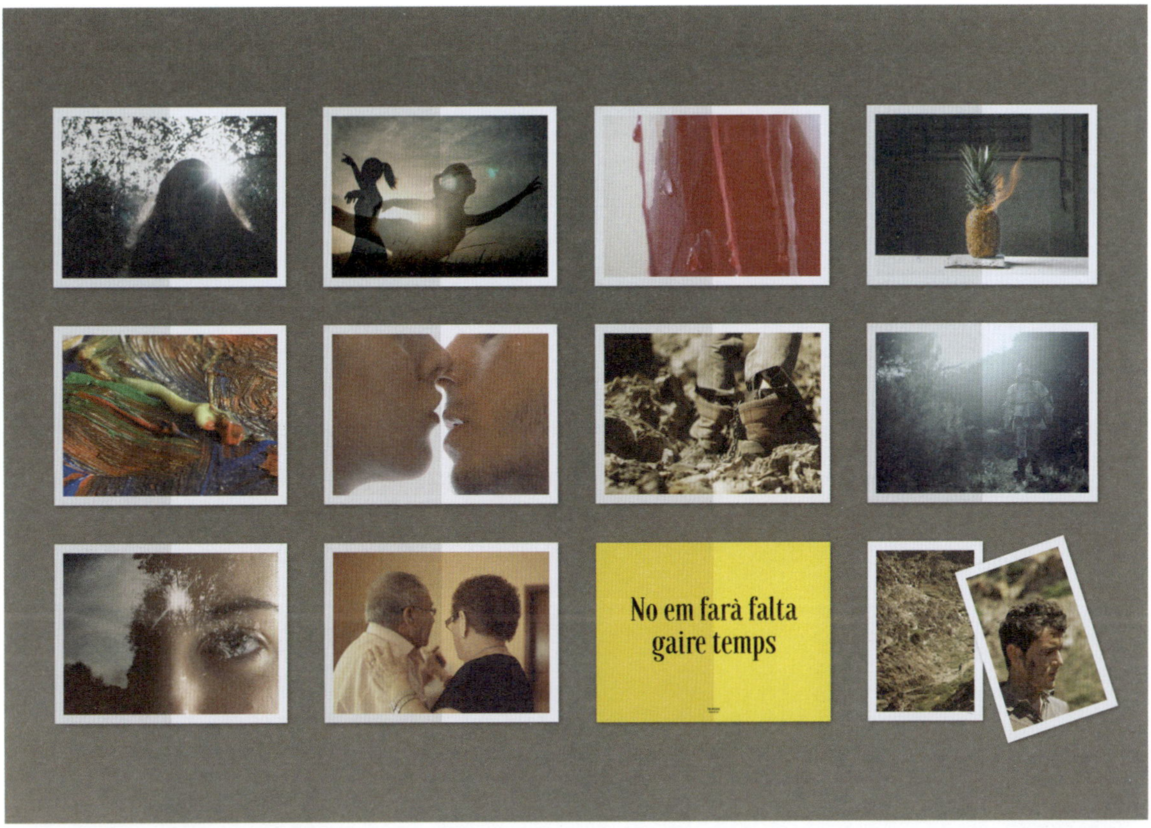

No em farà falta
gaire temps

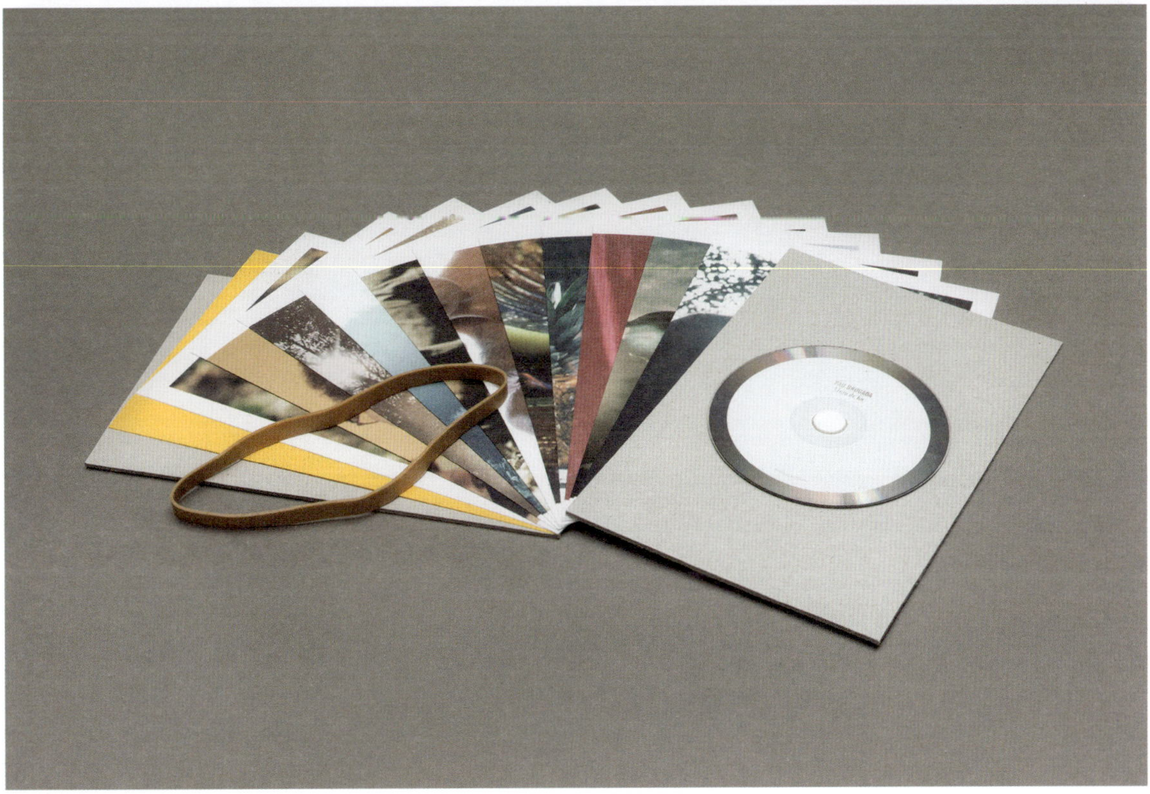

ON CHINESE TRADITIONAL FESTIVAL CUSTOMS

Designer : Chen Tianyou, Chen Yuexi

This is a handmade book on Chinese traditional festival customs, a limited edition with 18 copies. The designers innovatively combined old printed pictures with an extant manuscript of a book on festival custom from the Qing Dynasty. The effect of the combination of the two different types of paper texture and elements of different concepts has exceeded the designer's expectation.

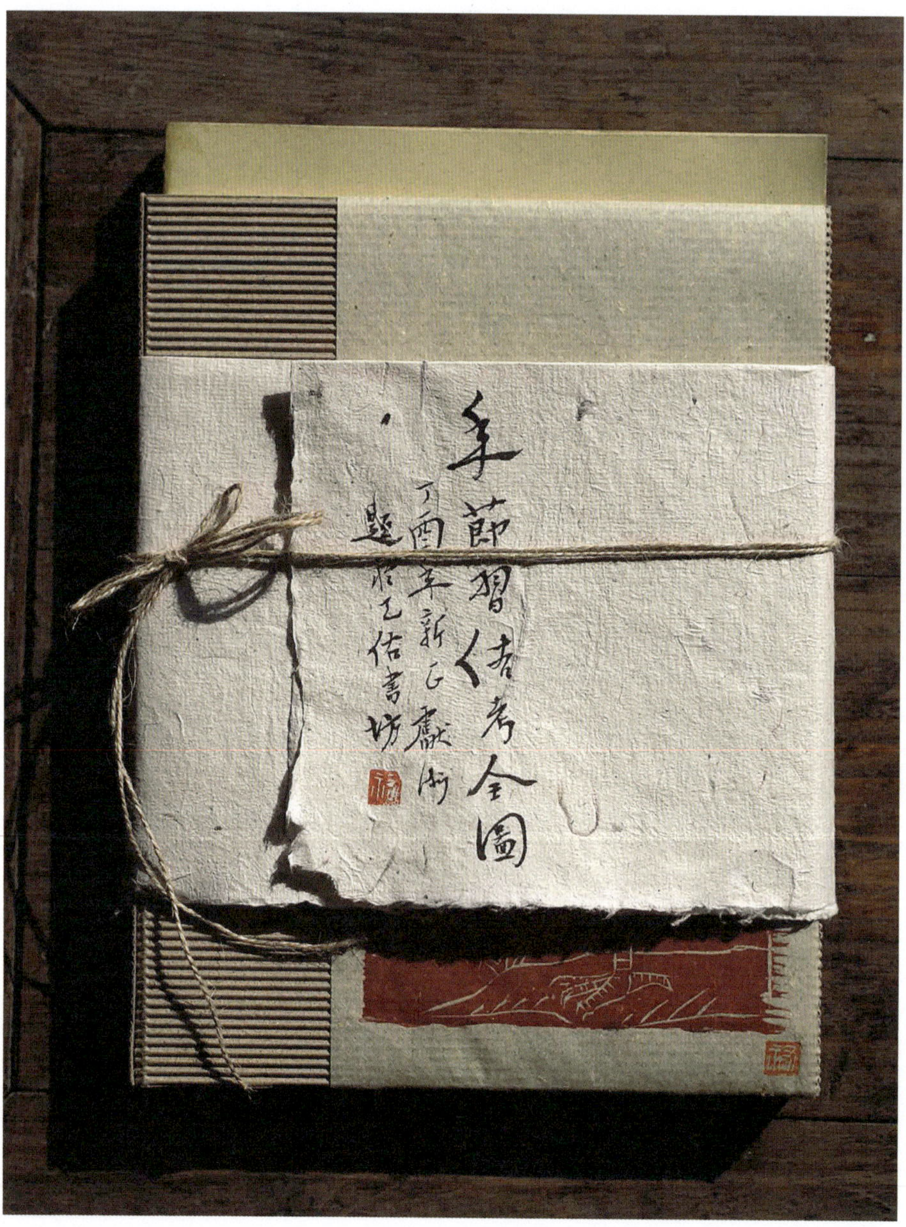

年節習俗考全圖
年節習俗攷全圖
喜神西南
辰司命天德黃道唐符鳳輦 空亡
巳國印 勾陳 空亡
午青龍天開黃道貴人太乙 上吉

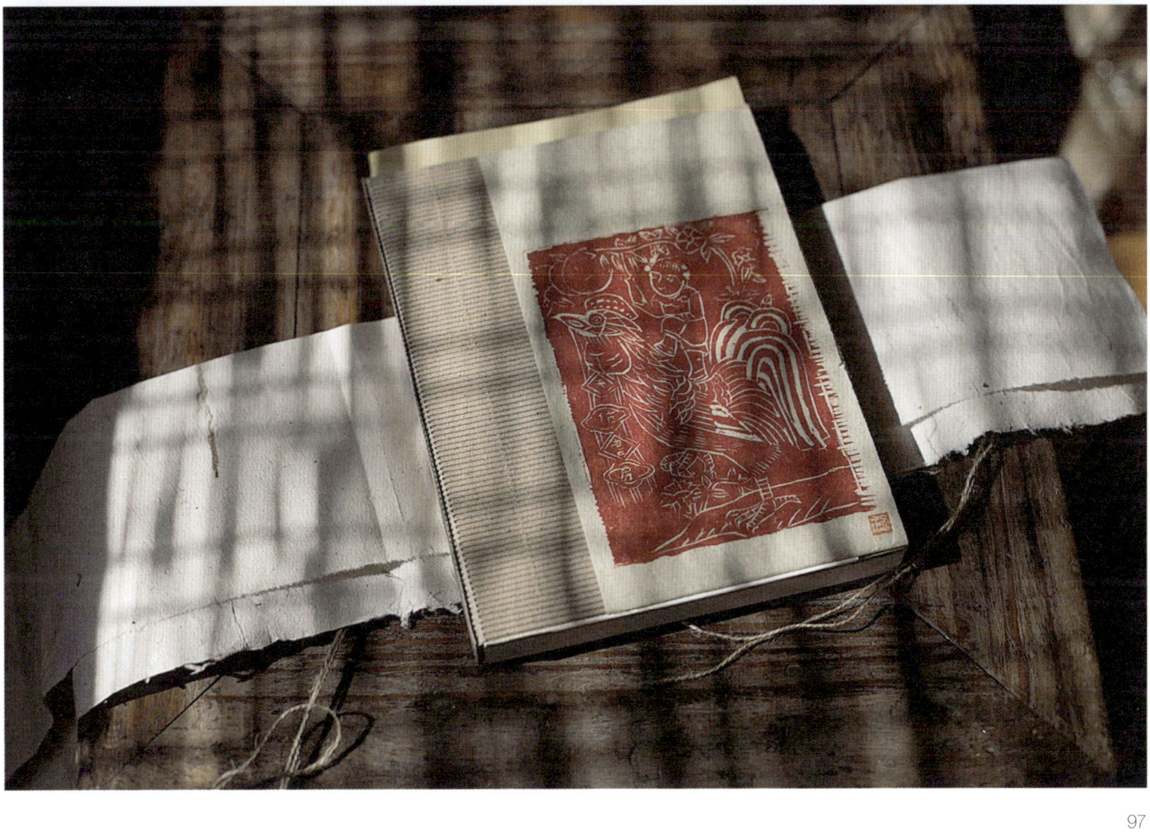

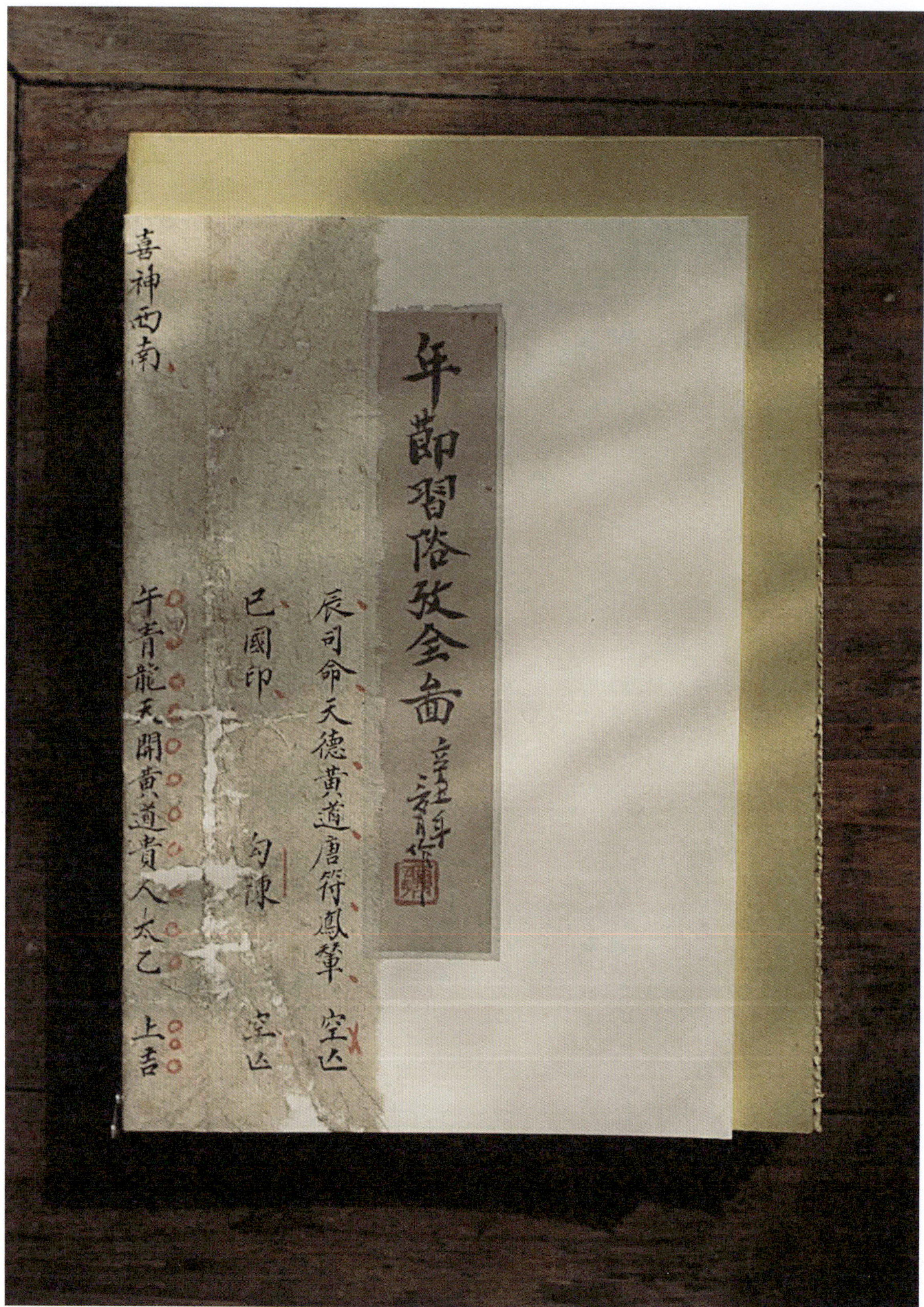
年節習俗攷全畫
辛社醇作
喜神西南
辰司命天德黃道唐符鳳輦 空亡
巳國印 勾陳 空亡
午青龍天開黃道貴人太乙 上吉

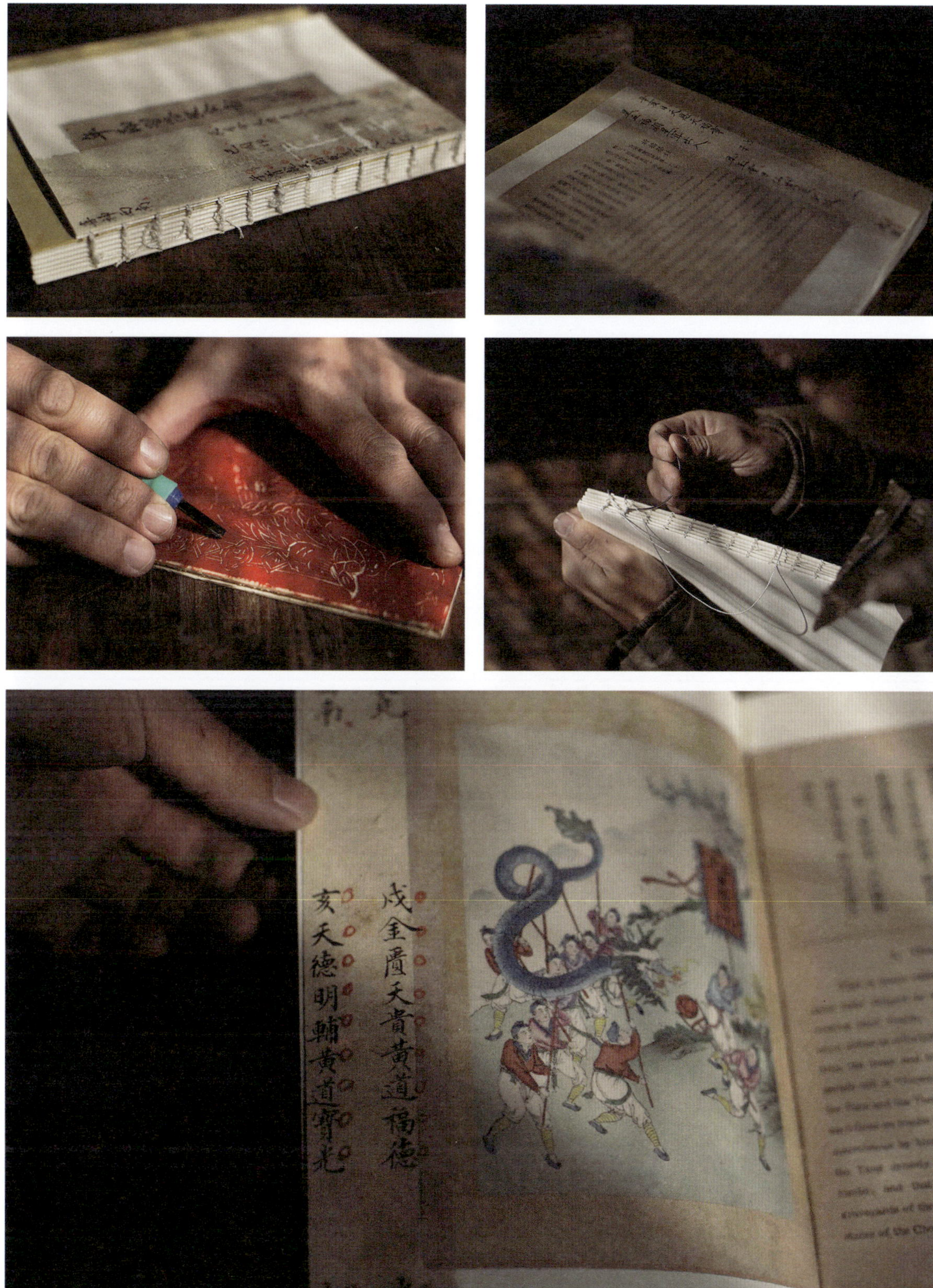
戌金匱天貴黃道福德
亥天德明輔黃道寶光

DA SHI TEA PAVILION

Studio : SHINYA OOYOSO DESIGN   Designer : Hongrui Shen, Fan Cao

The origin of Da Shi Tea Pavilion is revelant to a charitable monk. The packaging is a tribute to the monk's story, taking the Zen circle and teacup as the design elements to reflect the concept of combining Zen and tea. The brand logo is formed by dots to highlight the characteristics of Zen. The packaging is produced with handmade paper with a deckle edge to strengthen the visual and tactile experience.

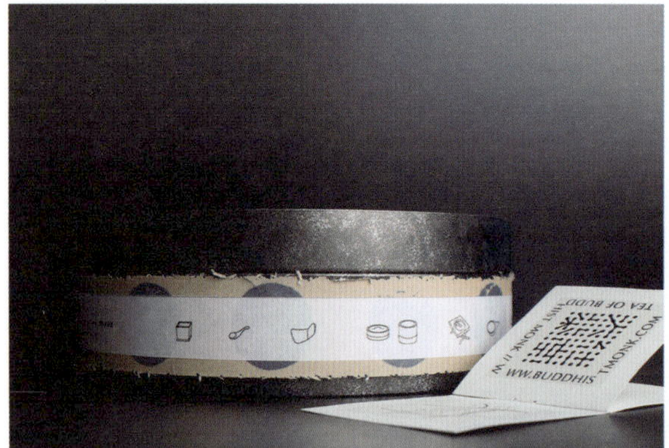

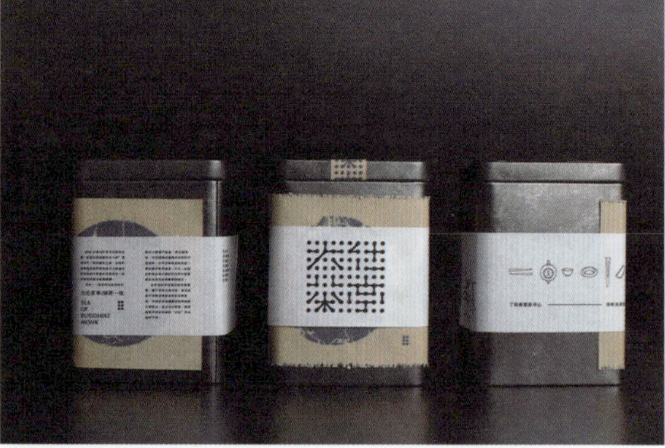

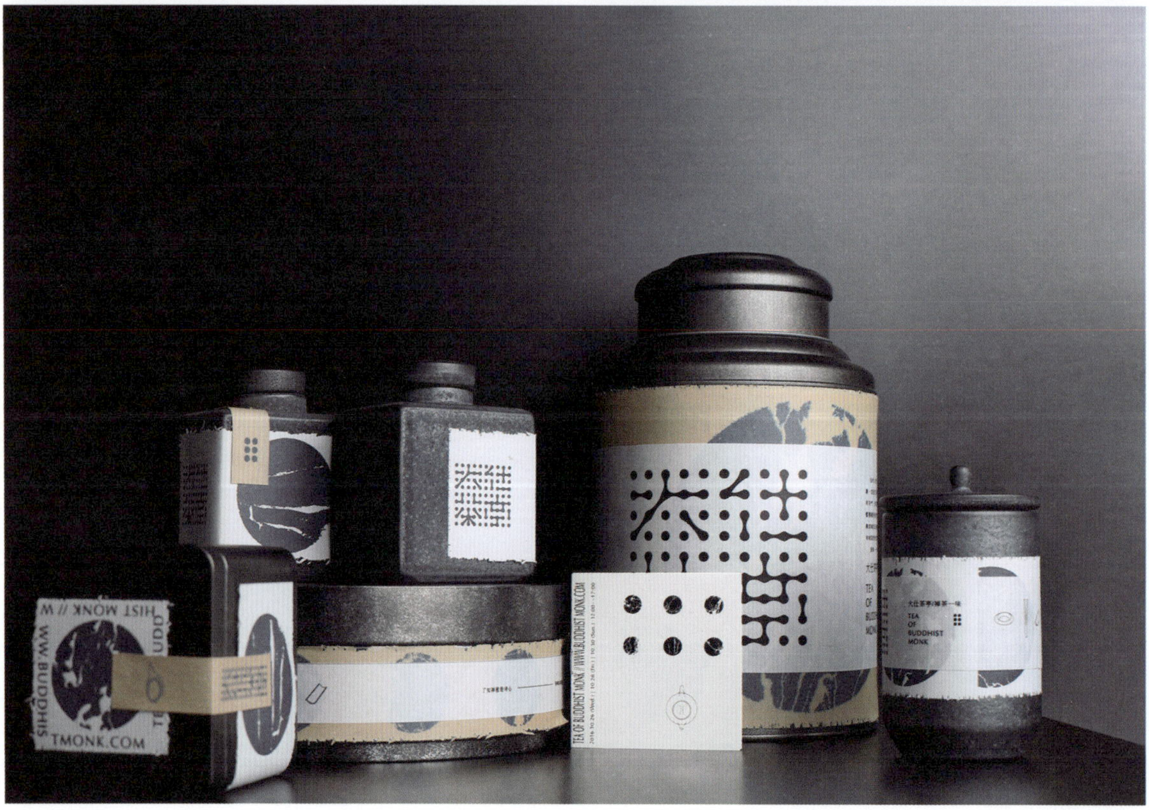

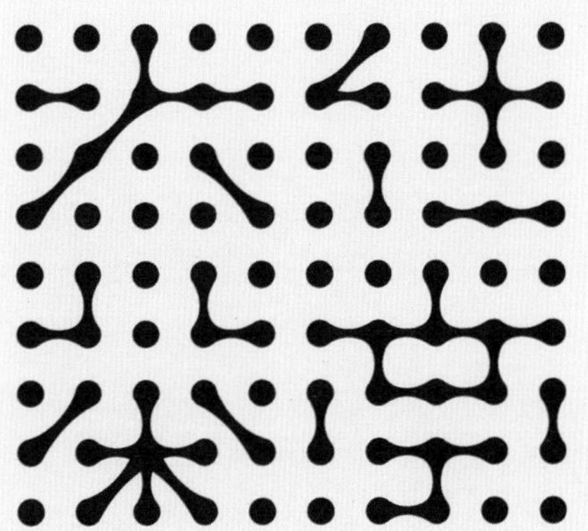
TEA OF BUDDHIST MONK

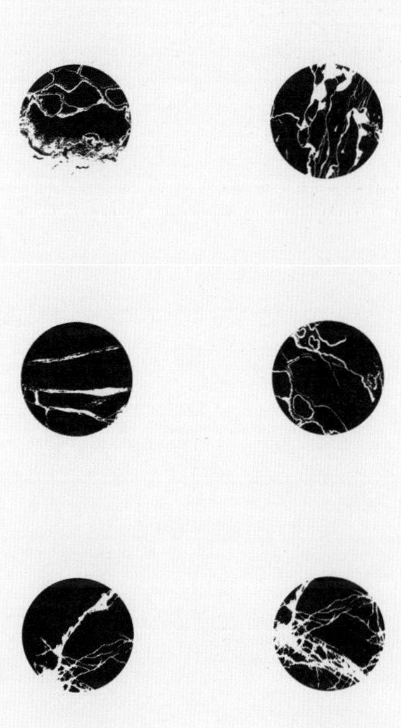

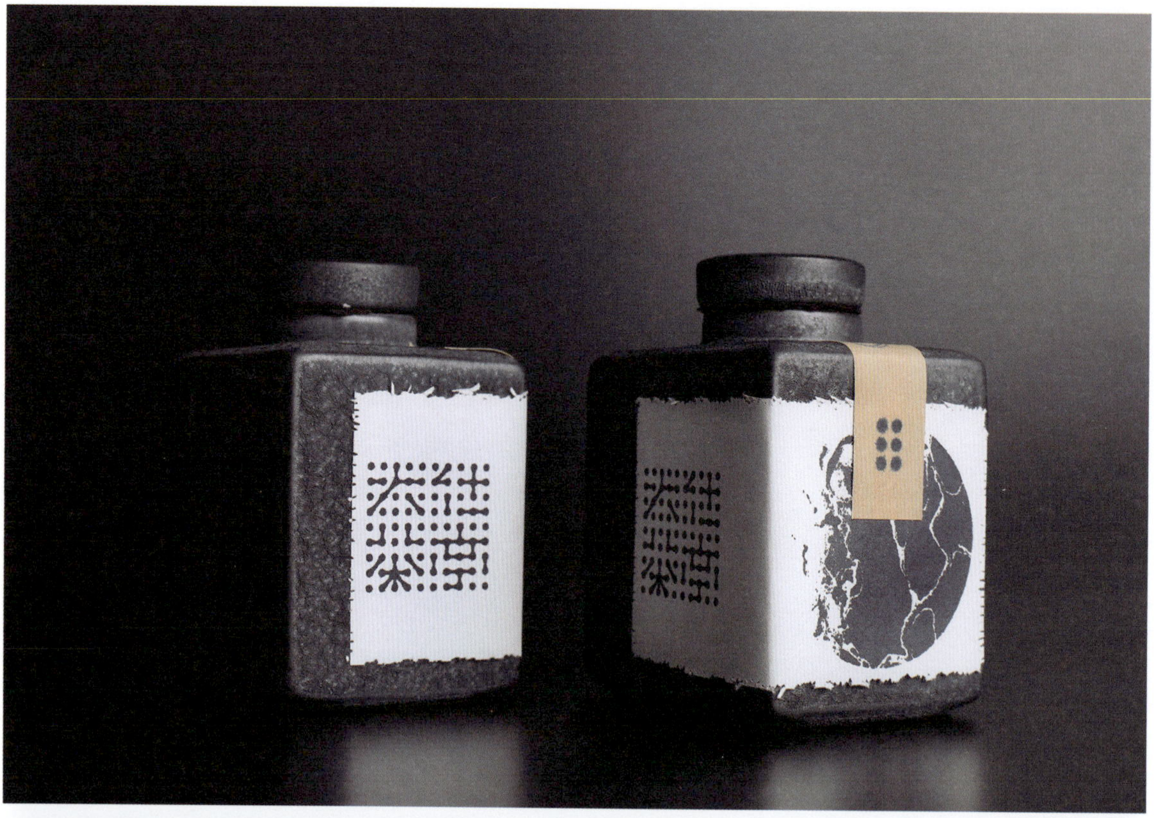

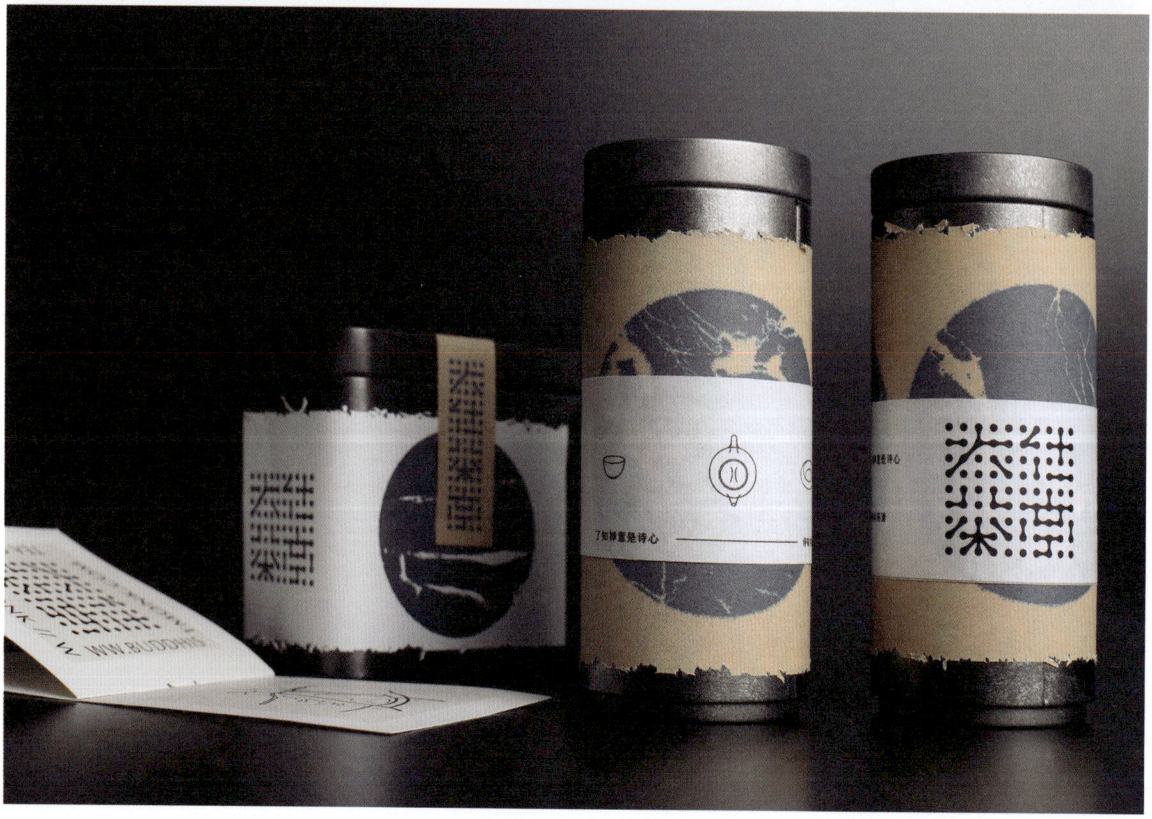

TEA OF BUDDHIST MONK // WWW.BUDDHIST MONK.COM

第 一 回

TEA OF BUDDHIST MONK

旧时，水西门外多为农田和水塘，这里农民种植的水八鲜"很有名气，每年夏秋之季，农民们都要挑担徒步将这些水八鲜送往南京城里出卖途中总喜欢在一块有树阴的地方换肩歇脚。

后来，一位名叫大仕和尚耳闻水八鲜盛产此地，便云游而来，可见到挑担歇脚的农民们汗流浃背、口干舌燥地在此休息，顿生建亭供茶慈念，不久，由这位和尚出资兴建的四方亭宇便落成在农民们经常歇脚的地方。

■ 展览日期

2016 / 12 / 26 (Wed)

12 / 28 (Fri)

12 / 30 (Sun)

12:00-17:00

■ 大仕茶亭水西门店

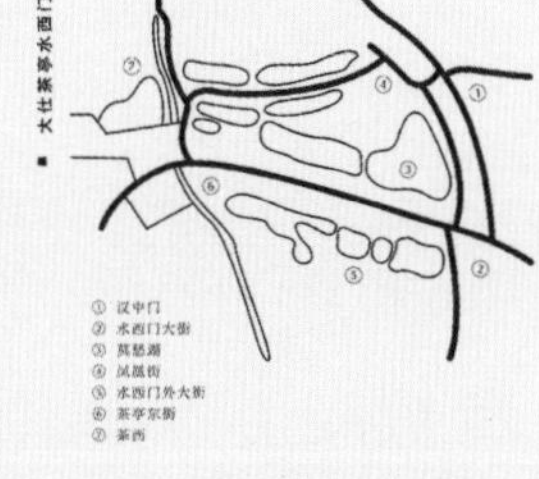

南京市八宝前街188号锦江丽舍809室

该亭当时为四顶立的无墙草篷，篷下设有石桌石凳，甚至还备下瓦钵凉茶供农民们免费饮用，农民们非常感激这位和尚的大慈善心，但又无以报答，便将这座茶亭以和尚的"大仕"号名称呼下来。

了知禅意是诗心 ——— 诗味共茶清

■ 大仕茶亭

色不异空 / 空即是色 / 水不是茶 / 茶就是水 / 本心念佛证菩提 / 用心泡茶得真味 / 明心见性 / 度化众生 / 是佛陀 / 舍己 / 济人 / 为茶饮 / 心就是佛 / 佛就是水。

茶禅一味，茶禅不二，以禅入茶，以茶会禅，鹅王择乳，香象渡河，同沾法味，明心见性。

大仕茶亭/禅茶一味

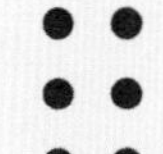

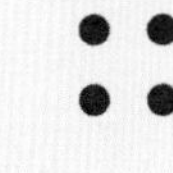

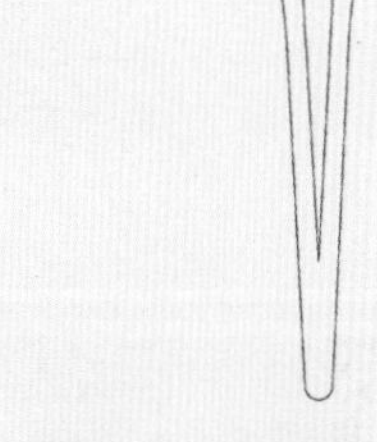

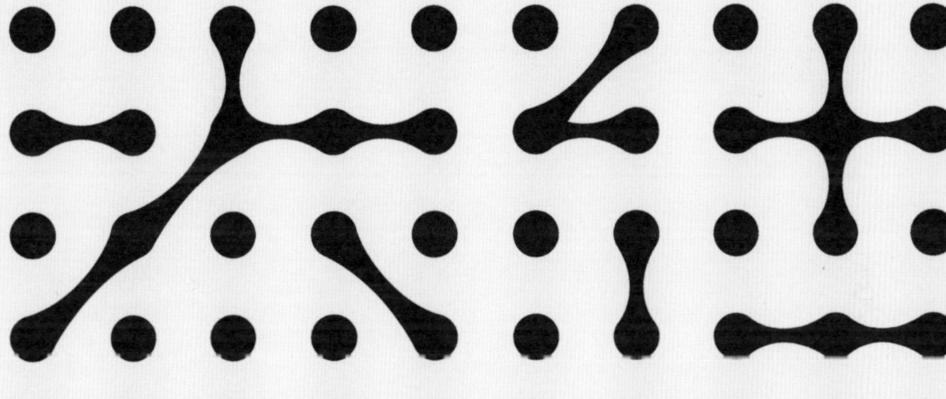

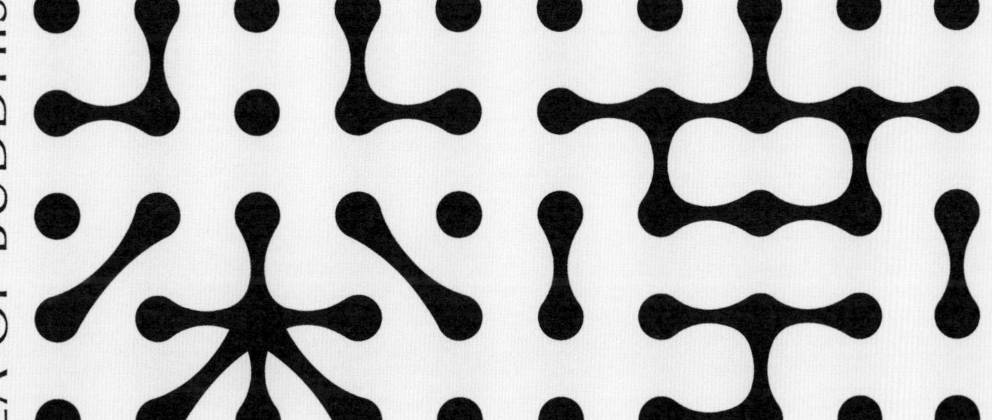

2016.12.26 (Wed.) | 12.28 (Fri.) | 12.30 (Sun.) 12:00~~17:00

NINIGI

Designer : Estudio Yeyé

In Japanese mythology, Ninigi no Mikoto, grandson of Amaterasu, was sent to earth to plant rice. The designer brought this myth into the NINIGI project which covers branding, packaging, furniture design, multimedia and interior design.

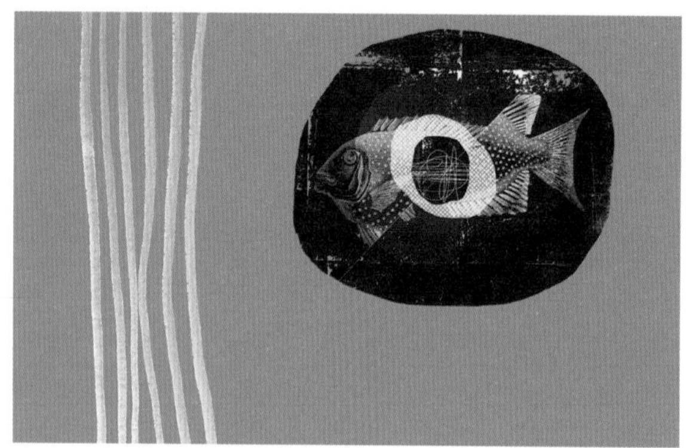

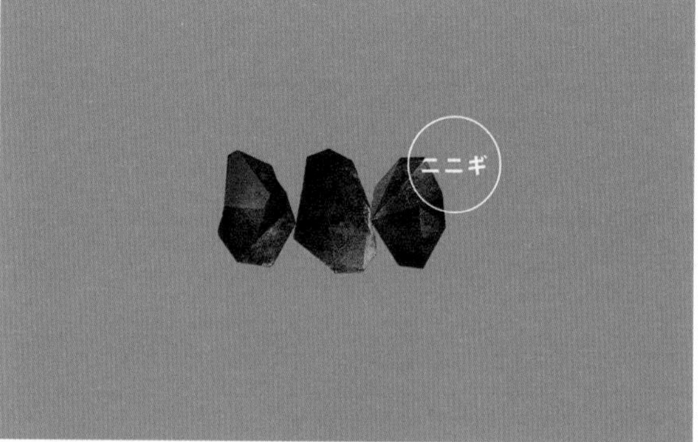

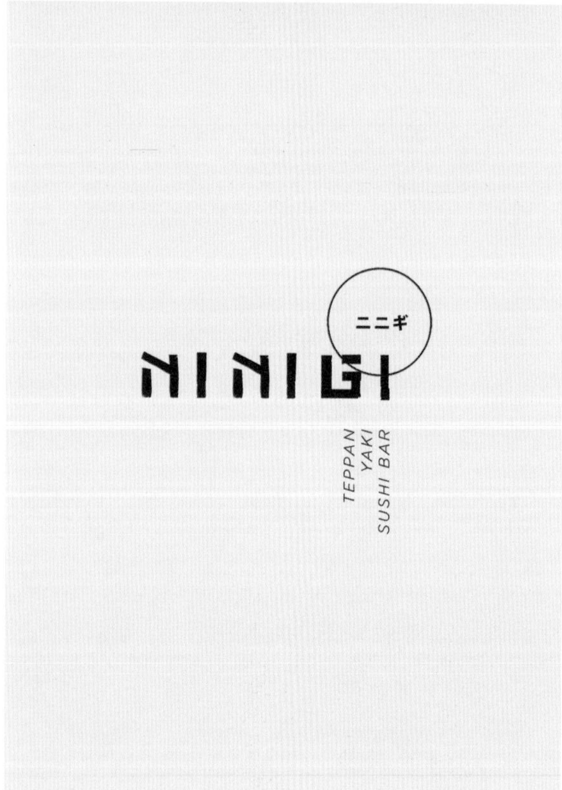

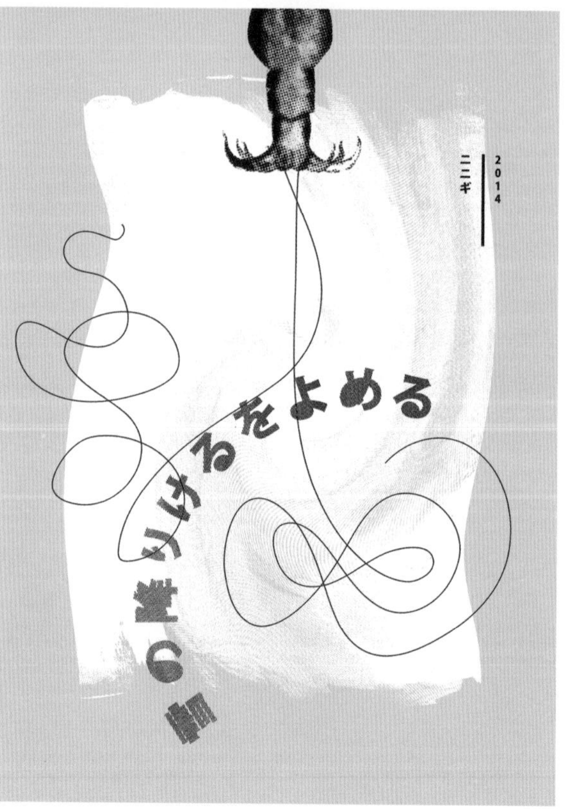

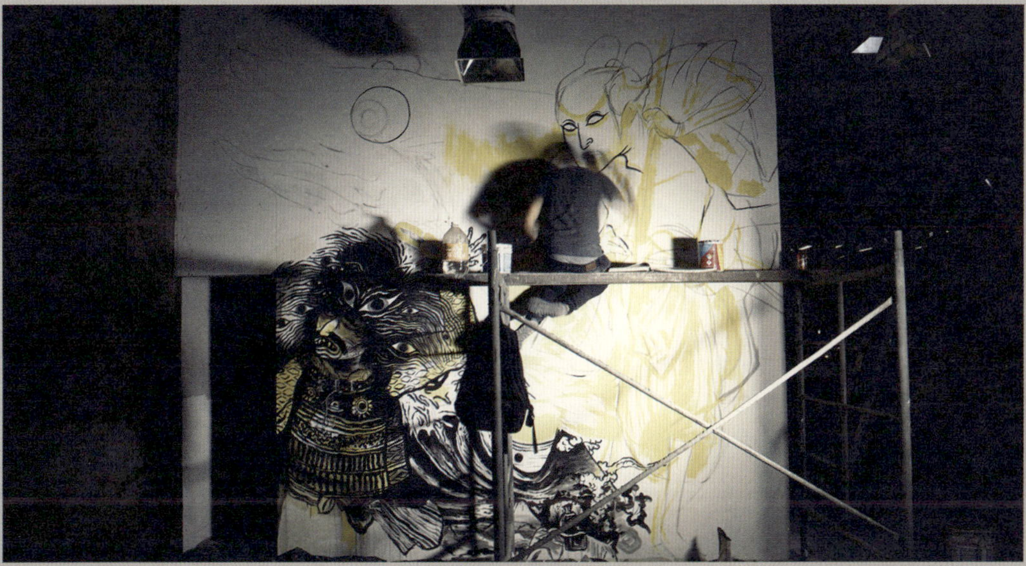

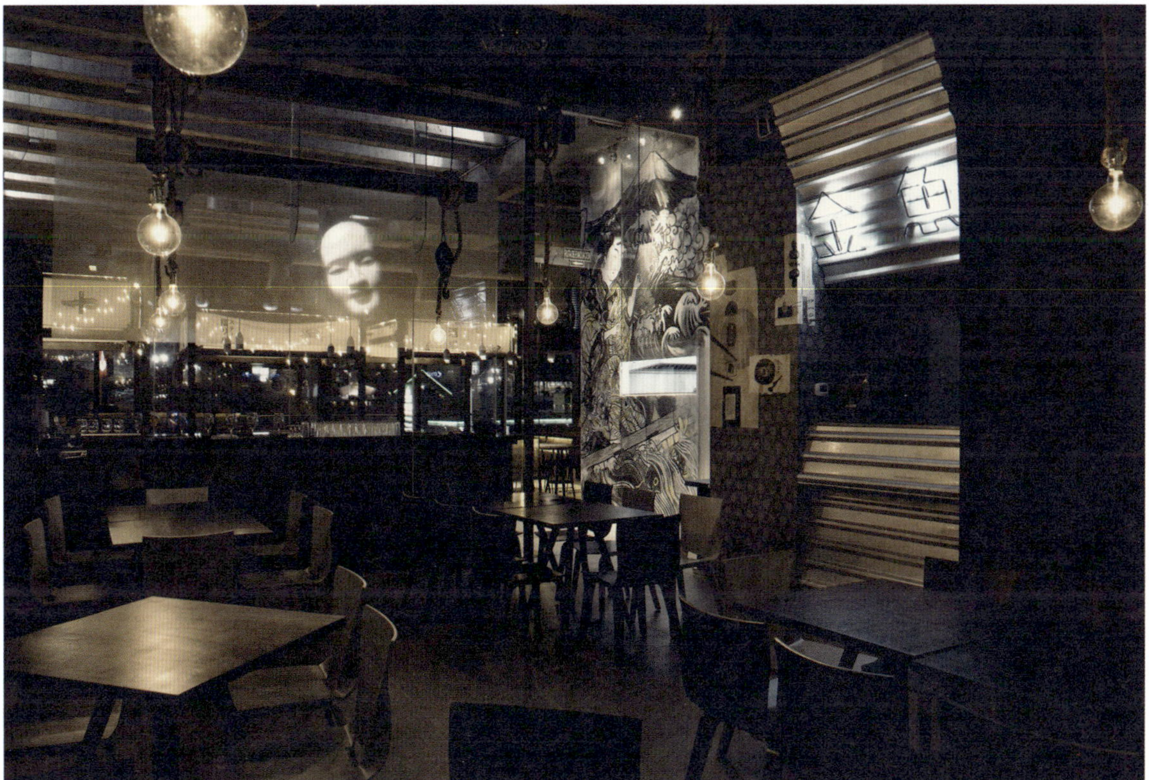

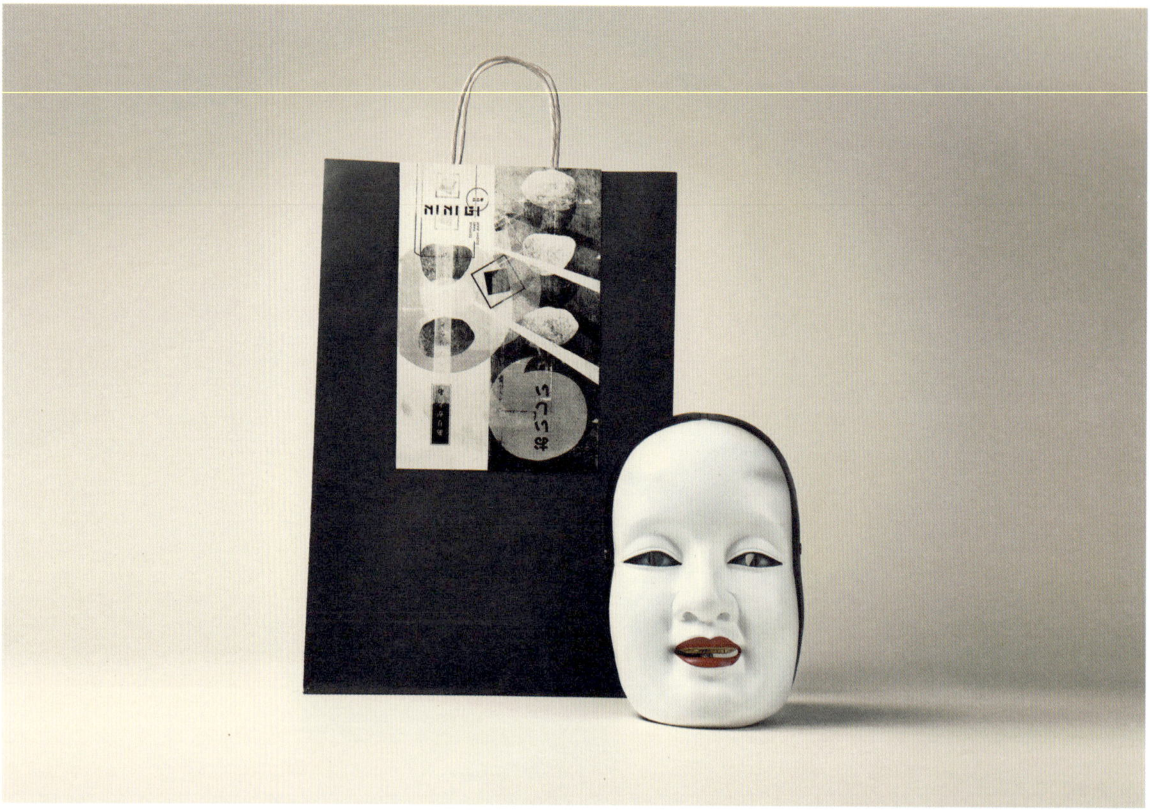

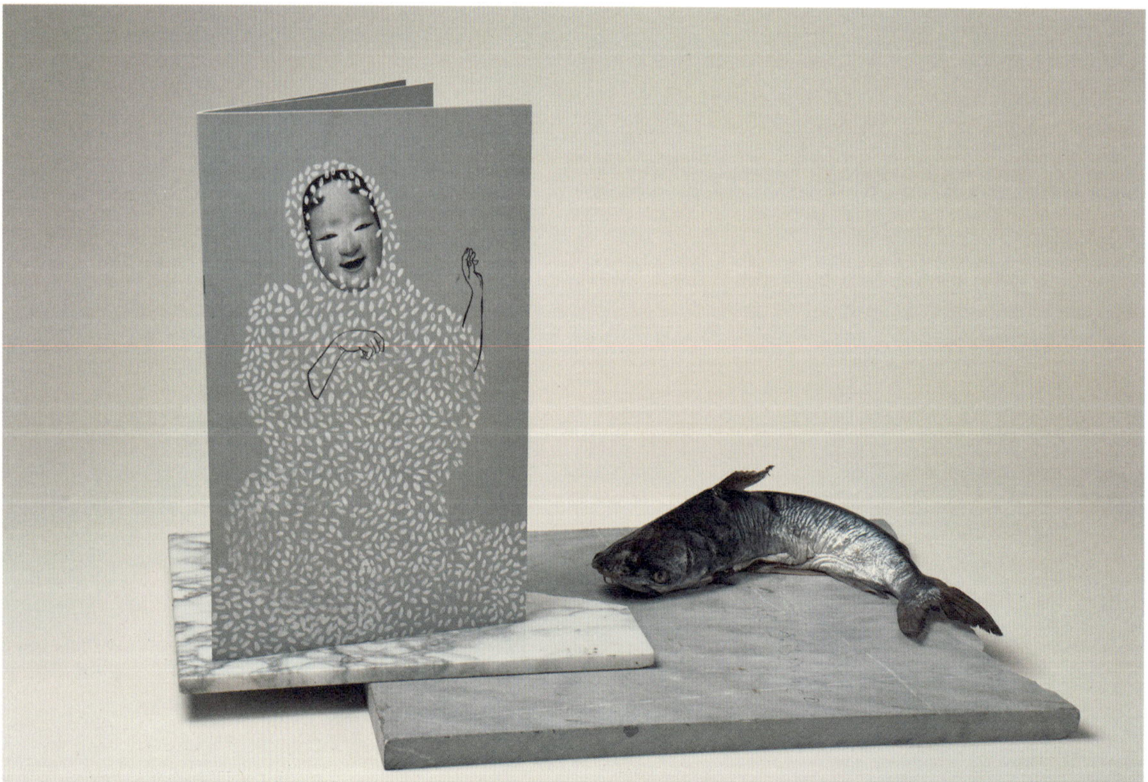

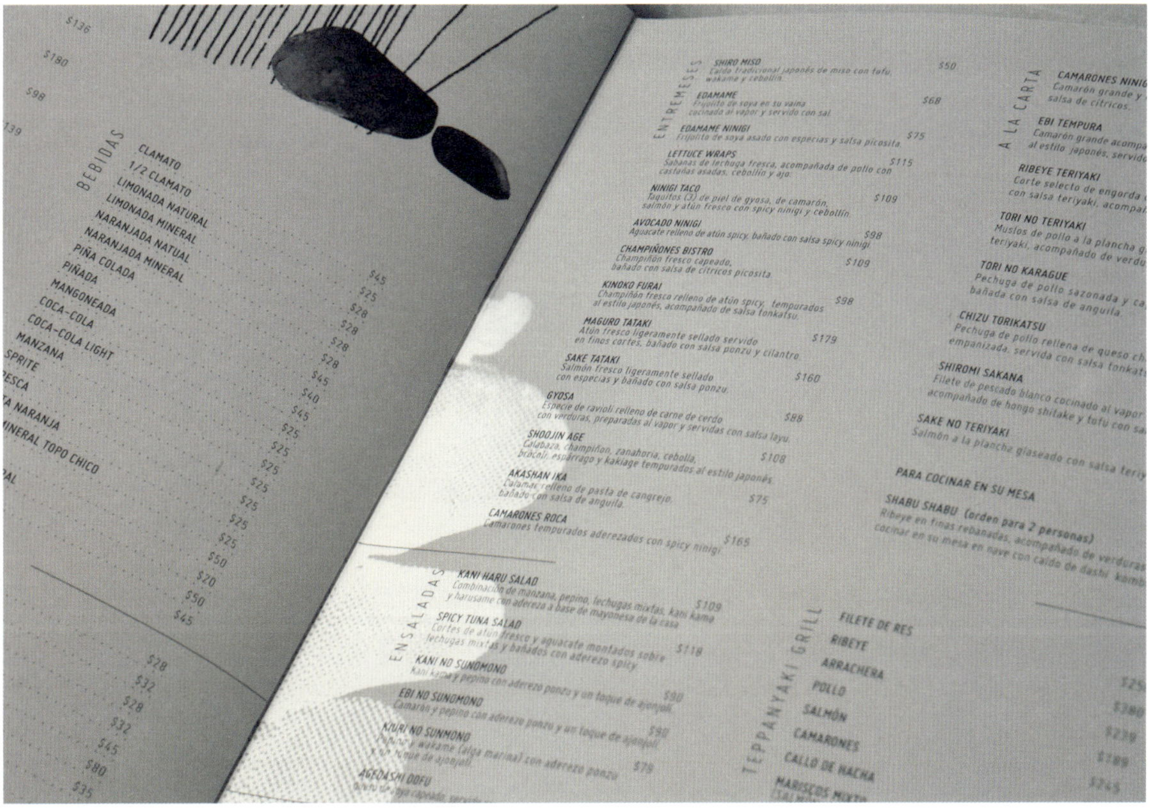

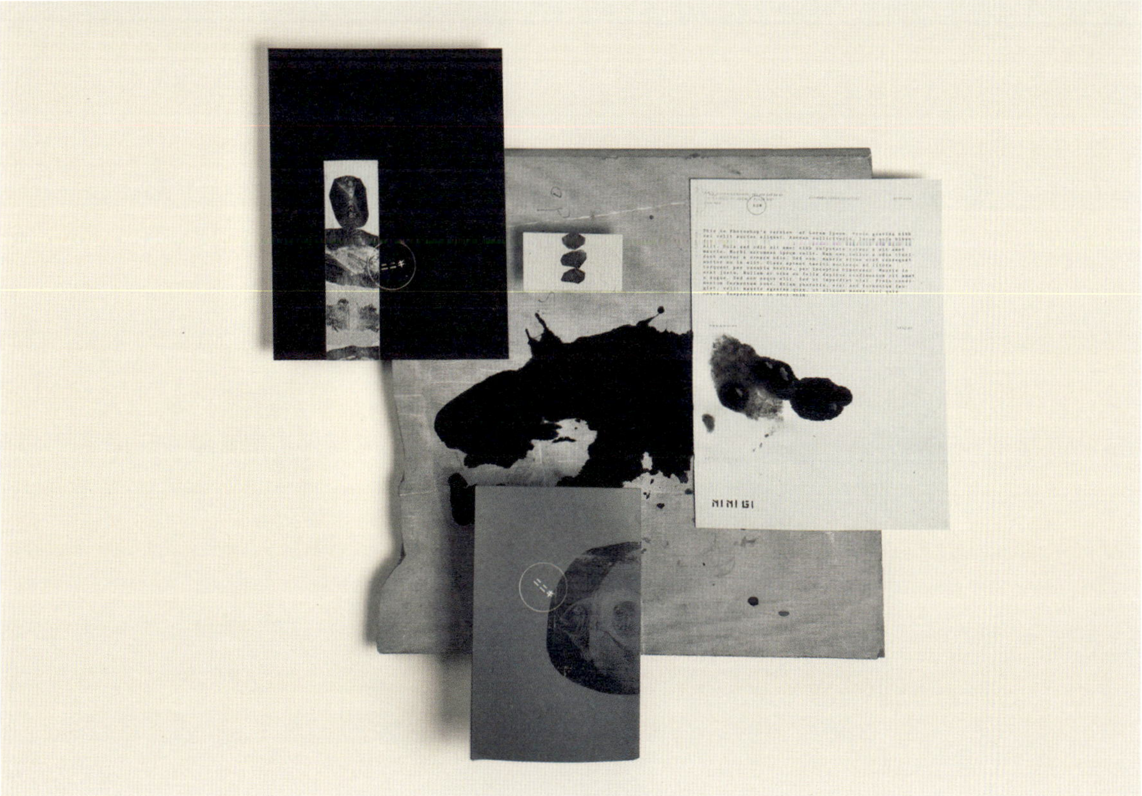

ACRE

Designer : Estudio Yeyé

Acre is a 25 acre piece of farmland adjacent to San Jose del Cabo, which will be developed as a space for people to relax, study, recuperate and celebrate. The design concept revolves around the culture of the farmers, freedom and flavors of Mexican land.

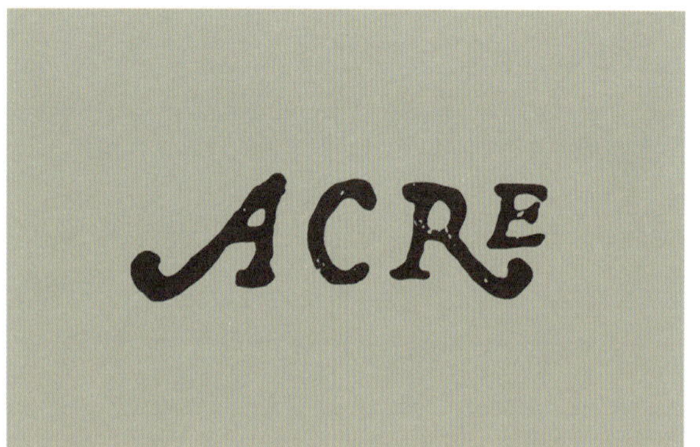

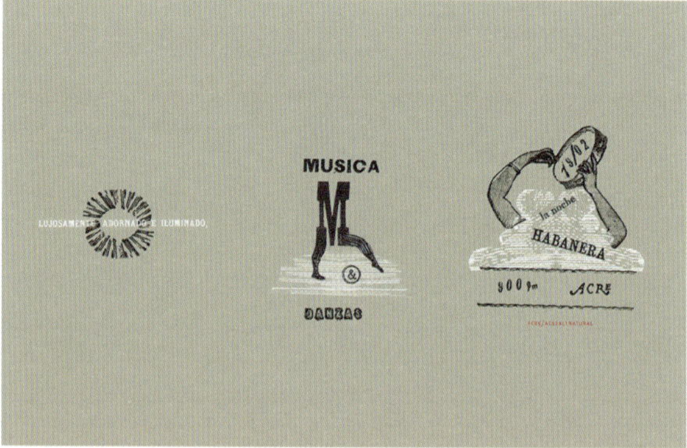

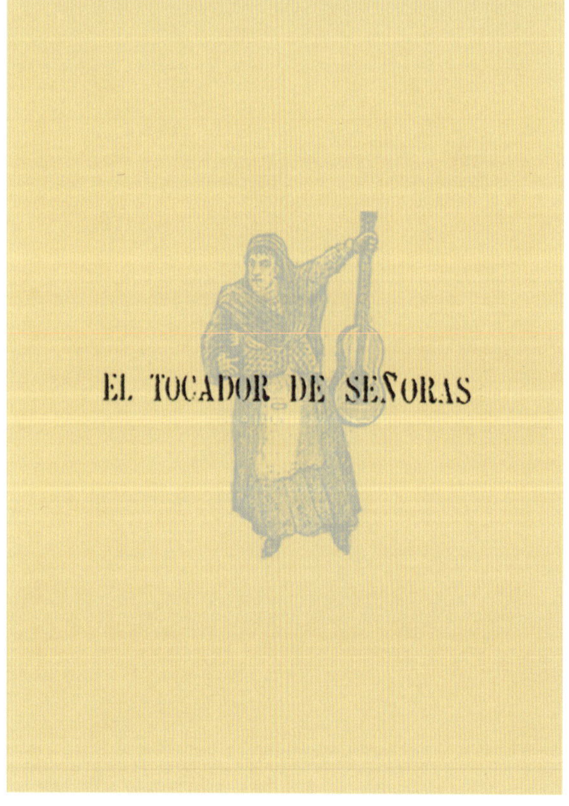

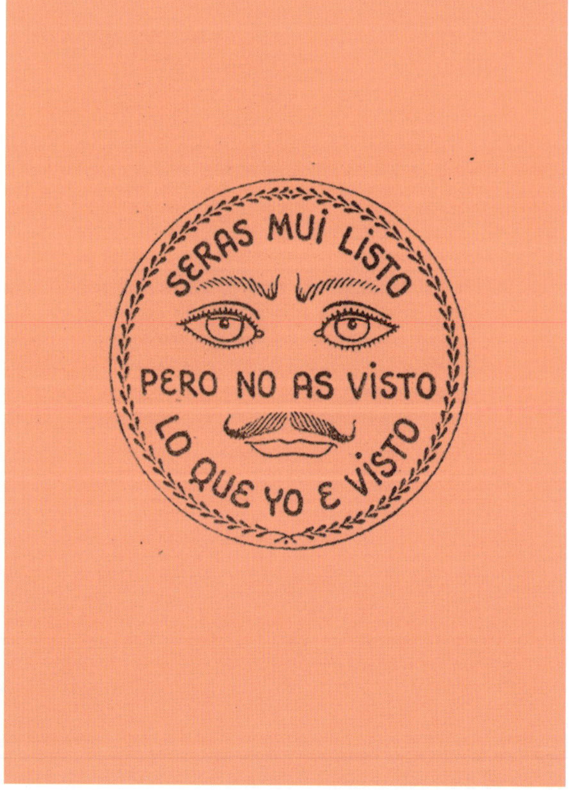

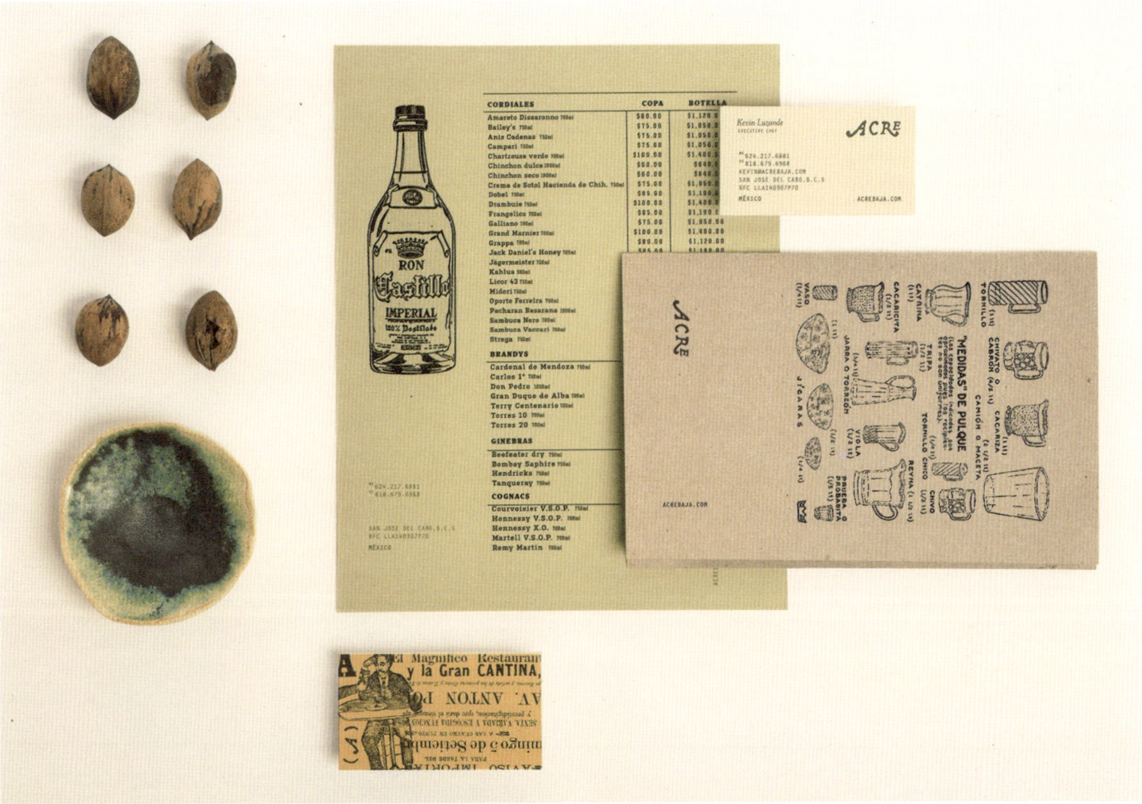

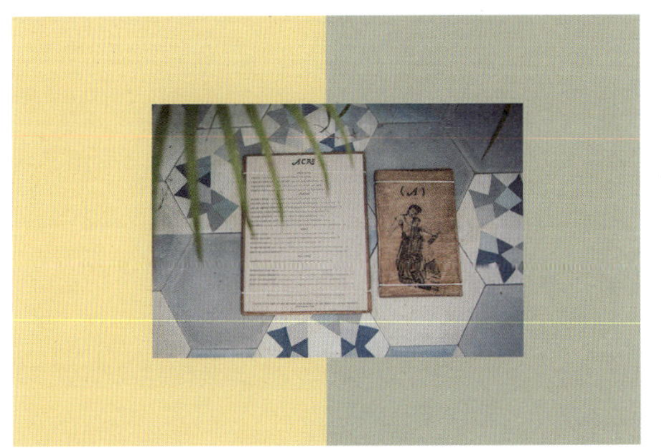

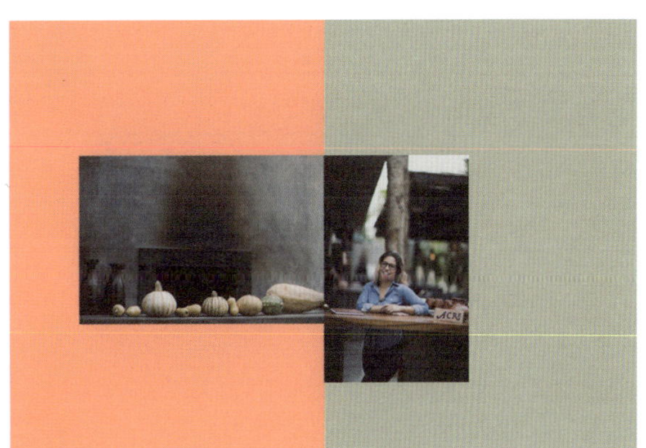

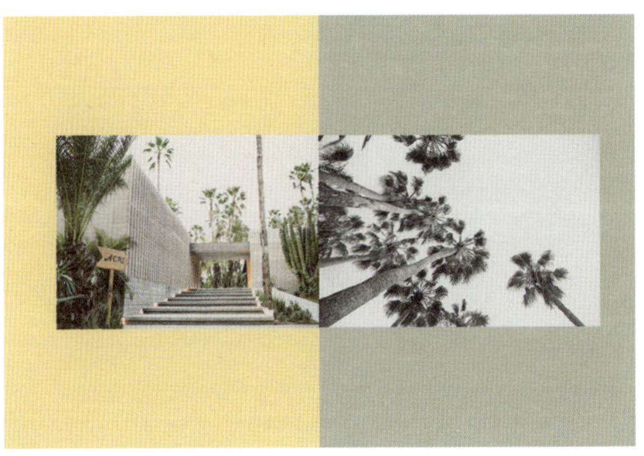

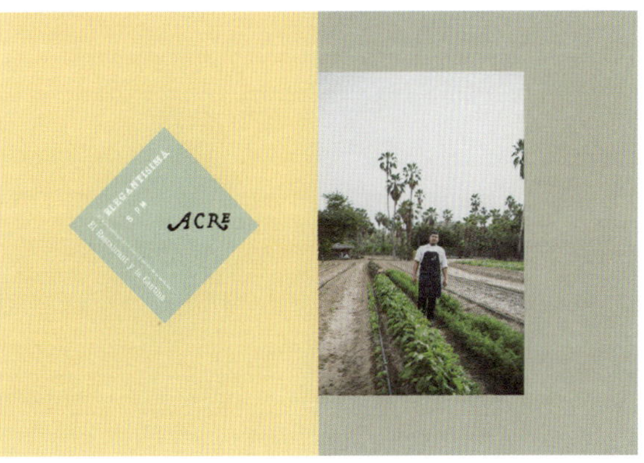
ACRE

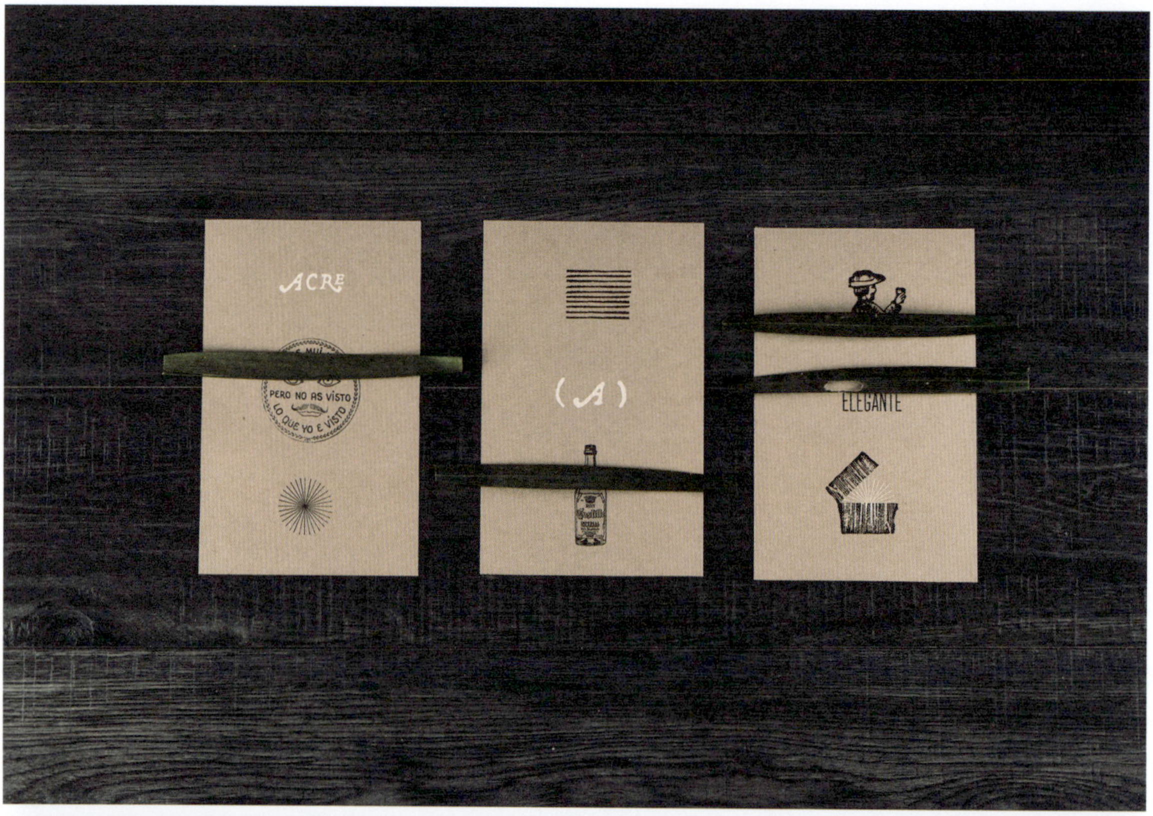
ACRE
PERO NO AS VISTO
LO QUE YO E VISTO
(A)
ELEGANTE

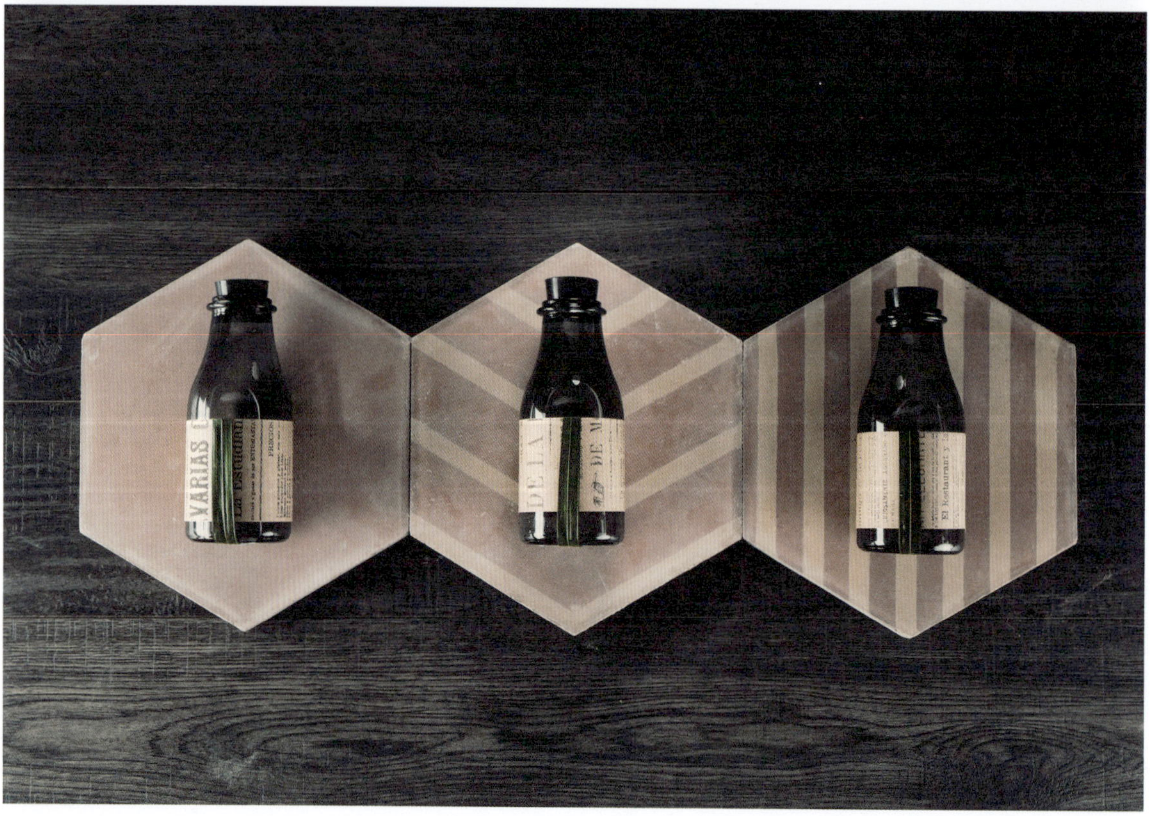
VARIAS
DE LA

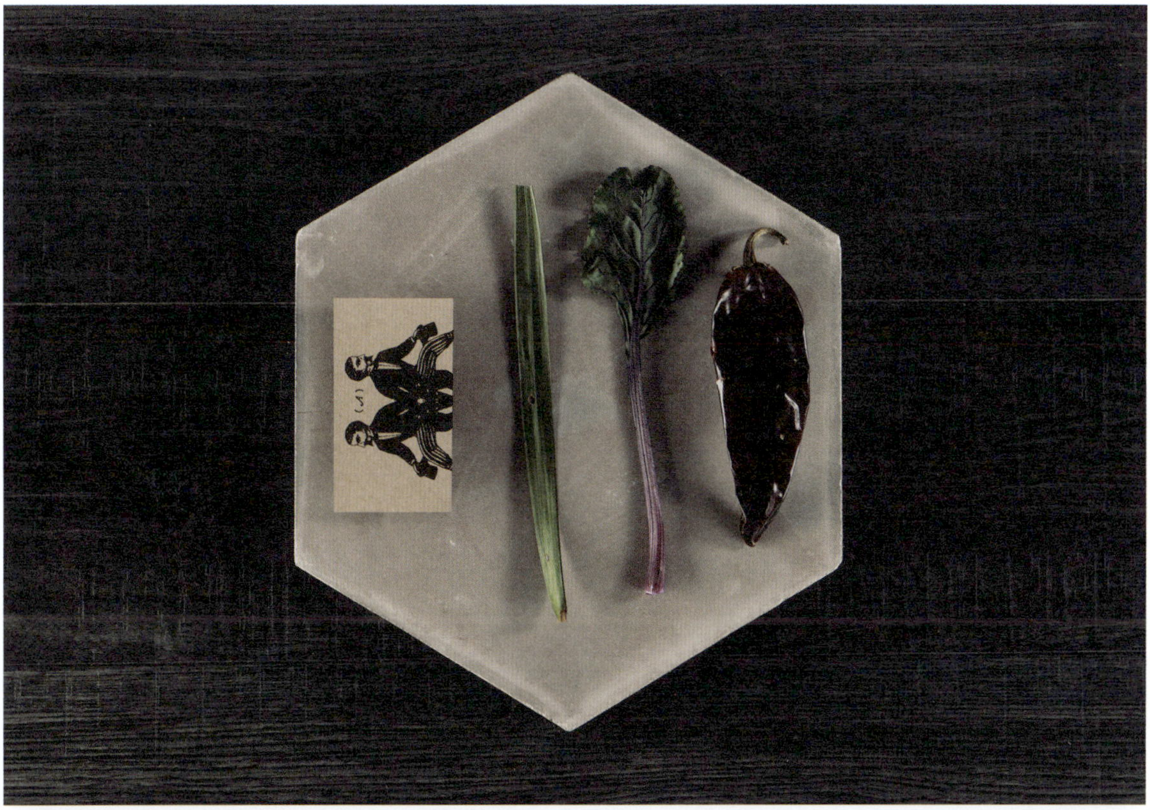

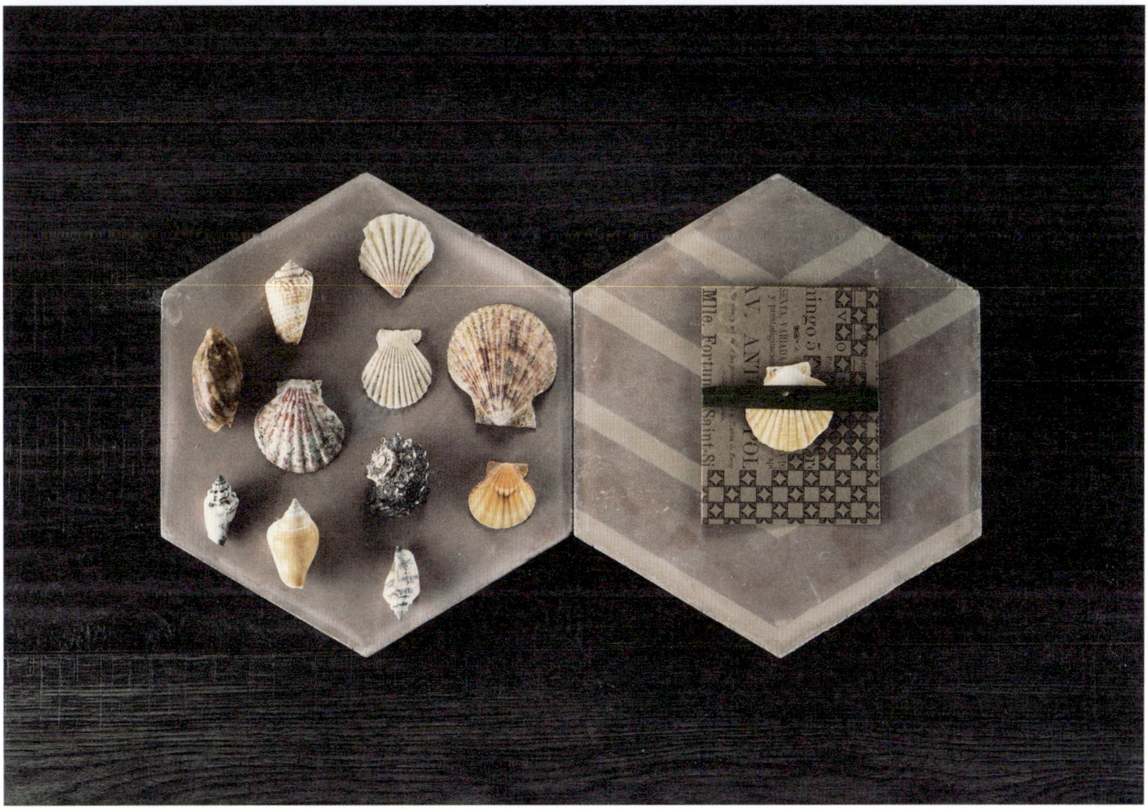

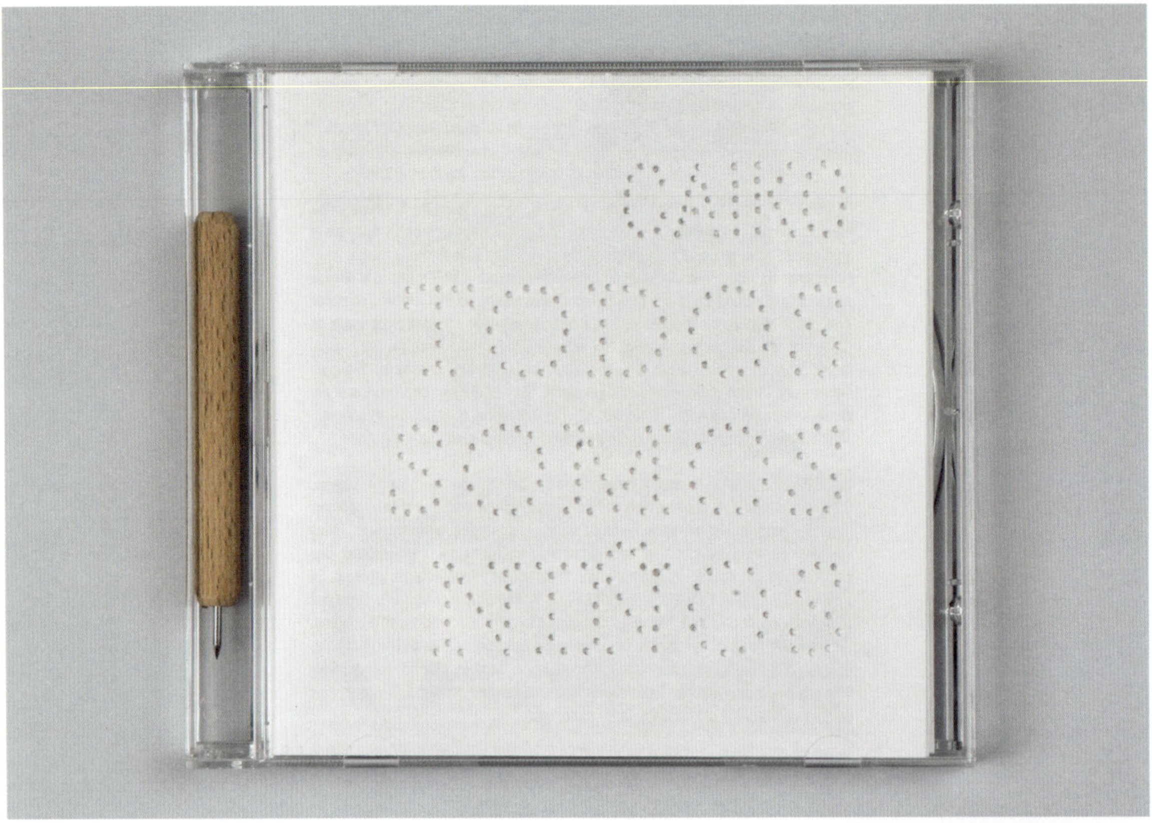

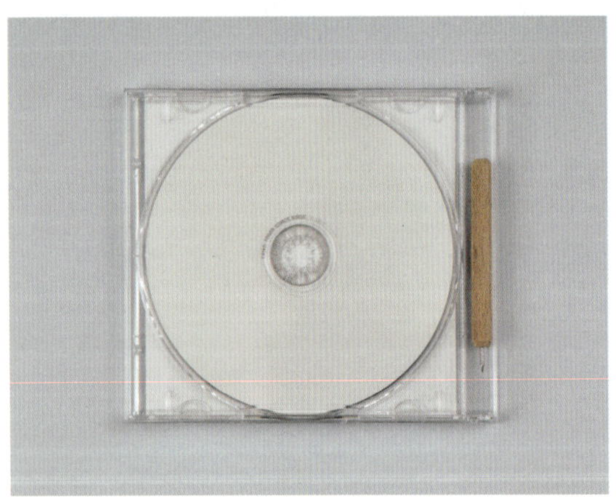

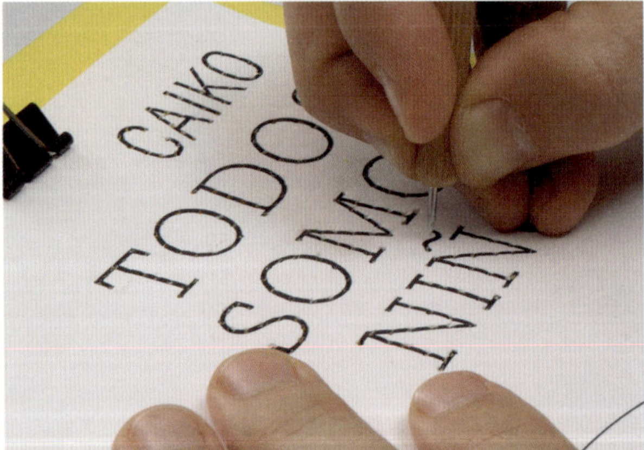

TODOS SOMOS NIÑOS

Studio : Enserio   Designer : Miquel Amela, Ferran Rodríguez

This was a poster designed for the band Caiko. Once folded, it served as a cover. The holes on this completely white poster were made with an awl.

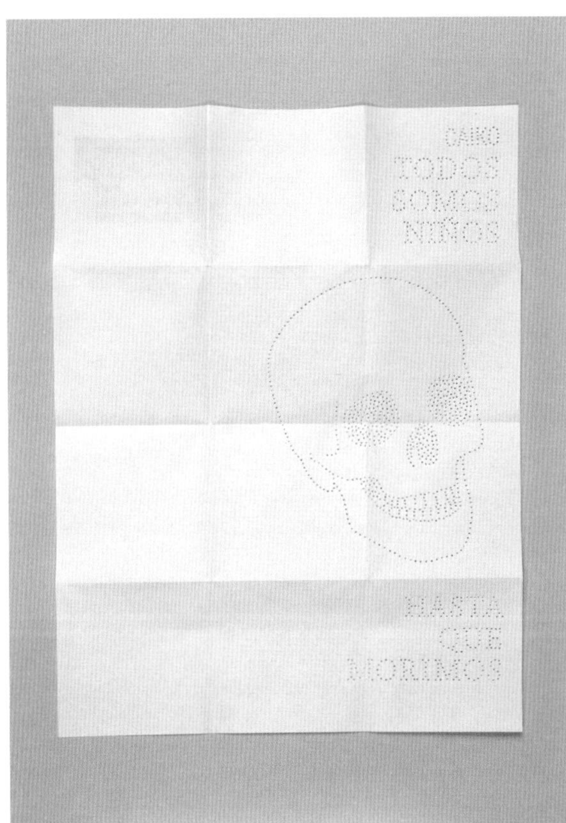
CAIKO
TODOS
SOMOS
NIÑOS
HASTA
QUE
MORIMOS

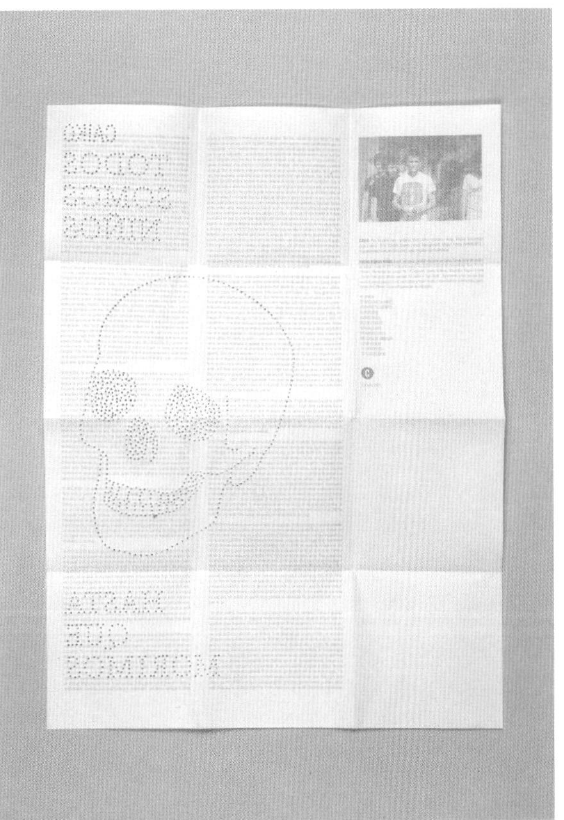

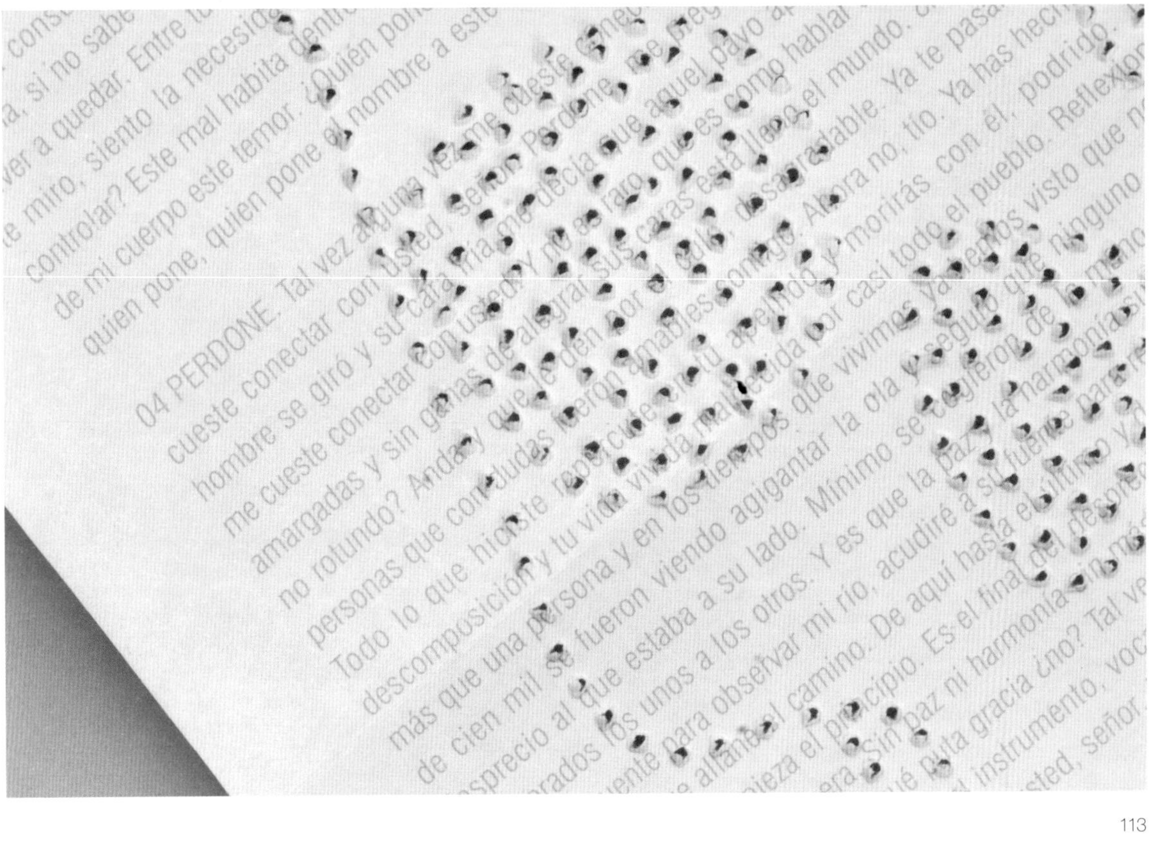

BI-CITY BIENNALE

Studio : Another Design

"Re-living the City" is the theme of the 2015 Bi-City Biennale, proposing that we should reuse, rethink and reimagine existing architectures and cities, and reshape daily lives through design. The identity concept was developed around the core theme of "Re-", by reusing and redesigning the patterns, typography and other visual elements of past biennale identities. After recollecting newspapers, planning maps, advertising banners, mosaic tiles, plastic woven bags and construction wastes from around the world, the studio reframed the materials and screen-printed biennale information on them, turning them into new promotional materials.

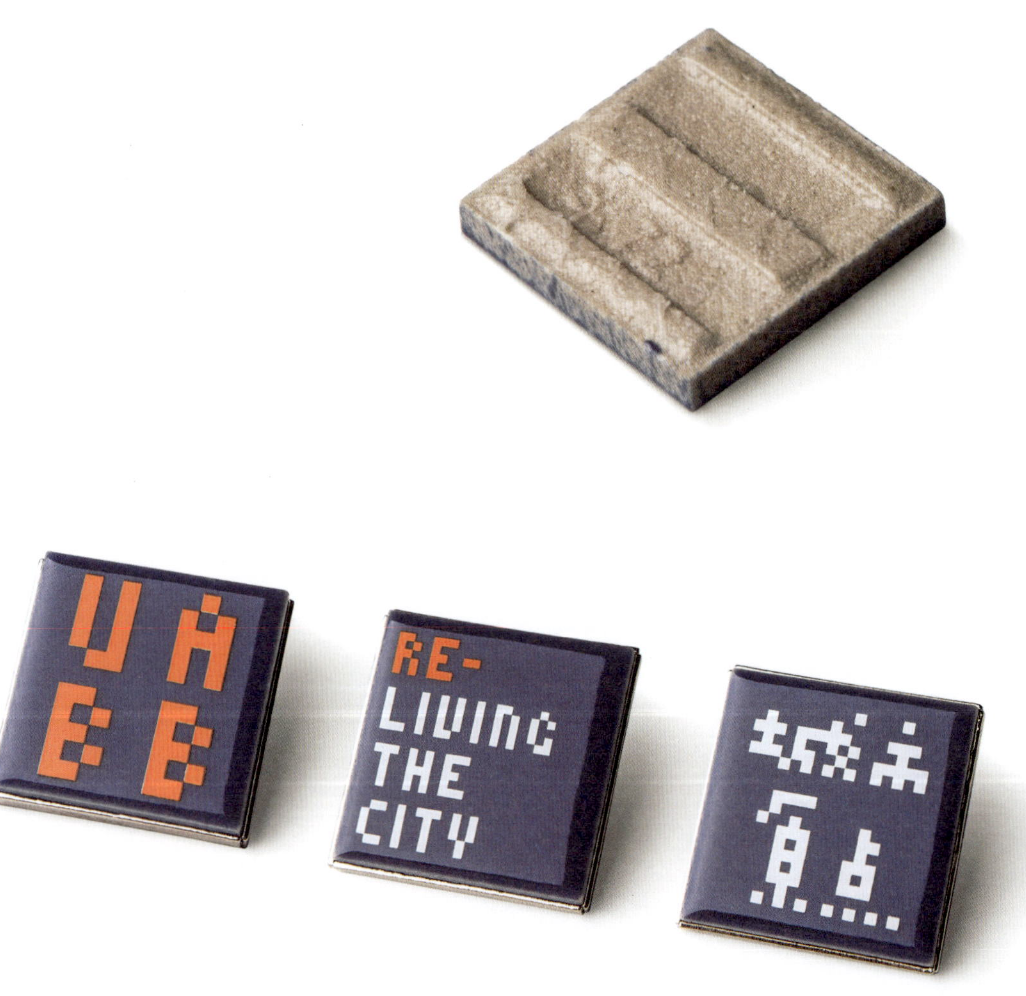

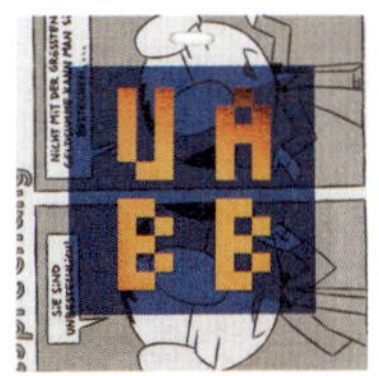
UA
BB
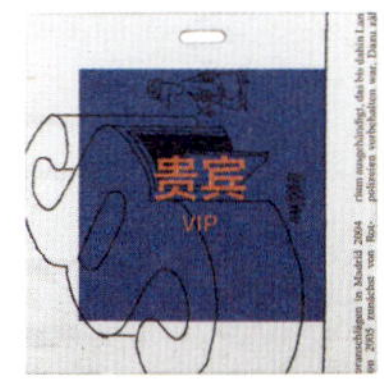
贵宾
VIP
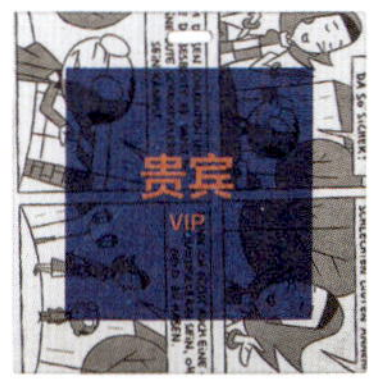
贵宾
VIP
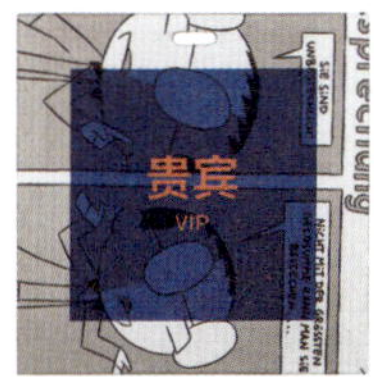
贵宾
VIP
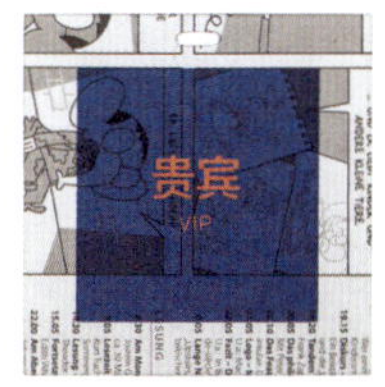
贵宾
VIP
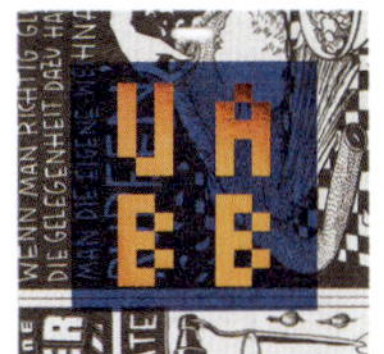
UA
BB
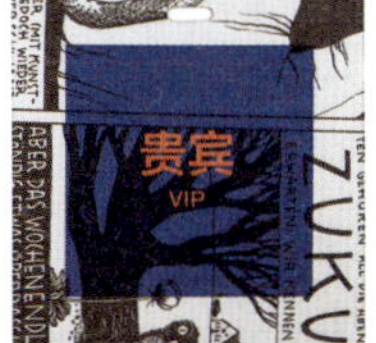
贵宾
VIP
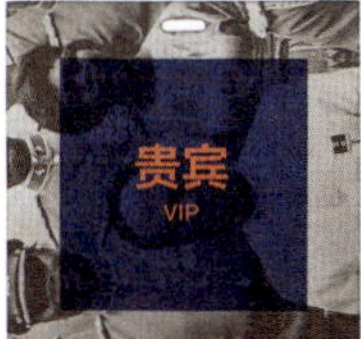
贵宾
VIP
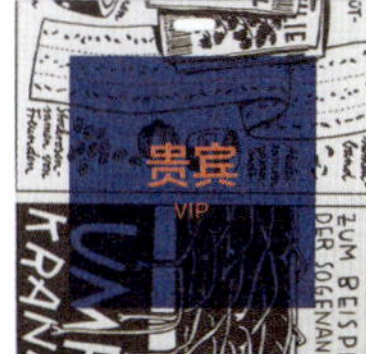
贵宾
VIP
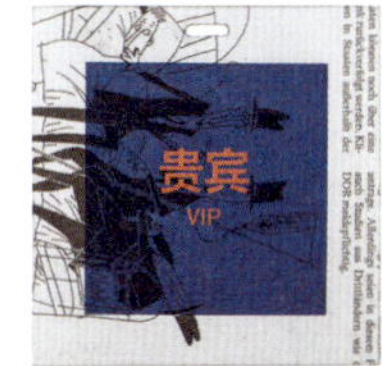
贵宾
VIP
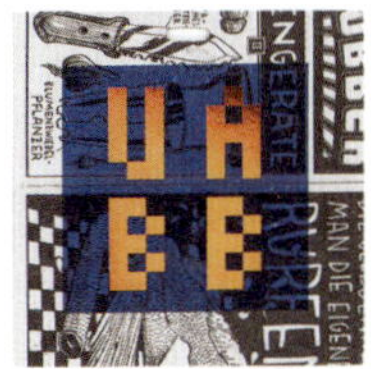
UA
BB
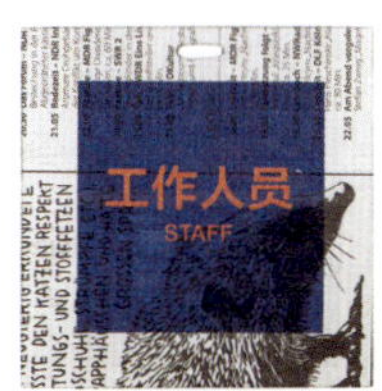
工作人员
STAFF
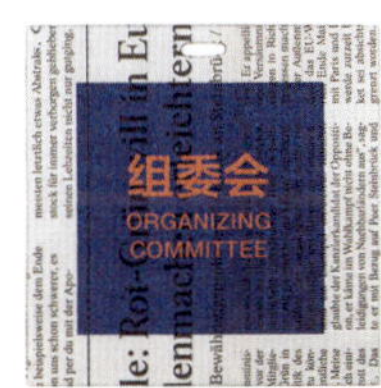
组委会
ORGANIZING
COMMITTEE
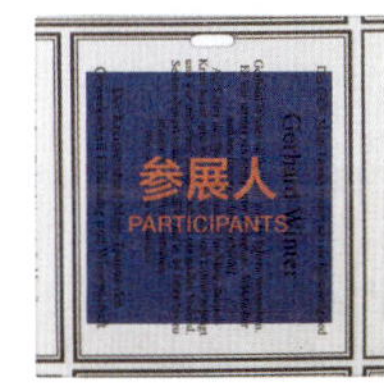
参展人
PARTICIPANTS
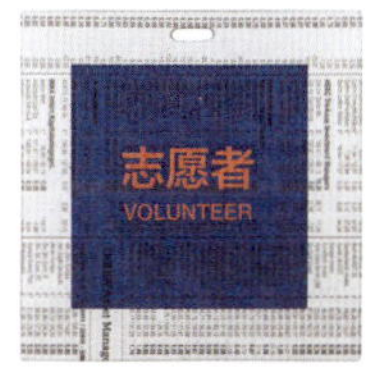
志愿者
VOLUNTEER
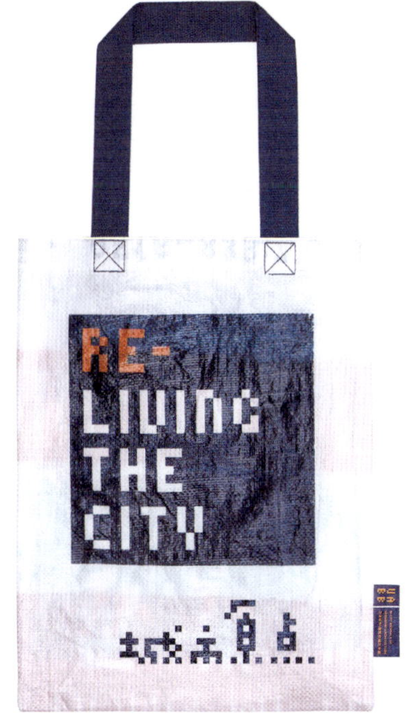
RE-
LIVING
THE
CITY
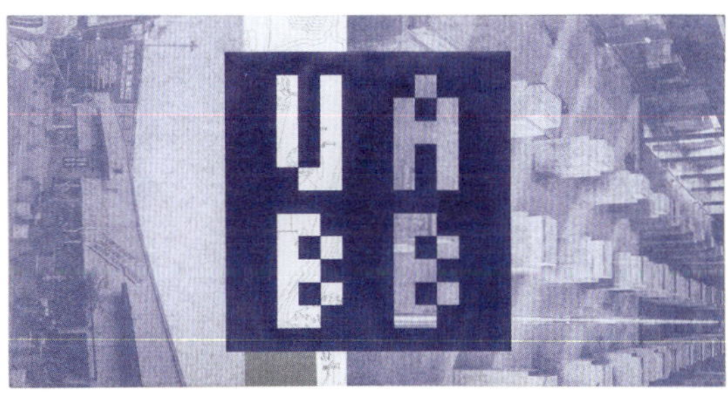
UA
BB
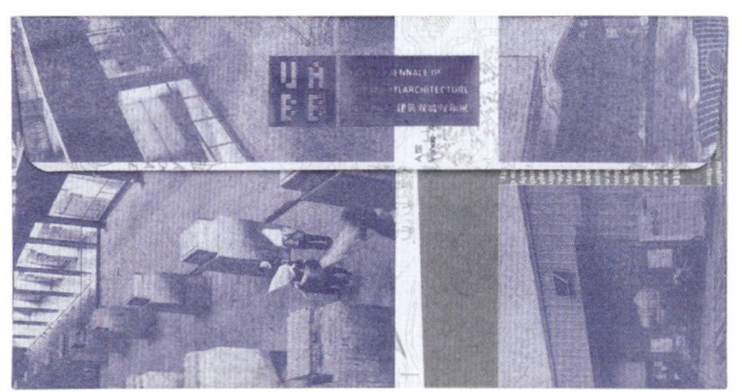
UA
BB

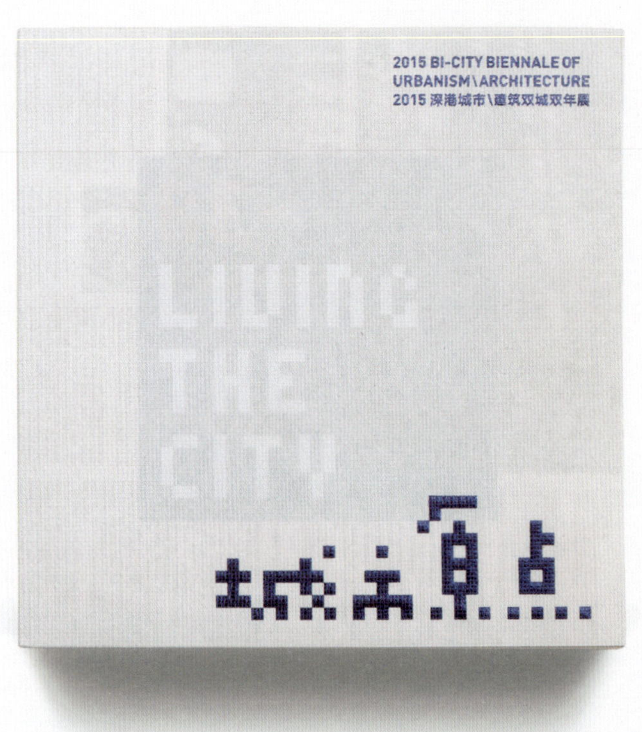
2015 BI-CITY BIENNALE OF
URBANISM\ARCHITECTURE
2015 深港城市\建筑双城双年展
LIVING
THE
CITY!

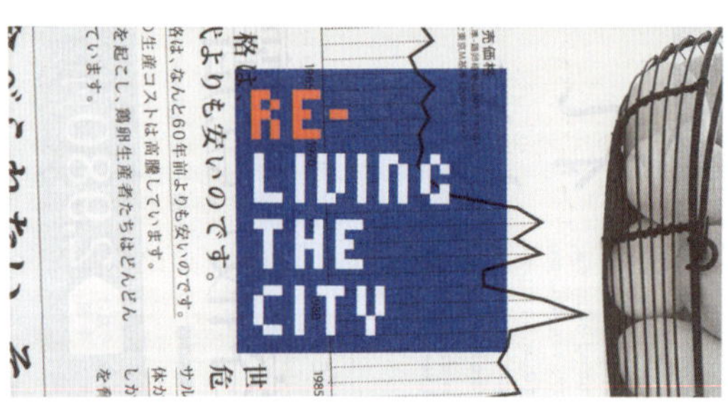
RE-
LIVING
THE
CITY

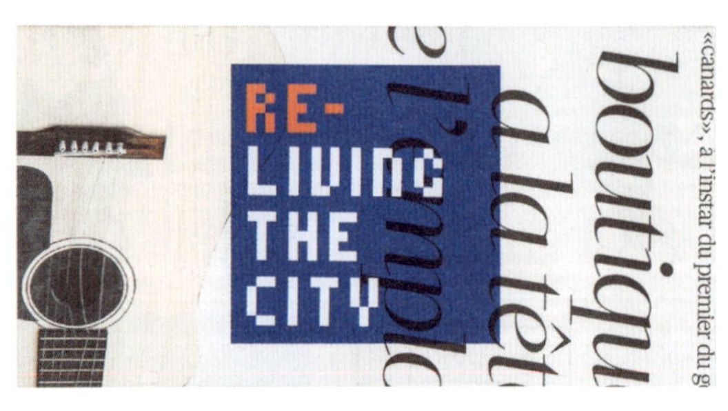
RE-
LIVING
THE
CITY

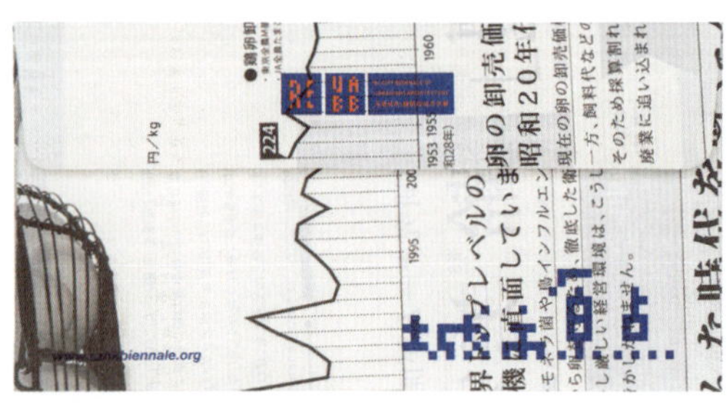
www.szhkbiennale.org

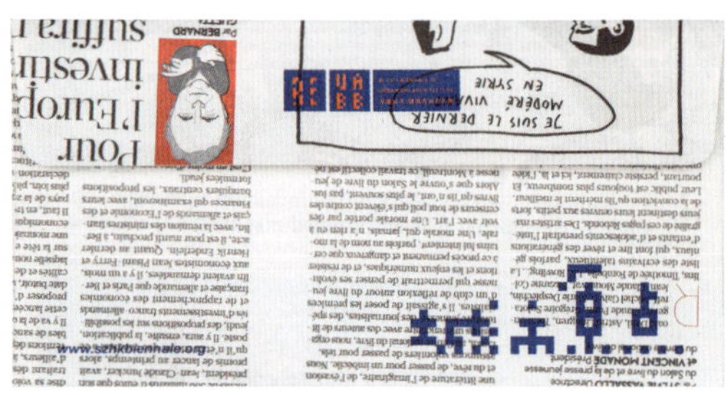
www.szhkbiennale.org

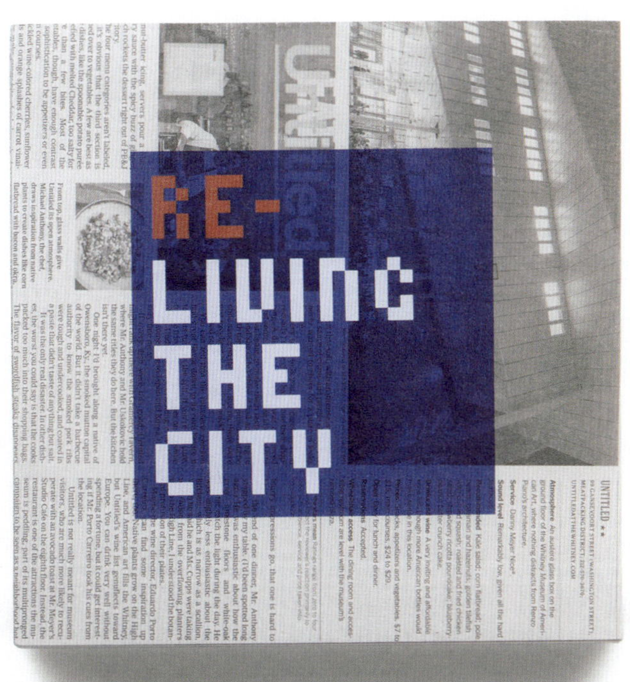
RE-
LIVING
THE
CITY

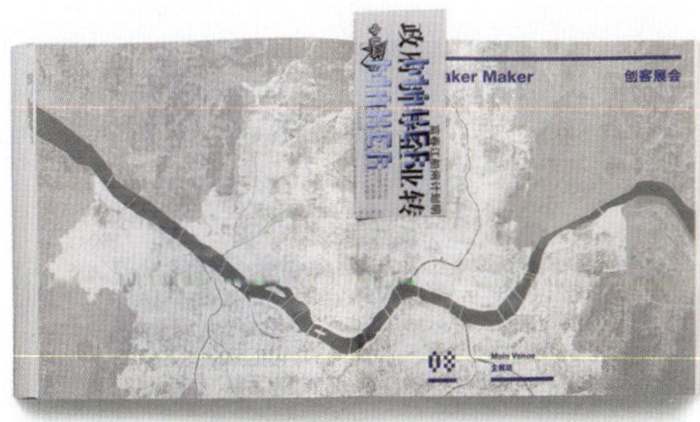
aker Maker
创客展会

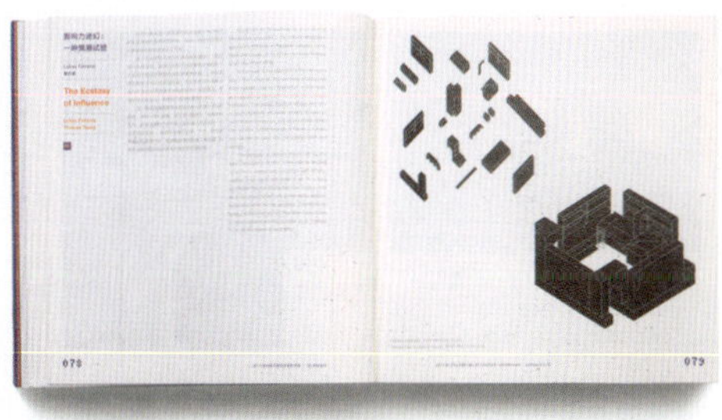

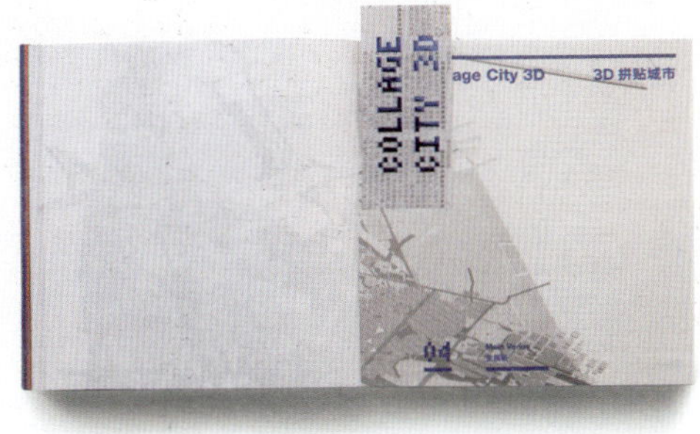
COLLAGE
CITY 3D
age City 3D
3D 拼贴城市

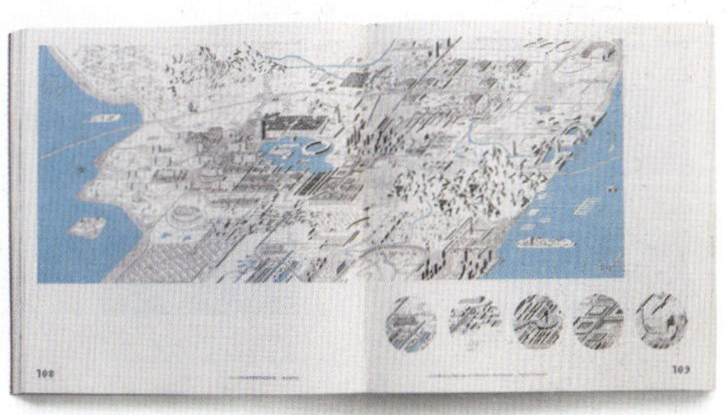

DE PETITS TOTS MATÀVEM FORMIGUES

Studio : Enserio Designer : Miquel Amela, Ferran Rodríguez

De petits tots matàvem formigues (When we were children we used to kill ants) is a theater play between the Western and film noir.

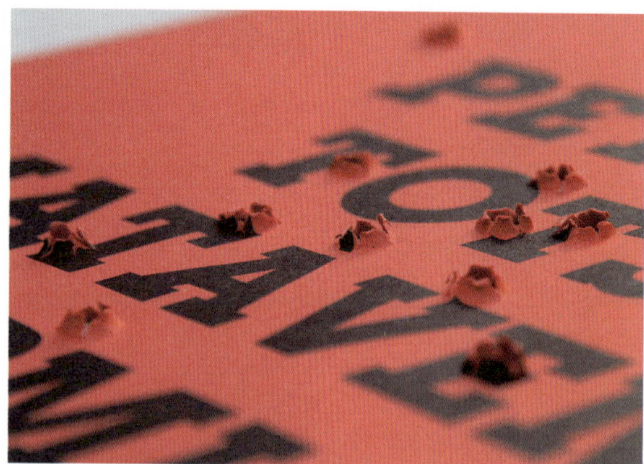

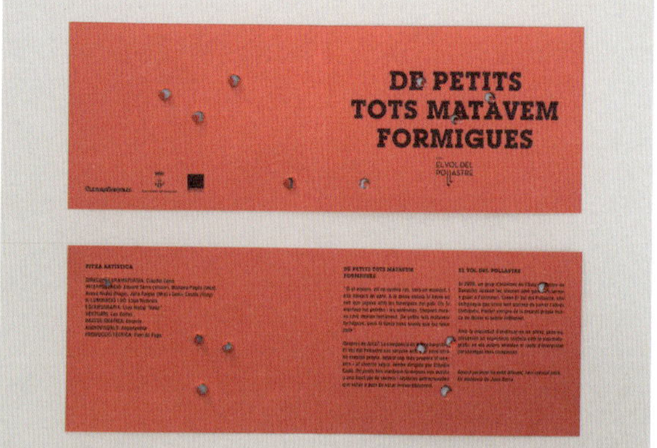

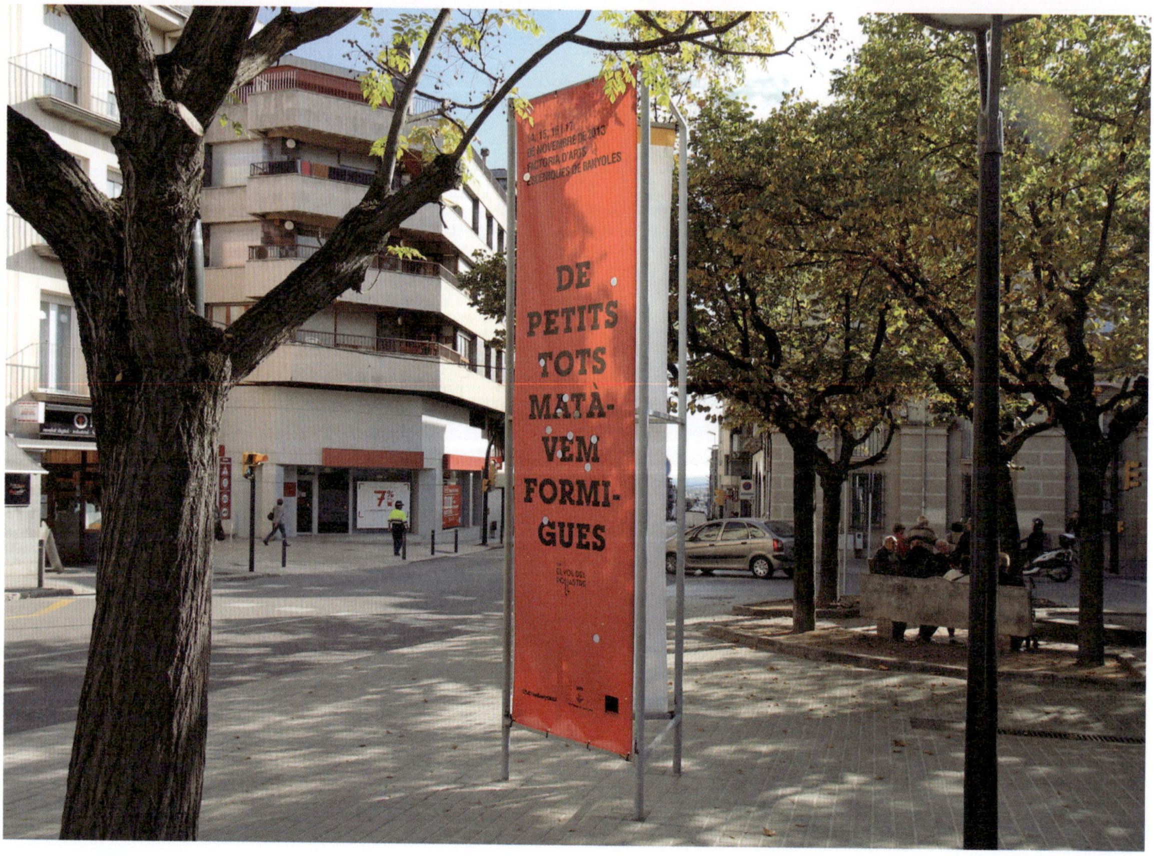

14, 15, 16 i 17 DE NOVEMBRE DE 2013
FACTORIA D'ARTS ESCÈNIQUES DE BANYOLES

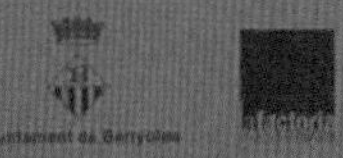

DE PETITS TOTS MATÀVEM FORMI- GUES

CIA.
EL VOL DEL POLLASTRE

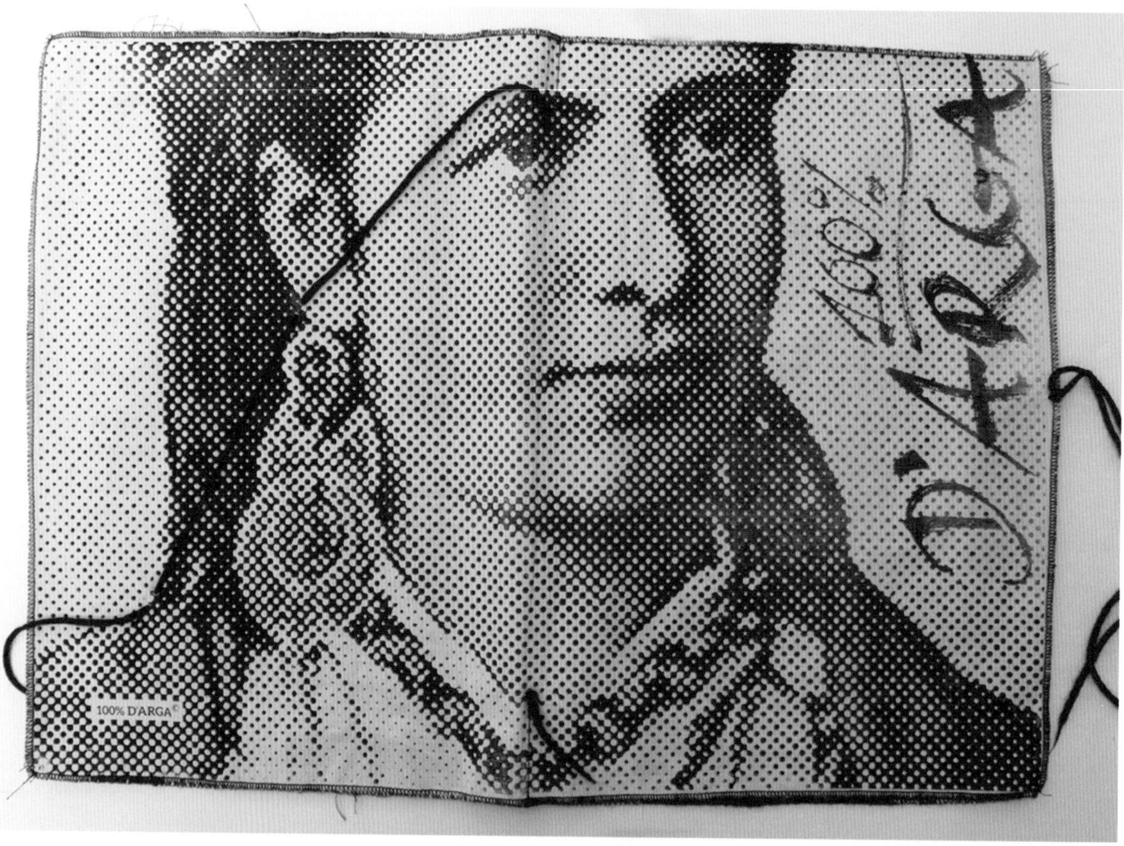

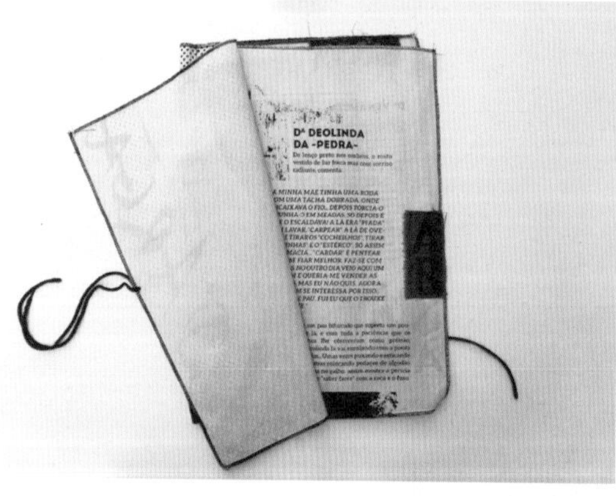

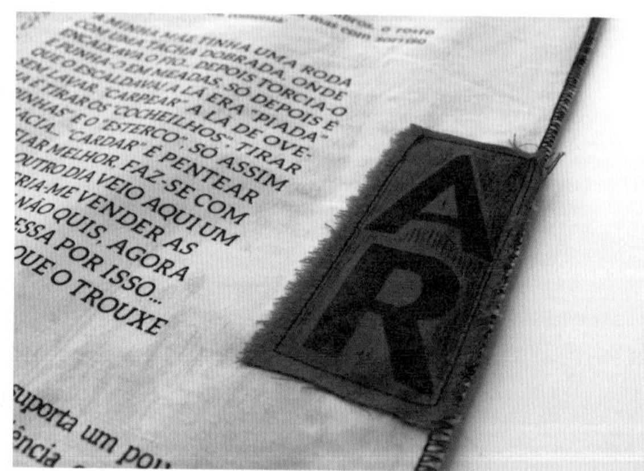

100% D'ARGA-TISSUE NEWSPAPER

Designer : Helena Soares, Sara Costta

"Senhora d'Arga" is a communitarian project of local development, which aims to recover the traditions of Serra d'Arga (located in north Portugal) such as the embroidery and weaving. Thus, a tissue newspaper named 100% d'Arga was made to present and promote the project.

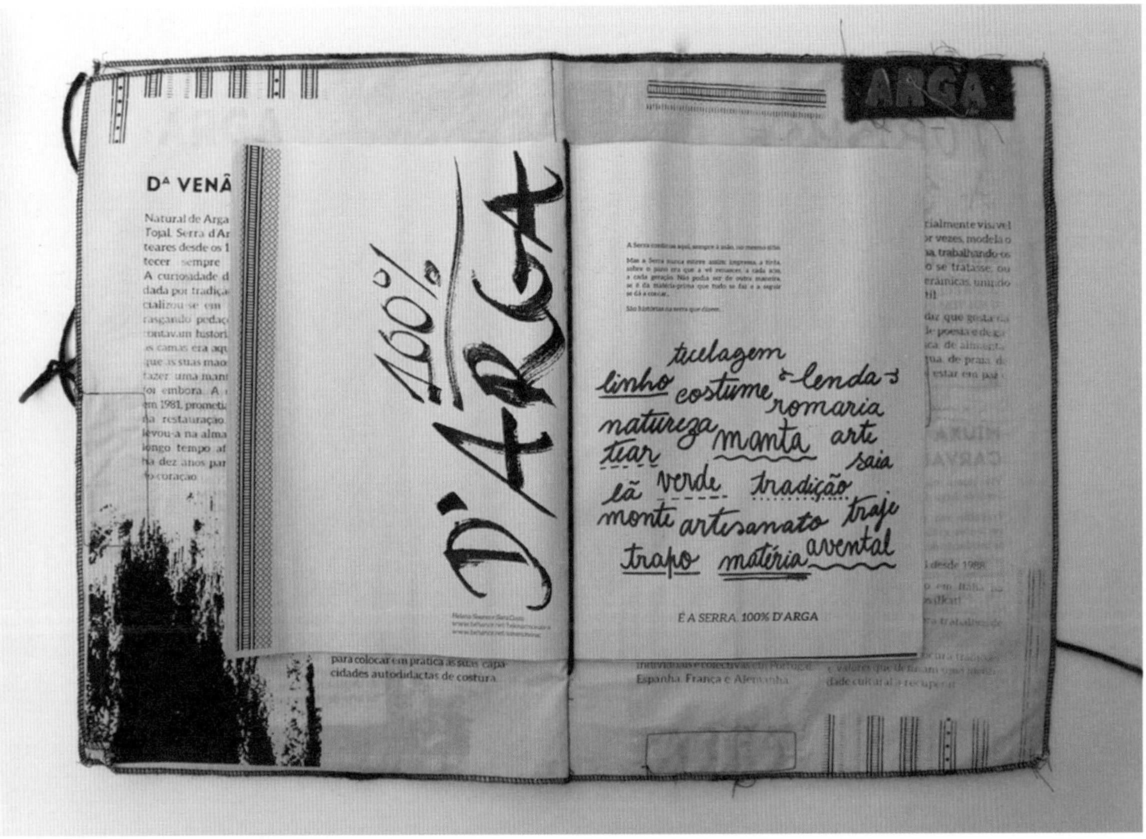

ARGA

Dª VENÃ

100% D'ARGA

tecelagem
linho costume lenda
romaria natureza
tear manta arte
saia lã verde tradição
monte artesanato traje
trapo matéria avental

É A SERRA. 100% D'ARGA

para colocar em prática as suas capacidades autodidactas de costura

Espanha, França e Alemanha

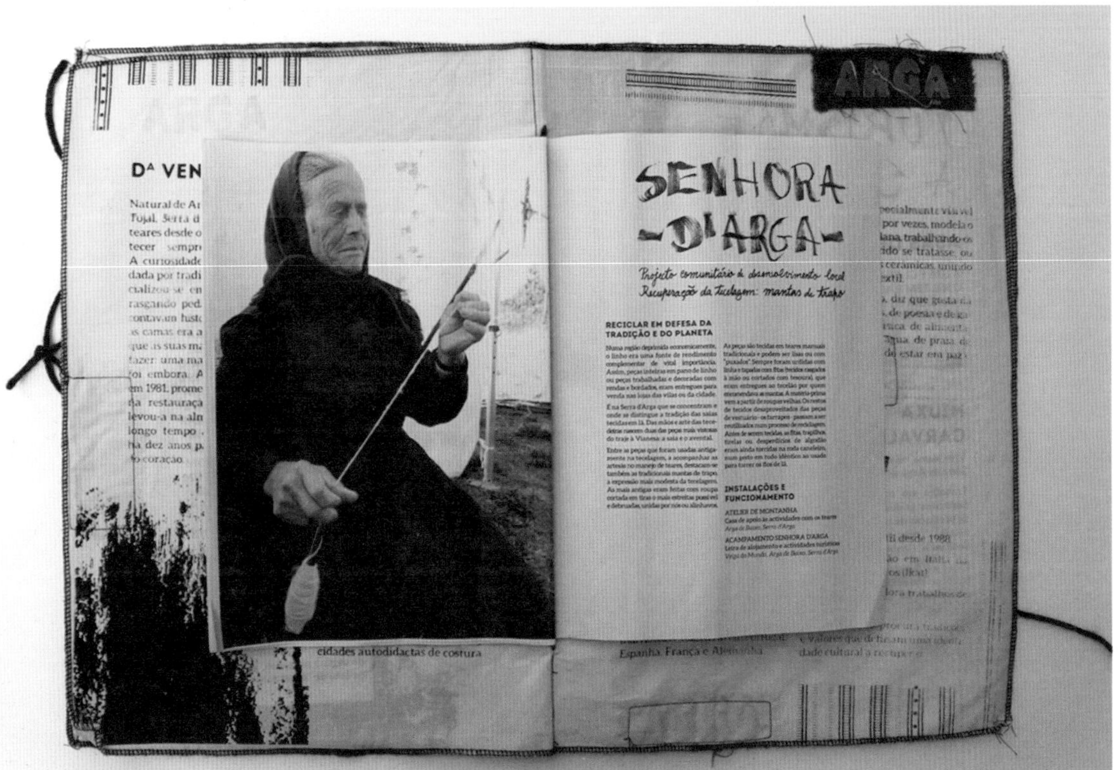

THE LOGBOOK

Designer : Cowei Liu

This book is a diary about the designer's experience as an actor. The words on the cover are convex and are accompanied by gold stamping in order to highlight the atmosphere.

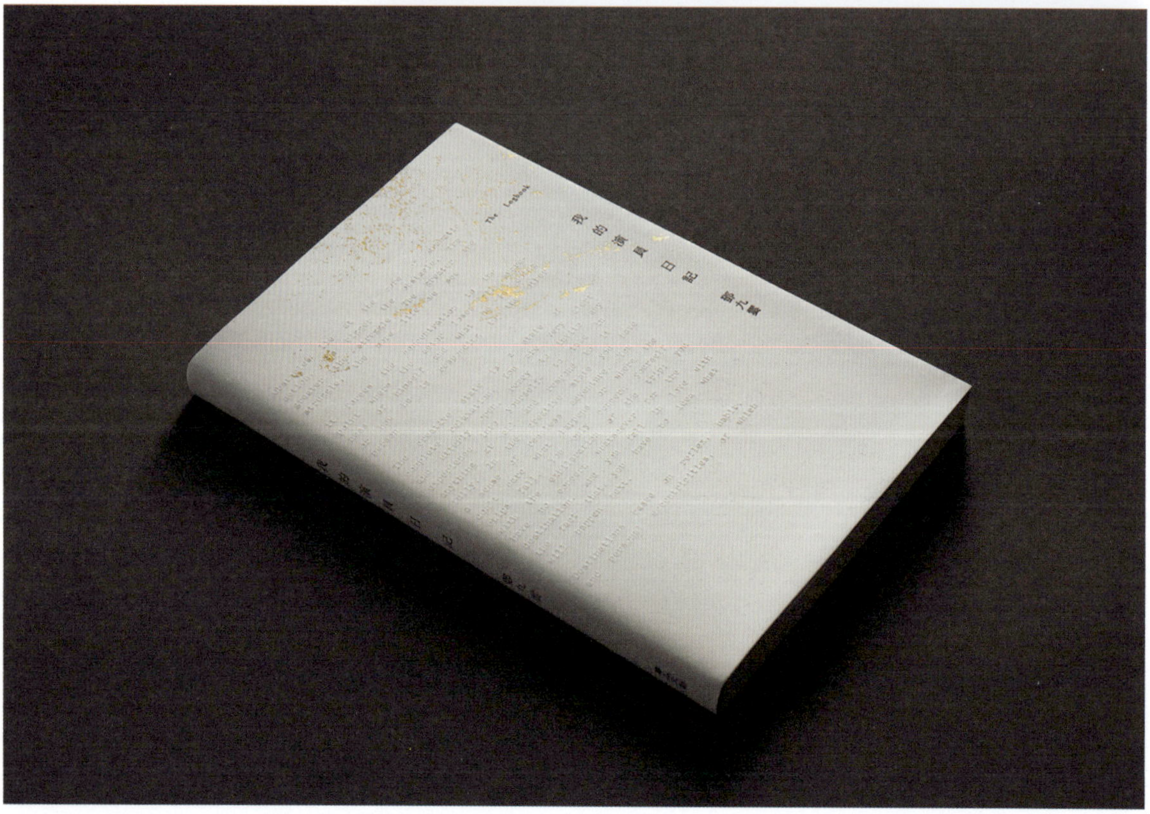

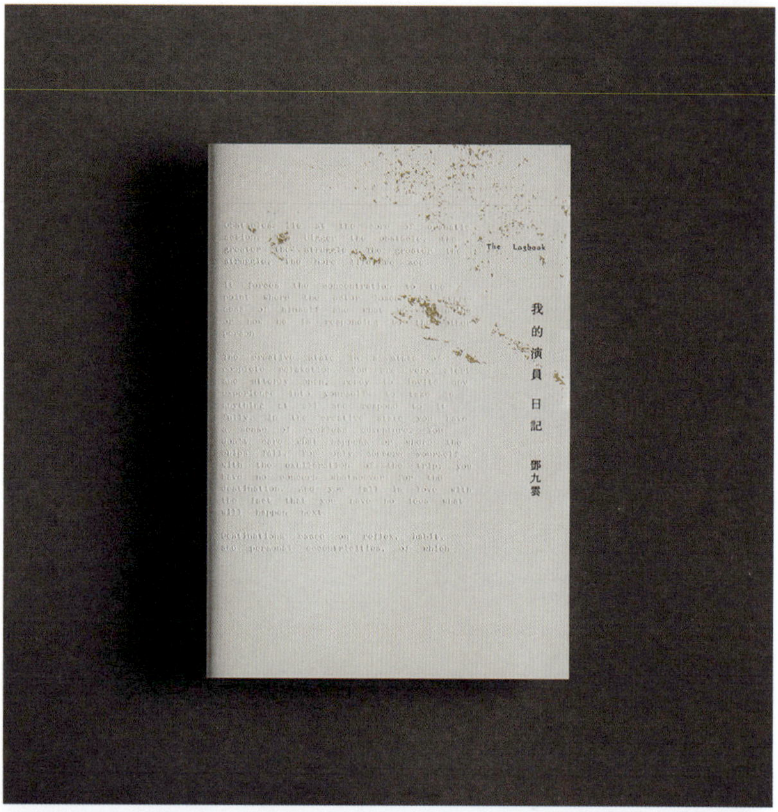

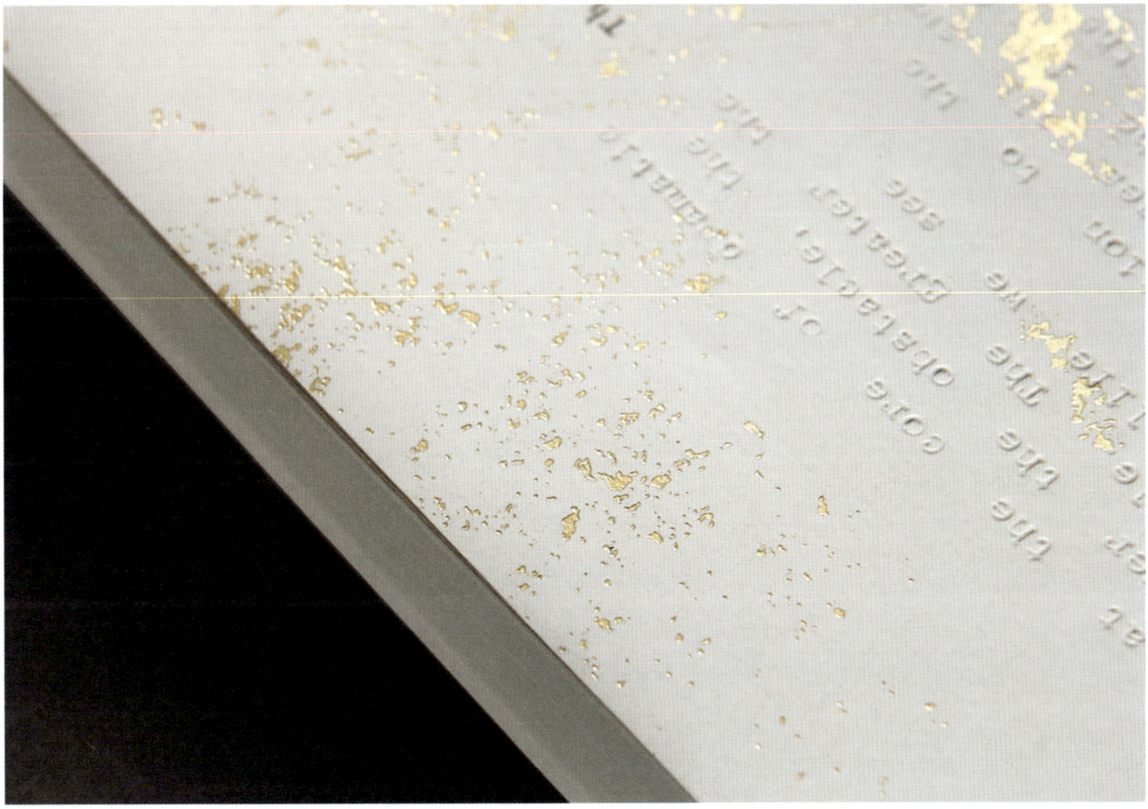

DOTYKY

Studio : Studio Goat s.r.o.   Designer : Miroslav Kozel

Ivan Mihok released his 3rd album named "Dotyky" (Touches), which was about the fact that people touch others less and less. The designer tried to find a metaphor to represent the barriers that hinder people from mutual contact. Parts of the visuals are protruding to show that through touch people can find something new that isn't evident at first glance.

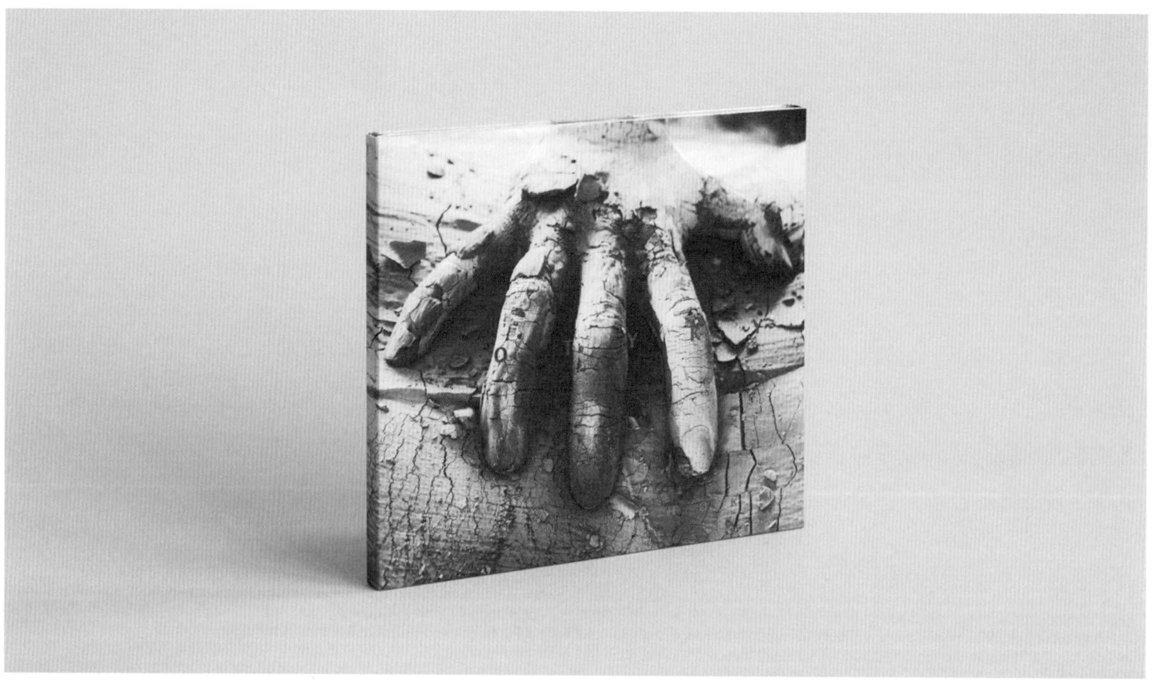

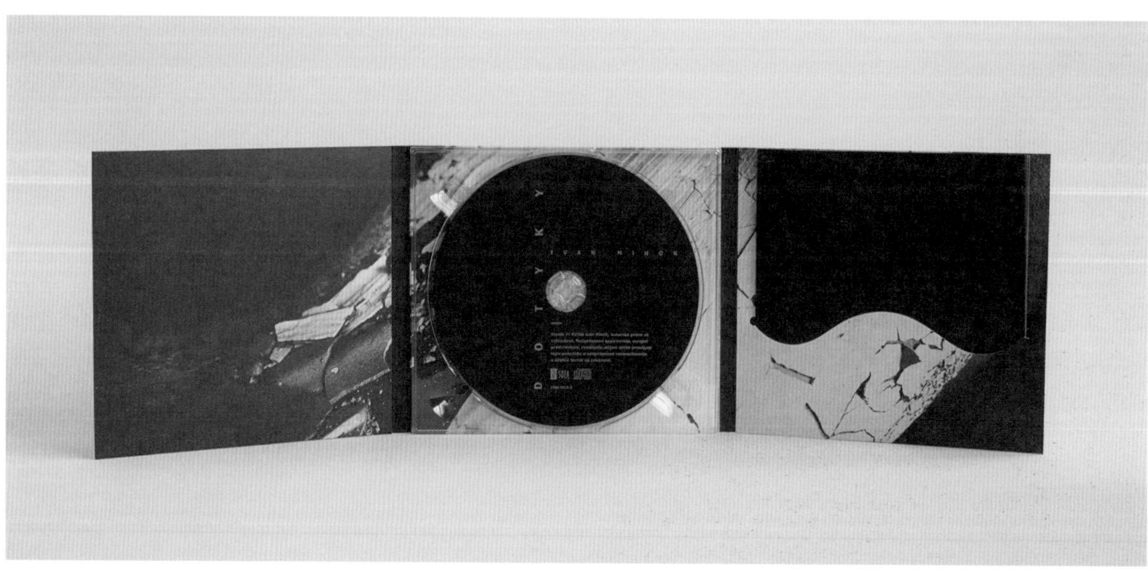

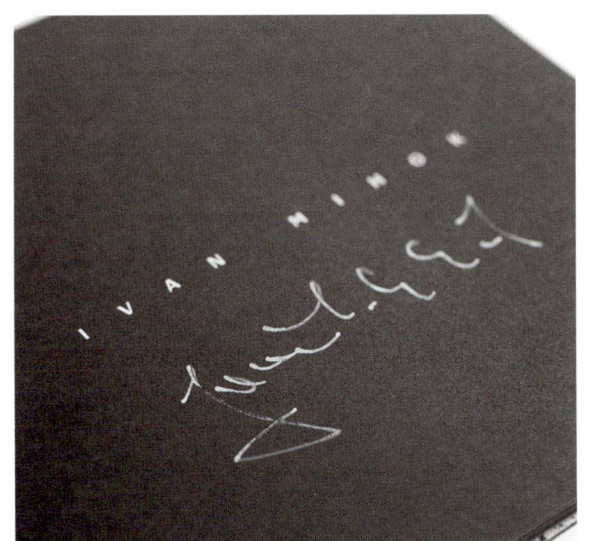
IVAN MIHOK

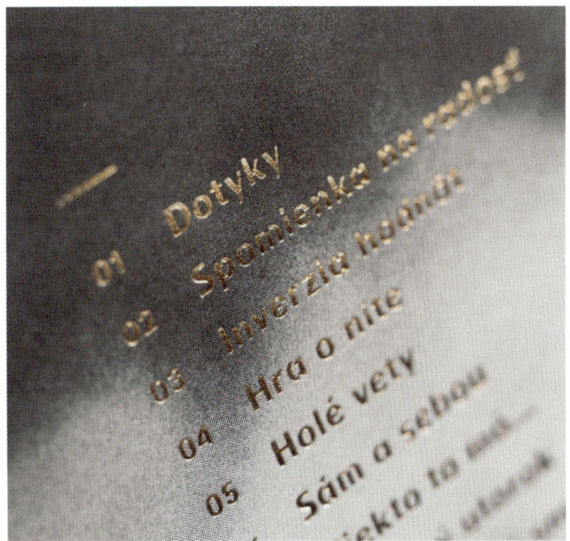
01 Dotyky
02 Spomienka na radosť
03 Inverzia hodnôt
04 Hra o nite
05 Holé vety
Sám a sebou

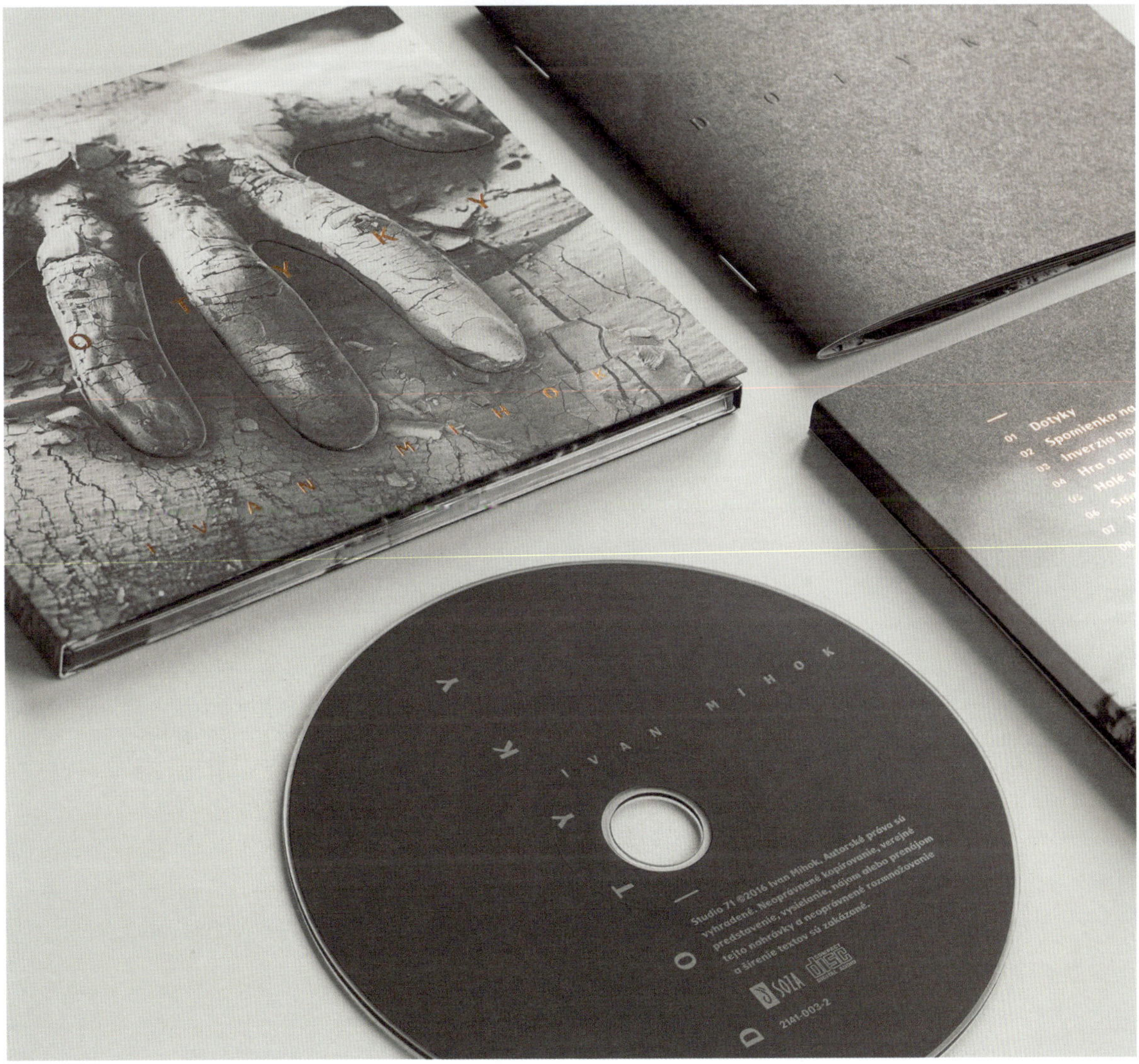

SEASIDE—UNSAID, UNHEARD EP

Designer : Tamas Birinyi

This is an album design for the Hungarian multi-intrumentalist producer, SEASIDE. The project includes Seaside logo design, CD cover design and packaging, digital cover variations for the songs, music video and social media.

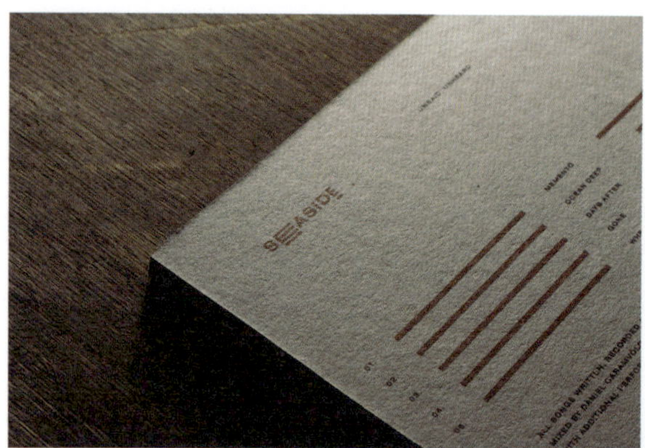

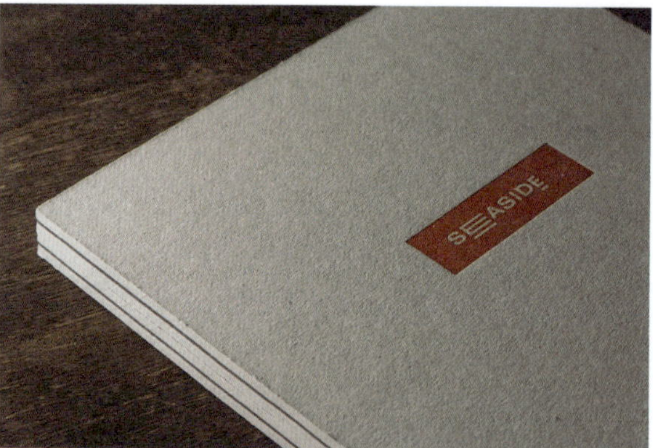

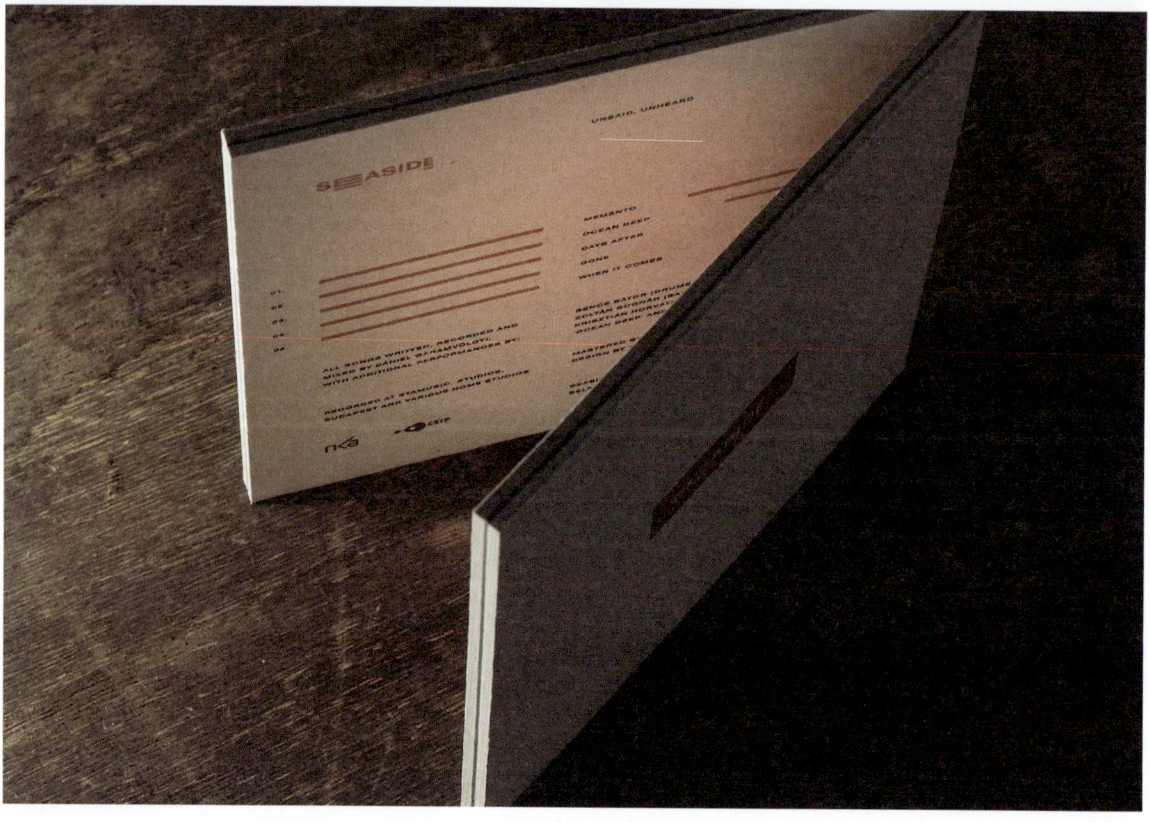

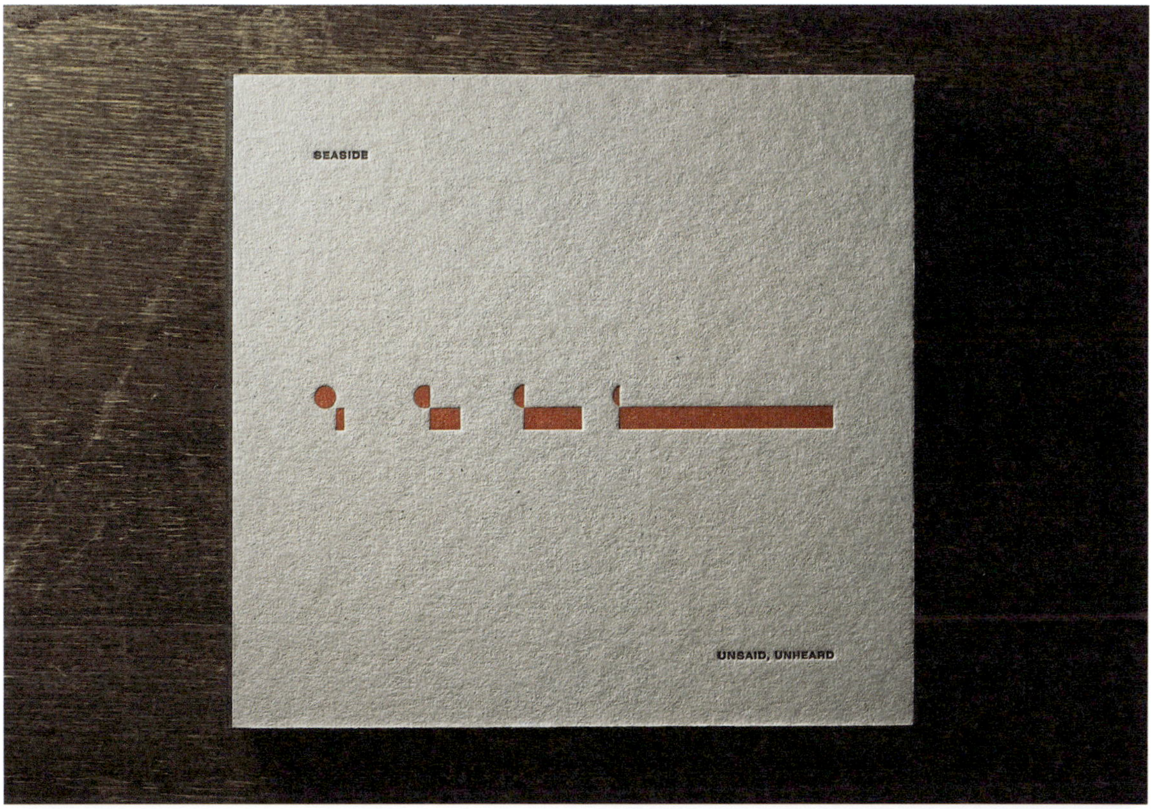

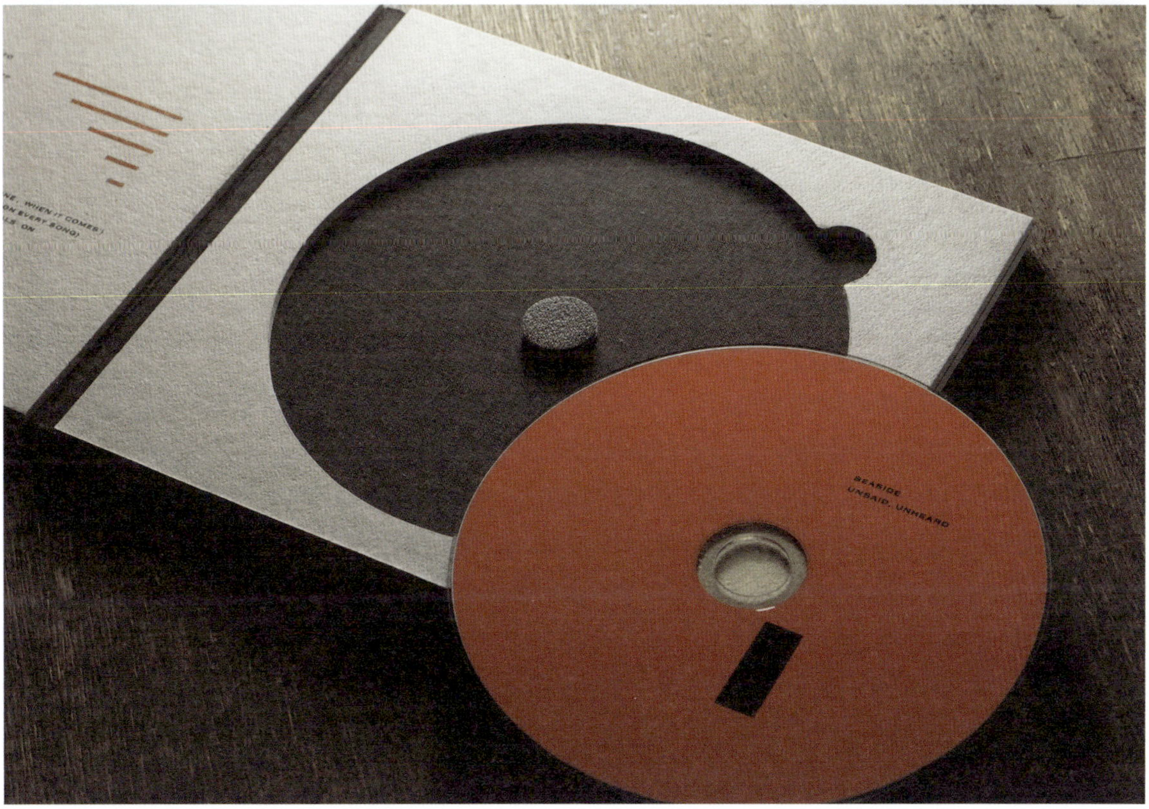

THE PAVILIA HILL

Studio : Toby Ng Design   Designer : Toby Ng, Ronald Cheung

The Pavilia Hill is a luxury bespoke residence in the heart of Hong Kong. Its interior and landscape designs are all based on Wabi-Sabi. Based on the principles of Wabi-Sabi, a visceral and texturally rich book is designed to reflect the serenity of the main feature of this residence.

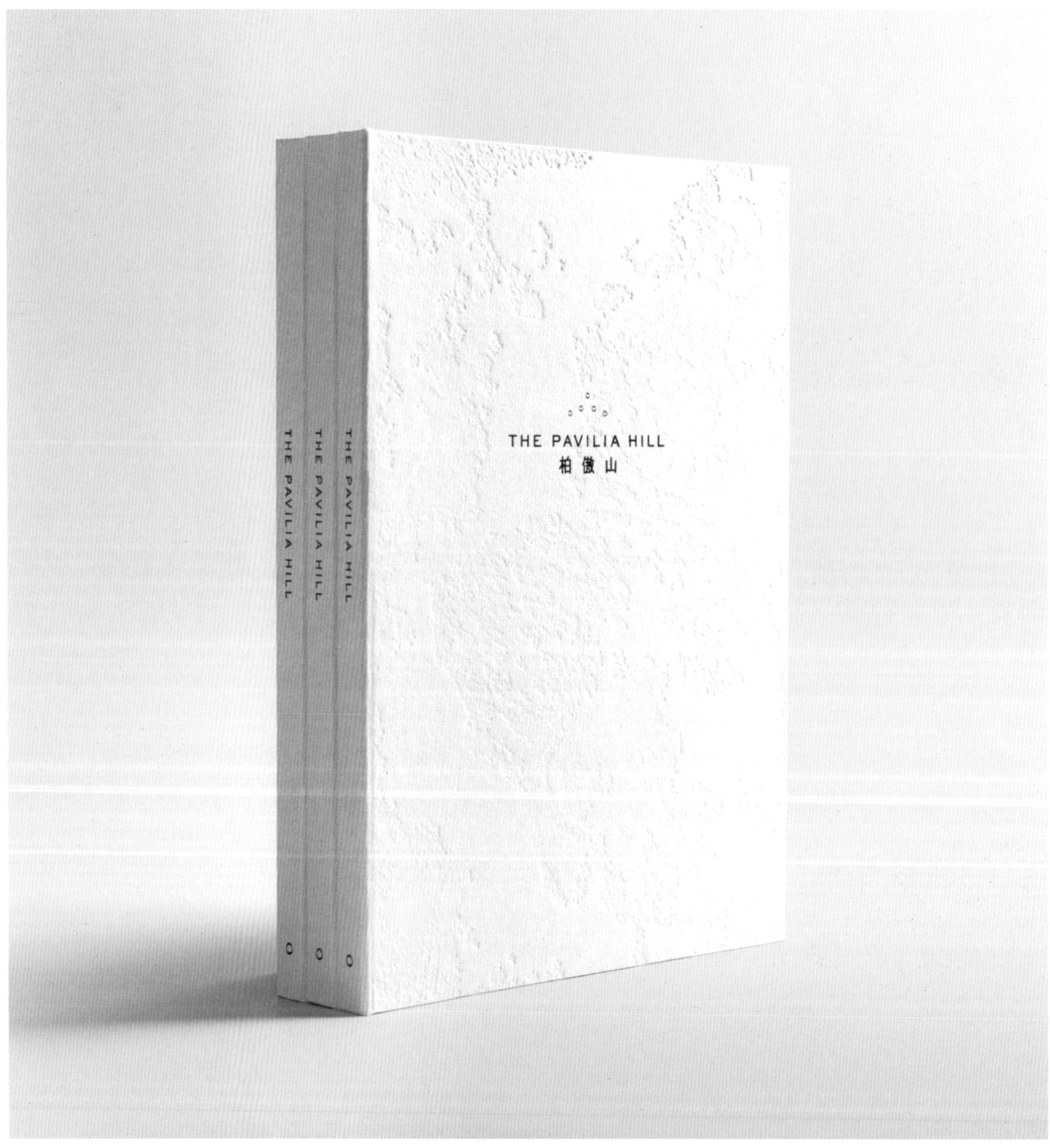

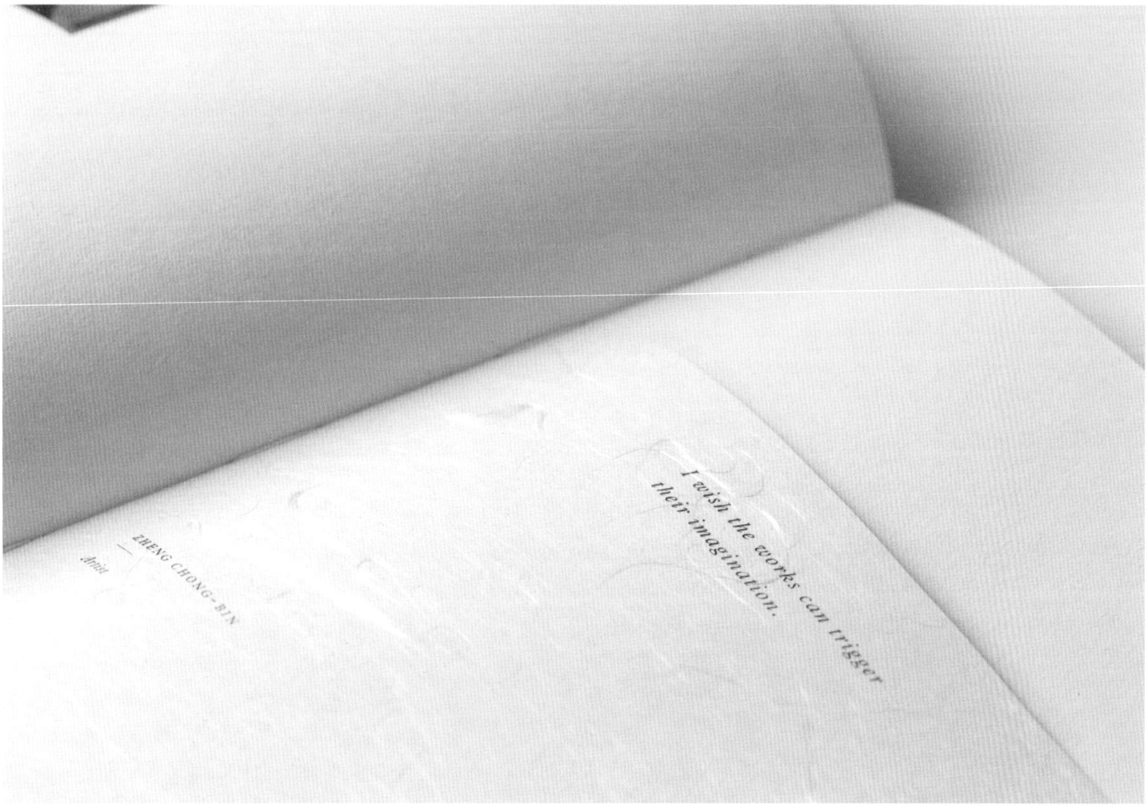

I wish the works can trigger their imagination.

ZHENG CHONG-BIN

—

Artist

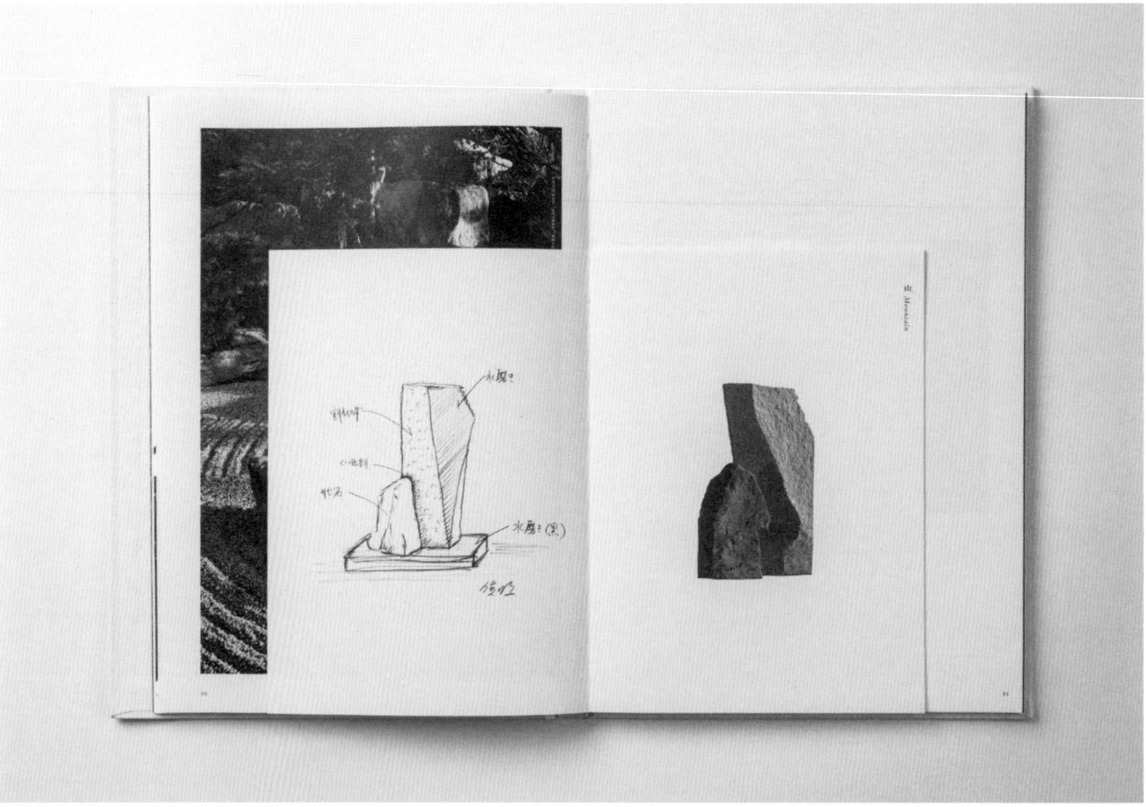

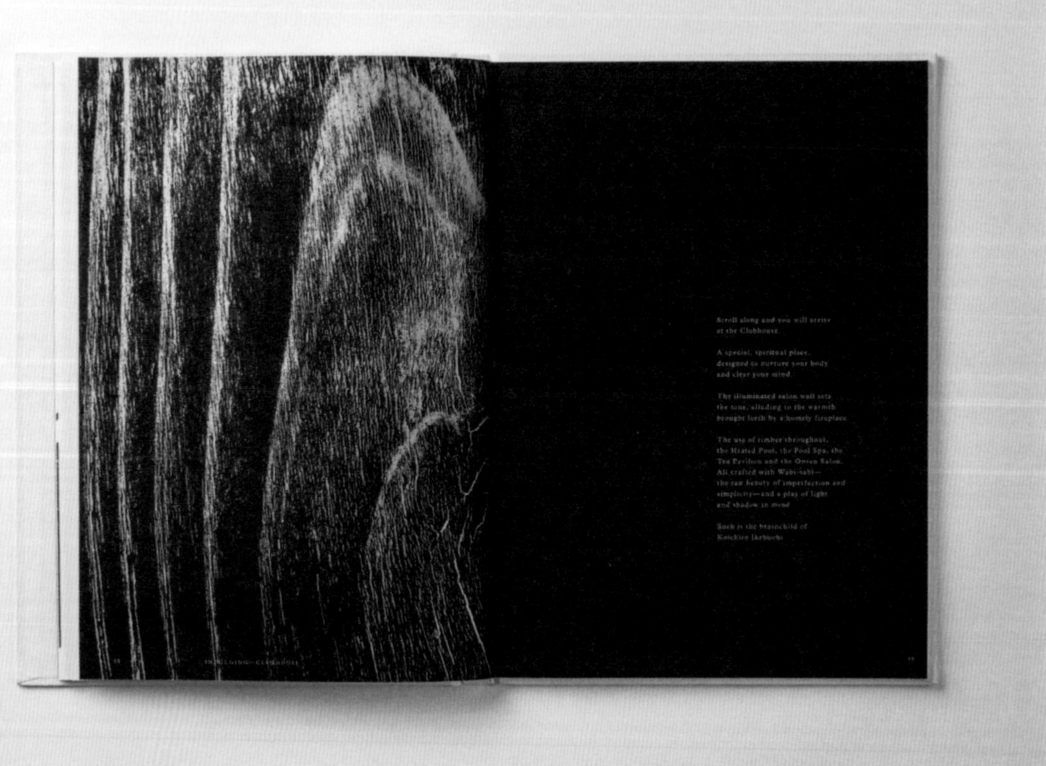
Stroll along and you will arrive
at the Clubhouse.
A special, spiritual place,
designed to nurture your body
and clear your mind.
The illuminated salon wall sets
the tone, alluding to the warmth
brought forth by a homely fireplace.
The use of timber throughout,
the Heated Pool, the Pool Spa, the
Tea Pavilion and the Onsen Salon.
All crafted with Wabi-sabi—
the raw beauty of imperfection and
simplicity—and a play of light
and shadow in mind.
Such is the brainchild of
Koichiro Ikebuchi

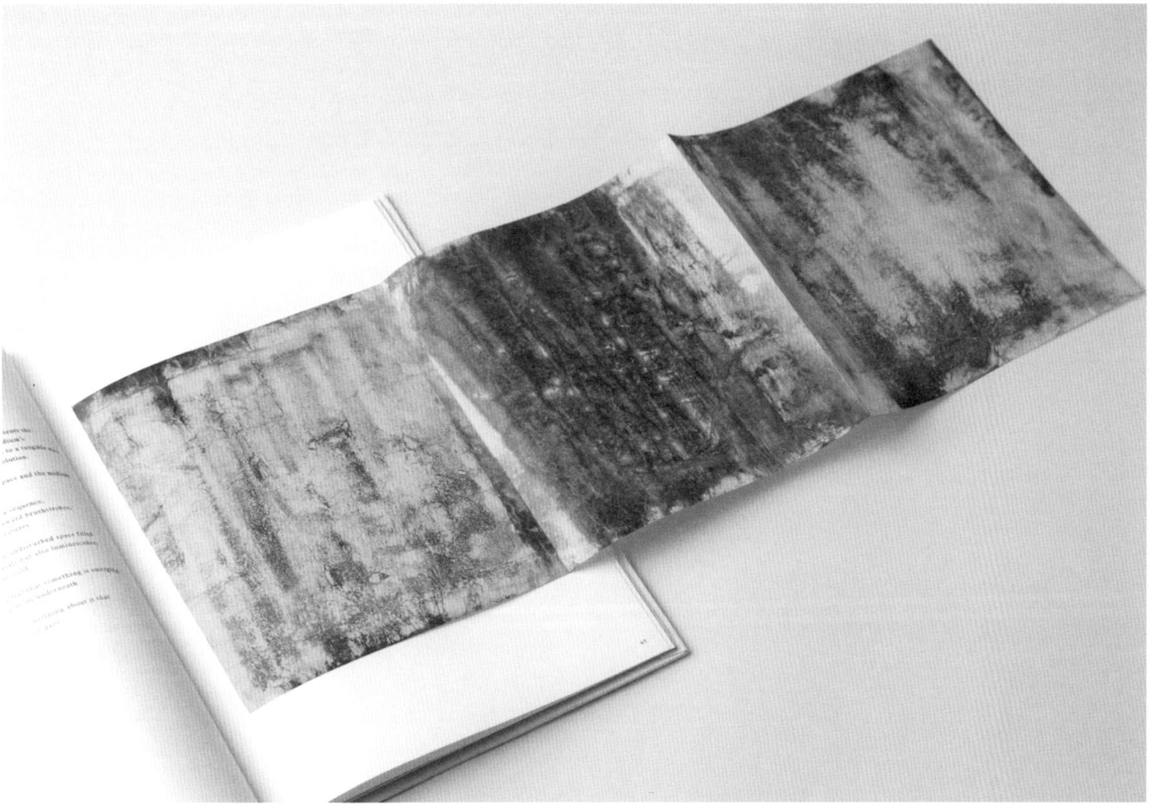

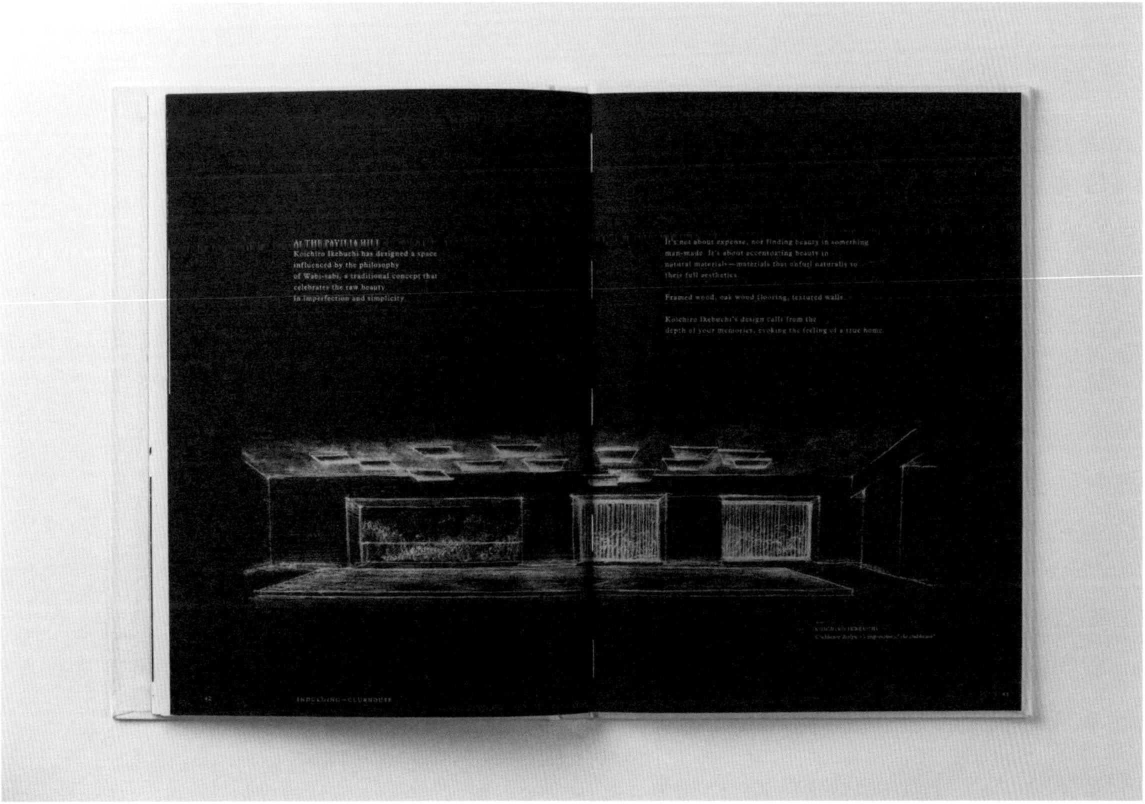
Koichiro Ikebuchi has designed a space
influenced by the philosophy
of Wabi-sabi, a traditional concept that
celebrates the raw beauty
in imperfection and simplicity
It's not about expense, nor finding beauty in something
man-made. It's about accentuating beauty in
natural materials — materials that unfurl naturally to
their full aesthetics.
Framed wood, oak wood flooring, textured walls.
Koichiro Ikebuchi's design calls from the
depth of your memories, evoking the feeling of a true home.

LIANZHOU FOTO

Studio : Another Design
Type Designer : Zhan Guodong
Photographer : A Rock

The theme of the 2016 Lianzhou Foto Exhibition is "As Entertaining as Possible", by which the curator intended to criticize the present consumption concept. "Homo faber" is fast disappearing and is being replaced by "homo consumer". Photography has witnessed this major transformation in contemporary society. For the visual identity, the curatorial theme was silk screen printed on gold foil papers which were torn, crumpled and poked as a way to demonstrate the core concept of the exhibition and to obtain pleasure.

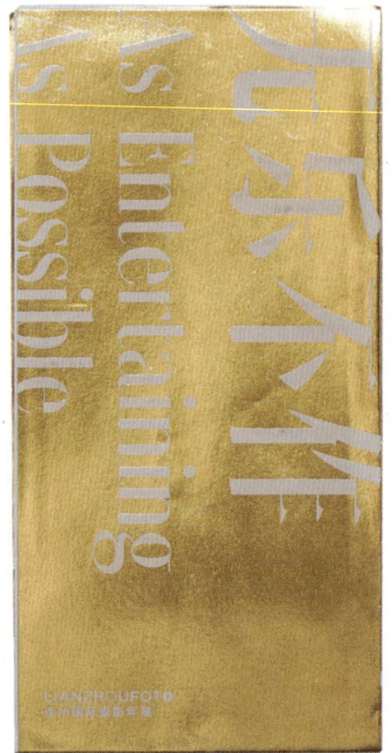

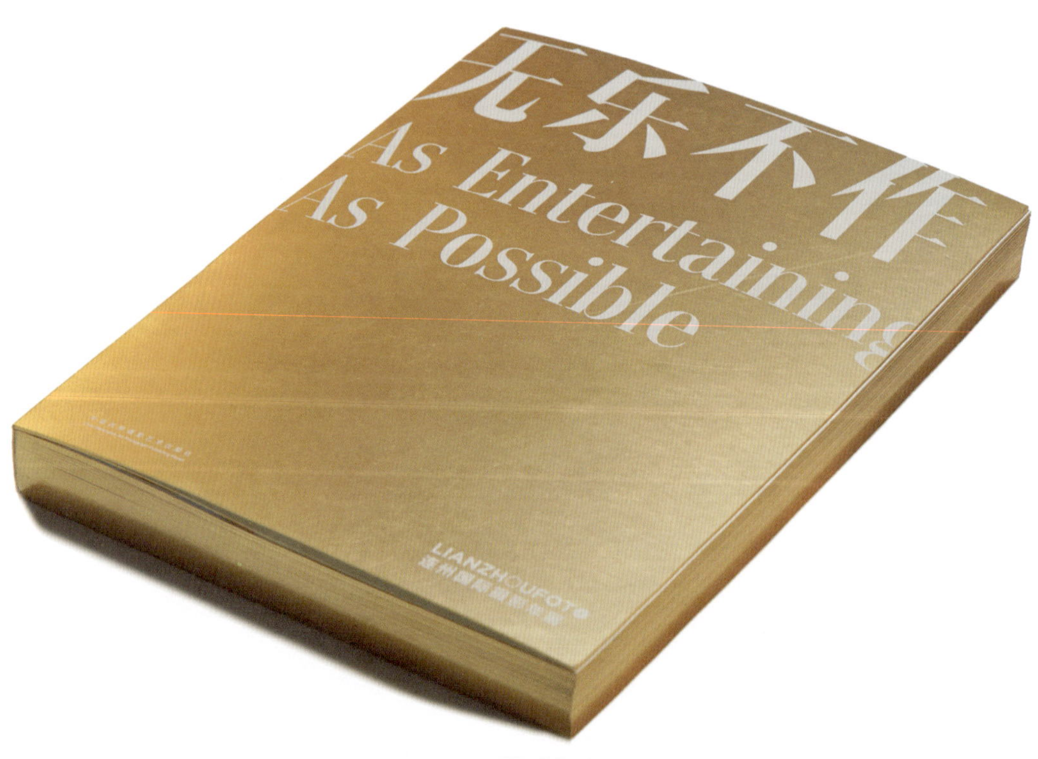

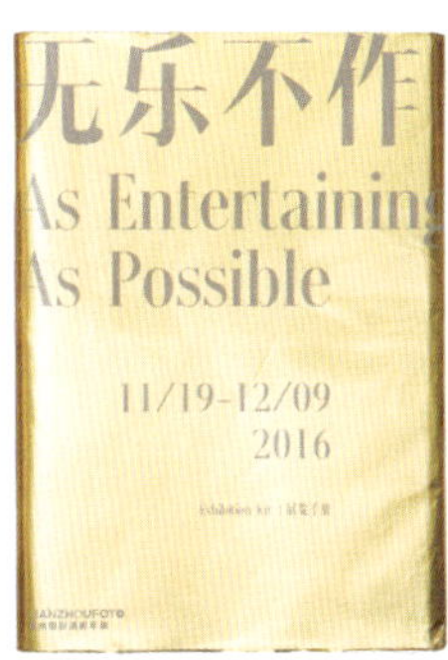
无乐不作
As Entertaining
As Possible
11/19-12/09
2016

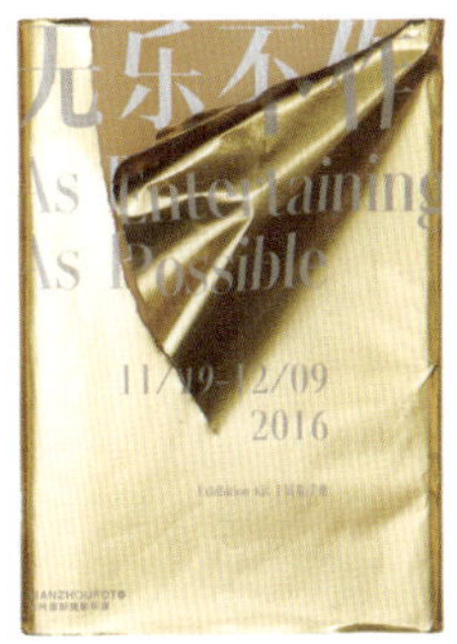

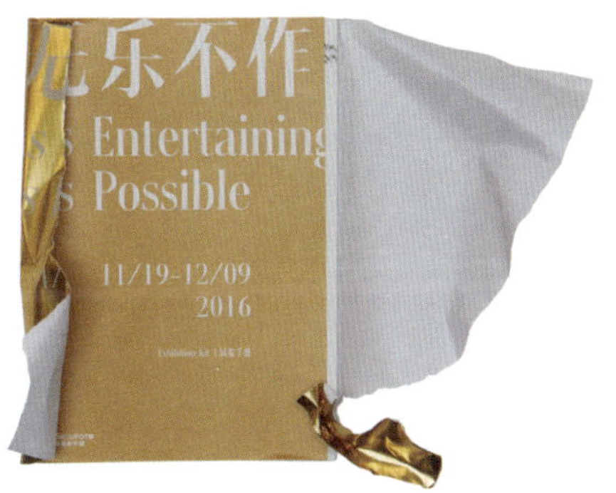
无乐不作
Entertaining
Possible
11/19-12/09
2016

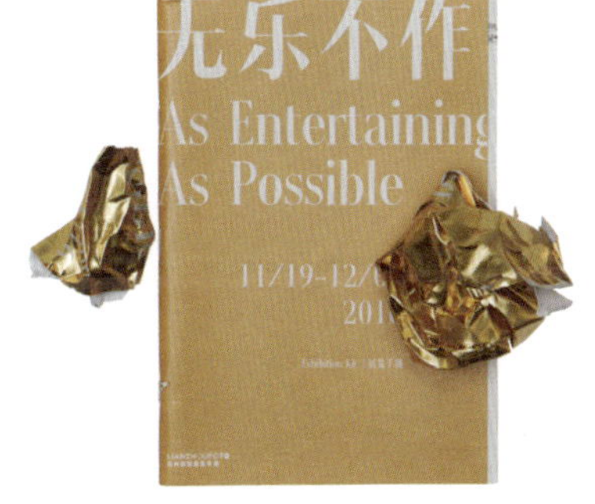
无乐不作
As Entertaining
As Possible

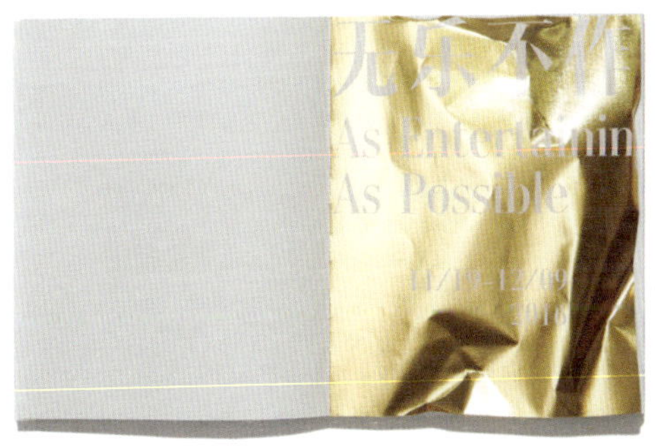

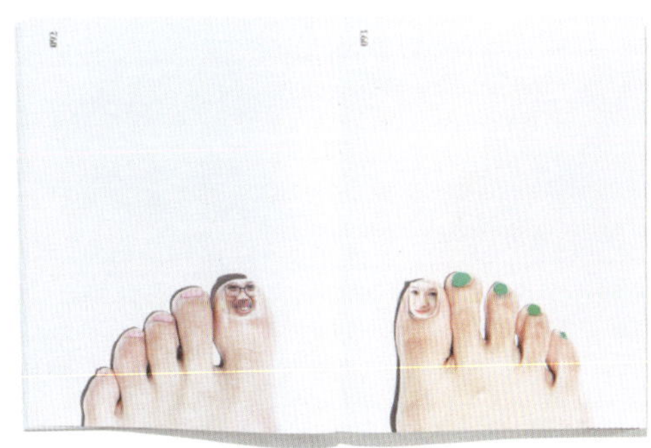

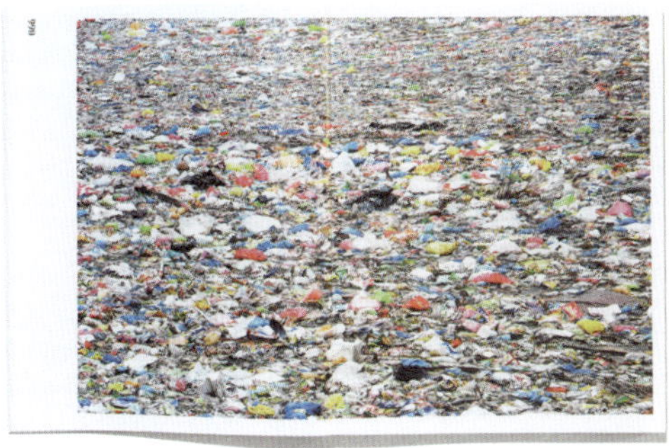

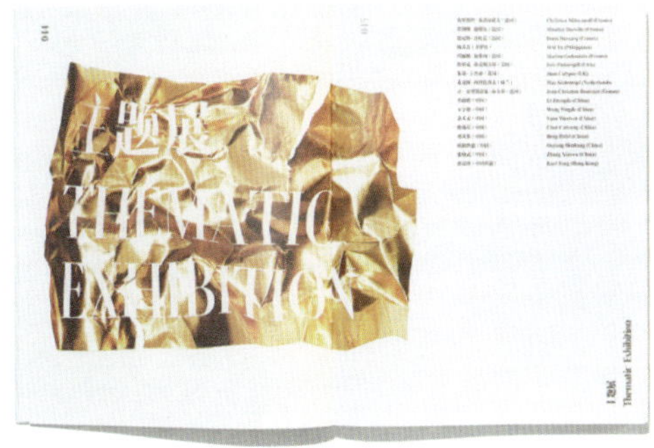

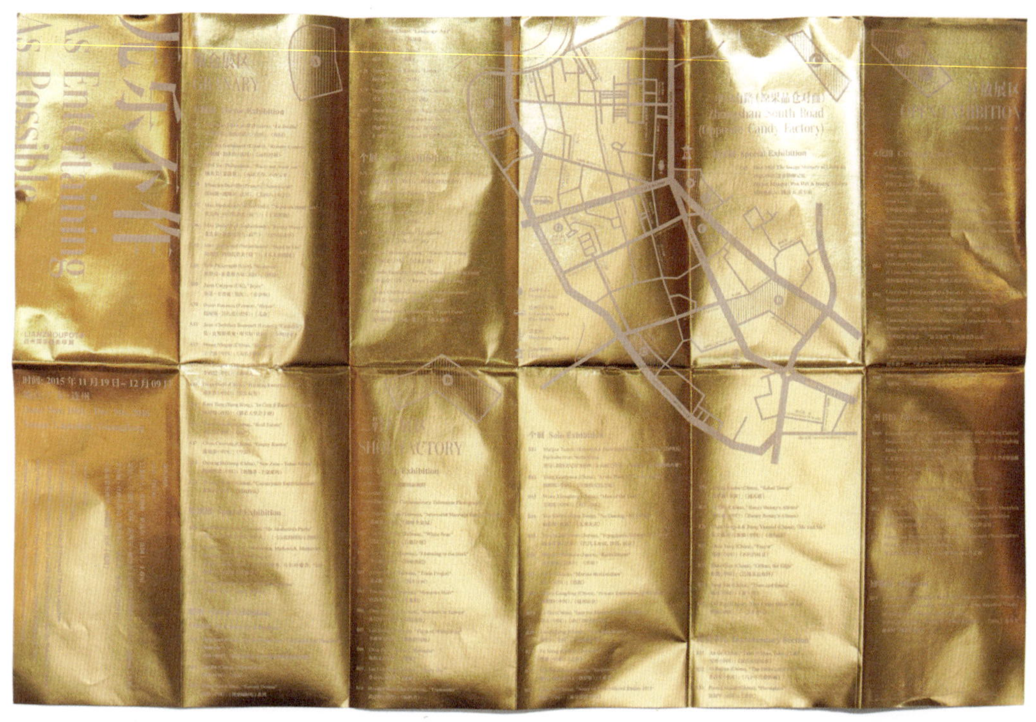

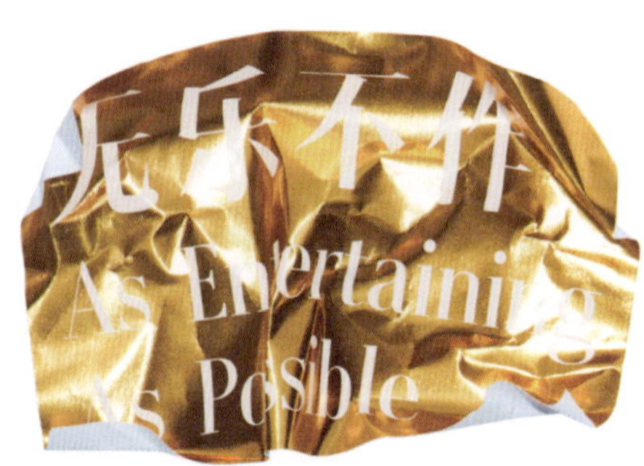

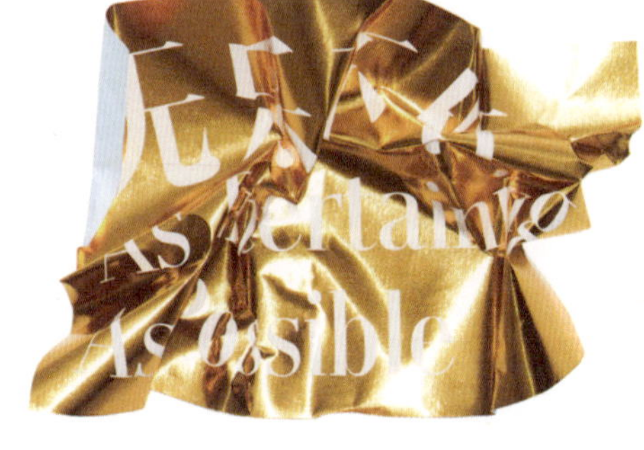

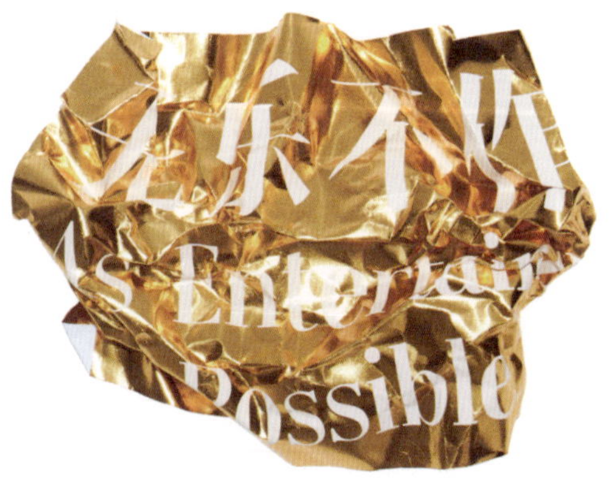

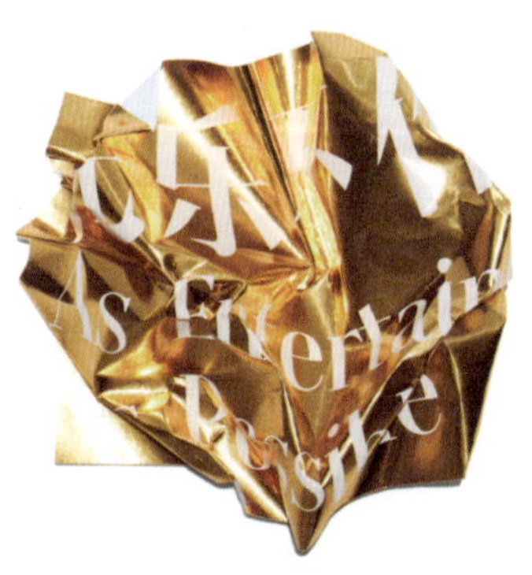

2016 连州国际摄影年展
LIANZHOU FOTO 2016

总监：段煜婷

总策展人：弗朗索·萨瓦尔（法国）/ 王春辰

策展人：章翔鸥 / 樊林 / 沈昭良（台湾）/ 露西尔·丽博芝（法国）/ 仲西祐介（日本）/ 奥尔加·丝维布洛娃（俄罗斯）/ 米歇尔·菲利博（法国）

Director: Duan Yuting

Chief Curators: François Cheval (France) / Wang Chunchen

Curators: Zhang Xiangou / Fan Lin / Shen Chao-Liang (Taiwan) / Lucille Reyboz (France) / Yusuke Nakanishi (Japan) / Olga Sviblova (Russia) / Michel Philippot (France)

无乐不作
As Entertainin As Possible

From the "Mr. Malhotra's Party" series © Sunil Gupta

11/19-12/09
2016

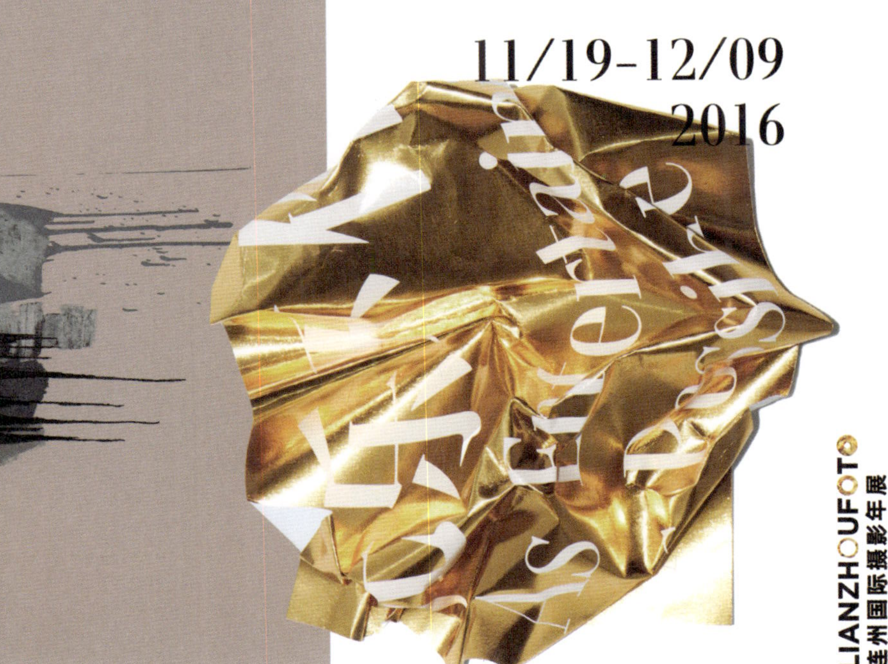

LIANZHOUFOTO
连州国际摄影年展

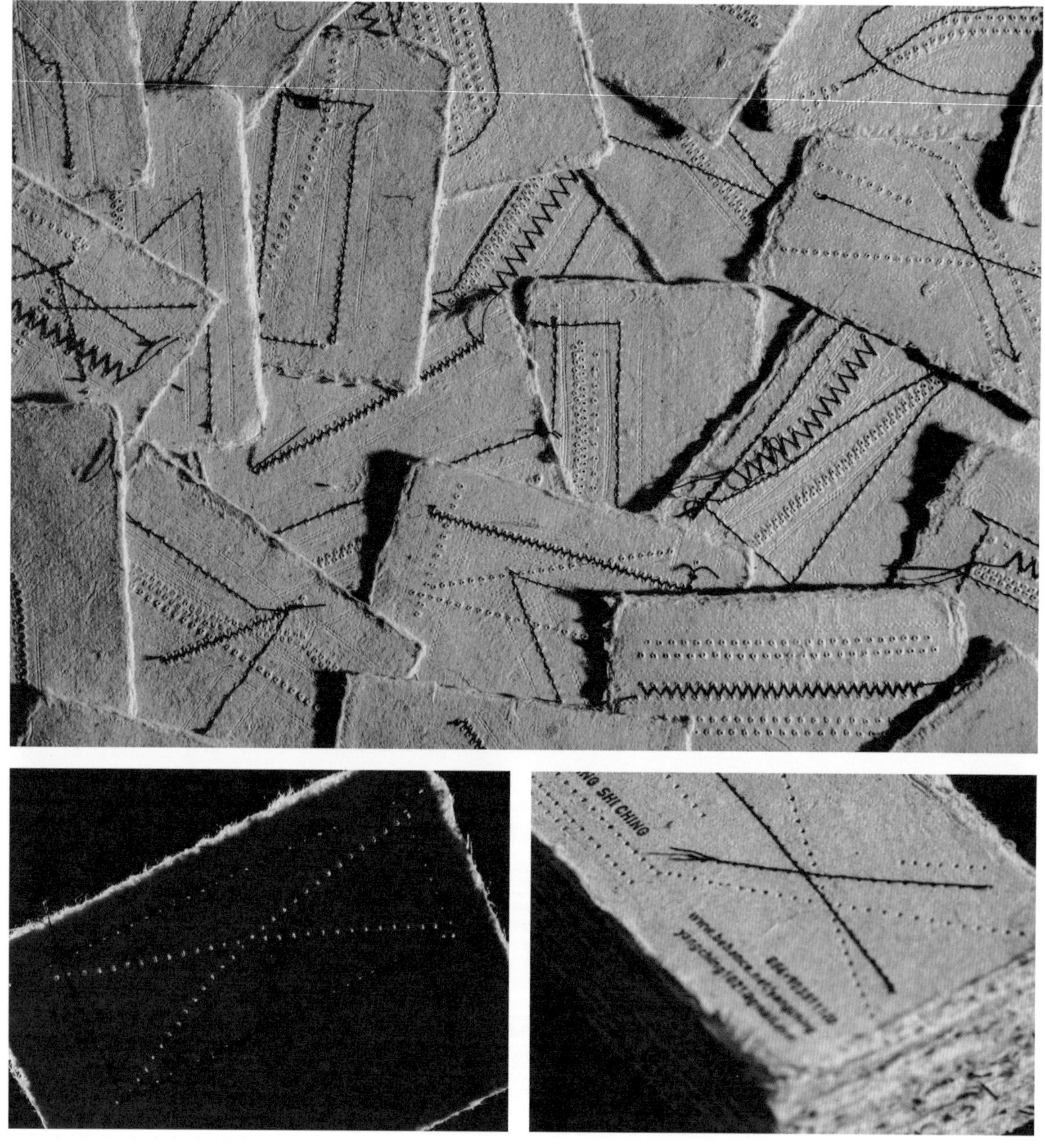

YANG SHI CHING WORKSHOP BUSINESS CARD

Designer : Yang Shi Ching

The designer believes that the design of a business card is vital for making a good first impression. He uses the stitch lines to draw different outlines on each card in order to show his infinite creativity in graphic designs.

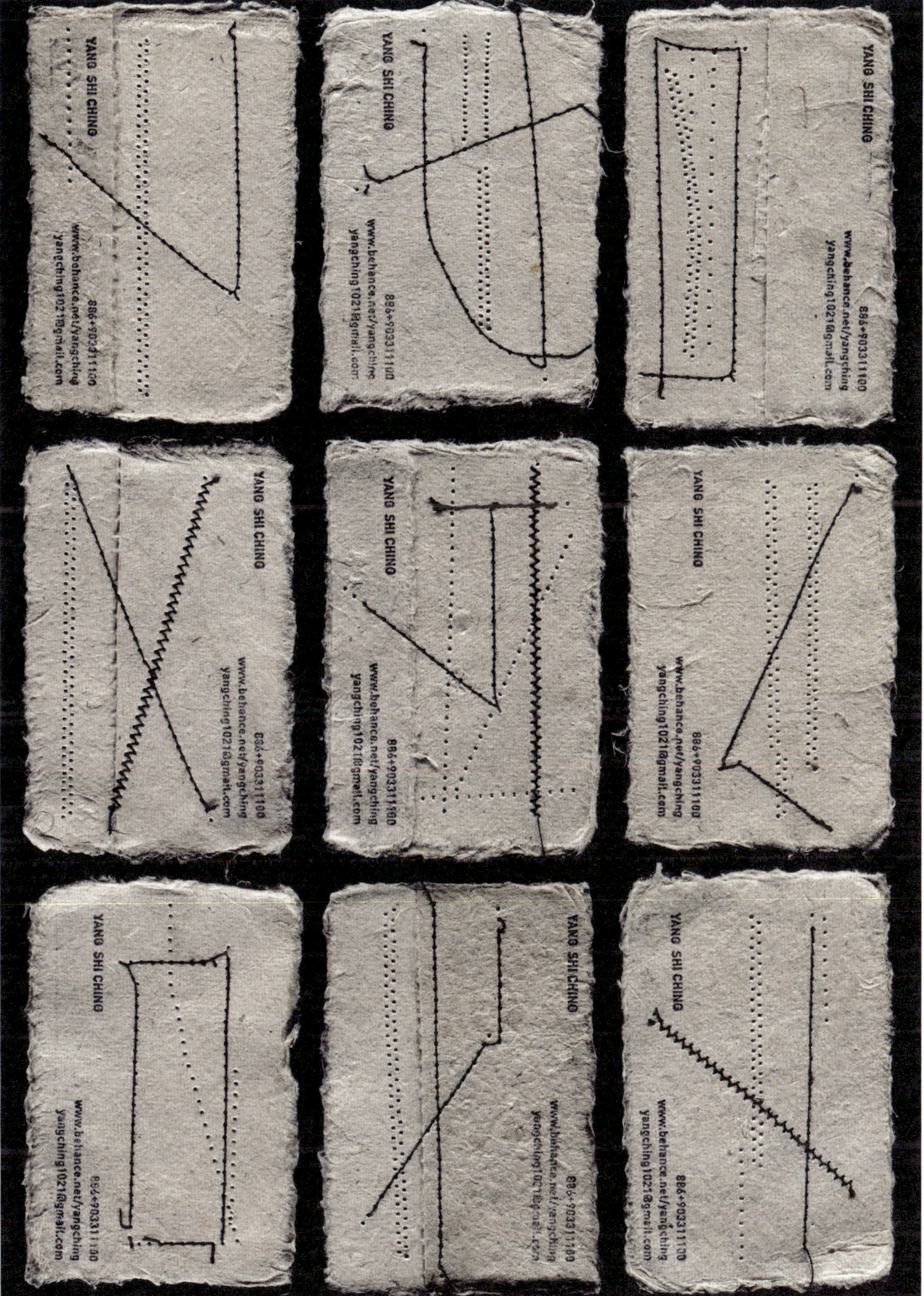
YANG SHI CHING
886+903311100
www.behance.net/yangching
yangching1021@gmail.com

OUMPH

Studio : Snask

Oumph is a new generation of innovative food company, producing eco-friendly vegetarian products 100% made of beans. Inspired by the look and feel of food trucks and chalkboard scribbles, all the product names and the majority of the typography for the graphic identity were hand painted.

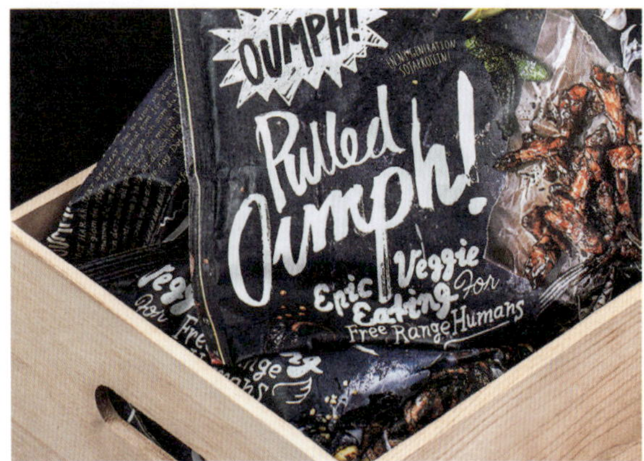

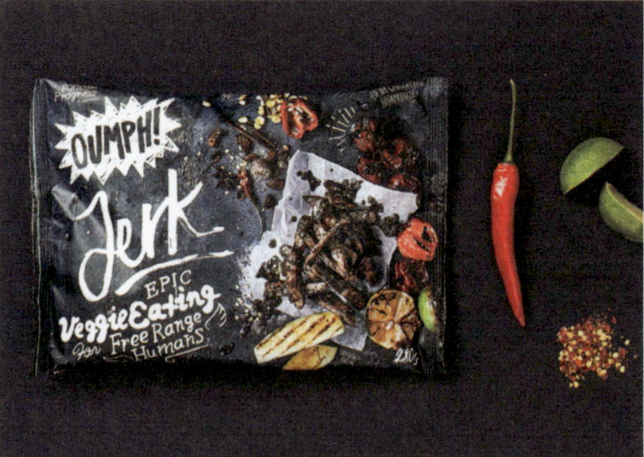

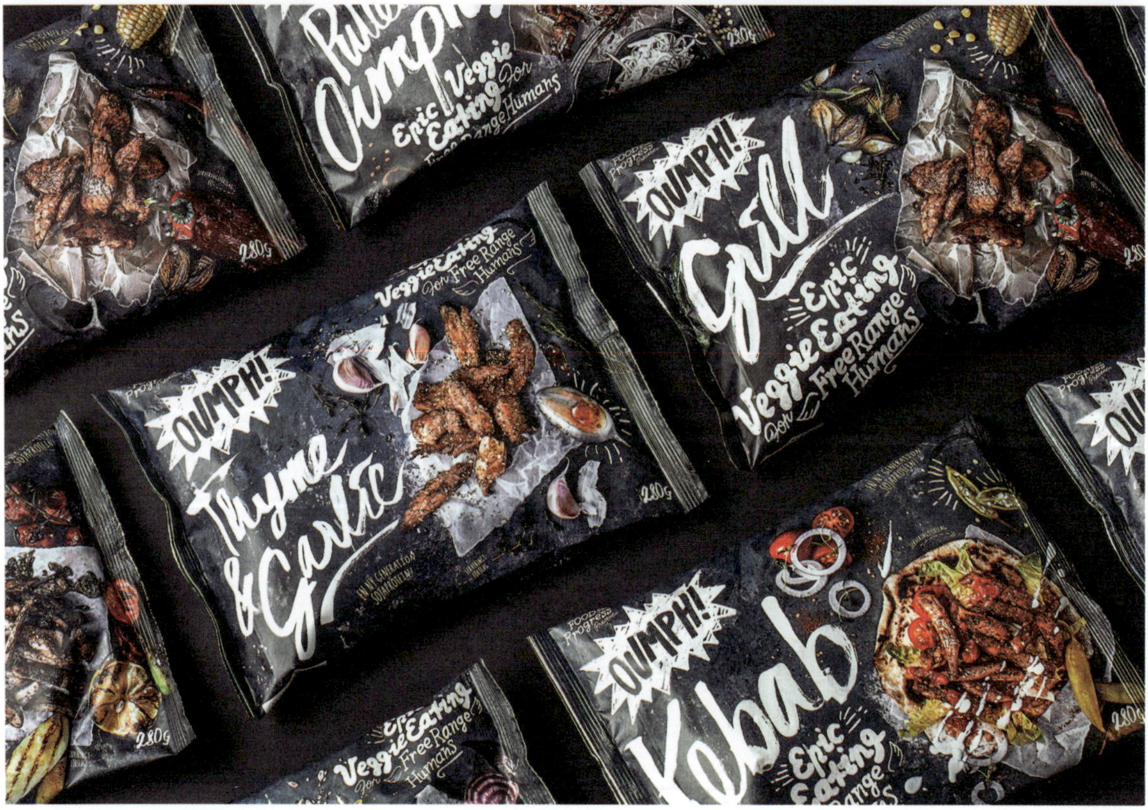

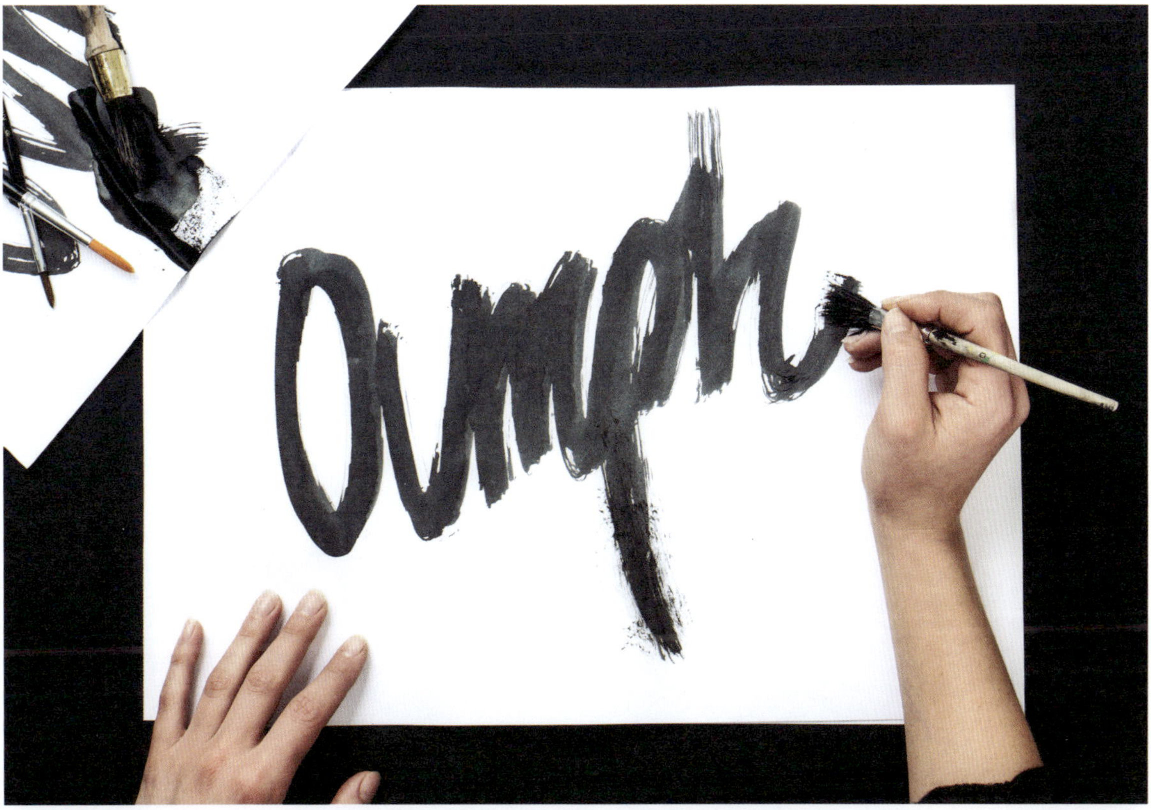
Oumph

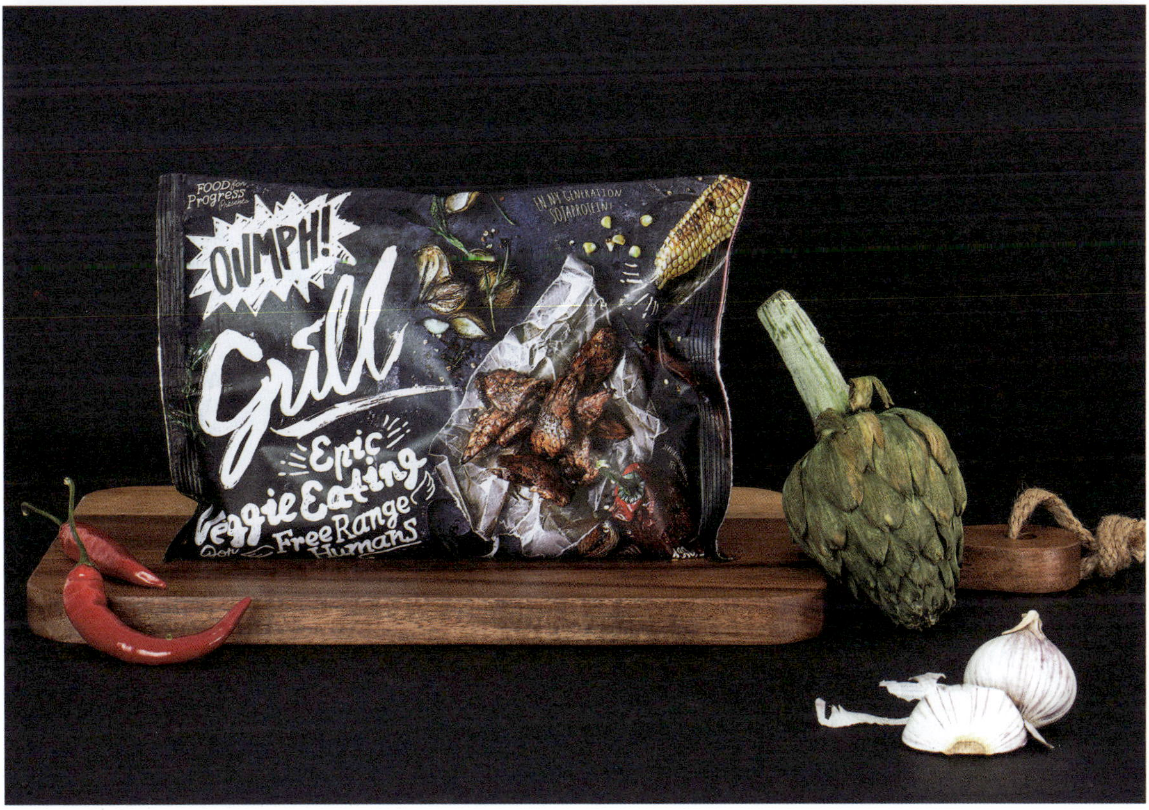
FOOD for Progress
OUMPH!
Grill
Epic
Veggie Eating
Free Range
Humans

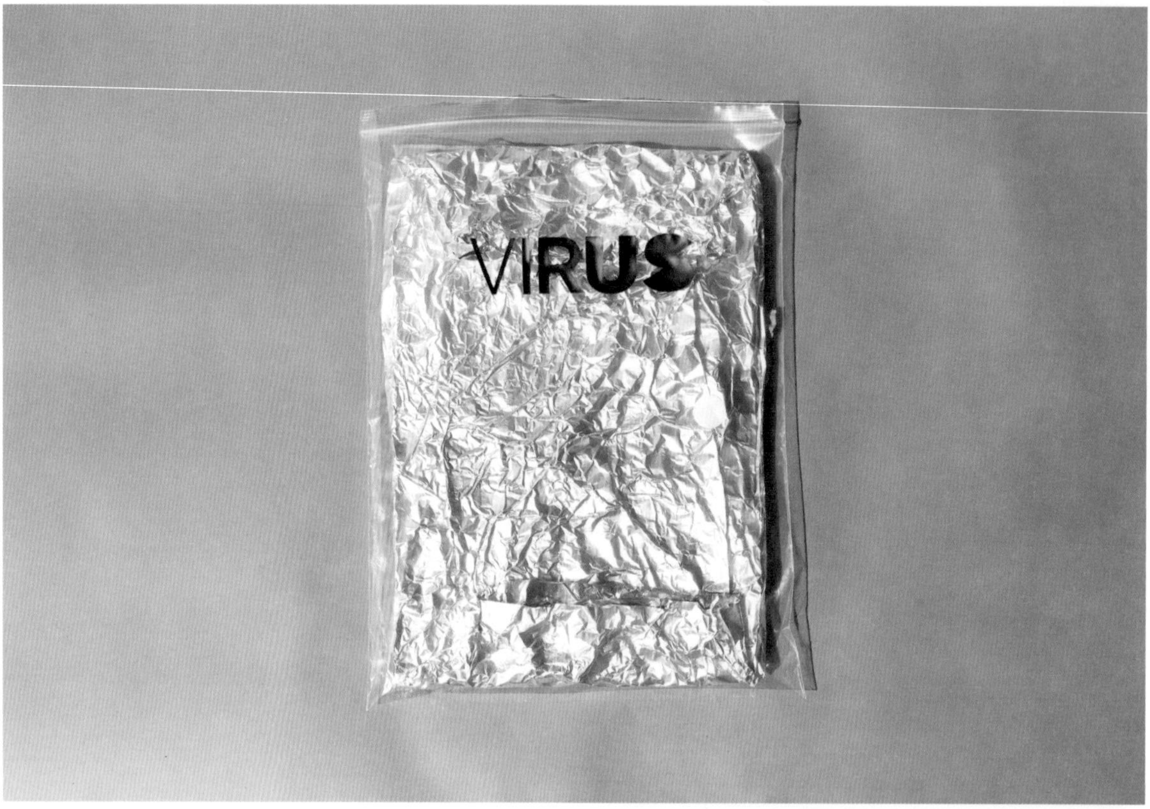

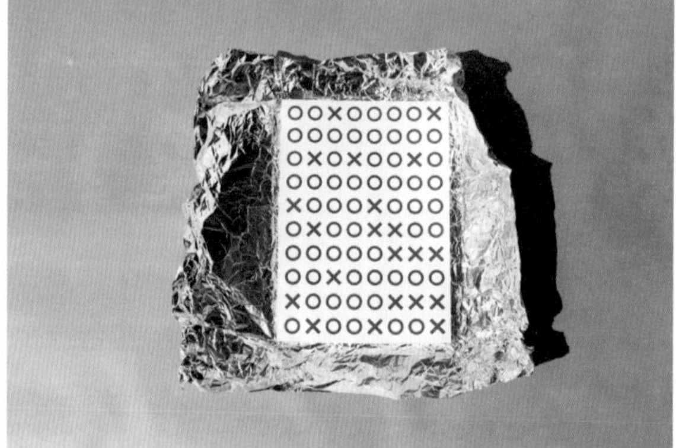

VIRUS

Studio : Fable   Designer : Jiahui Tan

This issue of VIRUS casts the spotlight on nostalgia, memories, stories, as well as the inherent imperfections they come with. Seeking to subvert the conventional definition of beauty, this issue is characterized by its planned disorder and intentional imperfections. Through random illustrations, multiple photo collages, graphic illusions intended to dilate the reader's eyes, and irregular page sizes in different signatures, VIRUS aims to evoke the raw and visceral nature of memories and emotions.

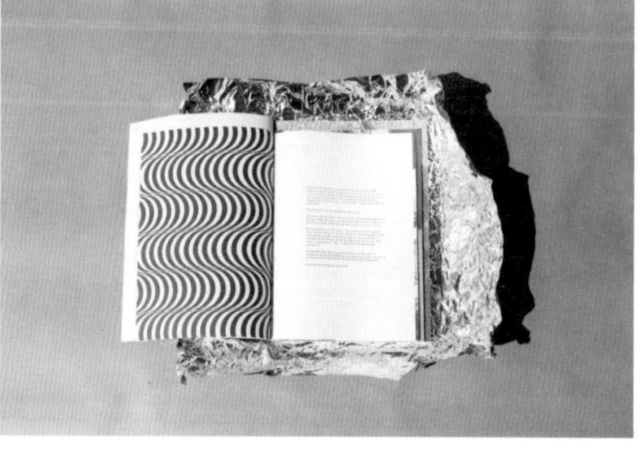

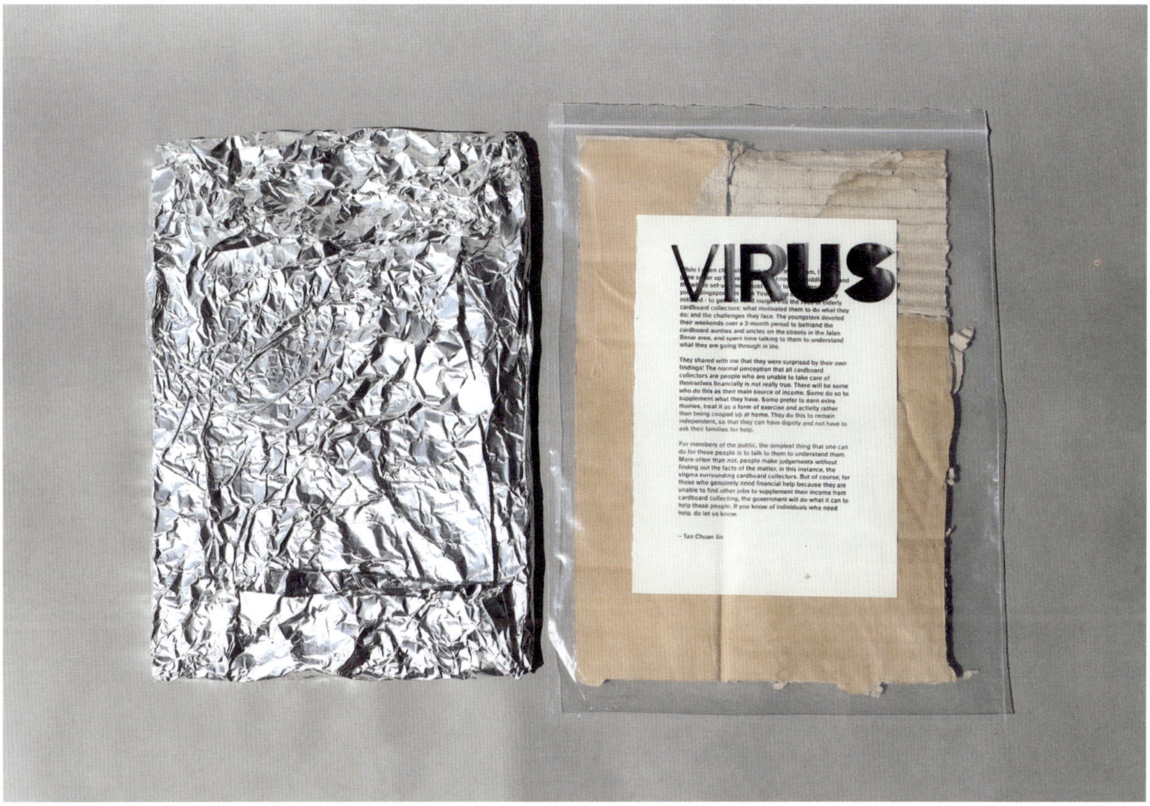

VIRUS

cardboard collectors: what motivated them to do what they do; and the challenges they face. The youngsters devoted their weekends over a 2-month period to befriend the cardboard aunties and uncles on the streets in the Jalan Besar area, and spent time talking to them to understand what they are going through in life.

They shared with me that they were surprised by their own findings! The normal perception that all cardboard collectors are people who are unable to take care of themselves financially is not really true. There will be some who do this as their main source of income. Some do so to supplement what they have. Some prefer to earn extra monies, treat it as a form of exercise and activity rather than being cooped up at home. They do this to remain independent, so that they can have dignity and not have to ask their families for help.

For members of the public, the simplest thing that one can do for these people is to talk to them to understand them. More often than not, people make judgements without finding out the facts of the matter, in this instance, the stigma surrounding cardboard collectors. But of course, for those who genuinely need financial help because they are unable to find other jobs to supplement their income from cardboard collecting, the government will do what it can to help these people. If you know of individuals who need help, do let us know.

– Tan Chuan Jin

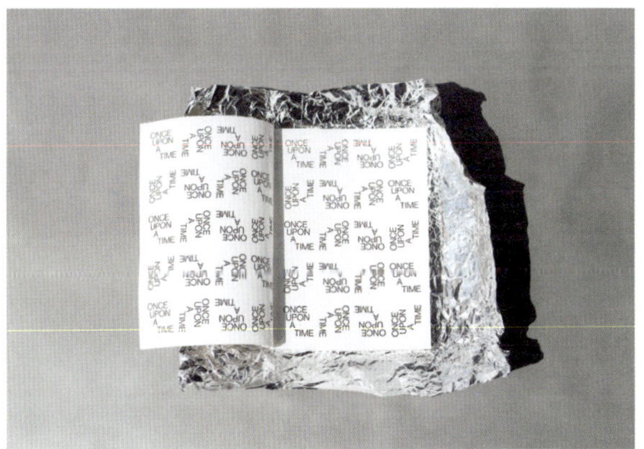

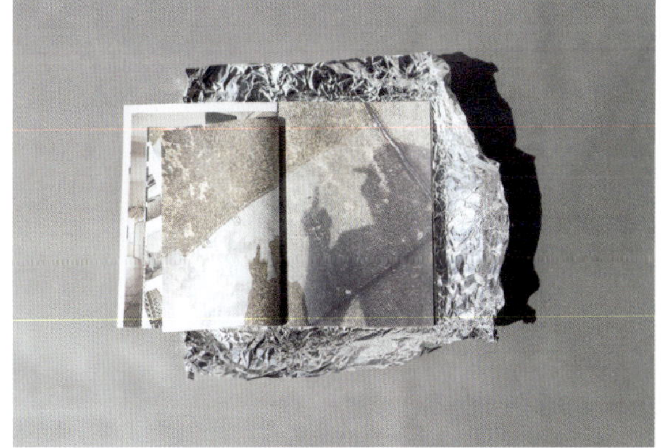

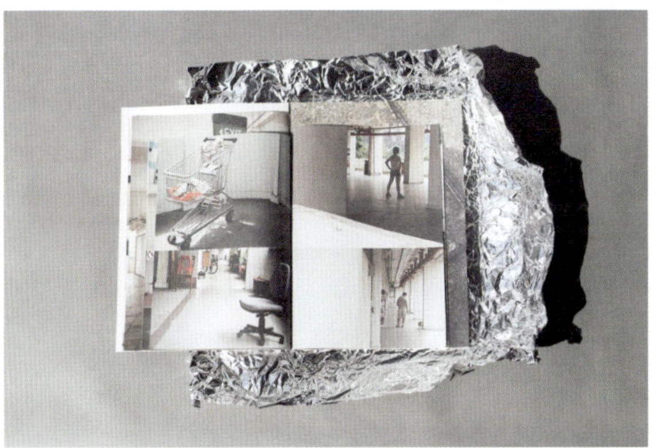

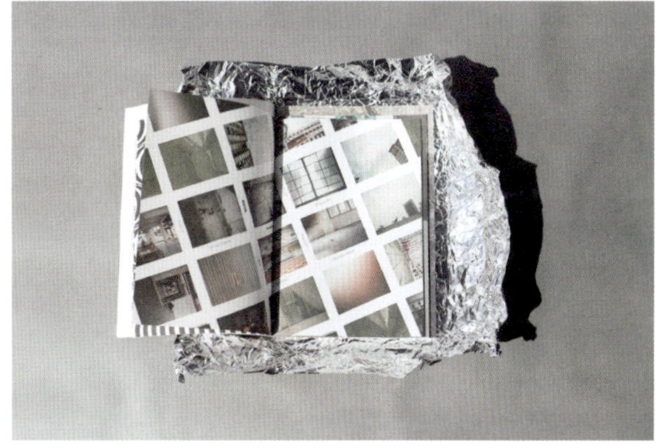

Studio : Studio Riebenbauer   Designer : Franz Riebenbauer, Almut Becvar

In order to translate the journey of the grain from field to bread into an olfactory experience, the designers created three fragrances that communicate the brand's comprehensive, philosophical approach to bread making.

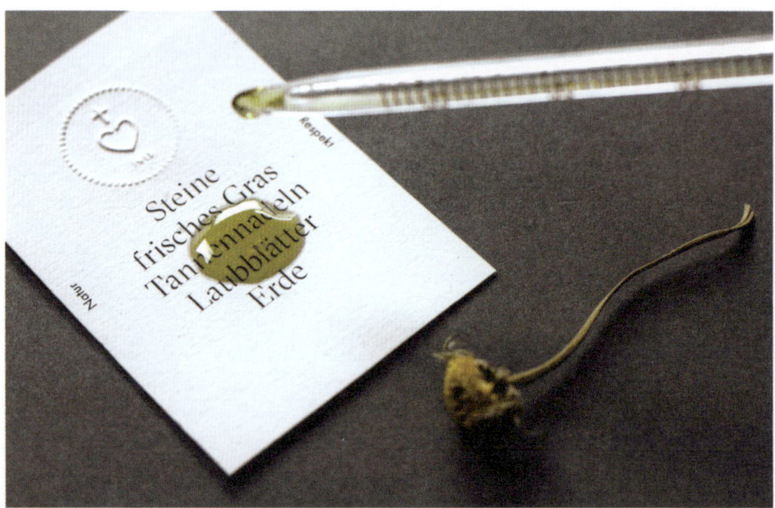

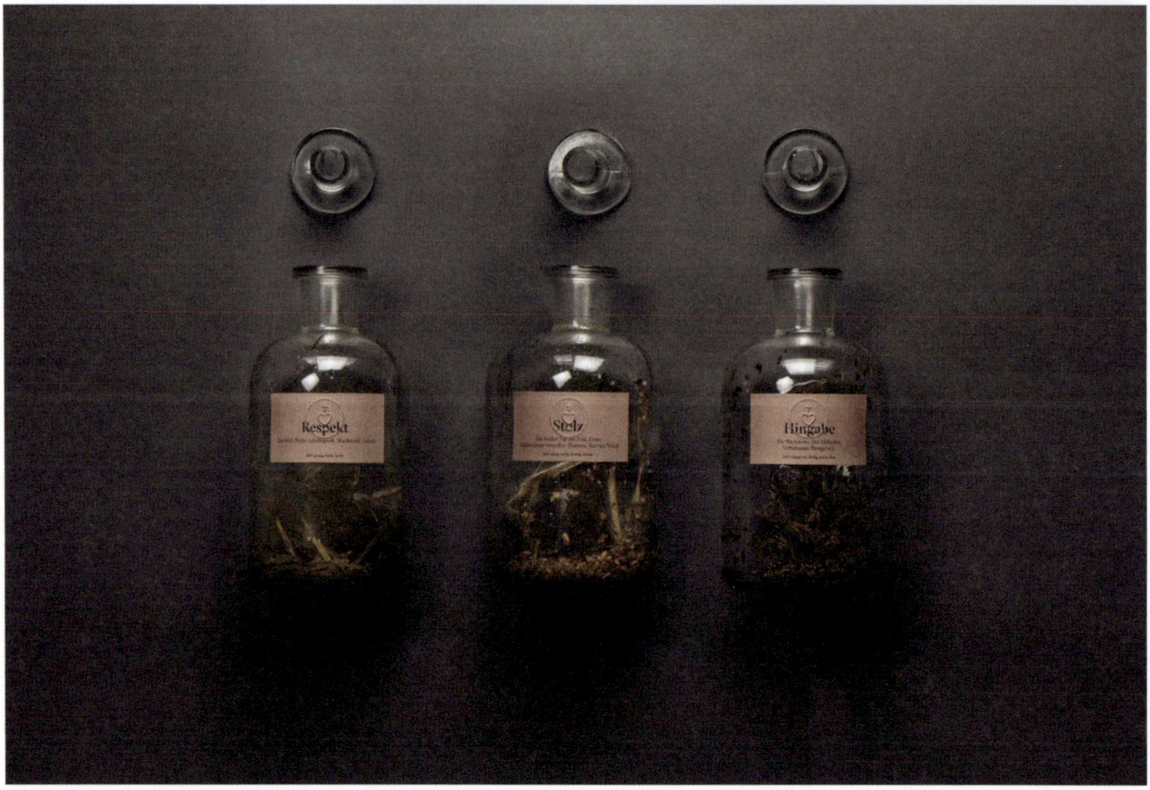

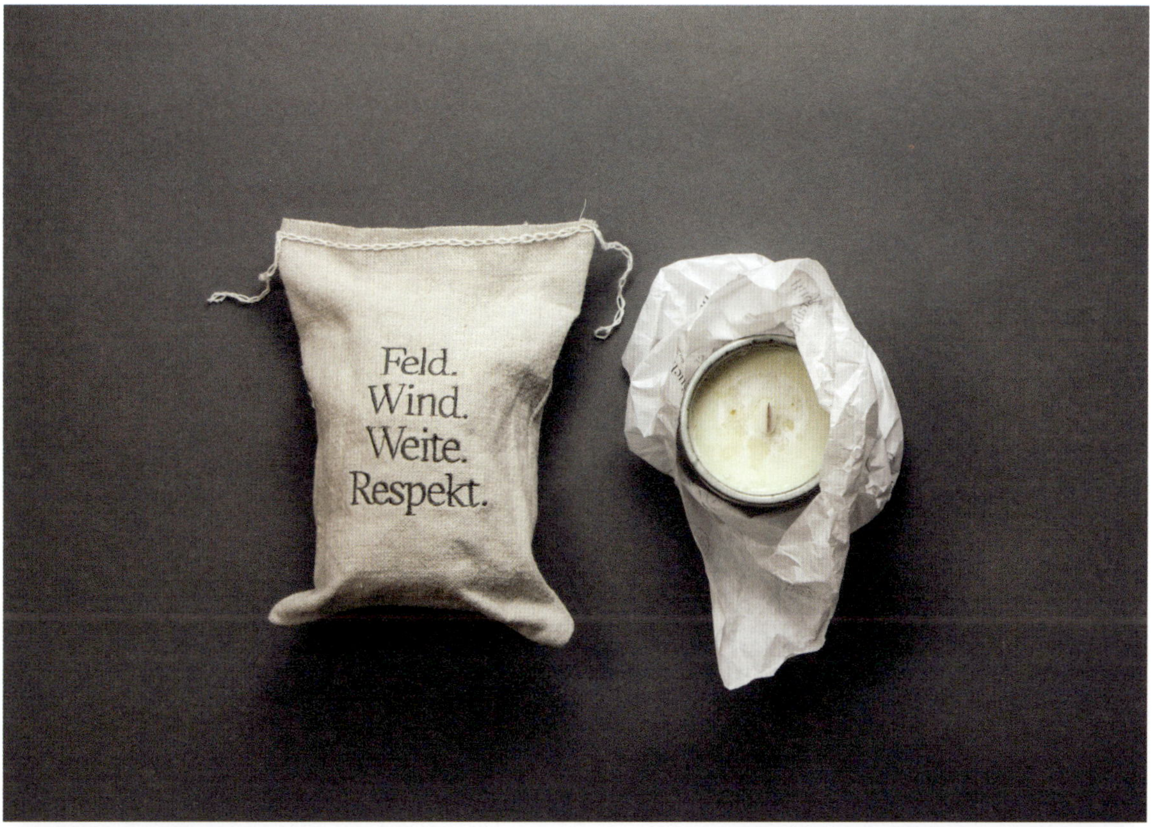
Feld.
Wind.
Weite.
Respekt.

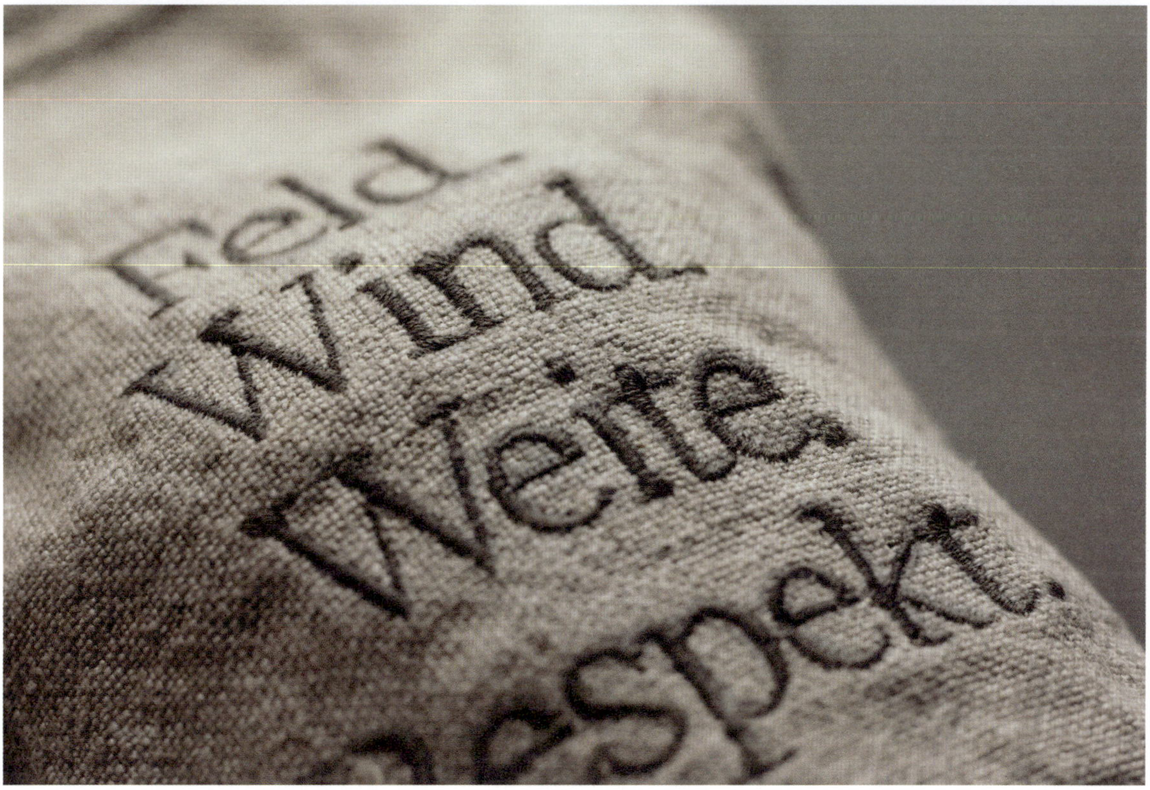
Feld.
Wind.
Weite.
espekt.

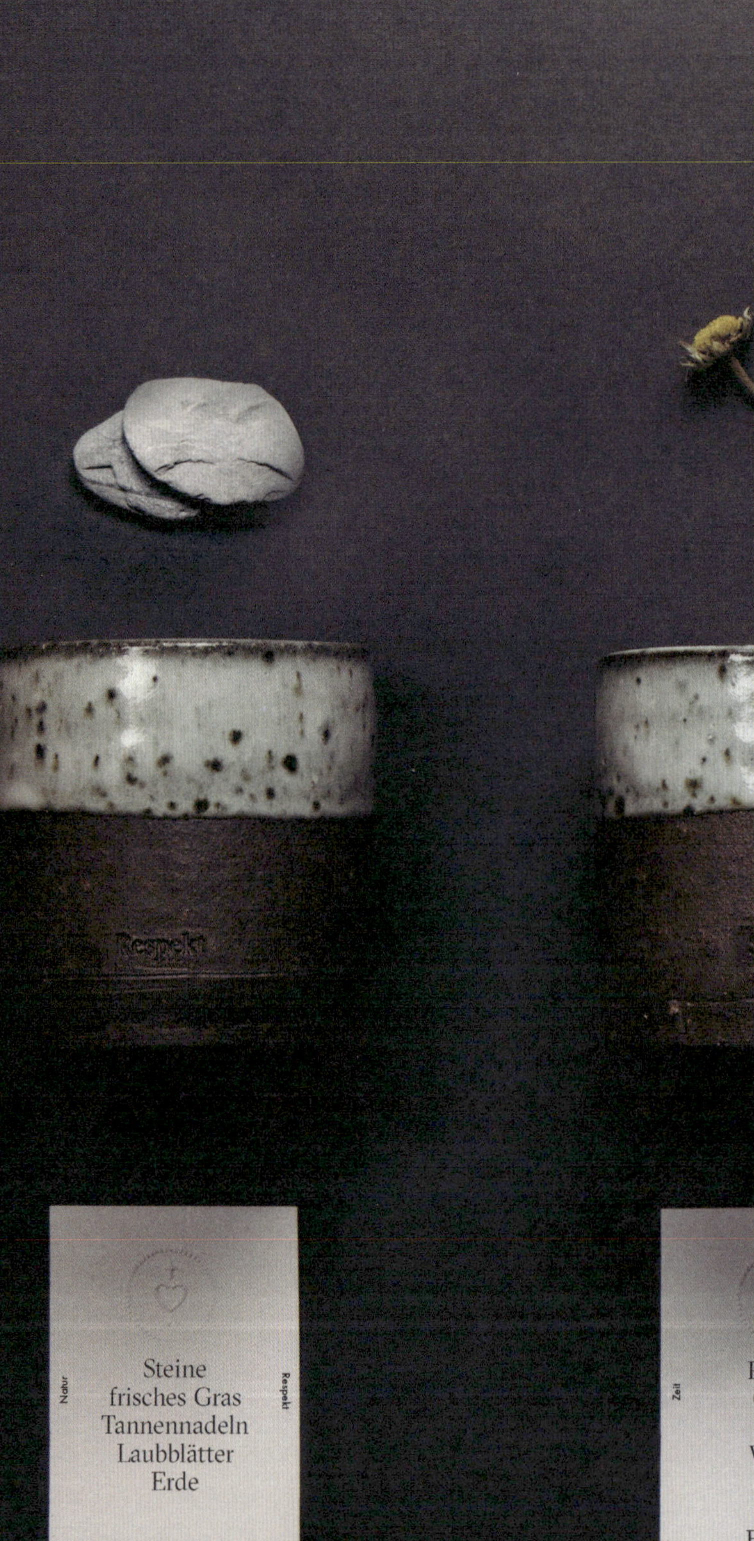
Respekt
Natur
Steine
frisches Gras
Tannennadeln
Laubblätter
Erde
Respekt
Zeit

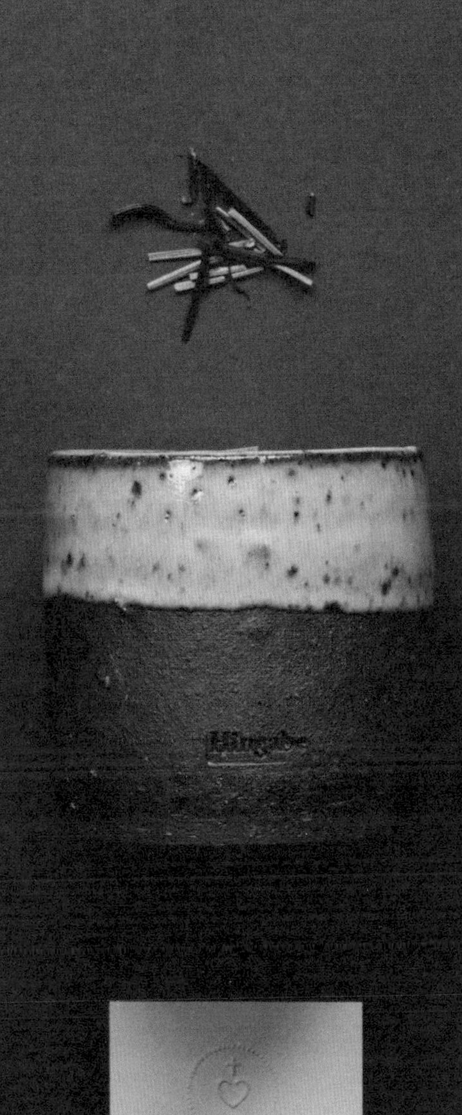
Hingabe
Stolz
Leidenschaft
Brot
Brotkruste
Kümmel
Fenchel
Brotpapier
Streichhölzer
Hingabe

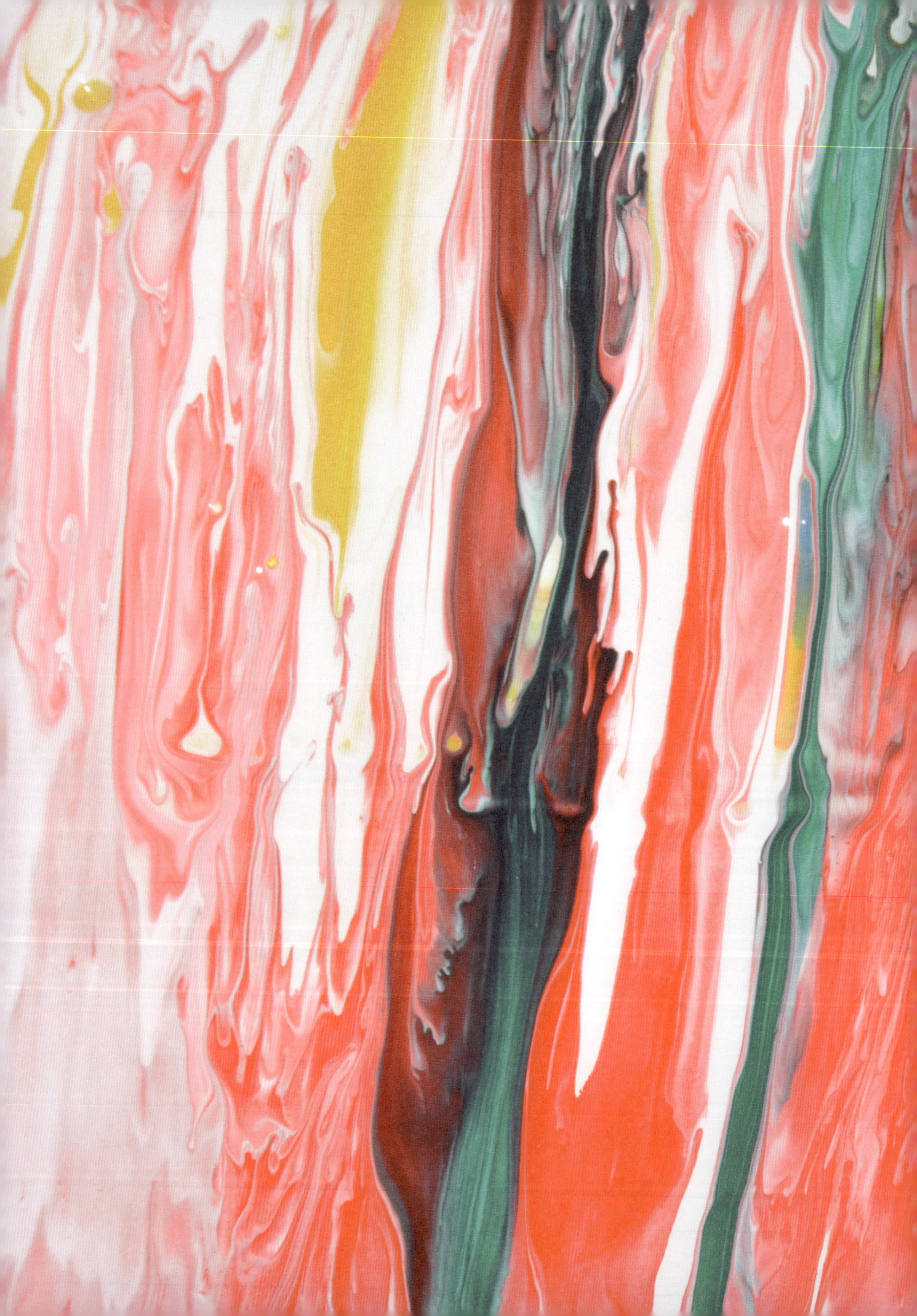

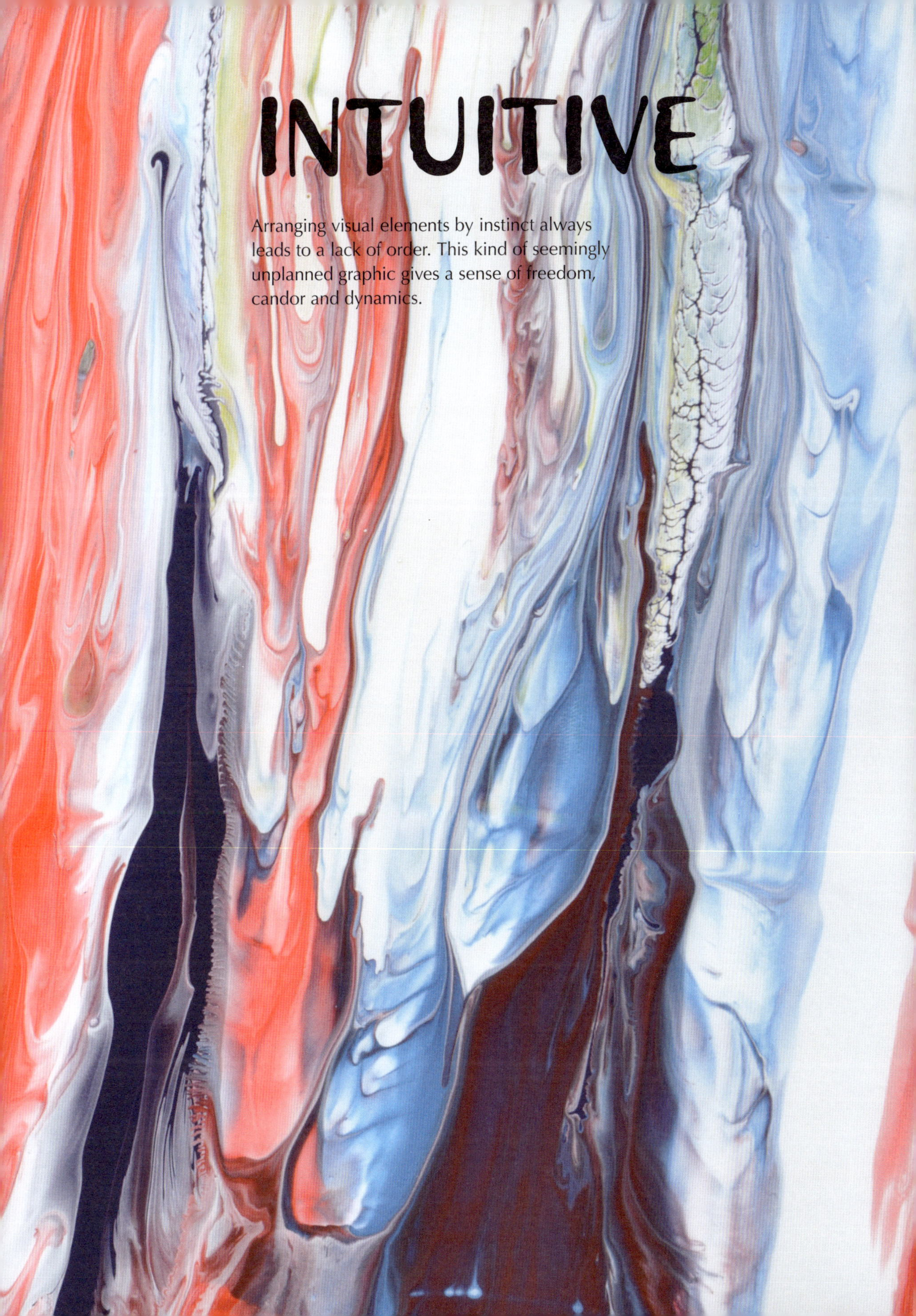

INTUITIVE

Arranging visual elements by instinct always leads to a lack of order. This kind of seemingly unplanned graphic gives a sense of freedom, candor and dynamics.

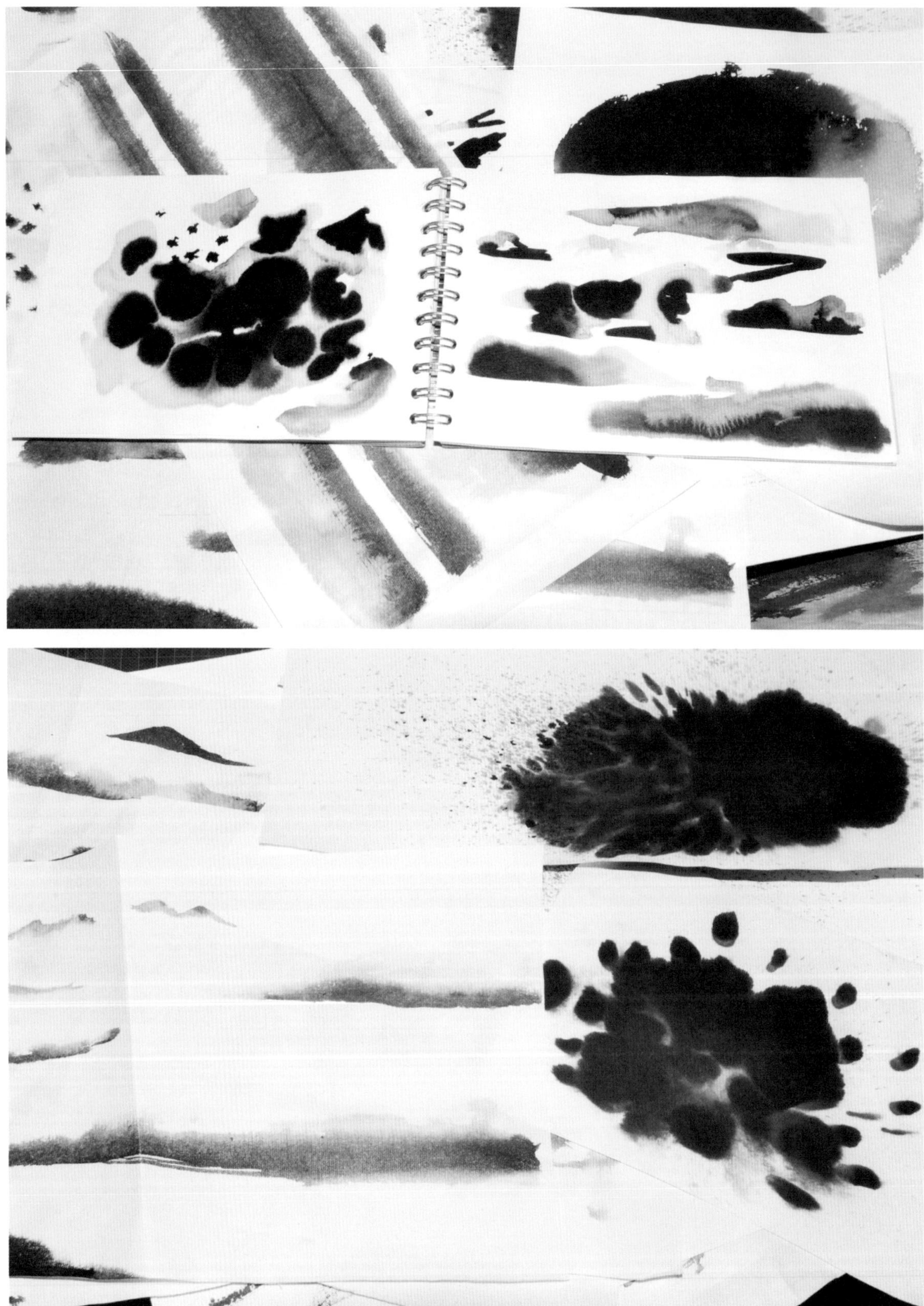

INK VISION

Designer : Leechiehting

The designer used 12 kinds of experimental skills to make this calendar, showing different perspectives of Chinese ink, in order to explore more possiblities of it.

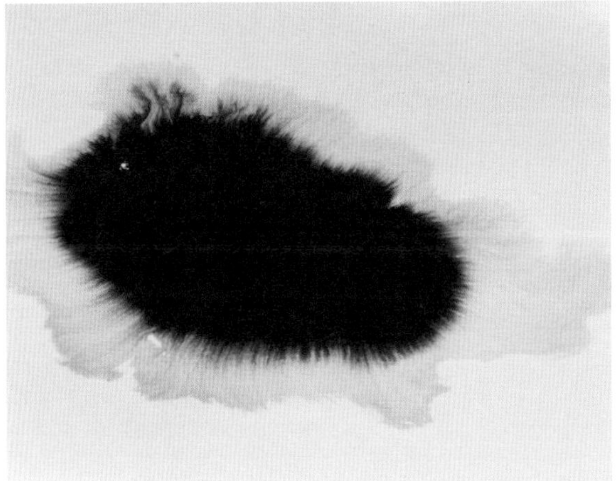

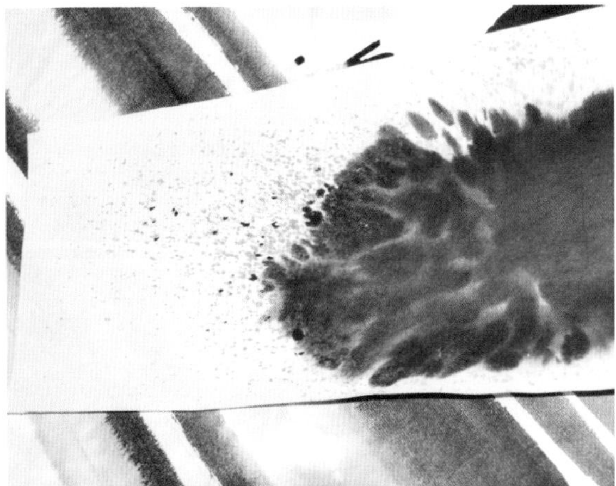

As a kind of visual experience, what do you think about the "roughness" in graphic design ?

In my view, the roughness in the art represents the worship of the original forms, and I divided it into three aspects: rough from tool, rough from skill, rough from thought.

1. Tool: take different tools as a kind of primitive exploration, like some artists love to create with stones, drinking straws, tree branches, needle and thread or other tools in their original state.
2. Skill: use the basic skills to present the primitive exploration. Some artists express the primitive concept of art by means of graffiti, rap or body language.
3. Thought: think in the most direct and simple way to present beauty. Let's say Joan Miro's *Blue II*, it is already a pure aesthetic experience without embellishing or adding anything.

I think every type of roughness has its own characters.
There is even a hybrid form in art; it depends on the artist's predilection. As for roughness in design, it should be presented appropriately based on client's requirement or goal, a natural and smooth process from the beginning to the end.

What are your common approaches to produce a "rough" visual effect ?

In INK VISION, I had tried to present the rawness as well as the variance of the materials in terms of skill (syphoning, blowing, smudging, rubbing, etc.). I think that the primitive materials, techniques and tools can directly show their own textures. So we could also say that "roughness" is the love for primitive materials. The appreciation of materials and the choice and application of them are both important parts of expression. I hope there would be a chance to experiment with the other two aspects.

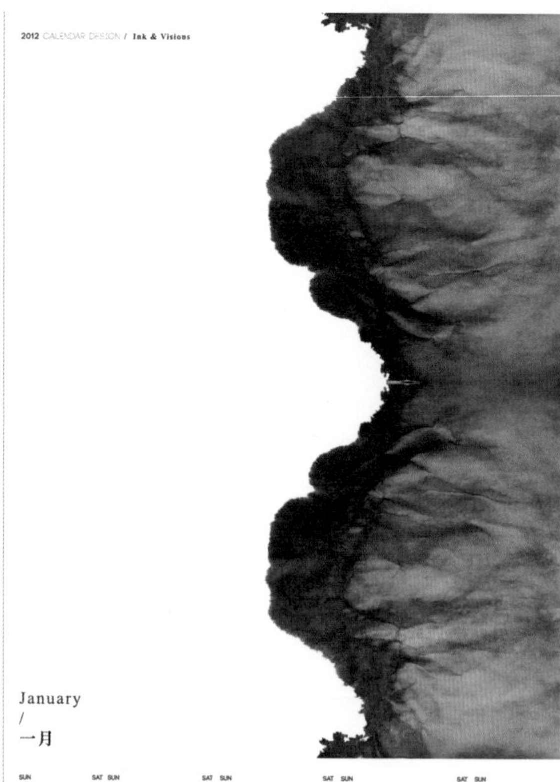
2012 CALENDAR DESIGN / Ink & Visions
January
/
一月
2 3 4 5 6 7 8 9 10 11 12 13 14 15 16 17 18 19 20 21 22 23 24 25 26 27 28 29 30 31

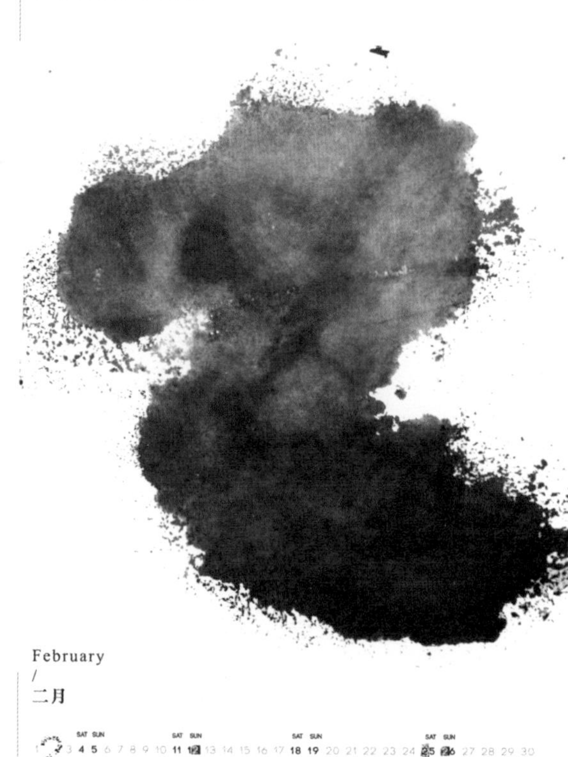
2012 CALENDAR DESIGN / Ink & Visions
February
/
二月
3 4 5 6 7 8 9 10 11 12 13 14 15 16 17 18 19 20 21 22 23 24 25 26 27 28 29 30

June
/
六月
2012 CALENDAR DESIGN / Ink & Visions
1 2 3 4 5 7 8 9 10 11 12 13 14 15 16 17 18 19 20 21 22 23 24 25 26 27 28 29 30

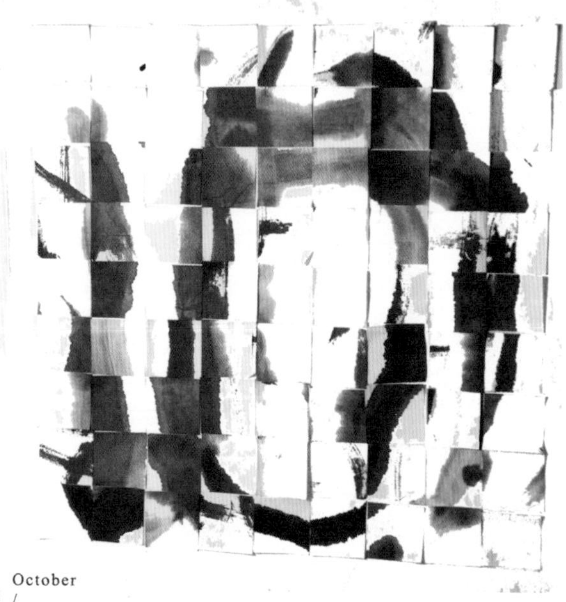
October
/
十月
2012 CALENDAR DESIGN / Ink & Visions
1 2 3 4 5 6 7 8 9 11 12 13 14 15 16 17 18 19 20 21 22 23 24 25 26 27 28 29 30 31

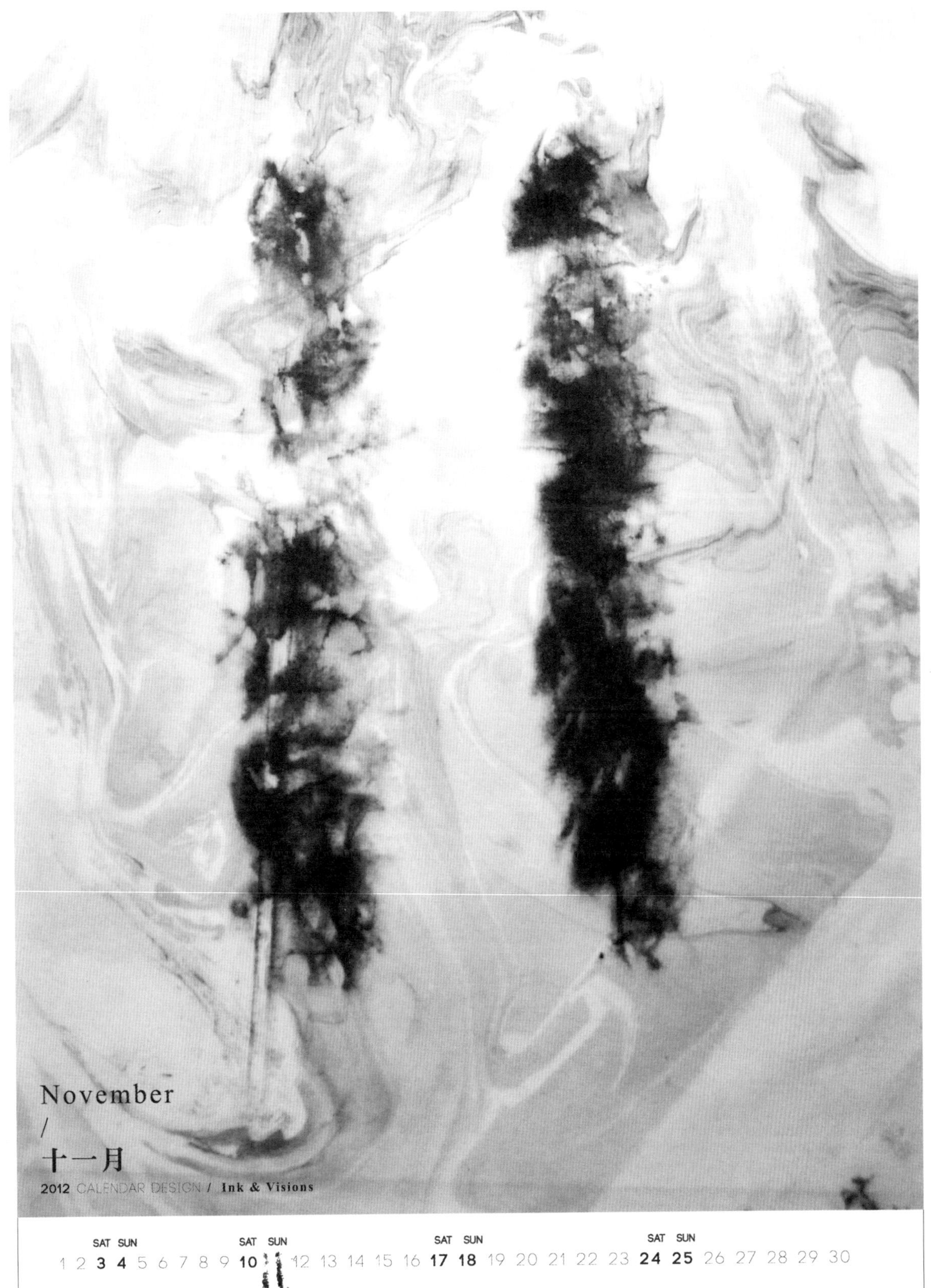

		SAT	SUN						SAT	SUN						SAT	SUN						SAT	SUN					
1	2	**3**	**4**	5	6	7	8	9	**10**	**11**	12	13	14	15	16	**17**	**18**	19	20	21	22	23	**24**	**25**	26	27	28	29	30

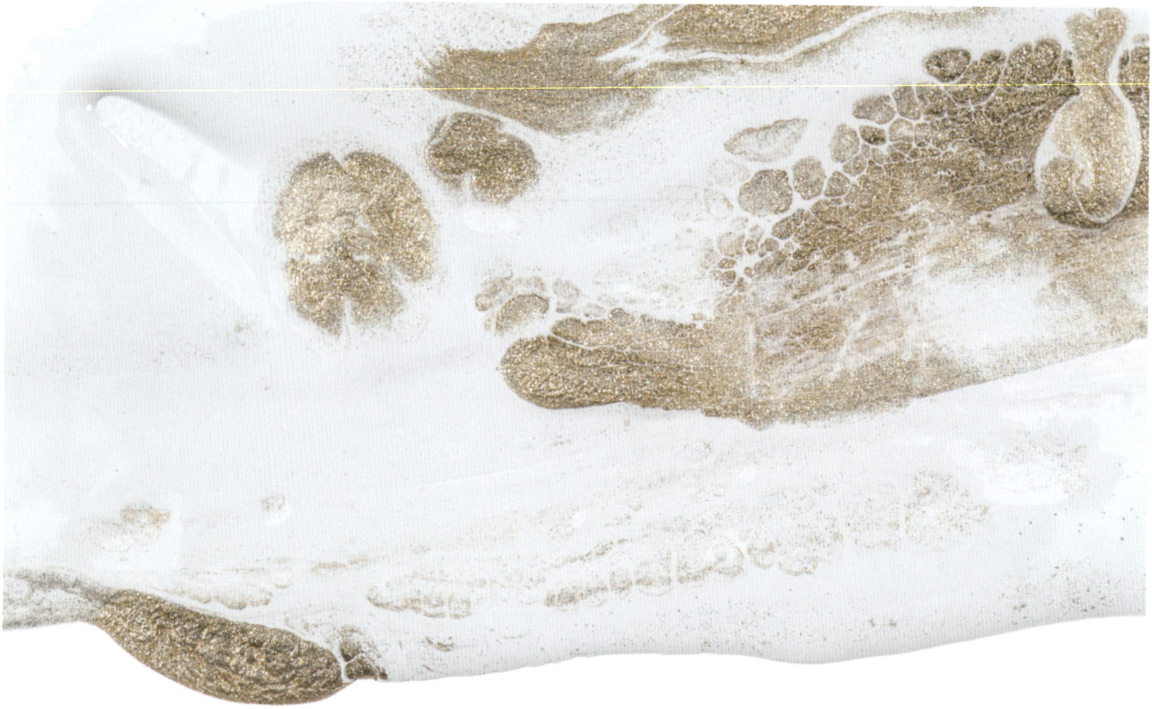

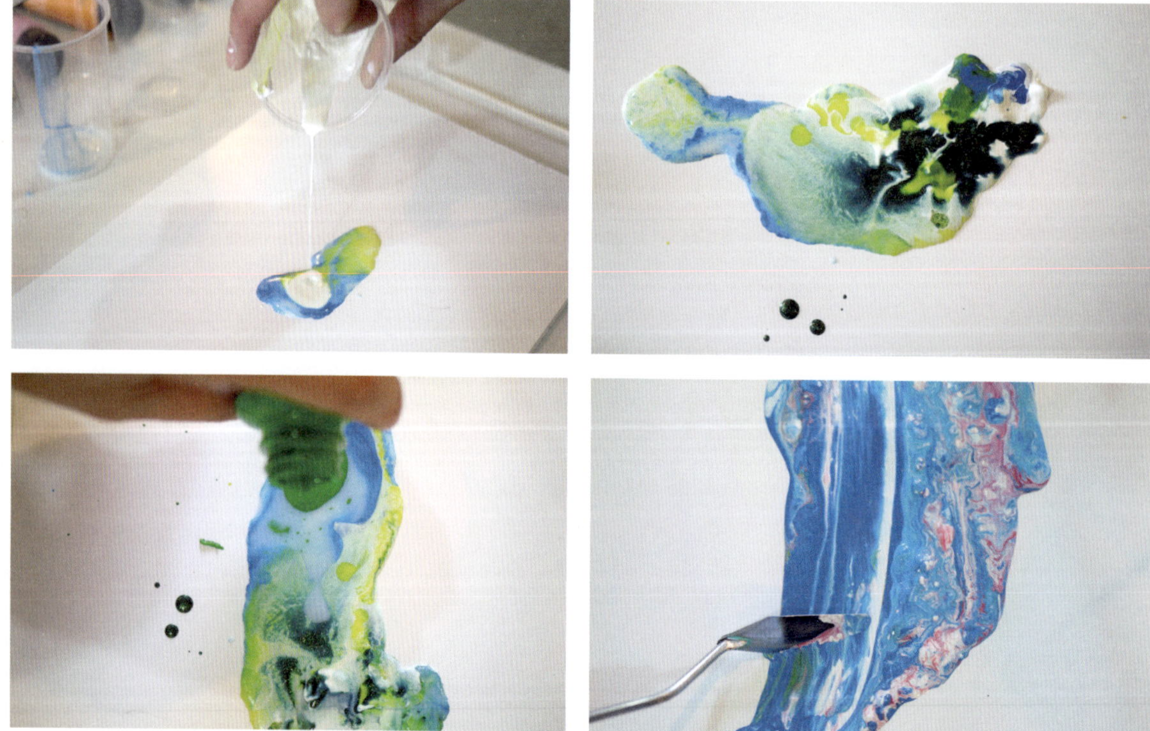

MORIARTY EVENTS

Studio : Bond Creative Agency   Designer : Hugh Miller, Tyrone Lou

This festive and fun identity was designed for the luxury event planning specialist Moriarty. Inspired by the spontaneity and energy of a party and exploring the notion that event curating is an art, Bond crafted a series of abstract textures for all communication materials.

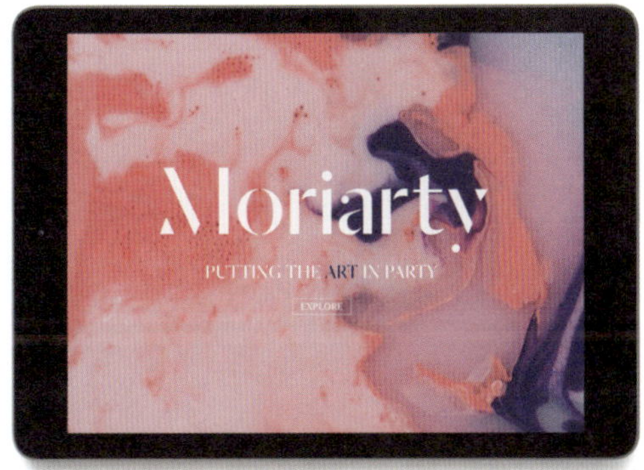

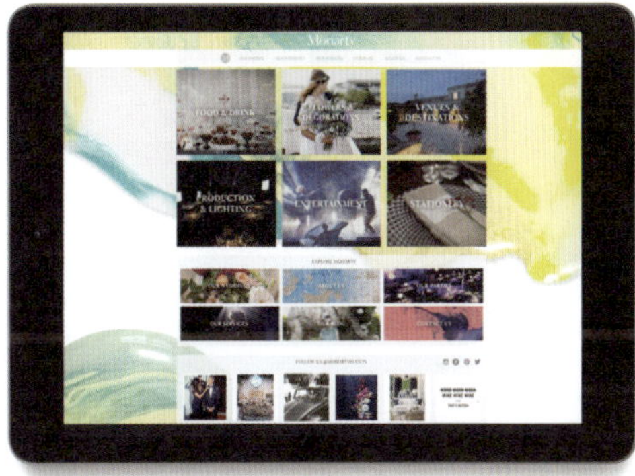

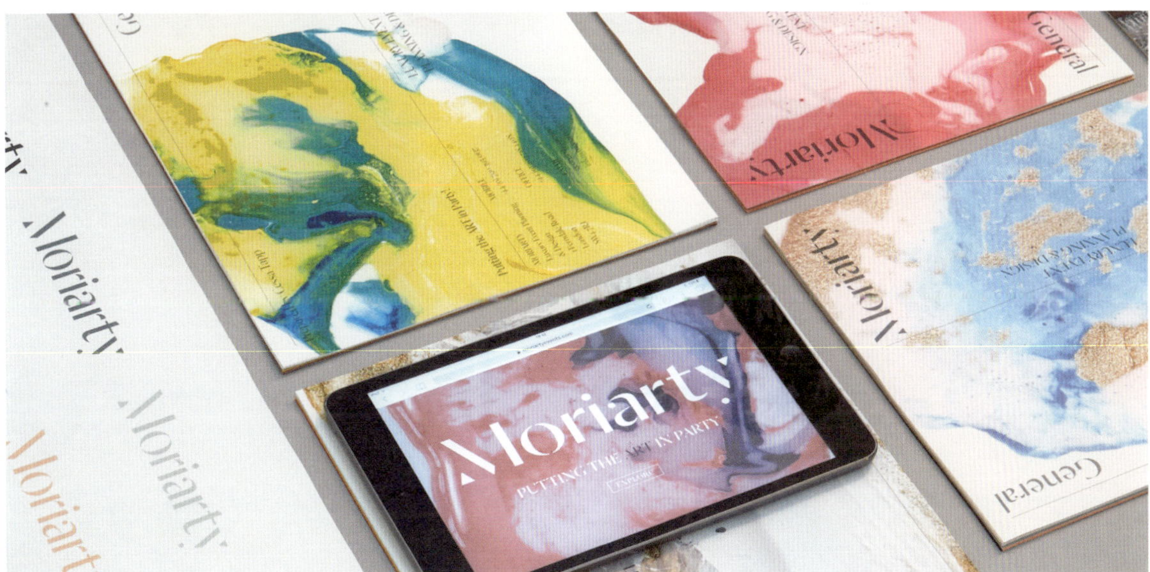

As a kind of visual experience, what do you think about the "roughness" in graphic design ?

Rough or raw graphic design captures expression and energy. It has a kind of punk spirit which we like. Allowing accidents to happen through mark making gives dynamic energy and a rebellious spirit.

What are your common approaches to produce a "rough" visual effect ?

Embrace mistakes and accidents. Be open to discover new ways to create and make marks. Through abstraction, sometimes the work itself is also open to interpretation.

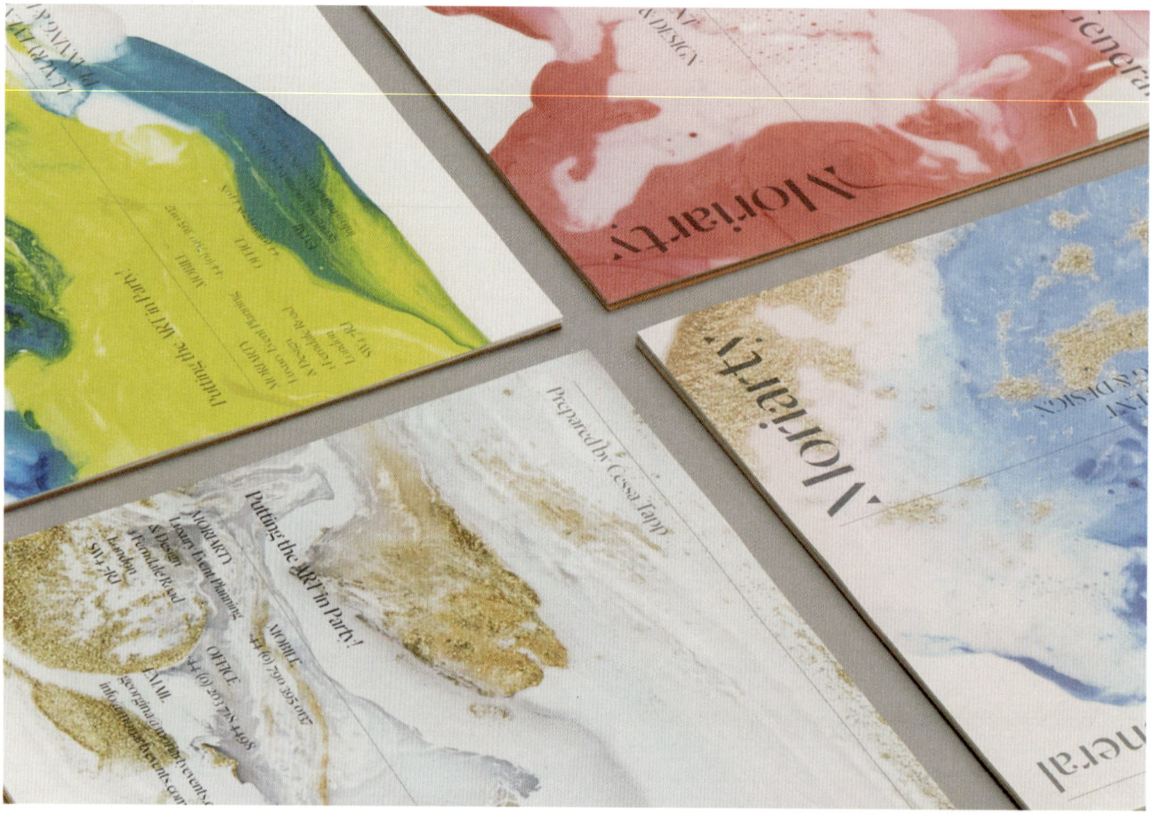

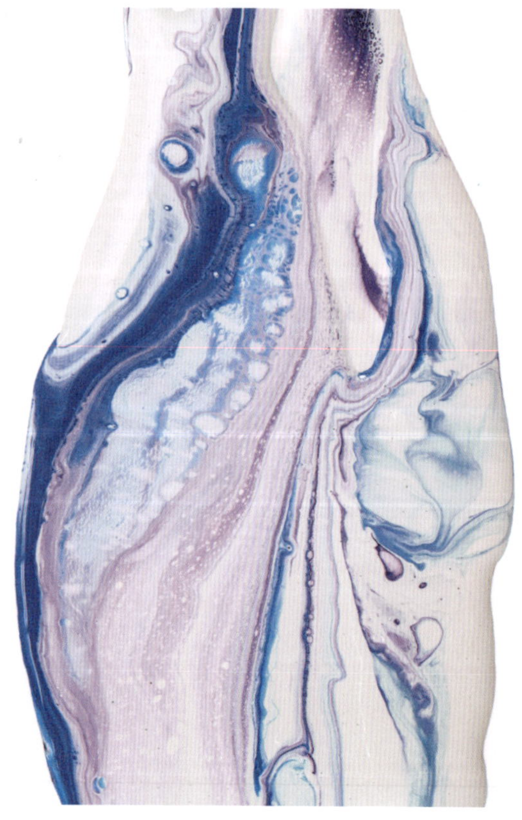

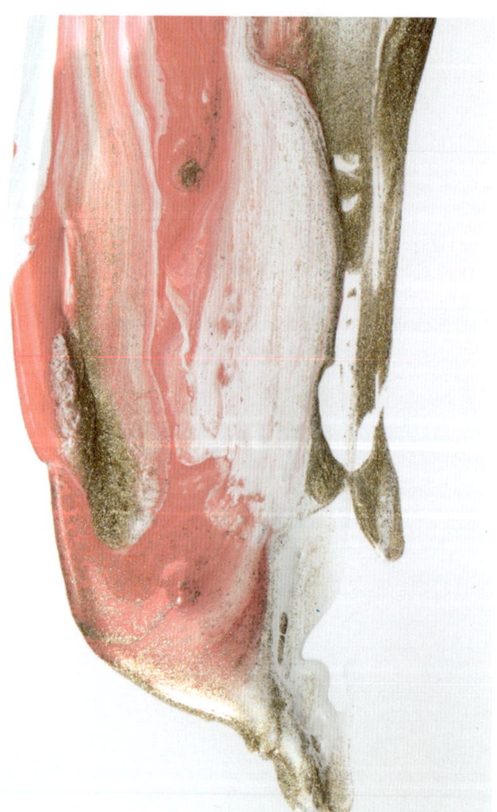

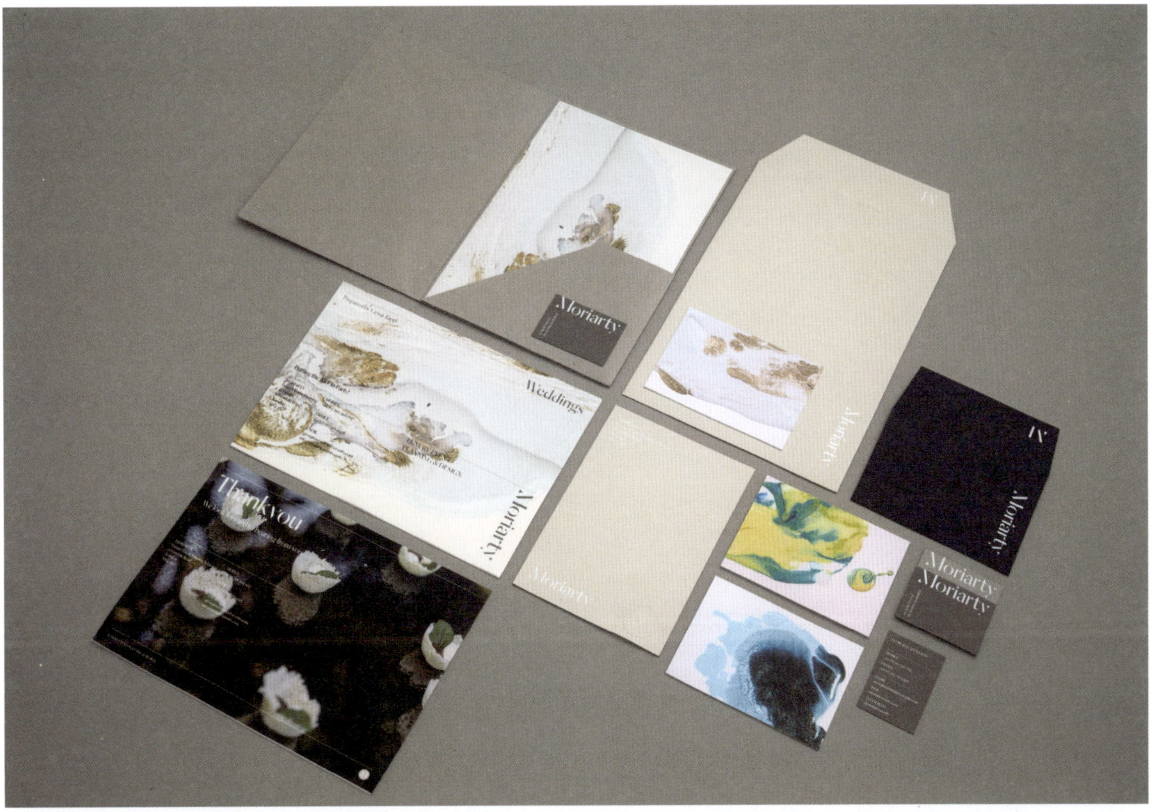
Moriarty
Weddings
Thankyou
Moriarty
Moriarty
Moriarty
Moriarty
Moriarty

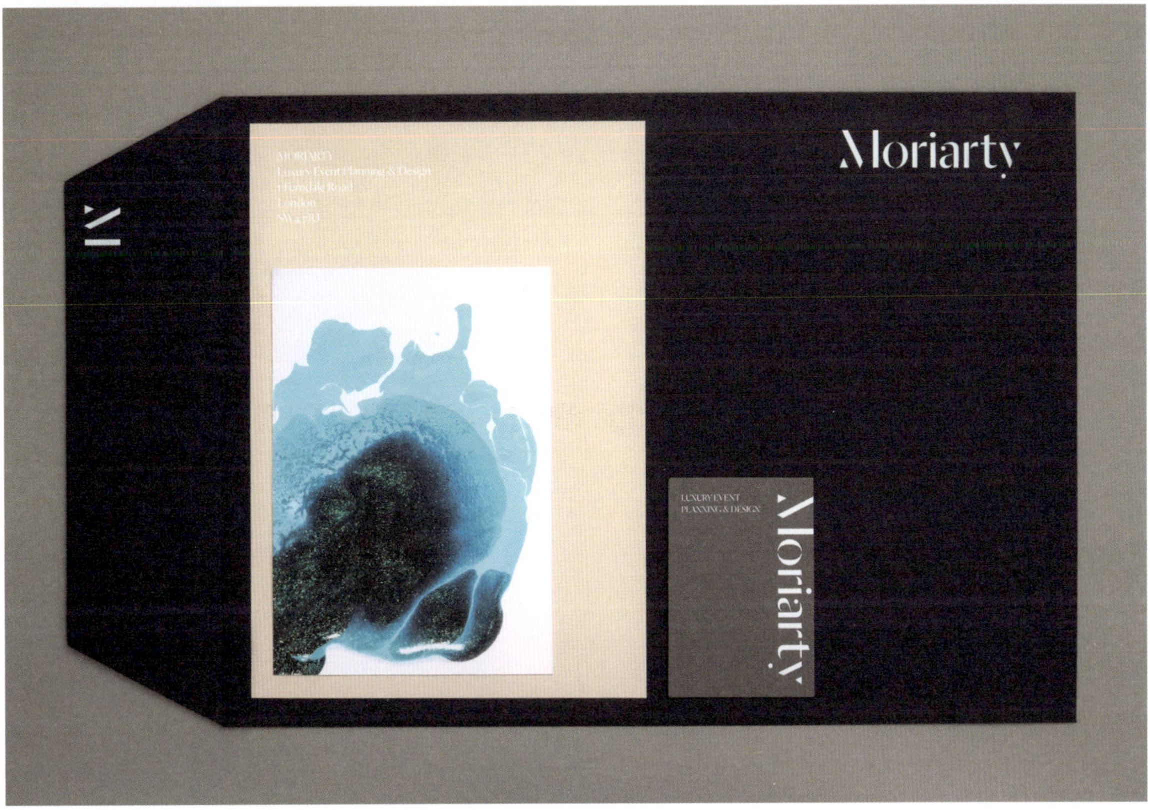
Moriarty
MORIARTY
Luxury Event Planning & Design
London
LUXURY EVENT
PLANNING & DESIGN
Moriarty

MINI - SYMPOSIUM

Designer : Leechiehting

This is visual communication designed for a symposium held in Taiwan Tech, focusing on communication and design practice. Acrylic paint was used to present the flow of visuals, and symbols to encourage people to observe and imagine, which is the first step of design practice.

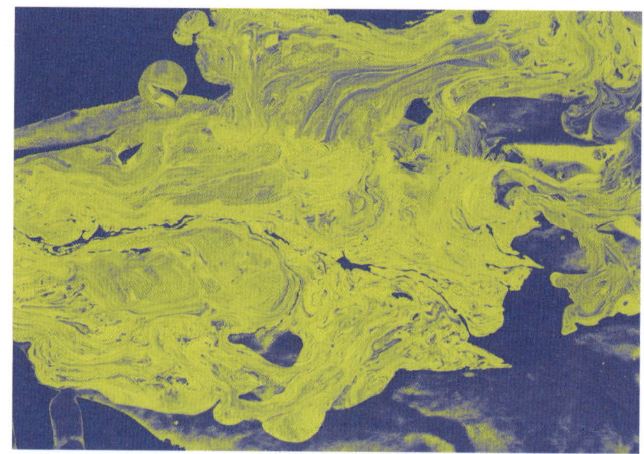

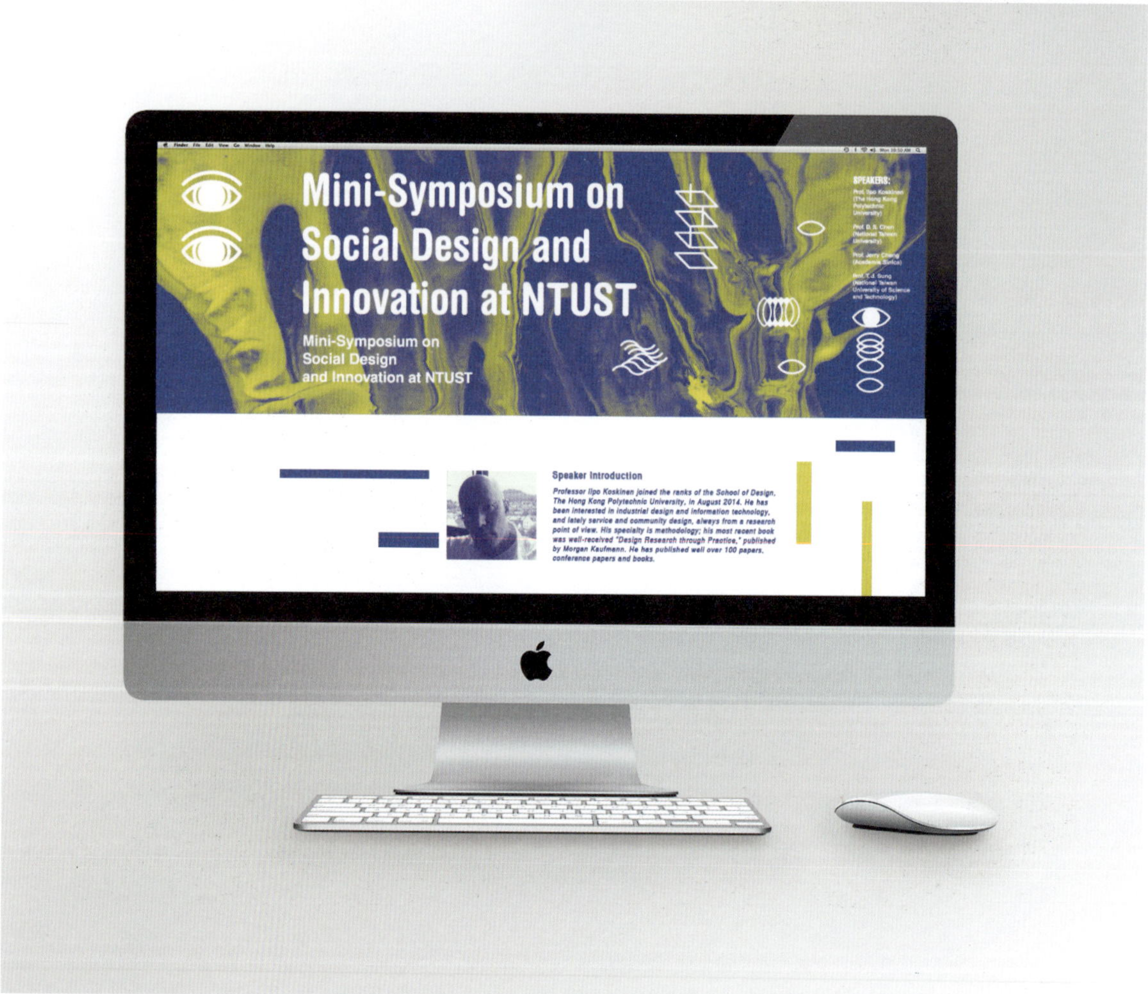

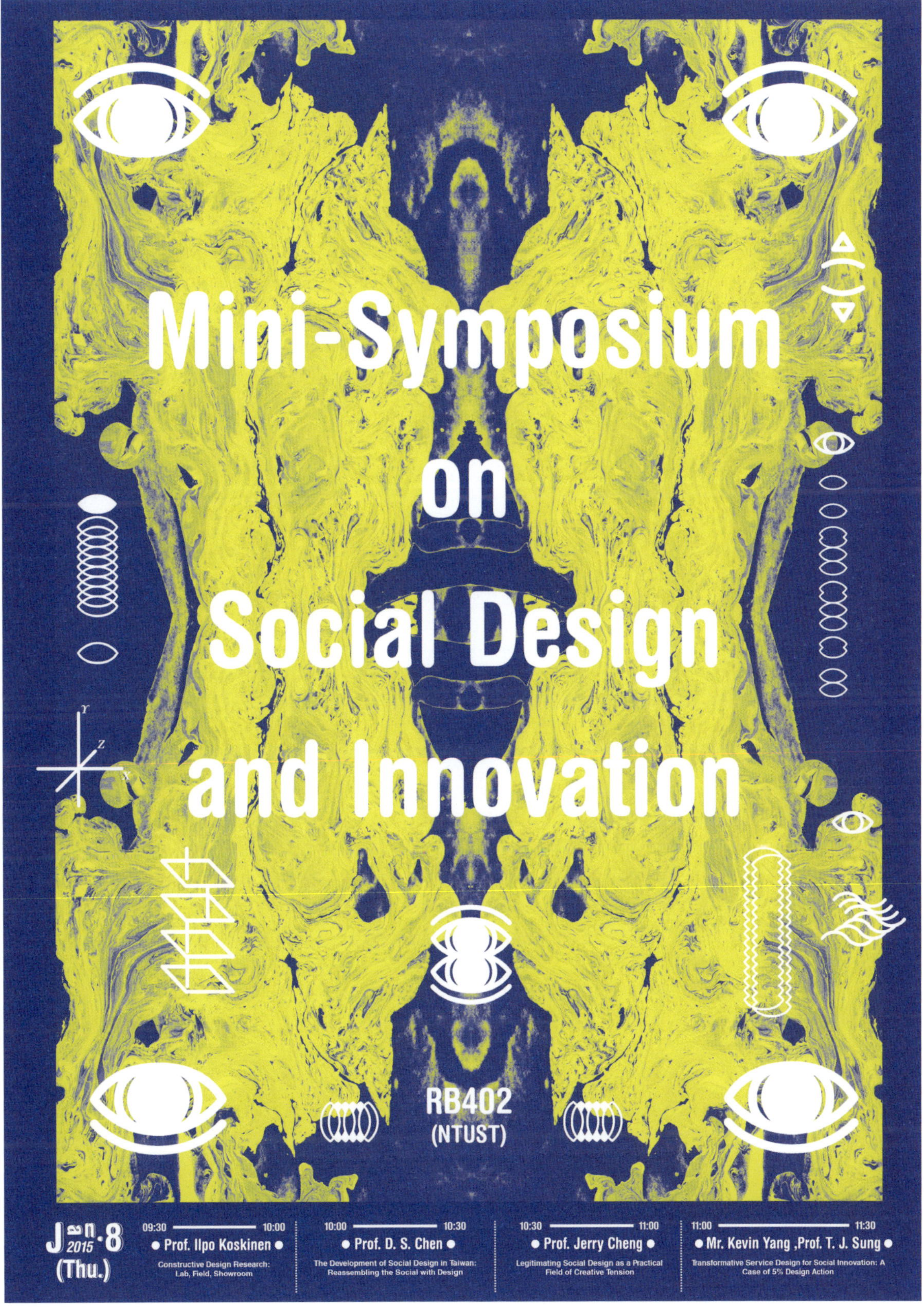
Mini-Symposium
on
Social Design
and Innovation
RB402
(NTUST)
Jan 2015 .8
(Thu.)
09:30 10:00
Prof. Ilpo Koskinen
Constructive Design Research: Lab, Field, Showroom
10:00 10:30
Prof. D. S. Chen
The Development of Social Design in Taiwan: Reassembling the Social with Design
10:30 11:00
Prof. Jerry Cheng
Legitimating Social Design as a Practical Field of Creative Tension
11:00 11:30
Mr. Kevin Yang ,Prof. T. J. Sung
Transformative Service Design for Social Innovation: A Case of 5% Design Action

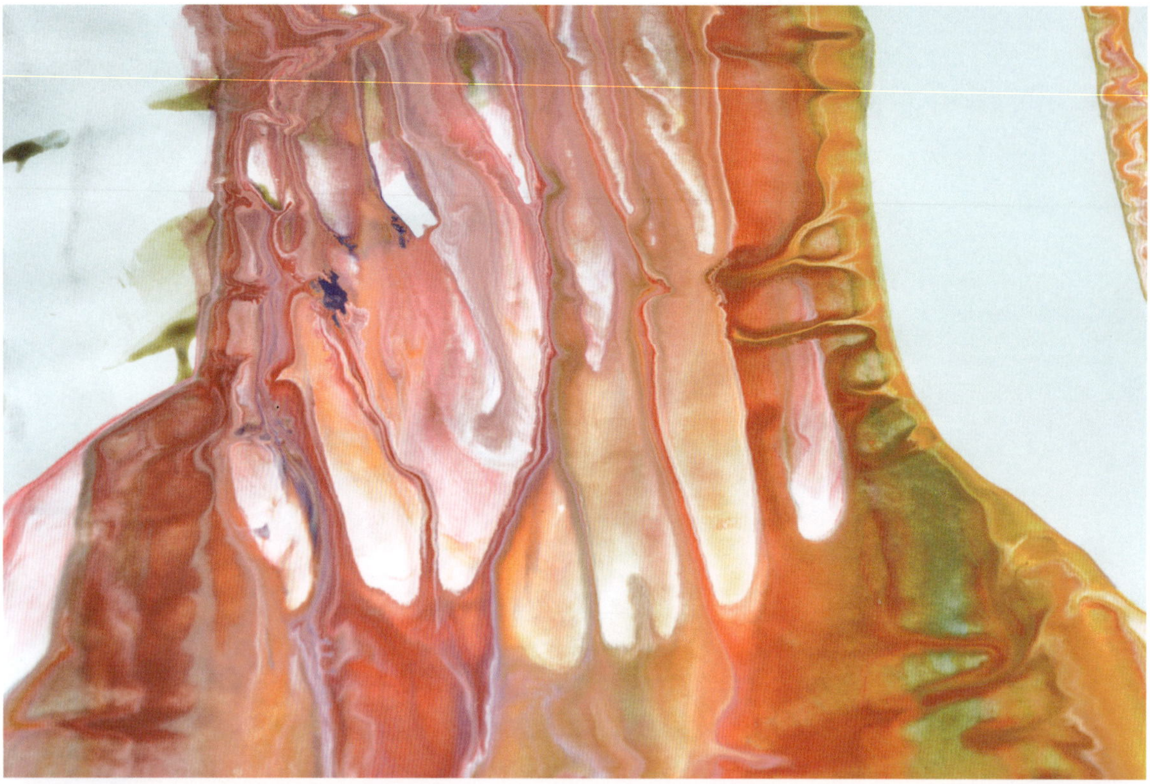

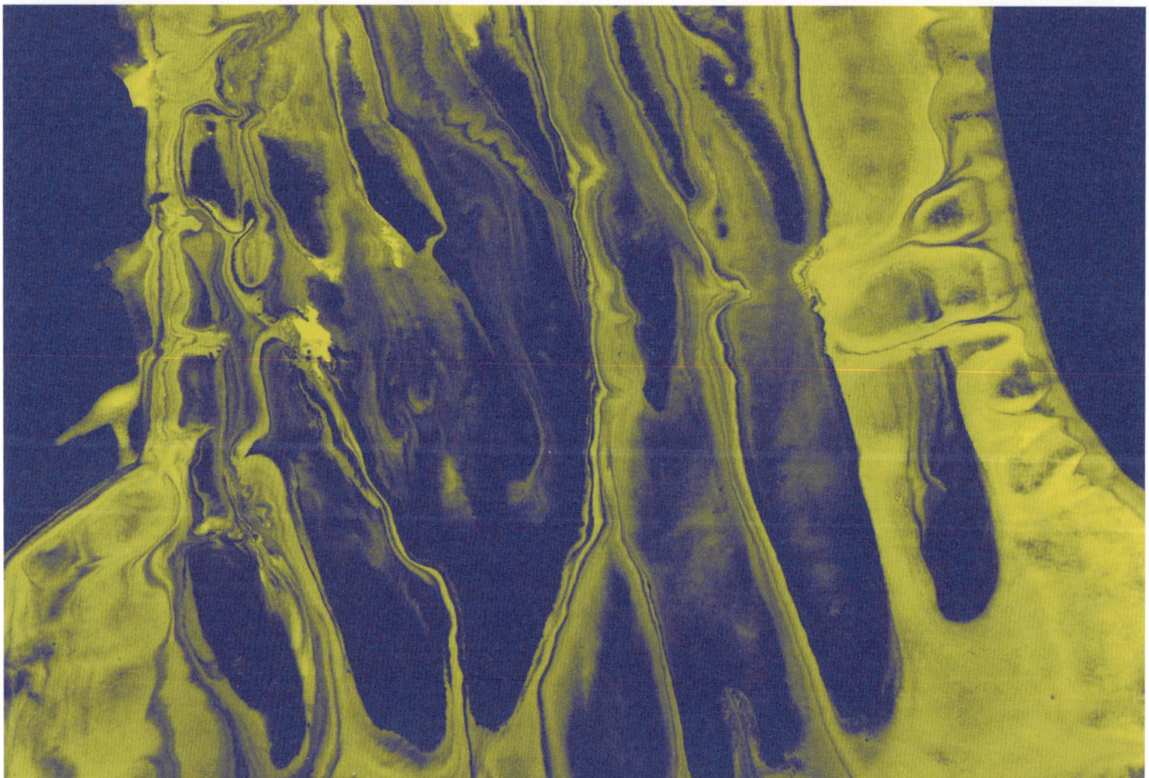

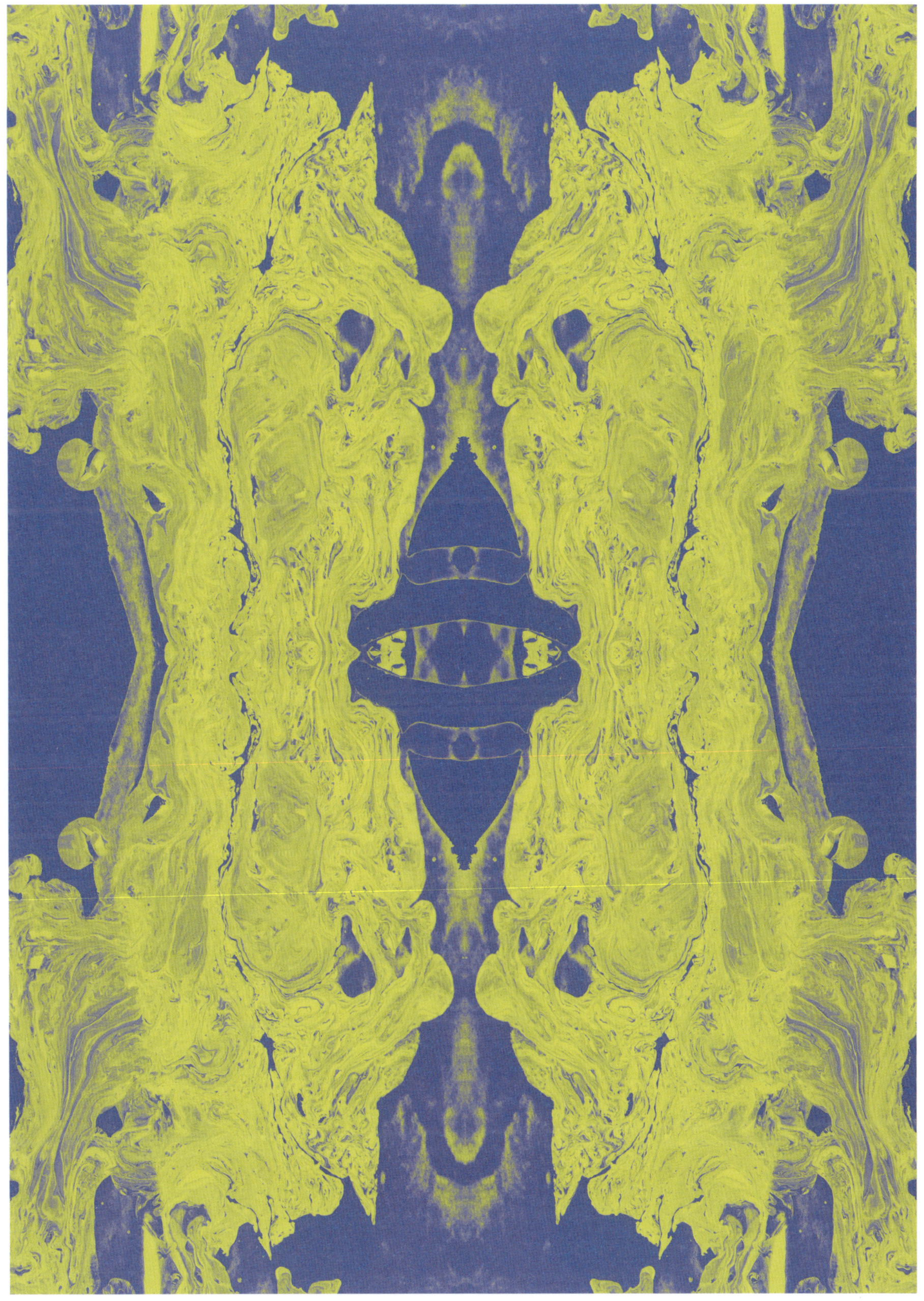

RGE

Studio : Moby Digg GmbH Designer : Maximilian Heitsch, Moby Digg

The minimalistic corporate identity is based on the three founding partners, who have been visualized by three top lines. The additional lines symbolize the numerous employees. The blue circle stands for the passion and emotion that the company puts in every project, having a strong influence on the design development and altering the lines accordingly. The lines not only connect a starting point with an ending point, but also symbolize the path of a project

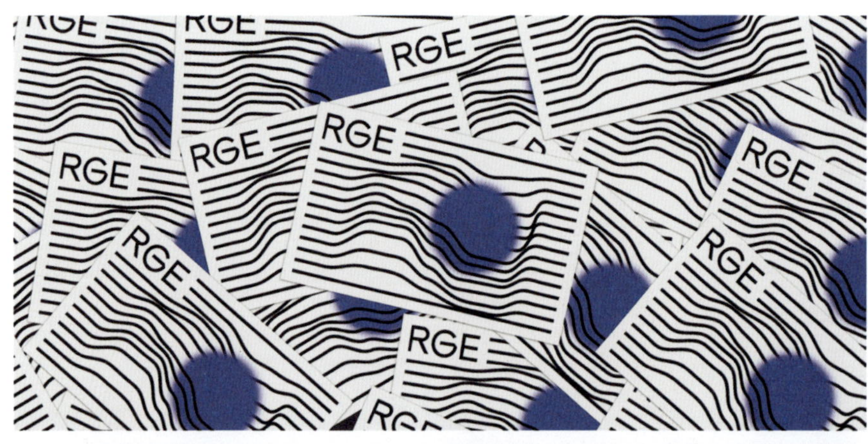

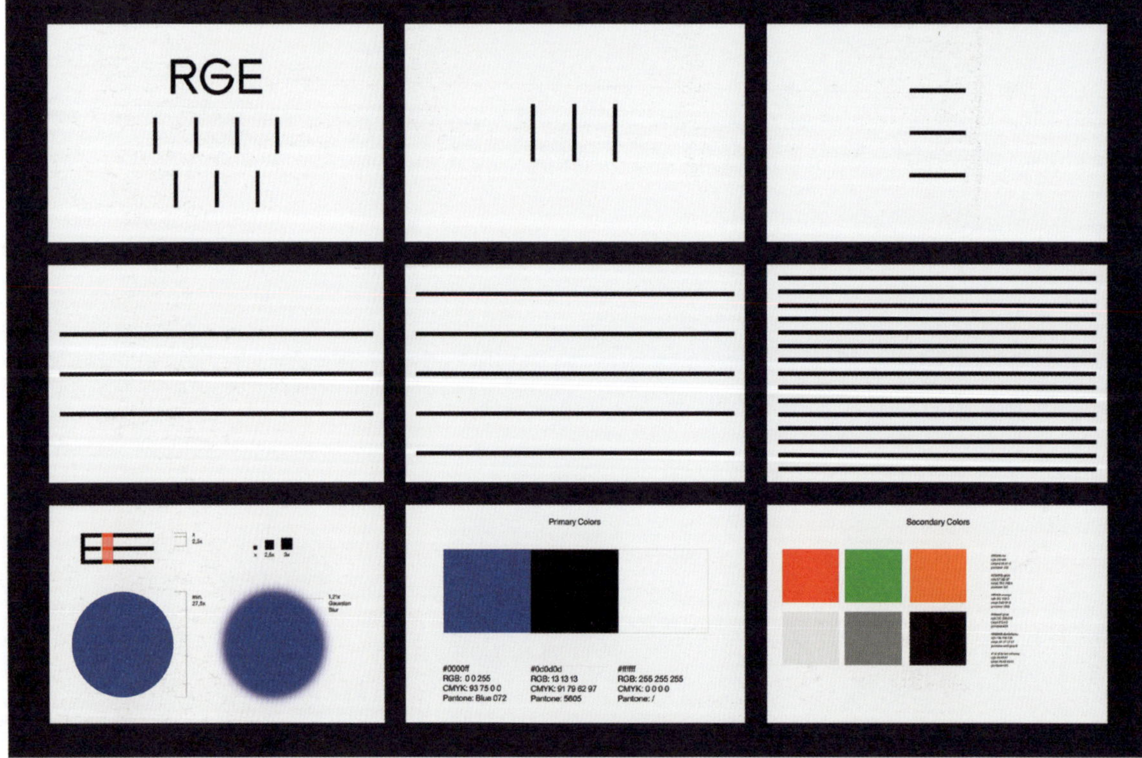

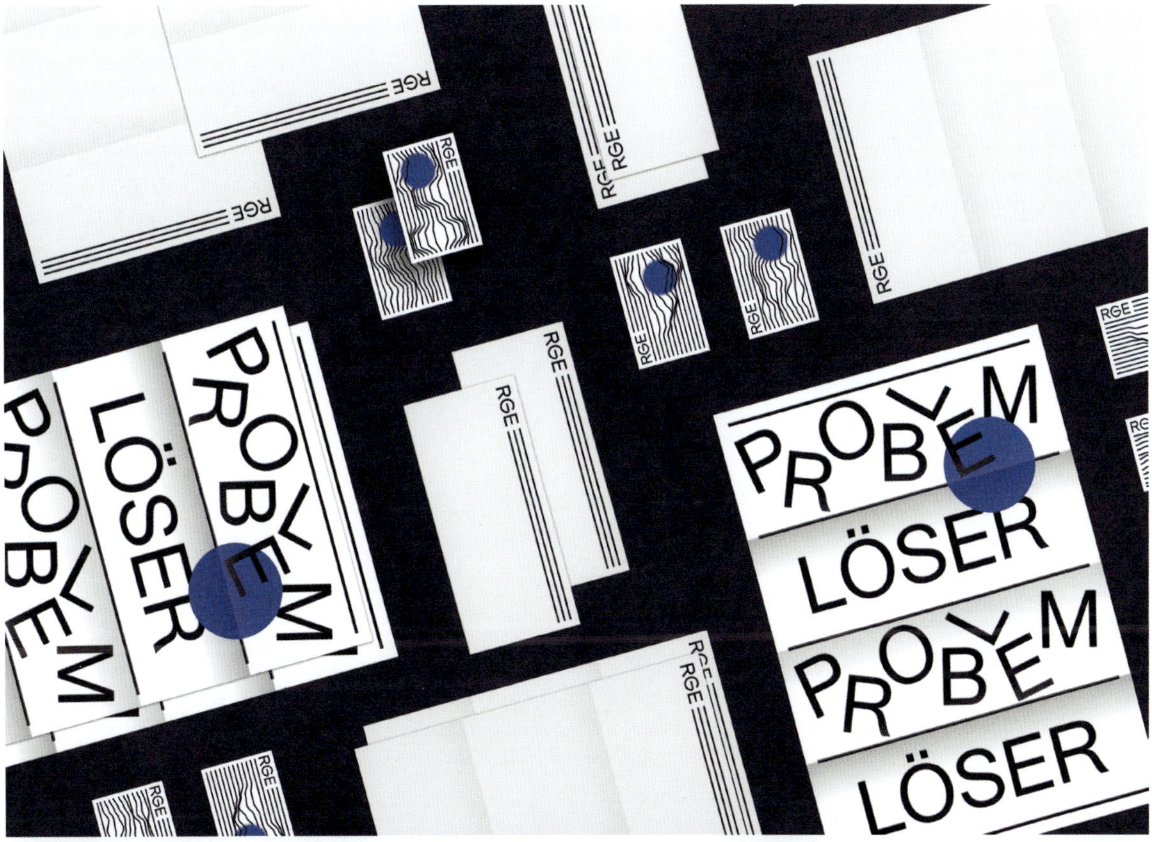

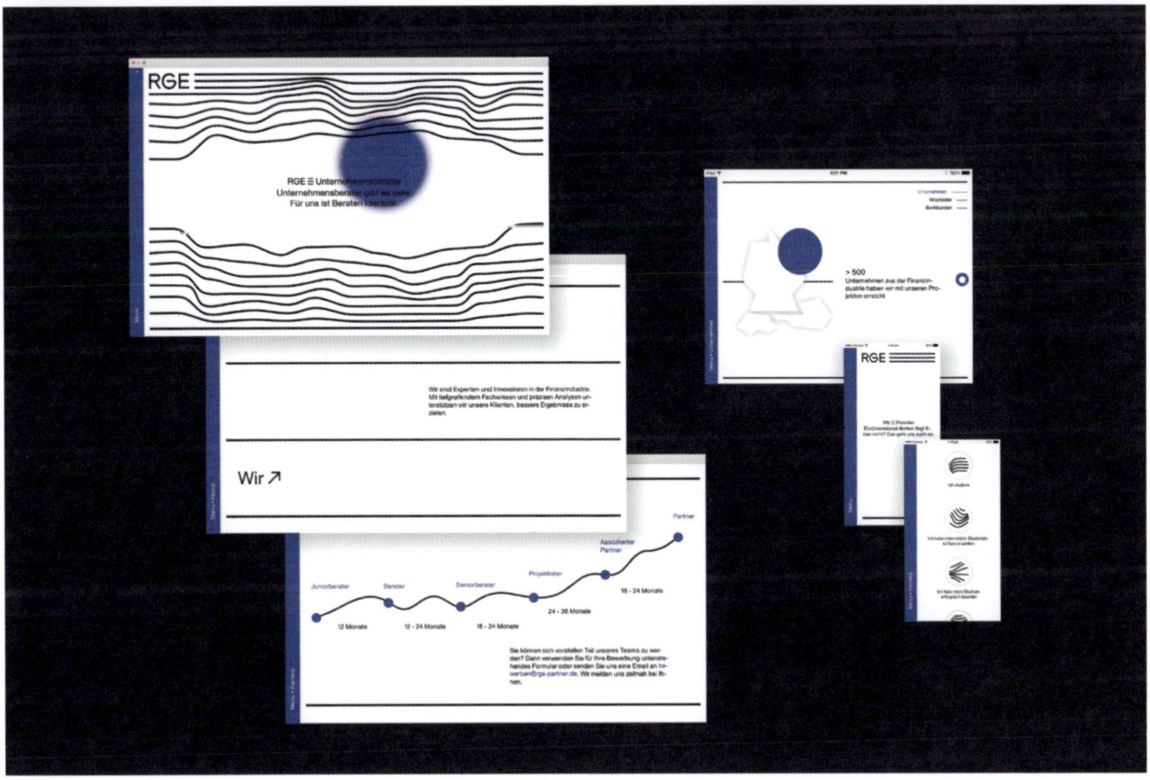

42X60

Designer : Marcelo Batista, Ricardo Donato

In this series of artistic posters, the designers suggested the development of skills and critical sense, taking intuition as the starting point of the creation process. They also presented a diversity of experimental techniques and the creative use of ordinary elements to enhance our eye towards our surroundings.

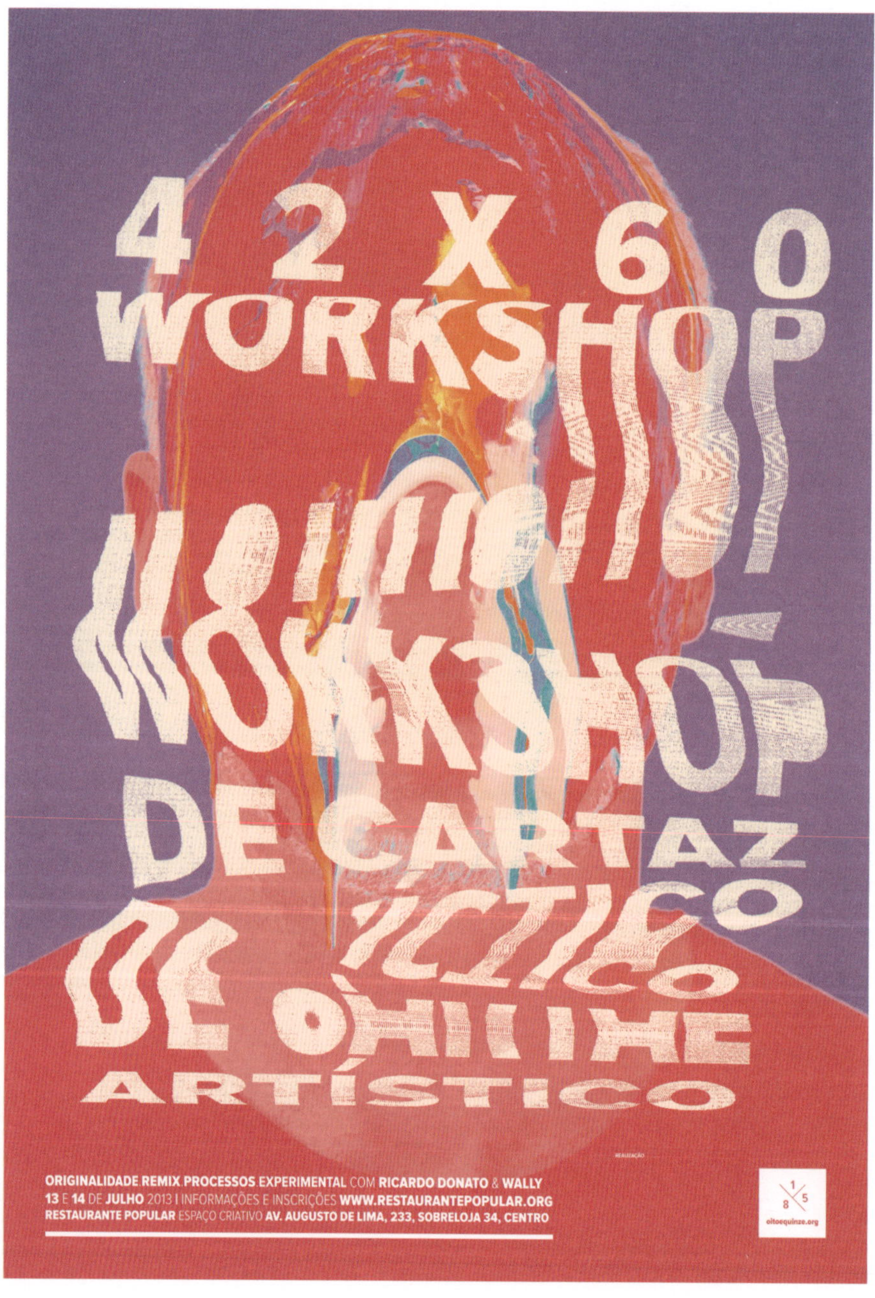

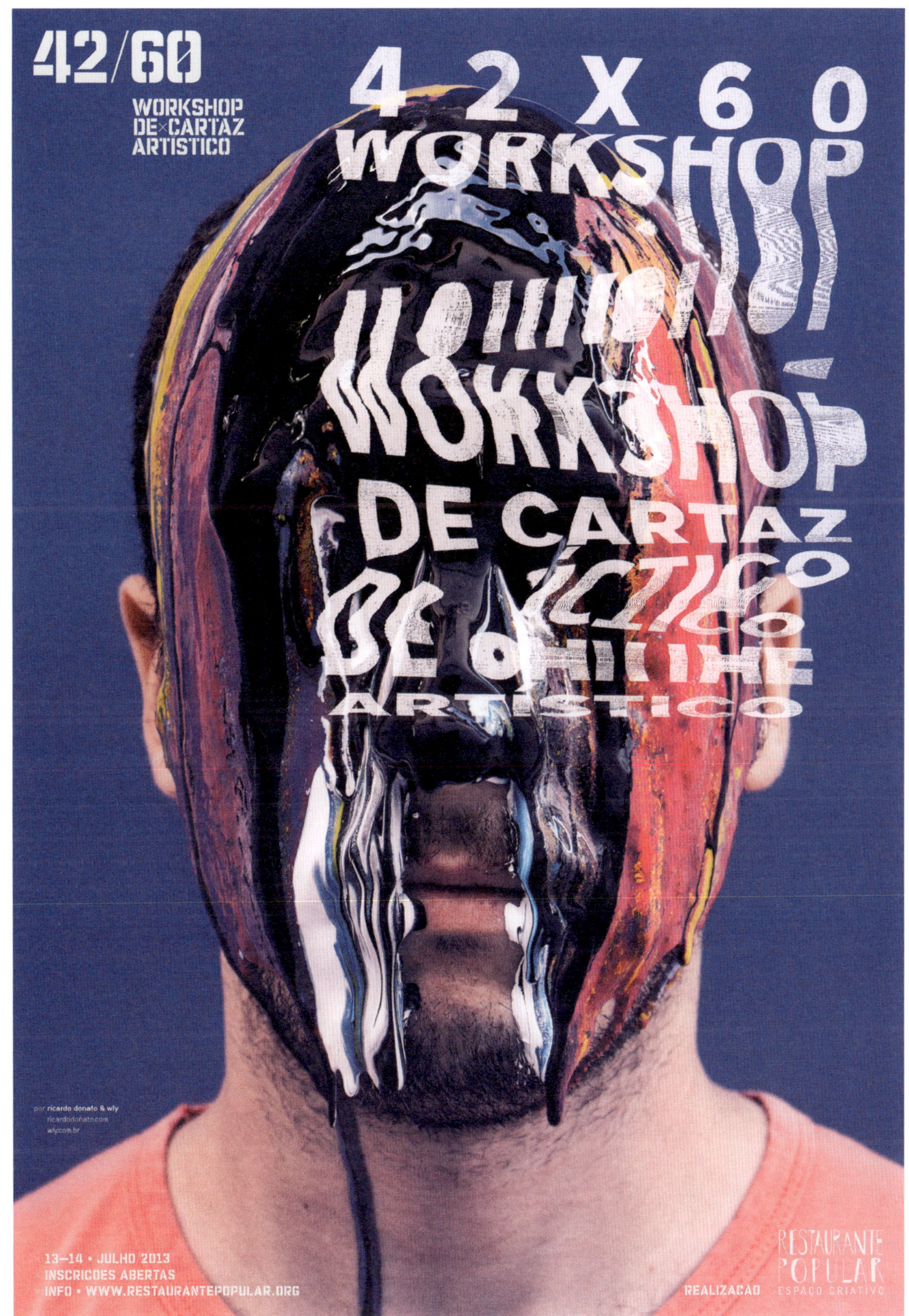
42/60
WORKSHOP
DE×CARTAZ
ARTISTICO
4 2 X 6 0
WORKSHOP
WORKSHOP
DE CARTAZ
ARTISTICO
por ricardo donato & wly
ricardodonato.com
wly.com.br
13–14 • JULHO 2013
INSCRICOES ABERTAS
INFO • WWW.RESTAURANTEPOPULAR.ORG
REALIZACAO
RESTAURANTE
POPULAR
ESPAÇO CRIATIVO

ASCENSORES

Studio : Amateur(dot)rocks   Designer : Ivo Pallucchini, José Bessega

Ascensores is a conceptual musical project led by Juan Pablo Lisi, a young Argentinian producer. Ascensores 017-25:57 is a lo-fi record adapted to a live format that combines more than 2 years of studio sessions, live recordings and other miscellany. For the album design, the designers translated all the universe of loops and hypnotizing sounds through a simple visual system using repetition as the main resource.

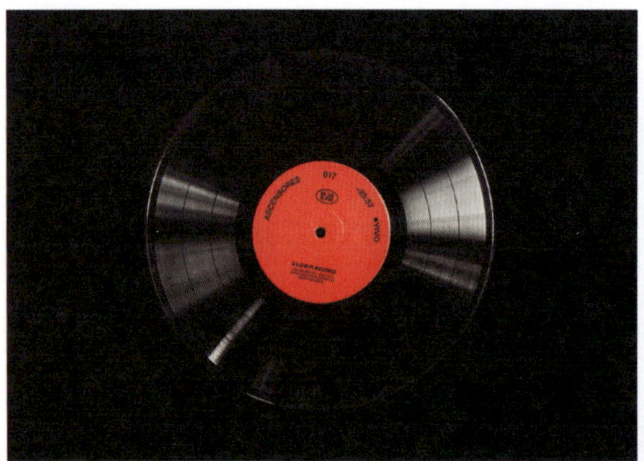

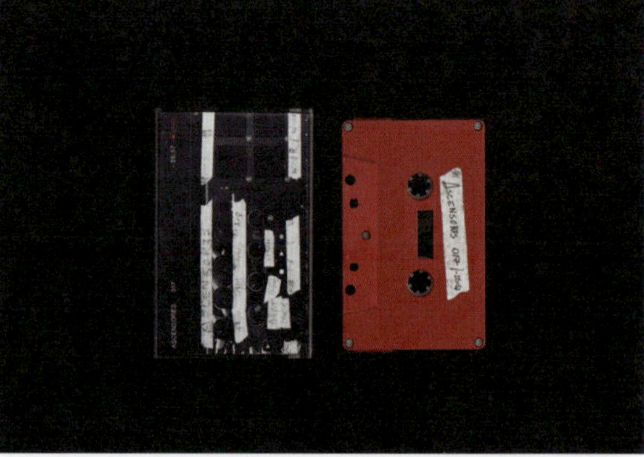

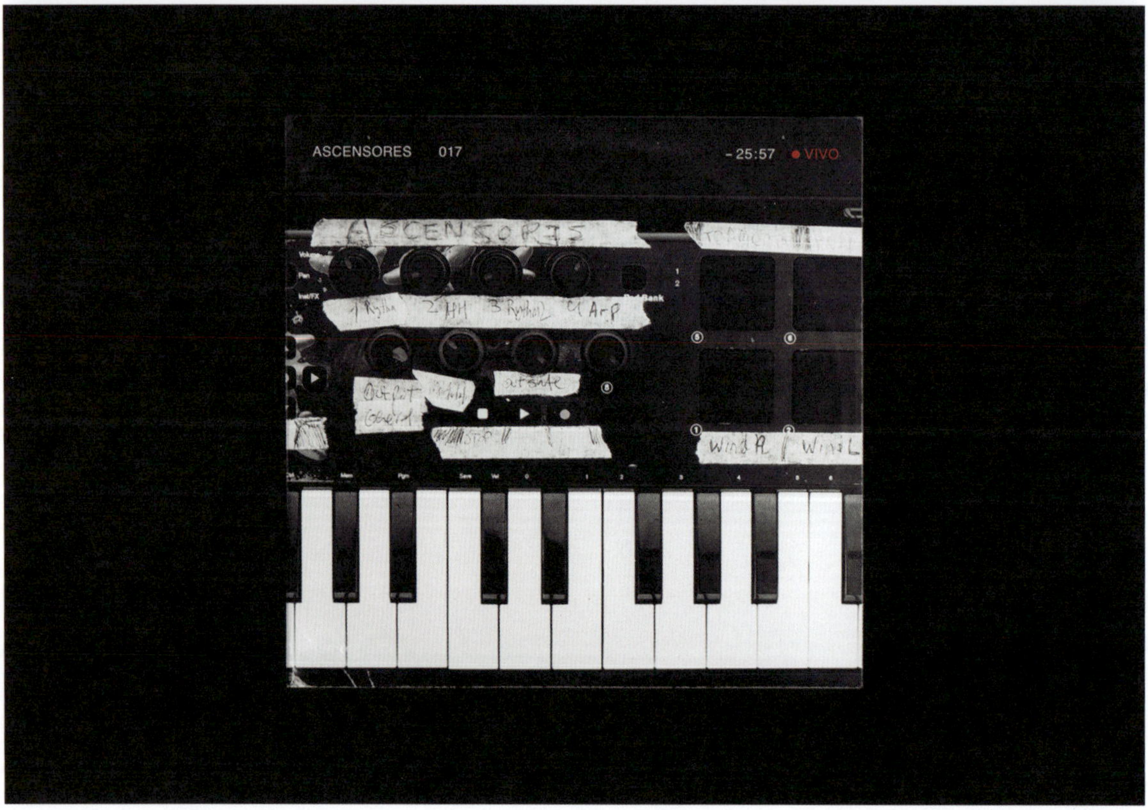

● LIVE -25:57 AS
AS CEN ○ VIVO RE
ASCEN SO S
PRE - 25:57 ASCNS
PRE ASCENSORES
SENTA. 017017017017 017
-25:57 AS
AS CEN ○ VIVO RE
ASCEN SO S
PRE - 25:57 ASCNS
PRE ASCENSORES
SENTA. 017017017017 017

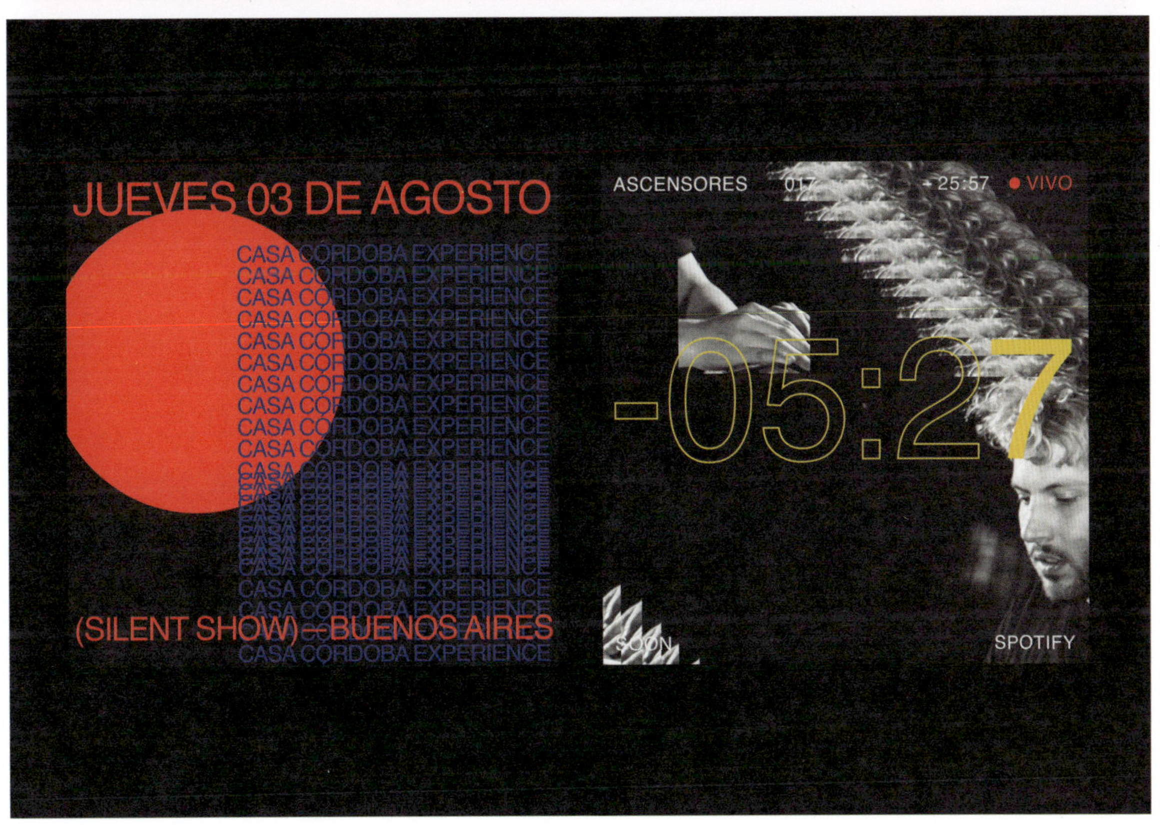

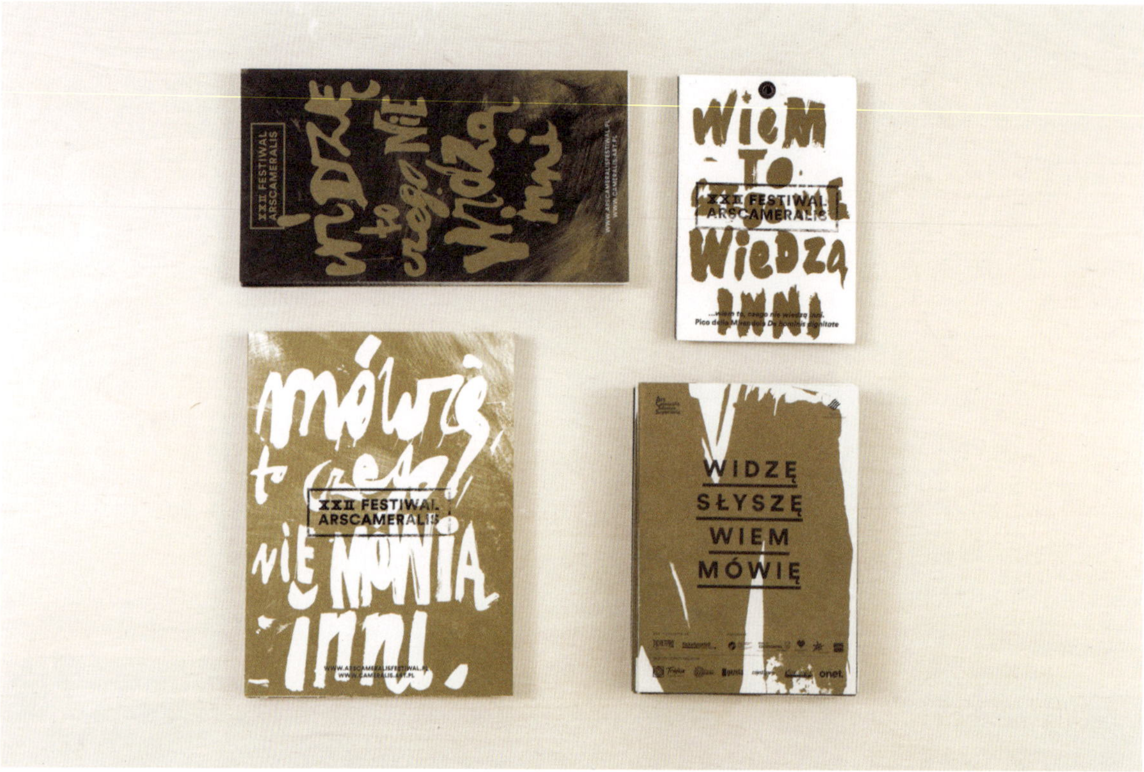

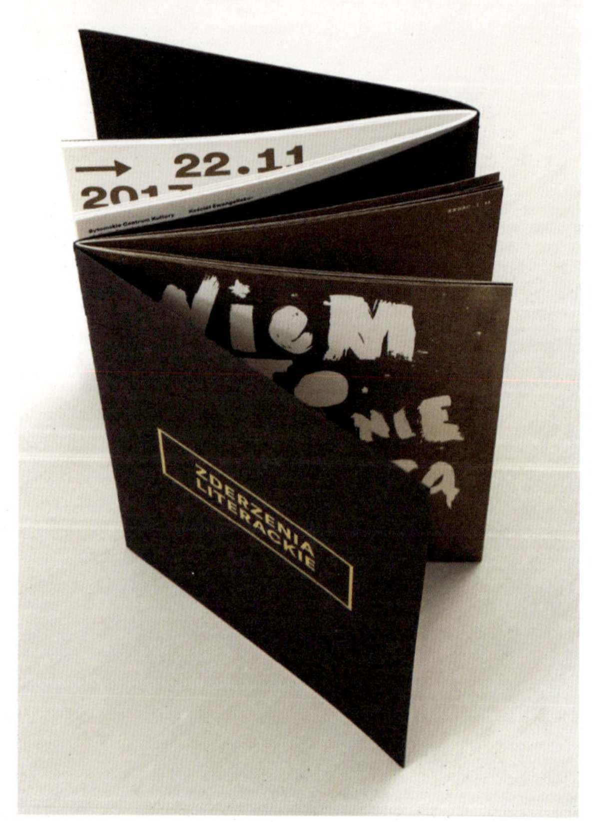

ARS CAMERALIS FESTIVAL

Designer : Marta Gawin

For this visual identity, some raw, clumsy handwritten letters were arranged to clash with the centrally positioned, rational typography. The posters were placed in public spaces in different configurations, sometimes arranged as clear message and sometimes as meaningless combination of words. This intensified the feeling of mystery and encouraged the discovery of meanings.

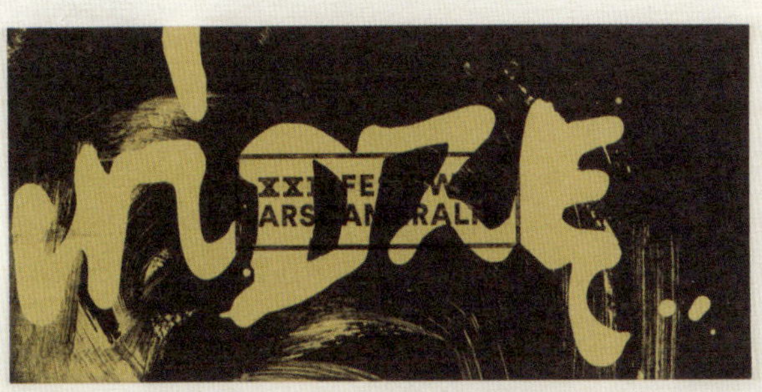
XXII FESTIWAL
ARSCAMERALIS

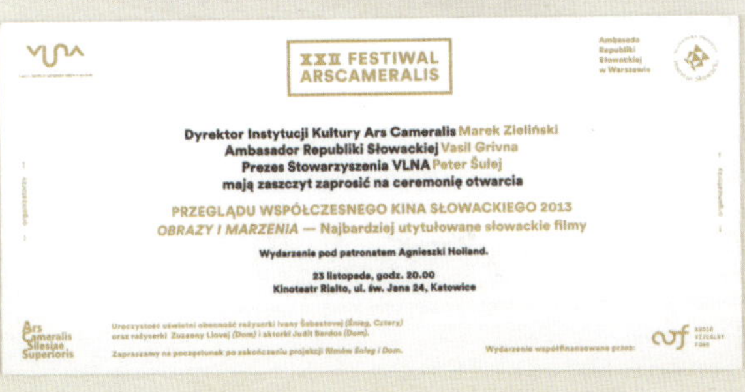
XXII FESTIWAL
ARSCAMERALIS
Ambasada
Republiki
Słowackiej
w Warszawie
Dyrektor Instytucji Kultury Ars Cameralis Marek Zieliński
Ambasador Republiki Słowackiej Vasil Grivna
Prezes Stowarzyszenia VLNA Peter Šulej
mają zaszczyt zaprosić na ceremonię otwarcia
PRZEGLĄDU WSPÓŁCZESNEGO KINA SŁOWACKIEGO 2013
OBRAZY I MARZENIA — Najbardziej utytułowane słowackie filmy
Wydarzenie pod patronatem Agnieszki Holland.
23 listopada, godz. 20.00
Kinoteatr Rialto, ul. św. Jana 24, Katowice
Ars
Cameralis
Silesiae
Superioris
Wydarzenie współfinansowane przez:

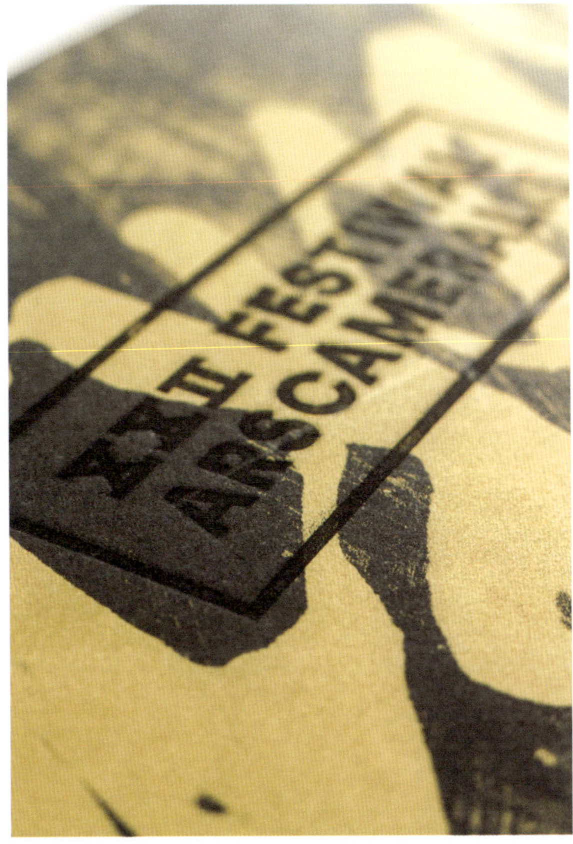
XXII FESTIWAL
ARSCAMERALIS

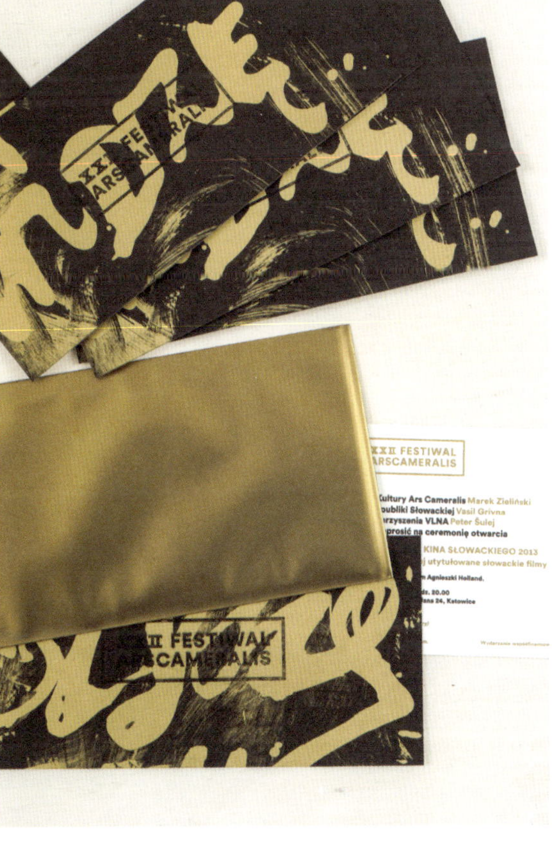
XXII FESTIWAL
ARSCAMERALIS

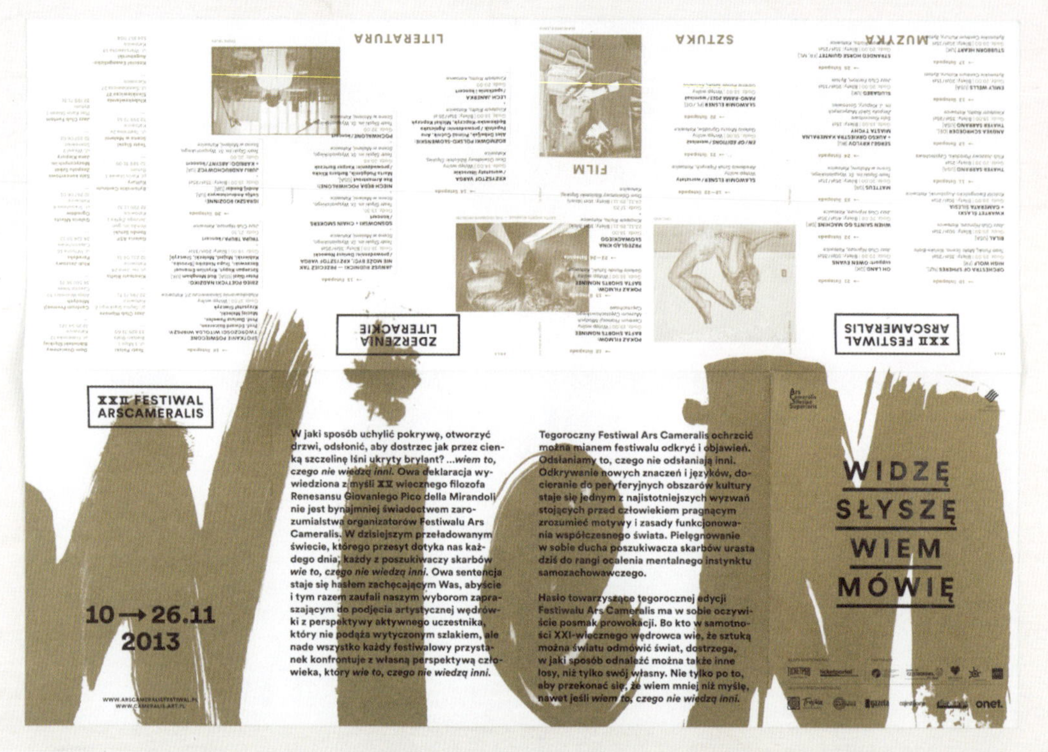
XXII FESTIWAL
ARSCAMERALIS
ZDERZENIA
LITERACKIE
LITERATURA
SZTUKA
MUZYKA
FILM
W jaki sposób uchylić pokrywę, otworzyć drzwi, odsłonić, aby dostrzec jak przez cienką szczelinę lśni ukryty brylant? ...wiem to, czego nie wiedzą inni. Owa deklaracja wywiedziona z myśli XV wiecznego filozofa Renesansu Giovaniego Pico della Mirandoli nie jest bynajmniej świadectwem zarozumialstwa organizatorów Festiwalu Ars Cameralis. W dzisiejszym przeładowanym świecie, którego przesyt dotyka nas każdego dnia, każdy z poszukiwaczy skarbów wie to, czego nie wiedzą inni. Owa sentencja staje się hasłem zachęcającym Was, abyście i tym razem zaufali naszym wyborom zapraszającym do podjęcia artystycznej wędrówki z perspektywy aktywnego uczestnika, który nie podąża wytyczonym szlakiem, ale nade wszystko każdy festiwalowy przystanek konfrontuje z własną perspektywą człowieka, który wie to, czego nie wiedzą inni.
Tegoroczny Festiwal Ars Cameralis ochrzcić można mianem festiwalu odkryć i objawień. Odsłaniamy to, czego nie odsłaniają inni. Odkrywanie nowych znaczeń i języków, docieranie do peryferyjnych obszarów kultury staje się jednym z najistotniejszych wyzwań stojących przed człowiekiem pragnącym zrozumieć motywy i zasady funkcjonowania współczesnego świata. Pielęgnowanie w sobie ducha poszukiwacza skarbów urasta dziś do rangi ocalenia mentalnego instynktu samozachowawczego.
Hasło towarzyszące tegorocznej edycji Festiwalu Ars Cameralis ma w sobie oczywiście posmak prowokacji. Bo kto w samotności XXI-wiecznego wędrowca wie, że sztuką można światu odmówić świat, dostrzega, w jaki sposób odnaleźć można także inne losy, niż tylko swój własny. Nie tylko po to, aby przekonać się, że wiem mniej niż myślę, nawet jeśli wiem to, czego nie wiedzą inni.
10 → 26.11
2013
WIDZĘ
SŁYSZĘ
WIEM
MÓWIĘ
onet.

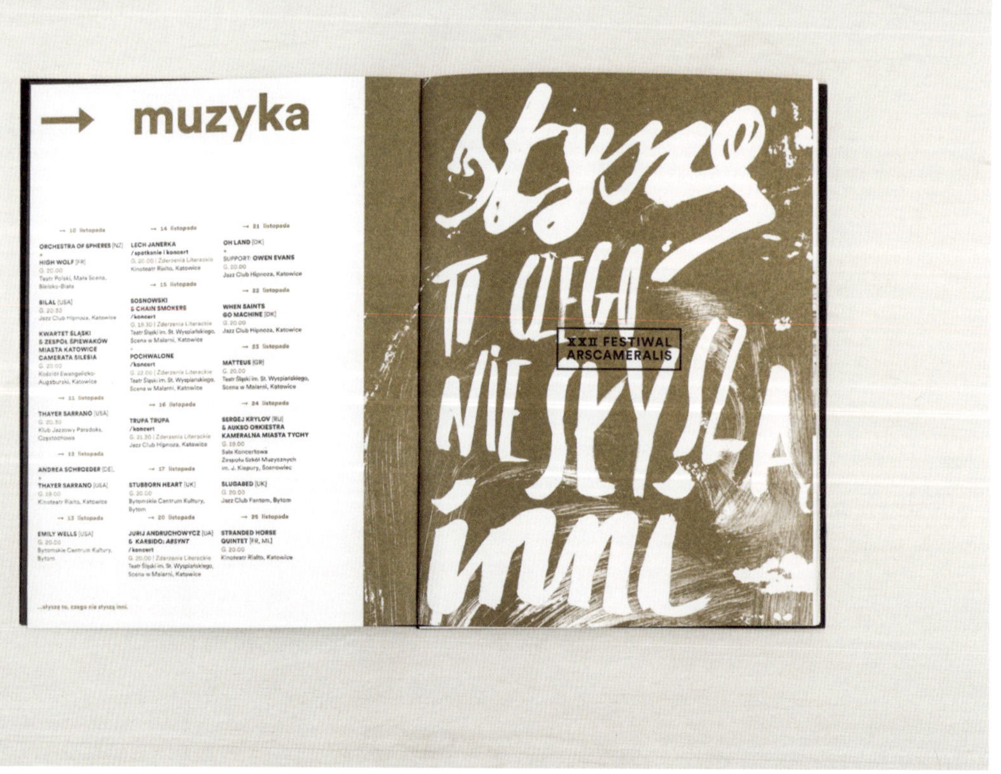
→ muzyka
→ 10 listopada
ORCHESTRA OF SPHERES [NZ]
+
HIGH WOLF [FR]
G. 20.00
Teatr Polski, Mała Scena, Bielsko-Biała
BILAL [USA]
G. 20.30
Jazz Club Hipnoza, Katowice
KWARTET ŚLĄSKI & ZESPÓŁ ŚPIEWAKÓW MIASTA KATOWICE CAMERATA SILESIA
G. 20.00
Kościół Ewangelicko-Augsburski, Katowice
→ 11 listopada
THAYER SARRANO [USA]
G. 20.30
Klub Jazzowy Paradoks, Częstochowa
→ 12 listopada
ANDREA SCHROEDER [DE]
+
THAYER SARRANO [USA]
G. 19.00
Kinoteatr Rialto, Katowice
→ 13 listopada
EMILY WELLS [USA]
G. 20.00
Bytomskie Centrum Kultury, Bytom
→ 14 listopada
LECH JANERKA
/spotkanie i koncert
G. 20.00 | Zderzenia Literackie
Kinoteatr Rialto, Katowice
→ 15 listopada
SOSNOWSKI & CHAIN SMOKERS
/koncert
G. 19.30 | Zderzenia Literackie
Teatr Śląski im. St. Wyspiańskiego, Scena w Malarni, Katowice
+
POCHWALONE
/koncert
G. 22.00 | Zderzenia Literackie
Teatr Śląski im. St. Wyspiańskiego, Scena w Malarni, Katowice
→ 16 listopada
TRUPA TRUPA
/koncert
G. 21.30 | Zderzenia Literackie
Jazz Club Hipnoza, Katowice
→ 17 listopada
STUBBORN HEART [UK]
G. 20.00
Bytomskie Centrum Kultury, Bytom
→ 20 listopada
JURIJ ANDRUCHOWYCZ [UA] & KARBIDO: ABSYNT
/koncert
G. 20.00 | Zderzenia Literackie
Teatr Śląski im. St. Wyspiańskiego, Scena w Malarni, Katowice
→ 21 listopada
OH LAND [DK]
+
SUPPORT: OWEN EVANS
G. 20.00
Jazz Club Hipnoza, Katowice
→ 22 listopada
WHEN SAINTS GO MACHINE [DK]
G. 20.00
Jazz Club Hipnoza, Katowice
→ 23 listopada
MATTEUS [GR]
G. 20.00
Teatr Śląski im. St. Wyspiańskiego, Scena w Malarni, Katowice
→ 24 listopada
SERGEJ KRYLOV [RU] & AUKSO ORKIESTRA KAMERALNA MIASTA TYCHY
G. 19.00
Sala Koncertowa Zespołu Szkół Muzycznych im. J. Kiepury, Sosnowiec
SLUGABED [UK]
G. 20.00
Jazz Club Fantom, Bytom
→ 25 listopada
STRANDED HORSE QUINTET [FR, ML]
G. 20.00
Kinoteatr Rialto, Katowice
...słyszę to, czego nie słyszą inni.
XXII FESTIWAL
ARSCAMERALIS

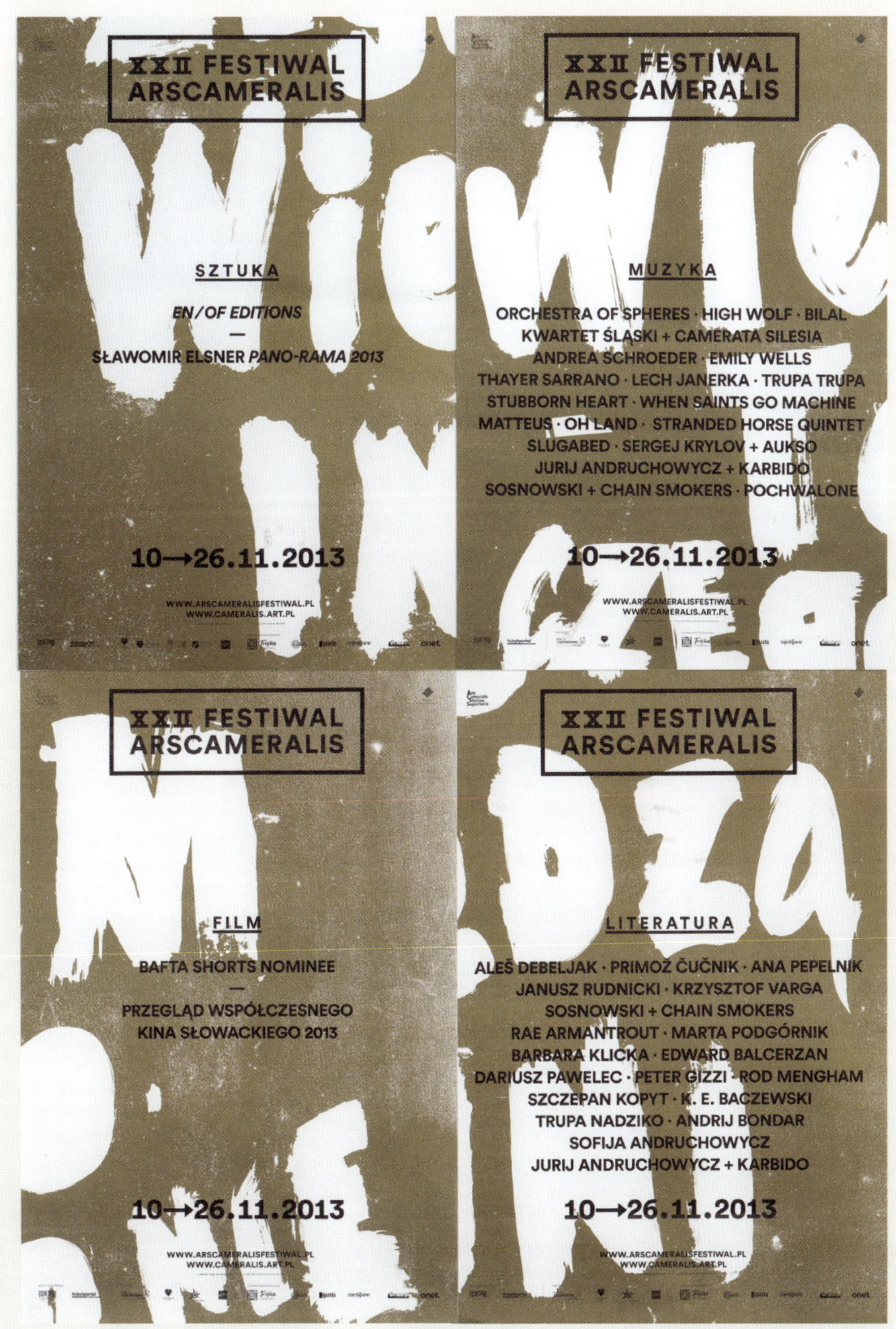
XXII FESTIWAL ARSCAMERALIS
SZTUKA
EN/OF EDITIONS
—
SŁAWOMIR ELSNER PANO-RAMA 2013
10→26.11.2013
WWW.ARSCAMERALISFESTIWAL.PL
WWW.CAMERALIS.ART.PL
XXII FESTIWAL ARSCAMERALIS
MUZYKA
ORCHESTRA OF SPHERES · HIGH WOLF · BILAL
KWARTET ŚLĄSKI + CAMERATA SILESIA
ANDREA SCHROEDER · EMILY WELLS
THAYER SARRANO · LECH JANERKA · TRUPA TRUPA
STUBBORN HEART · WHEN SAINTS GO MACHINE
MATTEUS · OH LAND · STRANDED HORSE QUINTET
SLUGABED · SERGEJ KRYLOV + AUKSO
JURIJ ANDRUCHOWYCZ + KARBIDO
SOSNOWSKI + CHAIN SMOKERS · POCHWALONE
10→26.11.2013
WWW.ARSCAMERALISFESTIWAL.PL
WWW.CAMERALIS.ART.PL
XXII FESTIWAL ARSCAMERALIS
FILM
BAFTA SHORTS NOMINEE
—
PRZEGLĄD WSPÓŁCZESNEGO
KINA SŁOWACKIEGO 2013
10→26.11.2013
WWW.ARSCAMERALISFESTIWAL.PL
WWW.CAMERALIS.ART.PL
XXII FESTIWAL ARSCAMERALIS
LITERATURA
ALEŠ DEBELJAK · PRIMOŽ ČUČNIK · ANA PEPELNIK
JANUSZ RUDNICKI · KRZYSZTOF VARGA
SOSNOWSKI + CHAIN SMOKERS
RAE ARMANTROUT · MARTA PODGÓRNIK
BARBARA KLICKA · EDWARD BALCERZAN
DARIUSZ PAWELEC · PETER GIZZI · ROD MENGHAM
SZCZEPAN KOPYT · K. E. BACZEWSKI
TRUPA NADZIKO · ANDRIJ BONDAR
SOFIJA ANDRUCHOWYCZ
JURIJ ANDRUCHOWYCZ + KARBIDO
10→26.11.2013
WWW.ARSCAMERALISFESTIWAL.PL
WWW.CAMERALIS.ART.PL

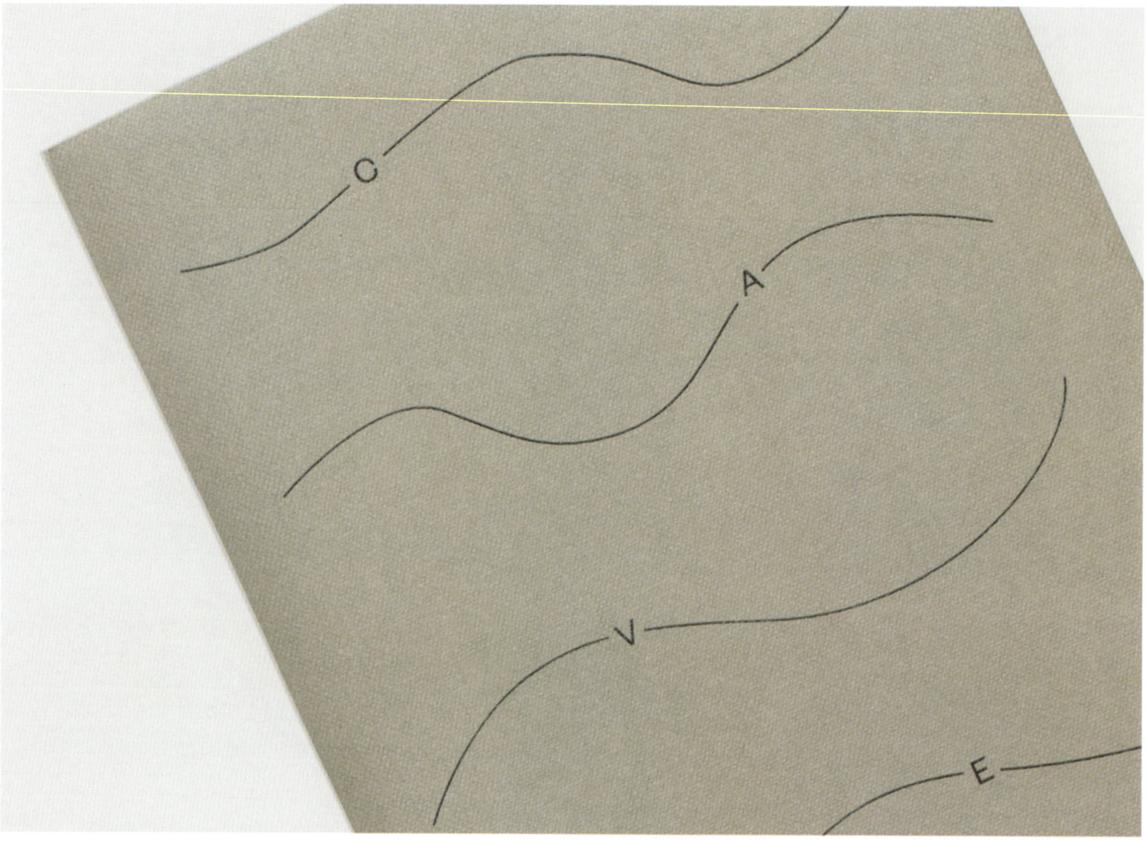

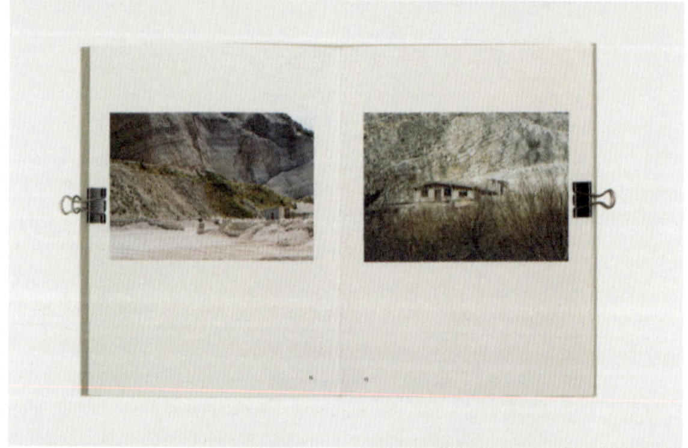

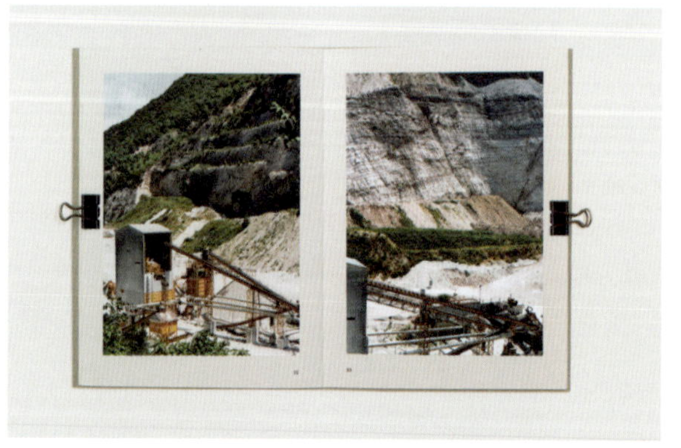

CAVE. LA PIETRA DENTRO

Designer : Gloria Maggioli

This analogical photographic project consists of a little book and three fine art prints. It was inspired by a personal observation of the environment of caves of limestones, near Gubbio, Italy.

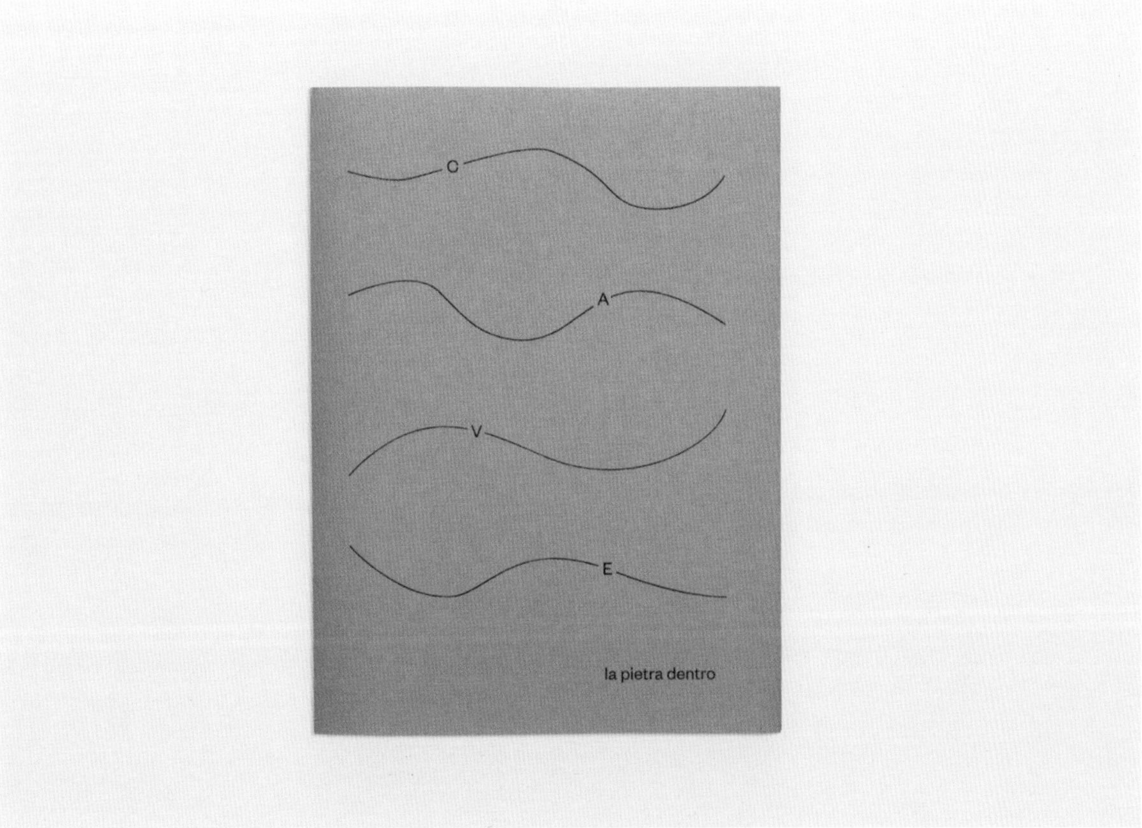

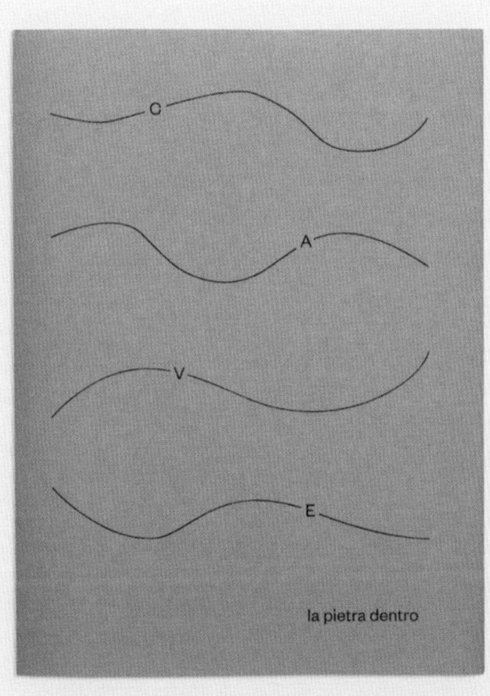

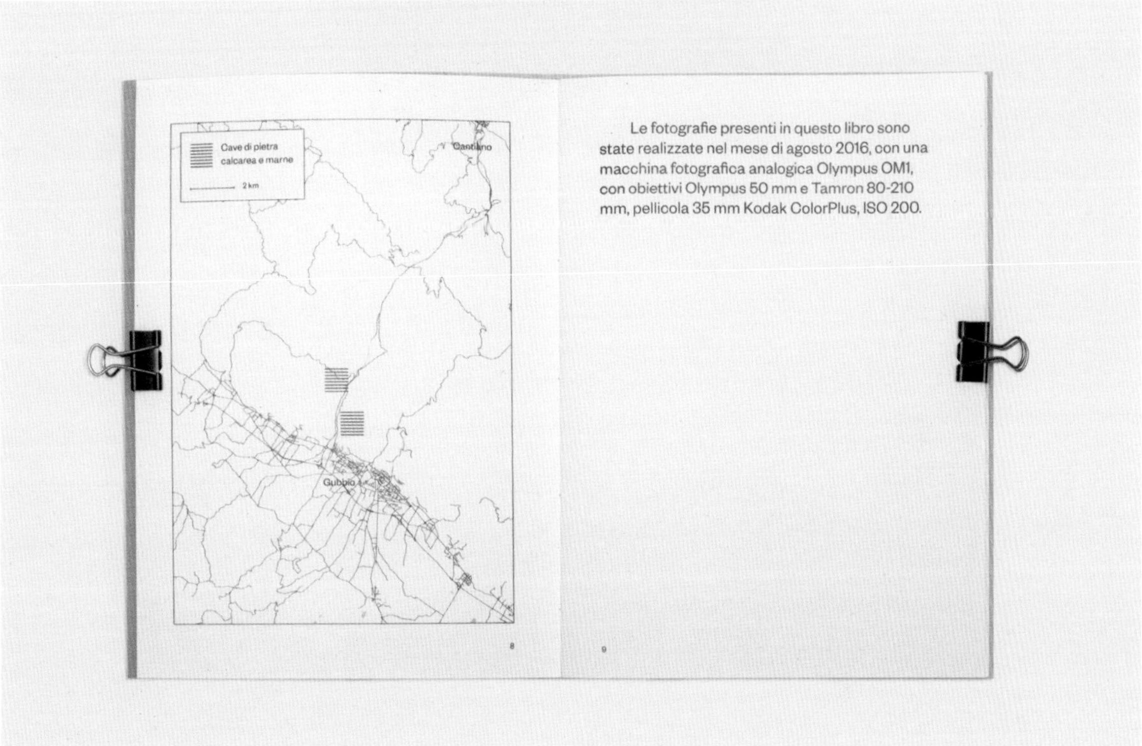

Cave di pietra calcarea e marne

2 km

Cantiano

Gubbio

8

9

Le fotografie presenti in questo libro sono state realizzate nel mese di agosto 2016, con una macchina fotografica analogica Olympus OM1, con obiettivi Olympus 50 mm e Tamron 80-210 mm, pellicola 35 mm Kodak ColorPlus, ISO 200.

THE NINETY-NINE HAND JOB POLITICS TO THE LITTLE DEATH

Designer : Cowei Liu

This book takes on both edgy and traditional qualities by using modern design languages and complicated binding techniques.

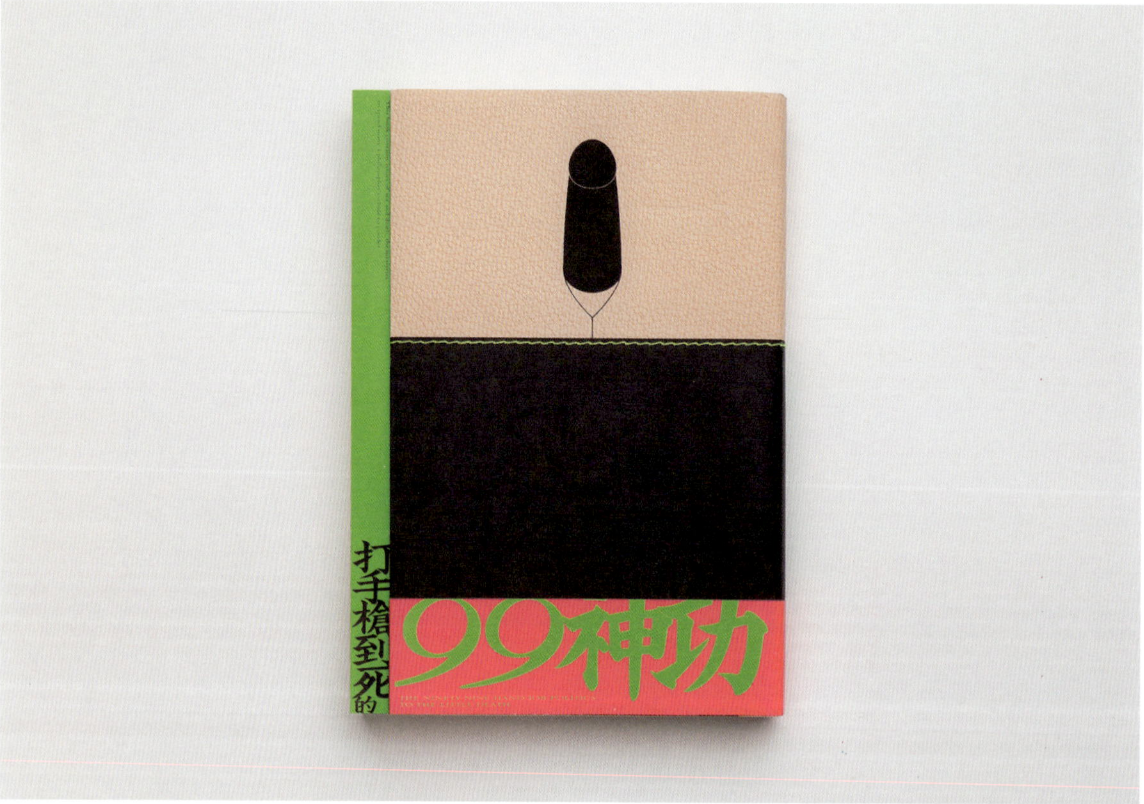

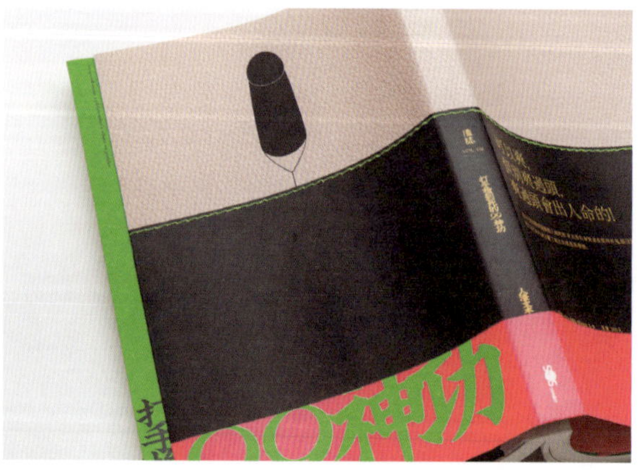

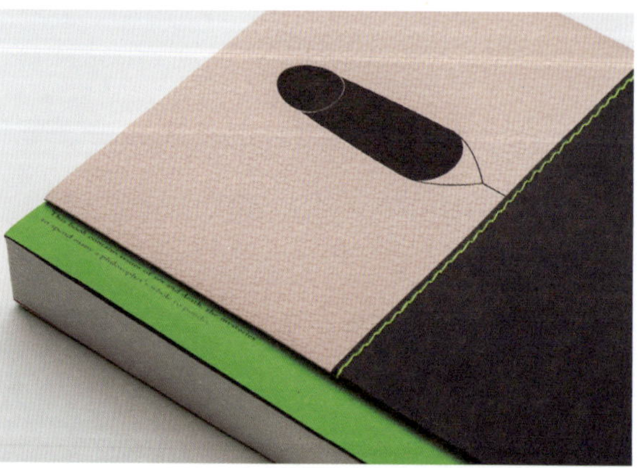

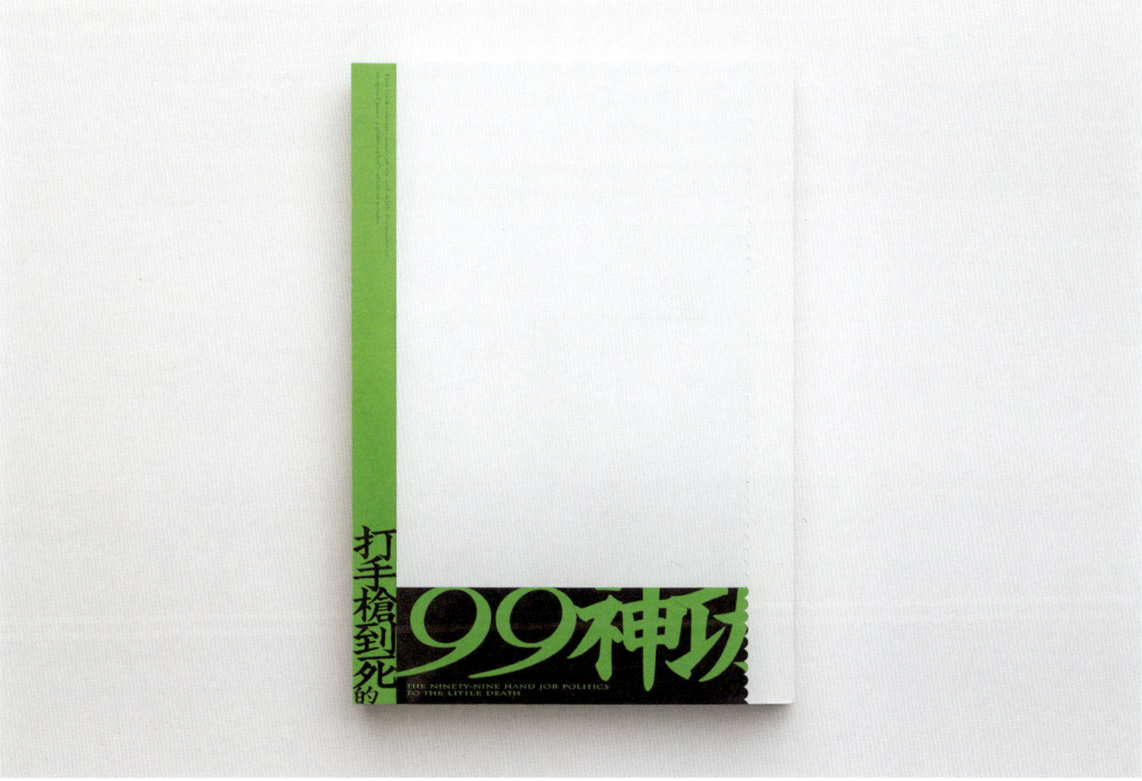

打手槍到死的
99神功
THE NINETY-NINE HAND JOB POLITICS
TO THE LITTLE DEATH

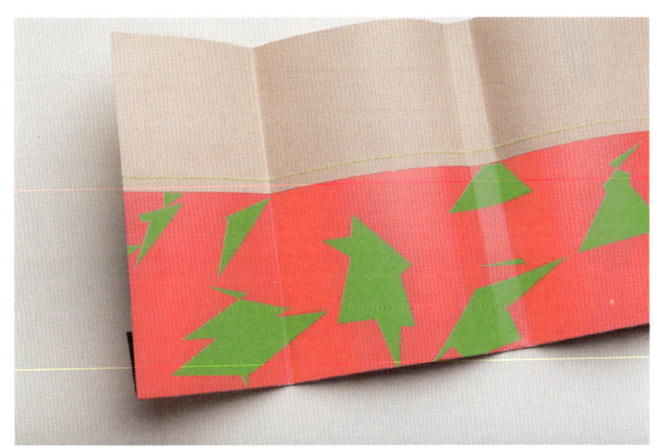

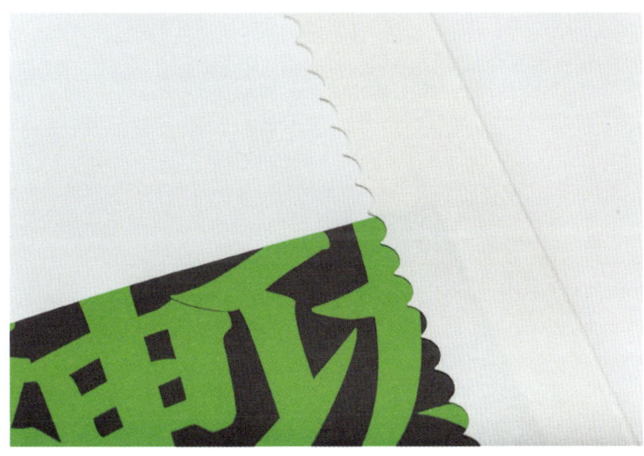

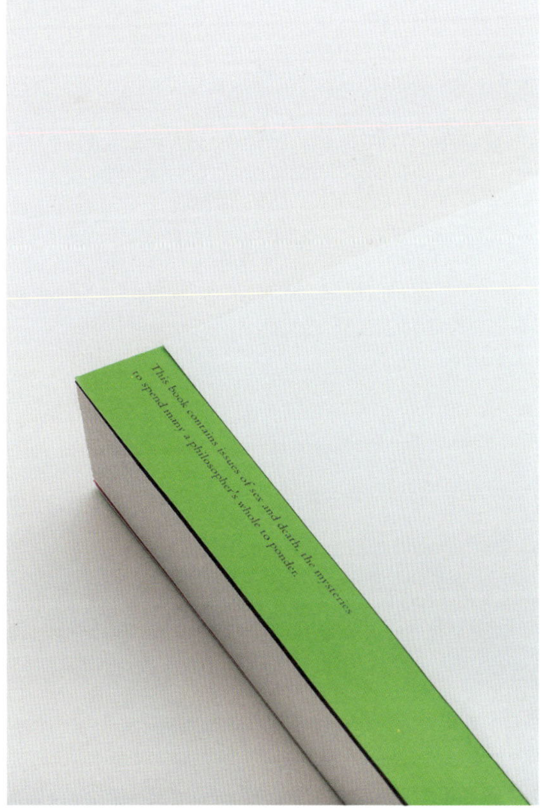

WELL... I JUST WANT TO MAKE A FANCY BOOK

Designer : YI-HSUAN LI

The designer collected images from her previous design works as well as her personal life to make this book, which is covered with foil to attract eyeballs. She believes that the coarse texture of the paper fits the "fancy" style perfectly and the texture can record the folding lines made by readers.

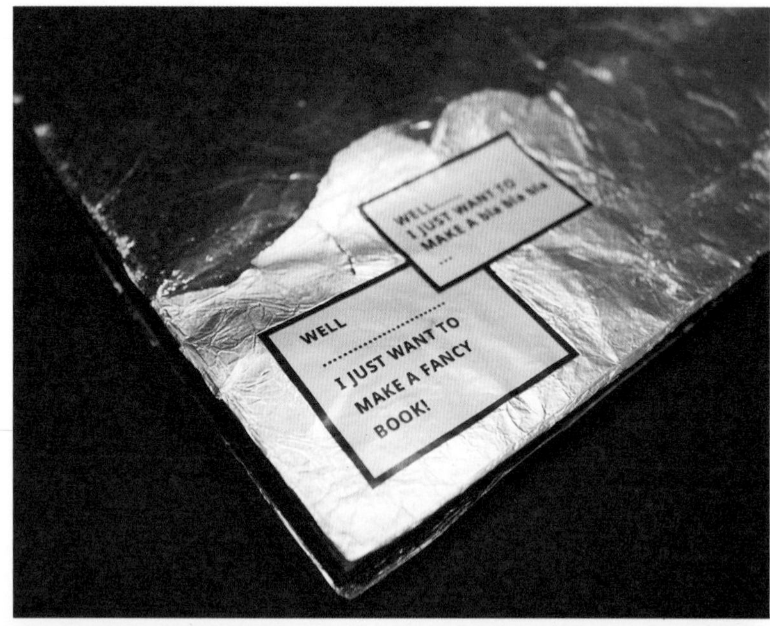

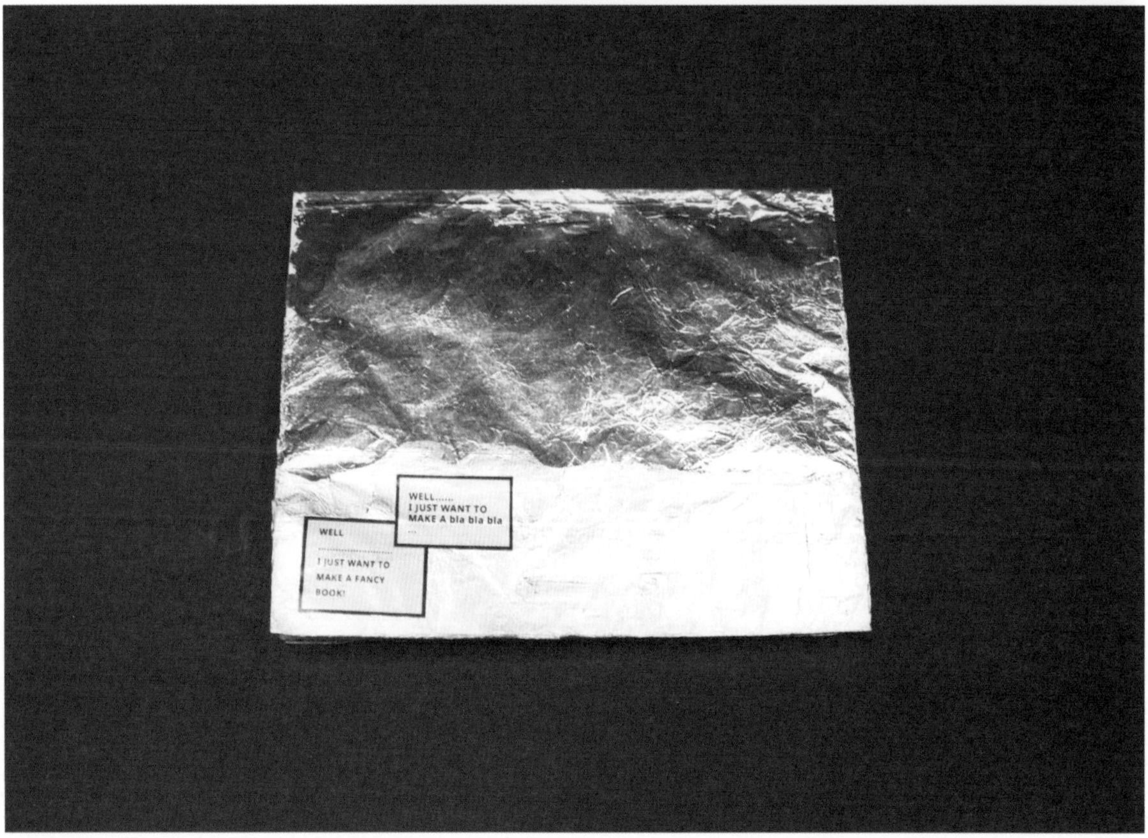

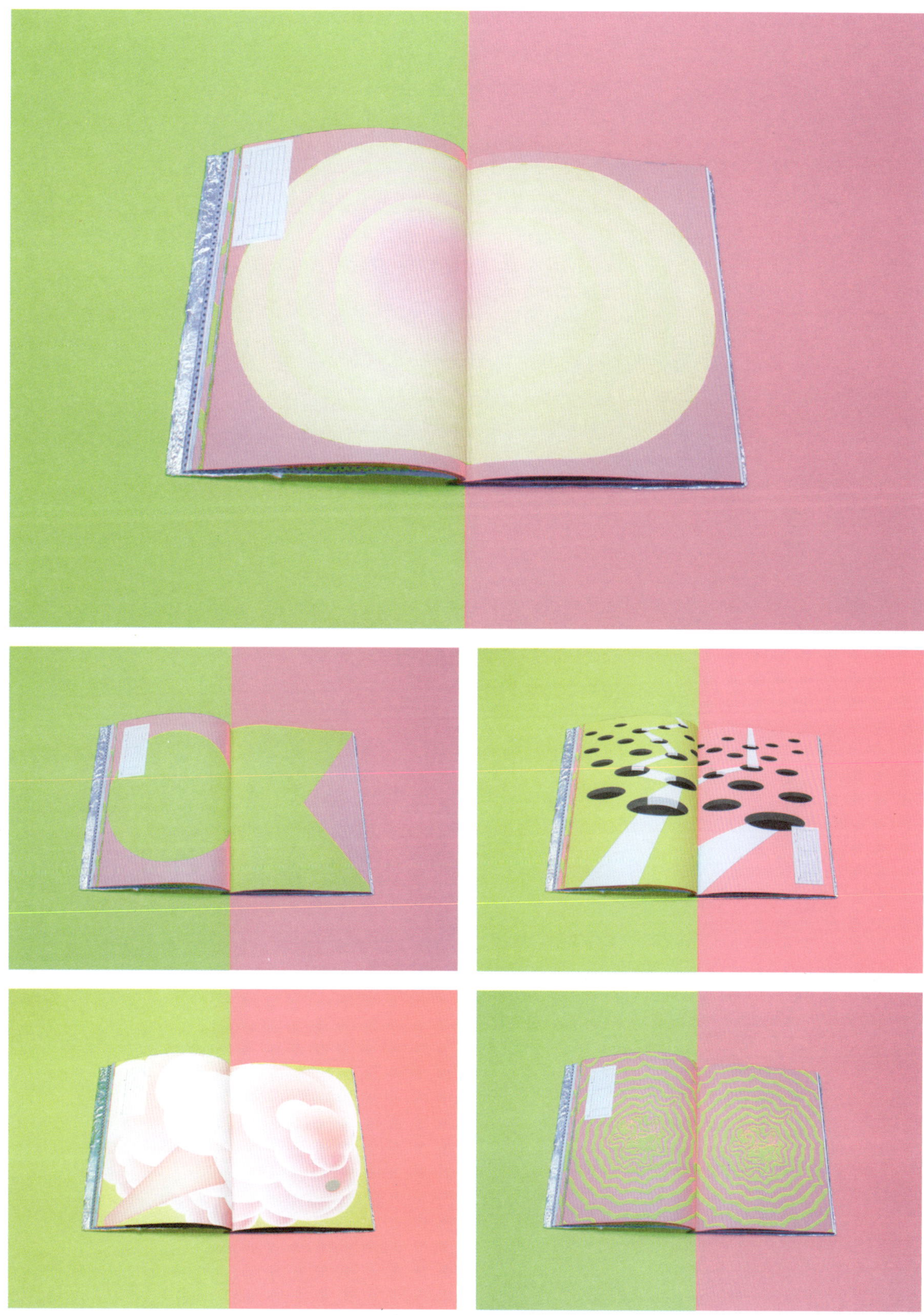

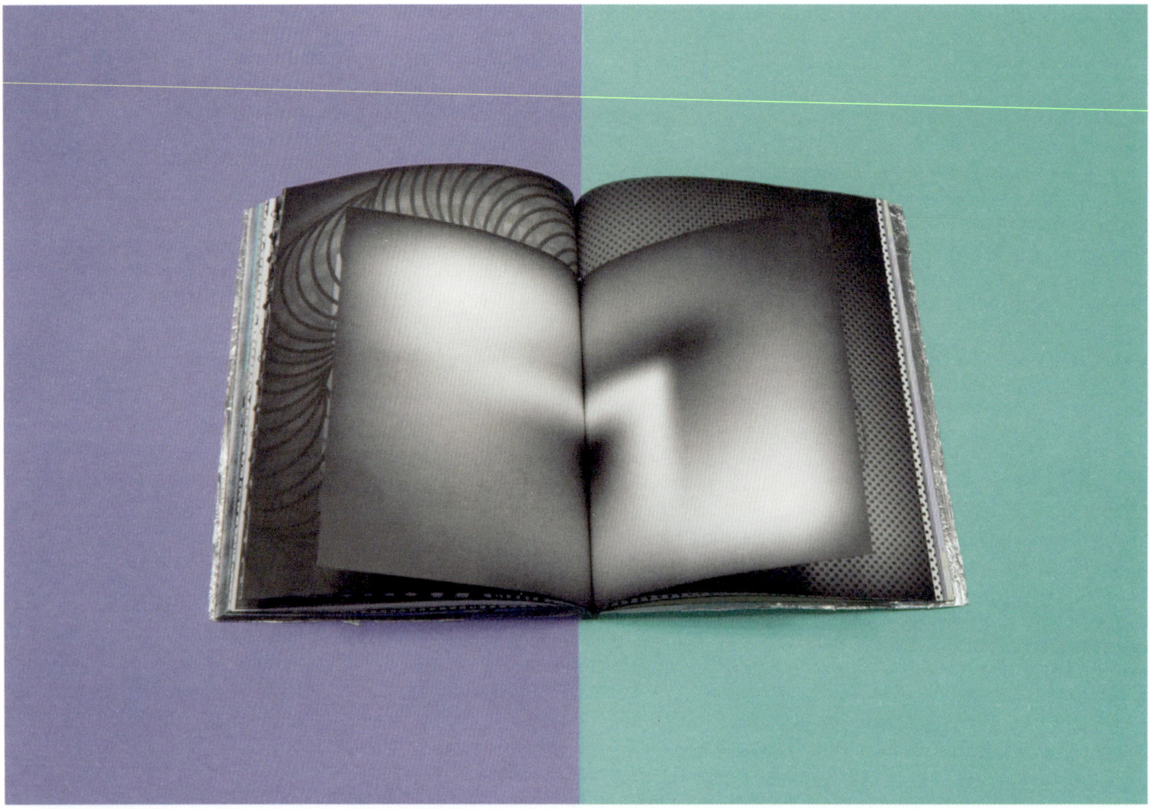

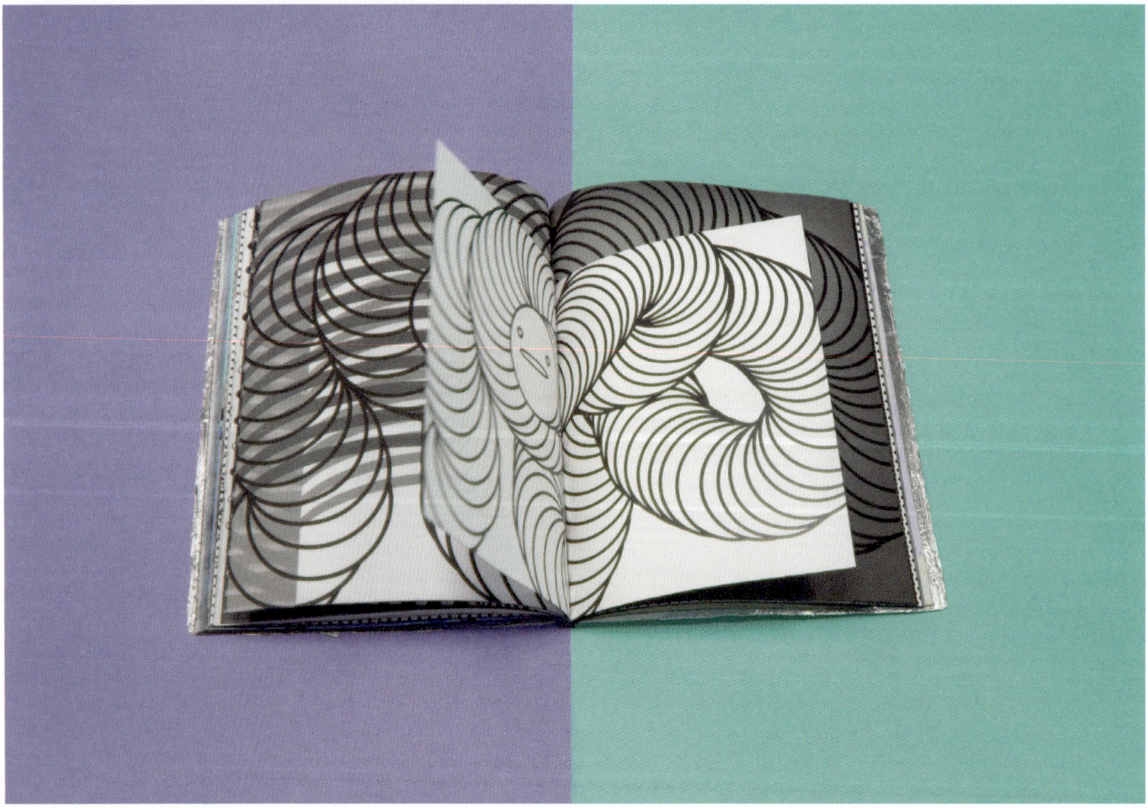

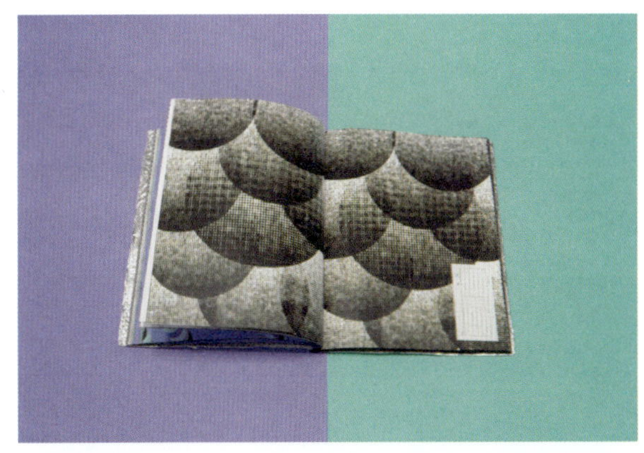

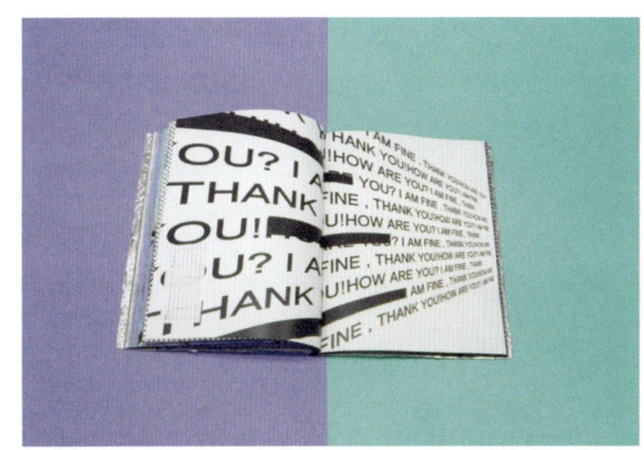
OU? I A
THANK
OU!
U? I A
HANK
FINE , THANK YOU!HOW ARE YOU? I AM FINE , THANK
U!HOW ARE YOU? I AM FINE , THANK
FINE , THANK YOU!HOW ARE YOU?

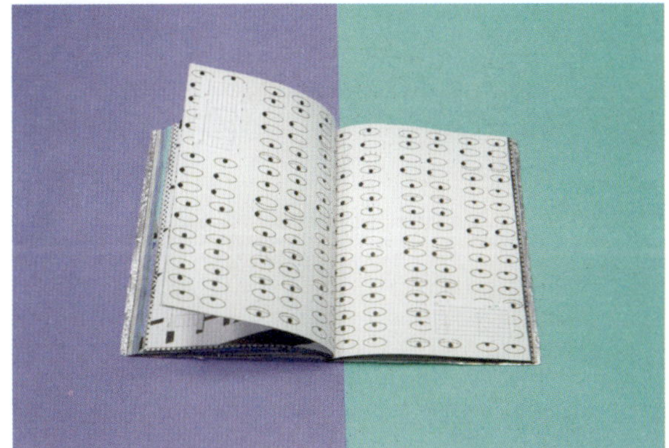

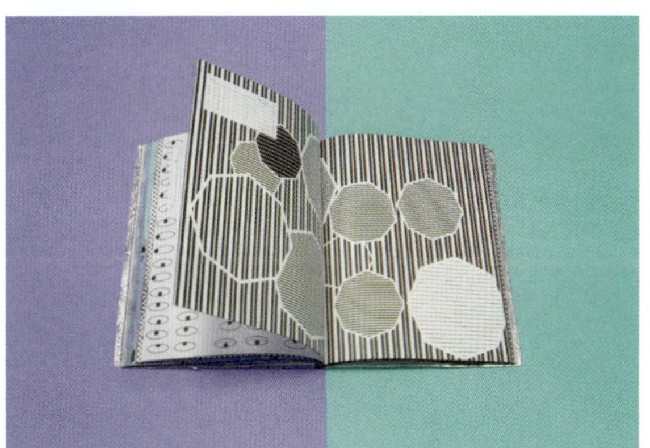

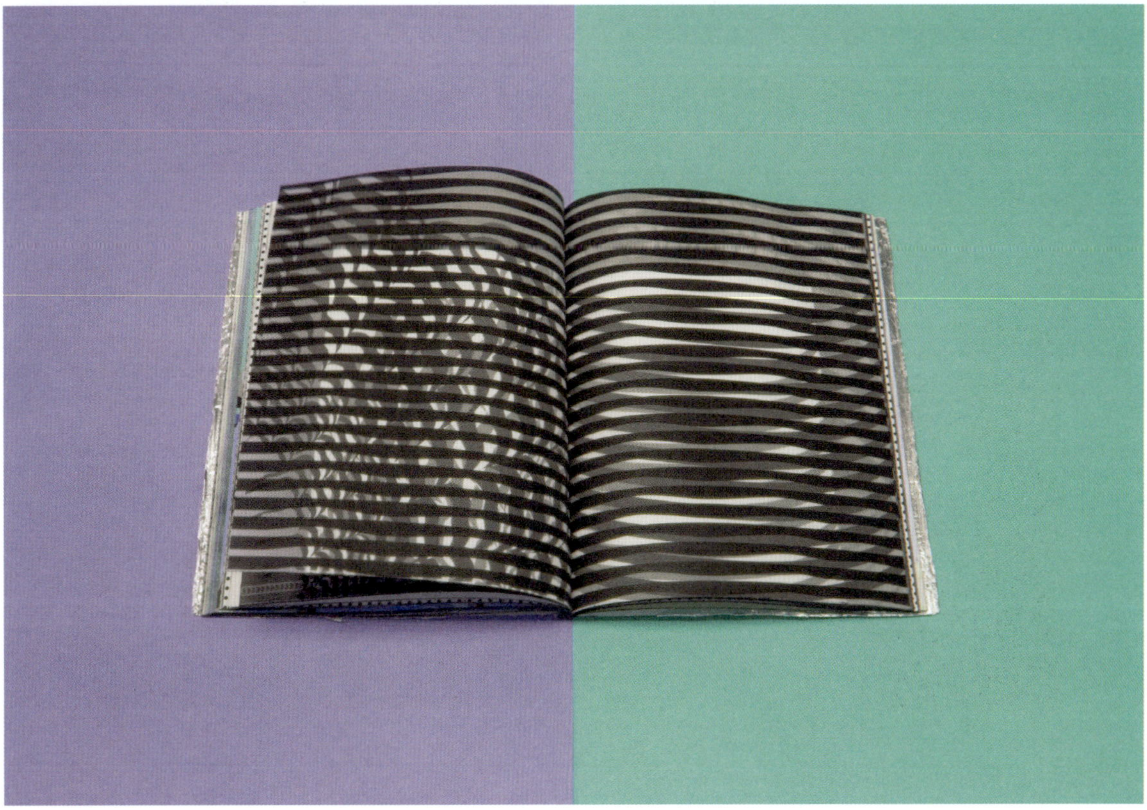

DON'T MAKE A SOUND

Designer : Shu Yu Tsai

"Don't Make a Sound" is a paradoxical and amusing name of this album. To correspond with this name, the designer reversed the shadow in the photograph of the cover. The shadow seems like holding talks with the singer, however, actually it cannot make a sound.

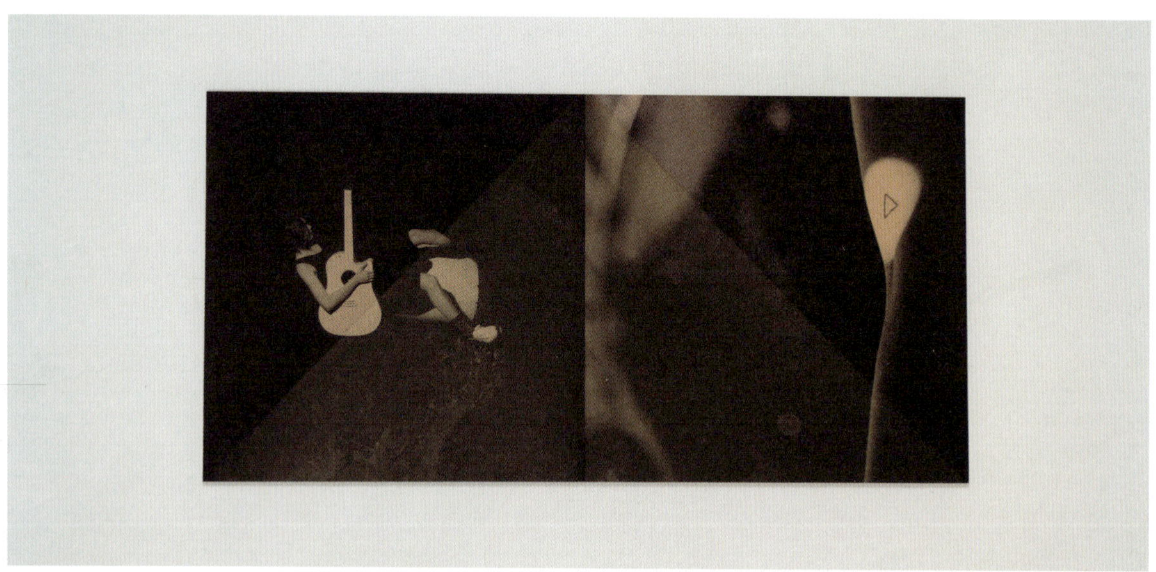

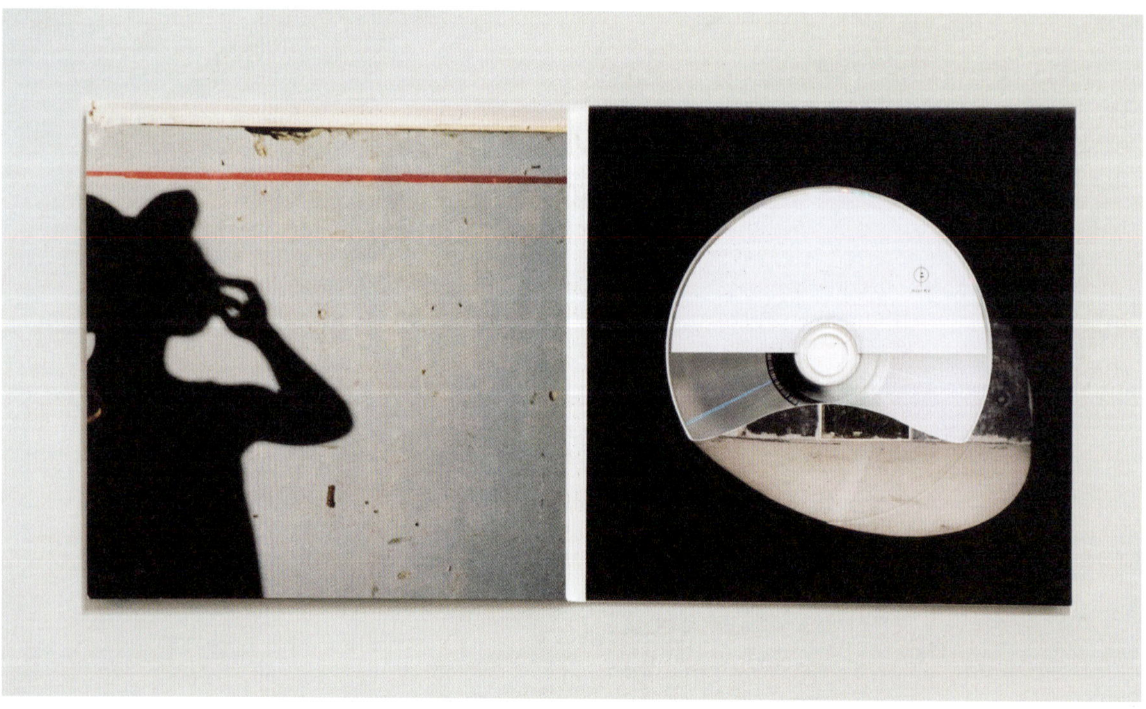

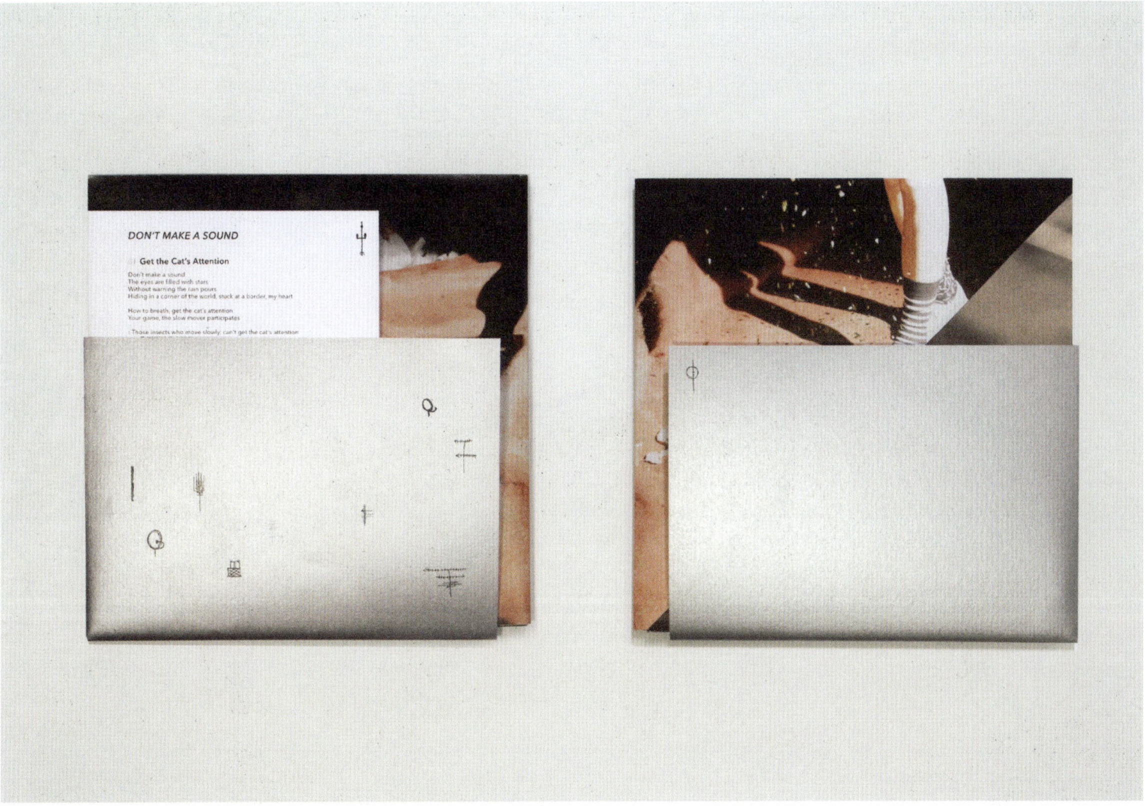

DON'T MAKE A SOUND
Get the Cat's Attention
Don't make a sound
The eyes are filled with stars
Without warning the rain pours
Hiding in a corner of the world, stuck at a border, my heart
How to breath, get the cat's attention
Your game, the slow mover participates
Those insects who move slowly, can't get the cat's attention

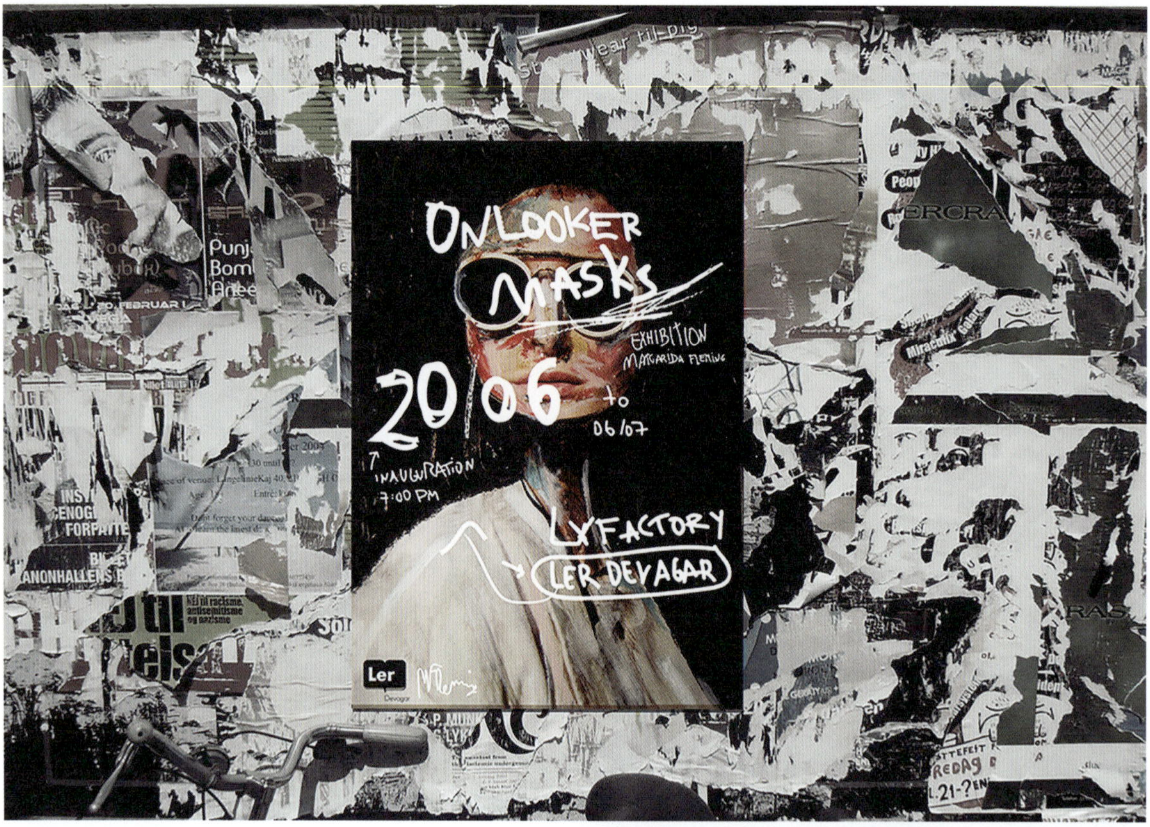

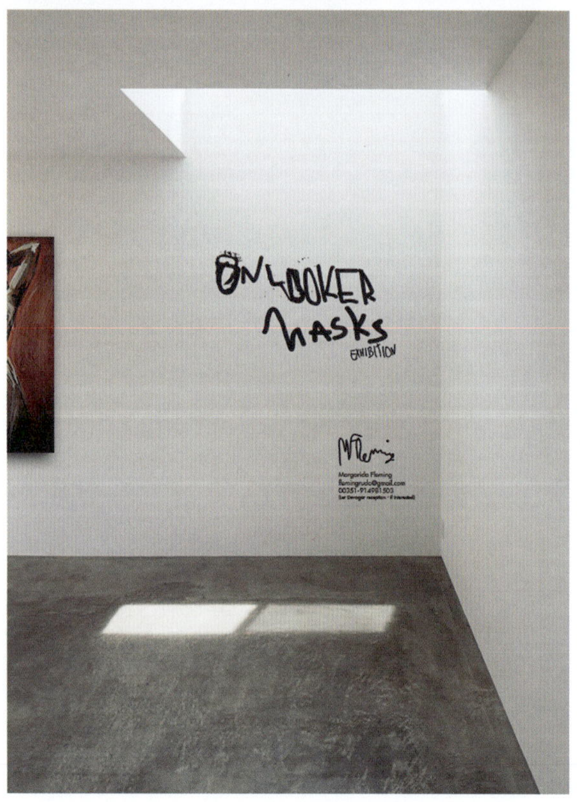

BRANDING EXHIBITION

Designer : Margarida Fleming

This work was designed for an individual painting exhibition of Margarida Fleming in Lisbon. The idea came from the painting style, which is very expressive and with fast brushstrokes.

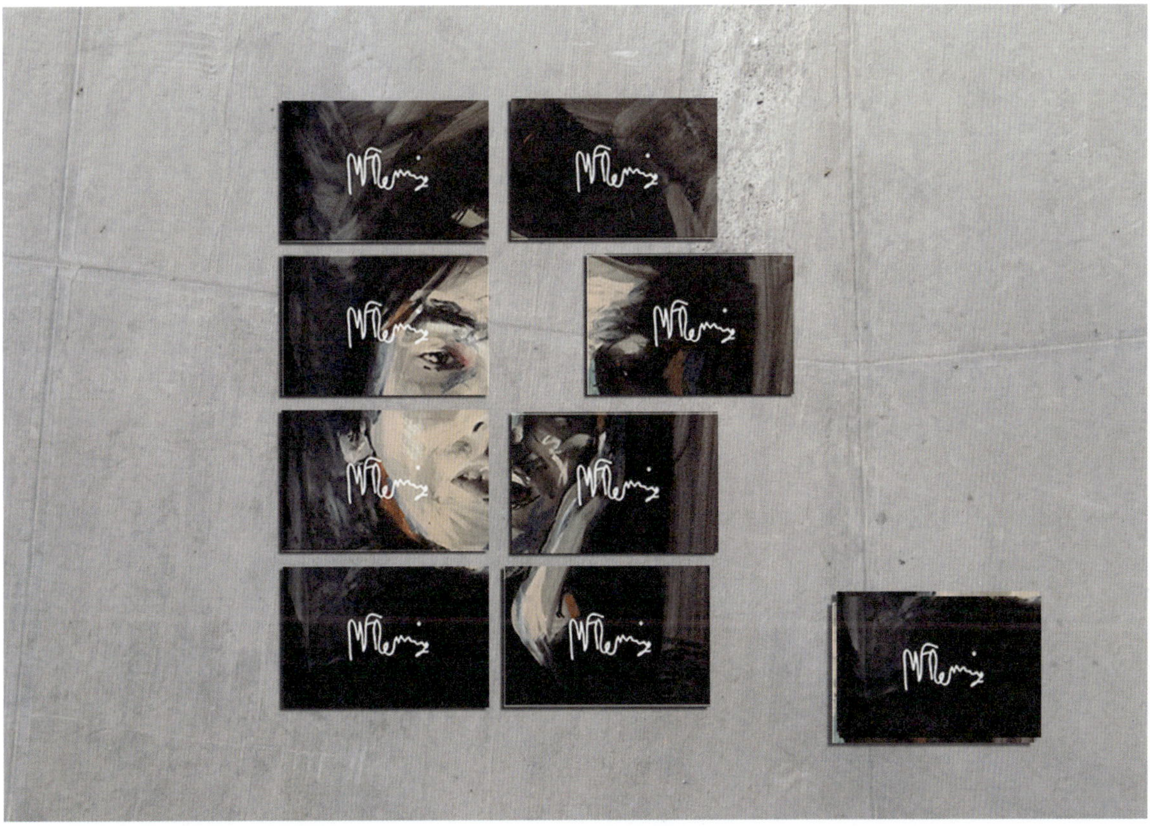

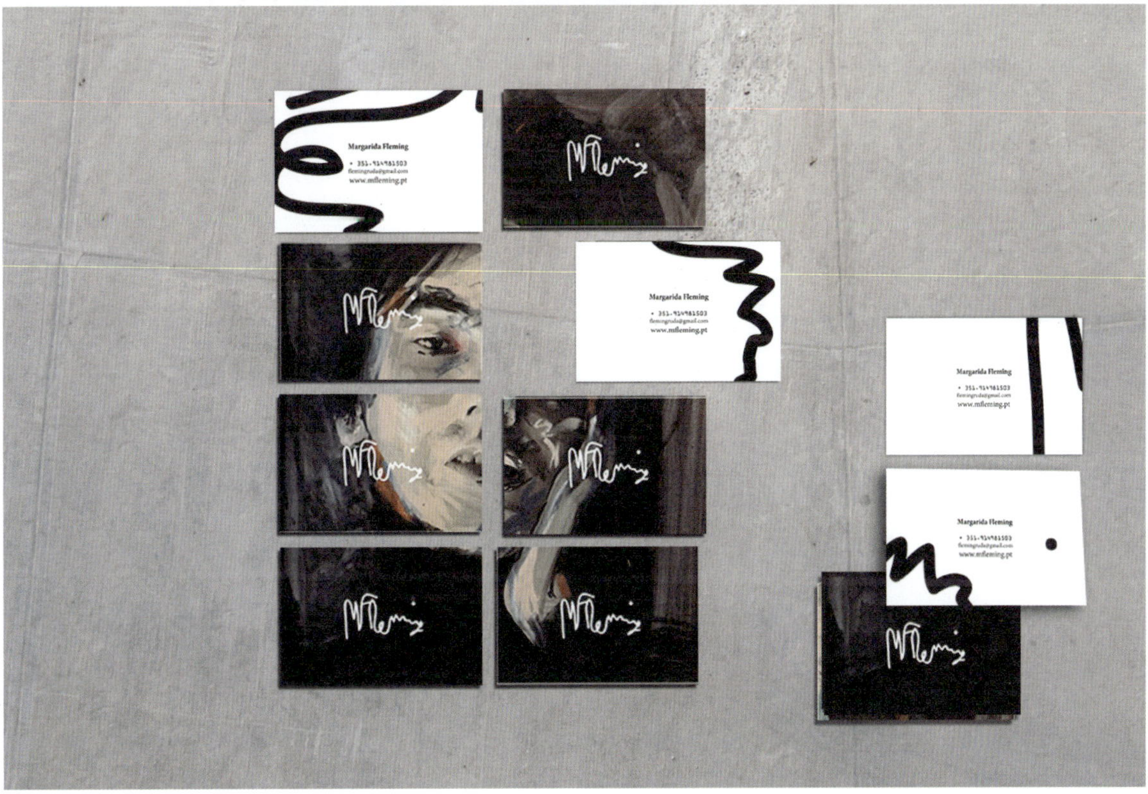

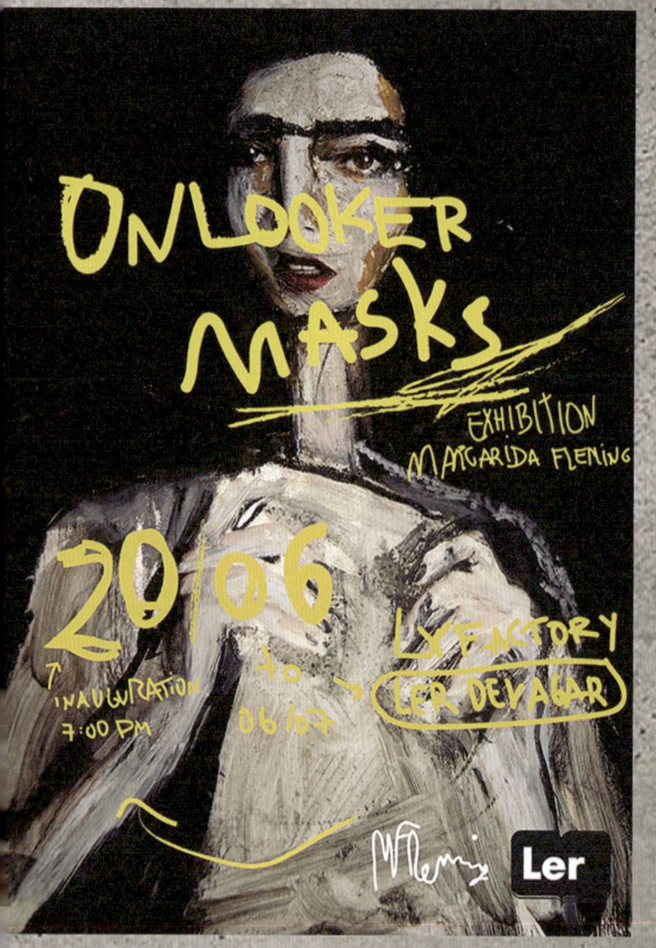
ONLOOKER
MASKS
EXHIBITION
MARGARIDA FLEMING
20/06
INAUGURATION
7:00 PM
to
06/07
LXFACTORY
LER DEVAGAR
Ler
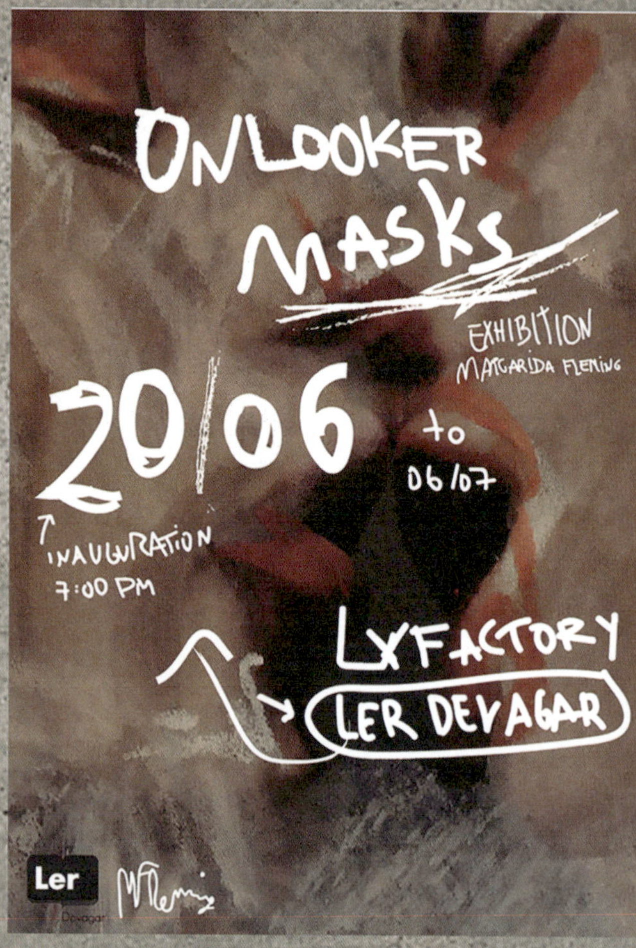
ONLOOKER
MASKS
EXHIBITION
MARGARIDA FLEMING
20/06
to
06/07
INAUGURATION
7:00 PM
LXFACTORY
LER DEVAGAR
Ler
Devagar

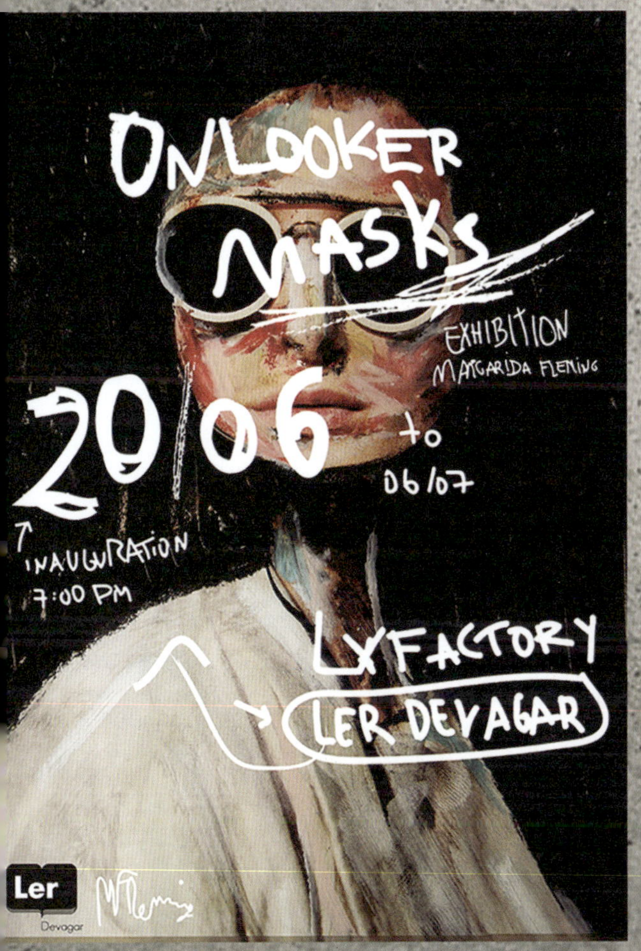
ONLOOKER
MASKS
EXHIBITION
MARGARIDA FLEMING
20/06 to 06/07
INAUGURATION
7:00 PM
LXFACTORY
LER DEVAGAR
Ler
Devagar

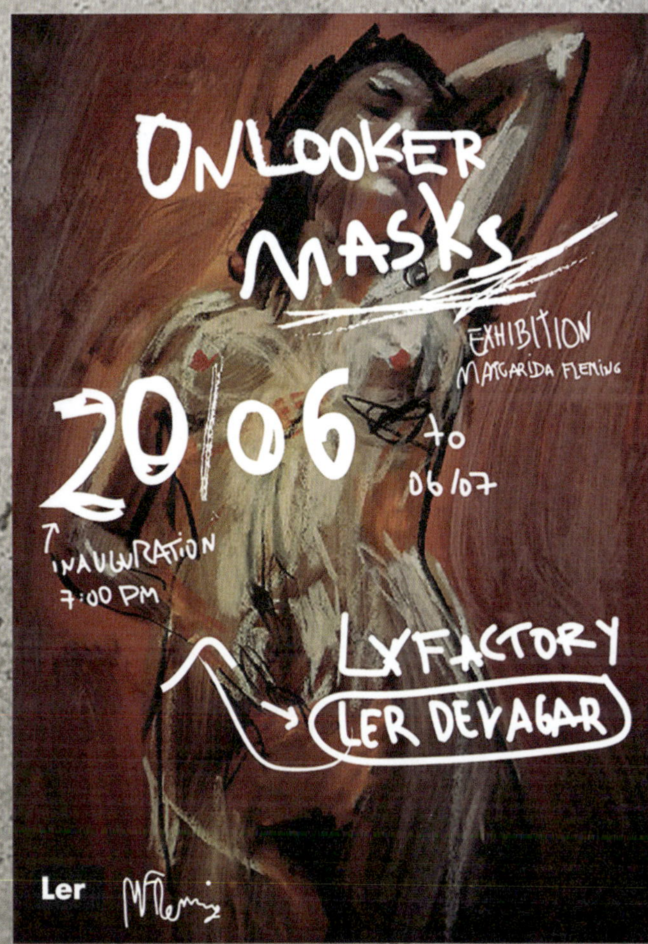
ONLOOKER
MASKS
EXHIBITION
MARGARIDA FLEMING
20/06 to 06/07
INAUGURATION
7:00 PM
LXFACTORY
LER DEVAGAR
Ler

CICLO DE CINEMA DAVID FINCHER

Designer : João Fonseca

One of the main features of director David Fincher's films is obscurity and this is used as the basic concept of the project. To represent this feature, the designer uses black ink spots and calligraphy.

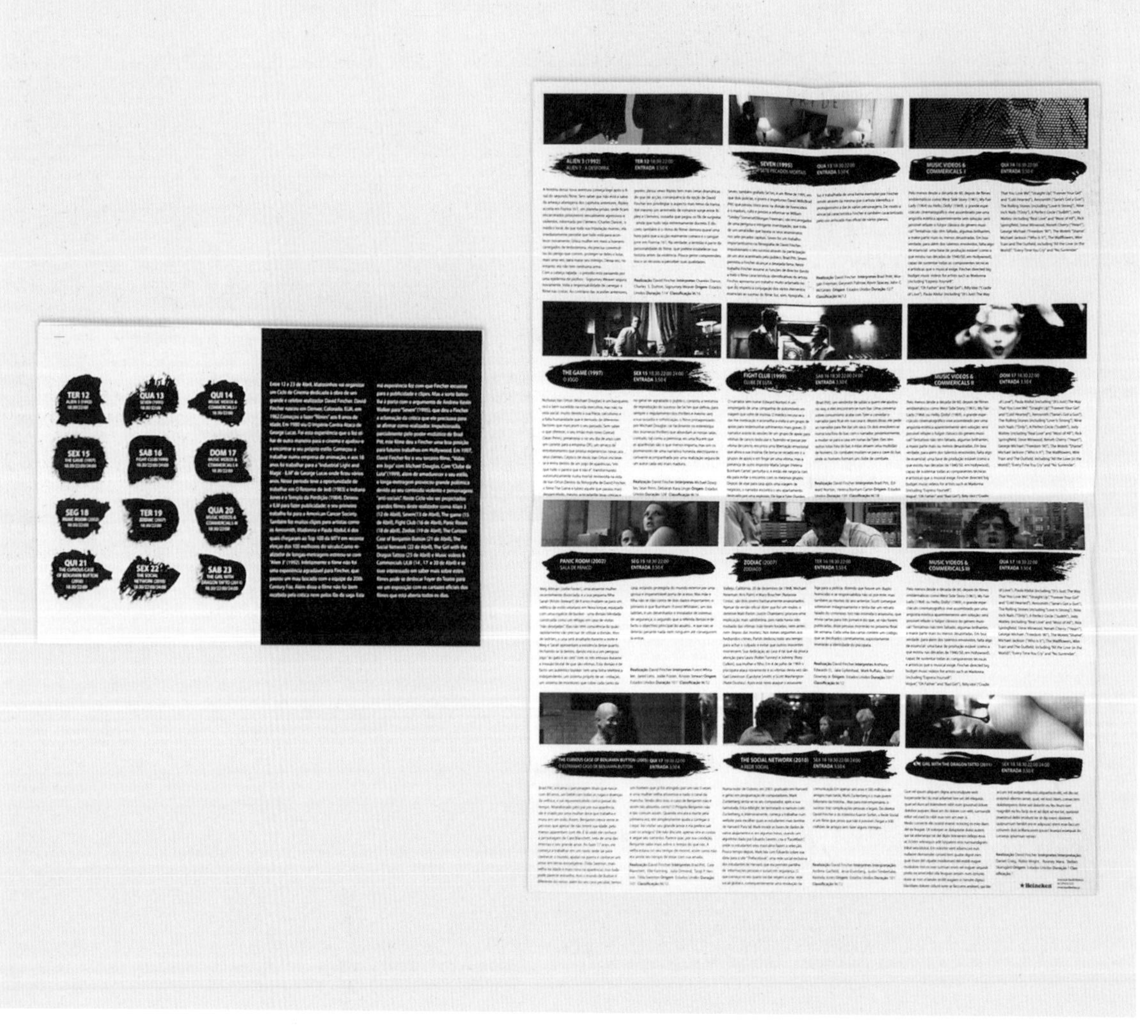

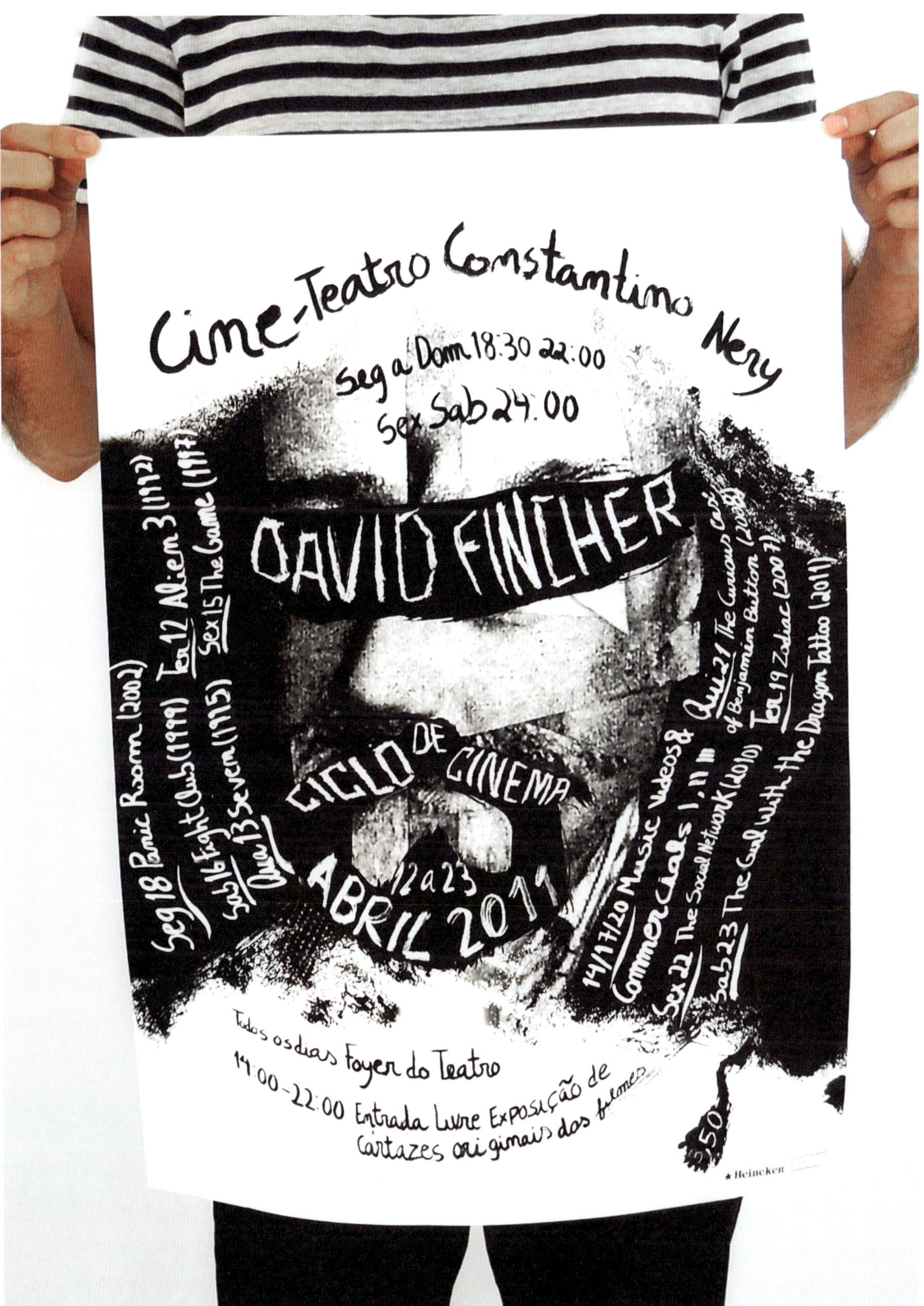

Cine-Teatro Constantino Nery
Seg a Dom 18:30 22:00
Sex Sab 24:00
DAVID FINCHER
CICLO DE CINEMA
12 a 23
ABRIL 2011
Seg 18 Panic Room (2002)
Ter 12 Alien 3 (1992)
Sab 16 Fight Club (1999)
Sex 15 The Game (1997)
Qua 13 Seven (1995)
Qui 21 The Curious Case of Benjamin Button (2008)
Ter 19 Zodiac (2007)
14/17/20 Music Videos & Commercials
Sex 22 The Social Network (2010)
Sab 23 The Girl with the Dragon Tattoo (2011)
Todos os dias Foyer do Teatro
14:00-22:00 Entrada Livre Exposição de Cartazes originais dos filmes
Heineken

LEAP DIALOGUES

Designer : TwoPoints.Net

LEAP Dialogues is a first of its kind book that explores new career pathways in social innovation for designers, with contributions from 84 thought-leaders from across disciplines and sectors. These contributors encompass critical and diverse points of view, stories and experiences about key issues direct from the field, creating a multilayered picture of how this field is being shaped.

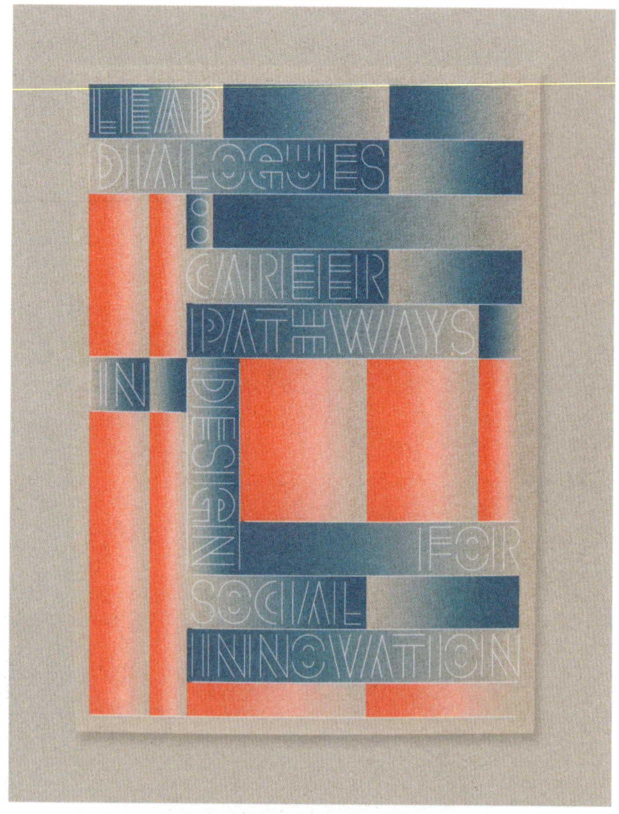

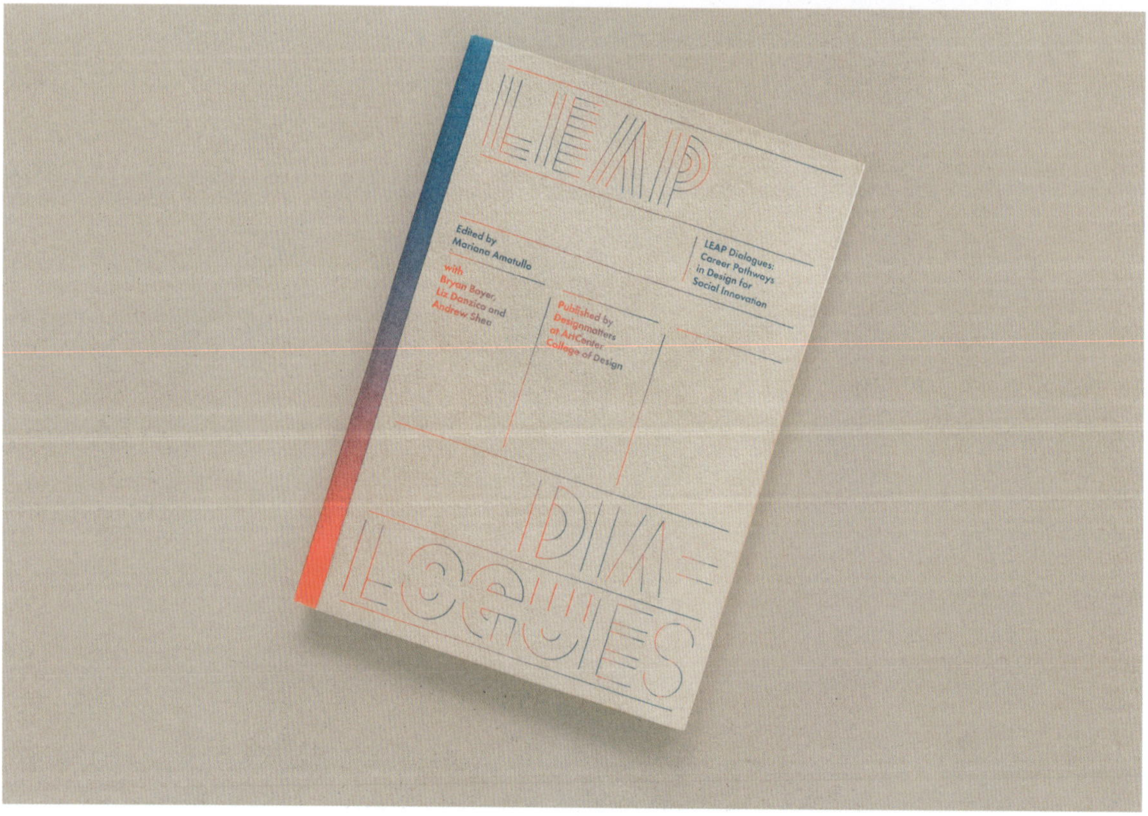

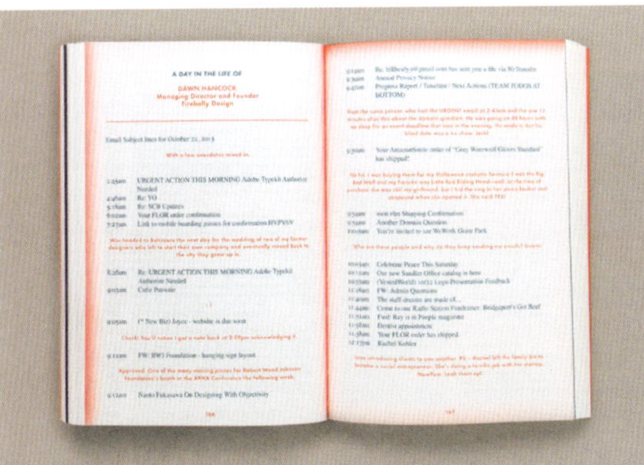

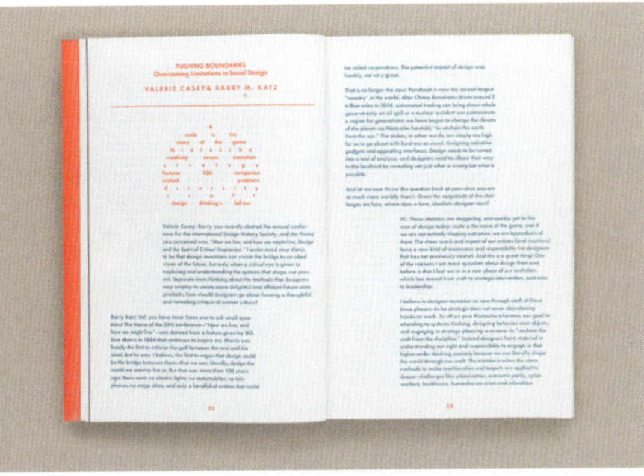

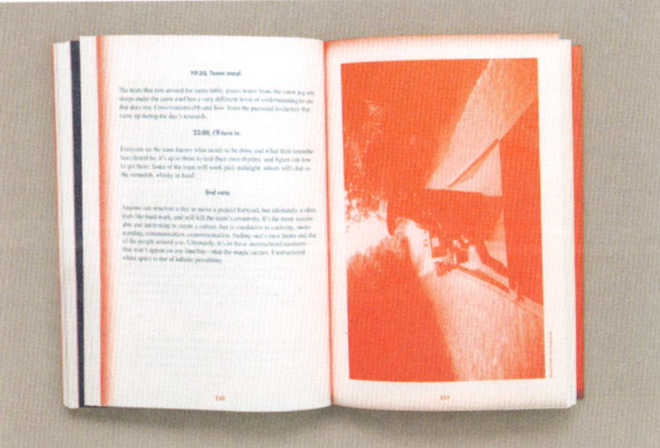

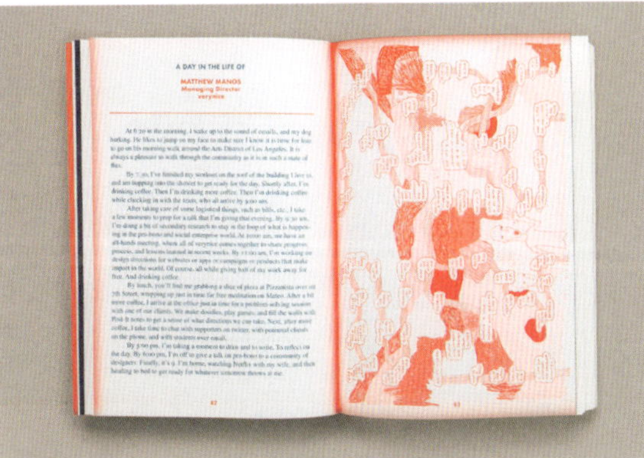

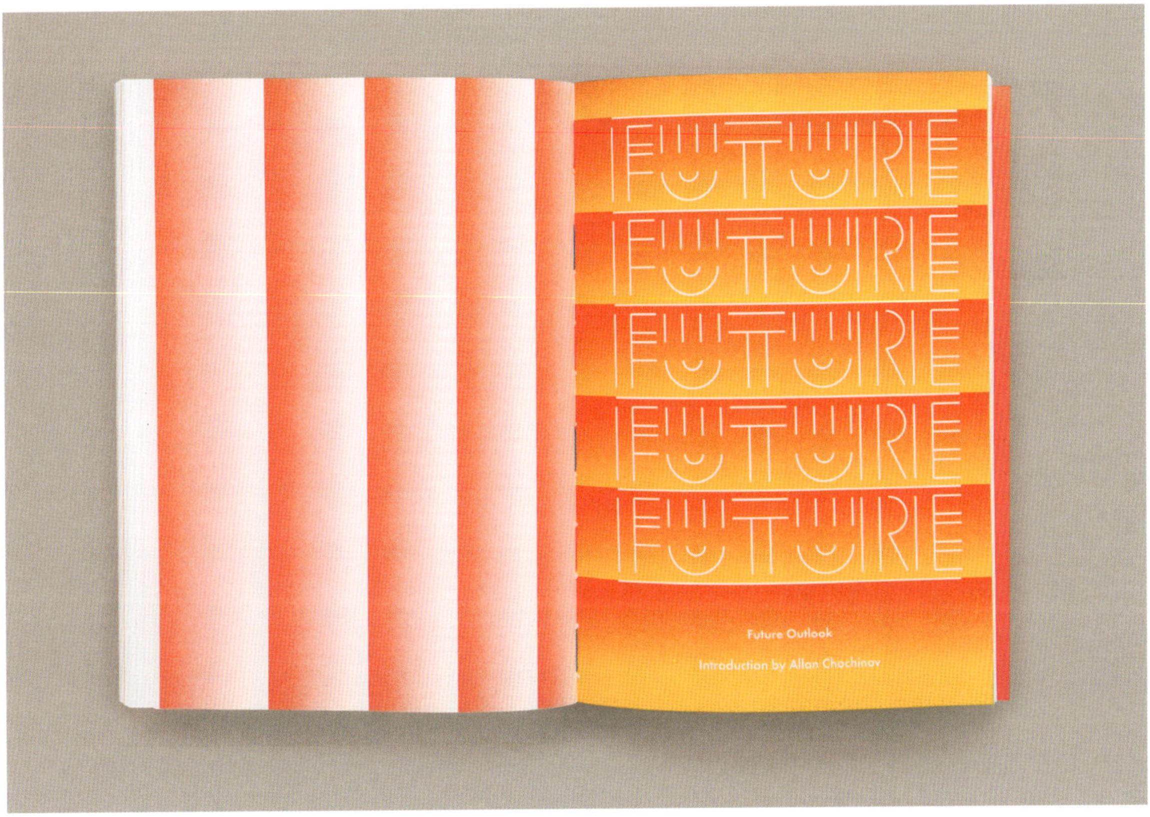

FUTURE
FUTURE
FUTURE
FUTURE
FUTURE

Future Outlook

Introduction by Allan Chochinov

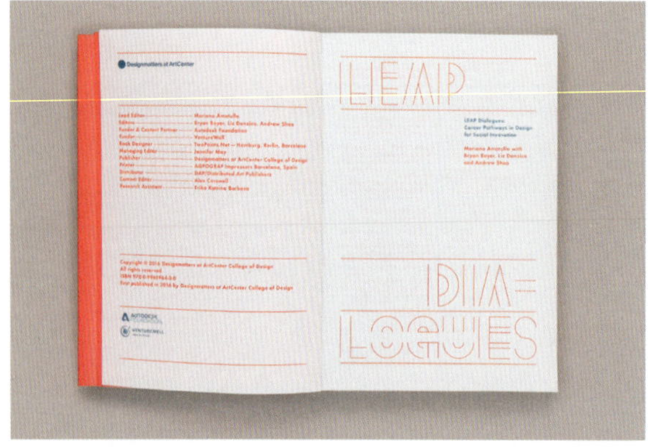
LEAP
DIA-
LOGUES

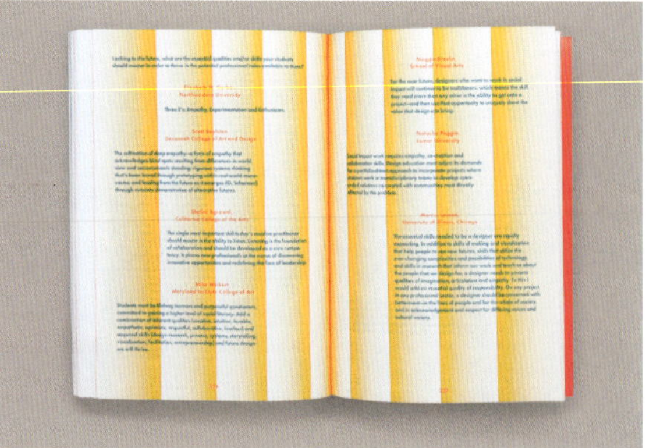

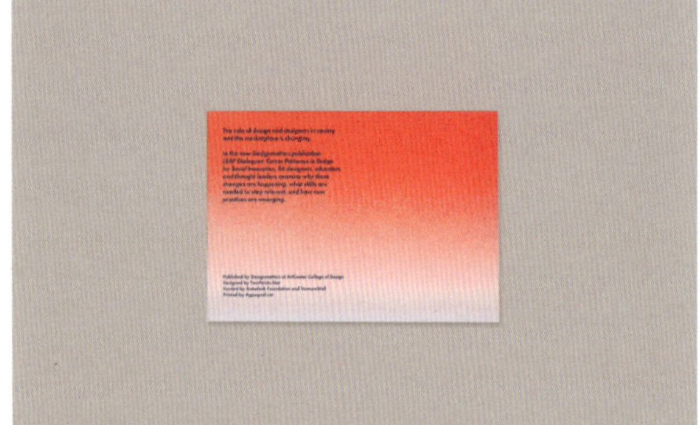

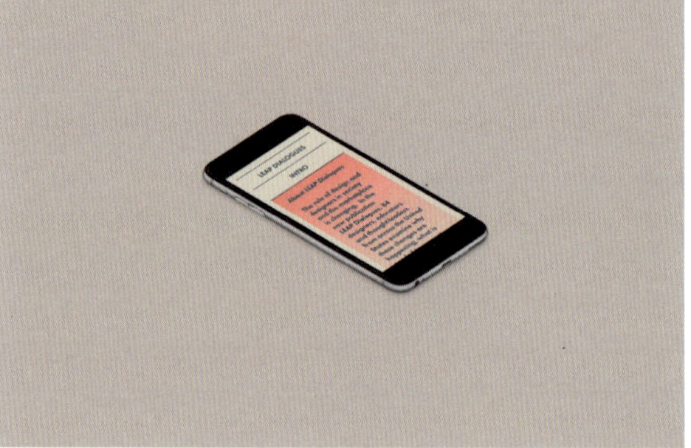

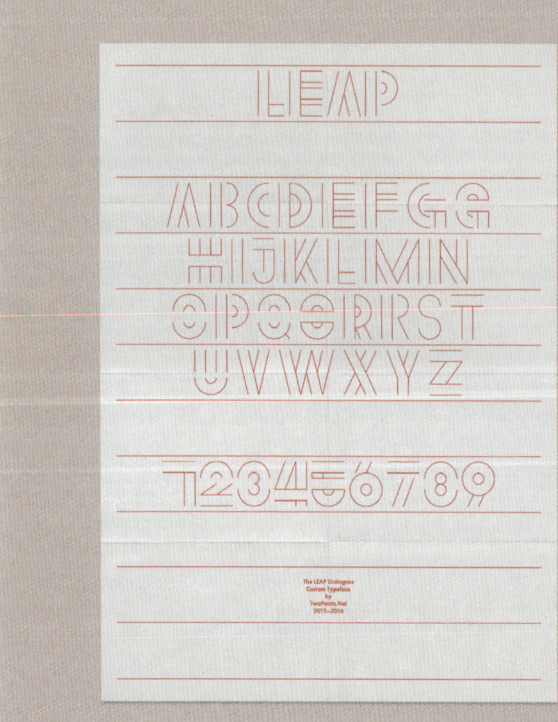
LEAP
ABCDEFGG
HIJKLMN
OPQQRRST
UVWXYZ
123456789
The LEAP Dialogues
Custom Typeface
by
TwoPoints.Net
2015–2016

WHY WHAT
WHY WHAT
WHY WHAT
WHY WHAT
WHY WHAT
HOW FUTURE
HOW FUTURE
HOW FUTURE
HOW FUTURE
HOW FUTURE

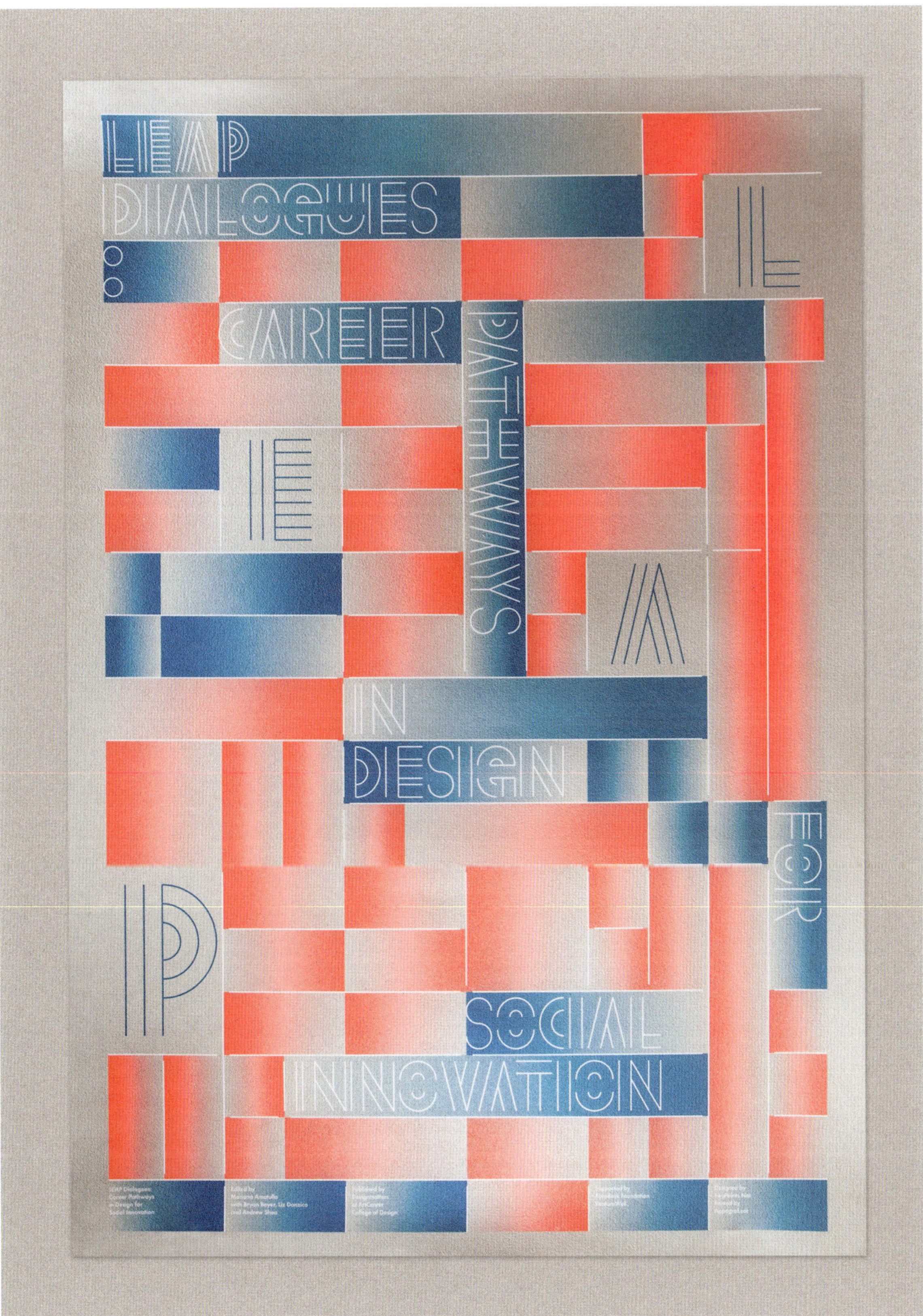
LEAP
DIALOGUES
:
CAREER
PATHWAYS
IN
DESIGN
FOR
SOCIAL
INNOVATION
Edited by
Mariana Amatullo
with Bryan Boyer, Liz Danzico
and Andrew Shea
College of Design

NATIONAL MUSEUM OF MORDOVIA

Designer : Tatiana Egoshina

The identity system for the museum is based on a play with iconic patterns and typography sets. The pattern was inspired by a photo of a rug from the museum exhibition, which has a traditional design of Mordovia Republic. In this project, the designer combined the strong forms of Helvetica, Brush Script and Bodoni fonts to attain a contrast and a feeling of fabric. The words "text" and "textile" have the same Latin root, which means "to weave". This is an interesting aspect of turning the combination of lines on carpet into the typographic part of the identity.

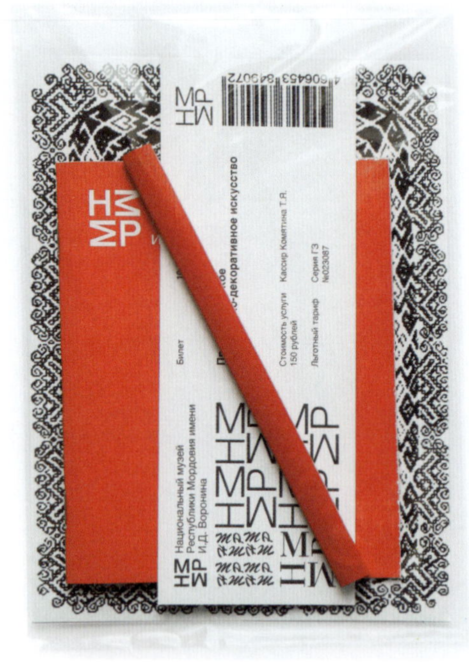

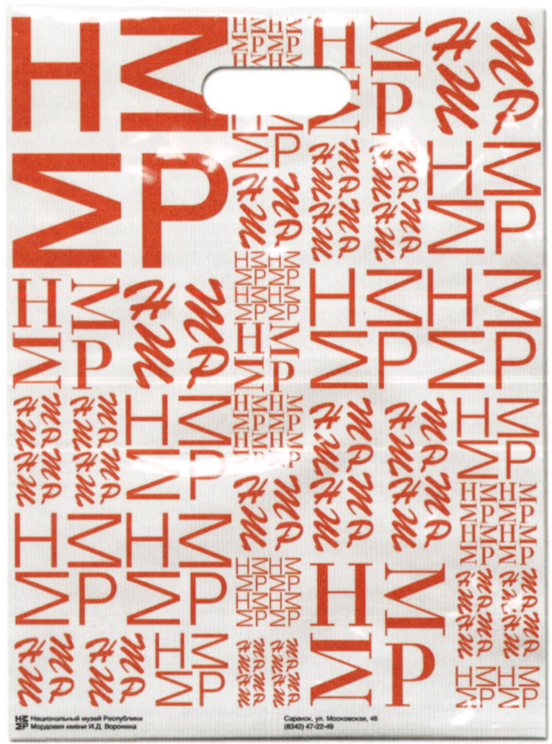

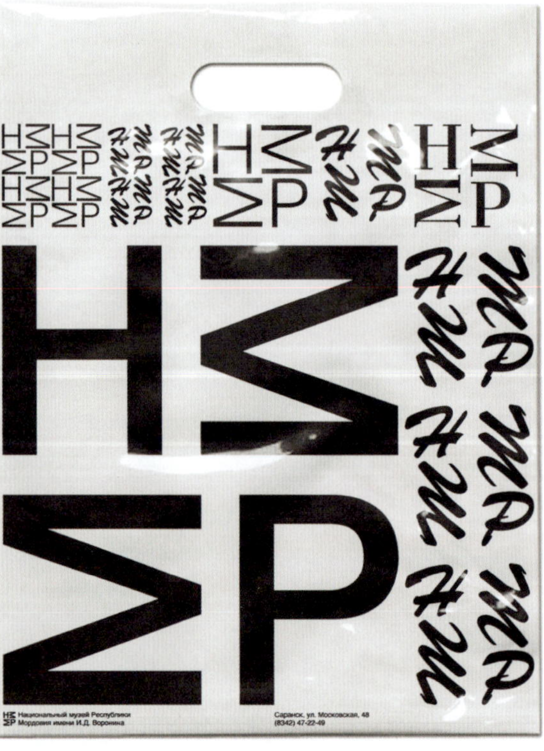

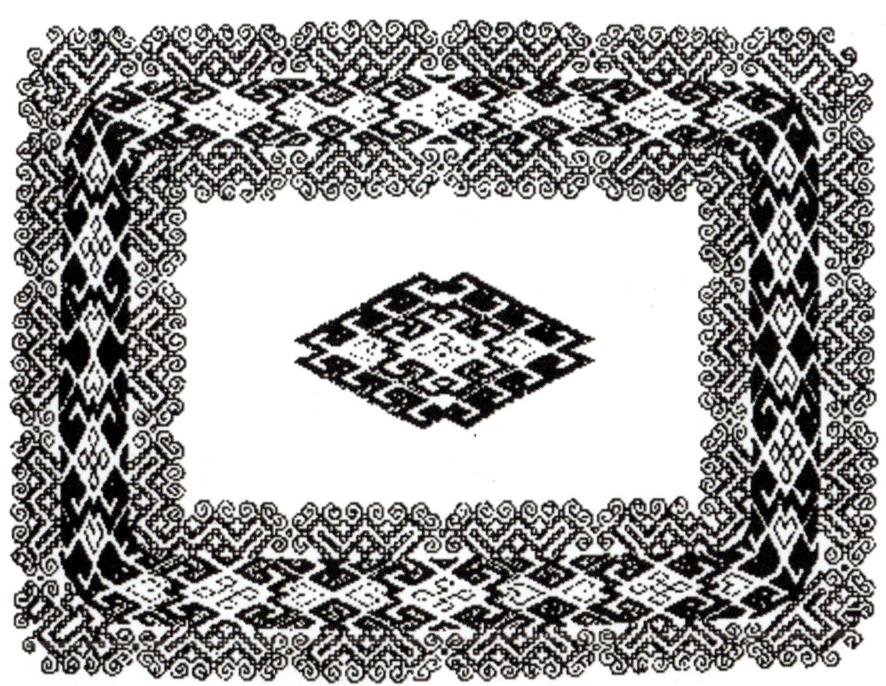

Национальный музей
Республики Мордовия
имени И.Д. Воронина

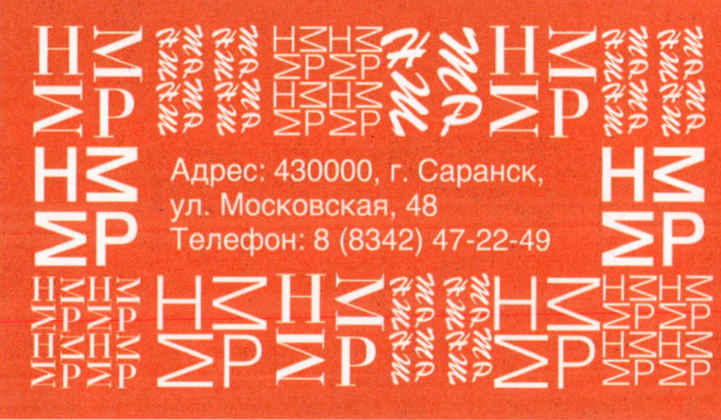
Адрес: 430000, г. Саранск,
ул. Московская, 48
Телефон: 8 (8342) 47-22-49

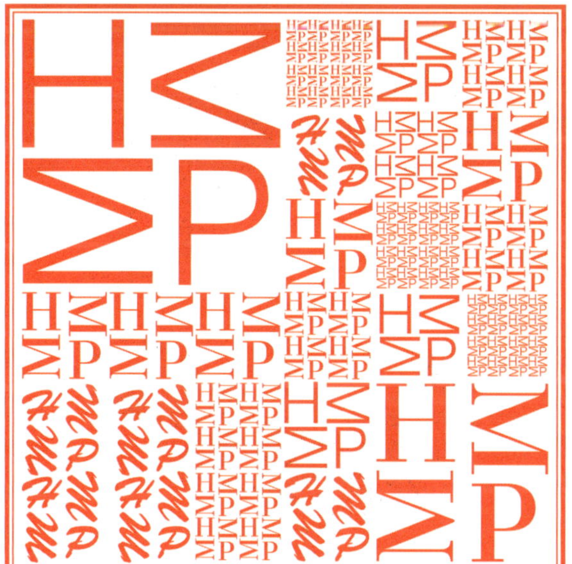

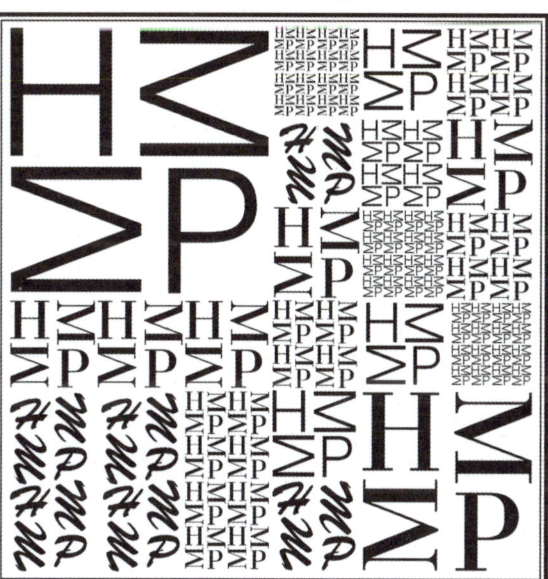

г. Саранск,
ул. Московская, 48
(8342) 47-22-49

Национальный
музей Республики
Мордовия имени
И.Д. Воронина

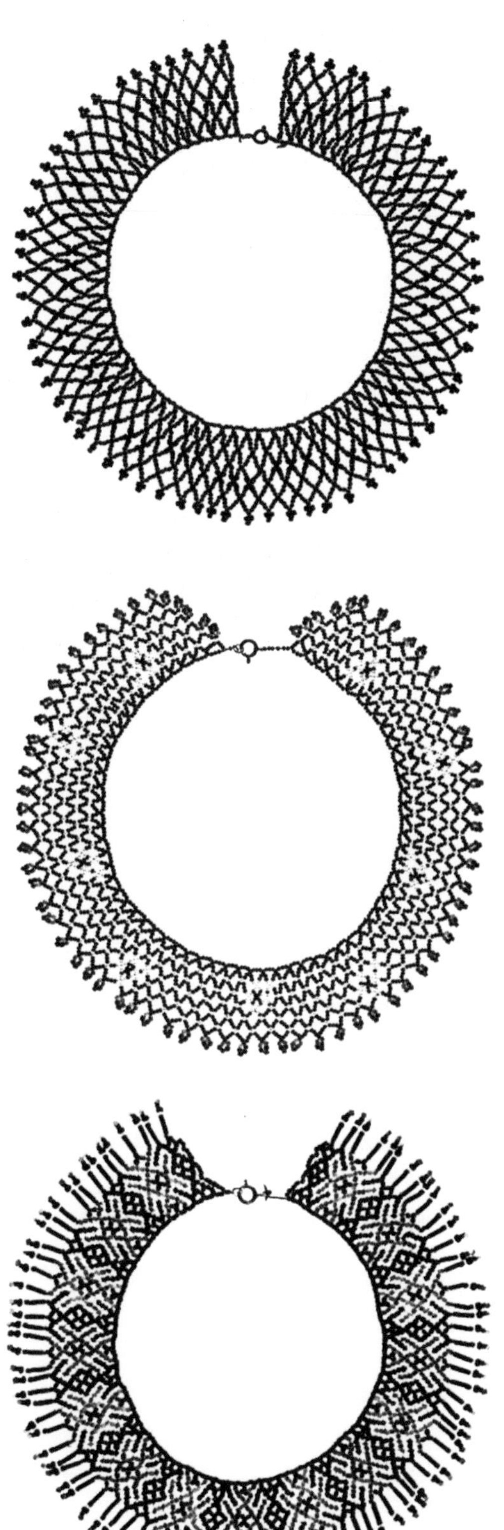

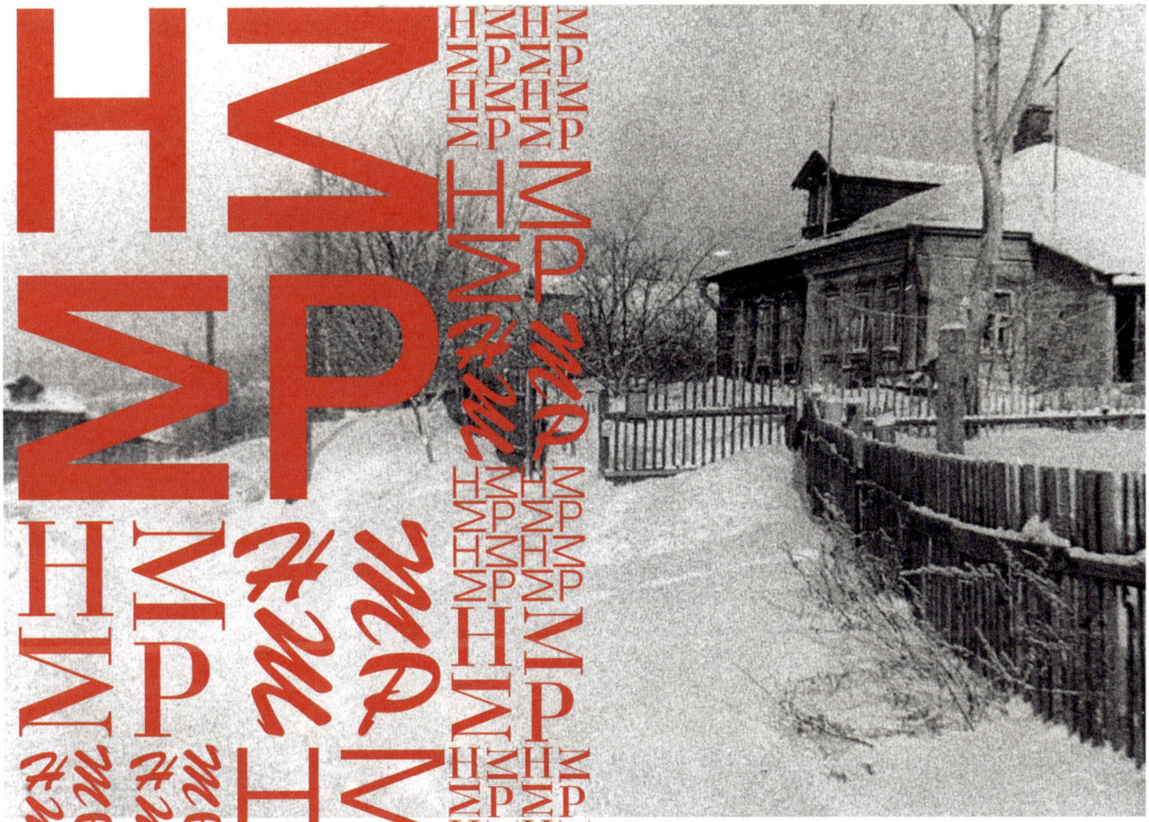

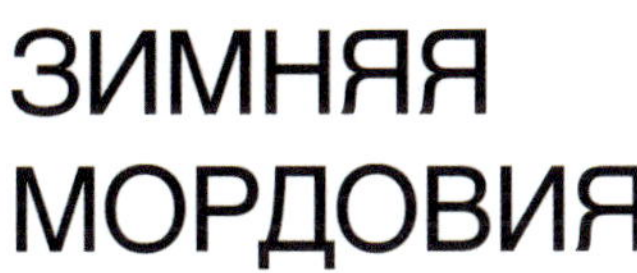

ЗИМНЯЯ МОРДОВИЯ

Выставка документальной фотографии местных фотохудожников

12.01-30.04.16

Режим работы:
10:00–18:00
Касса до 17:00
Понедельник – выходной

Адрес: Саранск, ул. Московская, 48
Телефон: (8342) 47-22-49

Национальный музей Республики Мордовия имени И.Д. Воронина

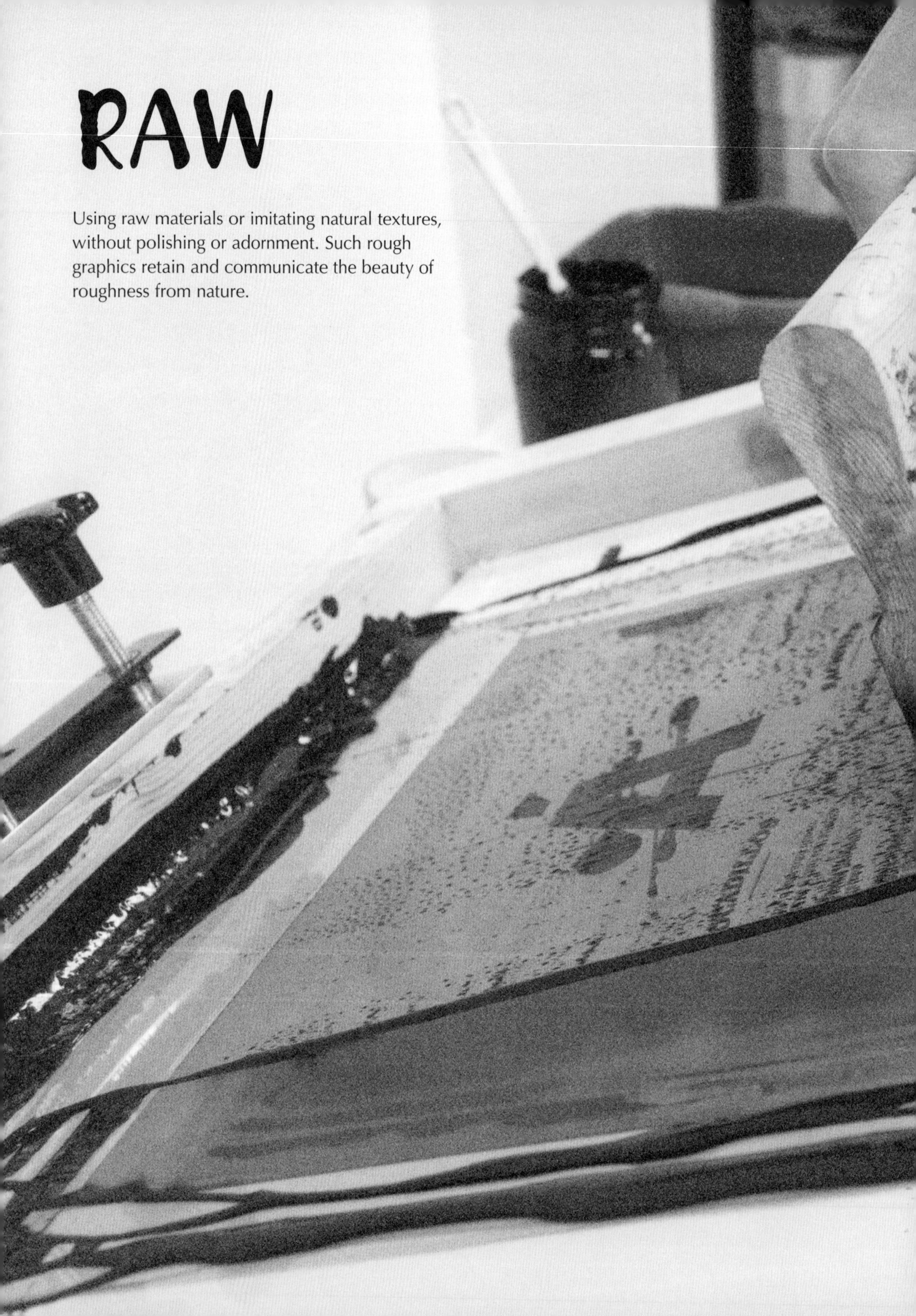

RAW

Using raw materials or imitating natural textures, without polishing or adornment. Such rough graphics retain and communicate the beauty of roughness from nature.

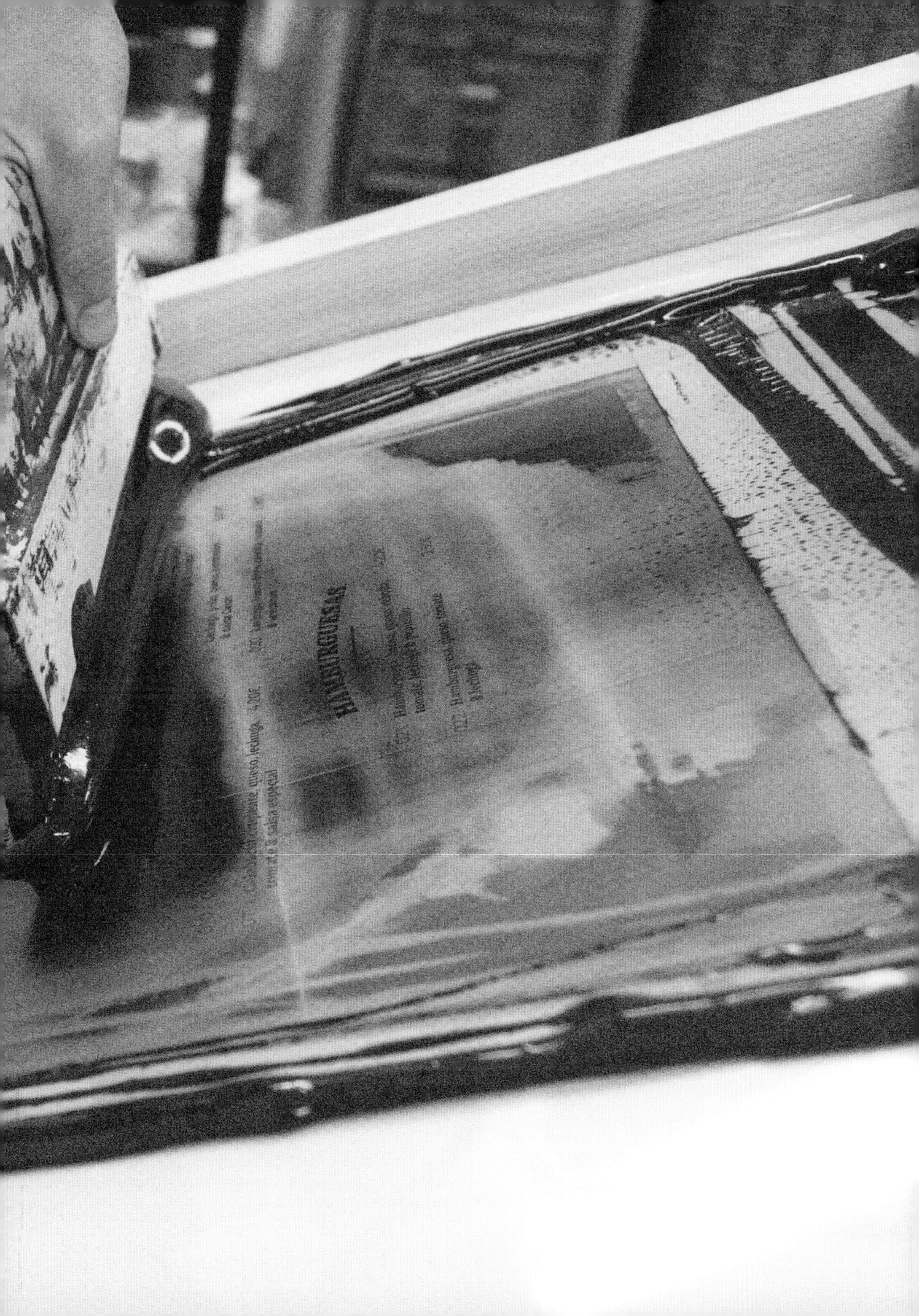
HAMBURGUESAS

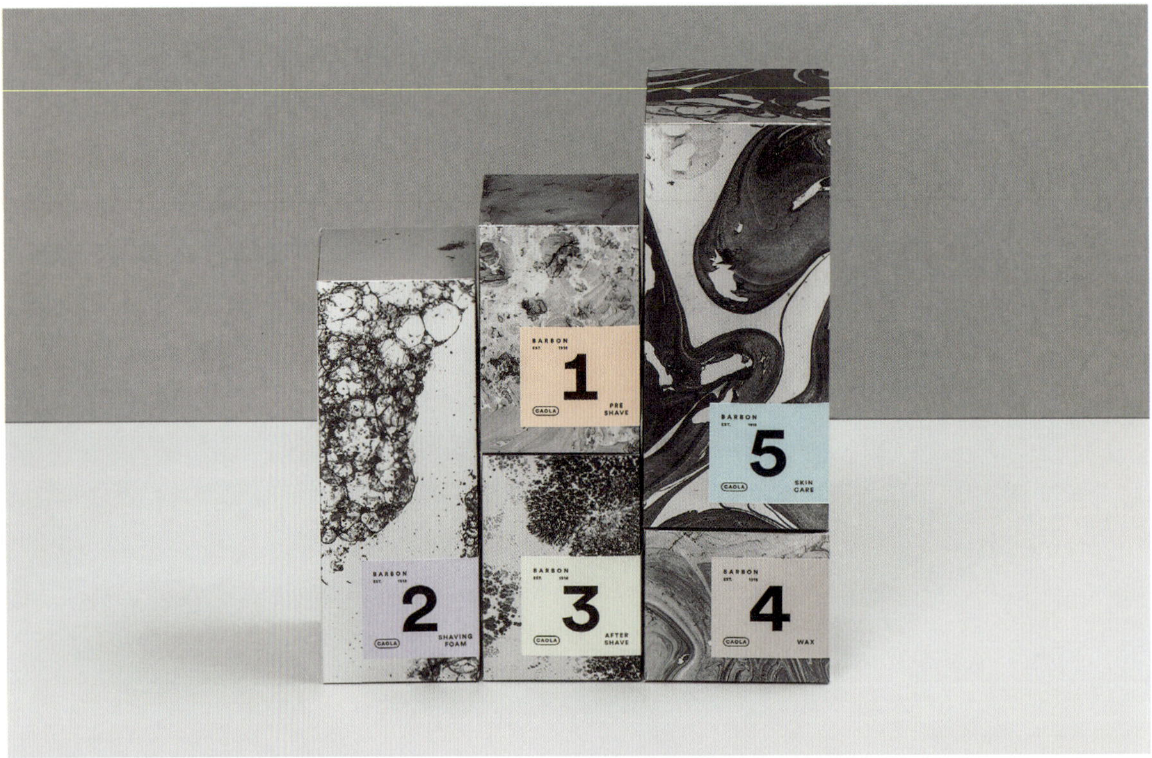
BARBON
1
PRE SHAVE
BARBON
2
SHAVING FOAM
BARBON
3
AFTER SHAVE
BARBON
4
WAX
BARBON
5
SKIN CARE

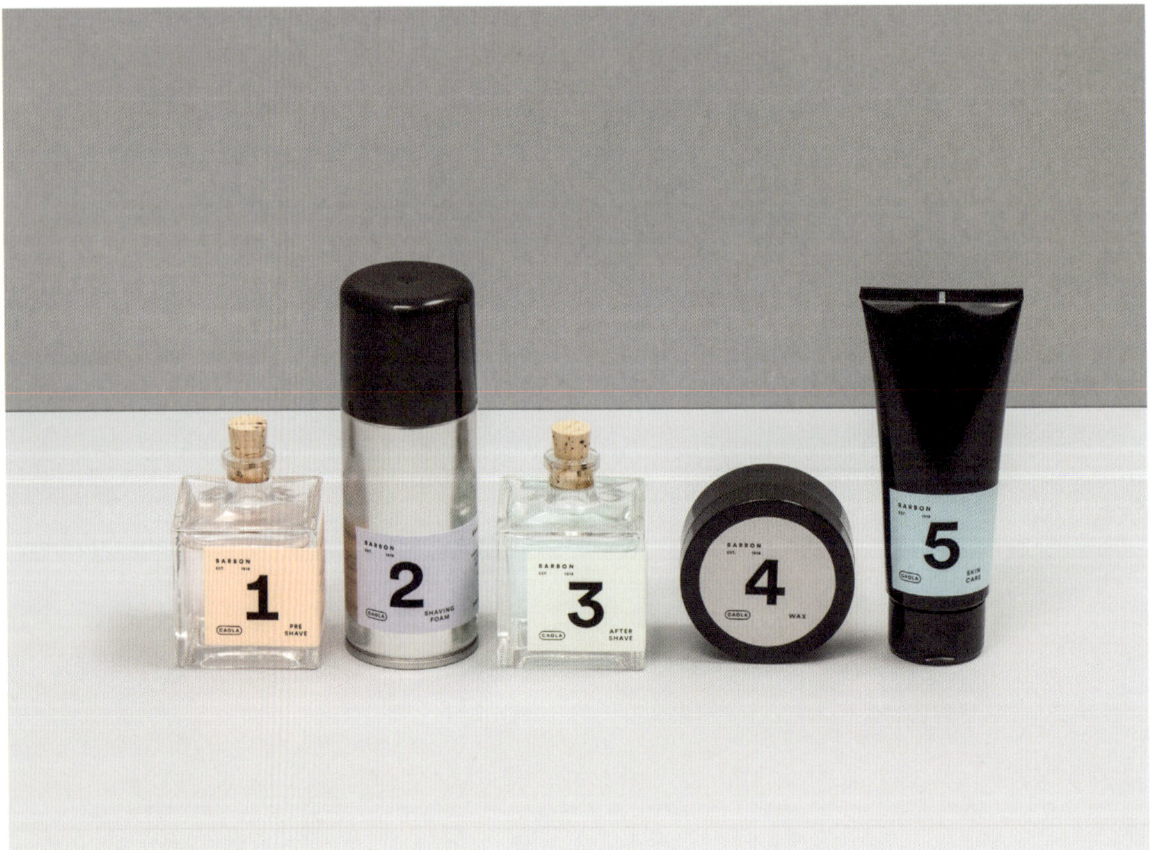
BARBON
1
PRE SHAVE
BARBON
2
SHAVING FOAM
BARBON
3
AFTER SHAVE
BARBON
4
WAX
BARBON
5
SKIN CARE

BARBON

Designer : Peltan-Brosz Roland

Barbon is Caola's range of products for men's shaving. The lineup consists of 5 cosmetic products, all of which are numbered and distinguished by pastel colors and patterns that suggest the content and purpose.

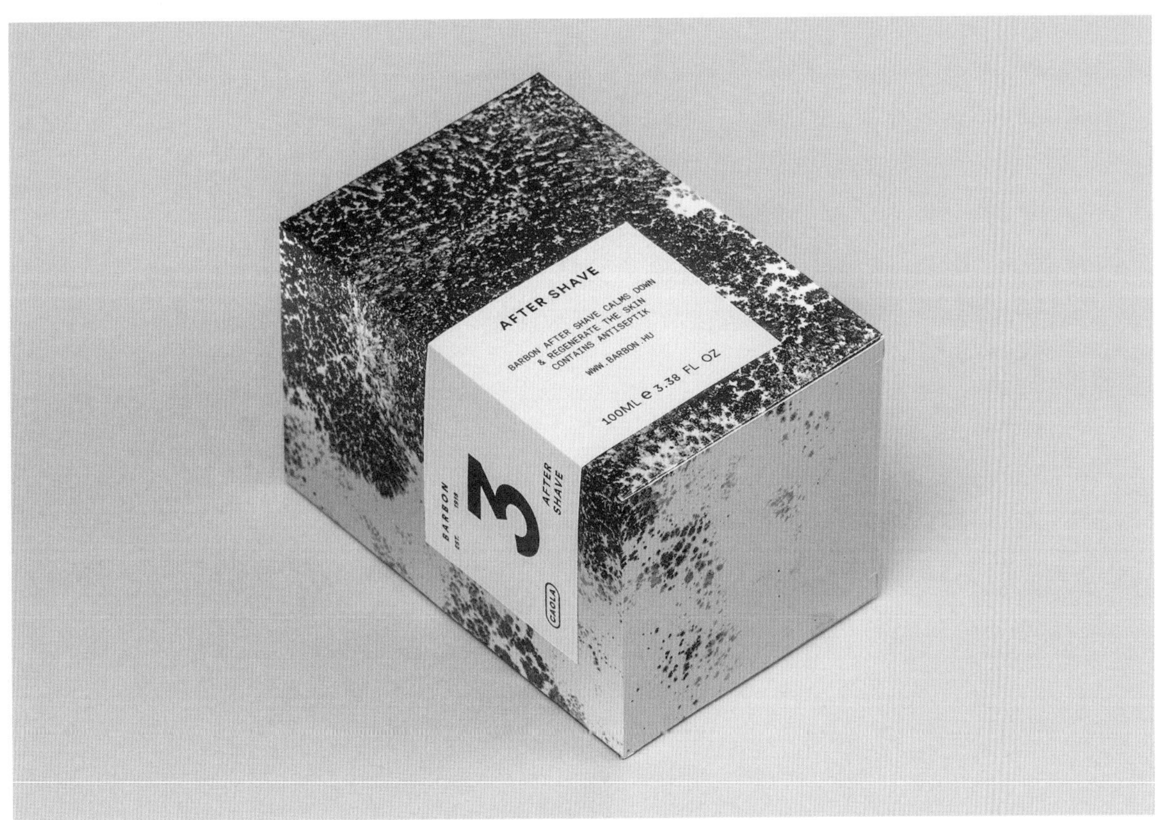

As a kind of visual experience, what do you think about the "roughness" in graphic design?

I think that in graphic design the approach to the "rough" concept can be a very creative and progressive experience. Take a frequently used font for example, you altering it based on your own perception as a graphic designer is a "rough" action, bold and courageous. I think that the "rough" effect is about the attitude that you want to take in graphics as well as the techniques outside the digital area. To be progressive in this field is all about taking courageous idea and pushing it with confidence.

What are your common approaches to produce a "rough" visual effect?

My vision as a graphic designer is based on the concept of timeless design. In my work "rough" is present in the usage of texture, manual technique and mediums outside the digital area. I often feel bold in my work and that is when the "roughness" and the energy is channeled in a creative way that complements the refined details. "Roughness" is also the base of the logos that I create, an unambiguous central element that is surrounded by the more polished details.

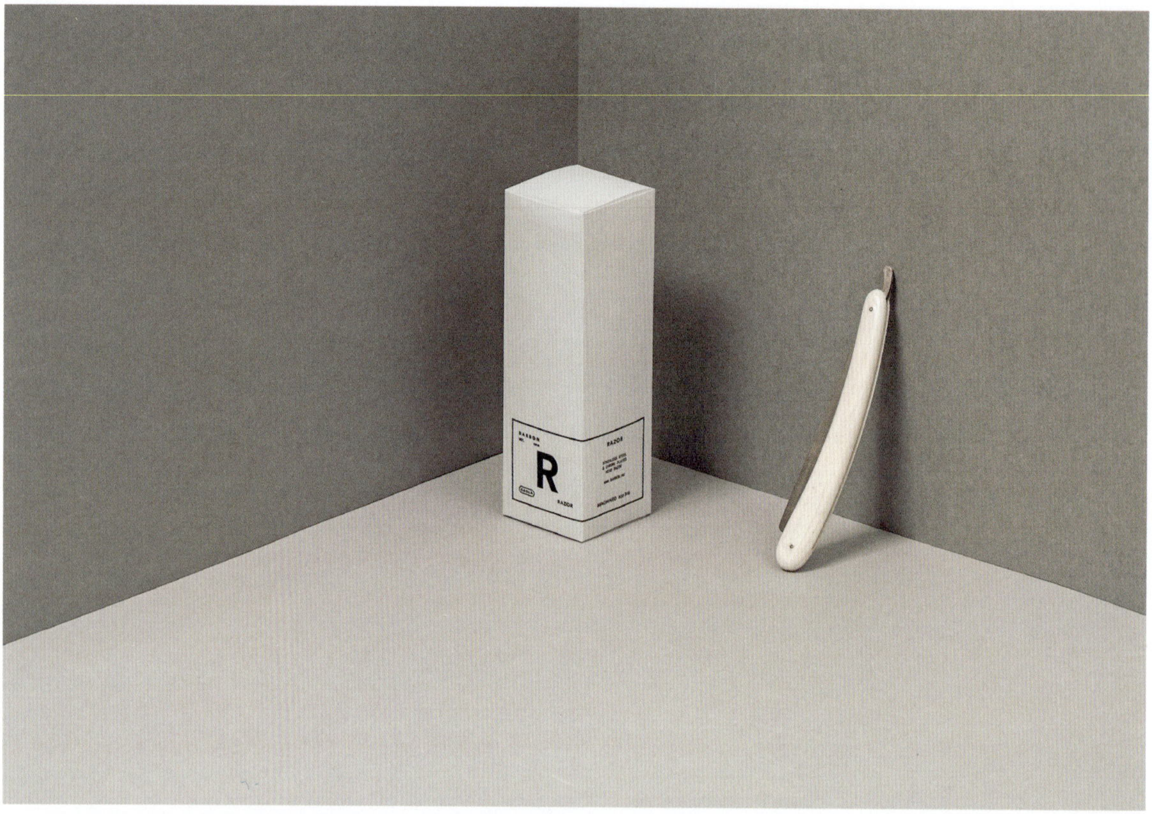
BARBON
R
RAZOR
RAZOR

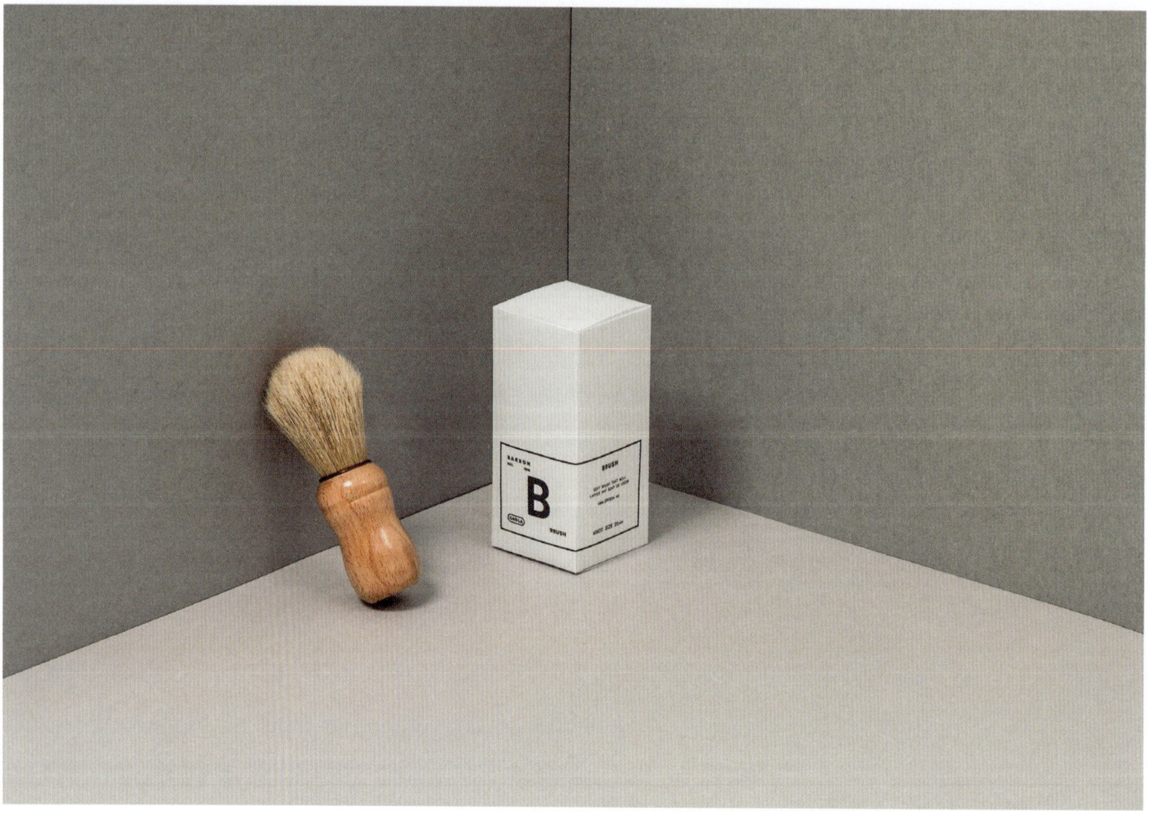
BARBON
B
BRUSH
BRUSH

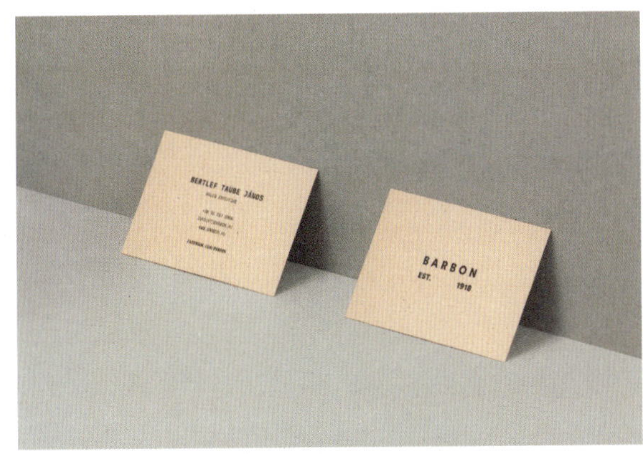
BARBON
EST. 1918

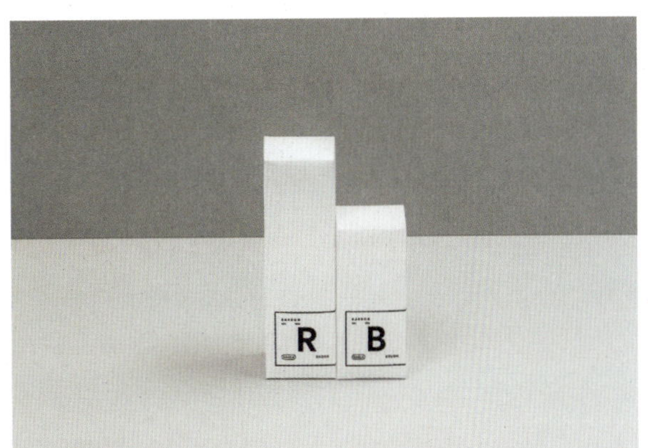
R
B

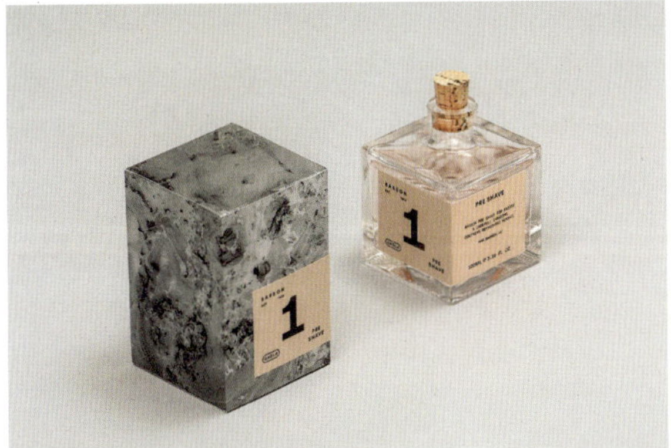
1
PRE SHAVE

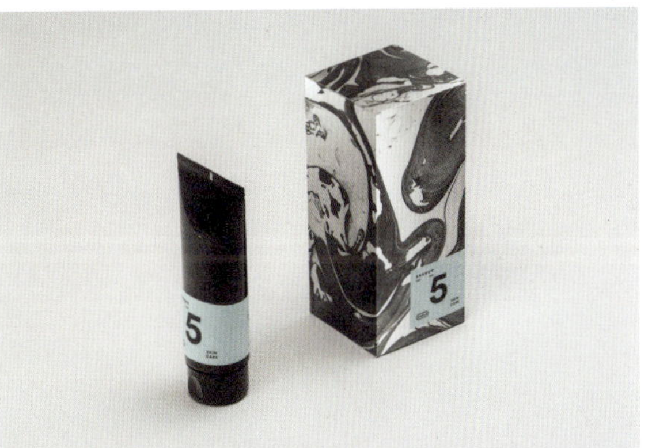
5

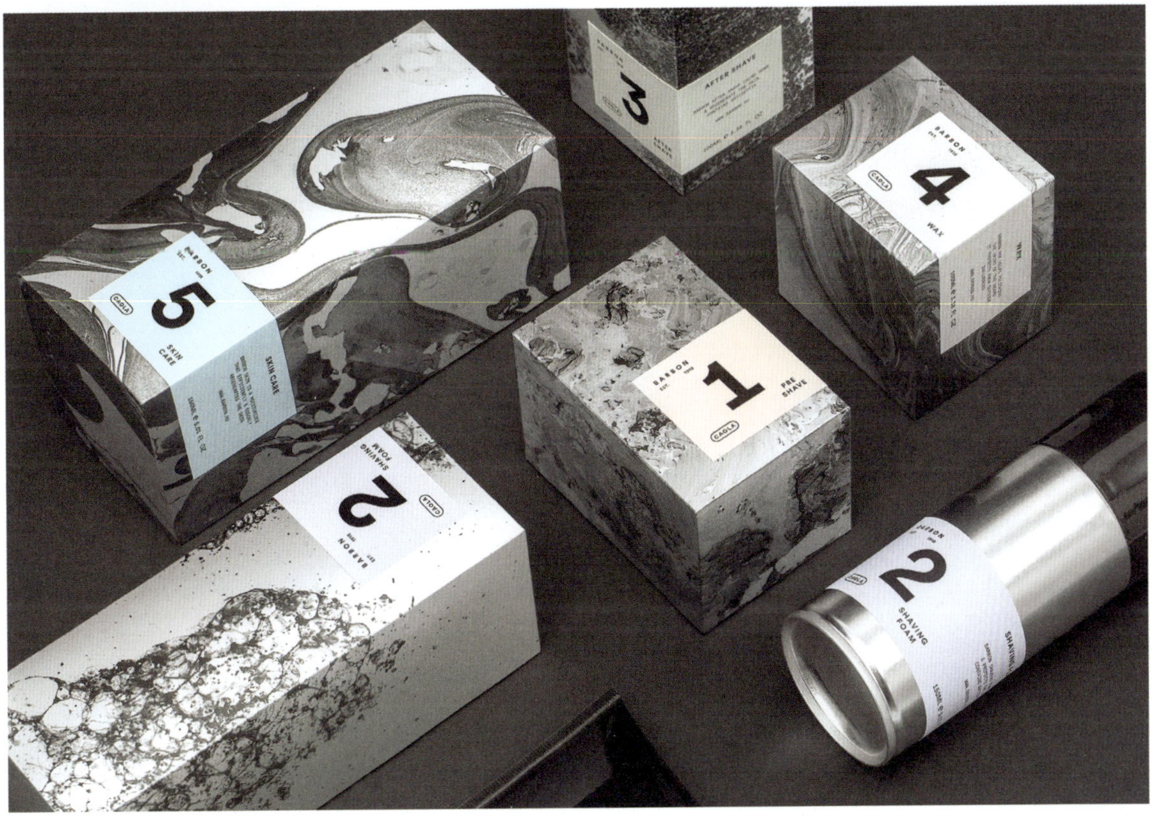

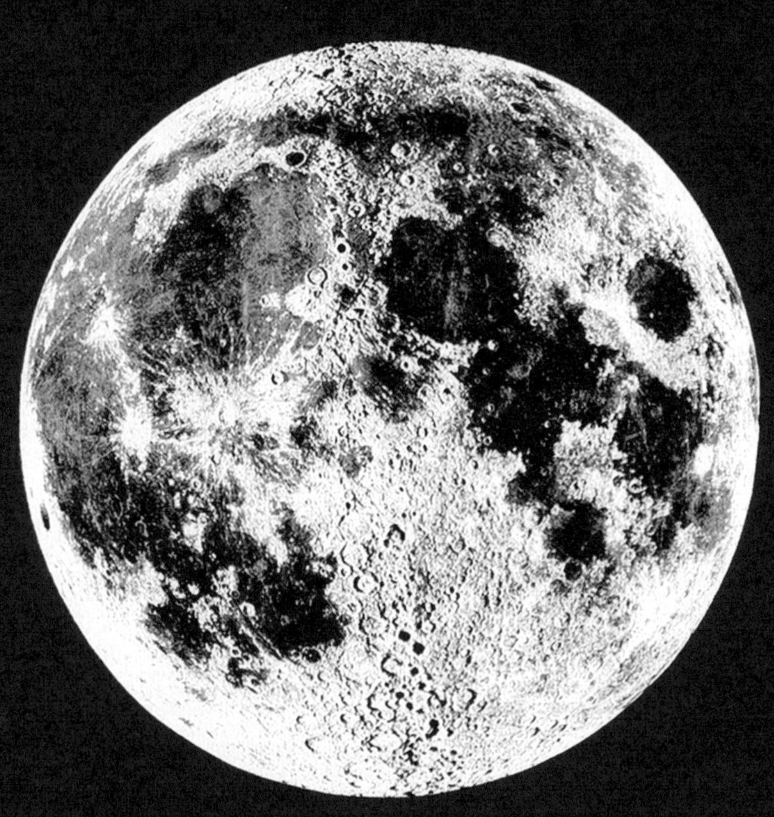

CATCHING MOONBEAMS

Studio : Toby Ng Design   Designer : Toby Ng, Fibi Kung

The light of the moon was chosen as a metaphor for Antalis paper printing effects project to promote their black, grey and sliver paper. The project is presented in a set of two volumes within a specially designed moon-textured case. The whole set is designed to capture the concept of "Catching Moonbeams", highlighting the ephermeral and illusory nature of light, darkness, colors.

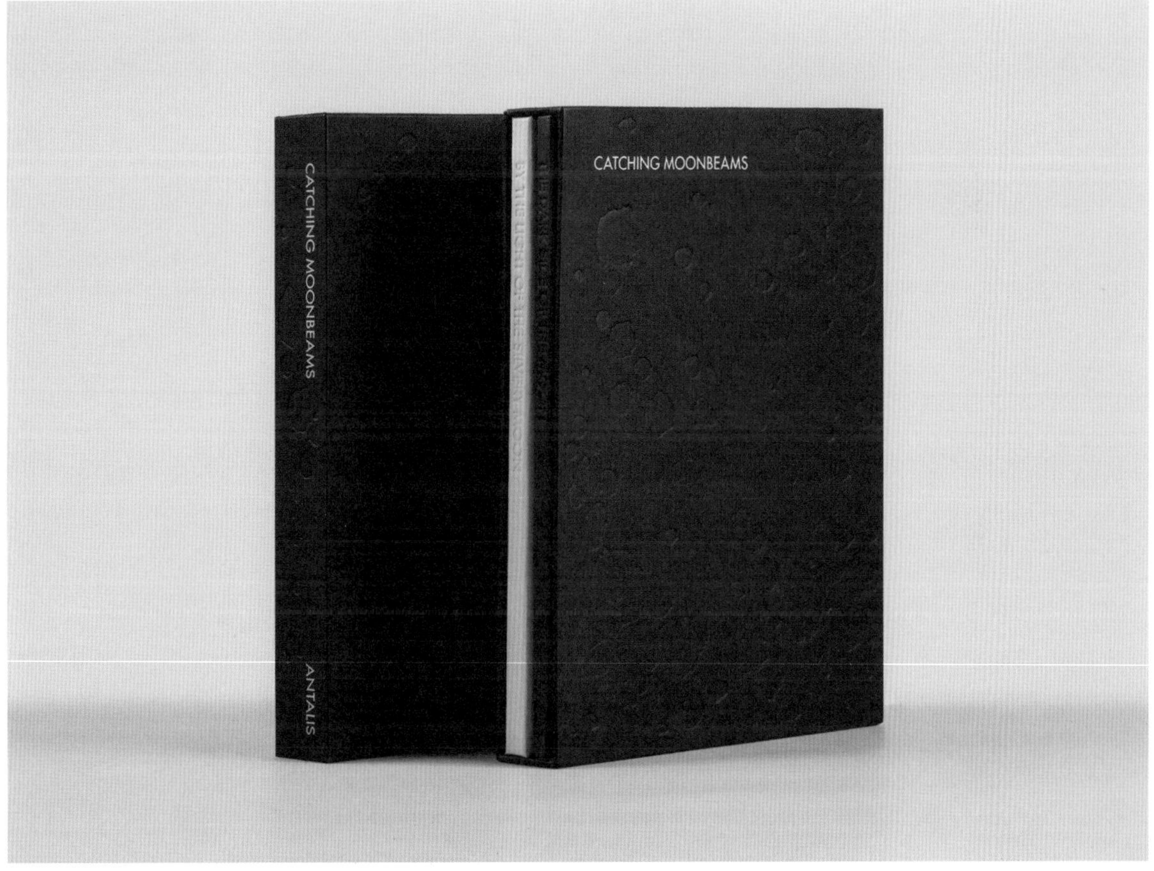

As a kind of visual experience, what do you think about the "roughness" in graphic design?

Roughness can refer to many different things in graphic design—the rough texture of printed matter, printing effects. An idea can be rough but nice when it is suitable.

What are your common approaches to produce a "rough" visual effect?

It mainly happens on the paper we select as well as the printing effect.

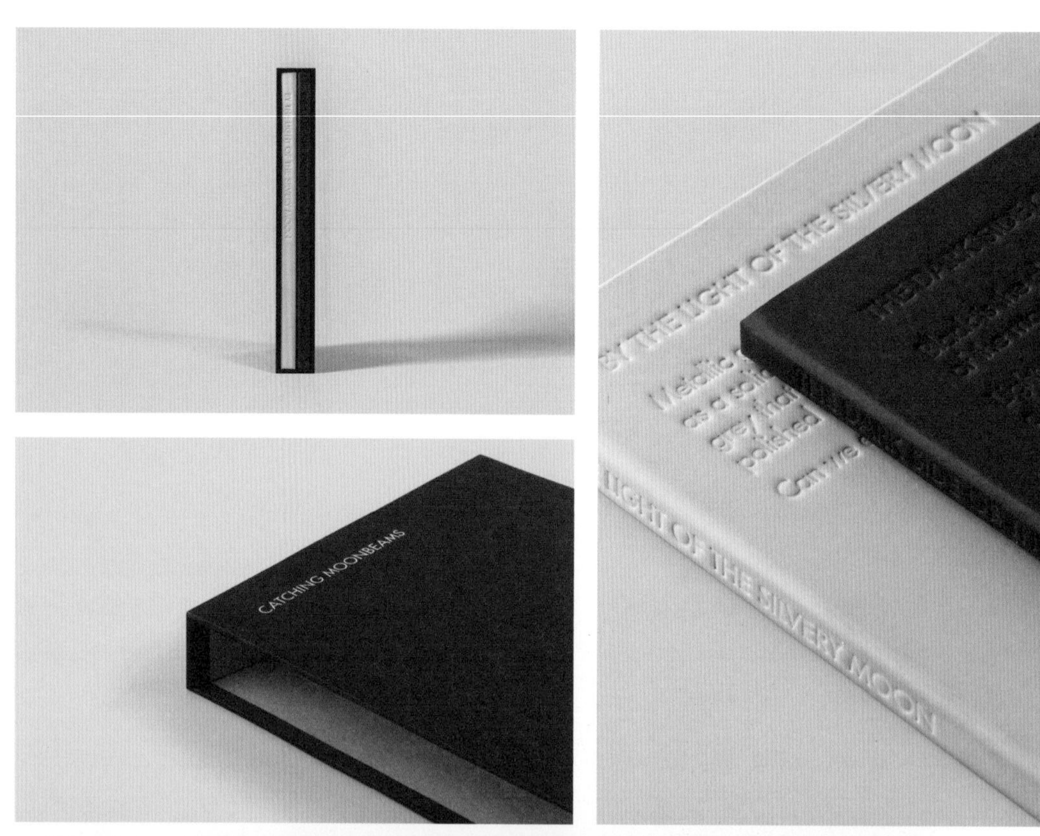
CATCHING MOONBEAMS
THE LIGHT OF THE SILVERY MOON

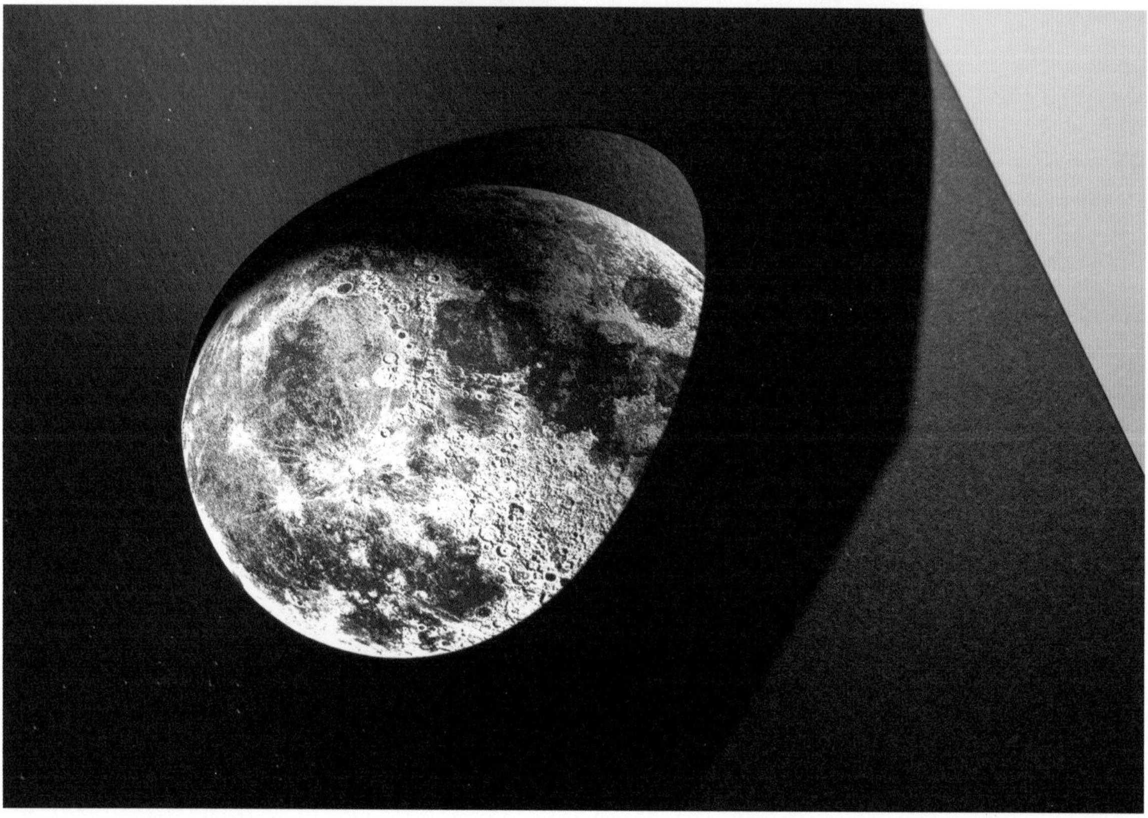

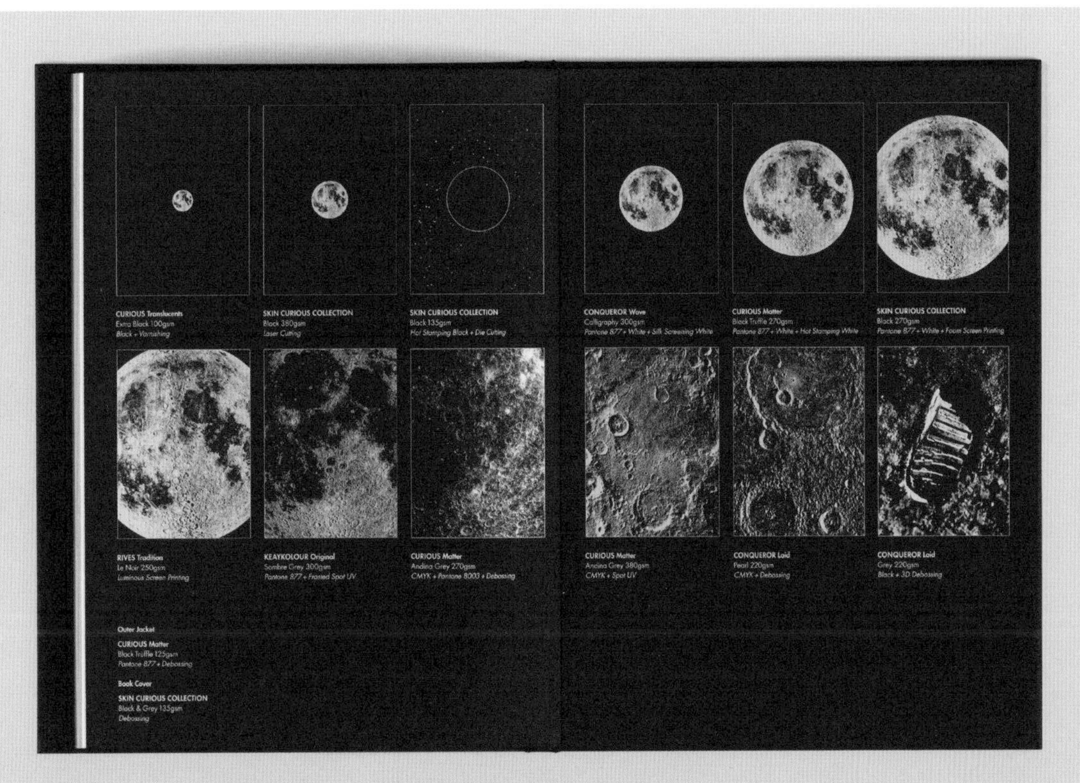
CURIOUS Translucents
Extra Black 100gsm
Black + Varnishing
SKIN CURIOUS COLLECTION
Black 380gsm
Laser Cutting
SKIN CURIOUS COLLECTION
Black 135gsm
Hot Stamping Black + Die Cutting
CONQUEROR Wave
Calligraphy 300gsm
Pantone 877 + White + Silk Screening White
CURIOUS Matter
Black Truffle 270gsm
Pantone 877 + White + Hot Stamping White
SKIN CURIOUS COLLECTION
Black 270gsm
Pantone 877 + White + Foam Screen Printing
RIVES Tradition
Le Noir 250gsm
Luminous Screen Printing
KEAYKOLOUR Original
Sombre Grey 300gsm
Pantone 877 + Frosted Spot UV
CURIOUS Matter
Andina Grey 270gsm
CMYK + Pantone 8003 + Debossing
CURIOUS Matter
Andina Grey 380gsm
CMYK + Spot UV
CONQUEROR Laid
Pearl 220gsm
CMYK + Debossing
CONQUEROR Laid
Grey 220gsm
Black + 3D Debossing
Outer Jacket
CURIOUS Matter
Black Truffle 125gsm
Pantone 877 + Debossing
Book Cover
SKIN CURIOUS COLLECTION
Black & Grey 135gsm
Debossing

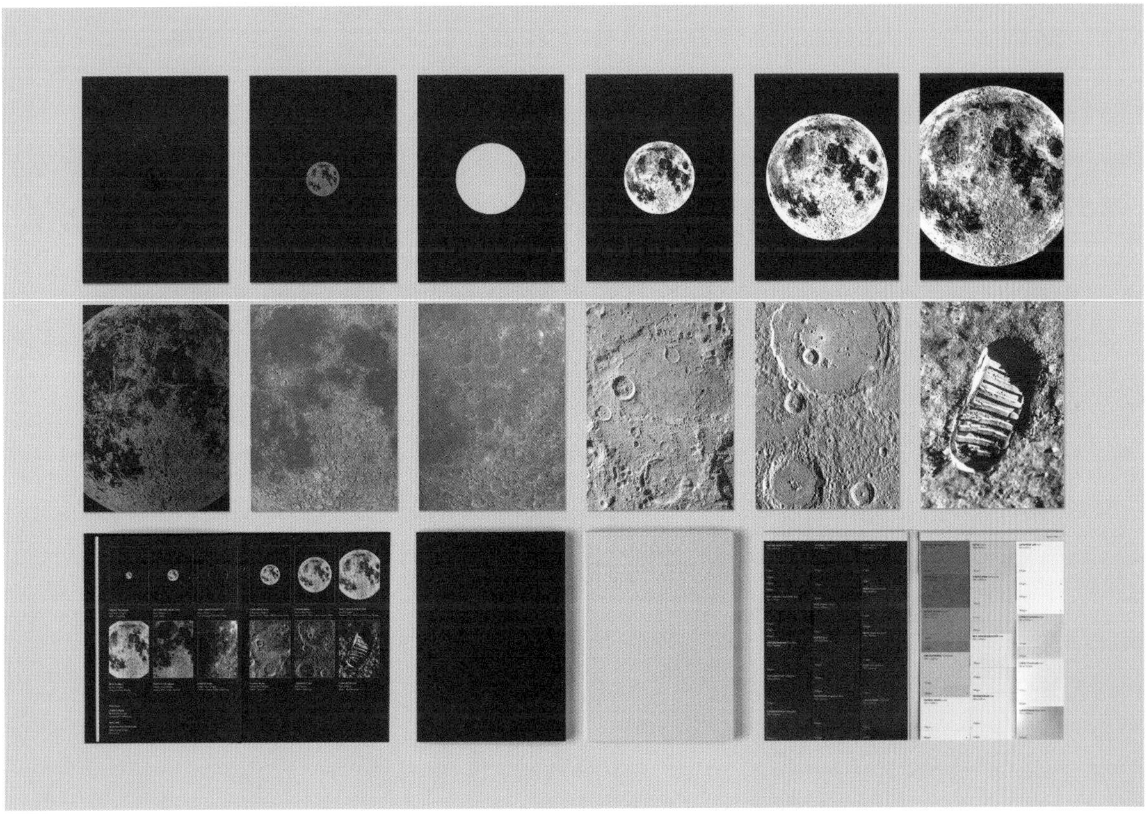

ILA BARÚ

Designer : Estudio Yeyé

This design project was to capture the spirit of nature that we see inside each fruit and each living being through raw and natural brand applications. The architectural part conveys a sincere and relaxing language through raw textures and terracotta tones.

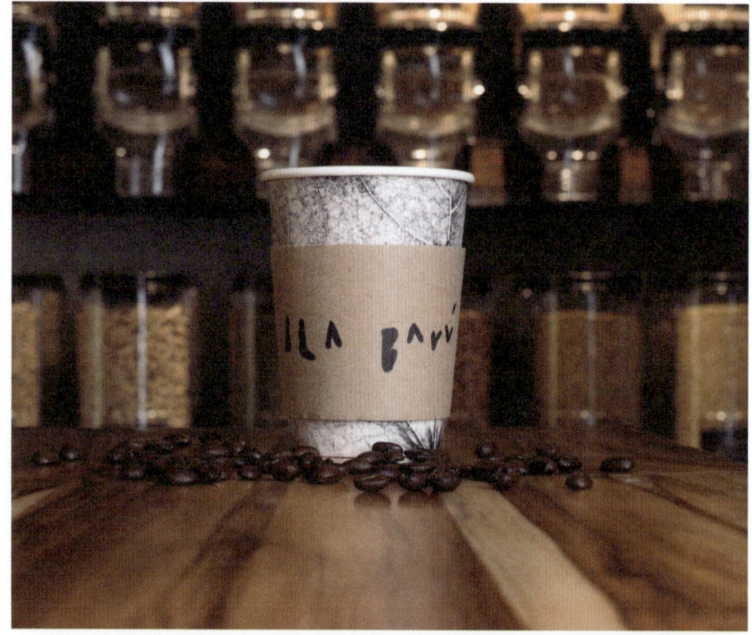

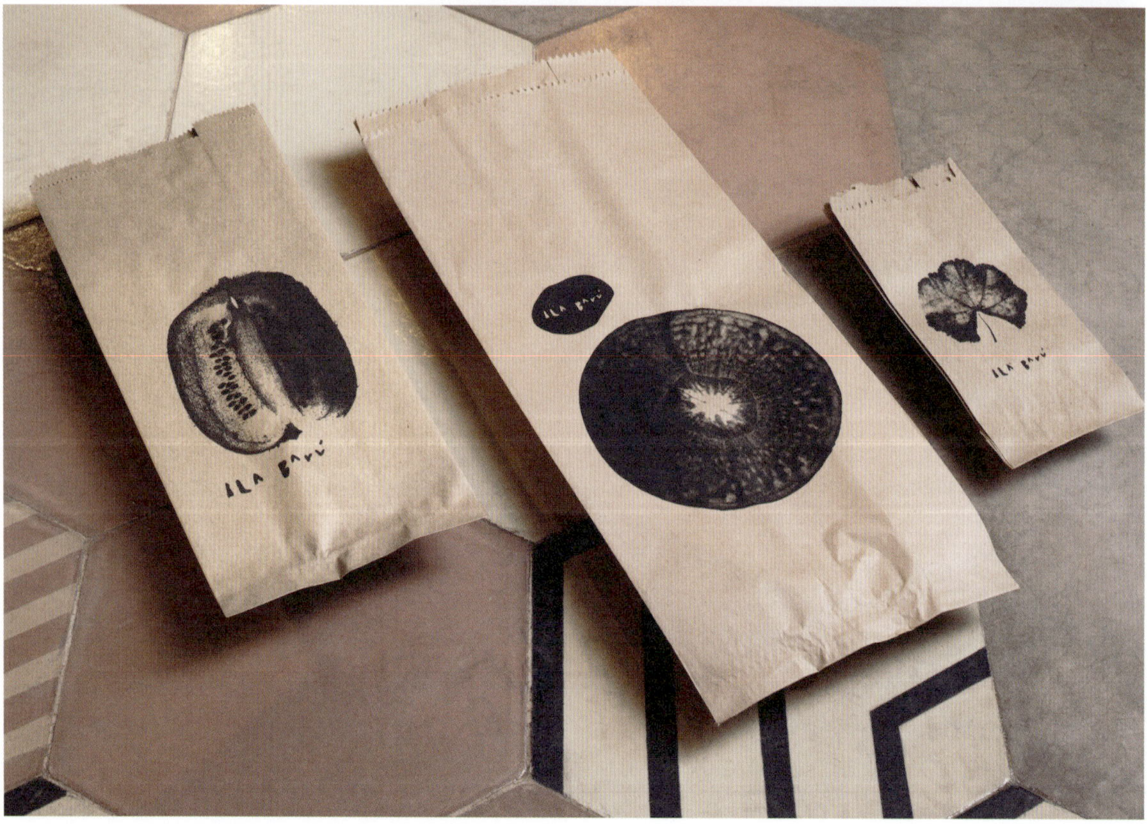

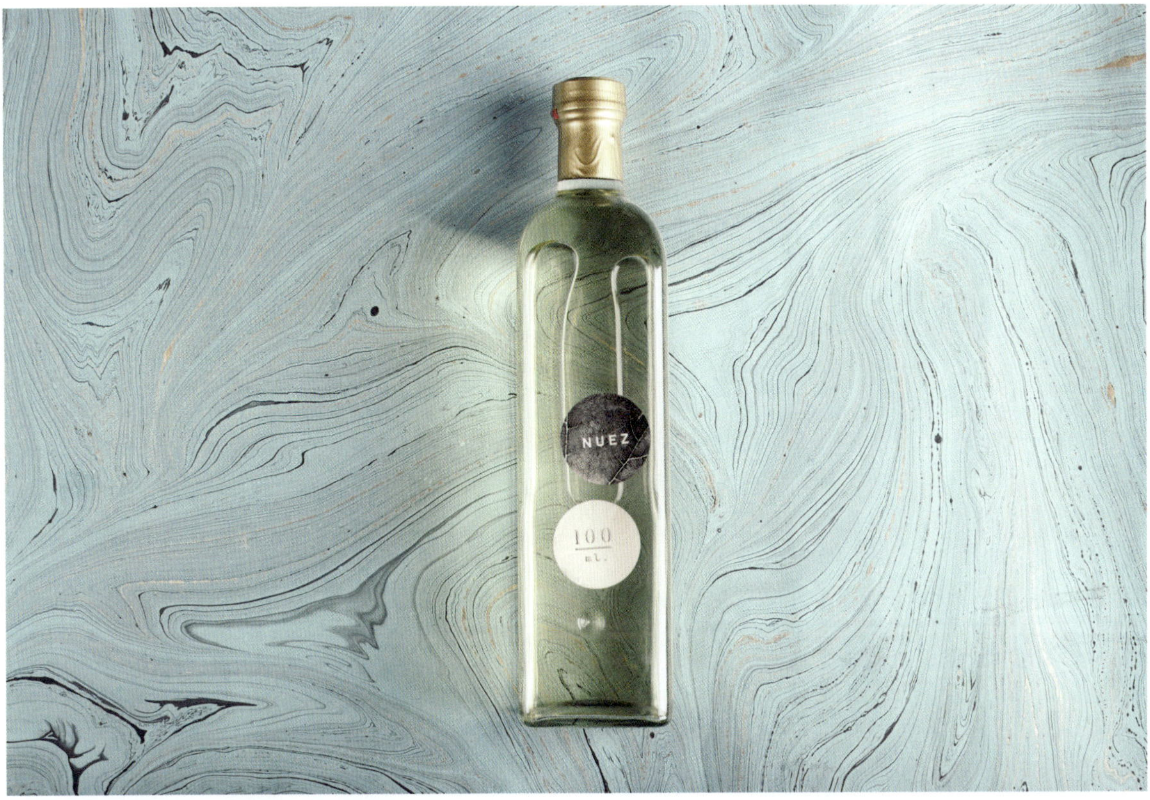

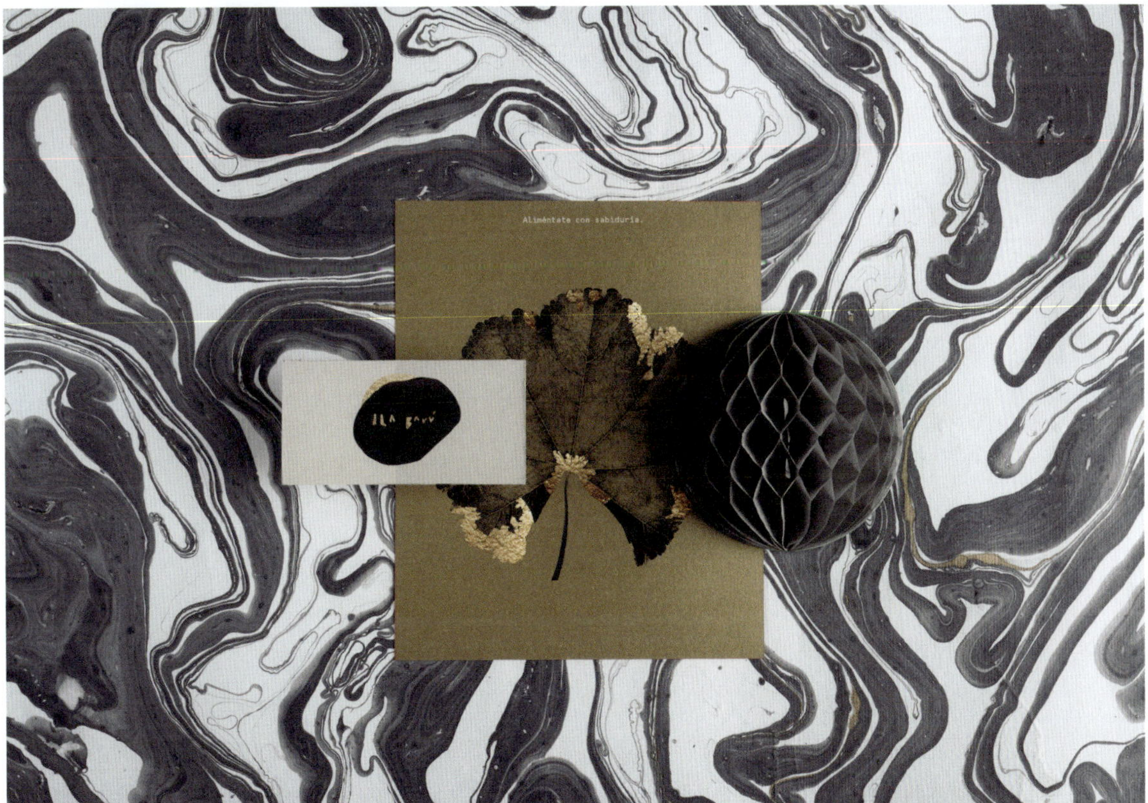

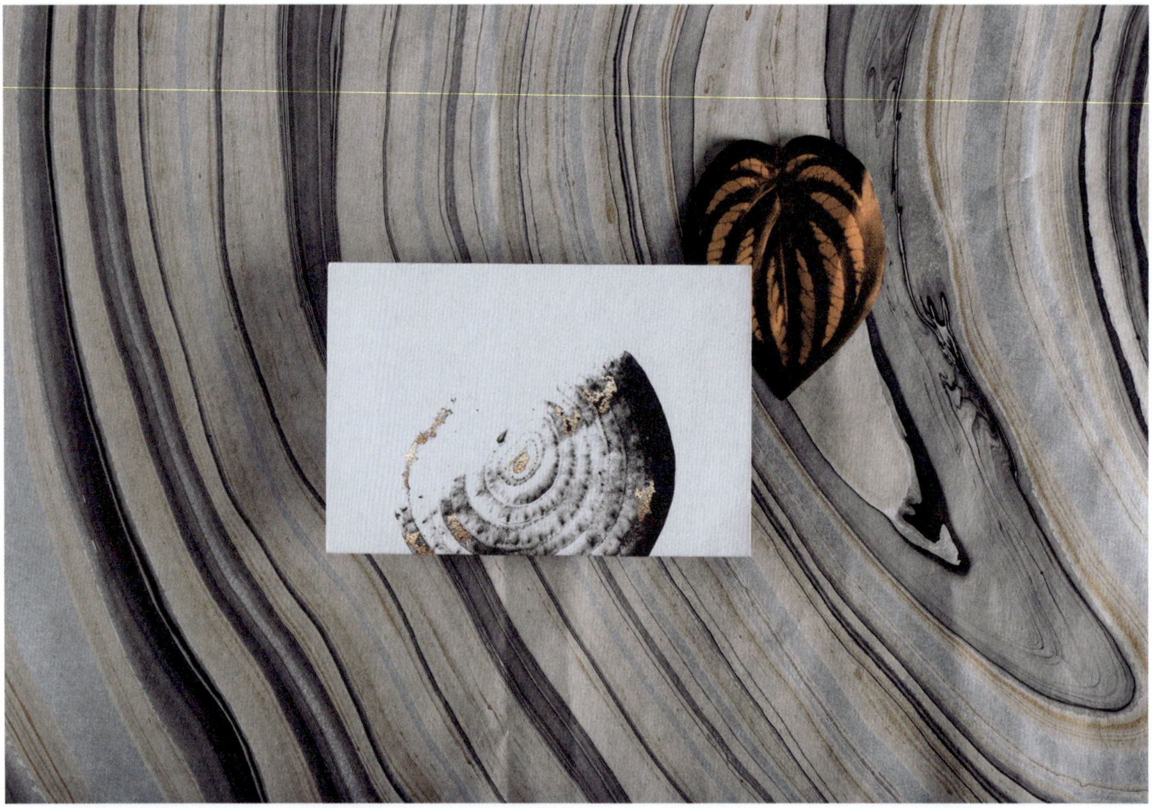

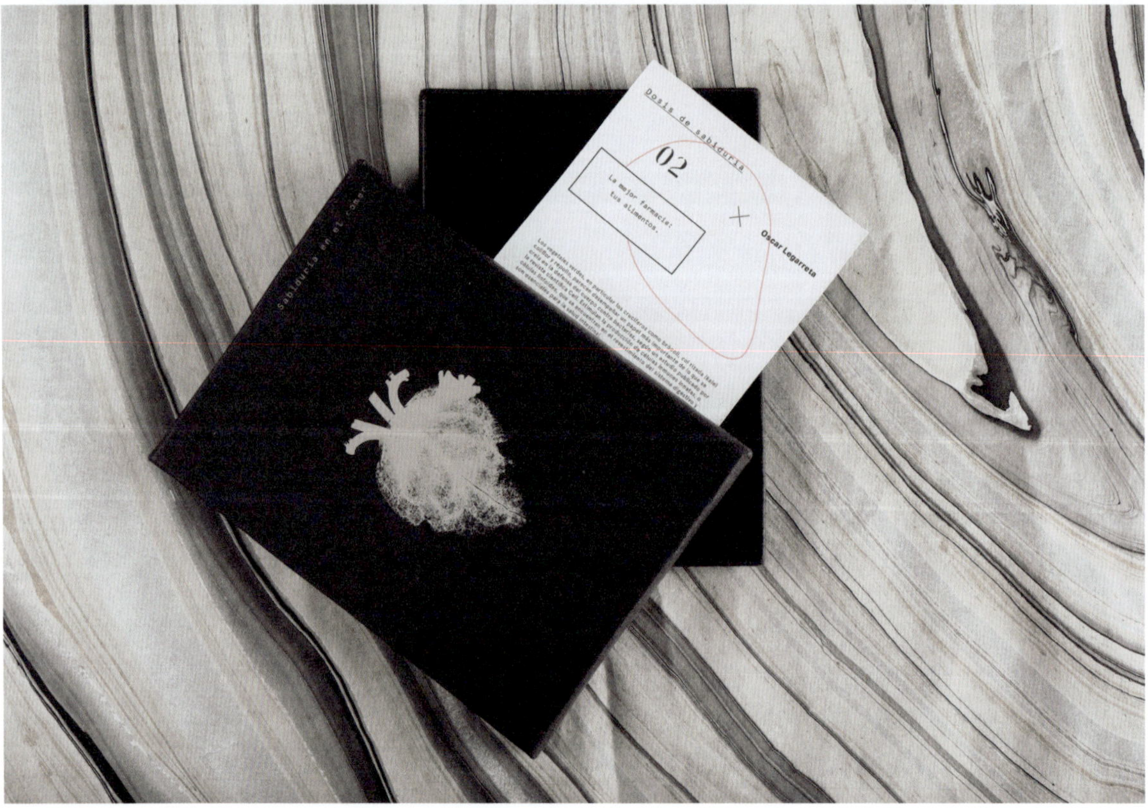

Dosis de sabiduría
02
La mejor farmacia: tus alimentos.
Oscar Legarreta

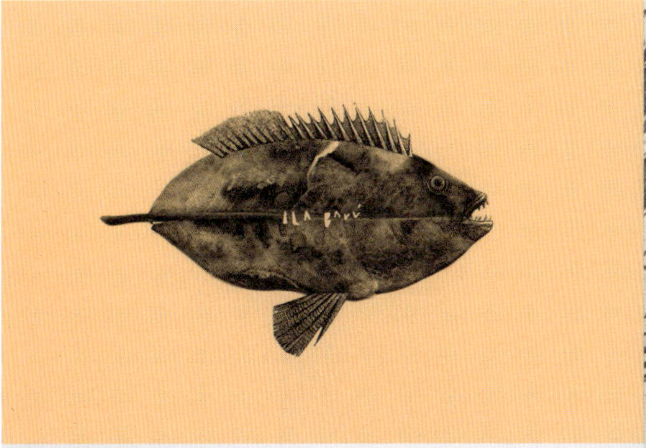

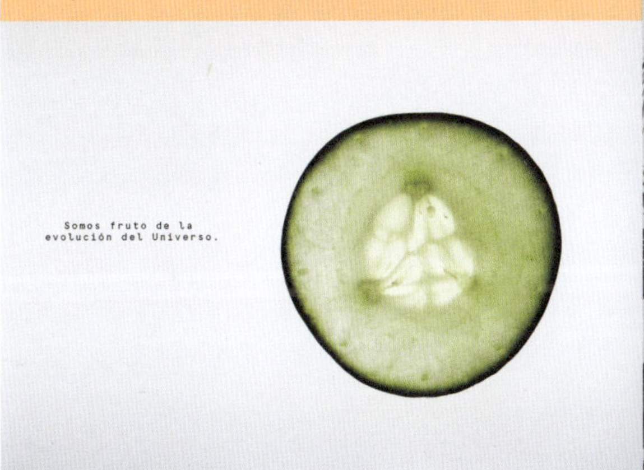

Somos fruto de la
evolución del Universo.

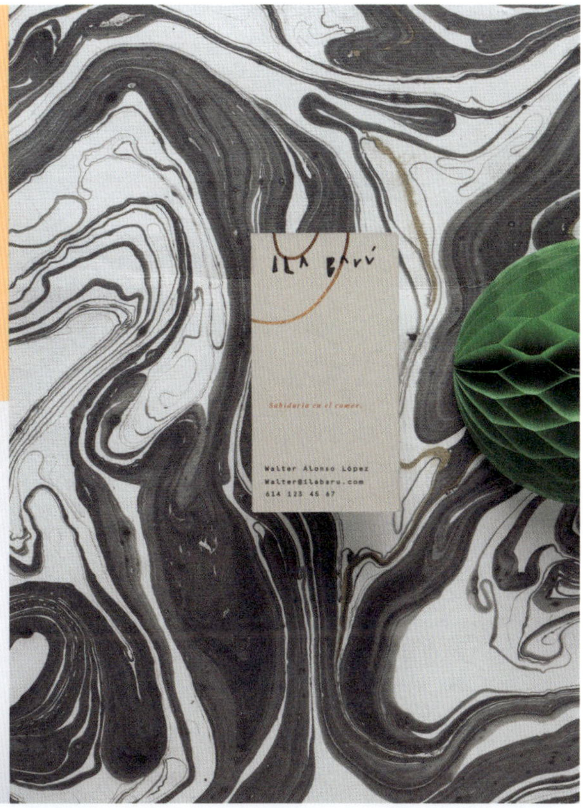

Sabiduría en el comer.

Walter Alonso López
Walter@ilabaru.com
614 123 45 67

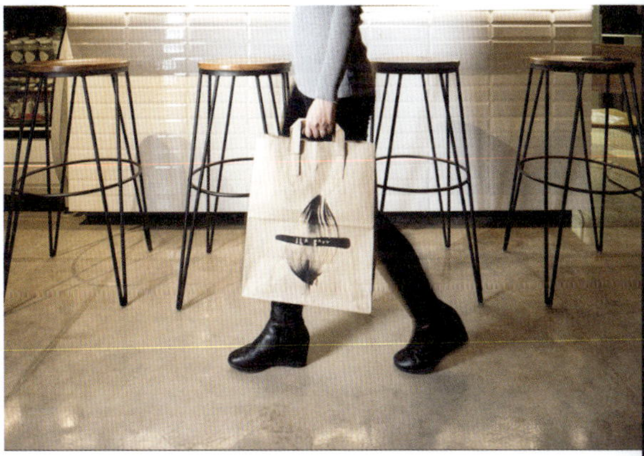

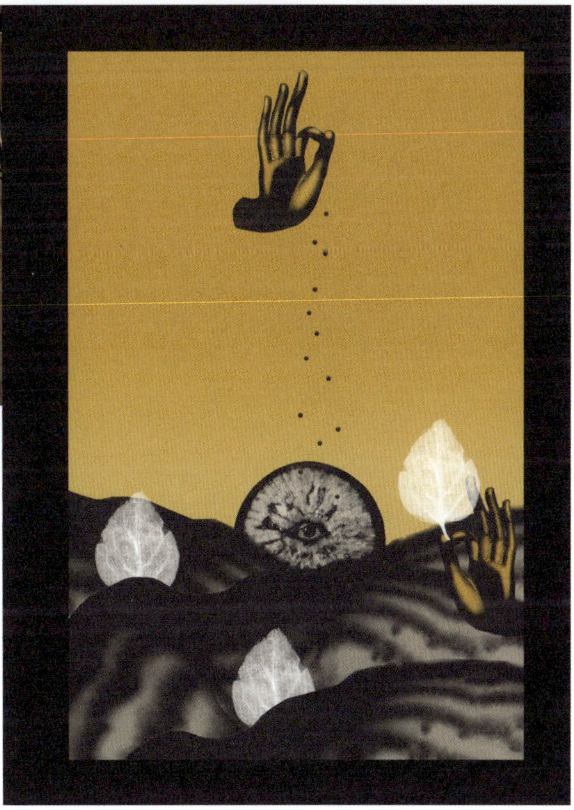

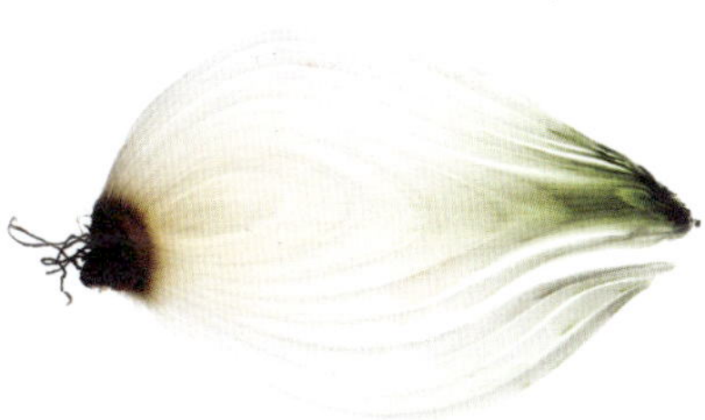

BLACK OIL

Studio : Studio Roniverony   Designer : Rony Schneider, Roni Ben Yosef

Black Oil is an olive oil which has a very bitter and dominant taste. The package design focuses on these specific "negative" features and turns them into "positive" ones. Therefore, its appeal is in its poisonous, seductive dark look, inspired by oil pollution and gold bars.

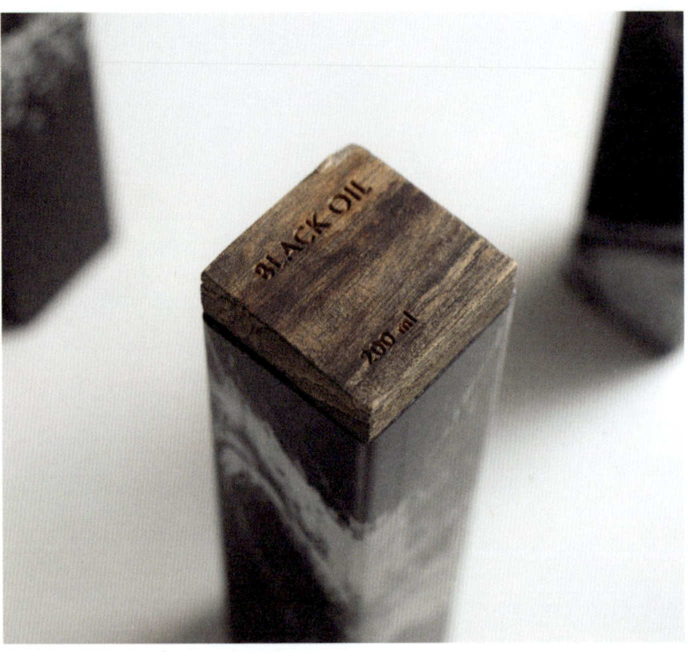

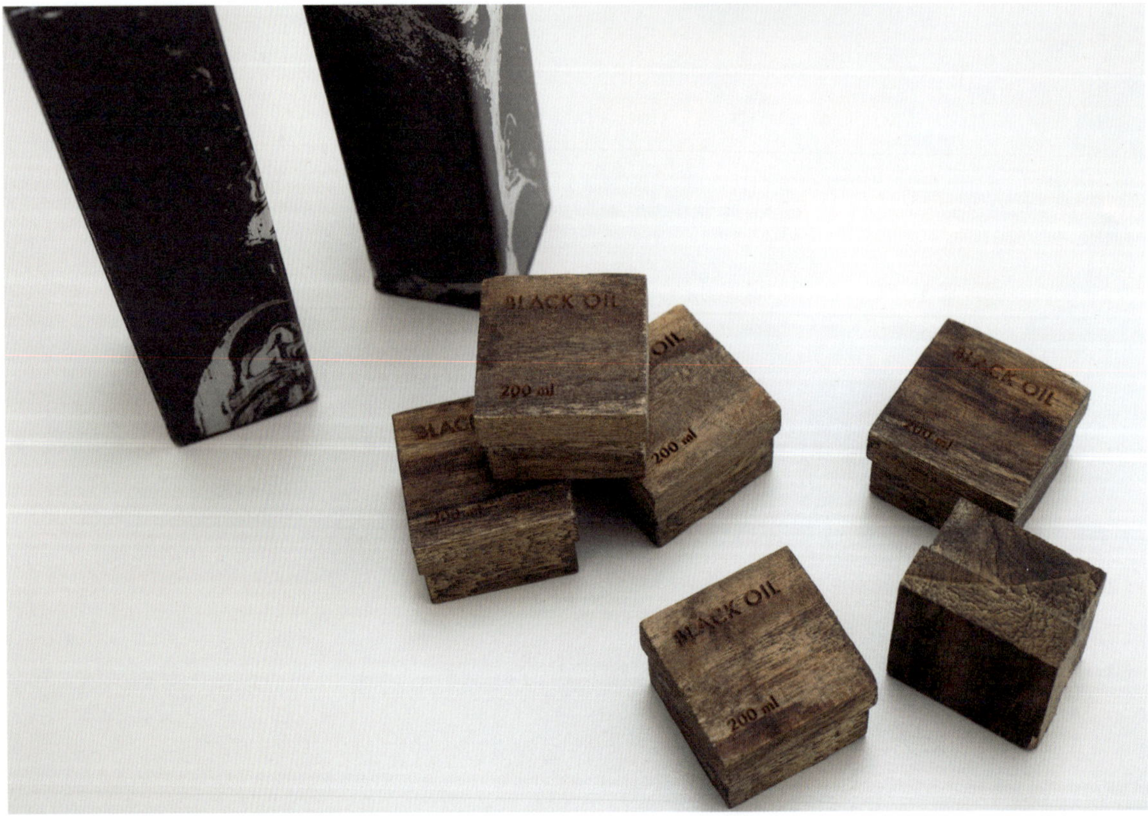

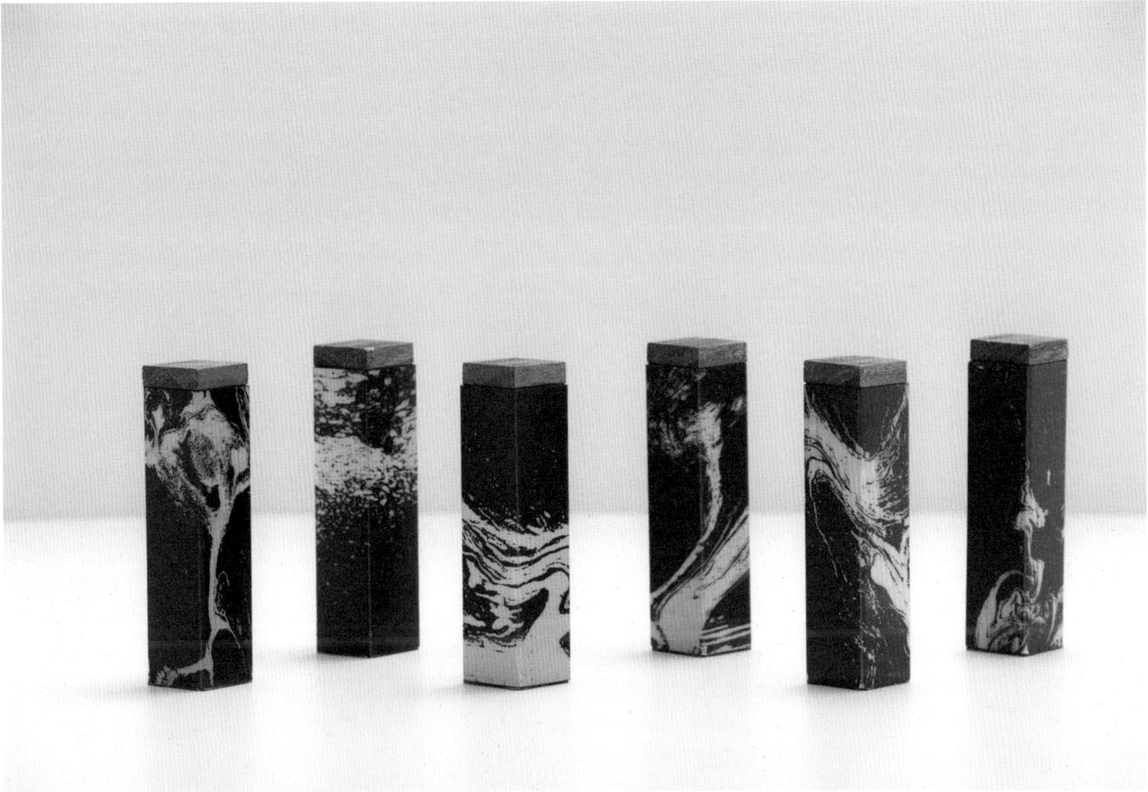

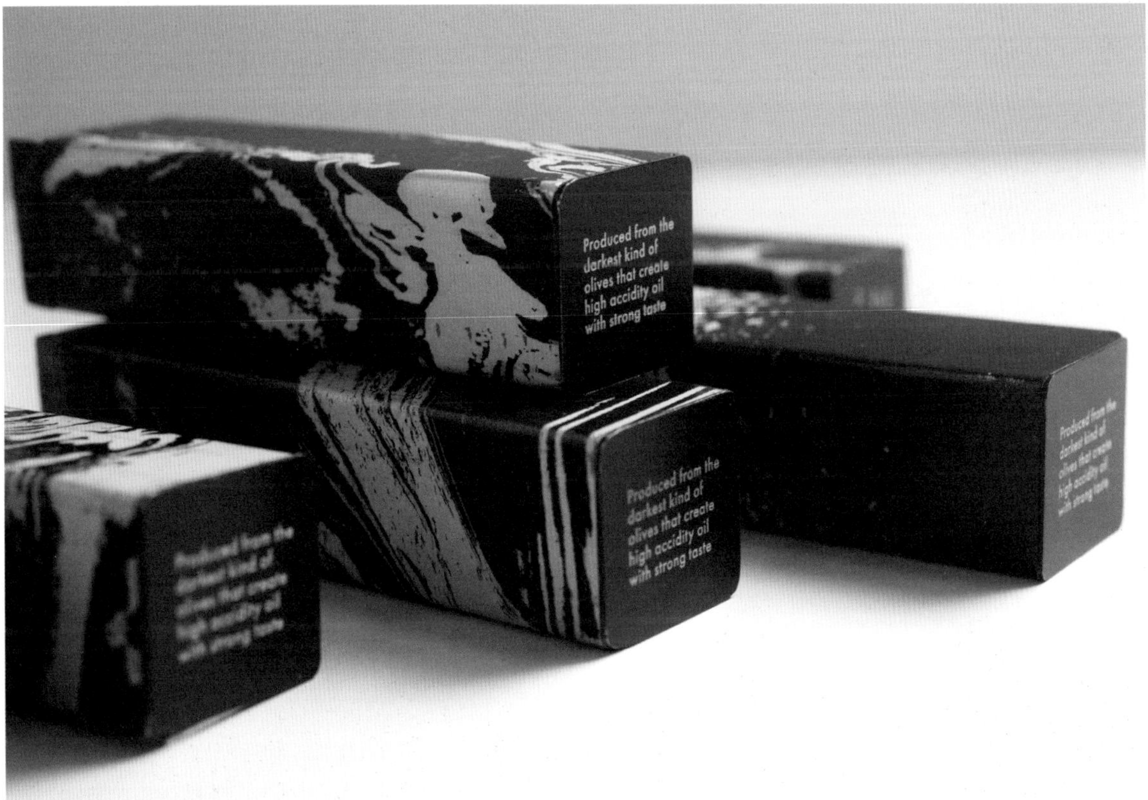

ÁLAMO

Studio : NOEM9 Studio   Designer : Jose Garrido, Fabiola Correas

ÁLAMO is a bar specialized in tapas and sandwiches in the city of Zaragoza, Spain. The joy of tasty homemade food with organic ingredients accompanied by a warm and homelike space was the main concept of this identity design.

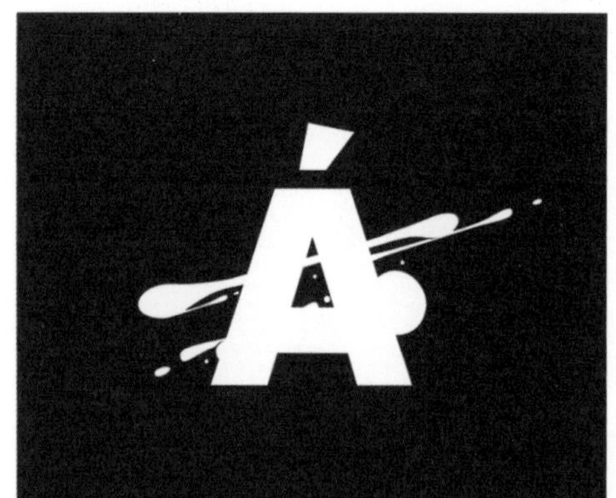

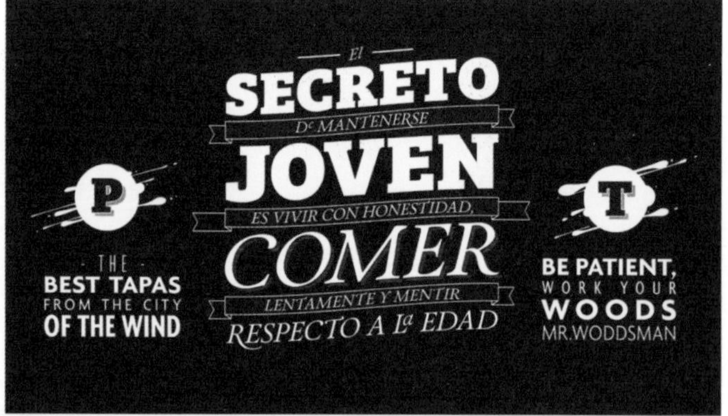

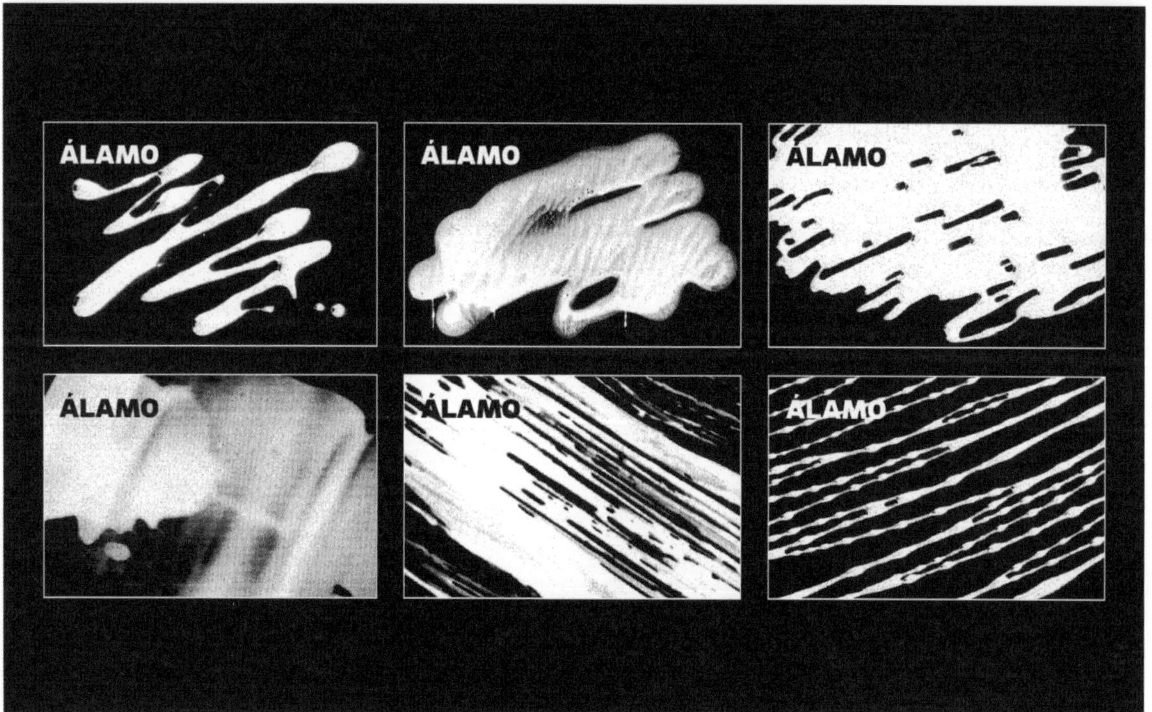

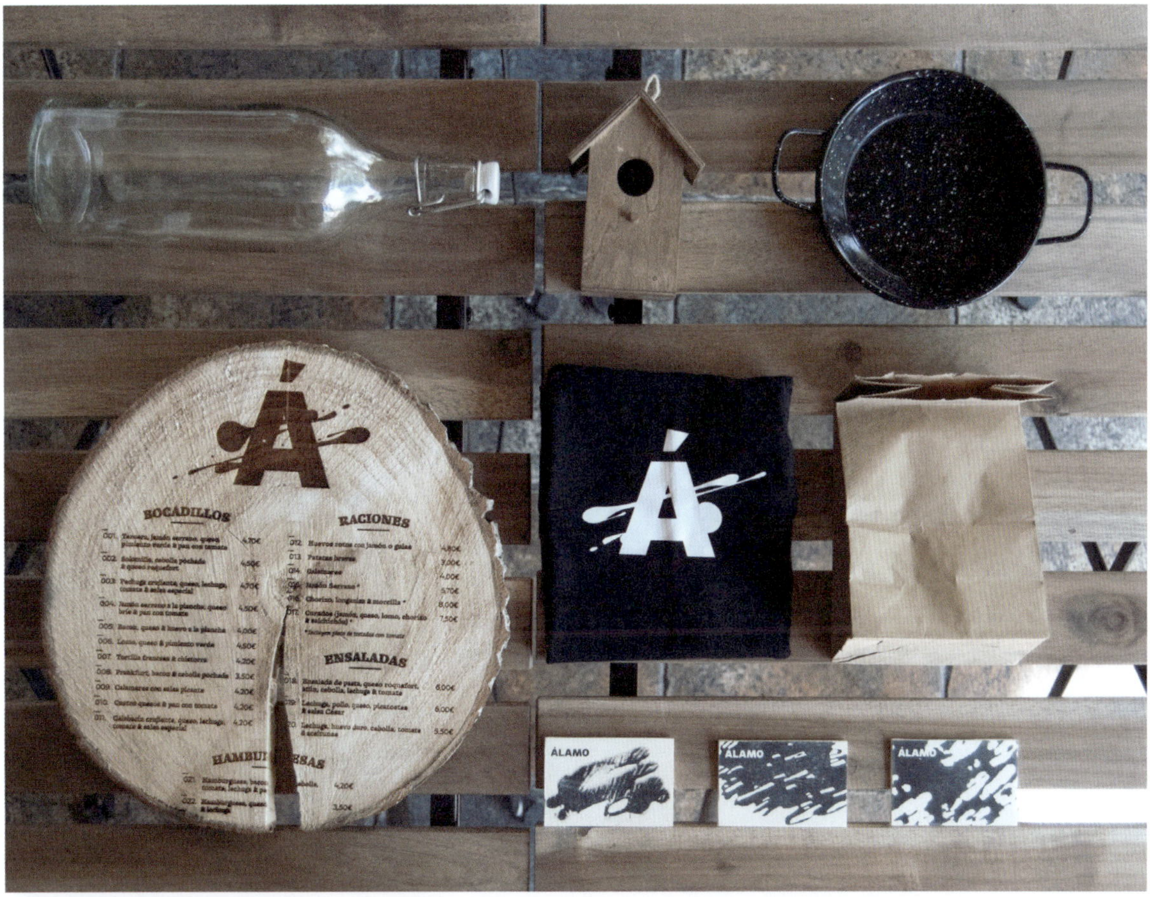

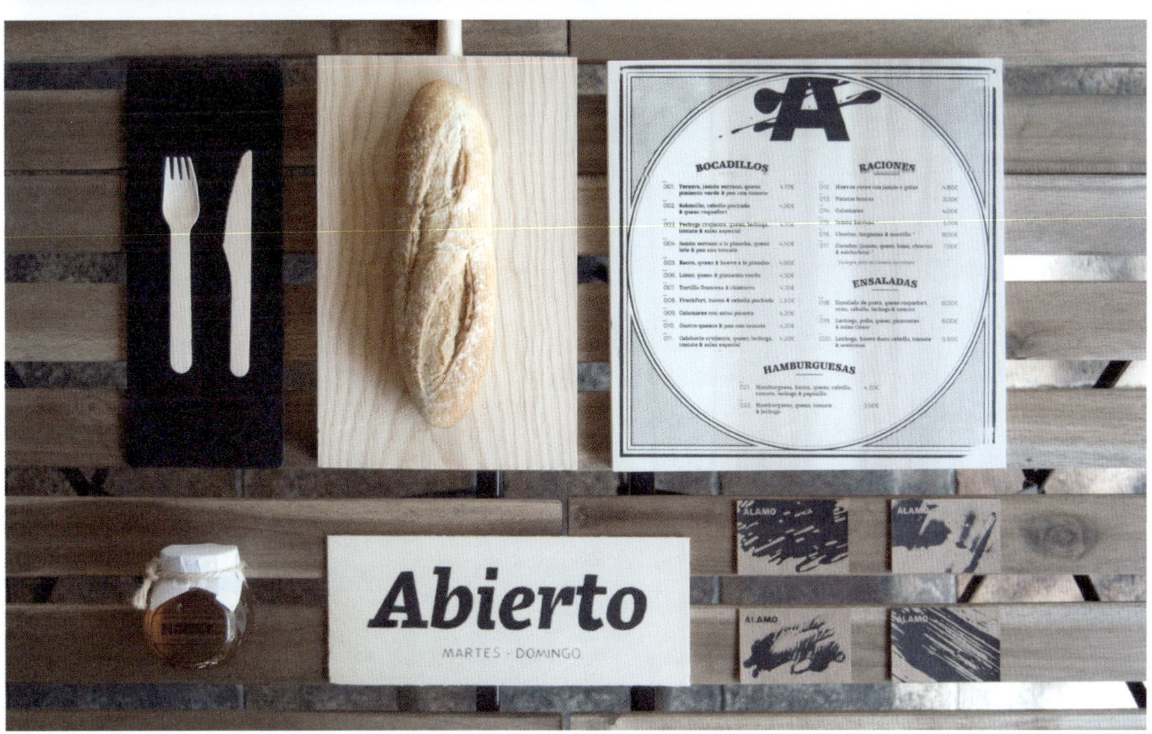
BOCADILLOS
RACIONES
ENSALADAS
HAMBURGUESAS
ÁLAMO
ÁLAMO
ÁLAMO
ÁLAMO
Abierto
MARTES - DOMINGO

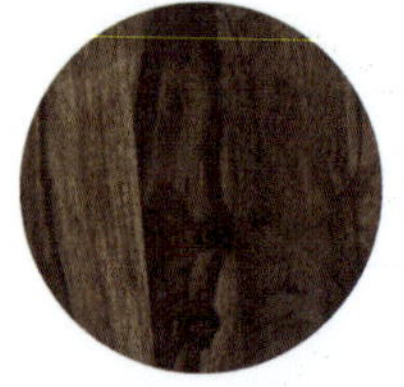

NEW YORK
WOOD TEXTURE

MADRID
STONE TEXTURE

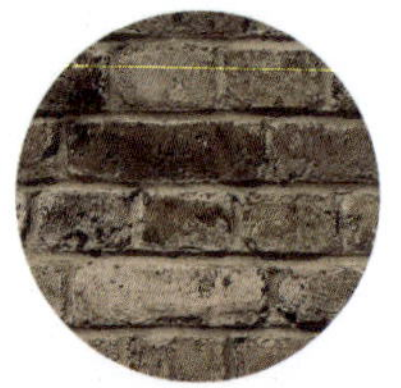

LONDON
BRICK TEXTURE

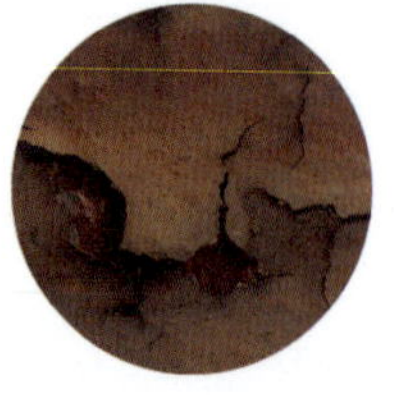

PARIS
METAL TEXTURE

CHOCO & CO SPECIAL EDITION

Designer : Isabel de Peque

The chocolate packaging for Choco & co based on common materials from some of the major cities in the world provides a unique interpretation of the cities it represents. The chocolate comes in different materials and flavors for each city, for example, stone and dark chocolate for Madrid, striking and profound.

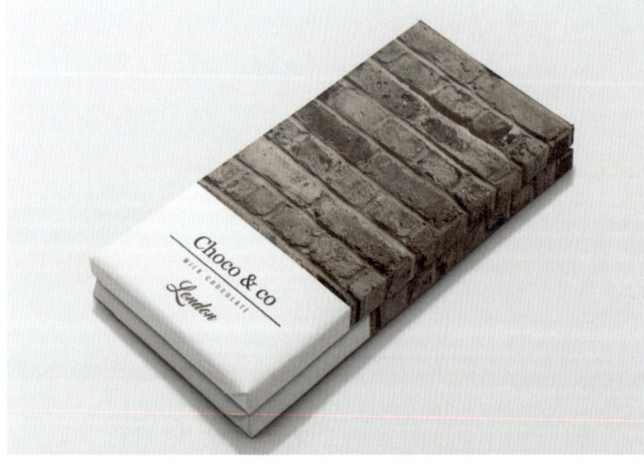

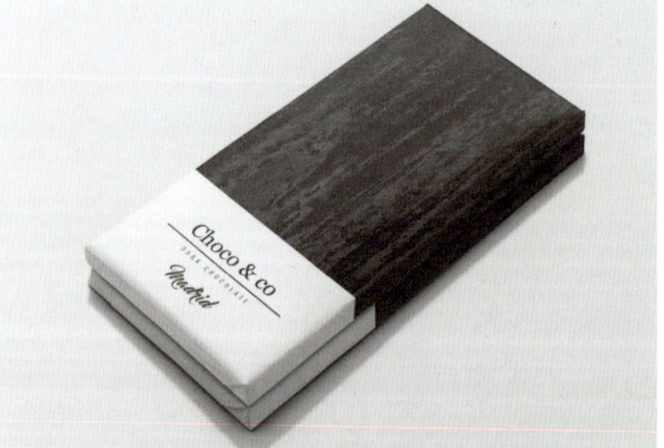

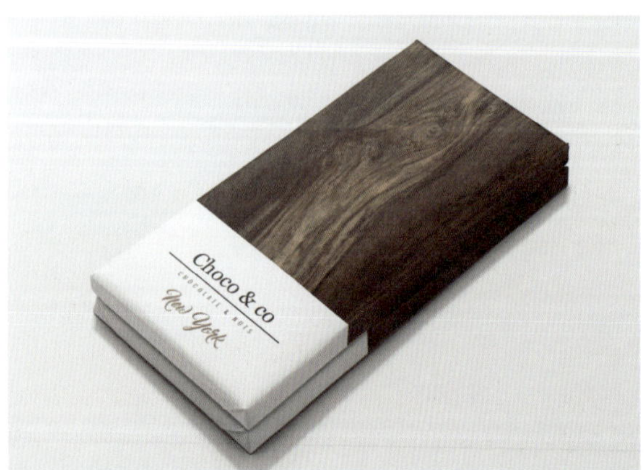

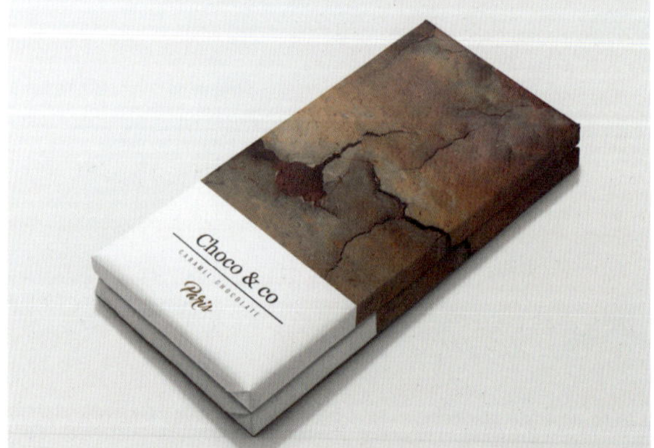

LOGO DESIGN

Choco & co

DARK CHOCOLATE

Madrid

Choco & co

CARAMEL CHOCOLATE

Paris

Choco & co

CHOCOLATE & NUTS

New York

Choco & co

MILK CHOCOLATE

London

PACKAGING

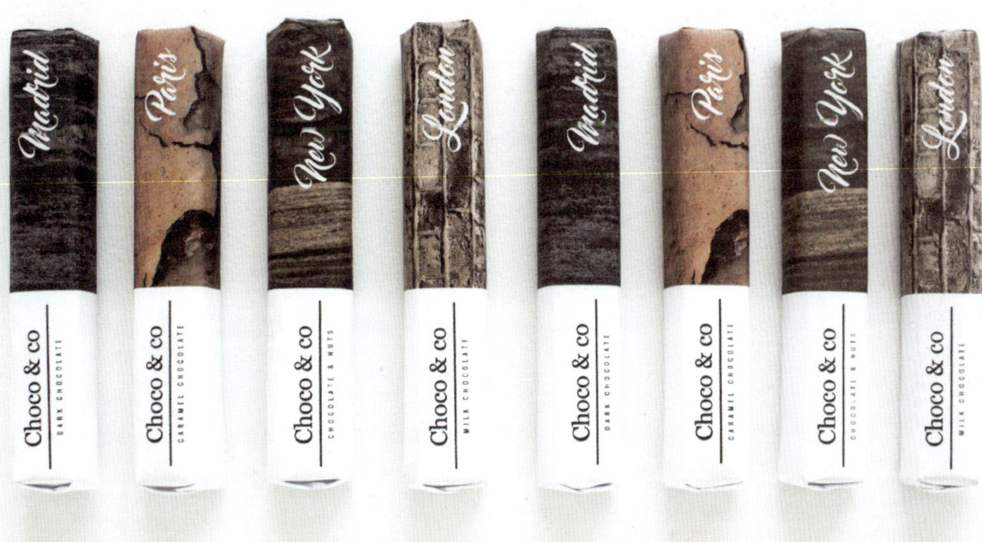

PACKAGING-ROS CAUBÓ

Studio : Zoo Studio   Designer : Gerard Calm, Xevi Castells, Maria Blanch

This is a packaging design for a special edition of Ros Caubó organic olive oil. The main parts of the package are two pieces of rectangular olive tree wood, a piece of handmade papier-mâché and a catalogue. These elements are fastened together with hemp twine.

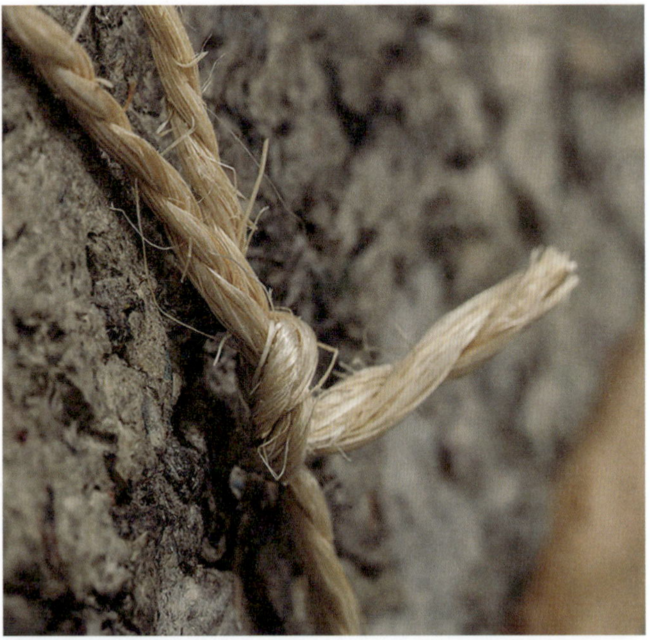

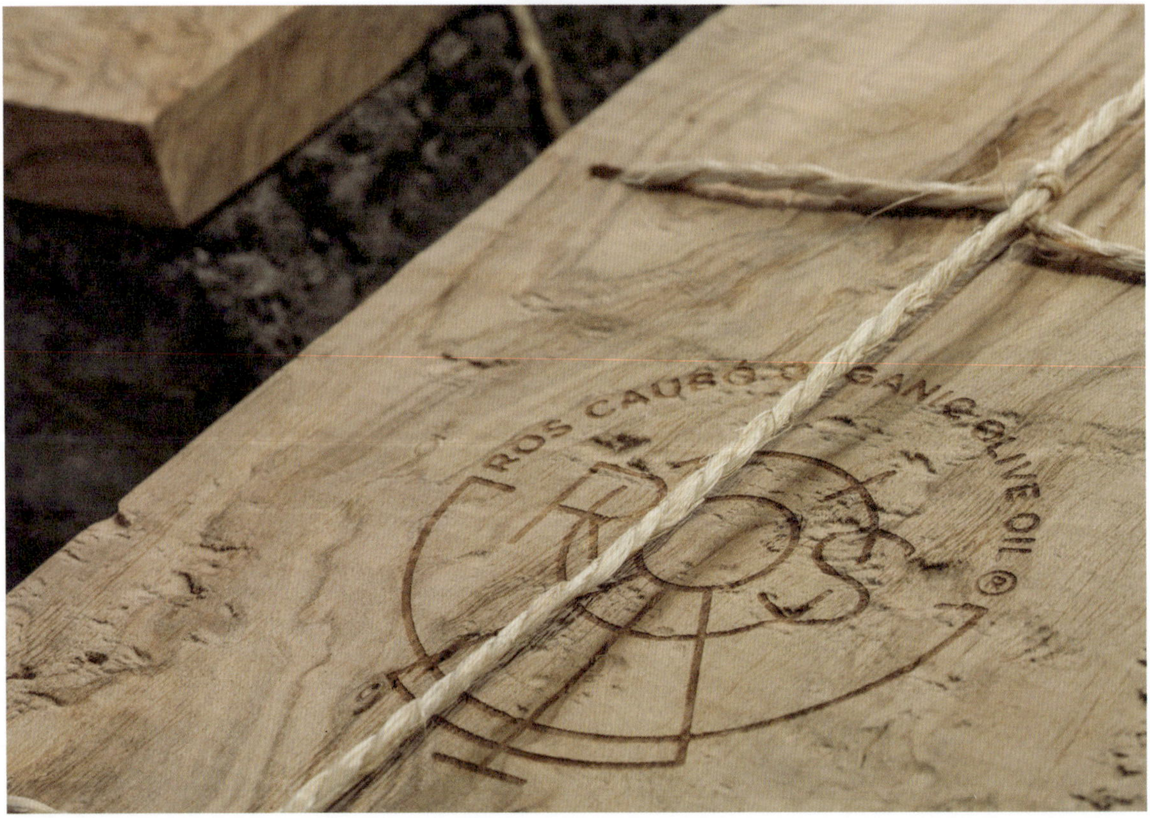

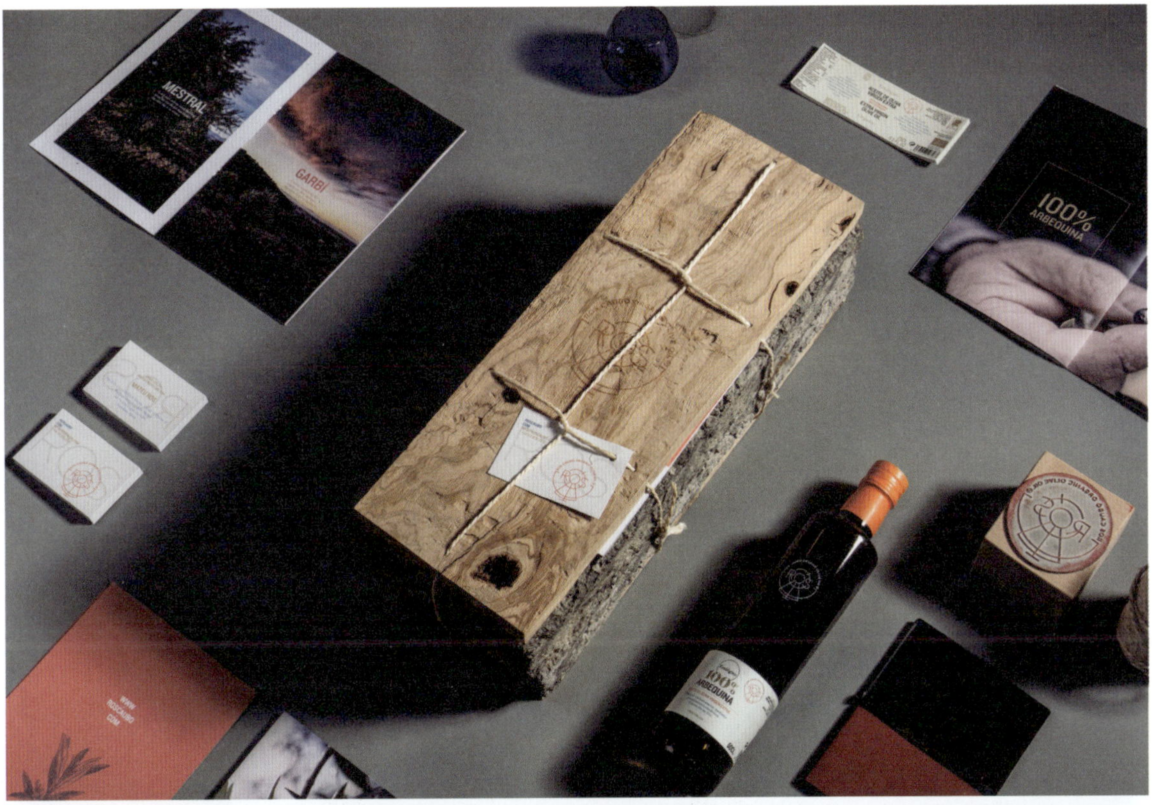

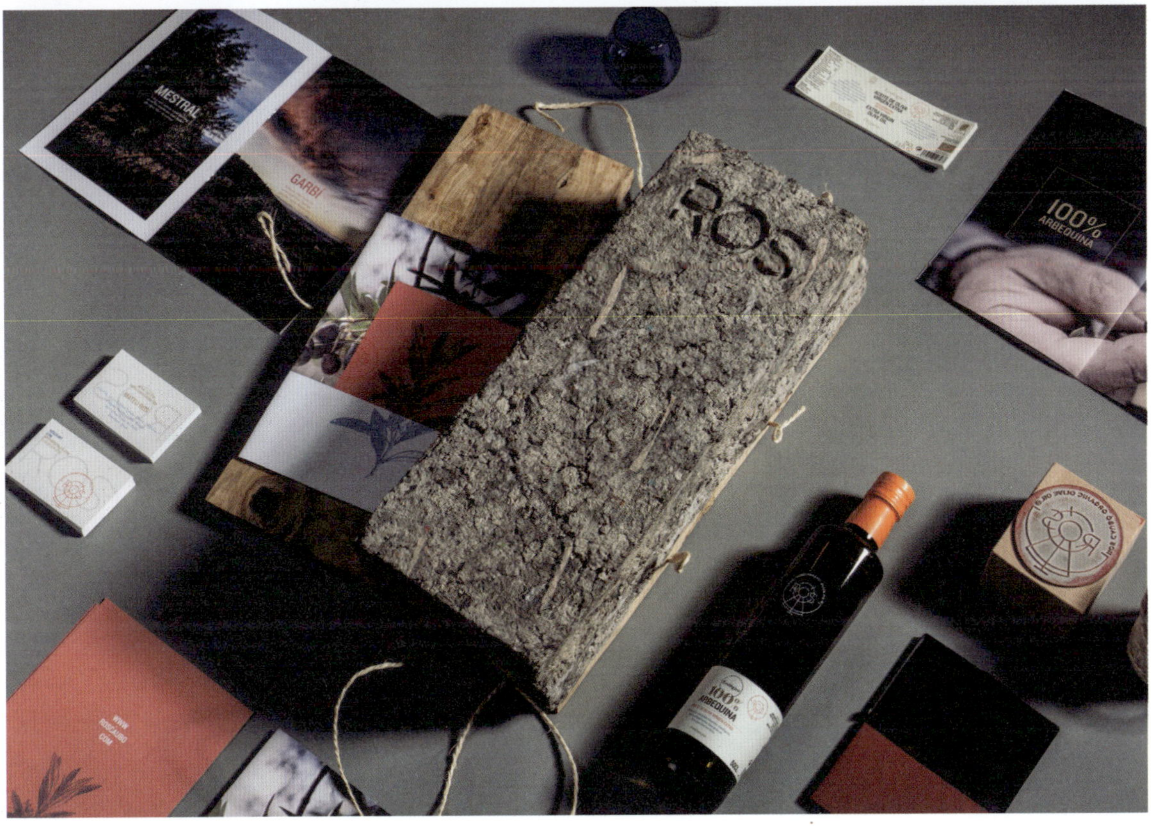

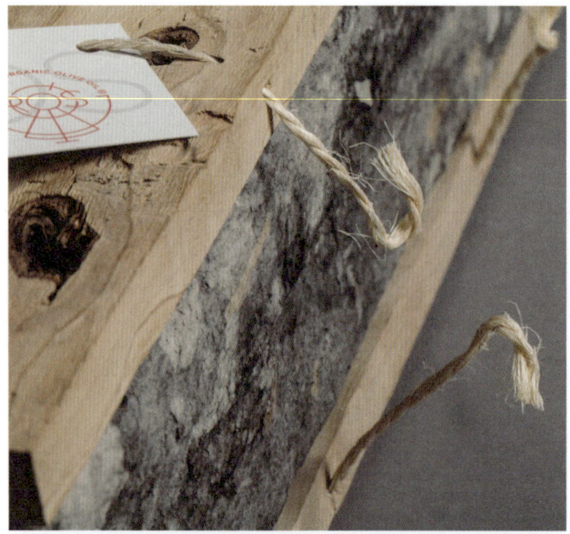

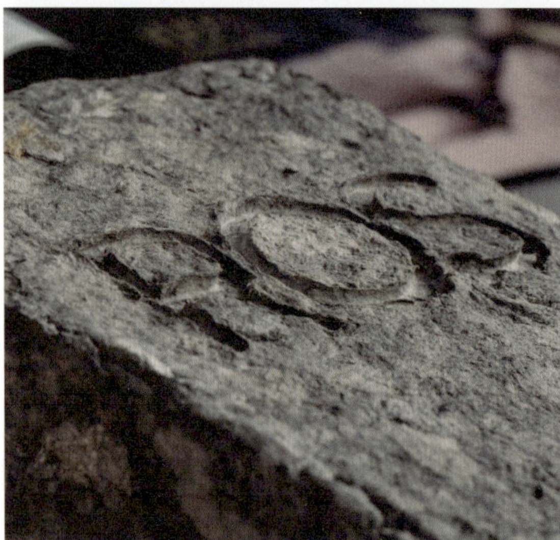

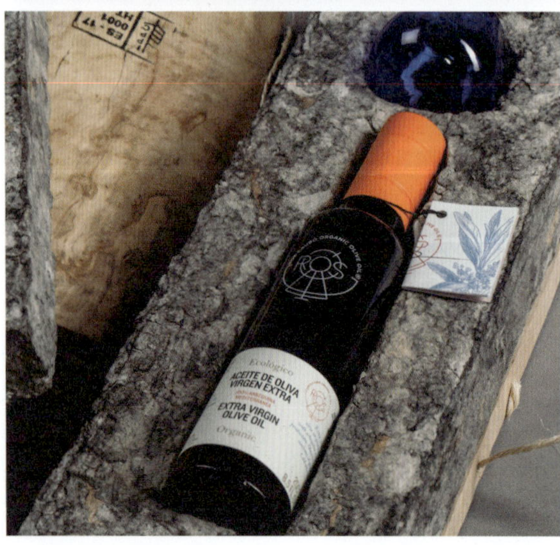
Ecológico
ACEITE DE OLIVA
VIRGEN EXTRA
EXTRA VIRGIN
OLIVE OIL
Organic

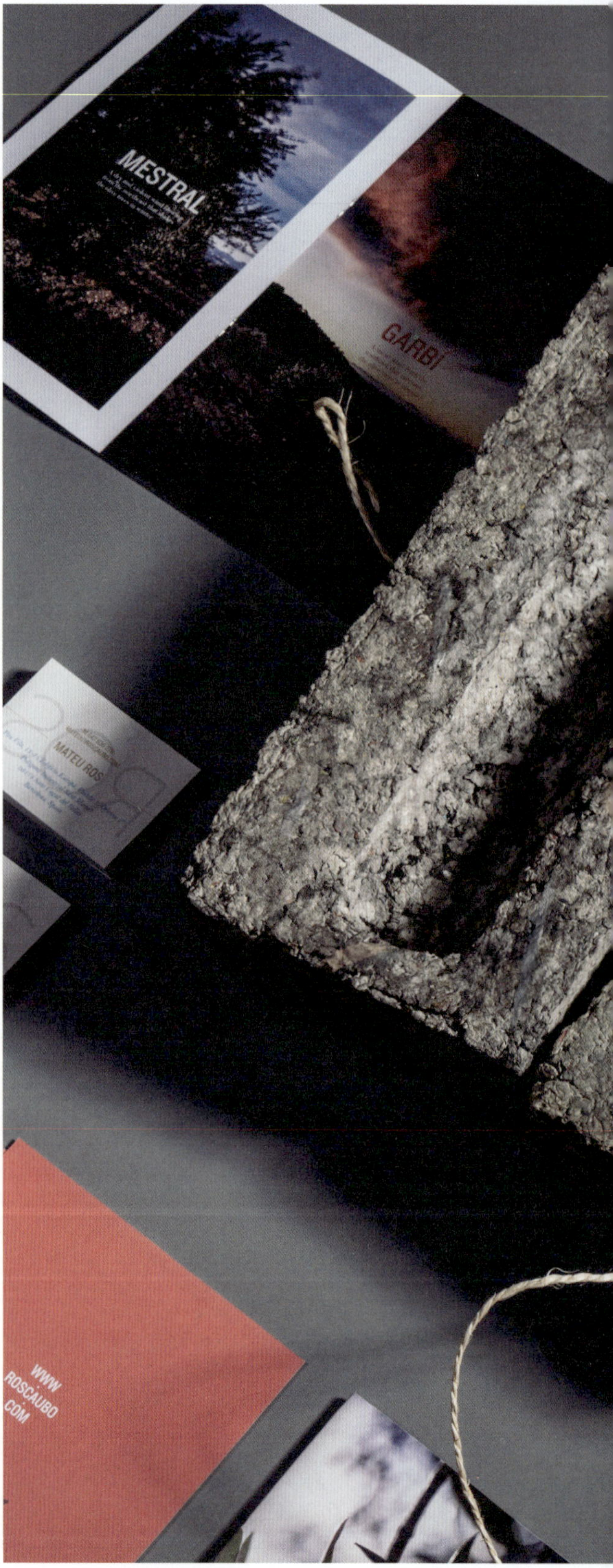

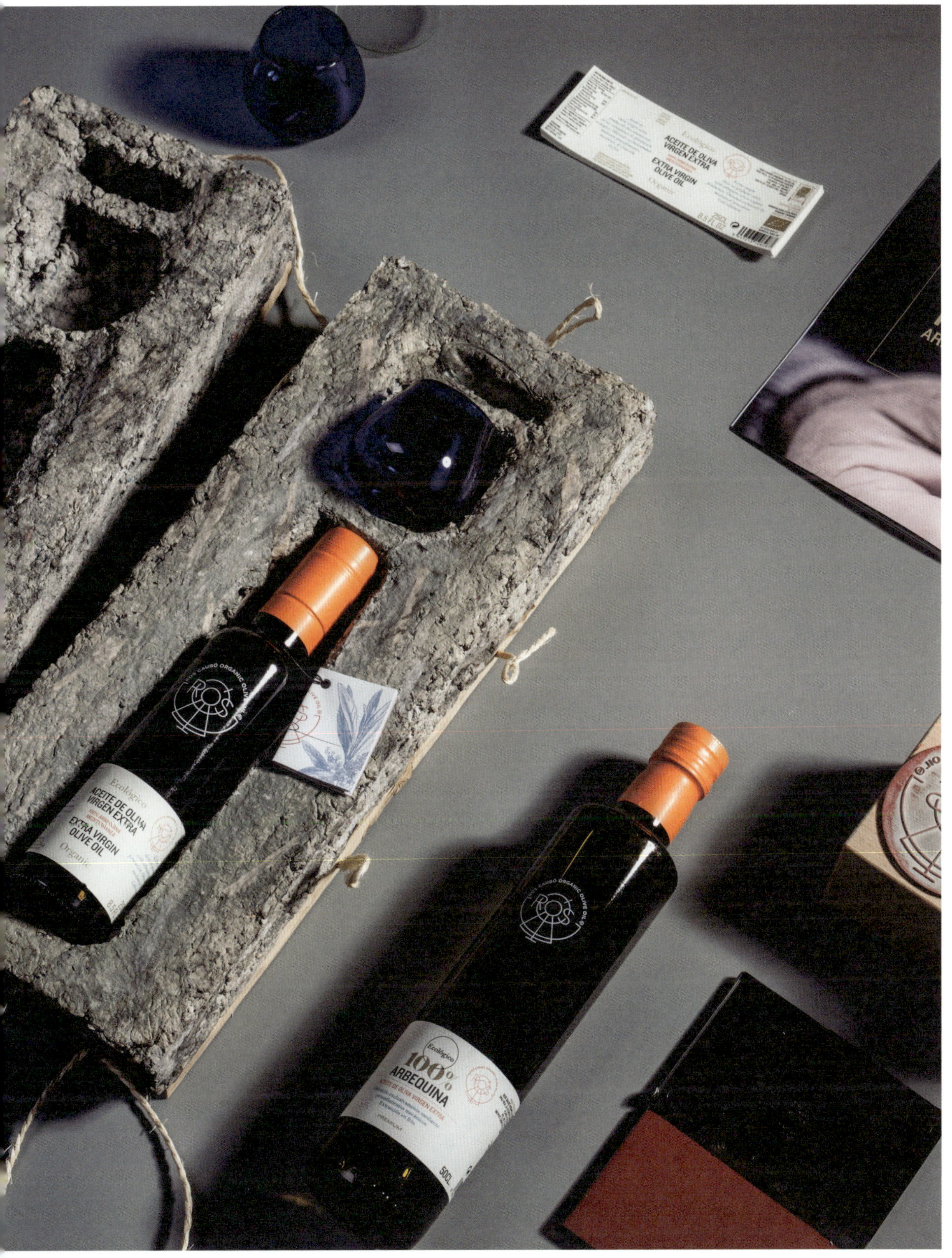
Ecológico
ACEITE DE OLIVA
VIRGEN EXTRA
EXTRA VIRGIN
OLIVE OIL
Organic
100%
ARBEQUINA

JAPANESE SAKE KOI

Designer : Aya Codama

This is the package design for the Japanese sake "KOI". The purpose was to create a sake packaging that represents Japan.

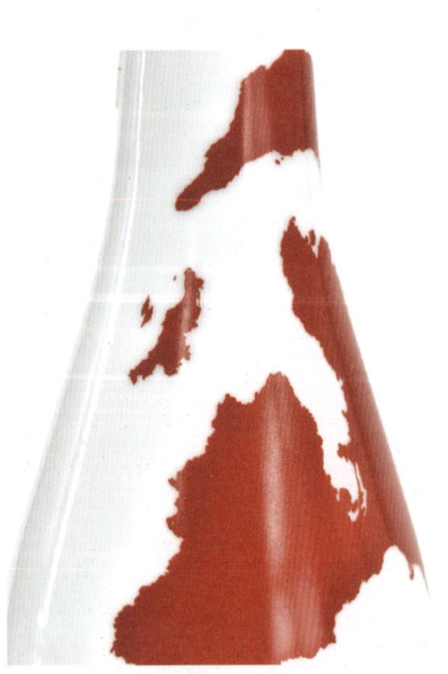

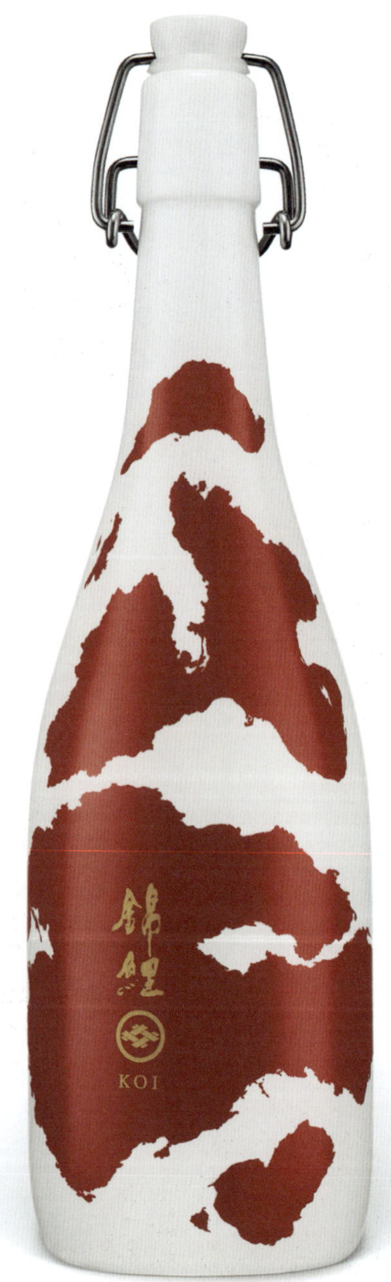

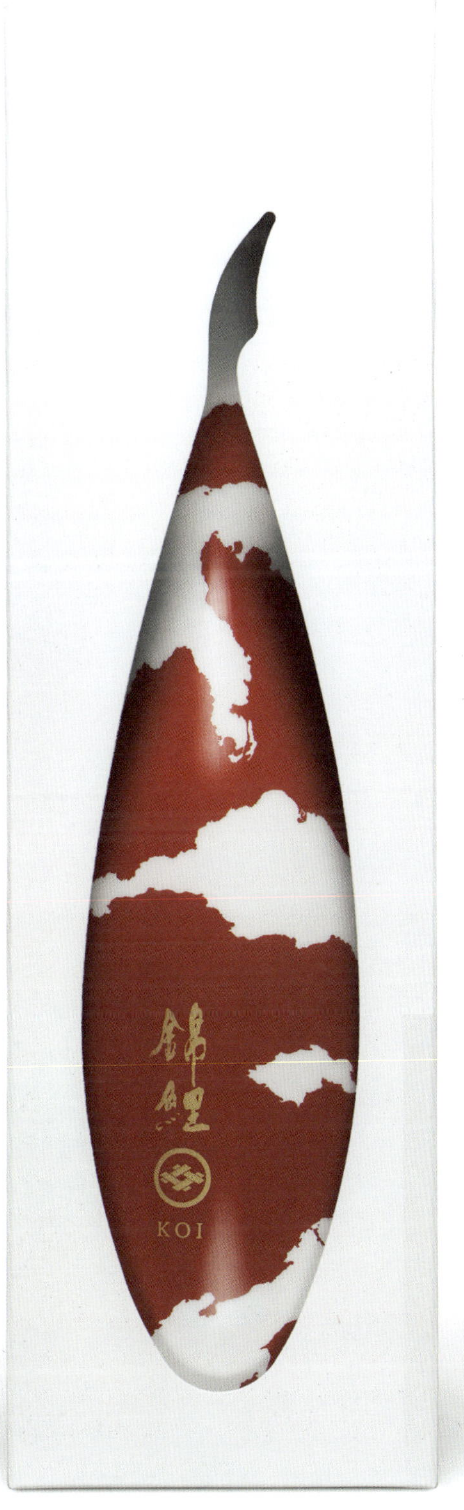
錦鯉
KOI

MISOMBER NUAN COLLECTION IV

Studio : Somewhere Else

With black being the main color, this fashion collection is a reflection of emptiness and void. The promotional literature created for Misomber Nuan is all directed to express their experimental approach towards materials and fabrics.

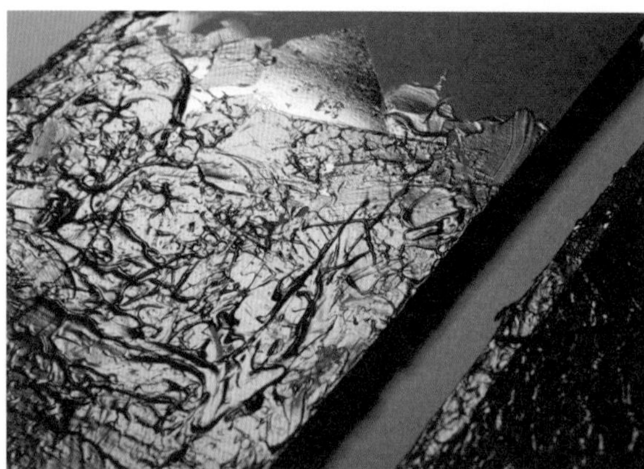

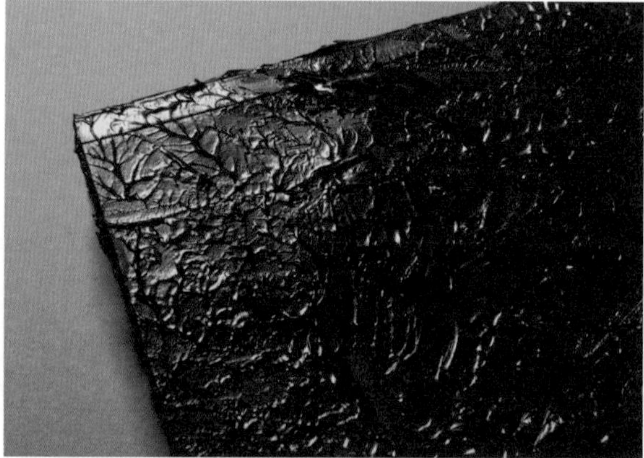

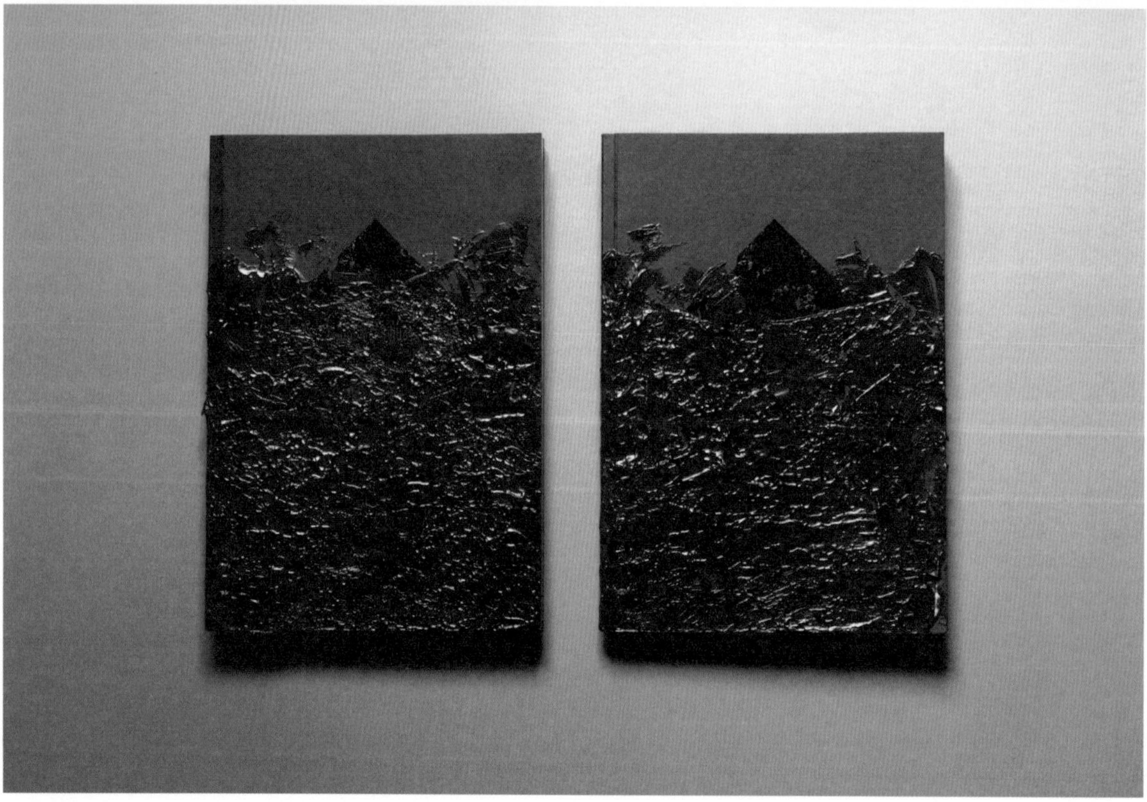

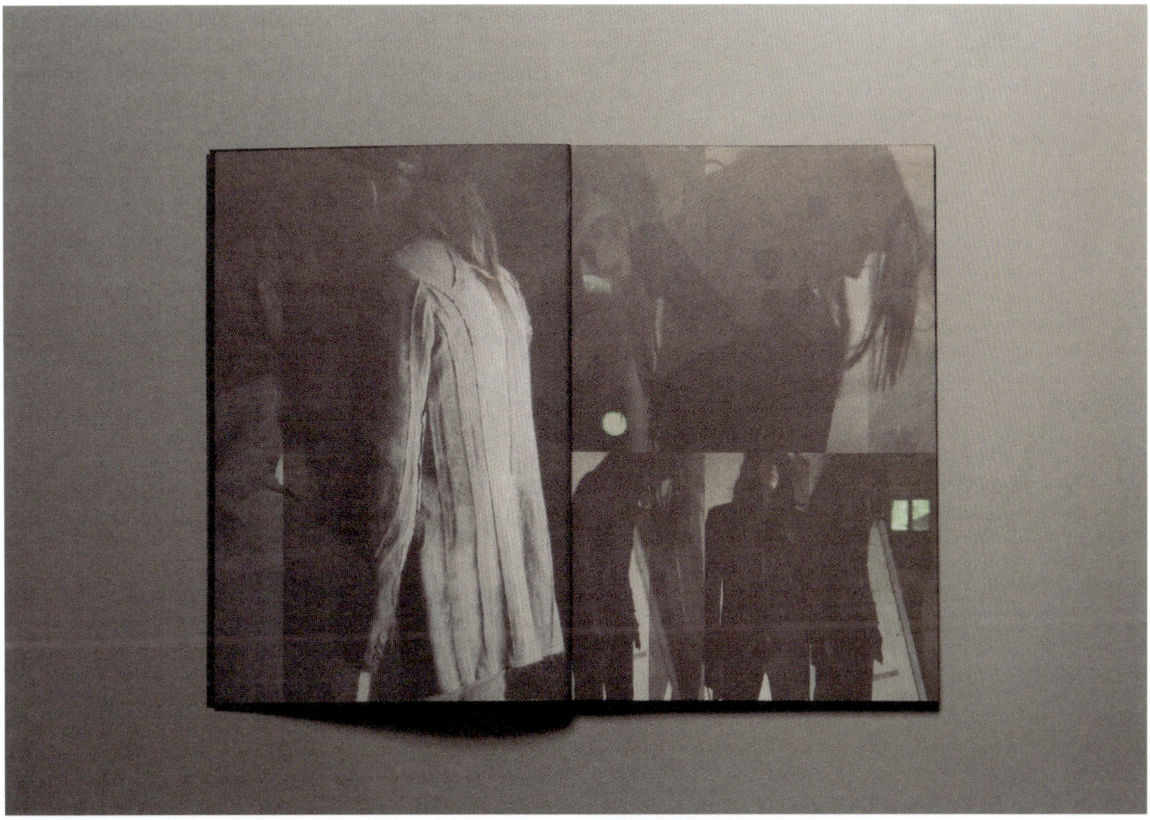

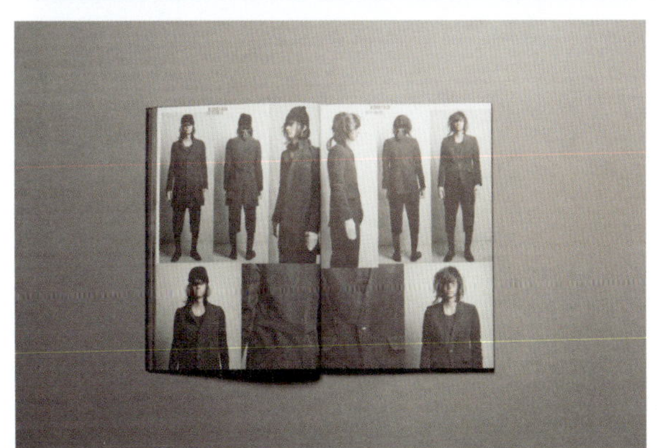

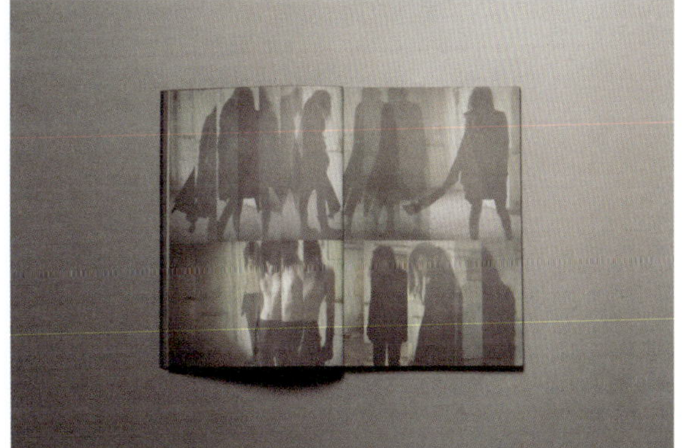

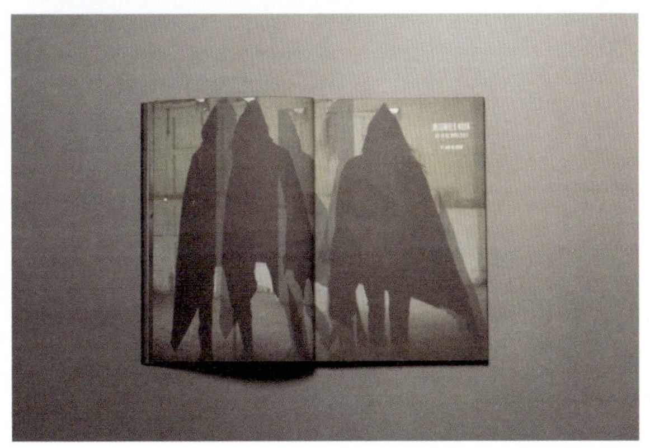

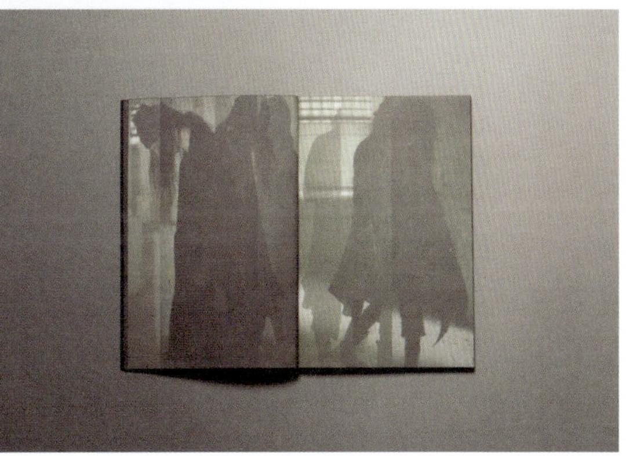

Index

ACKNOWLEDGEMENTS

We would like to thank all the designers and contributors who have been involved in the production of this book. Their contributions have been indispensable in its compilation. We would also like to express our gratitude to all the producers for their invaluable opinions and assistance throughout this project. And to the many others whose names are not credited but have made specific input in this book, we thank you for your continuous support.

FUTURE COOPERATIONS:

If you wish to participate in SendPoints' future projects and publications, please send your website or portfolio to

editor01@sendpoints.cn